FINANCE AGAINS'

Since the 1980s development theorists have increasingly argued for the provision of small loans to micro-entrepreneurs as an effective policy instrument in the fight against poverty.

In Volume 1 of *Finance Against Poverty*, David Hulme and Paul Mosley reviewed and extended the theory behind such ideas. In the present volume, they assess the effectiveness of the theory when put into practice, drawing on detailed comparative data from seven developing countries: Bangladesh, Bolivia, India, Indonesia, Kenya, Malawi and Sri Lanka.

Both volumes provide a wealth of information and research on the impacts of savings and credit on productivity, employment, poverty levels and sociopolitical relations. With its detailed assessment of both the benefits and the limitations of financial intervention, *Finance Against Poverty* is the most comprehensive study of microfinance to date. It is essential reading for all those interested in development, poverty-reduction, social welfare and finance.

David Hulme is Professor of Development Studies and Director of the Institute for Development Policy and Management at the University of Manchester. **Paul Mosley** is Professor of Economics and Director of the International Development Centre at Reading University.

FINANCE AGAINST POVERTY

Volume 2

David Hulme
and Paul Mosley

London and New York

First published 1996
by Routledge
11 New Fetter Lane, London EC4P 4EE

Simultaneously published in the USA and Canada
by Routledge
29 West 35th Street, New York, NY 10001

© 1996 David Hulme and Paul Mosley

Typeset in Garamond by
J&L Composition Ltd, Filey, North Yorkshire
Printed and bound in Great Britain by
TJ Press (Padstow) Ltd, Padstow, Cornwall

British Library Cataloguing in Publication Data
A catalogue record for this book is available from the British Library.

Library of Congress Cataloging in Publication Data
A catalogue record for this book has been requested.

ISBN 0–415–12430–1 (hbk)
ISBN 0–415–12431–X (pbk)

CONTENTS

CONTENTS

FIGURES

TABLES

NOTES ON CONTRIBUTORS

Debapriya Bhattacharya is a senior research fellow at the Bangladesh Institute of Development Studies, GPO Box no. 3854, Dhaka, Bangladesh.

Graeme Buckley is a research associate of the Institute for Development Policy and Management, University of Manchester, Oxford Road, Manchester M13 9GH, UK.

David Hulme is Professor of Development Studies and Director of the Institute for Development Policy and Management, University of Manchester, Oxford Road, Manchester M13 9GH, UK.

Richard Montgomery is a lecturer at the Centre for Development Studies, University College of Swansea, Singleton Park, Swansea SA2 8PP, UK.

Paul Mosley is Professor of Economics and Director of the International Development Centre at the University of Reading, PO Box 218, Whiteknights, Reading RG6 2AA, UK.

ABBREVIATIONS

ACCU	Asian Council of Credit Unions
ADAB	Association of Development Agencies in Bangladesh
ADB	Asian Development Bank
ADD	Agricultural Development Division (Malawi)
ADMARC	Agricultural Development Marketing Corporation (Malawi)
AO	Area office
ARDRS	Agricultural and Rural Debt Relief Scheme (India)
B	Boliviano (monetary unit of Bolivia)
BAAC	Bank for Agriculture and Agricultural Co-operation (Thailand)
BAB	Banco Agricola Boliviano
BAMIN	Banco Minero Boliviano
BancoSol	Banco Solidario (Bolivia)
BANEST	Banco del Estado (Bolivia)
BB	Bangladesh Bank
BBD	Bank Bumi Daya (Indonesia)
BBS	Bangladesh Bureau of Statistics
BI	Bank Indonesia
BIDS	Bangladesh Institute of Development Studies
BIMAS	Bimbangan Massal (Indonesia)
BKB	Bangladesh Krishi Bank
BKD	Bank Kredit Desa (Indonesia)
BKK	Badan Kredit Kecamatan (Indonesia)
BNP	Bangladesh Nationalist Party
BPD	Bank Pembangunan Daerah (Indonesia)
BPR	Bank Perkreditan Rakyat (Indonesia)
BRAC	Bangladesh Rural Advancement Committee
BRDB	Bangladesh Rural Development Board
BRI	Bank Rakyat Indonesia
BSBL	Bangladesh Sambaya Co-operative Bank
BUD	Bank Rakyat Indonesia Unit Desa

CB	Co-operative Bank (India)
CCA	Canadian Co-operative Association
CIDA	Canadian International Development Agency
CIGP	Credit-based income-generating project
CMA	Credit and Marketing Assistant (Malawi)
COP	Client Orientation Programme (Kenya)
CRB	Co-operative Rural Bank (Sri Lanka)
CRCS	Comprehensive Rural Credit Scheme (Sri Lanka)
DFI	Development finance institution
DTW	Deep tubewell
DU	District Union (Sri Lanka)
DYD	Directorate of Youth Development (Bangladesh)
EPA	Extension Planning Area (Malawi)
FAO	Food and Agricultural Organisation
FTCCS	Federation of Thrift and Credit Co-operative Societies (Sri Lanka)
GA	Group Animator (Bangladesh)
GB	Grameen Bank
GDP	Gross domestic product
GNP	Gross national product
GS	*Gram Shebok/Shebika* (local village worker, Bangladesh)
GTF	Group Trust Fund (Bangladesh)
GTZ	(German technical assistance agency)
HAT	Hadiah Angsuran Tepat Waktu (Indonesia)
HRM	Human resource management
HYV	High-yielding variety
IDA	International Development Association
IDSS	International Development Support Services (Australia)
IFAD	International Fund for Agricultural Development
IFM	Informal financial market
IGVGD	Income Generation for Vulnerable Group Development (Bangladesh)
IIC	Interamerican Investment Corporation
ILO	International Labour Organisation
INDEBANK	Investment and Development Bank (Malawi)
INDEFUND	Investment and Development Fund (Malawi)
INE	Instituto Nacional de Estadistica (Bolivia)
IPTW	Insentif Pembayaran Tepat Waktu (Indonesia)
IRDP	Integrated Rural Development Programme (India)
ISP	Informal Sector Programme (Kenya)
JLBS	Joint Loan Board Scheme (Kenya)
JTF	*Janasaviyar* Trust Fund
KCB	Kenya Commercial Bank
KIE-ISP	Kenya Industrial Estates–Informal Sector Programme

KIWA	Kikundi Cha Wanabiashara (Kenya)
KREP	Kenya Rural Enterprise Programme
KSh	Kenya shilling (monetary unit)
KUPEDES	Loan scheme for small rural enterprises operated by BRI, *q.v.* (Indonesia)
KURK	Kredit Usaha Raykat Kecil (Indonesia)
LDB	Land Development Bank (India)
LDC	Less-developed country
LLDP	Lilongwe Land Development Project (Malawi)
MHP	Million Houses Programme (Sri Lanka)
MK	Malawi kwacha (monetary unit)
MMF	Malawi Mudzi Fund
MPCS	Multi-Purpose Co-operative Society (Sri Lanka)
MRFC	Malawi Rural Finance Company
MUSCCO	Malawi Union of Savings and Credit Co-operatives
NABARD	National Bank for Agricultural and Rural Development (India)
NCB	Nationalised commercial bank
NCRCS	New Comprehensive Rural Credit Scheme (Sri Lanka)
NFPE	Non-Formal Primary Education Programme (Bangladesh)
NGO	Non-governmental organisation
NHDA	National Housing Development Authority (Sri Lanka)
NORAD	Norwegian International Development Authority
NRDP	National Rural Development Programme (Malawi)
ODA	Overseas Development Administration (UK)
OP	Outreach Programme (Bangladesh)
OTEP	Oral Rehydration Therapy Extension Programme (Bangladesh)
PL	Poverty line
PNN	Praja Naya Niyamaka (Sri Lanka)
PO	Programme organiser
PRIDE	Promotion of Rural Initiatives and Development of Enterprises (Kenya)
PRODEM	Fundación para la Promoción y Desarollo de la Micro Empresa (Bolivia)
PTCCS	Primary Thrift and Credit Co-operative Society (Sri Lanka)
R	Rupee (Indian movetary unit)
R&D	Research and development
RBI	Reserve Bank of India
RCP	Rural Credit Project (Bangladesh)
RCTP	Rural Credit and Training Programme (Bangladesh)
RDP	Rural Development Programme (Bangladesh)/Rural Development Project (Malawi)
RDRS	Rangpur and Dinajpur Rural Services (Bangladesh)

REP	Rural Enterprise Programme (Sri Lanka)
ROSCA	Rotating Savings and Credit Association
Rp	Rupiah (Indonesian monetary unit)
RRB	Regional Rural Bank (India)
RRDB	Regional Rural Development Bank (Sri Lanka)
SACA	Smallholder Agricultural Credit Administration (Malawi)
SANASA	Federation of Thrift and Credit Co-operative Societies (Sri Lanka)
SAP	Structural adjustment programme
SDI	Subsidy Dependence Index
SDR	Special Drawing Rights
SEDOM	Small Enterprise Development Organisation of Malawi
SEFCO	Small Enterprise Finance Company (Kenya)
SIDA	Swedish International Development Authority
SIMPEDES	Savings scheme organised by by BRI, *q.v* (Indonesia)
SLFP	Sri Lanka Freedom Party
SMI	Small and medium industries
SUSENAS	National social survey office (Indonesia)
T&V	Training and visit extension
TABANAS	Tabungan Nasional (Indonesia)
TCCS	Thrift and Credit Co-operative Society (Sri Lanka)
Tk	Taka (monetary unit of Bangladesh)
TRDEP	Thana Resource Development and Employment Programme (Bangladesh)
UNDP	United Nations Development Programme
UNP	United National Party (Sri Lanka)
UNRISD	United Nations Research Institute for Social Development
USAID	United States Agency for International Development
VO	Village Organisation (Bangladesh)
WOCCU	World Council of Credit Unions

PREFACE

In Volume 1 we presented an overview of the literature on microfinance, a theoretical structure designed to illuminate the reasons for the success of some of these institutions and the failure of others, and a comparative analysis of the performance of thirteen of these institutions in seven developing countries. On the basis of this analysis we discovered:

1 that each of market interest rates, intensive loan collection by mobile bankers, savings and insurance facilities and incentives to repay had a potential role to play in most environments, both in individual and in group-based schemes, to enable new financial institutions to overcome an inherent failure in developing-country financial markets, and to traverse the knife-edge between failure to reach the poor and financial collapse;
2 that most of the schemes examined had had positive effects on incomes and poverty, and also indirect positive effects on the behaviour of other providers of finance to the poor, but very restricted effects on employment and technology, possibly because the tendency of borrowing to augment the borrower's risk exposure had been overlooked;
3 that at any one time a trade-off existed between the income impact and poverty impact of schemes, a trade-off which could be moved by measures to improve institutions' financial performance, lower their transactions costs, or remove the demand constraints to which borrowers are subject;
4 that in the light of the above, a case existed for temporary, performance-related subsidies to innovative credit institutions; for such institutions to offer emergency consumption loans; and for them to consider introducing the design features listed in 1 above, if they are not already in force.

This volume presents the country case-studies on which the above conclusions are based, covering twelve institutions in seven countries (the thirteenth discussed in Volume 1, the Grameen Bank of Bangladesh, is already amply documented in the literature, in particular in the studies by Khandkhar *et al.* 1995 listed in the Bibliography). The original intention was to work only in Asia and Africa, and to study only 'exemplary' institutions; but the temptation to add BancoSol of Bolivia to the original list proved irresistible, and as noted in the introduction to the first volume, several of the case-study institutions were exposed by the research as being far from exemplary, thereby enlivening the research beyond measure. All of the studies follow a *broadly* similar format, intended to facilitate the comparisons of Volume 1: historical and institutional background (including a discussion of alternative financial models to those studied), financial performance over time, direct effects on incomes, employment and technology, indirect effects on other borrowers and lenders. But the balance between topics varies by case: the Bangladesh, Kenya and Sri Lanka studies have the most detail on group dynamics, the Bangladesh study of government–institution relationships, the Indonesia study of performance-related pay, and so on. In addition, as readers will discover, the studies diverge enormously from this common core in order to seek to understand unique features of the systems under review, not discussed in Volume 1, which need to be grounded in the local social and political context. Examples of these particularities are: the Indian tradition of 'social banking'; the role of local officials and 'incentives to repay' in bringing about recovery of individual-based loans in Indonesia; sponsorship of microbusiness lending by private macro-entrepreneurs in Bolivia; and the linkage of lending to specific agricultural technologies in Malawi. Whether these features remain unique or turn out to be capable of adaptation in other countries (an issue which we dodge) we believe that a study of their evolution will be valuable for students, designers and managers of financial institutions serving the poor in every country, and we present them in that spirit.

The authors are deeply grateful to the many hundreds of poor people in developing countries who consented to be interviewed, sometimes repeatedly, for this study, and to the individuals in each of those countries who as supervisors, enumerators or removers of bureaucratic obstacles made our research possible. Some of the more exceptional of these are named at the beginning of each country study; but to all of them, our warmest thanks, and our hope that we may be able to give back in terms of ideas some part of what we have taken in terms of labour.

10

METAMORPHOSIS FROM NGO TO COMMERCIAL BANK

The case of BancoSol in Bolivia

Paul Mosley

INTRODUCTION

Banco Solidario of Bolivia, popularly known (and hereafter described) as BancoSol, is the first non-governmental institution in the world to convert itself into a deposit-taking bank. It aims to lend exclusively to low-income people, and amongst the institutions studied in this volume, has the highest repayment rate of all. These facts alone justify the inclusion of BancoSol in any study of efforts to remedy poverty through the financial system. Both its institutional features and its achievements, however, owe much to the socio-economic conditions in which it was born, and we must therefore begin by describing these.

With a per capita income of $620, a life expectancy of sixty and an under-five mortality rate of 126 per thousand, Bolivia is not only a poorer country than any in Latin America, but also poorer than the average for less-developed countries as a whole.[1] From the 1950s through to the early 1980s a succession of governments had attempted to wrench Bolivia out of poverty through 'structuralist' policy measures, including a thoroughgoing land reform in 1952, nationalisation of the mines in the same year and of the country's natural gas reserves in 1965, and widespread controls on the exchange rate and other 'key prices'. Except under the impetus of petro-dollar inflows in the 1970s, however, the Bolivian economy did not respond well to these stimuli. Further, the government made no attempt to adjust to

This study could not have been completed without the help of the following people: in Washington – Maria Otero and Mohini Malhotra; in La Paz – Miguel Taborga, Sergio Ortiz and Paola Barragan. Particular thanks are due to Pancho Otero for accepting my intrusions with great warmth in the middle of an exceptionally hectic fortnight in late April 1993, and to the brave team of enumerators – Felipe Santos, Juan Charles Ascarrus, Waldo Carpio, Leopoldo Molinedo, Guadalupe Calderon, Maria Luisa Rea Machado and their supervisor, Bernardo Santa Maria – for carrying out a strenuous task with exceptional good humour and professionalism.

1

the collapse of world demand and of foreign investment in the wake of the 1980 international economic crisis, except by imposing controls on yet more prices. The consequence was a withdrawal from the country, after the collapse of an early structural adjustment programme, by the World Bank and IMF in 1981; six consecutive years of negative economic growth from 1981 onward; a public-sector budget deficit rising to 21 per cent of national income in 1984; and as a direct consequence of the decision to finance this deficit with the help of the printing-press, a hyperinflation reaching its climax at an annual rate of 24,000 per cent in August 1985.

This was a watershed. In that same month, a new government, under Victor Paz Estenssoro, who had previously been president from 1950 to 1958, committed itself to an unusually drastic stabilisation programme, involving the liberalisation of all prices (including interest rates), foreign trade and much state enterprise. This quickly restored stability to the financial economy; the rate of inflation fell to 14 per cent within two years, and it has remained in the range of 14–20 per cent since 1987. Growth in the real economy has been slower in coming, but it has been positive since 1987, and in 1991 Bolivia experienced its first year of positive growth in per capita income since 1981. What is particularly relevant to our present discussion are the social effects of the stabilisation programme and its effects on the banking system.

Having been delayed so long, the 1985 stabilisation hit hard when it came, and hit especially hard at low-income groups who were unable to defend themselves. In particular, in the wake of both stabilisation and a dramatic fall in tin prices in 1985, most of the tin mines operated by the state mining company, COMIBOL, were closed, and the majority of tin miners lost their jobs.[2] Nor was agriculture remotely able to take up the slack: between 1986 and 1988, when the rest of the economy was beginning to recover, agricultural GDP declined and yields for most crops (apart from soya and a few others produced in the fertile east of the country) are continuing to fall (Morales 1991: 12, 155). The consequence was a flood of migrants into La Paz, and to a lesser degree the other main cities. A few were able to find employment in the formal manufacturing and services sector, or in the relief projects set up by the government,[3] but the majority were forced into the 'informal' sector, operating mostly from squats in municipal property or shanty towns on the fringes of the main cities: one of these, El Alto on the *altiplano* outside La Paz, is estimated to have grown in size from 100,000 to 500,000 over the last ten years. A recent newspaper report suggests that 45 per cent of the population of La Paz may be living in illegal housing, some of it actually dangerous in that it is situated in areas of landslide risk on the near-vertical escarpments which surround the city.[4] This is exactly the catchment for one of the other credit schemes discussed in this volume (KREP Juhudi discussed in Chapter 15). As in Kibera, Nairobi, the circumstances of high population density give any

2

'innovative' operator the opportunity of being able to expand operations rapidly and at low cost. This advantage is compounded because, as we now discuss, there are few alternative credit outlets which a micro-entrepreneur can use.

Bolivia's banking system, even more than other parts of the economy, was characterised during the pre-1985 period by extreme inefficiency and, for the most part, by an inability to reach the small borrower. Both the three main state-financed banks and the twelve main commercial banks, before 1985, were hampered by the natural instinct of all Bolivians who could afford to place their money in overseas accounts at market interest rates rather than locally at controlled, and in real terms negative, interest rates. The consequent shortage of savings in total currency bred financial conservatism among Bolivian banks and, in particular, a reluctance to embark on high-risk projects such as lending to small farmers or micro-entrepreneurs. The squeeze on demand imposed by the 1985 stabilisation turned a number of the banks' good customers into bad customers and produced a situation which an AID report has described in the following way:

> The 1985–88 period had virtually eliminated every financial institution in Bolivia. In that period, the peso boliviano went from 6,000 to the dollar to 1,500,000 to the dollar. Savings disappeared: all banking transactions moved on to the street corners and the formal financial sector ceased to exist. The credit union system dropped from 300 credit unions to around 30.
>
> (Fischer *et al.* 1992: 2)

This is poetic licence. The twelve main private banks survived the crisis and the main state-financed banks clung on until 1992, at which point they were closed under major pressure from the World Bank and the IDB. What is true is that their portfolios were hopelessly contaminated before 1985, a state of affairs which the subsequent reforms exposed, and that this made any experiment in banking for low-income groups impossible for those

Table 10.1 Bolivia: performance of major banks, 1990 (end April)

	Public sector banks			Private commercial banks
	BAB	*BAMIN*	*BANEST*	
Administrative costs/ total assets (%)	5.8	4.3	10.5	4.5
Loans in default/ total assets (%)	64.4	41.8	61.3	12.2

Source: Müller and Associates (1991)
Note: BAB = Banco Agricola Boliviano; BAMIN = Banco Minero Boliviano; BANEST = Banco del Estado

houses (see Table 10.1). 'Quasi-formal' institutions did exist, namely the surviving credit unions and the Fondo de Desarollo Campesino; but for reasons to be discussed on pp. 20–4, these organisations did not contribute effectively to filling the vacuum which existed where the credit market for small rural and urban enterprises should have been. Consequently PRODEM – BancoSol's predecessor – on setting up operations in 1987, did so in an environment of pent-up concentrated demand from the informal micro-enterprise sector, widespread mistrust in the formal banking system, and little effective competition from the informal banking system. We shall now examine how these unique (in terms of our sample) initial conditions influenced the circumstances of PRODEM's foundation and its metamorphosis into a commercial bank.

PRODEM INTO BANCOSOL: DOES THE ENVIRONMENT CREATE THE INSTITUTION?

Like one of the other institutions studied in this volume (KREP Juhudi, Kenya), PRODEM (Fundación para la Promoción y Desarollo de la Micro Empresa, or Foundation for the Promotion and Development of Micro-enterprises) owed its origins to the midwifery, if not parenthood, of USAID. In late 1985, just as the Bolivian stabilisation programme was getting under way, that organisation funded a study by a staff member of the American NGO ACCION International of the possibility of establishing a micro-enterprise lending programme in Bolivia. However, the true father of PRODEM is a Bolivian businessman, Fernando Romero, chief shareholder in the Banco Hipotecário, who persuaded a group of Bolivian businessmen to invest in PRODEM alongside a contribution of PL-480 money from USAID.[5] PRODEM is the only one of the seven institutions under study here to be established by the local business community in this way. Romero was appointed in 1986 as managing director of the Emergency Social Fund, which then proceeded to invest in PRODEM consistently with its policy of supporting initiatives by local NGOs. By the end of 1988 PRODEM had an equity capital of $400,000, subscribed on concessional terms by the three agents mentioned above together with the Canadian Calmeadow Foundation. Table 10.2 summarises the main design features of PRODEM in relation to two of the main 'models' discussed elsewhere: the Grameen Bank of Bangladesh (Vol. 2, Chapter 12) and the Indonesian BKK (Vol. 2, Chapter 11). In terms of the 'group versus individual' spectrum, PRODEM stood (and BancoSol now stands) between the two: whereas BKK lends to individuals and Grameen lends to sub-groups of five within borrower centres of thirty, PRODEM lent to individuals within 'solidarity groups' of four to seven members.[6] All three use intensive loan collection methods never experimented with by commercial banks or specialist farm credit institutions and have been rewarded

Table 10.2 PRODEM and BancoSol: main design features

	PRODEM → BancoSol		*For comparison*	
			Grameen Bank	BKK
1 Collection method for loans	Fortnightly or monthly on bank premises		Weekly at or near borrowers' premises	
2 Borrower	Individual within 'solidarity group' of four to seven individuals	As PRODEM	Individual within group of five within centre of thirty	Individual
3 Interest rate (1992)		60%	24%	Various but average 45%
4 Insurance arrangements	Compulsory deposit, 5% of value of loan		'Emergency Fund' contribution of 25% of the interest payment	
5 Savings taken from general public	No	Yes	No	Yes
6 Incentives to repay	No	No	No	Yes
7 Collateral requirement	No	No	No	No
8 Criteria for loan approval	Existing businesses willing to join solidarity group		Owns $\frac{1}{2}$ acre of land and other criteria	Any borrower approved by village leadership

by consistently low default rates. All three seek to charge market interest rates but these vary enormously by country to reflect local financial market conditions: Grameen's lending rate is relatively low by virtue of the large quantity of concessional capital available to it, and PRODEM's is relatively high as a consequence of the initial breakdown of the Bolivian financial system in 1985–8, leading to a haemorrhage of confidence and savings from the formal financial system and the consequent need to pay a high supply price (in terms of the notation of Vol. 1, Chapter 3 above) for savings. Like Grameen, PRODEM insisted on a compulsory savings deposit (in its case, 5 per cent of the value of the loan), not returnable until the loan was fully paid up. Finally, and importantly, PRODEM, unlike

5

Grameen, imposed no maximum income requirement. The only criteria imposed were that loans would be given to an existing business, to persons over eighteen years of age willing to form a group. The low initial loan size ($200), split among five to eight persons, is intended to act as a self-targeting device precluding the non-poor from receiving credit. How far this has happened will be considered on pp. 14–18 below.

As it stood in 1988, PRODEM therefore satisfied one of Yaron's 'fundamental conditions' (1991: 36–7) for a successful poor-orientated financial institution – a commercial orientation – but not the other: effective outreach. The 3,300 borrowers PRODEM had signed up by December 1988 represented, in the view of both USAID and PRO-DEM, less than 2 per cent of potential demand,[7] and without a means of expanding lending rapidly the momentum for expanding loan size (given that only a small proportion of first-time borrowers could be expected to graduate to larger loans), and hence profitability would not exist. The solution initially adumbrated in 1988, and finally implemented on 24 January 1992, was the conversion of PRODEM into a commercial bank, BancoSol, financing itself by taking savings deposits: a highly traditional thing to do in terms of financial markets worldwide, but an unprecedented step for an NGO.

The main obstacles to such a process were three:

1 to build up PRODEM's capital to a point where it would satisfy the Bolivian Government's guidelines (recently tightened up in the light of the banking sector crisis of 1986–8) for incorporation as a bank. The threshold figure eventually agreed was $3.2 million:[8] but in 1988, as shown in Table 10.3, PRODEM only had $400,000 subscribed;
2 to select an appropriate blend of voluntary and compulsory saving, and to make realistic forecasts of the rate at which savings, on either model, could be built up. In spite of favourable experience in doing this at BKK and BRI unit desas in Indonesia, this represented a shot in the dark, especially in a still turbulent and, above all, savings-poor economy in which 'past bank scandals and fraud throughout Bolivia have left many with little reason to entrust a formal institution with their savings. The poor are left with no alternative but to store the value of their currency in assets such as livestock, inventory or consumer products, or to save it without the benefit of interest bearing accounts' (Glosser 1993: 8–9);
3 to overcome political opposition within Bolivia to a declared intention of changing market-determined interest rates – which were to rise to 60 per cent per annum by 1992 when BancoSol was finally incorporated. Such an intention ran up against the consensus of Bolivian opinion about how a bank – any bank, but above all a bank lending to the poor – should conduct itself. A number of 'not for profit' organisations, including the Fondo de Inversiones Economicas, and

Table 10.3 PRODEM/BancoSol: summary of lending activities

	1987	1988		1989		1990		1991		1992	1993	1994
		Jan–June	July–Dec	Jan–June	July–Dec	Jan–June	July–Dec	Jan–June	July–Dec			
Number of new borrowers	1,737	1,030	685	1,035	2,503	3,251	5,394	3,924	6,551	8,500	12,500	15,300
% women borrowers	81	67	70	75	79	71	73	76	74	72	71	71
Average loan size ($)	92	145	191	213	157	213	228	272	275	322	345	361
Amount disbursed ($ thousand)	462	665	687	1,107	1,872	2,680	5,040	5,750	9,050	16,500	24,700	—
Value of equity capital ($ thousand)	158	279	413	512	932	1,400	2,440	2,760	4,560	5,103	5,400	—
Value of savings deposits ($m)	0		0		0		0		0	0.9	2.0	3.05
Arrears rate (%)[a]	0		0.4		0.19		0.23		0.20	2.05	3.5	5.2
Number of offices	1		1		1		2		5	8	15	29
Number of staff	19		24		35		71		116			
Net profit (loss)			28		(13)		(19)	161		(397)	485	650

Source: PRODEM Annual Reports 1987–92 inclusive; BancoSol Annual Report for 1994.
Note: [a] 'Arrears rate' is defined as proportion of loans in arrears for three weeks or more

Table 10.4 BancoSol: composition of equity as at April 1993 ($'000)

Individuals (Bolivia)	52
Businesses (Bolivia)	1,025
Calmeadow Foundation	406
ACCION International	250
ECOS Holding (FUNDES group)	250
Rockefeller Foundation	250
Inter-American Investment Corporation	1,325
SIDI (France)	120
International Finance Corporation	800
DEG (Germany)	250
Total	5,178

Source: BancoSol (1993)

Table 10.5 PRODEM/BancoSol: portfolio structure, 1989 and 1992

Type of business	1989			1992		
	Amount of loan portfolio ($'000)	% of total clients	% of total loan portfolio	Amount of loan portfolio ($'000)	% of total clients	% of total loan portfolio
Commerce and services						
Food trading	296	23.0	18.5	3,663	47.9	39.0
Textiles and footwear	234	17.0	14.7	1,534	13.0	16.3
Consumer durables	52	7.5	3.3	740	5.8	7.8
Wholesaling	8	3.1	0.5	177	1.9	1.9
Miscellaneous services	200	14.5	12.4	429	5.0	4.5
Total	791	65.1	49.4	6,543	73.6	69.2
Industry						
Textiles	290	11.2	18.1	1,791	16.5	19.6
Food manufacture	133	8.2	10.5	248	2.5	2.6
Shoe making	100	5.0	6.8			
Carpets and furniture	85	3.3	5.4	429	63.7	4.6
Miscellaneous	200	7.2	9.8	371	3.4	4.0
Total	1,603	34.9	50.6	2,838	26.1	30.8

Sources: 1989, Inter-American Investment Corporation internal document; 1992, BancoSol analysis as at 30 November

8

Table 10.6 BancoSol: income statement, 1992–4 (current $'000, December)

	1992	1993	1994
[1] Income (*r*)			
Interest earned			
Loan portfolio	2,152	5,483	7,221
Legal reserves	17	39	69
Certificates of deposit	10	0	219
Total interest earned:	2,179	5,522	7,510
[2] Cost of funds (*i*)			
Savings deposits	210	544	1,010
Other short-term debt	246	374	19
Debt – PL 480	168	192	192
Fixed-term deposits	96	555	1,142
Total cost of funds	720	1,666	2,364
[3] Financial margin ([1] − [2])	1,458	3,856	5,146
Administrative spending			
Personnel	539	1,210	1,551
Contracted services	22	46	53
Communications	44	89	115
Maintenance	22	69	97
Other expenditures	87	263	325
National and branch office costs	766	1,058	1,269
Depreciation	118	170	206
[4] Total administration	1,599	2,908	3,618
[5] Loan loss provision (*p*)	17	17	17
[6] Tax payments	192	327	421
[7] Miscellaneous costs	48	87	108
[8] Total non-financial costs (*a*) ([4] + [5] + [6] + [7])	1,856	3,340	4,165
[9] Net profit/loss ([3] − [8])	(397)	516	981
[10] Return on equity (%)	4	6.7	11.2

Sources: Glosser (1993: Table 3) plus author's calculations; see also note 11

other church-sponsored organisations, were setting an 'appropriate' example by lending at rates of interest between 12 and 18 per cent.

The story of how these obstacles were overcome has been well told by Drake and Otero (1992: 88–98) and Glosser (1993) and we shall only summarise it here. In relation to obstacle 3 it was crucial for the purpose of piloting the BancoSol proposal through the legal and political minefield that the conception of the bank had support from Bolivian investors with appropriate political weight – one of them, indeed, a former Minister of Planning (Romero). In relation to obstacles 1 and 2 it was significant that PRODEM had not one, but four, fairy godmothers: USAID, ACCION, the

9

Calmeadow Foundation, and the group of Bolivian businessmen referred to earlier. The last three of these agreed to sponsor a planning authority, COBANCO, which developed a prospectus to sell the idea of the prospective bank to major investors. In 1990, crucially, the Inter-American Investment Corporation was persuaded to contribute a stake of $1.3 million,[9] and other European and North American foundations followed. The list of investors in BancoSol as at April 1993 is in Table 10.4. PRODEM appears in the list since a great part of its assets were transferred to the credit of the new bank at its inauguration in January 1992. PRODEM continues to exist, however, as the research and planning arm of BancoSol – in other words, the function which COBANCO occupied in relation to PRODEM – and retains 20 per cent of its former assets.

BancoSol's portfolio of activities in 1989 and 1993 are as set out in Table 10.5, and its income and expenditure account for 1992–4 are in Table 10.6. The bank's dependence on small-scale trading activities appears to be increasing sharply,[10] although it is greater in terms of total lending, that is, average loan size is bigger in manufacturing than in trade. The debt strategy for the bank is to replace more expensive debt such as bonds and inter-bank loans with client deposits, on which it currently pays interest at an annual rate of 21 per cent. By 1994 client savings, currently 25 per cent of the portfolio, were projected to represent 50 per cent of the bank's liabilities; by this time, also, it was expected to be sufficiently in profit to be able to declare a dividend.

INTERNAL EFFECTIVENESS AND 'ROLE IN THE MARKET'

In this section we examine the trend of costs and financial performance over time, and then proceed to examine the way in which PRODEM/ BancoSol have fitted in to the local capital market. All questions of impact will be deferred to the following two sections.

In Table 10.7 we examine the time trend of the three key elements of cost, borrowing cost (i), administrative cost (a) and default (p), as a proportion of the value of the total portfolio over the short time period that PRODEM/BancoSol have been in operation. It is notable that the expected negative relationship between loan size and the total cost of credit (see, for example, Mosley 1993) is scarcely in evidence. Instead of a decline in arrears rates (part 4 of the table) as the banker 'gets to know his market' what we have is minuscule arrears rates from the very beginning,[11] which are the result of (part 3 of the table) very heavy and very effective investment in mechanisms for loan recovery. These administrative expenses, after a sharp early fall, remain unchanged between 1990 and 1992, while the cost of funds borrowed (line 2) rises with the gradual reduction of the subsidy element in BancoSol's funding, so that the total

10

cost of credit (line 6) actually rises between 1990 and 1992, whilst average loan size is actually rising quite sharply. There is an 'upward bump' in what is expected to be a smoothly downward-sloping long-run cost curve, essentially because both the cost of borrowing and administrative costs are subject to an exogenous upward shock intended to achieve the transition from bank to NGO. After this rude shock which persisted through to 1994 as the voluntary savings schemes grew and replaced more concessional sources of borrowing from institutions, the smooth downward progression of total cost is expected to be resumed, always assuming that nothing untoward happens to overdues (see note 11) or the international or local financial markets (see Table 10.7 and Figure 10.1).

It is, of course, impressive that PRODEM managed to register a 'profit' in its first year of operation, that it returned to 'profit' in 1991 in the middle of the transition to bank status and that the newly ordained BancoSol returned to 'profit' by end 1993. Yet the meaning of the phrase is different in each case. At its inception PRODEM enjoyed the advantage not only of concessional PL-480 loan finance at an interest rate of 7 per cent (against a market rate of 9 per cent) but also of grants[12] from the USAID local office, USAID central funds, USAID operating through the NGOs ACCION International and Development Alternatives and the Calmeadow Foundation of Canada, and the Bolivian Emergency Social Fund. At the moment of PRODEM's handover of banking operations to BancoSol, a range of institutions, listed

Table 10.7 PRODEM/BancoSol: elements of cost as proportion of value of portfolio

	1988	1990	1992	1994	1996 predicted
1 Value of portfolio ($m)	0.4	2.4	7.0	14.0	24.0
2 Costs of funds borrowed (% of portfolio)	5.2	7.6	9.7	16.8	14.5
3 Operating expenses	37.5	22.9	22.8	17.9	14.1
4 (a) Amount overdue	—	—	1.4		
(b) (of which expected to be recovered)	—	—	1.3	—	—
(c) = (a) − (b) 'ultimate loss'	0.4	0.2	0.1		
(d) Loan loss provision	0.5	0.3	0.2	0.2	0.2
5 Other costs (taxes and miscellaneous)	0.5	1.0	3.4	3.6	3.2
6 Total cost of credit (2 + 3 + 4(d) + 5)	43.2	31.8	36.1	38.5	31.8
7 Memo item: average loan size ($)	168	220	322	352	382

Sources: PRODEM Annual Reports, Table 6; Inter-American Investment Corporation internal documents

11

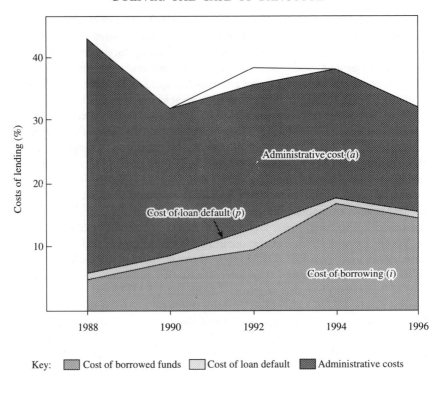

Figure 10.1 BancoSol: estimates of components of lending cost, 1988–96
Source: Table 10.7
Notes
1 Two alternative values of the cost of loan default are given for 1992; the lower one reflects the official loan-loss provision; the higher one, the actual rate of default (i.e. loans in arrears by more than six months).
2 The top line (the sum of i, a and p) should be seen only as an approximation of the total cost of borrowing. The precise value is defined by a non-linear relationship; see Mosley (1993).

in Table 10.4, took out equity stakes in the new bank, on which no dividend has so far been paid. An estimate of the degree of subsidy implicit in such operations is contained in the Subsidy Dependence Index devised by Jacob Yaron (1991), which blends together the elements of subsidy derived from below-market interest rates, concessionary equity stakes[13] and the provision of free services. On this measure, as shown in Table 10.8, PRODEM had a Subsidy Dependence Index which rose to nearly 200 per cent in 1989 and 1990 following the receipt of very large concessional grants in those years (see note 10), but then fell back sharply. If current profit forecasts are realised, the value of the index will be down to 12 per cent by the end of 1995, below (that is, better than) that achieved by BAAC in Thailand and

BKK in Indonesia, and only the bank's continuing access to concessional PL-480 credits will stand between it and the claim to be financially 'sustainable'.

A third potential indicator of the effectiveness of BancoSol in remedying market failure is the extent to which it was able to reach micro-entrepreneurs who had not previously been able to borrow from any other source. On this matter it is useful for the first time to draw on the results of our survey, the methodology of which is summarised in the following section. Table 10.9 shows, first of all, that the majority of BancoSol borrowers had not received, and indeed had not requested,[14] loan finance from any source.

Table 10.8a PRODEM/BancoSol: value of Yaron's Subsidy Dependence Index (%)

1987	74
1988	29
1989	198
1990	195
1991	68
1992	81
1993	12

Table 10.8b Comparative value of Yaron's Subsidy Dependence Index in other lending institutions (%)

BKK (Indonesia)		BRI unit desas (Indonesia)		BAAC (Thailand)		Grameen Bank (Bangladesh)	
1987	1989	1987	1989	1986	1988	1987	1989
23	32	5	−9	28	23	180	130

Sources: Table 10.8a: PRODEM/BancoSol Annual Reports; Table 10.8b: Yaron (1991: Table 4)
Note: The Subsidy Dependence Index is intended to be a measure of a financial institution's sustainability; it is the size of the percentage change in the on-lending interest rate which would have been required to eliminate all subsidies. It is calculated as

$$SDI = \frac{A(m - c) + (Em - P) + K}{Ln}$$

where:

A = value of institution's borrowed funds outstanding
m = interest rate the institution would be assumed to pay for borrowed funds on the open market, i.e. if access to concessional funds were eliminated
c = rate of interest paid by the institution on its average borrowed funds outstanding
E = average annual equity
P = reported annual profit (adjusted for loan loss provision)
K = value of non-interest subsidies received by the institution
L = value of institution's outstanding loan portfolio
n = institution's average on-lending interest rate

13

For those who had, the most popular source was borrowing from family and friends, followed by borrowing from other NGOs and traditional associations, from commercial banks and from moneylenders in that order. Such prior borrowing was almost entirely confined to the higher income groups within the sample. Within these higher income groups, however, *all* previous borrowing from family and friends had been done by women and *most* previous borrowing from moneylenders and commercial banks had been done by men. The picture which emerges is indeed that for the majority of the sample, including nearly all its poorer members, BancoSol did indeed unlock the door to the capital market; at higher income levels there was experience of previous borrowing but this was functionally divided by gender, with males doing most of the 'informal' borrowing. Many borrowers claimed not to know the interest rate they were paying, which may reflect the likelihood that in a situation known to be

Table 10.9 BancoSol borrowers: extent of previous borrowing by income and gender

Family income (Bs/month)	0–250	250–1,000	More than 1,000	Total
Previous participation in capital market				
No previous loan from any source	8 + 0	16 + 22	13 + 9	68
Loan from moneylender	—	—	3 + 2	5
Loan from commercial bank	—	—	0 + 6	6
Loan from other NGO including pasanaku[b]	—	—	8 + 0	8
Loan from family and friends	—	4 + 0	9 + 0	13
Total	8	42	50	100

Source: Author's survey, April 1993
Notes
Sample size: 45; $1 = Bs4.19 at time of survey.
[a] Figures in each cell are percentages of total sample; the number to the left of the + sign represents women and the figure to the right represents men.
[b] *Pasanakus* are traditional rotating savings and credit institutions.

monopolistic, the benefits from search aimed at finding the most competitive rate are likely to be relatively low.[15] A major contribution to the effectiveness of BancoSol in all of the senses discussed above was expected to be made by the device of requiring all borrowers to be members of 'solidarity groups' of between five and seven members. In a few cases (less than 10 per cent of those surveyed) these groups already existed in the form of traditional rotating savings and credit organisations (*pasanakus*)[16] but the size of BancoSol groups surveyed as shown in Table 10.10 was much smaller than the norm for a *pasanaku* and indeed smaller that the size intended by BancoSol itself, averaging 4.4 against a bank norm of 'five to seven persons'.[17] One-third of all groups surveyed did not meet at all 'except for casual encounters in the street'; but in the remaining two-thirds, attendance at group meetings was a very high proportion of the group membership. In twenty-one of the groups surveyed, or just under half, respondents claimed that there existed people either richer or poorer than themselves and in these groups, as shown in Table 10.11, there was a much higher likelihood that other group members would ask the respondent for financial help than in those groups where income was seen as being homogeneous. However, it did not follow from this – as has been argued *a priori*[18] – that 'non-homogeneous' groups are more likely to have arrears on their loans; indeed, the proportion of 'homogeneous' groups having arrears is slightly and insignificantly *in excess* of the proportion of non-homogeneous groups having arrears. What appears to be occurring is that in groups where intra-group income differences were significant, richer

Table 10.10 Characteristics of 'solidarity groups'

Average group size[a]	4.4
Average frequency of meetings (per month)[b]	0.9
Average proportion of members present at group meeting (per cent)[c]	65
Proportion of groups receiving:	
technical assistance (per cent)	17
assistance with voluntary savings mobilisation (per cent)[d]	34
Proportion of interviewees believing that:	
there are richer people in the same group (per cent)	16
there are poorer people in the same group (per cent)	27
everyone is in the same state (per cent)	57

Source: Author's 1993 survey
Notes
[a] Maximum = 6, minimum = 3.
[b] 24 groups met monthly, 7 fortnightly, one weekly and the remaining 16 did not meet 'except casually'.
[c] This figure covers all groups, including those which did not meet; 48 per cent of all groups reported that all members were present at every meeting.
[d] This excludes the compulsory savings mobilisation which is carried out to generate a loan insurance fund.

members were acutely aware of the need to help out if poorer members suffered a short-term fall in ability to pay; indeed, twelve out of the thirteen respondents who stated that there were poorer people in their own group also noted that other members of the group had asked them for help in occasional months of ill-fortune, and in nearly all cases had been willing to oblige them, sometimes by offering loans with a very short term (the period of a week was mentioned by two respondents). Respondents were explicitly asked about the strategy they would adopt if one member failed to pay his or her quota, but only two mentioned the possibility of taking a defaulter to court;[19] five mentioned moral pressure, but no fewer than ten suggested that any individual member's arrears problem was a group problem and better dealt with by a group meeting than by individual-to-individual pressure. In other words, although it certainly appears that the use of the group lending mode is enabling BancoSol to keep its arrears rates down, it is by no means obvious that effort put into creating homogeneous groups will necessarily pay off in terms of lower arrears rates. So strong is the sense of group obligation among richer group members to help the less well-off that any 'free-riding' which takes place appears to be rewarded through the medium of other richer members paying their share rather than countered by retaliatory measures leading to the break-up of the group. However, the share is itself often paid in the form of a *loan* to the group member who cannot otherwise pay, so we are not necessarily talking about altruism so much as a process which may well act to deepen intra-group inequalities as the price for keeping the group going.

Table 10.11 Frequency of arrears and 'requests for help' within groups, by composition of group

| Group type | Group performance | | | |
| | Has the group member been asked for financial help by other borrowers within his group? | | Does the group have arrears?[a] | |
	Yes	No	Yes	No
'Homogeneous' membership[b] (*n* = 27)	10	17	6	21
'Non-homogeneous' membership (*n* = 21)	12	9	4	17

Source: Author's 1993 survey

Notes

[a] 'Arrears' are defined as debts to BancoSol overdue for payment by 30 days or more.

[b] 'Homogeneous' groups are those where the group member interviewed denied that there existed others within the group richer or poorer than him (or her) self (question C-6 on questionnaire).

IMPACT ON INCOMES AND
PRODUCTION METHODS

In this section we seek to assess the direct impact of BancoSol lending programmes on the employment, technology and income levels of its borrowers. All of the results are derived from a survey of BancoSol borrowers conducted on 27 and 28 April 1993, already drawn on in the previous section, and we shall begin by describing this.

A sample of thirty-six borrowers was drawn from the register of the La Paz and El Alto offices of BancoSol. The sample frame consisted of six localities, four in La Paz and two in El Alto, and within each of these clusters a sample of eight borrowers was drawn at random. Of these eight borrowers, four would be 'old' borrowers (who had taken at least six loans from BancoSol) and four 'new' borrowers who had been approved for a loan but had not yet bought any supplies or equipment with it. The intention was that the 'new borrowers' would be able to act as a control group for the experiences of the 'old borrowers' whilst at the same time experiencing a higher level of motivation to answer questions than a completely extraneous control group.

A first estimate of the scheme's impact on income is given by Table 10.12: 91 per cent of borrowers had experienced increases in income since the previous year, and the effect was relatively more dramatic within the lower-income portion of the sample in the sense that nearly all (89 per cent) of this group experienced large (more than 50 per cent) increases in income, whereas the proportion receiving income increases of this size was only 28 per cent in the higher income groups. An income of 250 bolivianos per month is our best estimate of the Bolivian 'poverty line' in 1992,[20] and on this basis, just over one-quarter, or 29 per cent, of the sample crossed the poverty line between 1992 and 1993: the standard error for this sample is relatively low, at 17.5, and there is therefore only a 2.5 per cent chance that the income increase experienced by the population of BancoSol borrowers below the poverty line fell more than two standard errors below the sample average, in other words that it fell below Bs215. It is almost certain, therefore, that poorer BancoSol borrowers nearly doubled their monthly cash income between April 1992 and April 1993. It is, however, only a minority of BancoSol borrowers who appear to be below the poverty line as defined by INE.

The income changes over a time period recorded in the upper part of Table 10.10, in any case, do not necessarily imply causation, since they could have arisen from sources other than the BancoSol loan. To control for this it is useful to compare the income levels of experienced borrowers and those who have not yet benefited from BancoSol loans. This comparison (lower part of Table 10.12) suggests that experienced borrowers have income levels approximately $2\frac{1}{2}$ times as high as non-borrowers. This pattern of difference is reflected across all productive sectors except food trading, and a *t*-test suggests that the difference between the sample means is significant at the 95 per cent level.

Finally, it is useful to examine the range of incomes within the group or those borrowers who received their initial loan in a specific year – 1988. This is set out in the bottom part of Table 10.12. This part of the table confirms the impression given by part III that the ability to keep servicing a series of loans does not necessarily lead to a cumulative increase in income. Of those who took out first loans in 1988, 64 per cent were

Table 10.12 Loan impact on family incomes

I *'Before versus after'* [a]			
	Monthly income one year ago (Bs)		
	<250 [b]	250–1,000	>1,000
Income change since loan			
Decrease/no change	0	0	9
Increase/0–50%	3	25	17
Increase >50%	26	6	14
Average change since previous year	252	576	583
Standard error (Bs)	17.5	24.7	29.9

II *'With versus without'*		
Economic category	Monthly net income (Bs)	
	With	Without
Trade		
Food	876	787
Textiles	230	1,325
Other	320	2,000
Production		
Textiles	566	1,835
Other	962	2,633
Sample average	620	1,676
Standard error	290.9	570.5

III *Frequency distribution of current (1993) incomes for those borrowers receiving their first loan in 1988*	
Value of loan (Bs)	*Percentage*
Less than 600	41
600–1,200	23
1,201–3,000	23
More than 3,000	11

Source: Author's 1993 survey
Notes
[a] Figures in each cell are percentages falling within each category.
[b] That is, below the poverty line.

Table 10.13 Loan impact on employment

I *'Before versus after'*[a] Employment change since loan	Monthly income one year ago (Bs)		
	<250[b]	250–1,000	>1,000
Decrease	3	3	6
No change	22	26	11
Increase/0–50%	0	0	6
Increase >50%	0	6	27

II *'With versus without'* Economic category	Average employment levels	
	Recently approved borrowers (BancoSol loans, no previous)	Experienced borrowers (6 loans or more)
Trade		
Food	0	0
Textiles	0	1.2
Other	0	0.5
Production		
Textiles	2.0	2.4
Other	0.7	2.0
Sample average	0.7	1.4

Source: Author's 1993 survey

still, in 1993, below the sample average of just over Bs1,200 per month; 11 per cent had experienced spectacular income growth and now had monthly incomes over Bs3,000, and 23 per cent had above-average incomes of between Bs1,200 and Bs3,000 per month. Even these data give a rose-tinted picture, as they exclude those borrowers who go bankrupt and in consequence become ineligible for further credit. The data of part III of Table 10.12 are consistent with the verbal evidence of bank staff, which converged on the estimate that of any borrower cohort, about a quarter show spectacular growth; 10 to 15 per cent go bankrupt; and the remainder sustain their business at its existing level. Figures of this type need to be borne in mind when making financial projections based on an increase in average loan size over time, as will be done on pp. 27–8 below.

Table 10.13 examines the effect of BancoSol loans on employment, which interestingly turns out to be almost the mirror-image of their effect on incomes. Whereas large impacts on income were commonest amongst the poorer borrowers (with incomes below Bs250) increases in employment are literally non-existent among this group, which, on balance, actually had a small tendency to *shed* labour. Large increases in employment (large, that

19

Table 10.14 Loan impact on technology

I Quantitative analysis by economic category	*Experienced borrowers: % carrying out technical change with previous BancoSol loan*
Trade	
Food	None
Textiles	20
Other	20
Production	
Textiles	66
Other	14
Sample average	26

II Examples of technical changes came about with the help of BancoSol loans (number of cases)	
Mechanical cutting tools replaced by electrical	3
Purchase of sewing machine	4
Purchase of vehicle	2

Source: Author's 1993 survey

is, in relative terms: no enterprise surveyed here had more than six employees) were initially confined to richer micro-entrepreneurs with family incomes in excess of Bs1,000 per month. The 'with versus without' figures in part II of the table confirm that experienced borrowers had higher employment levels than those recently approved for loans. The general impression emerging from Table 10.13 is that any injection of capital made into a microbusiness is only used to take on labour *after* that business has grown to a certain critical size, which appears to be around Bs1,000 per month; before that point increases in employment in the microbusiness sector, and their consequent poverty-reducing effects, are *not* to be expected.

Table 10.14, finally, considers the extent to which BancoSol loans were used to implement technological change, defined as an alteration in the type of capital goods used by the micro-enterprise with the intention of raising productivity. As will be seen, only a quarter (26 per cent) of sampled borrowers used their loans to bring in new technology; such introduction of new techniques was heavily confined to the textile manufacturing sub-sector (which also took the largest loans) and was often associated with the replacement of hand-powered by electrical machines. In one case, the grant of a loan (again to a textile producer) was closely followed by the purchase of a taxi – a clear example of the exercise of fungibility by the client.

THE WIDER PICTURE

The economic and social impact of a lending institution is not confined to its effect on its customers, as examined in the previous section. Also relevant is its effect on the market for credit as a whole and in particular on smallholders' access to such credit; for the advent of an 'innovative' credit institution may lead other suppliers of credit to the same market either to increase or to reduce the availability or the price of that credit, and much depends on what their reaction actually is.

First, let us summarise the available evidence on the terms upon which credit is made available by informal moneylenders in Bolivia. As shown in Table 10.9, not many of our sample had used moneylender credit, but a high proportion were aware of its existence and its terms, and the general belief among both BancoSol staff and independent inquiries (Malhotra 1993) was that moneylenders existed within easy walking distance of all urban clients, although many rural clients would have difficulty gaining access to one. The price of their credit in La Paz and El Alto was generally quoted to us by both clients and moneylenders themselves at between 3 per cent and 5 per cent per month – in other words, highly competitive with the BancoSol rate, which is 4 per cent per month in local currency – although other sources cite

Table 10.15 BancoSol and informal moneylenders: transaction costs compared

| | BancoSol | | Traditional moneylenders | |
	Survey-based estimate	IIC estimate	Survey-based estimate	IIC estimate
(A) Direct financial costs	21	25	25	48
(B) Transaction costs				
Negotiation	9.1	—	9.6	—
Group information	5.6	—	—	—
Training	1.4	—	—	—
Total transaction cost	16.1	23	9.6	3
(C) Accessibility costs				
Travelling time	5.6	—	3.3	6
Asset pledge	—	—	20	20
Guarantee Fund Savings System	10	10	—	—
Total accessibility cost	15.6	10	23.3	26
Total cost (A + B + C)	52.7	58	57.9	77

Sources: IIC estimates from Inter-American Investment Corporation (1991); 'Survey-based estimates' from author's 1993 survey

Notes: All calculations are based on a US$200 two-month loan. BancoSol current interest rates are 4% per month in current bolivianos, and IIC estimates have been updated to use this figure. The survey asked for details of transactions and accessibility costs in loans and these have been valued at the level of the respondent's current cash income (average value: Bs5.41 per hour).

a much higher rate, going as high as 12 per cent per month or 200 per cent per year.[21] Our survey asked respondents to make an estimate of the non-financial costs associated with borrowing from both BancoSol and money-lenders, and the results are reproduced in Table 10.15 alongside a similar assessment by the Inter-American Investment Corporation made as a component of their initial appraisal of BancoSol. The two surveys concur that BancoSol has higher transaction costs than the moneylender (essentially because of the extra time occupied by training and group formation, and lower direct financial costs).

On accessibility, BancoSol emerges with a distinct advantage, but this is made up of several distinct components. There is little difference between the two suppliers on travelling time, but the cost which BancoSol inflicts on its borrowers by taking a compulsory deposit of 5 per cent of the value of the loan is more than counterbalanced by the asset pledge which money-lenders require of their clients, and which is clearly one of the reasons why many BancoSol borrowers were unable to take credit from moneylenders. Contrary to the standard picture which represents moneylenders as com-peting with 'quasi-formal' institutions like BancoSol in the market for small unsecured loans, all Bolivian moneylenders demanded collateral, often as a higher multiple of the loan than the commercial banks.[22] Taking all elements of the cost of borrowing together,[23] BancoSol emerges on the evidence of our survey respondents' evidence as slightly cheaper than the average moneylenders' terms, and on the evidence of the IIC survey it emerges as substantially cheaper. The difference between the two estimates is almost entirely due to a difference in assumptions about moneylenders' financial terms, as discussed earlier.

It may well be, however, that this difference reflects not just sampling error, but a systematic attempt by moneylenders to make their lending rates more competitive in areas where BancoSol is operative. It is important to know whether this is the case, and to shed more light on the matter. Ten moneylenders were interviewed, six of them in La Paz and four in El Alto. Each was asked what had happened to his volume of credit and his interest rate since the advent of competition from BancoSol (in La Paz from 1987, and in El Alto from 1990). The distribution of replies was as set out in Table 10.16. It suggests a general tendency for moneylenders to reduce their interest rates – sometimes quite drastically – and to increase their volume of lending when faced with competition from BancoSol, particu-larly in La Paz where, as we have seen, their competitive disadvantage in terms of transaction costs was greatest. Not only, therefore, did BancoSol confer the direct benefits to its borrowers recorded in Tables 10.12, 10.13 and 10.14, but also the indirect benefit of inducing moneylenders to make credit more cheaply and more generally available in a market previously characterised by oligopoly. The argument presented here can be clarified by reference to Figure 10.2, which owes some of its inspiration to the analysis of Indian informal credit markets by Bell (1990). Before the arrival of BancoSol, the market for small informal-sector loans was dominated by a group of moneylenders who, we may assume, were aware of one another's activities, and as consequence implicitly colluded to maximise joint profits: in Figure 10.2, this happens at a volume of lending OA, where the marginal

Table 10.16 La Paz and El Alto: moneylenders' responses to question 'How have your interest rates and volume of credit changed since 1988[a]?'

	La Paz (n = 6)	El Alto (n = 4)
Interest rates		
Raised	0	1
Kept the same	1	2
Reduced	5	1
Average change		
Volume of credit		
Increased	4	2
Kept the same	2	2
Reduced	0	0

Source: Author's 1993 survey
Note: [a] 1990 in the case of El Alto

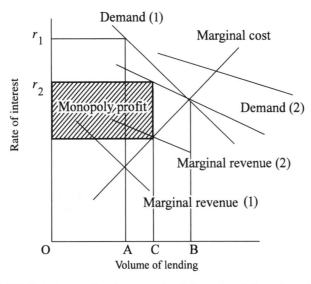

Figure 10.2 Bolivia: interaction between the informal and formal credit markets
Note: Demand (1) and Marginal revenue (1) are the relationships between price of credit, demand for credit, and supplier's marginal revenue which apply before the arrival of competition from BancoSol. Demand (2) and Marginal revenue (2) are the relationships which apply after BancoSol enters the market.

23

revenue curve intersects the marginal cost curve (and well short of the volume of loans where supply equals demand, which is OB), and a rate of interest r. When competition from BancoSol arrived, two things happened: first, the overall market for credit widened, at any rate at lower levels of borrowing cost, as a consequence of BancoSol's willingness to give loans without collateral; and second, demand became more sensitive to the cost of borrowing as for the first time it became possible for borrowers to exercise a choice among suppliers. The demand curve therefore rotated anti-clockwise, from Demand (1) to Demand (2). Marginal revenue now equalled marginal cost at a lower level of interest rate (r_2) and a higher level of output (OC) than that prevailing in the pre-BancoSol situation.

CONCLUSIONS

BancoSol's achievements during its short life of seven years are remarkable, particularly when one reflects that the premier 'poverty-lenders' in the world, the Indonesian BKK and BUD, 'took 10 years or more before the seeds produced flowers' (Boomgard *et al.* 1992: 15). In an atmosphere of national financial turmoil, an institution was created which aimed squarely at the urban poorest while charging commercial interest rates. It has grown faster than any institution of its type in Latin America, and has now diversified into deposit-taking and rural lending. Our survey work further suggests that it has had positive effects on incomes of the poor, employment and technology, and that its impact on the informal financial sector has been such as to motivate moneylenders to maintain their lending and cut their charges, thereby adding a 'multiplier' to the direct effects chronicled on pp. 18–19. BancoSol has now been widely imitated, and at a conference convened by it and its sponsors in April 1993 an 'Association for Sustainable Banking' was formed, whose members[24] – mainly NGOs involved in banking activities – committed themselves to adopt 'commercial' pricing policies and in most cases to incorporate themselves as banks on the BancoSol model.

In the process of these nine years, however, as with all successful institutions, a mythology has grown up around the organisation: for example, that it is entirely self-sustaining; that it has no arrears problems; that it invariably charges 'market' interest rates; and that all its loans go to very poor people.[25] The fact that none of these things is true should not blind the outside observer to the bank's extraordinary level of performance so far. But each of them raises a policy issue worth discussing at slightly greater length as it relates to the future policy decisions and expansion possibilities not only of BancoSol but of financial institutions for the poor in other developing countries.

Sustainability and 'market interest rates'

As Table 10.8 demonstrates, PRODEM (BancoSol) has throughout its life absorbed subsidy from international donors in the form of concessional lending, technical assistance grants and concessional equity. This rate of subsidy appears to be falling sharply, but much depends on performance matching expectations in 1993, and the level of subsidy is understated in the sense that everything that is experimental or not yet profitable about BancoSol – for example, its nascent rural operations – is intended to remain hived off within PRODEM, which is itself heavily supported by the international financial institutions and treated by them as a research laboratory rather than a commercial organisation.

There is a financial case for eliminating this subsidy immediately – for example, by raising the monthly interest rate to 5 per cent, which on the assumption of highly elastic demand would do the trick within 1993. Lending rates have, in fact, been frozen since 1991 'to build up confidence among depositors and borrowers during the transition period'[26] and the IIC, in particular, has been pressing both for higher average interest rates and for interest rates which vary according to the customer and the locality.[27] However, there is a more powerful economic case for retaining subsidy at a level determined by the level of external benefits which BancoSol confers on other institutions. To the extent that BancoSol is able to lower the costs of other banking institutions by providing them with information concerning which potential borrowers are good and which are bad lending propositions, or those of other non-governmental organisations by providing them with technical assistance which improves their efficiency, it creates an externality, and the economic optimum rate of interest will be less than the 'financial optimum', or profit-maximising, interest rate (Henderson and Khambata 1985). If the market worked well enough to enable the beneficiaries of such externalities to pay for the benefits which BancoSol provides by means of its pioneering activities,[28] the case for such subsidies would be weaker; but the market does not currently bring about this outcome, and until it does it is right that international donors should admit and defend the level of subsidy which BancoSol still receives, rather than pretend that it does not really exist.

Loan recovery, poverty impact and possibilities for expansion

The major premiss on which 'new' micro-enterprise lending practice has been based is that the exercise of commercial policies by lenders not only is compatible with poverty alleviation but may actively assist this process. Whereas BancoSol and several other institutions have achieved major success in both directions, this is not to say that the policy which maximises

25

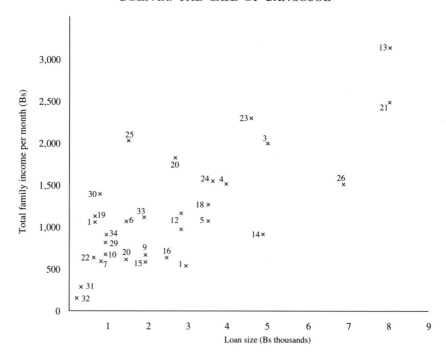

Figure 10.3 BancoSol: loan size in relation to borrower's family income

poverty reduction over any period is the same as the policy which max-imises profits. It is important, in conclusion, to get some idea of the extent of the trade-off between the two if BancoSol's possibilities for future expansion are to be assessed.

The crucial linking variable between the two is loan size. As loan size diminishes, the more attractive borrowing becomes to low income groups (Figure 10.3 for the BancoSol survey data); but as loan size increases, the lower become unit administrative costs, the higher, *ceteris paribus,* the margin that can be earned on lending. A group of AID consultants invited to consider the possibility of creating Indonesian-style 'village unit' banks under the BancoSol umbrella reported that:

> from our projections it is difficult for the units to be profitable unless [average] loan size reaches at least $500 unless interest rates or popula-tions are substantially higher. As loan size reaches $600 and above, units sharply increase in profitability.[29]

BancoSol's current average loan size is around $250. Any lender therefore has the choice between setting loan size so as to maximise poverty-impact and setting it so as to maximise profitability and future growth prospects, operating within the dual constraints that *some* poverty-impact must be

26

demonstrated and that sustainabiity must be achieved over a reasonable period.

To specify the optimum loan size in either sense requires us to make assumptions concerning the relationship between loan size, demands for loans, interest rate on loans and the default rate.[30] A formal model of the relationship between these variables is set out in Mosley (1993). If applied to Bolivia it yields the results depicted in Figure 10.4.

Poverty impact for a given size of lending programme peaks at a loan size of $100 and thereafter declines continuously, although it remains positive at any level, allowing for trickle-down effects. Profitability is negative, even allowing for 'commercial' interest rate policies, at a loan size below $200 and thereafter rises continuously, although levelling off at a loan size above $900. If we now introduce constraints of minimum profitability (say 5 per cent) and minimum poverty impact (say $200,000), these define a 'feasible range' of average loan sizes which in turn defines the range of acceptable options; given the parameters specified this goes from just under $400 to almost exactly $500. The optimum expansion path for the bank within this feasible range will depend on the relative weight it attaches to the two objectives, but unless it is completely heedless of poverty impact, it will not allow average loan size to grow to a point where such impact is insignificant or simply ignored, as it is in the consultancy report mentioned. The figures for 'graduation' of poor borrowers quoted above, with only 21 per cent of borrowers having doubled the real value of their assets five years later, warn

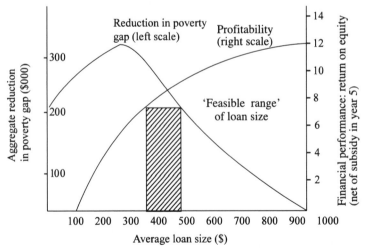

Figure 10.4 Financial performance and poverty reduction in relation to loan size
Notes
1 'Poverty-gap' is the sum of persons in poverty multiplied by the difference between their income and the poverty line (Bs250 per month).
2 Lending programme is assumed fixed.

us of the difficulty of expanding lending rapidly without deserting the originally specified target group. However, the voluntary savings scheme, now growing rapidly (Table 10.3), enables BancoSol to provide financial support to individuals currently too poor to borrow. There is now (June 1995) discussion of the possibility of creating a 'BancoSol 2', specifically for the requirements of 'graduating' clients who have grown through a series of loans and now need to borrow amounts in excess of $1,000 rather than the average $200–$500. So far, BancoSol has shown remarkable success at reconciling the objectives of growth and poverty reduction, and initial indications are that the experiment of extending its operations into rural areas is working well, although it is currently being consolidated rather than expanded; but nobody, even now, can know what kind of adult this remarkable seven-year-old will grow into.

NOTES

1 Comparative data are the following:

	Latin America	Developing countries
Under-5 mortality rate (1991)	57	101
Life expectancy (1991)	67	61
Per capita income (1990)	2,105	805

Source: United Nations, State of the World's Children, 1993.

2 Estimates of the number of tin miners made redundant vary; Chavez (1992: 6) puts the figure at 23,000 out of a workforce of 30,000, or about 80%, and Morales (1991) at 90%.

3 As a means of mitigating the social costs of adjustment, the Bolivian government, with the help of the World Bank and others, set up a number of relief funds, one of which, the Emergency Social Fund (ESF), has become famous through its practice of granting funds not to individuals but to entrepreneurs in the private and NGO sectors. There is no doubt that the effects of the ESF have been positive – and indeed have benefited poorer employees more than richer – but they have been mainly confined to the construction industry, and therefore to male beneficiaries (Newman et al. 1991). Another less-successful fund was the Fondo de Desarollo Campesino (Smallholder Development Fund): for discussion of this organisation, see below.

4 'En la cuidad de La Paz el 45% de la población tiene viviendas illegales' Presencia (La Paz, 18 April 1993, section 2, p. 10).

5 These are: the Banco Hipotecario Group; the BISA Group; the Banco Boliviano Americano Group; and the Compania Minera del Sur Group.

6 Although the Grameen Bank precedent was, of course, known when PRODEM began operations, the idea of a 'solidarity group' of flexible size comes from the quite distinct ACCION line of parentage. Micro-enterprise schemes involving 'solidarity groups' have been pioneered by ACCION in fourteen countries of Latin America since 1979.

7 Glosser (1993: 7).

8 In this respect, PRODEM was lucky. To set up as a bank in Colombia an

organisation requires paid-up capital of $15 million (personal communication, Lauren Burnhill, IIC).

9 With this new equity stake came additional conditionality (including, astonishingly, an upper limit of $35,000 on the size of loan that BancoSol was allowed to grant). This constraint will not bite for some time: maximum loan size is currently $5,000.

10 There is a risk, however, that the trend may appear sharper than it really is because of discrepancies between the classification of the earlier and the later survey.

11 However, arrears rates did rise to 2.05% in 1992 and averaged 4.03% for the first three months of 1993, in part as a consequence of difficulties associated with the opening of a new branch in Santa Cruz. These arrears rates are still low by comparison with those reported by other institutions in our sample, but the rise is worrying, as if not immediately stopped the possibility of default may get built into the expectation of borrowers. They are also inconsistent with loan-loss provisions of 0.7% and 0.3% for 1992 and 1993 respectively (see Table 10.6, lines 1 and 5).

12 Those we have been able to trace are the following (in US $):

		Loan	*Grant*	*Purpose*
1986	USAID via ACCION		150,000	Director salary and staff training
1986	USAID	410,000		PL-480 loan for credit fund and operational support
1988	Calmeadow Foundation		—	Technical assistance
1988	USAID	360,000		PL-480 loan
1989	Calmeadow Foundation		—	Technical assistance
1989	USAID		2,700,000	Donation to credit fund, operational support
1989	USAID	180,000		Capitalised interest
1990	Calmeadow Foundation			
1991	USAID through GEMINI		35,000	General and project support

13 Concessionary in the sense that no dividend is expected by the shareholders before the bank returns to profit, possibly in 1994.

14 The questionnaire contained a question 'Have you ever been refused a loan by any lender?' Only two borrowers – 4% of the sample – answered yes to this question.

15 Only a minority of borrowers knew accurately the interest rates they were paying.

16 *Pasanakus* are savings and credit groups of variable size, stretching up to thirty members as a maximum but more often numbering between seven and ten. The core of a *pasanaku* is usually an extended family. These are more common in the eastern part of Bolivia (around Santa Cruz) than in La Paz, and there is some anecdotal evidence that in La Paz they are larger than in Santa Cruz.

17 Glosser (1993: 3).
18 Mosley (1993: 18).
19 This is a more successful strategy in Bolivia than in many countries. In Santa Cruz (where BancoSol's arrears problems have been worst) it has often been possible to get a defaulting group member summoned to appear in court within a week of a case being lodged by the creditor (Interview, Pancho Otero, 20 April 1993).
20 The most commonly accepted definition of poverty (e.g. World Bank 1990) is an income level which allows a family to purchase 70% or less of a 'basic needs' basket of goods. On this definition the 1989 Integrated Household Survey (Government of Bolivia 1989) estimated the poverty line at 200 bolivianos per month, and on that basis, 51% of the employed population (including the self-employed) in Bolivia were beneath the poverty line in 1989 (Table 6). This 'poverty level' of 200 bolivianos of 1989 per month is equivalent, if indexed to the government's low-income price index, to 249 (say 250) current bolivianos per month in 1992. This accordingly is the concept of 'poverty line' used in Table 10. A more recent household survey (Government of Bolivia 1992) did not estimate a poverty line or levels of *rural* household income, but estimated that 21.5% of *urban* households were below this 250 bolivianos poverty line in 1992.
21 The rate quoted by Inter-American Investment Corporation (1991: annex) is 12% per month – which would approximate to 200% per annum for any borrower taking out a full-year loan. Malhotra (1993) quotes lending rates between 6 and 8% per month.
22 Malhotra (1993: 7) argues:

Unlike most informal financial arrangements which traditionally lend more on the basis of character than collateral, Bolivian informal moneylenders' collateral requirements equal or supersede formal bank collateral requirements, which average 2:1. Forty per cent of the lenders required a 3:1 guarantee to loan ratio; 20 per cent required a 2:1 ratio, and 40 per cent asked for 1.5:1. However, these moneylenders accepted different types of guarantees than the formal banks. For example, telephone lines (which cost $1,500) are acceptable collateral for a $750 or a $1,000 loan, depending on the collateral requirements of the lender. Other examples of commonly accepted collateral for loans under $5,000 are jewelry, vehicles, household electronic appliances, and in a few cases, personal cheques from a current account in a major bank or promissory notes.

23 It is not clear that all elements of cost have been included in the estimates of Table 10.13. The director of the El Alto office of BancoSol expressed the opinion, which was backed informally by several of the survey respondents, that the process of negotiation with BancoSol was a pleasanter and less humiliating process than negotiating with a moneylender, in part because it was governed by formal criteria rather than by person-to-person dependence relationships.
24 The conference was held in Santa Cruz, Bolivia, on 26–30 April 1993. There were representatives at the conference from Panama, Colombia, Argentina, Paraguay, Bangladesh (BRAC, examined in Chapter 12 of this volume), the Philippines, Nigeria, South Africa and Kenya (KREP), examined in Chapter 15 of this volume.

25   *Claims:*   *Contradictory evidence is presented here in:*
      Self-sustaining   Table 10.3 + note 11
      Market interest rates   pp. 10–14
      All loans to poor   Table 10.12

26 Interview, Miguel Taborga (Director of Finance, BancoSol), 29 April 1993.
27 Interview, Lauren Burnhill (Inter-American Investment Corporation), 15 April 1993.
28 There might, however, be a case for formalising the relationship between BancoSol and other Bolivian NGOs by allowing it to act as a channel for both money and formal technical assistance to NGOs, such as happens with KREP in Kenya (see Chapter 15).
29 Boomgard *et al.* (1992: 7). Boomgard and Patten are USAID-financed advisers to the Bank Rakyat Indonesia which sponsors the unit desa scheme.
30 The default rate comes into the story because if lending is expanded too fast, this may place a strain on loan-collection efforts and recovery rates. This appears to have happened with BancoSol (see Table 10.3 and note 11 above).

11

INDONESIA

BKK, KURK and the BRI
unit desa institutions

Paul Mosley

POLICY AND INSTITUTIONAL BACKGROUND

Economic background

The performance of the Indonesian economy over the last quarter-century has been remarkable, combining a per capita growth rate of 4.8 per cent between 1970 and 1991[1] with a reduction in the incidence of poverty from 60 per cent of the population to less than 20 per cent.[2] The development of its rural financial institutions has also been remarkable, providing what one commentator describes as 'the world's laboratory of rural financial market experiments' (Gonzales-Vega and Chavez 1992: 1). It is not impossible that these two facts are linked, and in this chapter we describe and, where possible, evaluate the contribution of three of these 'rural financial market experiments', namely the financial services offered by the Bank Rakyat Indonesia's unit desas (village units) and the BKK and KURK systems operated by the Development Banks of, respectively, Central and East Java. Each of these systems exhibits features not associated with successful performance in the other institutions examined in this study, such as state ownership and loans to individuals rather than groups. Furthermore, each of the systems studied here, as we shall see, underwent fundamental redesign in the course of its evolution: they did *not* produce healthy shoots on first appearance, and had they been impatiently torn up on that evidence, would not have yielded the fruit from which their customers and very many others now benefit.

My grateful thanks to the following for their advice and ideas: Professor Mohammed Arsjad Anwar, Jim Boomgard, Anne Booth, David Lucock, Richard Patten, Robert Rerimassie, Ichsan Semaoen and other staff of the Agricultural Economics Research Centre, Brawijaya, East Java.

Institutions to be studied in relation to national economic policy

The institutions studied here have their roots in the 1960s, a period of disequilibrium in both the economic sense (with 600 per cent inflation in the middle of the decade) and in the political sense, with an attempted communist coup in 1965. There was widespread despair among commentators of the time about the low level of agricultural productivity, prompting in particular Geertz's celebrated observation that Javanese peasant agriculture was doomed to experience 'involution', that is, the evolution of social mechanisms to share a stagnant level of subsistence output, and not technological dynamism in response to population pressure (Booth 1990: 1235). But at this time the incoming Suharto government initiated a pattern of fiscal conservatism, liberalised exchange rates and financial support[3] for 'key sectors', crucial amongst which was agriculture.[4] The terms of trade for agriculture were kept favourable by setting a floor price on rice and controlling the price of fertiliser to keep the growing of rice profitable. In addition, beginning in 1970, Bank Rakyat Indonesia (BRI), as the state-owned bank most involved with the agricultural sector, was mandated to channel the government's growing oil surpluses into creating a green revolution in Indonesia. An agricultural intensification programme (BIMAS, or Mass Guidance) was created, under which each 600–1,000 hectares of irrigated rice in Java and Bali and each 2,000 hectares in the outer islands was to be provided with, among other things, a new bank called the BRI Unit Desa (Village Unit), operating throughout Indonesia and intended to channel credit directly to participating farmers. The scheme was subsequently extended to cover other crops including maize, groundnuts, soya beans, sorghum and green peas. More than 3,600 unit desas were established throughout the country to service BIMAS credit between 1970 and 1983, most of them located in sub-district (*Kecamatan*) capital towns and serving on average eighteen villages. The government's combination of pro-agricultural policies (exchange rates, price support, subsidy, and directed credit) had by 1980 achieved not only the government's goal of self-sufficiency in rice, but also levels of agricultural productivity far ahead of those achieved in other green revolution countries.[5] To disentangle which of these policy influences was the key one is a major task and will not be attempted here, although the World Bank insists without proof that 'this was due to the favourable price incentives effected between 1976 and 1982, rather than to credit' (World Bank 1988: 6).

Like the Indian IRDP and the Malawi government's Smallholder Agricultural Credit Administration, BIMAS credits were provided primarily in kind, to farmers certified as efficient by the Agriculture Department's extension workers. While BRI, in principle, retained authority for loan approval there was major pressure from agricultural development officers

33

in the local administration to achieve lending targets, as in India and Malawi, with the consequence that many loans never received proper financial scrutiny. By 1984, unit desa overdue rates, which between 1970 and 1976 had never exceeded 10 per cent, had risen to 54 per cent (Table 11.4 below) and the system's losses, which before 1978 had never exceeded 2 billion rupiah ($1.8 million) had risen to Rp25 billion (Table 11.3 below). The number of farmers participating in the scheme fell by 60 per cent between 1975 and 1983, and according to Boomgard and Angell (1990: 5), 'those who remained in the programme were among the richest farmers who sought cheap credit and the poorest ones driven to borrow by their poverty'.

At this point the government of Indonesia, faced with falling oil revenues which had hitherto financed more than 60 per cent of the government budget, initiated a major liberalisation of the financial system under which Bank Indonesia (BI), the central bank, removed credit and interest rate ceilings and began to phase out the subsidised 'liquidity credits' which it provided to priority sectors of the economy.[6] It terminated a number of loss-making activities, including BIMAS (in 1984). Real interest rates on normal savings deposits[7] increased from 5.26 per cent in 1982 to 10.7 per cent in 1985, and nationally savings deposits more than tripled over those same three years (World Bank 1988: figure 1.2). For its part BRI, now free to set its own borrowing and lending rates and with external technical assistance from USAID, introduced new financial instruments for both savings (SIMPEDES) and lending (KUPEDES) through the unit desas; the distinguishing feature of the latter is that the unit desas may lend for any productive purpose, and as we shall see, agricultural lending now forms only a small part of their portfolio. The unit desa system is now highly profitable, and indeed since 1987 has yielded more than 30 per cent of the BRI's net income (Boomgard and Angell 1990: 31). The detail of the 1983–4 reforms has been excellently described from a participant's point of view by Patten and Rosengard (1991) and by Boomgard and Angell (1990).

The BKK and KURK systems both constitute initiatives of provincial governments – Central Java and East Java respectively – mediated through their respective provincial development banks (*Bank Pembangunan Daerah* or BPDs). The BKK programme (*Badan Kredit Kecamatan*, or sub-district credit agencies) was established in 1970 with the explicitly political objective of defusing potential subversion by providing economic opportunities for low-income groups through a programme of very small loans. It receives concessional credits from the Ministry of Finance through Bank Indonesia and from 1984 to 1992 from USAID under its Financial Institutions Development Programme. By 1975, there were units in all but six of Central Java's 492 sub-districts (*Kecamatan*) with each sub-district office having a network of between five and twenty village posts (*pos desa*), manned by travelling BKK staff once a week on average, usually on a local market day. Each BKK is a financially autonomous unit, and is shut down if it becomes insolvent; indeed, during the period which Goldmark and Rosengard (1983: 16) describe as 'survival of the fittest' between 1975 and 1979, 33 per cent of BKKs were closed down. And BKKs, being legally designated not as banks but as mere 'credit institutions', have from the start been able – indeed they were instructed by the Central Java BPD – to charge market interest rates (see p. 41 below). They were therefore treated as a 'special case' by the Indonesian government during its period of managed interest rates prior to 1983, and their period of major reform, unlike that of the BRI unit desas, came well before that. However, like the transformation of the BRI unit desas, this redesign involved a retreat from the agricultural sector, which now accounts for less than one-sixth of all BKK loans (Table 11.6 below).[8] Goldmark and Rosengard (1983: 48) describe this process as follows:

> To survive, the BKK program had to move out of the agricultural credit business. It only takes about three years for a BKK capitalised with 1 million rupiah (at that time, just over $1,000) to go bankrupt when seasonal loans are provided at the 2 per cent seasonal loan rate. Policy makers had intended to promote agriculture by providing farmers with low-interest loans; however, because these interest rates could not cover the risks of such loans, this policy almost caused the BKK programme to become bankrupt. The decision therefore was made to service off-farm activities that produced a steady cash income.

Does this process – which of course occurred in both BKK and the unit desas – reflect simply a failure to charge the right interest rate, or an iron law that credit programmes aimed at very small farmers always fail? The issue arises in many of the countries covered by this study, and it is of major importance to discover the answer. (A tentative answer is suggested below.) At any event, the reconstituted BKK system now trades profitably, although, as the next section reveals, it still depends, as the BRI unit desa system does not, on subsidised rates of interest. BKKs were granted permission to collect their own savings deposits in 1984, and BKKs have collected voluntary savings deposits over and above their normal practice of collecting a mandatory (and refundable) savings deposit of 10 per cent of the value of the loan.

Finally, the KURK system (*Kredit Usaha Rakyat Kecil* or 'Small Rural Credit') was established by the provincial government of East Java in 1979, in connection with the Provincial Development Programme funded by the Government of Indonesia and the US Agency for International Development. In the original design the employees of the KURK units – one book-keeper and one cashier for each village post – received no salary at all after the first year, as a device to keep down the fixed costs of the operation. Instead, they received a 4 per cent fee on any loan instalment or other cash inflows collected. They thus virtually fulfilled the Ohio School's dream of lending direct to the moneylender, the more so since the book-keeper (*komisi*) very frequently was a former 'traditional' moneylender now given the opportunity to legalise his position. The system grew in the first four years to 1,603 village units, but by 1987 45 per cent of these units were inactive, an unsurprising fact given that the East Java BPD was not able to provide substantial help with supervision. In 1987, the KURK units were incorporated into the USAID's Financial Institutions Development Project, and the 1,603 village-level units were consolidated into 222 entities with regular paid staff, operating at the *Kecamatan* or sub-district level, with village-level staff continuing to be paid on commission only; in other words, the structure of the organisation has evolved somewhat towards the BKK model. By 1992, the large majority of KURK units (215 out of 222) generated accounting profits, with an average return on assets of 16 per cent.

The structure of rural financial institutions in Indonesia

In Indonesia as a whole, the financial sector is dominated by a central bank (Bank Indonesia – BI) and five state-owned banks, each with primary responsibility for selected priority sectors.[9] Of these, however, only the BRI has responsibility for rural development at village level; there is a separate state bank, the Bank Bumi Daya (BBD), which finances plantation crops.

Within the rural areas, the system continues to be state-dominated right down to village level, but is complex, as portrayed by Table 11.1. One of the inevitable uncertainties in such a portrayal is that the activities of *private* moneylenders (*mendrings*) continue to be illegal under Indonesian law (Prabowo 1987: 8) and, in consequence, cannot be enumerated with accuracy. A now out-of-date sample survey of East and West Java by Prabowo and Sayogyo (1973) indicates that 46 per cent of the total sample are clients of state financial institutions or co-operatives, and of the remainder 'who do not have access to the formal credit market', about 30 per cent borrow from informal sources such as moneylenders or ROSCAs (*arisans*).[11] For want of better data these proportions have been assumed in estimating different institutions' shares of total loan volume in the final column of Table 11.1. From the table it is immediately apparent:

1 that in spite of the dominance of state-controlled credit outlets, there is competition at every level of rural credit provision in Indonesia. Indeed, under recent legislation known as PAKTO 88 together with Banking Law no. 7 of March 1992, the barriers to entry into rural credit markets have been further lowered: any institution able to demonstrate banking

expertise and put up initial capital of Rp50 million (about \$25,000) may now register as a bank in Indonesia. These requirements are low by international standards[12] and make the market for rural financial services more 'contestable' than ever. It is not clear, however, how effectively institutions at different levels (for example, the unit desa and BKK/KURKs) compete *with one another*, given the flexibility of their advertised product, and this issue will be taken up on pp. 54–5 below;

2 that the BRI unit desas have a very strong position in the middle of the rural credit market, with just over a third of all estimated rural credit flows (46 per cent if moneylenders and rotating credit societies are excluded). However, at the village level, institutions such as BKKs and KURKs are outnumbered, in terms of volume of loans granted throughout the country as a whole, by village credit institutions (BKD – *Badan Kredit Desa*), an institution inherited from the Dutch government, with surviving healthy remnants in some regions (East Java) but ailing in others. There are also village co-operatives (KUDs), providing an alternative to the generally individualistic orientation of credit in Indonesia;

3 what will, however, not be apparent from Table 11.1 is that, in spite of this profusion of credit-provision models and the openness of the market, the density of banking services in Indonesia is actually less than that obtaining in comparable, and indeed some poorer, countries of Asia: for example, populations per bank office in Indonesia are nearly twice those of India in rural areas, and nearly three times those of India in urban areas.[13] These data, together with the rapid increase in real per capita rural incomes in Indonesia since 1970, give reason to believe that scope still exists for a further widening and deepening of the country's rural financial institutions.

By way of introduction, it is necessary finally to discuss the role of external resources in Indonesia's financial development. Many of Indonesia's cabinet and state bank senior staff hold degrees from American universities, including one in particular (the so-called 'Berkeley Mafia') and, whether for this reason or otherwise, relations between Indonesian government institutions and the World Bank (at the macro level) and USAID (at the micro, or institutional, level) have been exceptionally harmonious and creative. The World Bank (which provided a \$100 million 'hard' loan for KUPEDES, and a series of adjustment loans in support of the government's financial reforms) had by 1986 grown so trusting of its economic policy as to be willing to grant it a \$500 million adjustment credit without policy conditions attached, a quite unprecedented move (Mosley *et al.* 1991: 105). And USAID, which had been supporting a regional development programme throughout Indonesia since the mid-1970s, has provided \$38 million at a highly concessional rate (forty years with ten years' grace: 2 per cent interest during the grace period, 3 per cent thereafter) for two separate

Table 11.1 Indonesia: institutional structure of the rural credit market

Level/type of institution	Ownership	Scope of operations	Loan size (Rp '000 1993)	Maturity	Collateral	Effective interest rate (%)	Type of borrowers	Number of loan approvals in 1992 ('000)	% of total loans outstanding[b]
Village									
Moneylenders (*mendrings*)	Private		200 max.	Up 6 months	Usually none	5–60 per month	Any		15.3
BKKs, KURKs, CDs	Provincial governments	Branch network; compulsory and voluntary savings	20–200 average = 80	Short-term, not exceeding 1 year	None	26–130 p.a.	Mostly rural traders	562[a]	3.8
BKDs, BKPDs, CDs	Local governments	Unit bank; compulsory savings	200 max. average = 40	Maximum of 10 weeks	None	25 for 10-week period	Mostly rural traders	710[a]	2.8
KUDs	Co-operative	Credit + savings	n.a.	Short-term	None	12	Rural manufacturers and traders	203	3.4
Arisans	Co-operative	Credit + savings	n.a.	Short-term	None	0	Any	n.a.	7.6
Sub-district									
BRI unit desas	State-owned	Branch voluntary savings	<5,000	Up to 3 years	Land, buildings, equipment	22–32 p.a.	Rural entrepreneurs and traders/a few farmers	992[a]	35.5
Bank pasar (market banks)	Private = 57% Govt = 34% Co-operative = 9%	Unit bank; voluntary	1,000 max. average = 735	1 year max.	Trading inventory, fixed assets	48–60 p.a.	Market traders	262[a]	26.1

Institution	Ownership	Structure/services	Loan size	Term	Collateral	Interest rate	Borrowers		
Pawnshops	State-owned	Unit bank; no savings	5–500	Up to 7 months	Consumer durables, jewellery	42–60 p.a.	Farmers	16,500[a]	5.0
District and province									
BPDs	Provincial governments	Branch network; voluntary savings and other services	150–3,370	Short, medium and long-term	Land, fixed assets	12–24 p.a.	Small and medium-scale entrepreneurs		
Branches of commercial and development banks	State and private	Branch network; voluntary savings and other services	No fixed ceiling	Short, medium and long-term	Land, fixed assets	12–33 p.a.	Public enterprises, medium and large-scale enterprises		
National									
Head offices of commercial and development banks; non-bank financial institutions in Jakarta	State and private	Branch networks; full banking and financial services	No fixed ceiling	Short, medium	Land, fixed assets	12–33 p.a.	Public large-scale and foreign enterprises		

Sources: Institutions named in column 1. Data for *artisans* and pawnshops are World Bank estimates

Notes
[a] 1986
[b] Excludes loans at district levels and above

projects, known as Financial Institutions Development I and II respectively: $22 million in 1984 to support the regional development banks in the replication (or improvement) of BKK-type systems in seven provinces of Indonesia, and $16 million in the form of an 'opportunistic intervention' (Boomgard's phrase) to relieve central government financial constraints in the expansion of the BRI unit desa system. The money was used not only to capitalise the systems but also for computers, staff training and technical assistance. A crucial aspect of the latter is that, again in sharp contrast to the position in other developing countries, it has been *demand-led* and *long term*. One description of the process by which the BRI unit desa system was turned from loss to profit in 1983–6 runs as follows:

> The Minister of Finance came to the Harvard advisory team in 1983 with the problem of the unprofitable unit desas and said, why don't you guys kick this one around. The Harvard team came up with an experimental solution within a few weeks, which eventually became the KUPEDES system.[14]

This willingness of the Indonesian government to treat foreign advisers as a think-tank – rather than as a last resort, a financial trigger or a scapegoat – is rare, and has had an enormous pay-off in terms of the ease with which quite complicated institutional reforms have been carried through. And the willingness of Indonesian government agencies and USAID to enter into a long-term relationship has reduced the costs associated with staff turnover and possible instability of policy advice. In a quite different context Lele and Goldsmith (1989) have ascribed the Rockefeller Foundation's success in catalysing the green revolution in India, and its relative failure in doing so in Africa, to the relatively long-term relationships which were formed in India between Indian agronomists and the foundation's own technical assistance personnel; it may well be also that similar conclusions for the success of external support for institutional reform may be extracted from the Indonesian experience. This point is pursued further on pp. 68–70.

DESIGN FEATURES OF CASE-STUDY INSTITUTIONS

The BRI unit desa, BKK and KURK systems have been selected for study here from the wide range of Indonesian rural financial institutions in Table 11.1 because (a) they are *prima facie* successful, and either actually or potentially may hold useful lessons for the design of financial institutions in other developing countries;[15] (b) they are relatively well documented; (c) they present a *diversity* of institutional models, albeit with some common features. Some of those common features have already been foreshadowed in Table 11.1: market interest rates, small loans rising progressively in size if repayment is prompt, initial sponsorship by state institutions followed by external technical support. Other distinctive features, however, vary across the three institutions studied, and are listed in Table 11.2.

Interest rates

Since 1983 the Indonesian government has allowed, and Indonesian rural financial institutions have taken advantage of, freedom to set their own interest rates, and the resulting room for manoeuvre has been described by Boomgard and Angell (1990: 63) as 'an absolutely essential precondition to the success of the system'. All the institutions studied here, although by no means all throughout Indonesia,[16] have taken advantage of it. With the BRI KUPEDES system, charges for credit are standardised, with one rate for loans of Rp3 million or less and another for loans in excess of Rp3 million.[17] In the BKK and KURK systems there are a variety of loan models involving payback periods ranging from twenty-two days to six months, repayment intervals from one day to six months, and nominal monthly interest rates from 2 per cent to 4.8 per cent,[18] a feature which has been praised as taking these institutions close to the flexibility provided by the moneylenders (Gonzales-Vega and Chavez 1992). The effective rates resulting from the variegated menu offered by the BKKs and KURKs range from 26 per cent to 130 per cent, but these of course only represent upper limits on the returns which banks actually earned from their lending: to the extent that there are either arrears or payment delays within the lending institution, actual returns will fall short of these effective interest rates. Indeed, as we shall see (pp. 47–55 below) the BRI unit desa system, which charged *lower* effective interest rates than the BKKs, earned a higher effective return on capital. All the institutions studied here, however, have charged highly positive real interest rates.

Collateral

In common with most of the institutions studied in this book, the BKK and KURK systems do not ask borrowers for collateral, which they are assumed too poor to be able to supply. Loan sizes are lowest of all in the KURK system, which may correlate with the fact that the system has the highest proportion of women borrowers (over 70 per cent). The BRI unit desas do require collateral to the extent of the loan; however (a) unit desa loans can be very small, with a minimum of only $15; (b) collateral does not have to be supplied in the form of land – many applicants use house plots, motor cycles or even consumer durables (Holt 1991: 10); (c) the threat to repossess and realise collateral is almost never invoked (Rhyne 1991: 8; Gonzales-Vega and Chavez, 1992: 8, 82), a fact which is known to borrowers and must reduce their perceived cost of transacting through the unit desa system. Indeed,

41

Table 11.2 KUPEDES, BKKs and KURKs: design features

	KUPEDES/ SIMPEDES (BRI unit desa)	BKKs (Central Java BPD)	KURKs (East Java BPD)
Loan size ($)			
minimum	15	5	5
maximum	2,700	550	550
average (1992)	625	38	30
Maturity	3–24 months (working capital loans) 3 years (investment loans)	3 months[a]	3 months[a]
Repayment frequency	Monthly	Weekly[a]	Weekly
Collection method	At branch office in *Kecamatan* principal town	At village office	Generally at village office, occasionally at borrower's door
Effective interest rate (%)	30	84[a]	84
Average range	22–32	26–130	26–130
Collateral?	Yes	No	No
Women borrowers (%)	24	55	27
Savings facilities			
Compulsory	None	Mandatory refundable deposit of 6–20% of loan value	Mandatory refundable deposit of 6–20% of loan value
Voluntary	Yes (balance must exceed Rp25,000 to earn interest)	Voluntary small-trade saver scheme (TAMADES) available in some BKK units	Voluntary savings scheme available in a few units
Borrower's eligibility	'Any productive enterprise'	'Any productive enterprise'	'Any productive enterprise'
Appraisal method	Collateral and assessment of business plan	Character reference from *Kepala desa*	Character reference from *Kepala desa*
Repeat loan eligibility	Linked to previous repayment performance	Linked to previous repayment performance	Linked to previous repayment performance

Table 11.2 Continued

	KUPEDES/ SIMPEDES (BRI unit desa)	BKKs (Central Java BPD)	KURKs (East Java BPD)
Performance incentives			
for borrowers	0.5% per month premium, refunded twice a month if all payments on time	5% of loan value refunded at loan maturity if all payments on time	5% of loan value refunded at loan maturity if all payments on time
for bank staff	Discretionary cash incentive for *village unit* staff (only) linked to profitability and growth rate of savings	Incentive payment of 7.5% of BKK's pretax profits	*For salaried staff:* incentive payment of 10% of KURKs pretax profits *For staff paid on commission:* entire income of staff member is linked to bank profits
for others	Incentive payment to *kepala desa* of 1.5% of BKK's pretax profits. Also 0.5% to subdistrict head (*camat*)		

Source: Sponsor banks as listed above
Note: [a] Average for scheme as a whole

data to be presented on pp. 61–3 below will suggest that the proportion of borrowers below the poverty line is (astonishingly) precisely the same in the unit desa and BKK systems and even that the proportion of landless and near-landless[19] borrowing from the unit desas, at 73 per cent, is almost as high as it is for the Grameen Bank of Bangladesh (Boomgard and Angell 1990: 34). Whereas, as we shall see, these statistics fall within the category of 'true but misleading', what is crucial, and not in doubt, is that the collateral requirement does not stop some very poor people from borrowing from the unit desas, and therefore fails to segment the market between these and BKK-type institutions. Many individuals, in spite of the large differences in loan terms, borrow from both.

Savings and 'insurance' facilities

The BRI's voluntary savings schemes have succeeded beyond all expectations, and as of December 1993 have just over 7 million savers – four times as many people as borrow from KUPEDES – and has accumulated Rp957 billion in client savings, or 113 per cent of KUPEDES loans outstanding. Nearly three-quarters of the resources available to the unit desa system derive from internal sources, and of these 60.2 per cent are savings deposits (Boomgard and Angell 1990: 13, updated). Interestingly, those branches which have a surplus of savings over lending come predominantly from the poorer parts of Indonesia: the provinces which are net savers are generally not on the island of Java while those provinces which are net borrowers are located, for the most part, on Java (Boomgard and Angell 1990: 15). The BKK and KURK systems, as previously described, demand a compulsory savings deposit of 10 per cent (on average) of the value of the loan, which is refundable on repayment of the loan. There is also a voluntary savings scheme, TAMADES, initiated in 1987, which it is intended to extend to all BKK and KURK units; however, at the time of writing (August 1993) the ratio of savings to deposits, although growing rapidly (Gonzalez-Vega and Chavez 1992: 272) was only 13 per cent and 24 per cent respectively (by contrast with over 120 per cent in the BRI unit desa system) and only a fraction of BKKs and KURKs actually pay interest to depositors on either voluntary or forced savings. The compulsory savings scheme of the BKKs and KURKs can be seen as a loan insurance premium, although it is never described as such: a loan-loss provision financed by the borrower rather than the lender. It has been deplored by Gonzales-Vega and Chavez (1992: 113) who argue that it discourages voluntary savings and requires two transactions rather than one. But the first of these problems could be removed by paying interest on voluntary savings deposits, and it will always be in the interest of an individual BKK or KURK manager, who is not 'insured' by his head office[20] and has no collateral to fall back on, to limit his exposure by demanding a loan insurance premium rather than depend on the growth of voluntary savings to do his insurance for him. Obviously the size of – and ultimately the need for – an insurance premium depends on the extent to which the loan supervision system is able to keep down overdues, and to this we now turn.

Appraisal, 'progressive lending' and loan supervision

In the BKK and KURK systems the process of loan approval is very rapid: the applicant fills in a half-page loan application form (see Appendix 1) or if he or she is illiterate bank staff fill it out. This form is then signed by the village headman (*kepala desa*) if he is willing to certify the applicant's good character.

Once approved, disbursement of funds usually takes less than a week. In the BRI unit desa system the application procedure is more complicated only to the extent that the borrowers must provide proof of collateral: in particular, the need for elaborate project appraisal is obviated by the fact that the loan may be for 'any productive purpose', with borrowing for consumption discouraged but by no means forbidden. Once a loan is approved (and initial loans are always near the minimum of the permissible range) larger repeat loans, if requested, are granted if and only if repayment performance on the previous loan has been satisfactory.[21] Finally, as in a majority of the institutions studied in this project, loan instalments are repaid at frequent intervals: the frequency varies according to the loan type, but the commonest pattern is for BKK and KURK loans to be repaid weekly in the local village post (*pos desa*) and for BRI unit desa loans, in spite of their name, to be repaid monthly in the BRI branch of the nearest *kecamatan* (sub-district principal town). In the KURK system it is not uncommon for the loan instalments, and indeed savings, to be collected literally at the customer's door, which reduces the borrower's but increases the lender's transaction costs. The data to be reported on pp. 66–7 below suggest that transaction costs within the KURK system compare favourably with the other systems discussed in this book. In general the three measures described – approval by the village chief, progressive loan amounts and intensive supervision – enable the screening and enforcement problems to be dealt with even in the absence of peer pressure and (in the BKK and KURK systems) in the absence of collateral as well. Particularly interesting is the way in which the making of a *public* commitment to repay a loan, which is what making a commitment in the presence of the village chief amounts to, substitutes for pressure to repay from the member of a 'peer group': an incentive to good behaviour is provided by the behaviour taking place, as it were, in front of the whole village.[22] Of course, if the system is to work the *kepala desa* needs to be committed to making it work; but then his commitment is made more likely by the fact that he is himself co-opted by a unique system of financial incentives to repay, which we now describe.

Incentives to repay

In Indonesian rural financial institutions incentives to repay operate at three levels. The borrower not only gets an increase in his or her credit limit for repayment on time, as previously described, but also an incentive for timely loan repayment, the magnitude of which is indicated in Table 11.2.[23] Second, a proportion of bank staff's take-home pay is dependent on the institution's performance; in the case of KURK staff paid on commission the proportion is 100 per cent. Third, not only bank staff but also those officials of the local administration whose screening of borrowers is crucial to the success of the loan (notably the *kepala desa*) receive a bonus proportional to the institution's pretax profits. In this way all those on whom the system depends receive an incentive to keep the system functioning as it was designed to function rather than to exploit it for their own personal benefit. These incentives to repay constitute the truly distinctive

45

feature of the Indonesian rural credit system studied here, and are the more remarkable for the fact that they have been designed and implemented by government bodies rather than by the invisible hand of the market. The question which naturally arises is the level at which these incentives should be set to optimise performance. The question is tackled formally in Appendix 2, and is only examined superficially here. In the case of the borrower and the village headman there is relatively little flexibility concerning the size of bonuses; village headmen, after all, have other responsibilities beyond credit administration, and borrowers can only be given incentives to repay to the extent that the banks which offer them still have break-even interest rates below those of their competitors.[24] But in principle there is no upper limit to the proportion of an employee's pay that can be made performance-related, and for some employees of East Java's KURKs (in the early stages of the project), there is salary only in proportion to the institution's earnings from loan repayments. The constraint to this process is the number of competent individuals who are willing to bear the risks associated with this form of payment: for if bank staff are risk-averse, they will leave for other jobs offering a more certain income if their average earnings from bank employment, net of the risk premium which they require, fails to match the certain salary which they could expect to receive in alternative employment. As the performance-related element in employees' pay rises, therefore, losses from loan default may be expected to fall, as depicted in Figure 11.1, but the salary which the bank must pay to compensate employees for their uncertainty of their income also rises. The 'optimum incentive', shown as point A in Figure 11.1, is that which minimises the sum of costs from these two sources: after this point is

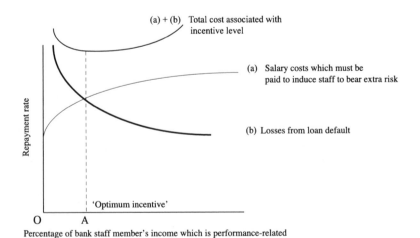

Figure 11.1 The optimum incentive to repay

46

reached the bank has to pay more in risk premia for its employees[25] than it gains from reduced default. But before this point is reached, the incentives provide their sponsor with a net dividend, which enables the Indonesian rural financial institutions to score over their counterparts in other countries.

INTERNAL EFFECTIVENESS AND 'ROLE IN THE MARKET'

In this section we examine the trend of costs and financial performance over time, and then proceed to examine the way in which the institutions under study have fitted into the local capital market. All questions of economic impact will be deferred to the next two sections.

Table 11.3 presents data on bank income, various components of bank expenditure, and profitability (essentially the difference between the two).[26] Each of the three banking systems has been consistently profitable in an accounting sense throughout the period under examination, which represents a remarkable turn-round for the BRI unit desa system.[27] Uniquely amongst all the institutions covered by this study, the BRI unit desas have since 1988 been profitable even net of the subsidies which they still receive on their long-term investment lending, from Bank Indonesia, in the form of concessional liquidity credits.[28] The BKK and KURK systems still receive highly concessional credits from their sponsor banks[29] and also technical assistance from USAID; as a consequence their 'subsidy dependence index', or percentage changes in on-lending interest rates required to eliminate subsidies, is positive for the BKK and KURK systems, even though it is negligible in relation to the subsidy currently provided to micro-enterprise and small-farm credit institutions elsewhere in the world.[30]

According to the hypothesis sketched out in Mosley (1993), the classical route by which a nascent rural financial institution traverses the 'knife-edge' between financial collapse and desertion of its target group is by gradually building up its loan size to trusted clients, so that in the process bad debts (p) are reduced (as a proportion of the portfolio) by the screening out of bad borrowers, and administrative costs (a) – and possibly even interest costs (i) – are brought down by an increase in average loan size. It is easiest to observe this process in respect of the BKK system, for which we have twenty years' more or less comparable data, as set out in Table 11.4. As average loan size rises, between 1972 and 1991, from \$9 to \$78 (or from Rp18,000 to Rp35,000 in terms of constant 1980 rupiah) administrative expenses, as a proportion of the portfolio, decline from over 20 per cent to 12.8 per cent and overdues from 7.1 per cent to 2.1 per cent. The cost of interest paid out to savers and the BPD *rises* over the same period from 0.5 per cent to just under 3 per cent, in part as a consequence of the BKKs' decision to accept savings during the later part of the period, but this trend

47

Table 11.3 KUPEDES, BKKs and KURKs: profitability, cost breakdown and subsidy dependence, 1985–92

	1985	1986	1987	1988	1989	1990	1991	1992
BRI unit desas								
Average loan size ($)	—	199	294	377	391	468		625
Interest income as % portfolio	28.9		38.7		35.9			
Expenses as % portfolio:								
Interest payment (i)	8.0		11.1		11.3			
Administrative expenses (a)	15.2		12.0		12.5			
Bad debts (p)								
long-term loss ratio	1.6		2.5		3.2	2.6	3.2	3.3
Profitability		2.7	4.8	4.9	3.6	3.5		
(return on average assets)								
Subsidy Dependence Index (%)			5.0		−9.0			
BKKs								
Average loan size ($)	52	57	62	66	75	103	157	133 (Jun)
Interest income as % portfolio	16.0	14.0	12.0	12.0	14.0	13.0	15.0	15.0
Expenses as % portfolio:								
Interest payments (i)	1.9		2.2		2.9			
Administrative expenses (a)	10.4		11.8		12.8			
Bad debts (p)	1.8		2.0		2.1			
Long-term loss ratio arrears rate	15.9	16.5	18.8	23.5	19.71	15.0	10.9	11.0 (Jun)
Profitability	8.3	7.9	6.2	1.6	4.0	6.8	7.3	4.5 (Jun)
(return on average assets)								
Subsidy Dependence Index (%)			23.0		32.0			

KURKs

Average loan size ($)	11	9	30	87	97	66 (Jun)
Interest income as % portfolio			27.0	26.0	23.0	37.0
Expenses as % portfolio:						
Interest payments (i)						14.0
Administrative expenses (a)						12.0
Bad debts (p)						
long-term loss ratio			9.7	12.7	14.9	17.3
Profitability				0.8	0.9	1.0
(return on average assets)						

Sources: All data are from the annual balance sheets and profit and loss statements of Bank Rakyat Indonesia (for BRI unit desas), Central Java BPD (for BKK) and East Java BPD (for KURK). For BKK and KURK the data have been abstracted from quarterly reports of USAID, Financial Institutions Development Project.

Notes

Administrative expenses (a) are defined as the sum of salaries and wages, administration, transport and depreciation.
Interest payments (i) are the sum of interest paid on borrowing from sponsor bank and interest paid on savings.
Arrears (p) are given in two forms:
  the *long-term loss ratio* is the ratio of cumulative overdues to cumulative lending;
  the *arrears ratio* is the sum of delinquent, doubtful and bad debts as a ratio of loans outstanding.
Profitability is declared pre-tax profits as a ratio of loans outstanding.
The *Subsidy Dependence Index* is a measure of the increase in the institution's on-lending interest rate which would be required to eliminate subsidies. For details of its calculation see note 30.

Table 11.4 BKK system: components of cost in relation to average loan size, 1972–92

Year	Average loan size				Components of cost		
	No. of BKK units	Current Rp '000	1980 Rp '000	Current US $	Interest paid to savers and BPD/ loans outstanding (i)	Administrative expenses (a)	Cumulative overdues/cumulative lending (p)
1972	200	4	18	9			7.1
1973	350	4	14	9			5.5
1974	432	5	18	12			4.9
1975	465	7	14	17			4.0
1976	486	9	16	22			3.7
1977	486	11	17	27			3.1
1978	486	14	20	31			2.5
1979	485	17	20	27			2.5
1980	485	26	26	41			2.3
1981	486	28	25	44	0.8	13.5	2.1
1982	486	34	30	51			1.9
1983	493	40	29	44			1.7
1984	496	47	31	51			1.7
1985	496	52	34	47	1.9	10.4	1.8
1986	497	57	34	44			1.9
1987	497	62	34	37	2.2	11.8	2.0
1988	497	66	33	39			2.4
1989	499	75	35	42	2.9	12.8	2.1
1990	499	103	46	55			
1991	499	157	51	78			
1992	499	133 (Jun)	38	64			

Sources: Development Bank of Central Java; deflator used to compile constant-price index in column 4 is the consumer price index as published in IMF, *International Financial Statistics*

is outweighed by the fall in administrative costs, so that the total cost of borrowing, administration and lending as a proportion of the portfolio falls over the period from 28 per cent to 17 per cent. It is notable that at the outset of the programme resources invested in administration (setting up *pos desas*, loan supervision, administration of the compulsory savings scheme, and so on) was far higher than the average reported for rural credit schemes by the World Bank, and no doubt as a consequence, the level of overdues even at the outset of the BKK scheme was *far* lower than the average.[31] The merit of this 'good start', from the BKK's point of view, is that in a majority of units it has quashed expectations amongst borrowers that they could get away with loan default.

For the BRI unit desa and KURK systems it is less easy to observe the long-term trend in components of cost, in the former case because KUPEDES is a relatively new scheme, only seven years old, and in the latter case because no reliable data for the KURKs are available before 1989. However, even over this relatively short time period it is possible to observe a decline in the administrative costs of the unit desa system as loan size increases over the late 1980s, a trend approvingly commented on in USAID's 1990 performance review (Boomgard and Angell 1990: 51). Arrears rates in the BPD and the BKK system, although not in the KURKs, are on a declining trend. Interestingly, by contrast with the position in other countries, there is no correlation whatever between gender and propensity to pay on time: across the BPD system as a whole, women account for 60 per cent of the borrowers and 60 per cent of the clients in arrears (Holt 1991: 13). The trend of the different components of cost over time is graphed in Figure 11.2.

It is notable that for both BRI and the BKK system subsidy dependence does not decline monotonically, but rises before it eventually falls, reflecting the fact that the principal external sponsor – USAID – did not become involved in supporting these schemes until they had established themselves (Patten and Rosengard 1991: 102). In relation to the other institutions covered by this study, this is similar to the experience of the Grameen Bank of Bangladesh but contrasts with the experience of the Kenya Rural Enterprise Juhudi Programme and PRODEM/BancoSol in Bolivia. Patten and Rosengard argue that this timing was crucial, but such an observation may distract attention from the role played by internal Indonesian government subsidy, which for both organisations was substantial until the 1980s, and for the BKK and KURK systems remains so. It is fashionable to rubbish credit subsidies in general (see, for example, von Pischke 1992; Adams and von Pischke 1992) and the BIMAS system in particular (see, for example, Patten and Rosengard 1991; Boomgard and Angell 1990) as undermining the screening function of credit programmes and providing a rent to rich borrowers. However, it is very possible that without the subsidised credit provided by the BIMAS programme, many poor

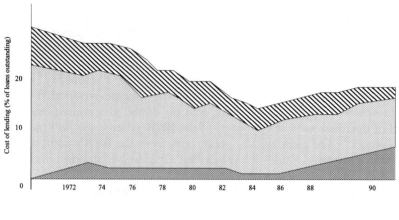

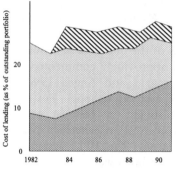

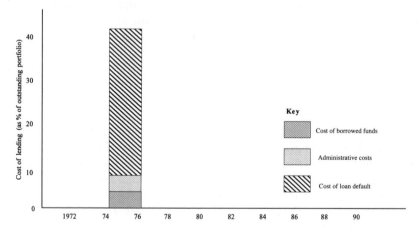

Figure 11.2 Time trend of intermediation costs for BKK, BRI unit desas and 38 developing-country credit schemes

Sources: Tables 11.3 and 11.4
(a) BKK
(b) BRI unit desas
(c) Average of 38 Third World Schemes (as reported by World Bank)

52

Indonesian farmers would not have been able to raise crop yields, providing the rural dynamism which underpins the crucial success of the unit desa programme; likewise the resources invested in the creation of the unit desa system in the 1970s must be seen as a hidden subsidy (hidden because its set-up costs are now written off) from the past to the present, which likewise is crucial to present success. The absence of anything like BIMAS in Africa in the 1970s or 1980s is one reason why credit institutions

Table 11.5a Proportion of borrowers 'new to the capital market'[a]

	BRI unit desa (1990)	BKK system (1983)	All FID-1[b] institutions (1990)	KURK system (1990)
No previous source of credit used	20	66	86	77

Table 11.5b Alternative credit sources for systems studied (%)

Source named by borrower	BRI unit desa (1990)	BKK system (1983)	All FID-1[b] institutions (1990)	KURK system (1990)
Rotating savings and credit associations	16	13	Insignificant	1
Co-operative	—	6	2	2
BRI unit desa	—	7	3	2
Moneylender	4	2	2	14
Neighbour, family	28	2	3	6
Private bank	2	1	Insignificant	Insignificant
Suppliers	30	—	1	1
Other government bank (including BPD-sponsored institution)	1	—	1	1
Other	—	2	—	2

Sources: BKKs (1983): Goldmark and Rosengard (1983: table 20); BRI (1990): Bank Rakyat Indonesia (1990: table 6); FID-1 institutions (1990): MSI/HASFARM (1990: table 3-19); KURK (1990): obtained from original questionnaires collected by MSI/HASFARM (1992). Data kindly made available by Dr Robert Rerimassie, Managing Director, P.T. Hasfarm Konsultan

Notes

Column totals may add to more than 100% on account of some respondents using multiple sources of credit.

[a] In response to question: 'Have you previously taken out loans for this business from other sources?'

[b] 'FID-1 institutions' consists of all rural financial institutions supported by USAID under its Financial Institutions Development Program. The category sampled by MSI/HASFARM (1990) includes BKKs and KURKs together with other systems of village banks in West Java and West Sumatra.

operating in Africa in the 1990s now experience such high fixed costs and such a relatively stagnant market.

Finally, it is useful to see to what extent the systems studied here substituted for existing sources of credit or alternatively were able to reach entirely new clients. Table 11.5 summarises survey results spread over a period of ten years, which show the proportion of borrowers from our three systems who at the time of survey were completely new to the capital market, and where the others got their credit from. It is apparent that the BRI unit desas serve as a point of entry to the capital market only for a minority of borrowers, as one would expect given the higher average loan sizes in which they deal. Rotating savings and credit institutions (known as *arisans*) are an important alternative source of credit for borrowers in all the systems studied here, and much more important than moneylenders. Some BKK and KURK borrowers make fairly substantial use of BRI credit, but the effect was less pronounced the other way about; finally, BRI unit desa borrowers also make substantial use of borrowings from suppliers and family members.

IMPACT ON INCOMES AND PRODUCTION METHODS

As a prelude to the examination of programme impact, it is useful to recall that both the BRI unit desa scheme and BKKs were switched midway through their evolution so as to divest them of much of their agricultural portfolio. As a consequence, as depicted in Table 11.6, their centre of gravity is now small-scale trade in rural areas, although this remains dependent on agriculture for its supplies, its market and indeed its survival.[32]

Table 11.6 Lending patterns by sector

	KUPEDES 16 sample unit desas (%)	BKK and KURK, 1990 sample survey (%)
Agriculture	7.4	13.0
Trade	68.1	70.6
Manufacturing	13.3	3.5
Services	2.4	8.0
Others	8.8	0.8

Sources: KUPEDES: Boomgard and Angell (1990); BKK and KURK: MSI/HASFARM (1992: table 3-42)
Notes
1 Includes agroprocessing.
2 This table gives details of 'principal activity' for which loans were ostensibly made. In practice, loans may have supported other activities. See note 8.

Incomes and employment

The impact of the three programmes studied here on family incomes and employment is compared in Table 11.7. Comparison is fraught with difficulty, since not only were the studies carried out over different time periods and different recall periods, but the study of BKK by Goldmark and Rosengard (1983) uses no control group at all, whereas the study of all USAID-supported village financial institutions works with a control group which is by its own admission flawed (MSI/HASFARM 1992: preface) containing (in particular) fewer women and less access to formal financial services than the borrower population as a whole. None the less, it can be said that across all the institutions examined there was a tendency for both employment and incomes to be increased in the period following the loan programmes to a greater extent than employment and incomes in the control group where one existed. The increases both in income and in employment are most dramatic in the BRI/KUPEDES scheme which reports a doubling of employment across the sample as a whole over the recall period (by contrast with the MSI/HASFARM study which suggests an employment increase of about 4 per cent per year for borrowers) and an average income increase of 20.7 per cent per year (by comparison with an increase in rural per capita incomes of 3.8 per cent across the same period). When the BRI unit desa sample is broken down by loan size (Table 11.8) the increase in household income is seen to be substantial across all loan size groups, but not to vary systematically by loan size. The largest increases in both enterprise and household income appear to have been obtained by borrowers operating just below the median loan (and income) level and borrowing between 250,000 and 100,000 rupiah.

Poverty impact

Before assessing the impact of specific programmes on poverty it is helpful to provide some background data about the distribution and definition of poverty in Indonesia, both contentious matters. Figure 11.3 gives the pattern of incomes by major occupational group and source for 1980, and shows that the poorest people in Indonesia are found amongst agricultural labourers and small operators owning less than 0.5 hectares; within the rural areas, as landholdings diminish so the proportion of income derived from labour increases, and the thrust of the rural finance institutions analysed here could reasonably be described as efforts to increase the capital base and diversify the income pattern of these poorer groups. The regional distribution of poverty is illustrated by Table 11.9; this shows that poverty in Indonesia is still highly concentrated in East Java (the target area of the KURKs) and Central Java (the target area of the BKK).[33] This regional distribution is correlated with the functional distribution of

Table 11.7 Family incomes and employment: summary of impact study findings

	BRI (KUPEDES)		BKKs	All FID-1 institutions		KURKs	
	Borrower group	Average all rural households	Borrower group	Borrower group	Control group	Borrower group	Control group
Recall period	Previous three years		'Since receiving first BKK loan'	Previous year		Previous year	
Investigator	BRI (1990)		Goldmark and Rosengard (1983)	MSI/HASFARM (1990)		MSI/HASFARM (1990); additional calculations by present author	
Control group?	No		No	Yes		Yes	
Family incomes: % whose income:							
had increased over recall period	—	—	88	41	26	30	26
remained the same	—	—	12	43	61	55	61
decreased over recall period	—	—	1	15	12	15	12
Average level at time of sample (Rp '000/month)	287	179	—	117	95	121	137
Average change (% per year)	20.7	3.8	—	5.2	2.4	3.9	2.1

Employment: % of sampled borrowers whose employment had:

increased over recall period	—	17	—	24	—
remained the same	—	82	—	64	—
decreased over recall period	—	1	—	12	—
Average level at time of sample	5.6	—	2.8	2.3	—
Average change (in person-years)	2.2	—	0.1	0.3	—

Source: Goldmark and Rosengard (1983: tables 24 and 26); MSI/HASFARM (1992: 78–81 and table 3-47); BRI (1990: table 4)
Notes: * Household income from enterprise only

Table 11.8 BRI unit desa borrowers: changes in employment and family incomes by loan size

	Loan size (Rp '000)				
	<250	*251–500*	*501–1,000*	*>1,000*	*All borrowers*
Sample size	35	51	54	52	192
%	18.2	26.6	28.1	27.1	100
Employment (persons)					
all workers	5.4	4.5	4.7	7.4	5.6
unpaid family workers	2.1	2.6	2.3	2.3	2.3
hired workers	3.3	1.9	2.4	5.1	3.3
Enterprise income (monthly)					
prior to loan (Rp '000)	52.3	82.4	165.9	234.3	141.1
annual change (in real terms) (%)	25.9	34.4	17.9	25.4	24.6
Household income (monthly)					
prior to loan (Rp '000)	124.9	159.1	267.1	383.6	244.0
annual change (in real terms) (%)	12.2	24.2	14.9	25.1	20.7
Wage share of enterprise income					
prior to loan (%)	17.3	23.1	21.9	7.8	13.6
Annual change (in real terms) (%)	11.4	−12.5	−18.2	−8.5	−7.4

Source: Bank Rakyat Indonesia (1990). Data extracted by Boomgard and Angell (1990) and reproduced as their table 5.2

Figure 11.3; it is in Java that the highest concentration of very small landholdings is found, with 60 per cent in East Java having less than half a hectare of land, by comparison with 47 per cent for Indonesia as a whole (IFAD 1987a: table 11.7). There is now outward migration from Java to the outer islands, which the Government of Indonesia actively encourages.

We now consider the poverty line which is to serve as a threshold. The Central Bureau of Statistics, on the basis of its own household expenditure surveys (usually referred to by their Indonesian acronym, SUSENAS) has defined a national poverty line for 1987 of Rp10,294 per capita per month, based on the cost of a daily 'necessary minimum' intake of 2,100 calories. This amounts to Rp57,852 at 1987 prices ($32) per household per month for an 'average' household of 5.6 people; about 30 million people, or about 16.4 per cent of the rural population, were below it in 1987. On that definition the percentage of BRI unit desa and KURK borrowers who fall below that line is close to the Indonesian rural average, but the percentage of BKK borrowers who do so is well above (Table 11.10).

Table 11.9 People in poverty and incidence of poverty, rural areas of the Indonesian provinces, 1980

Province	Total population ('000)	People in poverty ('000)	Incidence of poverty (%)
Central Java	20,387	12,594	61.8
East Java	23,223	13,713	59.1
West Java	21,315	7,312	34.3
D.I. Yogyakarta	2,131	1,465	68.8
Total Java	67,056	35,084	52.3
Other provinces	44,496	13,164	29.5
Total Indonesia	111,552	48,248	43.3

Source: IFAD (1987a: table 4.14)

Booth (1992: 637) has however argued that this line is 'extremely low' in relation to other countries in Southeast Asia, and indeed in other parts of the developing world, a statement apparently borne out by other component case-studies of this research project, all of which report rural poverty lines substantially higher than the Indonesian one.[34] To fix ideas and because important research on poverty impact has already been done using the SUSENAS poverty line, we shall begin by taking it as a datum, and then examine the sensitivity of the results to changes in that assumption.

We examine first data from the BRI unit desa system (Bank Rakyat Indonesia 1990: 7). The survey summary states that:

> Participation [in the KUPEDES scheme] is associated with both increased employment for hired workers in borrower enterprises and increased incomes for borrower families who were below the poverty line. For 1986, the average year that KUPEDES borrowers in our sample received their first loan, 15.1% of them fell below the poverty line. Thus, we can conclude that KUPEDES borrowers in our sample were not significantly different from the general rural population at the time they entered the programme. After an average three years of programme participation, however, only 4.17% of KUPEDES borrowers are still below the poverty line. While caution must be exercised in generalising from sample data to the national scale, it appears that an estimated 186,000 participating families have moved out of the seriously poor category.

However, these data take no account of dropouts from the survey between 1987 and 1990, and even if this problem is ignored, the sampling errors with a sample of 192 are such that the number of BRI borrowers who crossed the poverty line during the investigation period could plausibly be anything between 110,000 and 250,000.

We now consider the sensitivity of these assumptions to variations in the

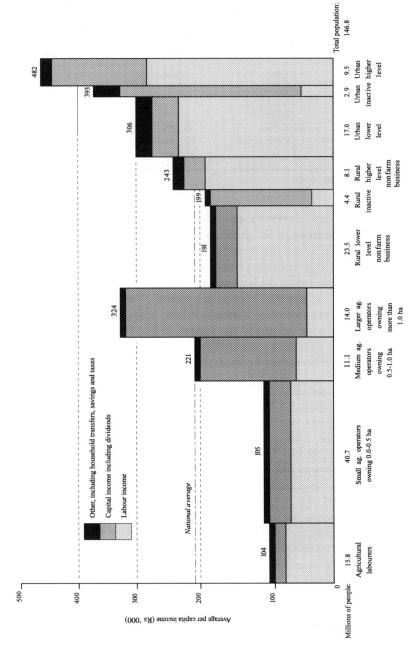

Figure 11.3 Indonesia: per capita income distribution, by household group and source, 1980

Table 11.10 Percentage of study population in relation to the poverty line

Bank: Sponsor:	KUPEDES BRI	BKK Central Java BPD	KURK East Java BPD
Percentage of target population: below SUSENAS poverty line in 1990	4.2	31.5	22.4
below $39 poverty line in 1990	6.6	38.4	29.4
Recall period	Three years (1987–90)	One year (1989–90)	One year (1989–90)
Percentage of sample (standard error in brackets) who crossed the poverty line during last year of the recall period: using SUSENAS poverty line	10.7 (3.9)	8.8 (2.7)	4.9 (2.9)
using $39 poverty line	8.4 (4.4)	6.6 (3.0)	3.3 (1.9)
Absolute numbers in target group who crossed the poverty line during last year of recall period (standard errors in brackets): using SUSENAS $32 poverty line	62,000 (23,000)	32,455 (15,108)	5,600 (3,300)
using $39 poverty line	48,670 (25,900)	36,932 (16,789)	3,753 (2,160)

Sources

Percentage below poverty line: BKK and KURK, MSI/HASFARM (1992: table 3-15, p. 47);
KUPEDES: BRI (1990: 7). Both studies use the SUSENAS poverty line of Rp10,294 per
month per individual in 1987 (Rp11,679 or $32 per household in 1990). For derivation of the
SUSENAS poverty line and comments, see p. 59. The alternative ('$39') poverty line is based
on the expenditure to buy 70% of a 'basic needs basket' of goods and services; for the
contents of this basket, see note 35.
Percentage who crossed the poverty line during sample period: KUPEDES: BRI (1990: table 5). BKK
and KURK: extracted from questionnaires used to compile MSI/HASFARM (1990) questions
502 and 504. For KUPEDES, proportions who crossed the poverty line between 1987 and
1990 are assumed to be evenly spread between the three years.

poverty line. Let us use as the definition of poverty not the SUSENAS
concept of a daily intake of 2,100 calories, but rather the United Nations
definition of 'an income level which allows a family to purchase 70% or less
of a basic needs basket of goods'. Using this definition and data on
household consumption patterns from the Central Statistical Office, we
reach a 1990 poverty line of $39 (Rp72,345) per household per month, or
$7 (Rp12,918) per individual per month.[35] If this poverty line rather than
the SUSENAS one is used as the benchmark, the proportion of borrowers
who crossed the poverty line shrinks to 8.4 per cent, or nearly 49,000

Table 11.11 Decomposition of poverty reduction in the BPD systems (BKK and KURK)

Bank: Sponsor:	BKK Central Java BPD	KURK East Java BPD
Average household income per month – whole sample	117,849	121,398
Number of sampled households with incomes below $39 (Rp72,345)	181 (38.4%)	71 (29.4%)
Average income increase (1989–90) for sampled households with income below $39 (Rp72,345)	12,963	1,478
Proportion of income *increase* (%) derived:		
from assisted business	60.8	52.8
from employment *outside* assisted business	31.5	45.5
from other sources (e.g. remittances)	7.7	1.7

Source: Calculated from data used to compile MSI/HASFARM (1990), questions 502 and 504

persons per annum: still a substantial number for an organisation not conceived as poverty-focused.

In Table 11.11 this analysis is repeated for the BKK and KURK organisations, examining only the income change between mid-1989 and mid-1990. On this basis, the proportions of the sample who crossed the poverty line in that year are slightly lower for BKK and KURK borrowers than for KUPEDES borrowers; furthermore, because KUPEDES borrowers are much more numerous the *absolute numbers* estimated to have crossed the poverty line are very comfortably highest for KUPEDES, the least ostensibly 'poverty-focused' of the three institutions. The sampling errors attached to these estimates, however, are such as to make comparisons of this type extremely hazardous. What appears to be not in doubt is that a significant number of borrowers were assisted to cross the poverty line by the organisations under study, although not so large a proportion of borrowers as in – for example – BancoSol and the Grameen Bank.

Not all the increases in borrowers' household income, of course, derived in the typical case from the assisted business; some came from other sources, including labour, secondary businesses and remittances. We did not have access to the questionnaires used to compile the BRI survey, but analysis of those used in the survey of BKK/KURK borrowers suggests that such 'non-assisted enterprise' income is significant and, indeed, may be more significant the poorer the borrower. We are reminded of the data in Figure 11.3 which suggest that the poorer the rural group studied, the higher proportion of its income which derives from the sale of labour services. The policy implication is that anything which can be done either by national government or by the lending institutions themselves to maximise the labour-intensity of assisted enterprises is likely to be poverty-reducing in its effect. We return to this issue in the concluding section.

It is finally necessary to stress that the relatively small proportions of individuals 'below the poverty line' reached even by the BKKs and the KURKs (top line of Table 11.10) represent an indication of the challenge, or alternatively the opportunities, which still lie in front of these institutions. Analysis of a 'control sample' of families who did *not* borrow from the BPD institutions in Central and East Java (that is, BKK and KURK) is presented in Table 11.12. It suggests that as income fell, the proportion in the category 'not having a loan but would like one' rises steadily, even though at the bottom of the income scale it is only 44 per cent. Not all of this 44 per cent, of course, are credit-worthy individuals; but it would be quite out of keeping with past experience if none of them were. What is much more likely is that the majority of them have been 'adversely selected' not to receive credit by the conventional banking system, and these are

Table 11.12 East and Central Java: sample of non-borrowers. Distribution of respondents by source of credit and household income level[a]

| Income bracket (Rp per month) | None | | Source of credit | | Other | Total |
	and does not want a loan	and would like a loan	Neighbour, friend or moneylender	BRI unit desa		
0–50,000	12 (31.5)	17 (44.1)	9 (23.3)	—	—	38
50,001–100,000	29 (39.1)	28 (37.8)	11 (14.8)	2 (2.7)	4 (5.4)	74
100,001–150,000	40 (39.6)	32 (31.6)	21 (20.8)	5 (4.9)	3 (2.9)	101
150,001–200,000	40 (48.7)	12 (14.6)	15 (18.2)	9 (10.9)	6 (7.3)	82
>200,000	12 (27.9)	—	8 (18.6)	18 (41.8)	5 (11.6)	43
Total	133	89	64	34	18	338

Source: Calculated from answers to questions 301, 302, 313 and 502 of USAID Rural Financial Institutions Loan Beneficiary and Household Survey. Blank questionnaire is reproduced as annex B of MSI/HASFARM (1992). New data kindly made available by Dr Robert Rerimassie, Managing Director, P.T. Hasfarm Konsultan

Notes
[a] Absolute numbers (percentage of row total in brackets).
1 Sample size = 338 interviews conducted.
2 Official (SUSENAS) poverty line for 1990 is Rp11,679 per individual (Rp65,402 for average family of 5.6 individuals).

precisely the individuals whom the BKK and KURK systems, for profitability as well as equity reasons, most need to supply.

Gender implications

As shown in Table 11.13, there is enormous variation across institutions in the frequency of women borrowers, with the ratio being lowest in the BRI unit desas and extremely high, at 72 per cent, in the KURKs. It is not, of course, the case that all loans are *used* by the person who takes them out; for example, in the BRI unit desa it quite frequently happens that the husband – in whose name the collateral is often registered – takes out a loan on his wife's behalf. None the less, the data in Table 11.13 do appear to reflect also a significant variance in access for women across the three systems, and this in turn appears to be due to:

1 *Transactions costs*: Systems with greater outreach to smaller villages appear to be ones that are most effective in reaching women. The majority-female systems, KURK and BKK, have respectively 7.6 and 5.9 village posts to every town unit. In contrast, the systems with fewer female clients (BRI and West Java) have lower ratios of respectively 0.2 and 0.1 to 1.[36] In addition, the BRI system, which requires collateral, is more complex and forbidding, albeit only slightly, than the BKK/KURK application procedure which requires only the filling in (often by a bank official) of a half-page form, reproduced as Appendix 1 to this chapter and a guarantee of good character from the *lurah*. The question of transaction costs is taken up further in the next section.

Table 11.13 Percentage female, geographical focus and loan size in the BRI and BPD systems

System: Sponsor	BKPD and LPK West Java	KUPEDES BRI	BKK Central Java BPD	KURK East Java BPD
Ratio of village posts to town units	0.1:1	0.2:1	5.9:1	7.6:1
Total number of borrowers	122,949	2,400,000	498,591	157,938
Percentage female	40[a]	24[b]	55[a]	72[a]
Average loan outstanding ($)	77	600	59	35

Sources: Development Alternatives (1993: attachment B); MSI/HASFARM (1990)
Notes
[a] 1990 sample data from MSI/HASFARM (1990)
[b] End 1992 data from Holt (1991)

2 *Loan size*: Across Table 11.13, and indeed across sampled villages as well, there is a strong and significant negative correlation between average loan size and the percentage of women borrowers. It seems very clear that women, although remarkably similar to men in the reasons they gave for preferring one source of credit to another, do lay more emphasis on being able to borrow small amounts,[37] especially in respect of their first loan.[38] (One element in this may be that women, who are heavily involved in expenditure decisions in Indonesian households, may wish to borrow for consumption more than men.[39]) As we have seen, small loans of this type are particularly easy to obtain from the BKKs and the KURKs.

THE WIDER PICTURE

It is clear that the institutions under study have exhibited better performance *both* in loan recovery *and* in reaching the poor than other formal financial institutions in Indonesia. The World Bank's (1988: xiii) review of Indonesia rural credit, for example, reported that:

> The KUPEDES and BKK loan programs have performed well compared to the KIK/KMKP and Bank-assisted tree crop credit schemes. Given the small loan sizes of the BKK and KUPEDES schemes, the absence of collateral requirement of BKKs, and accessible locations of the BKKs and BRI unit desas, they have provided wide access to credit for the rural population. In contrast, most KIK/KMKP lending has been in large loans to established entrepreneurs with proven experience. Small borrowers have effectively been screened out by banks that are unable to cover their lending costs by altering the administered price of credit. The loan repayment rates under the KUPEDES and BKK programs have been high. [By contrast] the low collection rates (40–70%) of KIK/KMKP and tree crop credit schemes have undermined their viability and sustainability. The dependence [of these programs] on low cost government funds has not provided any incentive for the banks to recover payments and maintain the financial viability of the programs.

We sketched on pp. 45–7 an answer to the question of how the BKKs and KURKs, themselves still dependent on 'low cost government funds', have been able to provide such an incentive. But our assessment of them cannot be complete until we have examined also their interactions with the informal end of the market for financial services: the moneylenders, savings clubs and other institutions that they were explicitly designed to replace.

First let us recapitulate the evidence concerning the terms on which informal finance is available to farmers and micro-entrepreneurs in Java. It will be recalled from Tables 11.1 and 11.5 that the principal sources of informal finance in Indonesia are (a) family and friends; (b) rotating savings and credit institutions (*arisans*); and (c) moneylenders, whose activities are illegal but who none the less thrive. There is some evidence that women borrowers are more dependent than men on these informal sources (Holt 1990: 22).[40] The first two of these credit sources charge no or extremely low rates of interest, and because of their informal procedures and closeness to the borrower, transaction costs are also low; it is, therefore, natural to take credit from these institutions rather than any other if it is available.

Table 11.14 BRI unit desas, KURKs and informal moneylenders: transaction costs compared (% per unit of principal per annum)

	See note	BRI unit desas	KURKs	Traditional moneylenders
Direct financial costs	2, 6	30	85	120
Transaction costs	3			
Negotiation	3	10	9	8
Obtaining necessary documents	3, 4	9	0	0
Total transactions costs		19	9	8
Accessibility costs	3			
Travelling time	3	10	5	3
Asset pledge	7	12	0	0
Interest forgone on compulsory savings	5	0	7	0
Total accessibility cost		22	12	3
Total cost		71	106	129

Sources: Survey of 30 borrowers in Samaan village (Klojen sub-district), Ngegong village (Mangunharjo sub-district) and Tingkis village (Singgahan sub-district), 19–20 August 1993
Notes
1 All calculations are based on a loan of Rp200,000 (⌐ $100). This is well above the average size for KURKs and well below the average size for KUPEDES (see Table 11.2 above).
2 For KURKs, average financial cost is that on a three-month loan (*mingguan*).
3 The survey asked for details of transactions and accessibility costs in hours and these have been valued at the level of individual respondents' cash income (*average* value: Rp638, or $0.31 per hour).
4 Documents are required only for BPI (KUPEDES) loans. They may include: business licences, insurance certificates, tax certificates, a mortgage or collateral posted, loan agreement certified by a lawyer, authority to sell collateral certified by a lawyer, and financial statements on the business to be supported.
5 In principle, KURKs (and BKKs) should pay interest on the second week's repayments, which are taken as an 'insurance premium' against default; in practice, such interest is seldom paid, nor can such compulsory savings be drawn on. It is assumed here that no interest is paid on such compulsory savings deposits: for some KURKs this will be inaccurate, and the cost associated with borrowing for KURKs will be *pro tanto* lower.
6 A quarter of this (the IPTW) is repayable at the end of the loan term if all repayments are made on time.
7 The notional interest that is forgone on financial asset (savings balance) of equivalent value to the collateral pledged.

The constraint is on the supply side: such sources may not be able to supply credit on demand in the needed quantity. For credit which is available instantly and can be spread over several months, the choices (recall Table 11.1) are: the informal moneylender; the BPD systems; the co-operative system; and (if collateral is available) the BRI unit desas. We now compare the terms on which their credit can be accessed. Table 11.14 presents estimates of average transaction costs for a sample of thirty borrowers spread across a range of villages in East Java in which the survey work reported in MSI/HASFARM (1990) had already taken place. It is immediately apparent that:

1 absolute levels of transaction costs are high even for those lucky enough to satisfy the criteria for borrowing from the unit desas. It is evident from the buoyant demand, however, that there is no shortage of projects offering a rate of return of 70 per cent per annum or more;

2 although the BRI unit desa system has lower *financial* costs, it has on average higher *transaction* costs on account of the greater distance of borrowers from bank staff (recall Table 11.12), the more complex application procedures and the need for an asset pledge;

3 although especially in East Java the transaction costs associated with KURKs are higher than those associated with borrowing from moneylenders (many *kecamatans* still do not have KURKs, and the village posts in those which do are only open once a week), the KURK still has an overall cost advantage over the informal moneylenders, on the evidence available to us, because of its lower financial charge for credit. However, this margin of advantage is being shaved on account of the recent adoption of more competitive charges by moneylenders to meet the challenge posed by the KURKs' invasion of their market. The fact that moneylenders have been induced to reduce their charges for credit in this way, whilst maintaining if not increasing their overall credit volume, must be accounted as one of the pecuniary external benefits arising from the creation of the BPD institutions.[41]

It should be noted that, because of difficulty of quantification, the above calculations omit two considerations which on the evidence of our interviews and those of others bear with borrowers: the likelihood that it is psychologically pleasanter to deal financially with an impersonal institution than with somebody you know[42] (who may in addition be in an oppressive relationship with you) and the fact that transactions with moneylenders are technically illegal, although in practice prosecutions for usury in Indonesia are extremely uncommon.

The BRI and especially the BPD-sponsored institutions, then, have already made an indirect contribution towards changing the terms on which access to financial markets is offered by suppliers other than themselves. Additionally, they have supplied an externality to rural lenders in Indonesia and other countries, not only by showing that the provision of financial services to the poor can be profitable, but also by showing how this can be achieved even without the conventional 'collateral substitute' of peer-group pressure. The range of performance-related incentives, in particular, have already been copied from BRI to BKK (in the case of the prompt repayment incentive) and vice versa (in the case of the staff bonus) and are just beginning to be diffused internationally.[43] Such diffusion cannot come too soon.

CONCLUSION

The evolution of Indonesia's micro-enterprise finance institutions, and KUPEDES in particular, lends itself naturally to analysis in puritanical and even moralistic terms. Collapsing oil revenues, on this interpretation, forced the Indonesian government to withdraw from the rural finance system an apparatus of subsidy and regulation which it could not afford; but necessity (together with a little friendly support from USAID) proved to be the mother of institutional innovation, and the results have been good for poverty relief and for profitability alike. The story has been described in this way, with an insider's insight but inevitably also with an insider's gloss, by Patten and Rosengard (1991), Snodgrass and Patten (1991) and by Boomgard and Angell (1990: 1) who describe the KUPEDES experiment specifically as 'one of the most ambitious experiments of modern economic development theory and practice'.

In many ways, this triumphalism is vindicated by the analysis of the preceding pages. The institutions reviewed here have created financially sustainable structures, opened the door to the capital market for many, created employment, and in the process reduced poverty. Further, they have influenced the terms on which credit is made available and the design of financial institutions in the wider economy both inside and outside Indonesia.

However, our analysis has also exposed worrying tendencies, specifically:

1 rising arrears within the KURK system (Table 11.3);
2 less than satisfactory progress with savings institutions in both the BKK and the KURK systems;
3 the fact that, both in the case of the BRI and BKK systems, loans to agriculture have had to be severely cut back to make the system viable;
4 a tendency for many very poor borrowers still to be unable to get credit, even within systems designed to help them (Table 11.12).

The first two of these tendencies has already caused anxiety to aid donors, and the USAID Financial Institutions Development Programme was unexpectedly terminated in June 1993. The euphoric tone of the late

1980s and early 1990s, well captured by Rhyne (1991) and Patten and Rosengard (1991), has vanished, at least as far as the BPD-sponsored schemes are concerned.

It is our belief that problems 1, 3 and 4 could be tackled by a simul-taneous policy of vigorously extending the network of village units (*pos desas*)[44] and *raising* interest rates on smaller (say, below Rp200,000) loans. The administration of loans from a village unit rather than from the individual would facilitate tighter supervision and bring down arrears, whereas the opening of new village posts would bring in savings, bearing in mind that 'closeness to home' of bank branch is the most important factor cited by rural Indonesians for saving in financial form.[45] At the same time, the raising of interest rates on the smallest loans is not likely to bring the BPD institutions up against a demand constraint, given that the available data (see, for example, Table 11.14) suggest that they still have a major transaction-cost advantage over the moneylenders. What it will do is to increase the unit profit which the lending unit can derive from making small loans rather than large, and, since there is a direct correlation between loan size and the poverty of the recipient, increase the profit which can be derived by lending to poor rather than middle-income people. And since in

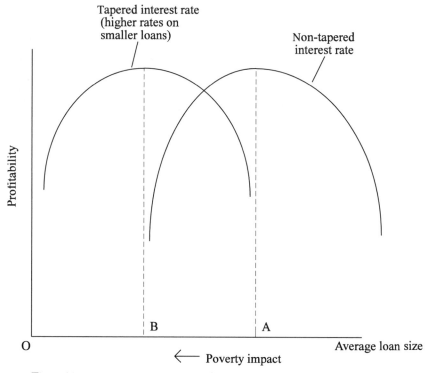

Figure 11.4 Interest rate taper, profitability, loan size and poverty impact

all the BPD institutions the staff and their helpers in the local administration are paid by results (Table 11.2), they too will receive an incentive to lend to the poorest. The general argument is conveyed by Figure 11.4. The more interest rates are tapered so that loan charges fall with loan size, the higher the profit margin on smaller loans will become, and the more motivated bank staff will be to make small (poverty-focused) loans, so that the 'optimum loan size' falls, for example from A to B on Figure 11.4. The advantage of an arrangement of this type is that it does not require any explicit poverty targeting, earmarking of funds or any other restrictive devices of this type; it simply uses the profit motive to bring about a *reduction* in average loan size rather than the secular increase – and inevitable diminution in poverty impact – which is observable in the unit desa system. It is not appropriate for the BRI unit desa system to go any further than it has with differential pricing; it has successfully found its market niche, and it is right for the BPD systems to stay as far away as they can from its competition and thereby intensify their poverty focus.

Such modifications might constitute a useful extension of an ambitious experiment now in progress for nearly a quarter of a century. The irony is that this experiment has throughout been sponsored by public-sector authorities at both national and local level. While private banks in Indonesia and elsewhere reward neither prompt repayment nor direct contributions to profitability, nor the provision of information which will assist the bank in its screening function, the public-sector authorities considered here provide incentives towards all three. In the circumstances, the common view that 'keeping government influence out of the business of lending to the informal sector is probably the most serious challenge that has to be addressed' (Salloum 1993: 10) is one that deserves re-examination.

APPENDIX 1   KURK LOAN APPLICATION FORM

[SFI Name:_____]

Borrower No._____

1 *PERSONAL DATA*

1. Name:_____	2. Status: M C B 3. Age:___ yrs
4. Address:_____	5. No. in household:____ persons
6. Employment:_____ 7. Land status: (i) Owned:___ M2 (ii) Used:___ M2	

2 *LOAN DETAILS*

3 *BUSINESS ACTIVITY*

2 LOAN DETAILS	3 BUSINESS ACTIVITY
1. No. of loans received:_____	1. Importance of activity: U S1 S2 other_____
2. Loan use code:_____	2. Turnover period: H M B other:____ months
3. Expected use of loan:	3. Income estimate per turnover:
a. _____ Rp._____	a. Sales Rp._____
b. _____ Rp._____	b. Expenses (−) Rp._____
c. _____ (+) Rp._____	c. Profit Rp._____
Total use: Rp._____	4. Wage expenses per month: Rp._____
Own contribution: (−) Rp._____	5. Total workers (i) In family_____ persons
Total loan: Rp._____	(ii) other_____ persons

AGREEMENT

_____   _____

Village Head   Borrower

4 *DECISION*

1. Rejection with reasons:	2. Agreement
	a. Loan amount Rp._____
	b. Interest rate_____ % per_____
	c. Loan term_____
	d. Loan repayment Rp._____ per____
	e. Collateral_____ Value Rp._____

_____

SFI Manager

APPENDIX 2 THE 'OPTIMAL INCENTIVE TO REPAY'

Introduction

What is unusual about the success of the Indonesian rural financial institutions studied here is that it was achieved within a context of lending to *individuals*. The best-known cases of schemes which achieve high repayment while targeting the very poor are group schemes (see Chapters 10, 12, 13 and 15) which can add peer pressure to the pressures to repay emanating from the lender. Individual schemes cannot do this, and in this volume we have reported a number of such individual schemes which have been unable to overcome the associated moral hazard problems (Bangladesh Krishi Bank, Indian Regional Rural Banks, Kenya Agricultural Finance Corporation, Sri Lanka's New Comprehensive Rural Credit Scheme). It would be more than useful to define what it is about the Indonesian schemes which sets them apart from others. In Table 11.2 we identified two incentives to repay which may provide the key:

1 loan size tailored to repayment performance on the previous loan (for details see note 21);

and, distinctively to Indonesia:

2 material incentives not only to borrowers who repay on time, but also to those members of the local administration who may be able (through the rigour of their loan screening or through subsequent informal pressure on borrowers) to influence by their behaviour the repayment performance of borrowers.

Of interest to those involved in designing financial institutions is not only how these incentives work, but how they could be optimised. Up to what point should they be pushed in different contexts? What counter-productive elements do they contain? Could they be adapted to provide not only an incentive to *repay*, but also to *reduce poverty*? These questions have not been investigated in previous writing on Indonesia and are only sketched in the main text above (see, for example, Figures 11.1 and 11.4). In this appendix we consider them formally, using a game-theory approach to examine the incentives operating on the lender to screen or on the borrower to repay, more or less effectively.

Theory

We examine the case of a development bank which is seeking to maximise net profit P, which is the difference between revenue E and costs C:

$$P = E - C \qquad\qquad [11.1]$$

The bank's revenue derives from loan income – the earning of interest r on that part of its portfolio $(1 - p)$ which is paid back – and non-loan income Y from sources such as asset sales and consultancy fees:

$$(1 + r) \sum_{j=i}^{n} (1 - p_j)X_j + Y \equiv E \qquad [11.2]$$

We may divide its costs, meanwhile, into four components: interest paid on borrowing i, wage costs w, other administration costs a, and non-loan expenditure such as training and outreach work z:

$$C = \sum_{j=1}^{n} (i + a_j + w_j)X_j + z \qquad [11.3]$$

An element α of wage costs is performance-related, i.e. indexed to the bank's overall profits, and probability of repayment p is sensitive to this proportion:

$$p = p(\alpha) \qquad [11.4]$$

Finally, both the interest rate r that the individual pays and the size of the repeat loan X which he or she gets (if any) are indexed to the repayment rate. Let us assume that this indexation, as in the case of the Indonesian BKKs and unit desas, takes the form of a discount d specific to individuals, such that for every individual j the interest rate $r_j = r - d_j$ and

$$d_j = \beta(p_j) \qquad [11.5]$$

whereas

$$x_{j(t)} = \gamma (p_j - 1) \qquad [11.6]$$

Notation

E   Bank revenue
C   Bank costs
P   Net profits (E – C)
p Proportion of bank's loans which are not repaid (default rate)
r Interest rate *charged* by bank on its lending
s Rate of return achieved by borrower on project
i Interest rate *paid* by bank on its borrowing
w Wage costs
a Administrative costs other than wages
α Performance-related element of pay

X   Loan size

β_j 'Discount' on interest rate received by individual j

γ_j Increment on loan size in previous period received by individual j

λ Percentage of loan repaid $(1 - p)$

Π Donor's expectation of loan repayment (i.e. his subjective forecast of p)

μ Recipient's loss of reputation from non-repayment

The bank's task is to set the staff incentive α, the borrower's incentive to repay β and the 'progressive lending' rule γ so that (in the first instance) they maximise profits P; at a later stage we shall consider other lender objectives, including poverty reduction.

In essence the lender is involved in two games, an internal one with his or her employees to persuade them to maximise supervision effort and an external one with the borrower to persuade him or her to repay. We consider these in sequence, but for the moment we shall simplify the first of these games by treating employee reactions as being predictable.

Payment by results (α)

First of all let us note, almost trivially, that under the assumptions so far made it is rational to increase the share α of the wage that is 'performance-related' without limit so long as that reduces the probability of default p.[46]

This requires us to focus on relationship [11.4], the nexus between the 'flexible' element in pay α and the repayment rate p. If it is continuously downward-sloping as in Figure 11.5a, then the condition that $\partial p/\partial\alpha = 0$ (Equation [11.1″]) is only satisfied at $\alpha = 1$, i.e. if *all* pay is performance-related. This was the solution originally adopted by the KURKs of East Java, for all staff in 1983, but it has subsequently been modified by allowing head office and regional office staff to receive fixed salaries subject to a performance-related bonus.

Is the assumption of a positive monotonic relationship between performance incentive and repayment probability (or as it is depicted in Figure 11.5a, a negative relationship between performance α incentive and default rate p) a reasonable one? The empirical data for Indonesia between 1989 and 1992, superimposed on Figure 11.5a, by no means confirm the hypothesis, in the sense that there is no observable relationship between the two variables, although it has to be remembered that in the real world many variables other than the pay structure (such as project rates of return and the level of bank supervision) determine repayment rates, and these may be 'disturbing' the partial relationship between repayment rates, and pay flexibility depicted in Figure 11.5a.

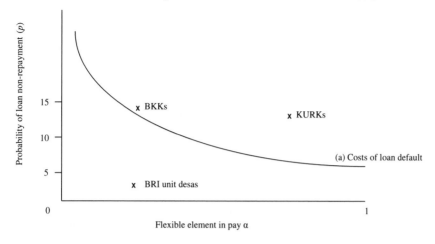

Figure 11.5a Possible relationships between pay flexibility and loan repayment – wage effects excluded

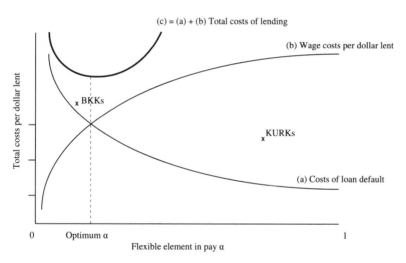

Figure 11.5b Possible relationships between pay flexibility and loan repayment – wage effects included

Even if these variables are held constant, a closer examination of the relationship between the performance-related element in pay α and repayment probability p suggests that it breaks down into two elements:

1 an influence of α on the efforts of staff to monitor loan performance and chase up such loans when they become overdue. Performance-related pay, in other words, acts as a deterrent to the moral hazard that bank staff

may get away with slack monitoring of loans. This effect is likely to be wholly positive (i.e., high α leads to high monitoring effort) although a saturation point may be reached before α reaches one, as in Figure 11.5a;

2 an influence of α on the stability and thence on the level of the average wage w. The reasoning runs as follows: the more staff are paid by results, the greater the instability of their earnings by comparison with their salaried counterparts; if they are even moderately risk-averse, they will demand a risk premium to compensate them for this increased instability.[47] This risk premium will push up the wage cost of lending w in [11.3], which now needs to be written as $w(\alpha)$. Once account is taken of the wage effect 2 the optimal performance-related element in pay α is no longer 1 unless staff are risk-neutral or risk-loving; it is that level of α which, as in Figure 11.5b, minimises the total level of costs associated with pay flexibility, that is, minimises the vertical sum of the 'loan default' and 'wage cost' curves.[48]

Borrower incentives to repay (β) and 'progressive lending' (γ)

Both of these are devices designed to increase the reward to the borrower from repaying rather than not repaying loans, and thereby encourage him or

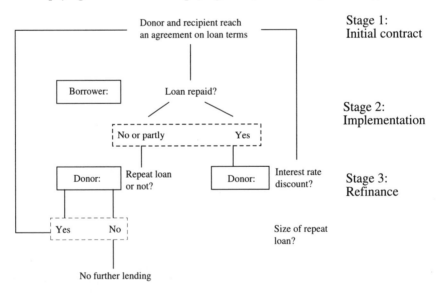

Figure 11.6 Incentives to repay and 'progressive lending': the game in extensive form

Note: The decisions which have to be taken at each stage, with the identity of the relevant actor, are in solid boxes. Information unavailable to the other actor is indicated in the dotted boxes.

76

her to repay in a situation where (because of the asymmetry of information about intentions between the borrower and the lender) the borrower may be tempted not to. The situation may be modelled in extensive form according to the game tree of Figure 11.6.

In principle the game may take place over an indefinite number of periods (and many BKK and BRI borrowers whom we interviewed had received over thirty loans from the same lender) but for analytical simplicity it can be visualised as a game in three stages which may or may not repeat themselves: initial agreement, implementation, decision on whether and on what terms to grant repeat finance. Henceforward, we refer to these stages as Acts I, II and III respectively. To gain a first foothold on the way in which incentives to repay may influence the pay-offs that may accrue to the two protagonists under different strategies, let us suppose that in Act I the lender makes a loan of standard size X at a standard interest rate r. In Act II the borrower receives a return s on the project which the loan is being used to finance and either (let us assume for the moment) repays the loan in full or not at all. In the event that repayment is not made, the lender either punishes this behaviour by refusing repeat finance, or not. The pay-offs in the absence of incentives are as set out in Table 11.15a.

It will be noted that in the bottom left-hand corner of the table the pay-offs for the case where the recipient does not repay the loan in Act II but the lender still provides a further loan in Act III (which we shall call the 'exploitative solution') are given in two different forms. This is because the lender's strategy of 'lending into the recipient's arrears'[49] is a gamble which may or may not come off in the sense of persuading the borrower to use the increased liquidity made available by the loan to pay back the arrears on the previous loan. The result of this gamble turns out to be crucial to the outcome of the game.

If it is successful, the game has a dominant strategy equilibrium in this bottom left-hand corner, since the lender has no incentive to deviate from the strategy *Refinance* and the borrower has no incentive to deviate from the strategy *Not repay* (the Act I loan) as long as $rx > \mu$, that is, the short-term financial gain from default exceeds any financial loss to the borrower from loss of reputation.[50] If however the gamble is foreseen as being unsuccessful the game has no equilibrium at all since the *Refinance* strategy is no longer dominant for the donor. In other words, under the assumptions of Table 11.15a the equilibrium of the game is either perverse, in the sense that it involves exploitation of the lender by the borrower, or non-existent. It is, of course, to prevent this kind of breakdown of trust and to channel the game into a stable '*Refinance, Repay*' equilibrium at the top left-hand corner of the table that incentives to repay were introduced in Indonesia. We now consider the circumstances in which they may be expected to work.

In Table 11.15b we introduce a premium β which, like the Indonesian

Table 11.15 Payoffs in the all-or-nothing repayment case

(a) Without incentives

Recipient strategies (Act III)	Donor strategies (Act II)	
	Refinance	No refinance
Repay 100 per cent of Act I loan	Act II Donor: $r\,x$ Recipient: $(s - r)x$ Act III Donor: $r\,x$ Recipient: $(s - r)x$	Act II Donor: $r\,x$ Recipient: $(s - r)x$ Act III Donor: 0 Recipient: 0
Not repay	Act II Donor: $-x$ Recipient: $s\,x$ Act III Donor: $-x$ or $r\,x$ Recipient: x or $(s - r)\,x$	Act II Donor: $-x$ Recipient: $s\,x$ Act III Donor: 0 Recipient: $-\mu$

(b) With incentives

Recipient strategies (Act II)	Donor strategies (Act III)	
	Refinance	No refinance
Repay 100 per cent of Act I loan	Act II Donor: $r\,x - \beta$ Recipient: $(s - r)x + \beta$ Act III Donor: $r\,(1 + \gamma)x - \beta$ Recipient: $(s - r)(1 + \gamma)x + \beta$	Act II Donor: $r\,x - \beta$ Recipient: $(s - r)x + \beta$ Act III Donor: 0 Recipient: 0
Not repay	Act II Donor: $-x$ Recipient: $s\,x$ Act III Donor: $-x$ or $r\,x - \beta$ Recipient: $-x$ or $(s - r)(1 + \gamma)x + \beta$	Act II Donor: $-x$ Recipient: $s\,x$ Act III Donor: 0 Recipient: $-\mu$

HAT or IPTW,[51] is refunded to the borrower in the event that a loan is paid back in full and on time, and an increment γ which is the percentage by which the borrower's credit limit in Act III is expanded in the event of successfully paying back the Act I loan.[52] These devices may secure the desired result of a dominant strategy equilibrium in the top left-hand corner of the table, but not automatically. The recipient will prefer to *Repay* as long as the net financial advantages conferred by the bonus and by the loss of reputation on the decision to repay $(\theta[\beta + \gamma x - rx] + (1 - \theta)\beta + \mu - rx]$, where θ is the likelihood of refinance and μ is the loss of reputation deriving from failure to repay) are positive. The lender will unconditionally prefer to *Refinance* if, in the event of the borrower implementing *Not repay*, his gamble of lending into the borrower's arrears is successful in eliciting repayment.[53] But we can already see the key determinants of the 'effectiveness' of the bonuses β and γ, apart from their magnitude: namely the interest rate r, the loss of reputation μ and the loan size X. These will re-emerge as crucial parameters when we come to calculate the 'optimal incentive to repay' on pp. 81–5 below.

It remains to introduce the possibility that the borrower, in Act II, will implement an option intermediate between zero and complete repayment. Let us specifically suppose that he or she chooses to repay a portion λ of the loan instalment due; the cases we have so far examined, total and non-repayment, are simply the points at the two extremes of this continuum, $\lambda = 1$ and $\lambda = 0$ respectively. The new pay-offs under this more general set of assumptions are set out in Table 11.16. By inspection of the final column it can be seen that the recipient will, if the donor chooses *not* to refinance, prefer total repayment if

$$\beta + \mu > \lambda rx$$

whereas, if the donor chooses partial or total refinance, the recipient will prefer total repayment if

$$\beta + \lambda x > \lambda rx$$

Hence the recipient will unconditionally prefer total repayment if

$$\theta[\beta + \gamma x - \lambda rx] + (1 - \theta)[\beta + \mu - \lambda rx] > 0 \qquad [11.7]$$

Meanwhile the donor, once again, will unconditionally prefer to refinance fully if and only if (in cells [7] and [8] of the table) such refinance is expected to be successful in securing repayment of previous lending[54] and the bonus for prompt repayment is less than the loan instalment due, that is:

$$(s - r)(1 + \gamma)x > \beta \qquad [11.8]$$

Conditions [11.7] and [11.8] between them constitute the requirement for the game between donor and recipient to converge on a dominant strategy equilibrium in cell [1] of the table, where the borrower always repays and the lender always refinances. As before, the incentives β and γ will be effective to a degree depending partly on their size and partly on determinants of the borrower's financial environment such as the interest rate, the loan size and the expected loss of reputation from non-repayment. As was pointed out in note 21, the 'progressive lending coefficient' γ varies between 50 and 100 per cent of the previous loan size according to the promptitude with which the previous loan was paid back whereas the 'incentive to repay' β is currently about 12 per cent in the BRI unit desas and 5 per cent in the BKK system. It seems more than likely that, set at

Table 11.16 Payoffs in the partial repayment case

Recipient strategies (Act II)	Donor strategies (Act II)		
	Refinance	Partial refinance (repeat loan, but no increase in size)	No refinance
Repay 100 per cent of Act I loan ($\lambda = 1$)	[1] Act II Donor: $r\,x$ Recipient: $(s − r)x + β$ Act III Donor: $r(1 + γ)x$ Recipient: $(s − r)(1 + γ)x + β$	[2] Act II Donor: $r\,x$ Recipient: $(s − r)x + β$ Act III Donor: $r\,x$ Recipient: $(s − r)x + β$	[3] Act II Donor: $r\,x$ Recipient: $(s − r)x + β$ Act III Donor: 0 Recipient: 0
Partial repayment: repayment percentage $0 < \lambda < 1$	[4] Act II Donor: $λ\,r\,x$ Recipient: $(s − λ\,r)x$ Act III Donor: $λ\,r\,x$ Recipient: $(s − λ\,r)(1 + γ)x$	[5] Act II Donor: $λ\,r\,x$ Recipient: $(s − λ\,r)x$ Act III Donor: $λ\,r\,x$ Recipient: $(s − λ\,r)x$	[6] Act II Donor: $λ\,r\,x$ Recipient: $(s − λ\,r)x$ Act III Donor: 0 Recipient: 0
Act I loan not repaid	[7] Act II Donor: 0 Recipient: $s\,x$ Act III Donor: 0 or $r\,x$ Recipient: $s\,x$ or $(s − r)(1 + γ)x + β$	[8] Act II Donor: $−x$ or $r\,x$ Recipient: $s\,x$ or $(s − r)(1 + γ)x + β$ Act III Donor: 0 or $r\,x$ Recipient: $s\,x$ or $(s − r)x + β$	[9] Act II Donor: $−x$ Recipient: $s\,x$ Act III Donor: 0 Recipient: $−μ$

their present level, these incentives play a vital part in ensuring that the Indonesian banks surveyed here, unlike most individual lending schemes, have high repayment rates. But could their efficiency be further increased by setting them at a different level, and if so, what criteria should be used to determine the size of the incentive? The next section considers these issues.

The optimal incentive to repay

We define the lender's optimal incentives to repay β and γ as those values of β and γ which maximise the lender's utility from the game depicted in Figure 11.6 given that the borrower is assumed to calculate his or her level of Act II repayment λ (or slippage $(1 - \lambda)$) so as to maximise his or her own utility.[55] We begin therefore by calculating the borrower's optimum slippage. We note from Table 11.17 that the recipient's utility from Act II can be generalised as

$$(s - \lambda r)X + \beta(\lambda) \qquad [11.9a]$$

whereas in Act III it is

$$\Pi(s - \lambda r)(1 - \gamma(\lambda)X) + \beta(\lambda) - \mu(\lambda) + (1 - \Pi)sX \qquad [11.9b]$$

where Π is the probability that any Act III refinance is used to pay off any outstanding loans in default, as discussed in cell [7] of Table 11.17.

The total utility which the recipient has to maximise across Acts II and III combined is then the sum of [11.9a] and [11.9b]:

$$V = (s - \lambda r)X + \beta(\lambda) + \Pi[(s - \lambda r)(1 + \gamma X\beta - \mu) + (1 - \Pi)sX] \qquad [11.10]$$

Differentiating this expression with respect to λ and setting it equal to 0 we have

$$\frac{\partial V}{\partial \lambda} = -rx + \beta'(\lambda) + \Pi[(s - \lambda r)\gamma x + \beta'(\lambda) - \mu'(\lambda)] \\ - r(1 + \gamma x + \beta - \mu) = 0 \qquad [11.11]$$

whence,[56] solving for the optimal level of repayment λ^*,

$$\lambda^* = \frac{\beta' - rx + s\gamma x + \Pi(\beta' - \mu' - r(1 - \gamma x + \beta))}{\Pi r \gamma x} \qquad [11.12]$$

Referring back to Table 11.17, we note that the donor's pay-off may be generalised as γrx for each of Acts II and III (recalling that if $\lambda = 0$, then the entire pay-off for that 'act' is zero); hence the pay-off for Acts II and III together is $2\lambda rx$. Substituting into this the recipient's optimal repayment percentage, λ^*, from [11.12], we have for the donor's maximand

81

$$W = 2\lambda^* rx = 2rx \frac{\beta' - rx + s\gamma x + \Pi(\beta' - \mu' - r(1 - \gamma x + \beta))}{\Pi r \gamma x}$$

[11.13]

whence, differentiating with respect to β,

$$\frac{\partial W}{\partial \beta} = \frac{(2rx + \Pi)}{\Pi r \gamma x} \beta'' - \Pi r = 0$$

[11.14]

Integrating [11.14] twice we have

$$\tfrac{1}{2}\Pi r \beta^2 - \left[\frac{2rx + \Pi}{\Pi r \gamma x}\right] \beta = 0$$

[11.15]

a quadratic equation which (if we disregard the negative root) solves for β as:

$$\beta^* = \left[\frac{2rx + \Pi}{\Pi r \gamma x}\right] + \frac{\left[\dfrac{2rx + \Pi}{\Pi r \gamma x}\right]}{\Pi r}$$

[11.16]

or in everyday language: the optimum incentive to repay is determined by the interest rate r, the donor's expectation Π of being able to claw back overdues by further lending to those who have already defaulted, and the coefficient of 'progressive lending' γ. If γ is already pre-determined (for example, by means of a rule such as that defined for the BRI unit desas in note 21) then this given value may be inserted into [11.16] to solve for the optimum value of the incentive to repay β. If, on the other hand, γ is free to vary, then the appropriate step is to differentiate [11.13] with respect to γ to derive an expression for the optimum value of γ:

$$\frac{\partial W}{\partial \gamma} = \frac{\gamma[sx - \Pi\gamma] - \beta' - rx + s\gamma x + \Pi(\beta' - \mu' - r[1 - \gamma x + \beta])}{\Pi \gamma^2}$$

[11.17]

which, after some rearrangements, once again yields a quadratic equation which can be solved as

$$\gamma^* = - \left\{ \left[\frac{2}{\Pi}s - 1\right]x + \tfrac{1}{2}\left(\left[\frac{2}{\Pi}s - 1\right]^2 - 2[r + \beta + \beta' rx - \Pi(\beta' - \mu')]\right)\right\}$$

[11.18]

so that the optimum values of β and γ are derived by solution of the simultaneous equations [11.16] and [11.18]. We shall work with this latter approach through the applications which follow.

We can solve [11.16] and [11.18] as simultaneous equations for the optimal 'incentives to repay' β^* and γ^*, if we are willing to make estimates of the key parameters which influence these solution values: the interest

Table 11.17 Actual and 'optimal' values of incentives to repay

Symbol	Meaning	Actual value	Optimal value US $	Optimal value % of loan value	Source
β	'Incentive to repay': proportion of loan which is rebated in return for 100% on-time repayment	0.12 (BRI system) 0.05 (BKK system)	42 4	0.12 0.11	Substitution in equation [11.16]
γ	'Coefficient of progressive lending': factor by which loan value is increased if previous loan was paid on time	0.5–1 (BRI system) 0.5 (BKK system)	282 3.1	0.47 0.69	Substitution in equation [11.18]
r	Interest rate on borrowing (% p.a.)	30 (BRI system) 84 (BKK system)	—	—	Table 11.2 above
x	Average loan size ($)	600 (BRI system) 38 (BKK system)	—	—	Table 11.2 above
Π	Lender's expectation that refinance will be used to pay back arrears on previous debt	0.9 (BRI and BKK systems)	—	—	Actual repayment data, see Table 11.3
μ	Value attached to loss of reputation if recipient is excluded from further borrowing from this lender	46 (BKK system) 600 (BRI system)	—	—	Value of average loan
μ', β'	Assumed zero since μ and β constant				

Table 11.18 BKK system: sensitivity analysis of 'optimal incentives to repay' to parameter changes

Impact of		'Incentive to repay' (β)	'Coefficient of progressive lending' (γ)
Interest rate on	up 25%	−8	−2
borrowing (r)	down 25%	+11	+3
Lender's expectation of	up 25%	−8	−2
borrower's repayment	down 25%	+11	+3
rate (Π)			
Borrower's expectation	up 25%	+4	−6
of loss of reputation (μ)	down 25%	−7	+6
Average loan size (X)	up 25%	+5	−9
	down 25%	−9	+12

Source: The values in this table are obtained by substitution of the parameter changes listed in the first columns into equations [11.16] and [11.18] above. They are expressed as percentage deviations from the 'base run' consisting of the current values for the BKK system as expressed in Table 11.6 above.

rate *r*, the average loan size *x*, the rate of return *s*, the expectation of loan repayment Π and the loss of reputation μ. The first two of these can be taken from current data for the institution under study (Table 11.2 above); the lender's expectation of loan repayment Π is estimated at the average arrears rate of the institution under examination; the value attached by borrowers excluded from further borrowing to 'loss of reputation' μ is assumed to be the average value of one loan from the institution under examination. The rate of return, *s*, is arbitrarily set at five percentage points above the rate of interest *r*. Using these estimates, the current values of the 'optimal incentives to repay' β^* and γ^* are as set out in Table 11.17. According to these data the BKK and KURK systems could benefit from stepping up the β incentives from 5 to 11 per cent of the loan value and the γ incentive from 47 to 69 per cent of the loan value, whereas the BRI system has its γ incentives about right but would benefit (in terms of current cash flow) from a *cut* in its β incentive. In general, as we shall see, when the coefficient of progressive lending (the γ incentive) is stepped up, the optimal level of the incentive to repay, or β incentive, declines very slightly. Table 11.18 gives estimates of the sensitivity of the optimal β and γ incentives to changes in the key parameters listed in Table 11.18. In general, the optimal values of the incentives β and γ rise, the lower the lending interest rate and the smaller the lender's trust in the borrower Π (formally, his expectation that, in the absence of incentives to repay, further lending would be applied to the repayment of overdues). The response of β and γ to loss of reputation μ and to average loan size X is more complex: as loss

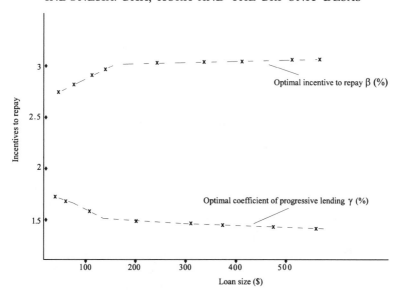

Figure 11.7 Optimal incentives to repay β and γ in relation to loan size

of reputation and loan size increase, optimal γ (the coefficient of progressive lending) diminishes, but optimal β (the bonus for on-time loan repayment) rises. This latter effect is of particular importance, since loan size is likely to be inversely correlated with the poverty of the borrower,[57] and the best way of simulating the effects of an attempt to enhance poverty-impact for any given institution is to imagine a sharp reduction in loan size with an associated increase in loan administration costs and therefore in interest rates.

Figure 11.7 illustrates the relationship between actual and optimal β and γ as average loan size is varied. As loan size is expanded from $30, the average size for the KURKs, to $600, the average size for BRI unit desa loans, the optimal progressive lending coefficient γ falls from 0.69 to 0.32; the optimal incentive to repay β rises from 11 to 12 per cent of loan size or from $40 to $42 on a loan of average size. At low loan sizes, an expansion in loan size is the most effective method of expanding profitability; a high level of γ automatically secures such expansion, hence its high optimal value when loan size is small, as it has to be in institutions lending primarily to the very poor. As loan size expands, it becomes necessary for optimum effect to increase the incentive to repay β, in part to counteract the 'temptation' which is conveyed by a rapid increase of loan size. But this incentive to repay does not itself benefit from being expanded without limit; beyond a certain point, which we have sought to identify, it adds more to the lender's costs than it adds to revenues by combating moral hazard.

85

Conclusion

We have sought to analyse how, in a situation such as that prevailing in Indonesia where lending to the poor is mainly to individuals rather than groups, a system of material incentives to borrowers and bank employees can none the less help to defend lenders against the predicament of asymmetric information against which they (usually) cannot defend themselves by taking collateral. We have visualised borrower and lender as seeking to optimise their pay-off from a game which has many analogies with the classical 'lemons' model (Akerlof 1970) in which the quality of the good or service being traded is unknown to one of the parties. But unlike the buyer of a used car in that model, lenders such as the Indonesian BKK and BRI do have a sanction against moral hazard, namely the potential loss of 'reputation', that is, creditworthiness, which a defaulting borrower will incur in future periods. This loss of creditworthiness, which we have characterised as μ, is reinforced by the judgement of the *lurah*, the local official who has to countersign all applicants for BKK and KURK loans as being of good character and who is himself co-opted into the system by being paid a 'performance bonus' which is dependent on the level of the BKKs' and KURKs' profits. In many ways, the performance incentives which we have characterised as β and γ are nothing more than an attempt to add to the weight which this potential loss of reputation occupies in the calculations of loan recipients. The incentive α, meanwhile, constitutes an attempt to maximise the effort which bank staff put into combating the threat of default by linking their pay packets to bank profits, which are at least partly a result of that effort.

A measure of the success of these devices is that nowhere else in the world has a scheme for lending to low-income individuals without collateral been financially viable on a long-term basis. This in turn has prompted the present investigation into how such devices can be used to maximum effect. It has illustrated that, effective though such devices are, they all have their costs, which are different in each case: risks to the labour supply in the case of α; a straightforward financial cost in the case of β; increased exposure to default in the case of γ. For each incentive, therefore, there is a 'golden mean' level, which we have sought to quantify in the case of β and γ in Indonesia. Such estimates, are of course, sensitive both to the specification of the model and to the assumptions made in calculating its parameters, and further research on the effectiveness of such incentives both in Indonesia and in other environments is therefore badly needed.

APPENDIX 3   GLOSSARY

BI	Bank Indonesia – the Indonesian Central Bank
BIMAS	Bimbangan Massal (Mass Guidance) – the Indonesian rice intensification programme
BKK	Badan Credit Kecamatan (sub-district credit institution), financed by Central Java BPD, *q.v.*
BPD	Bank Pembangunan Daerah (Regional Development Bank)
BPR	Bank Perkreditan Rakyat – institution licensed to trade as a bank since the new banking regulations of 1988
BRI	Bank Rakyat Indonesia (Indonesian People's Bank)
Desa/Kelurahan	Village/neighbourhood (the former in rural areas and the latter in urban areas)
HAT	Hadiah Angsuran Tepat Waktu (rebate for timely BKK loan repayment)
Kepala desa/lurah	Village/neighbourhood chief
KUPEDES	Kredit Pedesaan Umum (General Rural Credit), financed by BRI, *q.v.*
KURK	Kredit Usaha Rakyat Kecil (Small Rural Credit), financed by East Java BPD, *q.v.*
ROSCA	Rotating Savings and Credit Association (in Indonesian: *arisan*)
Rp	Indonesian Rupiah (August 1993: Rp2,096 = $1)
TABANAS	Tabungan Nasional – the national small savings programme

NOTES

1 World Bank (1993b).
2 World Bank, *World Development Report 1990*, p. 1.
3 Not only financial support; there was also widespread tariff protection and price control.
4 Patten and Rosengard (1991: 23) ascribe the origins of the BKK programme in Central Java (see pp. 33–5) to a desire by the provincial government to counter a potential communist threat by building up individual agricultural prosperity.
5 Grain crop output (kilograms per hectare), 1988–90 average:

Indonesia	3,843
India	1,861
Pakistan	1,744

Source: FAO *Statistical Yearbook, 1991*

6 These liquidity credits carried an interest rate of 3%. Some of them are still provided for specific agricultural and rural programmes, including BRI.

87

7 The rates quoted are for deposits of less than Rp1 million under the National Small Saving Programme (TABANAS).

8 However, note that it is very common for poor rural people in Indonesia as elsewhere to derive income from several enterprises. Borrowers from the BKKs and BRI unit desas are, however, required to fill in one enterprise on the application as the source of their repayments (see p. 71). They are advised to choose the one with the most stable cash flow – which is generally trade rather than agriculture, if the choice exists. Hence the figure of one-sixth given here may understate even the proportion of BKK loans which directly support agriculture – to say nothing of the ubiquitous indirect farm–non-farm linkages.

9 In 1986, the five state-owned banks controlled 72% of Indonesia's bank assets. The banks and their primary sectoral division of responsibility are Bank Bumi Daya (large farms and plantations); Bank Degang Negara (trade finance); Bank Export Import Indonesia (export credits); Bank Negara Indonesia 1946 (industrial finance) and Bank Rakyat Indonesia (agriculture, fisheries and co-operative credit).

10 Prabowo (1987: 1) accuses the Indonesian government of having 'attempted the eradication of some of the informal credit systems'. This can be seen as a more drastic version of the policy of the Reserve Bank of India in its rural credit market interventions, which was 'to provide a positive institutional alternative to the moneylender himself, something which will compete with him, remove him from the forefront and put him in his place' (Reserve Bank of India, *All India Rural Credit Survey* (1954: II. 481–2)).

11 This is broadly consistent with another more recent sample-based finding, that 57% of all Indonesian households borrow money from some source, while 43% report they have never taken loans (MSI/HASFARM 1992: 51).

12 For example, the minimum capital requirement to set up a bank in Bolivia is $3 million, and in Colombia $15 million (see Vol. 1, Chapter 7).

13 The data for selected Asian countries in 1988 are:

	Population per bank office	
	Urban	*Rural*
Indonesia[a]	18,287	40,220
Philippines	5,900	18,100
Thailand	9,826	20,278
India	16,910	23,449
Pakistan	6,910	22,497

Source: World Bank (1988: annex 1, table 14).
Note: [a] Outside Java.

14 Personal communciation, Richard Rosengard, USAID, 27 April 1993. The process of institutional reform in BRI is discussed, with inside knowledge, by Snodgrass and Patten (1991); but in spite of the publication date, they do not take the story beyond 1987.

15 For the application of the BRI unit desa model to the rural operations of BancoSol in Bolivia, see Chapter 10 above, and also Boomgard *et al.* (1992).

16 Schemes such as the World Bank/Indonesian government-financed KIK/KMKP scheme continued to lend at a flat 12% nominal interest rate (for a table of comparative lending rates, see World Bank 1988: II. annex 1, p. 7).

17 For loans of Rp3 million or less the rate is 1.5% per month, calculated as a flat rate on the original principal. For loans of more than Rp3 million 1.5% is charged, as before, on the first Rp3 million borrowed and 1% on the balance of

the loan, so that effective interest rates range from 32% for less than 3 million to 23% on a maximum loan of Rp21 million.

18 For the full range of BKK lending terms, see Patten and Rosengard (1991: 27, 37, tables).
19 Ownership of less than 2,000 square metres of land.
20 See discussion on earlier pages.
21 In the BRI unit desa system the linkage between loan repayment and subsequent loan eligibility is the following:

Rating	Criteria	Subsequent loan ceiling
A	All payments made on time	Increase of 100% over previous loan amount
B	Final payment on time, one or two late payments	Increase of 50% over previous loan amount
C	Final payment on time, two or more late instalments	Loan amount as for previous loan
D	Final payment late, but paid within his month of due date	Reduction of 50% over previous loan amount
E	Final payment more than two months late	No new loan

22 Village elders are also involved in certifying loans within the Indian Regional Rural Bank system but that this procedure has met with far less success.
23 This is described as IPTW in KUPEDES and HAT within the BKK system (see Glossary, Appendix 3); the HAT was only introduced in 1986 following pressure from USAID.
24 If the demand for loans is interest-inelastic, however, there may be substantial scope for increasing interest rates beyond their current levels.
25 Assuming, of course, that it is unable to draw on a catchment of enthusiastic gamblers.
26 'Essentially' because certain erratic items of expenditure (e.g. debt write-offs covering many past years) and income (e.g. asset sales) have been excluded from Table 11.3 as distorting the trend which we wish to observe.
27 The BRI unit desa system was consistently in deficit and made annual average losses of Rp11.5 billion over the years 1979–84; it was consistently profitable and made annual average profits of Rp25 billion over the years 1986–9. The reforms which achieved this turn-round are described above, and in more detail by Patten and Rosengard (1991: 61–76). A number of other Indonesian government-financed schemes of assistance for small producers, notably the KIK/KMKP (subsidised schemes for indigenous small-scale labour-intensive enterprises) and the tree crop lending schemes financed through BBD. These have been consistently unprofitable and have reported delinquency rates in excess of 30% (World Bank 1988: xii, 22, 24, 33).
28 As of 1987, however, investment lending only comprised Rp13.6 billion, or 3.9% of the KUPEDES portfolio.
29 The BKKs' and KURKs' principal source of finance is borrowing from the Central Java and East Java Development Banks, respectively, in the form of twenty-year loans at 1% per month, with a three-year grace period on principal payments. As yet savings play only a minor role in financing these banks, by contrast with the BRI unit desa system.
30 The Subsidy Dependence Index was devised in 1990 by Jacob Yaron and is measured for any given institution as:

$$SDI = \frac{A(m - c) + (Em - P) + K}{Ln}$$

where

A = borrowed funds outstanding
m = interest rate the institution would have to pay if access to concessional funds were eliminated
c = interest rate actually paid by the institution on its borrowed funds
E = average annual equity
P = reported annual profit (adjusted where necessary for loan loss provisions)
K = sum of all other subsidies (e.g. training, technical assistance, coverage of operational costs by government)
L = value of loan portfolio
n = institution's average on-lending rate

Subsidy Dependence Indices as calculated for 1989 in respect of institutions in our sample are:

BRI unit desa	−9%
BKKs	32%
Grameen Bank (Bangladesh)	130%
PRODEM (Bolivia)	198%

31 This statement is based on the following data for 1974:

	BKK system	Average of 38 rural development banks worldwide
Administrative expenses as % of portfolio	21.4	4.8
Cumulative overdues as % of portfolio	4.9	38.0

Sources: For BKK data: Table 11.4 above; for average of other rural schemes: World Bank, *Sector Policy Paper: Agricultural Credit* (Washington, DC: World Bank, 1975), annexes 10–12.

32 Bear in mind also the potential distortion introduced to the figures by the fact that poor rural borrowers typically derive income from several sources: see note 8 above.

33 The balance is however changing as a consequence of industrialisation and migration out of Java. Booth (1992: 639) estimates that if this continues the majority of the poor will be found in rural areas outside Java by the early years of the next century.

34 The average across all our seven country case-studies is a poverty line of $45 per household per month at 1987 prices.

35 The 'basic needs basket' includes the following items:

Item	Value	% of total expenditure
Rice, corn, cassava	1,753 cals	43.8
Other starches	283 cals	7.9
Fruits, vegetables	49 cals	2.6
Meal, eggs, fish,	51 cals	2.3
Oils and fats, pulses	322 cals	6.2
Housing improvement	Rp.7,264	5.7

Transport	Rp.5,318	4.1
Clothing and footwear	Rp.5,842	4.6
Education	Rp.11,265	8.8
Health	Rp.3,851	3.0
Utilities	Rp.4,249	3.5
Others		2.5

36 Bennett and Goldberg (1992: 3) also argue that degree of access to women depends on the availability of enterprise training services which takes women's needs and constraints into account and the salience of female staff members in the promotion and implementation of project services.

37 For example, the sample cited by MSI/HASFARM (1992) gave the following reasons for preferring the source from which they usually take their loans:

	Male borrowers %	Female borrowers %
Close to home	20	22
Know the lender	13	12
Institution isn't formal	10	8
Loans provided quickly	15	13
Small loans available	6	8
No collateral required	9	11
Others	27	26

Source: MSI/HASFARM (1990: table 3-23)

38 Average loan size across all borrowers in the MSI/HASFARM sample was $87 for men and $57 for women.

39 This idea is supported by a study of three West Javanese villages cited by the World Bank (1988: 46) which showed a larger proportion of women (61%) than men (41.5%) devoting loans to consumption.

40 In Holt (1990: table 7) it is shown that 3.4% of men and 4.9% of women cited the moneylender as 'the source of credit most frequently chosen'.

41 Both the thirty borrowers in East Javanese villages mentioned in the sources to Table 11.13 and a sample of four moneylenders were interviewed to establish what change in moneylenders' terms had occurred since the advent of the KURKs. There was no significant discrepancy between borrowers' and lenders' replies. The average of all responses was that moneylenders' lending rates had come down by an average of 2% (from 11% to 9% per month) as between the arrival of the KURKs in the villages in 1989 and August 1993. All the moneylenders interviewed stated that their loan volume had either stayed constant or increased.

42 This was mentioned by 10% of male respondents and 8% of female respondents to the MSI/HASFARM survey (MSI/HASFARM 1990).

43 One example of this is the influence which Indonesian institutions have exerted, especially on savings mobilisation, in BancoSol and other financial institutions in Bolivia; for more detail of this see Vol. 1, Chapter 7, also Boomgard *et al.* (1992).

44 And in East Java, where only a limited proportion of sub-districts are covered by KURK offices, increased coverage at sub-district level also.

45 See note 37.

46 Formally, combining [11.1]–[11.4]:

$$P = (1 + r)(1 - p(\alpha)X) + Y - (i + a + w)X - z \qquad [11.1']$$

Hence, differentiating [11.1′] with respect to α and setting $\partial p/\partial \alpha = 0$, the first-order condition for a maximum is

$$\frac{\partial p}{\partial \alpha} - X \frac{\partial p}{\partial \alpha} (1 + r) = 0$$

Hence, since by assumption $X \neq 0$ and $r \neq 0$, the condition for a maximum is that

$$\frac{\partial p}{\partial \alpha} = 0 \qquad\qquad\qquad [11.1'']$$

and P can be increased by an increase in α as long as $\partial p/\partial \alpha < 0$.

47 Binswanger and Sillers (1983: table 1) empirically demonstrate moderate levels of risk-aversion amongst the rural poor across a wide range of Asian countries.

48 Under the new assumption that wage levels are sensitive to the flexible element in pay α, the profit function becomes

$$P = (1 + r)(1 - p(\alpha)X + y - (i + a + w(\alpha)) - z \qquad [11.1''']$$

and the first-order condition for a maximum is

$$\frac{\partial \Pi}{\partial \alpha} = -X \frac{\partial p}{\partial \alpha} (1 + r) - \frac{\partial w}{\partial \alpha} = 0$$

To make further progress we must attach specific functional forms to the functions $p(\alpha)$ and $w(\alpha)$. We do not have enough empirical evidence to do this in the Indonesian case.

49 We borrow this phrase from staff of the World Bank and IMF who encounter a similar dilemma when deciding whether or not to extend a further loan to a client already in arrears.

50 If (as may often be the case for a poor unsecured borrower) the borrower cannot borrow from any source other than the banks under examination, then his or her reputation with other lenders will be of no account, and $\mu = 0$ by definition.

51 HAT = Hadiah Angsuran Tepat Waktu = rebate for timely BKK loan repayment. IPTW = Insentif Pembayaran Tepat Waktu = incentive for timely repayment of BRI (KUPEDES) loans.

52 In the BRI unit desa system the linkage between loan repayment and subsequent loan eligibility is the following:

Rating	Criterion	Subsequent loan ceiling
A	All payments on time	Increase of 100% over previous loan amount
B	Final payment on time, two or more late instalments	Increase of 50% over previous loan amount
C	Final payment on time, two or more late instalments	Loan amount as for previous loan
D	Final payment late, but paid within one month of due date	Reduction of 50% over previous loan amount
E	Final payment more than two months late	No new loan

53 We assume that $\beta < rx$, i.e., the bonus for prompt repayment is less than the loan instalment due.

54 It will be noted that a successfully operating compulsory savings or insurance scheme would raise, possibly to 100%, the likelihood of arrears being repaid to the lender and hence the likelihood that this condition will be fulfilled.

55 This is a loose analogue to the 'Stackelberg' approach to price and output decisions in oligopoly theory, in which one duopolist (the 'follower') chooses his price on the premiss that the other (the 'leader') has already selected a price–output combination which maximises his own utility. But the analogy must not be taken too far, since the protagonists in this game are on opposite sides of the market, not on the same side as in oligopoly theory.

56 The derivation is contained in an appendix available from the author.

57 A regression conducted by OLS on a sample of 146 borrowers from the East Java KURKs (selected at random by a USAID evaluation mission) gave the result:

$$\text{Loan size} = 45.9** + 0.15* \text{ income}, \; \bar{r}^2 = 0.22$$
$$\phantom{\text{Loan size} = } (3.98) \quad (2.07)$$

where both loan size and income are measured in thousands of current rupiah, figures in brackets below coefficients are Student's t-statistics, and ** and * denote significance at the 1% and 5% level respectively. The original data are reproduced in MSI/HASFARM (1992).

12

CREDIT FOR THE POOR IN BANGLADESH

The BRAC Rural Development Programme and the Government Thana Resource Development and Employment Programme

Richard Montgomery,
Debapriya Bhattacharya
and David Hulme

INTRODUCTION

The Bangladesh context

This chapter examines the performance and impact of the Bangladesh Rural Advancement Committee's (BRAC's) Rural Development Programme (RDP), and the Government of Bangladesh's Thana Resource Development and Employment Programme (TRDEP) (under the Ministry of Youth), based on a three-month field study in 1992–3. Both schemes have similarities with the model of credit delivery first developed by the Grameen Bank in the late 1970s – perhaps the best-known credit institution in the country, and one of the most renowned across the developing world.

Like the Grameen Bank, BRAC's RDP and TRDEP are targeted at the 'functionally landless' rural poor; they issue mostly small, uncollateralised one-year term loans to individuals belonging to jointly liable peer groups; and they use similar on-site loan disbursement and weekly collection methods by forming village organisations (VOs) or centres (*kendras*). However, both BRAC and TRDEP have operational elements which are distinct, as discussed below; and they are, in their own right, part of Bangladesh's diversity of innovative credit schemes.

We are grateful to our interpreter, Tomann A. Siddique, Syed Hashemi, Lynne Paquette and the interview team and staff at the Bangladesh Institute of Development Studies.

Credit as a development strategy has gained particular prominence in Bangladesh because of a long-running concern with the difficulties of providing formal finance to rural areas, and the dominance (and perceived exploitative operations) of informal credit markets. Recent commentators such as Atiq Rahman (1992) maintain that there is little evidence that Bangladesh's informal financial markets are exploitative; but low national growth and investment rates suggest that the rural economy does suffer severe capital shortage. State-sponsored employment and land reform schemes have had limited success in altering the socio-economic structure of poverty and the poor's continuing inadequate access to resources (see Osmani 1991 for a general discussion of past policies).

The Bangladesh economy has recovered only slowly from the aftermath of the 1971 war and subsequent famine. Decadal inflation in the 1970s averaged over 20 per cent, falling to an average of just over 10 per cent in the 1980s. By the early 1990s the rate had fallen to around 5 per cent per year. GDP growth rates have averaged around 4 per cent since independence, but have fluctuated quite severely due to import shocks and the frequent flood and cyclone disasters. Even though some sectors such as the textile and garment industry have seen marked growth in recent years, the general picture has been poor. As many as 80 per cent of the population depend on the agrarian economy, though slightly less than 50 per cent are directly involved in agriculture, many of whom are share-croppers. An increasing number of the rural population has to rely on the non-farm sector. Population, which was approximately 120 million in 1991–2, has been growing rapidly, and the farm sector is absorbing a falling proportion of new entrants into the labour market. Low growth and underemployment in rural areas remains a chronic structural problem.

One factor underlying low growth is a depressing domestic investment rate – only 10 per cent of GDP in 1991 (World Bank 1993c). This is the lowest domestic investment rate in South Asia – indeed, one of the lowest in the world – and has remained at this level for most of the past decade. No upward trend is discernible: private investment has yet to pick up, and public investment has decreased with the budgetary constraints imposed by IMF conditions (ADB 1993). Structural adjustment policies (SAPs) started in the Ershad dictatorship and continued by the post-1991 BNP democratic government, have included industrial, trade and financial reforms; but these reforms have been slow and piecemeal. Given the experience of SAPs in other countries, the prospects for poverty alleviation in the 1990s look less favourable than donor rhetoric might suggest.

Aid dependence, like poverty, is one of the defining components of Bangladesh's image. By 1989–90, the end of the Third Five-Year Plan, aid constituted 99 per cent of the Government's Annual Development Plan, and a large proportion of the recurrent budget is funded by import duties (often on aid-financed commodities). Such development assistance has been described as a double-edged sword, securing the survival of country in meagre conditions, but strengthening the power of a centralised, inefficient and elitist bureaucracy and allowing the Government to ignore the crucial structural problems of poverty (see Billetoft and Malmdorf 1992).

According to the most recent analysis of poverty trends, the percentage of the population below the conventional income-nutritional poverty line (PL) has fallen from around 70 per cent to 40 per cent between 1973 and 1990 (Rahman and Hossain 1992). Yet this same study also notes that since the mid-1980s 'no serious dent has been made into the situation of the extreme poor'. Indeed, there is evidence to show that this category of the poor has increased, and that four out of every ten people below the poverty line are still subsisting on 40 per cent or less of this income level.

There is a strong correlation between poverty (as defined by insufficient food access) and landlessness. The bottom 50 per cent of the population control only 4 per cent of the land – such households having either less than 5 decimals (16 per cent) or under 50 (33 per cent) (see Sen, in Rahman and Hossain 1992). This recent study, based on 1989–90 data, showed that 'being land-poor is not significantly compensated by the ownership of non-land assets either', but that there are differentials within the bottom half of the population which suggest that poverty alleviation strategies need to be suitably devised to address the different needs of particular 'poverty-groups' (an issue relevant to our concern with targeted credit programmes). The broad conditions of landlessness and poverty have been the main stimulus for the provision of off-farm credit to provide productive employment for the growing rural population. This rise of microcredit schemes has to be seen in the light of the biases in the operation of existing rural financial markets.

The formal financial sector

Formal rural finance is primarily provided by branches of the nationalised commercial banks (NCBs), the Bangladesh Krishi (Agricultural) Bank (BKB), the Bangladesh Samabaya Co-operative Bank Ltd (BSBL) and the Bangladesh Rural Development Board (BRDB – formerly the IRDP, it originated in the Comilla co-operative development of the 1960s). Four of the NCBs dominate the banking system, operating 63 per cent of total branches in the country, holding 60 per cent of all deposits and having 50 per cent of all outstanding loans.

In the post-Independence era, banking policy has been under the jurisdiction of the Bangladesh Bank (BB), and the formal system has been highly regulated, including clearly stipulated non-negotiable interest rates (for example, the BB offered funds to rural banks and other credit programmes at 8 per cent per annum at the time of this study). The Bank has only recently begun to relax interest rate rules – since this study was carried out (ADB 1993). As the central bank, the BB is the conduit for the government and donor funds which have been necessary to recapitalise poorly performing NCBs and other rural credit institutions in the 1980s and 1990s.

During the 1970s, loan recovery by the NCBs, the BKB, BSBL and IRDP averaged 65 per cent of the amount repayable from predominantly agricultural loanees (Sadeque 1986). This repayment situation changed little during the 1980s (though some individual schemes did better). For example, the BKB, lending mostly to farmers with land as collateral, has had overdues running at 30 per cent, and was severely affected in the run-up to the 1991 election when rival parties vied to offer the highest rate of loan forgiveness for farmers (Rutherford 1993). Not surprisingly, such politicised offers have undermined repayment discipline across the formal sector. These conditions, along with clientelist lending practices and the lack of an adequate legal framework for loan recovery, have undermined the financial health of the system. A new loan classification procedure introduced by the BB in 1990 unmasked that fact that by mid-1991 around 25 per cent of the NCB's loan portfolios were non-performing.

Apart from some individual schemes, the rural banking institutions have concentrated on lending to collateralised businesses and farmers. Credit for enhancing agricultural production through green revolution technology and especially irrigation was emphasised throughout the 1980s. Despite significant successes in this agrarian strategy (Hossain 1989), the national banking system has still been unable to replace a substantial informal financial market, and has largely failed to address the needs of the off-farm micro-enterprise sector.

The informal sector

Various estimates of the size of the informal financial market (IFM) in Bangladesh have been made. Atiq Rahman (1992), reviewing the various data from the mid- and late 1980s, suggests that the IFM constitutes approximately two-thirds of the volume of credit in the countryside. Furthermore, he presents evidence showing that the IFM has contracted and expanded in relation to the volume of business undertaken by the formal sector banking institutions. This complementarity between the formal and informal leads him to argue that Bangladesh's IFM is largely efficient and potentially 'developmental' rather than monopolistic and exploitative. However, this does not deny the fact that informal interest rates are both high and difficult to afford for many amongst the poorest 50 per cent of the population.

The rural IFM comprises a range of lenders – landlords, richer cultivators, traders and brokers, and some specialised moneylenders. There is also ample literature on the range of contracts existing, including various types of cash and kind (such as paddy) transactions, and land or asset mortgaging. In the highly unequal social and economic environment of the countryside, most forms of credit which are not directly cash-for-cash are explicitly or implicitly 'tied' to additional conditions (including clientelist ones). Hierarchies of lenders appear to exist, connected to both landholding and trading patterns, with those at the top of these hierarchies heavily involved in the formal financial sector (see, for example, Sen 1989; Rahman 1992; Crow 1992).

Given the diversity of informal sector credit contracts and notable regional differences, it is difficult to specify real interest rates. Atiq Rahman settles on a modal interest rate of 10 per cent per *month* for most loans, both large and small (a rate which when compounded is equivalent to 214 per cent per year). Formal sector lending rates in the past decade have been between 12 per cent and 20 per cent per year, with only a few experimental schemes using higher rates (for example, 36 per cent under the USAID-sponsored Rural Finance Experimental Project in 1978–80).

The large proportion of informal credit which Rahman estimates is interest-free (between 35 per cent and 45 per cent) is mostly attached to non-financial conditions (such as harvest-time crop selling, pledges of labour and political support, mortgaging of land or other assets, and so on). Other authors, such as Sen, have also found significant amounts of non-tied interest-free credit circulating on the basis of kith and kin (and neighbourhood) relations. However, these loans are normally small and confined to the consumption and contingency needs of households rather than providing 'productive' investment capability.

Overall, the informal sector is unable to satisfy the credit needs of all the poor. In the high-risk natural and economic environment, informal lenders are as keen to screen borrowers as are formal institutions, and high interest rates – which to some extent reflect high risks – are not affordable by most landless families without cashing in their existing assets. Debt at high interest rates, whether deemed as 'efficient allocation' or 'exploitation', remains one of the downward pressures which, along with other structural social and economic conditions, constitute the deprivation 'trap'; and various anthropological studies have shown that the many of the poor are not deemed creditworthy by informal lenders, and are thereby denied access to such financial assistance (see, for example, White 1992; Casper 1992).

The rise of microcredit programmes

The rise of targeted microcredit programmes over the last two decades, both state- and NGO-sponsored, derives from the various factors outlined above: capital scarcity, the inability of the formal system to reach the functionally landless (uncollateralised) poor, and the limited ability of the

IFM to meet the needs of the majority of poor people striving to survive in the off-farm sector.

Holtsberg's (1991) overview of credit programmes in the 1980s identifies at least 140 NGO schemes, in addition to at least twenty government projects aimed at promoting off-farm employment; and forty special credit programmes run by the NCBs – though not all these latter schemes are 'targeted'. Of course, many of these 200 programmes were (and are) small in scale, and only some have geographical spread. Of particular note amongst government targeted credit schemes is 'RD 12' (run by the BRDB) which covered a third of the *thanas* in the country by 1991 (139 out of the total of 460). Programmes such as BRAC's have comparable geographical coverage but are more concentrated (BRAC's membership was almost three times that of RD 12 in 1991). The largest single targeted credit scheme is the Grameen Bank, as illustrated in Table 12.1.

Just these selected targeted programmes, as of 1991, claimed to be reaching two and a half million people in a target group consisting of between ten and twelve million households. Although there are overlaps in membership and many programmes encourage several members to join from any single household, these particular programmes are all expanding – and are indicative of the extent to which targeted credit has become a prominent feature of the Bangladesh rural economy.

Most credit programmes for the poor have now adopted the main lessons from the Grameen Bank's pathbreaking work:

- the use of social rather than economic collateral through the formation of jointly liable borrowing groups;
- the formation of centres (*kendras*) or village organisations (*shomitis*) made up of joint-liability groups;
- high number of field staff and good outreach, disbursing loans and collecting repayments in borrowers' villages;
- a reliance on 'group' or 'provisional' savings funds, which are often made up of deductions from loans, are not immediately accessible to group

Table 12.1 Comparison of selected large-scale GoB and NGO credit programmes, 1991

	RD 12	Grameen Bank	BRAC	Proshika	RDRS
No. of *Thanas*	139	200+	120	70	28
No. of members	236,551	1,066,426	598,136	406,855	93,874

Sources: BRAC reports; Proshika Co-ordination Officer; Grameen Bank, *1991 Annual Report*; Holtsberg (1991) for RD 12; and Maloney (1989) for the Rangpur-Dinajpur Rural Service

members, providing an insurance mechanism for the programme if defaults do occur;

• and increasingly, since successive floods and other natural disasters, the use of additional 'insurance' deductions to help the programme or institution cope with the high risks of lending to the poor and vulnerable.

Despite these similarities, individual programmes have operational differences, and there is some 'competition' between both government and NGO agencies to claim particular success for 'their' model of credit delivery. One of the major debates has been that of whether credit should be accompanied with additional inputs (such as skills training, functional education and institution building), or whether the more limited supply-side intervention of 'credit alone' is more appropriate (and cost effective). The Grameen Bank claims the latter; BRAC attempts to supply additional inputs; and the government case-study in this volume (TRDEP) is somewhere in between.

The next section provides a more detailed background to the BRAC and TRDEP, a summary of their main design features, and a brief comment on the field methodology. A consideration of the financial performance of the two institutions and a brief outline of their role in the market and their transactions with borrowers then follows. After presenting evidence on the impact of the programmes, the overall performance and some comparative issues are discussed.

THE CASE STUDY PROGRAMMES

The Bangladesh Rural Advancement Committee (BRAC), formed in the early 1970s, is now the largest NGO in the country, and runs a range of programmes in various sectors. Credit provision has become one of its core activities, primarily under its Rural Development Programme (RDP) which attempts to integrate credit with other forms of support (both institutional and technical).

The Thana Resource Development and Employment Programme (TRDEP) was initiated by the Government in 1987, to reproduce and adapt the Grameen Bank and its methods. TRDEP operates on some of the *laissez-faire* principles of the latter organisation, including the assumption that people know their economic environment and priorities best, and therefore need little direction on loan use (Yunus 1987: 4). But like Grameen (and BRAC), TRDEP requires borrowers to state a specific 'productive' loan purpose, and does not provide credit for consumption needs. Initially, member education and skills training were to be part of the TRDEP approach, but in practice such inputs have been rare.

Apart from the different emphases on integrated versus minimalist credit provision, there are other major differences. TRDEP claims to concentrate on forming 'family-based' joint-liability groups, and will only give four loans to each individual member; after this, the *kendra* is closed down and membership ceases (and the programme moves on to another village or hamlet). Thus, TRDEP has an explicit concept of withdrawal, and hopes to enable borrowers to graduate out of poverty by providing several members of a single family with four loans in rapid succession (that is, over a four-year period). BRAC, however, has no firm concept of withdrawal from its members, and places no limit on the number of loans allowed to members (as long as their repayment performance has been good). Unlike TRDEP, RDP seeks to establish a long-term presence by creating village organisations, and by local area offices generating interest income on their loan portfolios, thereby sustaining the programme in the long term. As analysis later in this chapter shows, not all the components in these ideal models of the two programmes have yet materialised. Before this analysis, this section provides more background details on each of the institutions; a summary of the main design features is provided in Table 12.4.

The BRAC RDP

BRAC achieved national and international recognition in the 1980s primarily through its activities in the health sector. The Oral [rehydration] Therapy Extension Programme (OTEP), initiated in 1979, fulfilled its stupendous target of reaching thirteen million households in 1990 (see Lovell 1992). The OTEP had several consequences for BRAC. First, organisational capacity was vastly enhanced in the early 1980s. Second, it encouraged management personnel to be more ambitious in their planning of other field operations in various sectors. Third, the credibility acquired through the OTEP's coverage and success opened up new prospects for donor funding in the future. The result of the 1980s expansion of BRAC's education and credit programmes with donor assistance now makes it Bangladesh's largest development NGO in terms of staffing, funds deployed and clientele.

During the first half of the 1980s, concurrently with the OTEP, BRAC was experimenting with organising low-income groups, and rural training and credit extension (Lovell 1992: 75–80). These two pilot projects (the Outreach Programme (OP) and Rural Credit and Training Programmes (RCTPs), respectively) epitomise two central, intertwined strands of BRAC's development ideology and aims: to 'empower' low-income groups and to alleviate poverty.

The Outreach Programme concentrated on forming male and female village organisations (VOs), as permanent rural institutions. While the OP encouraged savings, it purposely avoided providing external loans to the

VOs. Instead, programme staff concentrated on education and on getting members to identify and mobilise their existing resources for self-reliance. In contrast, the Rural Credit and Training Programme provided loans, close supervision, technical assistance, and also attempted to identify market openings for income-generating activities – so it was more interventionist and 'patronal' towards its members.

The present RDP, initiated in 1986, was a merger of the principles of the OP and the RCTP. While the OP had failed to generate significant changes in members' access to tangible resources, the RCTP's limited emphasis on education and awareness-raising was seen as insufficient for enhancing group stability and performance. Combining these lessons in phase I of RDP (1986–9) led to the philosophy that (a) motivated and well-supported village organisations were a precondition for credit delivery, discipline and effective loan use; and (b) VOs are potential mutual support institutions to enhance the status of the rural poor.

RDP has been financed by a large donor consortium, which granted approximately US$50 million for the expansion of the programme over the 1990–3 period. Two donors, the Dutch NOVIB and the British ODA, have contributed around half the total funds, with seven other bilateral and northern NGOs contributing the rest. A further donor financial commitment for the 1993–5 phase III period, similar in size to the first consortium agreement, was agreed after our fieldwork. Donor funds for RDP include finance for a transition in the programme, under a sub-component called the 'Rural Credit Project' (RCP). This RCP hopes to transform the RDP into a self-sustaining banking institution, by building a network of branches which generate sufficient income from their loan portfolios alone, thereby eradicating the long-term need for donor support. However, given the resources which BRAC is pouring into RDP's expansion process, this overall RCP transition is being delayed.

By the end of 1992, RDP was operating across the country under the direction of a Dhaka head office with nearly 400 staff. A further 3,200 field staff were employed in the network of fifteen regional offices and 140 area offices (AOs). Each AO, twenty of which were established in 1992 alone, oversees approximately 120 village organisations (VOs), formed for men and women separately. Each VO consists of an average of forty-six persons (see Table 12.2).

Since 1990, as new AOs have been created, old and more financially mature AOs have been renamed branches in preparation for the RCP transition to the 'BRAC Bank'. However, the organisation and operation of branches differ little from those of AOs, and they are differentiated according to financial maturity only. Ideally, when an AO's outstanding loans have reached Tk8 million (at 1991 prices), the interest income is hypothetically sufficient to cover most of the AO's operating costs, and it is renamed a branch. This financial status is estimated to take six years

Table 12.2 Growth in BRAC's RDP/RCP membership and area offices/branches

Year	Number of members	% of women	RDP area offices (RCP branches)	Total AOs/ branches
1986	148,000			
1987	200,000		40	40
1988	251,668	58	56	56
1989	355,675	61	81	81
1990	460,764	64	90 (10)	100
1991	598,125	68	90 (30)	120
1992	649,274	74	90 (50)	140

Source: BRAC Statistical Reports and project documents: various years

(though many AOs have been renamed after four years in preparation for the real financial change). In fact, recent indications of membership turnover (in 1993) suggest that the older AOs have lost a substantial proportion (perhaps 25 per cent) of their membership, implying that many have experienced a slower growth in their loan portfolios than previously hoped. This study concentrates on RDP, because out of the four area offices in which the field study was carried out, only two have a financial maturity of five to six years, and the others have statuses of three to four years.

Apart from credit delivery, RDP consists of several other components. One of the most visible ones is the Non-Formal Education Programme (NFPE) which establishes schools primarily for the children of VO members; but there are also additional inputs for the VO members themselves. Unlike the more minimalist Grameen Bank approach, BRAC has a range of specific 'sectoral programmes' providing training for poultry, livestock, sericulture and fisheries enterprises. All such component programmes which make up the overall RDP are run at field level by a professionalised staff known as Programme Organisers (POs), with the help of locally recruited village workers (*Gram Sheboks* and *Shebikas* (GSs)). Since early 1992, all AOs are supposed to have at least twelve GSs and three POs: one for the sectoral programmes, one for institution building, and one for credit. Additional specialist POs are seconded from the regional offices on temporary assignments (that is, they circulate across the region). Such staff are unevenly represented and severely stretched in relation to the number of RDP members, and the actual amount of technical assistance to members should not be overestimated. For example, the single institution-building PO in each area office has responsibility for 120 VOs, which means he (or rarely she) is unlikely to spend, on average, more than two days every year with a single VO.

Men and women from the target group (see Table 12.4) are mobilised separately into Village Organisations by either credit or institution-building

POs. VO members take part in the functional education courses run by special teachers or GSs (some new VOs visited during fieldwork had not received full courses, because of the staff constraints which have arisen due to BRAC's continuing expansion). Once a VO is formed, members begin to save Tk2 per week, learn seventeen 'promises' which have to be ritualistically repeated in chorus at every weekly meeting, and are instructed on credit rules. Most VOs become eligible to start taking loans after three to six months, when savings discipline and some form of group identity have been established.

In procedural terms, BRAC is similar to the Grameen Bank and many other targeted Bangladeshi credit schemes in 'taking the bank to the people'. Weekly meetings are held in the villages to collect savings and evaluate loan proposals. In principle, each loan application is cleared by the VO members and its management committee, the VO's GS, the AO's credit PO and manager, and the local regional manager. Although the results of members' loan applications are conveyed by GS staff at these weekly meetings, borrowers have to collect their credit from the area office on designated days.

In principle, each VO is made up of borrower sub-groups, each of between five and seven members, who are jointly liable for each other's loans; members of a sub-group are not allowed to take loans at the same time – the repayment of the initial borrowers is a condition for disbursement to other sub-group members. By far the majority of loans are for a one-year term, to be paid back in fifty-two weekly instalments. Apart from the 20 per cent per annum interest rate (in late 1992), other direct costs to the borrowers are incurred through a 10 per cent deduction from the principal amount. This deduction is made up of a security deposit (5 per cent), a compulsory deposit (4 per cent) and a life insurance contribution (1 per cent). While the security deposit is nominally part of a borrower's savings (also comprising weekly Tk2 deposits), the compulsory deposit is placed in the Group Trust Fund (GTF) – a fund which is held and overseen by the area office for all the VOs. However, none of these deductions from the loan principal are effectively accessible by members, since no savings are on open access, and the GTF is totally controlled by the AO manager. In practice, such deductions are a part of the insurance arrangements for the AO's overall loan portfolio, and outstanding loans of defaulters can be covered by these various types of cash 'being held on behalf of the borrowers'. The strict deposit rules also mean that members perceive all savings as part of the cost of borrowing (even though they technically own such savings, and are supposed to have access to them after several years or when they leave the VO).

By the end of 1992, the estimated number of borrowers was well over 600,000 persons, 70 per cent of whom were women, and RDP–RCP credit operations were active in over a hundred *thanas* (sub-districts) out of the total of 460 in Bangladesh. In other words, BRAC was providing credit to the same number of borrowers as the Grameen Bank did in 1989. As an organisation, it is far from the 'committee' which was formed in response to relief and rehabilitation needs after the 1971 war. Its institutional framework is highly stratified, its staff professional, and its culture 'corporate'. While it continues to push for greater rural intervention in the health sphere (such as through its separate Women's Health Development Programme), and in education (under an expanded NFPE), the main transition which BRAC hopes to accomplish in the 1990s is the expansion and transformation of RDP into RCP – or the 'BRAC Bank'.

The Government's Thana Resource Development and Employment Programme (TRDEP)

TRDEP is a project overseen by the Government's Ministry of Youth and Sports and run by the Directorate of Youth Development (DYD) in Dhaka. It originated in negotiations between the Government and the World Bank in the mid-1980s. The latter proposed a preparatory project with a budget of Tk288 million (about US$6.5 million at the time). In 1986, the Government rejected this proposal due to its high cost, but decided to go ahead without any donor involvement. The Ministry modified the project design and appointed the DYD as the executive agency. The initial budget was scaled down to Tk20 million (US$0.5 million). At this time the project was called the 'Upazila Resource Development and Employment Project'; *upazilas* (sub-districts) were renamed *thanas* by the 1991 BNP government. The project started with a head office staff of fifteen, which had risen to only twenty-six by the end of 1992.

TRDEP was initiated by four newly created branches in two *thanas* in 1987, and expanded to a further five *thanas* in 1989. Each *thana* has an area office (not to be confused with BRAC's AOs) which administratively oversees two branches – the key field-level financial unit, comparable in role to BRAC's AOs. Thus, as of 1992 there were fourteen branches in total.

To date, TRDEP has been little studied. To our knowledge there are only four documents in existence, all unpublished (Bhattacharya 1990; Talukdar and Mafizul Islam 1992; a recent Asian Development Bank project document (n.d.); and Rutherford 1993). The Government has claimed remarkable success with the scheme as measured by indicators such as targeting and repayment ratios.

As a result of this success, the Asian Development Bank has recently agreed to provide a concessional credit of approximately US$30 million to enable the project, as 'TRDEP III', to expand to around sixty branches in twenty-five to thirty *thanas*. The reorganisation of branches into four zonal offices occurred after our 1992–3 fieldwork.

Table 12.3 TRDEP membership and branches, 1987–92

Year	No. of current borrowers	No. of branches
1987–8	3,068	4
1988–9	4,555	4
1989–90	4,791	14
1990–1	10,049	14
1991–2	10,288	14

Source: TRDEP head office files

As of mid-1992, TRDEP had over 10,000 current members reached through the network of fourteen branches and village 'centres' (*kendras*), of which there are about sixty under each branch (Table 12.3). Each branch has approximately twelve staff, five or more of whom are Group Animators carrying out the savings and loan operations in the *kendras*. Thus, the programme's clientele (and staff) is tiny compared to BRAC's. However, because TRDEP is a three to four year 'rolling programme', approximately 15,000 people had received their limit of three (now four) loans prior to 1992, and their *kendras* had been closed down. Of TRDEP's membership, 71 per cent are men, a proportion which is the reverse of BRAC's gender ratio.

Procedurally, TRDEP *kendras* consisting of thirty to fifty members from the target group are organised into five to seven member sub-(joint-liability) groups. While the programme officially stipulates a 'youth' age limit of thirty-five years, this appears to be relaxed in the field. TRDEP encourages the sub-groups to be 'family-based'. This is a contrast to the Grameen Bank and BRAC, which bar kin from membership of the same sub-group – to ensure more peer pressure, and partly to reduce the risks which a single family may represent. At first, TRDEP assumed that such a stipulation would ensure the participation of women in the programme – though this has not always been the case. More often male household heads dominate, and as our survey shows, while kin relations may play a part in forming sub-groups, few are truly 'household'-based.

TRDEP has also adopted an identical joint liability mechanism to that of the Grameen Bank: apart from the sub-groups, centre members are liable for the outstanding loans (cf. Hossain 1988). (This contrasts with BRAC's group trust fund arrangement, which is based at the area office.)

Like the Grameen Bank, TRDEP provides a short but supposedly intensive induction course for new members. This includes issues of family planning, health and hygiene, immunisation, the advantages of savings, and credit procedures; but it is a shorter process (one or two weeks) than the more gradual approach of BRAC. In addition, TRDEP differs from BRAC in two other key respects: skills training and institution-building provision. Although TRDEP's original mandate allowed for skills

106

training, this has not materialised in practice – there are simply not enough staff at branch level to provide such integrated inputs. Also, because of the way in which the credit delivery system is limited to four loans per member (see pp. 100–1), after which *kendras* are closed down, TRDEP is not attempting to create village-based institutions for the rural poor. This more limited approach means that *kendras* come into contact with fewer and less-specialised staff than in the case of BRAC's VOs.

A single Group Animator (GA) oversees a centre during its lifetime and conducts weekly meetings to collect savings and loan repayments. In fact, savings are a minor part of TRDEP's operations – members have only to save Tk1 per week, which after one year constitutes only 2 per cent or 3 per cent of the value of their first loans of approximately Tk2,000. Members do not have to save a set amount before applying for their first loan.

Each loan is of fifty-two weeks' duration, and is offered at an interest rate of 16 per cent per year (in 1992). The only other direct cost to the borrower is a 5 per cent deduction from the loan principal which is a forced deposit into the branch Provisional Fund (similar to the BRAC GTF in the way it is managed, but ultimately refundable to the member).

Loans are disbursed to all sub-group members within a much shorter time period than in BRAC VOs, and sometimes GAs allow all members of a sub-group to take out loans at the same time. However, TRDEP stresses to its clients that it is only prepared to provide credit over a limited period. Originally, members were allowed three successive loans, though this has now (since 1992) been increased to four. After the programme's four loans a person ceases to be eligible for any more credit, and once loans have been repaid the centre is closed down and savings are returned to the members. The *ideal* underlying TRDEP's loan cycle is that economic graduation can be achieved due to the rapid way in which successive credit is provided to whole families or households.

The credit delivery procedures effectively allow for substantial injections of capital into families and households. Even though the loans are individually taken and listed for each sub-group member, if they are taken simultaneously they can be pooled in one family-group enterprise. Additionally, the four loans which each member is allowed by the programme occur in quick succession: on repaying their first loans, members are immediately eligible to apply for the second, and so on. Successive loans can, in principle, be increasingly large (Tk2,000 – Tk2,500 – Tk3,000 – Tk4,000). In this manner, TRDEP's lending procedures theoretically allow a household or family to borrow nearly Tk60,000 over a four-year period, progressively re-investing in an enterprise, thereby greatly enhancing the potential for the programme's overall aim: the clientele's 'graduation out of poverty'.

The formation of family-based groups which can pool loans is a procedure which theoretically can overcome the constraints of microcredit, a

Table 12.4 Comparative summary of features of BRAC RDP and TRDEP in 1992

	TRDEP	BRAC
I Organisation and scale of operations at end of 1992		
Date of origin	1987	1986
Organisational units	Dhaka head office, 7 area offices, 14 branches, approximately 750 village *kendras*	Dhaka head office, 15 regional offices, 140 area (branch) offices, 14,000 village organisations
Number of members	10,000 present members, 15,000 past members (30% women)	650,000 (75% women)
Source of finance	Government allocations	9-member donor consortium – bilateral and northern NGO
II Definitions of target groups		
Land-holding	Under 50 decimals	Under 50 decimals
Income	An unrealistic stipulation that family income is under Tk6,000 per annum	A general principle that the main household worker sells at least 100 days of labour over year previous to joining
Assets	Borrower households must have less than Tk50,000 value of assets	Vague, but several documents mention target criteria of persons owning 'no implements of production'
Age	70% of clientele must be between 15 and 35 years	Men between 18 and 55 years; women between 16 and 55 years
Other	Must not be a defaulting borrower of any other bank or NGO; should not be indebted to informal lenders	Must not be a member of any other credit programme
III Borrower eligibility conditions		
Group discipline	Join a *kendra*, form a 5-person group, attend regularly. Loan must be approved by other sub-group members; family groups allowed	Join a VO, men and women separately; form a 5–7 sub-group; attend regularly; loans should be approved by VO membership; family sub-groups not allowed

Table 12.4 Continued

	TRDEP	BRAC
Training	Should complete a week-long awareness-raising induction course	Should complete a 3–6-month functional education and conscientisation period (e.g. learning the 17 promises)
Savings	Tk1 per week savings; but no minimum deposits before taking loans	Tk2 per week savings which must accumulate to be 5% of the value of the first loan, 10% of the second, and 15% of the third

IV Credit system features

	TRDEP	BRAC
Loan size	First loans Tk2,000 (US$50) to 2,500; successive loans are large – up to Tk4,000	First loans Tk2,000, graduation to larger loans
Maturity	All 1-year term	Majority of loans 1-year term; some loans 3–5-year duration
Repayment frequency and collection methods	Weekly in 52 instalments, collected by Group Animator at village *kendra* meeting	In weekly instalments (52 for 1-year term loans), by GSs and POs at village meetings
Interest rates	16%	20%
Collateral arrangements	None, but a 5% deduction from loan principle; sub-group joint liability	None, but 4% compulsory deposit in group trust fund, and 5% security deposit in personal savings account; sub-group joint liability
Insurance	None	Life insurance, paid up through 1% deductions on loans received; Tk5,000 paid out on death of member to relatives; BRAC has right to deduct any outstanding loan amount from insurance lump sum
Incentives to repay	Peer-group pressure; future loans (pressure from local government officials?)	Peer-group pressure; promise of further loans

Table 12.4 Continued

	TRDEP	*BRAC*
Repeat loan eligibility	Maximum of four	Unlimited – if borrower's repayment record is good
Loan use	Must stipulate a productive use; consumption loans not allowed	Must stipulate a productive use; consumption loans introduced in 1992 – but provided extremely rarely due to staff perceptions of high risk and the prolonged application process which makes this facility inappropriate for any urgent contingencies

constraint mentioned by other analysts of Bangladeshi schemes lending small amounts of money to individuals (see, for example, White 1991). In contrast, the Grameen Bank and BRAC place no limit on the number of loans which members can take over their lifetime, but are orientated to individual borrowers only. While BRAC establishes both male and female VOs in some villages, enabling both men and women from the same households to take credit, this situation has become increasingly rare over the last few years as the proportion of women making up the membership has increased.

In reality, loan-pooling amongst TRDEP's clientele is much less prevalent than might be expected. Family-based groups seem to be not as common as we were initially led to believe. Even where there are kin relations amongst a group, this does not ensure loan-pooling – two brothers may keep their monetary affairs largely separate, effectively being two households in the same *bari* (domestic compound). Additionally, a husband and wife may feel it less risky to invest in several small-scale activities, rather than putting 'all their eggs in one basket'. These different family states and strategies may also, of course, be influenced by local marketing and infrastructural constraints on ambitious entrepreneurial projects. The ideal of family graduation from poverty through multiple pooled loans is extremely attractive – especially for a government implementing agency. Ideologically, it is relatively conservative in the sense that it is supporting the family, and aiming to increase employment amongst the younger half of the population – theoretically those less likely to have gainful occupations in contemporary rural labour markets. Unlike BRAC, it does not attempt to mobilise men and women separately, so as to provide women with better access to official field staff (and therefore other services as well as loans).

110

TRDEP's clear cut-off point, after four loans, ensures that the agency can aim to cover an increasing number of borrowers: as each centre closes down, the Group Animator moves on to another village to start a new one.

Study methodology

Research in Bangladesh was carried out over three months, starting in December 1992. After recruiting a team of graduates and testing the Bengali questionnaire, surveys of 156 BRAC and 160 TRDEP members were carried out simultaneously over a five-week period. Informal field-work by the authors was also carried out in numerous VOs and *kendras*, to establish group histories and experiences, and to discuss the local conditions in which people were working.

The survey methodology was designed to capture the quantitative impact of credit on borrowers' enterprises and households. Interviewees were asked a range of questions about their use of loans, and how their enterprises had changed – for example in terms of marketing, technology and labour use. Also, enterprise and household asset details were elicited, as were income and expenditure data. Many of the questions were asked in two parts, the first asking respondents to describe the present-day situation, and the second asking them to recall the situation in the month before they took their last programme loan.

Apart from the recall methodology, a tripartite survey sample was selected for comparisons between types of members. These member categories were defined in terms of length of association with the credit programme and the number of loans they had received, as follows:

1 people who had been members for between three and five years, and had taken three loans;
2 members who had been borrowing for at least a year, and should technically have completed repayment of one loan;
3 newly recruited members of the programme, who had not yet taken any loans.

Comparison of groups 1 and 2 provides a basis on which to evaluate the impact of serial as opposed to individual loans. The third group was intended to act as a control ('without loans').

The sample frame for each programme was drawn up after selecting four research areas. These were situated in Rajbari and Sherpur districts (for the BRAC survey) and Faridpur and Comilla districts (for the TRDEP survey). In each district area offices or branches were chosen after discussion with head office staff. The intention was to select one 'vibrant' local economy and one relatively 'depressed' local economy for each programme. The Faridpur–Rajbari area, just south of the Ganges river, is comparatively advanced: green revolution agriculture, good communications, and with an important trade-route running through it connecting Dhaka with India. The AOs and branches in both Sherpur and Comilla district are serving less-well-developed areas: relatively more isolated, poorer communications and less market access.

Once the research sites had been purposively chosen, VOs and *kendras* were classified according to their age (that is, three to five years old, one to two years old, and recently formed). Once this had been done, the members were stratified according to the borrower types listed above to create a sampling list. This was a labour-intensive task which would not have been possible without the patience and help of the field staff in both organisations. The final sample was then drawn up by a random selection from these lists.

In addition to these surveys, during the final month in Dhaka various discussions were held with head office staff of the two organisations, academics working in the field of poverty alleviation, and donor representatives. These contacts also provided us with access to a number of unpublished documents which would otherwise have escaped our notice.

THE FINANCIAL PERFORMANCE
OF BRAC AND TRDEP

BRAC and TRDEP staff point to their high loan repayment rates as a key indicator of their successful operations. Both programmes use repayment calculations which allow for one year beyond due date before classifying a loan as 'late'; TRDEP claims 100 per cent repayment, while BRAC in 1992 claimed 97 per cent repayment.

This oft-cited indicator of success does not tell us much about the viability of the programmes – a more detailed assessment of income and costs is required. As with many targeted programmes, BRAC and TRDEP both use intensive loan-delivery, supervision and collection methods; also, the reliance on groups as vehicles for disbursement incurs mobilisation, training and institutional support costs. These intensive activities can be expected to have both high staff and general administration costs relative to more conventional banking schemes. Apart from income and expenditure ratios, other key indicators of performance include the unit costs for servicing each programme participant, and the delivery cost of loaned funds. These efficiency indicators help to place the official repayment rate statements in perspective.

Yet even such analysis, based on branch and head office level accounts, gives us only a nominal statement of profitability and efficiency. Both programmes have been, and remain, massively dependent on external funds, in both cases on a grant basis. The extent of this funding has been influenced by the objective of expansion, which has been particularly important for BRAC in recent years. For TRDEP as well, although small compared to BRAC, the extension from merely two to seven *thanas* in 1989 has determined a crucial reliance on government allocations (and the present 'going to scale' to establish a national network of TRDEP branches is reliant on a major concessional credit from the ADB). Such expansions imply major start-up and staff training costs. Thus, neither of the programmes has reached a 'steady state' at which an assessment of financial viability and sustainability would be more clear.

However, this section investigates financial data and several performance indicators for branch and programme-level operations to assess performance. The Subsidy Dependence Index (SDI) is also applied in order to indicate the degree to which the institutions are underwritten by external funds, and to provide a comparative perspective of the two organisations.

For programme-level analysis, data were collected from the respective head offices. It should be noted that BRAC's audited accounts were readily available, while TRDEP and the Ministry of Youth were unable to provide more than raw data from which the following summary of financial figures is constructed. Also, for branch-level analysis, BRAC's accounts were more easily extracted (for different area offices: Ahladipur, Baliakandi, Sherpur and Tinani), while in the case of TRDEP we have to rely on information from one branch (Debidwar). The latter was the only one out of the four branches on which our field study focused where the manager was able to provide acceptable accounts. (For the purposes of this comparative discussion BRAC's 'area offices' are classed as branches.)

Branch-level financial operations

The viability of branches is a necessary condition for the overall viability of a rural banking system or programme. The data from our field study indicate that branches under both programmes depend on annual allocations from head office to make up significant shortfalls between expenditure and locally generated resources (interest income earned on loans disbursed; and in the case of TRDEP interest on funds held by branches in local banks). While a brief comment on trends in the case of the four BRAC branches is made, there are serious problems with the TRDEP data available. Even in the case of the single branch for which some form of accounts was provided, these accounts were cumulative over a four-year period, and thus do not provide annual income figures (pp. 114–15). Tables 12.5 and 12.6 collate the available data, and show that BRAC's branches (area offices) are on average much larger than those of TRDEP. In terms of income, the former are over five times larger than the latter, and in terms of expenditure RDP branches are 8.5 times larger.

Income data for BRAC's RDP AOs/branches show that interest (and penalties) constituted 95 per cent of income over the four-year reporting period. Expenditure was substantially higher than income in all four years,

Table 12.5 BRAC branch (AO) level income and expenditure structure, 1989–92 (Tk'000)

	1989	1990	1991	1992	Total (all years)
I Income					
Head office allocations	—	118.60 (47.13)	—	—	118.60 (5.41)
Interest income	24.67 (100)	133.05 (52.87)	565.50 (99.78)	1,340.74 (99.43)	2,063.96 (94.18)
Penalities realised	—	—	1.24 (0.22)	7.73 (0.57)	8.97 (0.41)
Total income	24.67 (100)	251.64 (100)	566.74 (100)	1,348.74 (100)	2,191.52 (100)
II Expenditure					
Staff costs	406.19 (43.85)	740.62 (55.38)	1,518.14 (46.86)	1,856.88 (43.85)	4,521.84 (46.43)
Training & institution-building	389.98 (42.10)	377.36 (28.22)	1,029.82 (31.79)	1,488.72 (35.15)	3,285.88 (33.74)
Rent and accommodation	48.95 (5.28)	60.15 (4.50)	177.33 (5.47)	243.37 (5.75)	529.80 (5.44)
Stationery & supplies	61.30 (0.66)	30.23 (2.26)	147.35 (4.55)	167.93 (3.97)	351.64 (3.61)
Equipment	12.74 (1.38)	12.85 (0.96)	87.49 (2.70)	104.88 (2.48)	217.96 (2.24)
Other recurring expenditure	62.43 (6.74)	116.10 (8.68)	279.53 (8.63)	373.15 (8.81)	831.20 (8.54)
Total expenditure	926.42 (100)	1,337.31 (100)	3,239.66 (100)	4,234.93 (100)	9,738.32 (100)

Source: Annualised averages based on accounts provided by RDP area office (branch) managers in Ahladipur, Balliakandi, Tinani and Sherpur
Note: Figures in brackets are percentages

but the falling trend in the expenditure to income ratio is notable (see Table 12.7). Despite this favourable trend, the annual operational costs of BRAC's branch-level units are still more than three times their locally generated income.

In the case of TRDEP, interest on loans disbursed constituted only 57 per cent of branch-level income, while interest on funds held in local banks made up the bulk of the rest (36 per cent). This high share of bank interest, if replicated across the other branches, suggests an operational inertia in terms of capital turnover, and perhaps a managerial risk-aversion strategy (a preference amongst managers for gainful deposits to offset potential or real short-term losses from borrowers). It is not possible with the data available

Table 12.6 TRDEP branch-level income and expenditure structure, 1989–92
(Tk'000)

I Income	Total amount (Jan '89 to Dec '92)
Interest income on funds held in local banks	154.93 (36.04)
Interest income realised on disbursements	247.15 (57.49)
Provisional Fund	27.84 (6.47)
Total income	429.93 (100)

II Expenditure	1989–90	1990–91	1991–92	Aug '92– Dec '92	Total
Staff costs	134.12 (72.16)	289.21 (90.74)	433.91 (95.38)	193.27 (100)	1,050.51 (91.13)
Office rent	6.00 (3.23)	12.00 (3.76)	9.00 (1.98)	—	27.00 (2.34)
Stationery supplies	8.47 (4.56)	3.45 (1.09)	4.0 (0.88)	—	15.92 (1.38)
Furniture	31.09 (16.73)	—	—	—	31.09 (2.70)
Other recurring expenditure	6.17 (3.32)	14.08 (4.41)	7.98 (1.76)	—	28.23 (2.45)
Total expenditure	185.85 (100)	318.74 (100)	454.89 (100)	193.27 (100)	1,152.75 (100)

Source: Data supplied by TRDEP Branch Manager, Debidwar
Note: Figures in brackets are percentages

Table 12.7 Comparative branch-level income: expenditure data for BRAC RDP
and TRDEP (Tk'000)

Years	BRAC RDP			TRDEP		
	Income	Expenditure	Exp. as % of income	Income	Expenditure	Exp. as % of income
1989	24.67	926.42	3,743		185.85	
1990	251.61	1,337.31	531	(n.a.)	318.74	(n.a.)
1991	566.74	3,239.66	572		454.89	
1992	1,348.47	4,234.93	314		193.27	
Total (all years)	2,191.52	9,738.32	444	429.93[a]	1,152.75[a]	306[b]

Notes
[a] Amount for the period July 1989 to December 1992.
[b] Adjusted for the differences in reporting period for income and expenditure.

115

to make any assessment of the trends in the TRDEP branch's income to expenditure ratio. However, the average ratio for the last four years appears to be similar to the most recent figures for the BRAC branches.

The budgetary balances presented in Table 12.7 show that BRAC's RDP branch-level costs over the past four years are 4.5 times more than income, and for TRDEP the ratio is three to one. In other words, from locally generated income over the last four years BRAC's branches have covered 22.5 per cent of their costs, while TRDEP branches have covered 37.3 per cent of costs. In both cases, these major shortfalls in income have been covered by allocations from the respective head offices. Thus, the available data suggest that branches in both programmes are unlikely to be able to operate exclusively on the basis of local-level income in the foreseeable future. The lack of branch-level independent viability is not surprising given the overall financial efficiency of the two programmes, as the following sub-section illustrates.

Programme-level income and expenditure

The general financial data indicate the contrasting scale of the two programmes over the last five to six years (1988–92 for BRAC; and 1986–7 to 1991–2 for TRDEP). In 1992, BRAC's total income amounted to Tk346 million, while TRDEP's was only Tk20 million (seventeen times smaller than BRAC). However, over a similar period, TRDEP's annual income has expanded seven times, while BRAC's has increased four times (see Tables 12.8 and 12.9). Thus, TRDEP's relative rate of expansion is still significant, and should be borne in mind during the following analysis.

Table 12.8 Programme-level income structure: BRAC RDP (Tk million)

Year	Donation	Interest income	Internal resources	Training income	Total
1988	67.25 (80.08)	16.73 (19.92)	—	—	83.98 (100)
1989	138.71 (89.62)	11.02 (7.12)	5.04 (32.6)	—	154.77 (100)
1990	268.33 (89.1)	27.92 (9.29)	3.86 (1.28)	1.00 (0.33)	301.16 (100)
1991	382.32 (90.34)	39.01 (9.22)	—	1.87 (0.44)	423.20 (100)
1992	306.72 (88.70)	39.06 (11.30)	—	—	345.78 (100)
Total (all years)	1,163.33 (88.88)	133.79 (10.22)	8.90 (0.68)	2.87 (0.22)	1,308.89 (100)

Source: BRAC Audit Reports, various years
Note: Figures in brackets are percentages

116

Table 12.9 Programme-level income structure: TRDEP (Tk million)

Year	Government allocation[a]	Interest on loan	Bank interest	Provisional Fund	Total
1986–7	2.97	—	—	—	2.97
	(100)				(100)
1987–8	9.05	—	—	—	9.05
	(100)				(100)
1988–9	4.43	0.47[b]	0.52[b]	0.06[b]	4.38
	(80.84)	(8.58)	(9.49)	(1.09)	(100)
1989–90	1.99	0.93	1.10	0.08	3.1
	(64.19)	(30.0)	(3.23)	(2.58)	(100)
1990–1	33.10	1.28	1.02	0.11	35.51
	(93.21)	(3.60)	(2.87)	(0.31)	(100)
1991–2	17.70	1.75	0.85	0.17	20.47
	(86.47)	(8.55)	(4.15)	(0.83)	(100)
Total (1986–7	69.24	4.43	2.49	0.42	76.58
to 1991–2)	(90.42)	(5.78)	(3.25)	(0.55)	(100)

Source: Compiled from TRDEP head office file data
Notes
Figures in brackets are percentages.
[a] Including allocation for Revolving Fund.
[b] Cumulative for 1987–8 and 1988–9.

Both programmes have relied extensively on external financing (for approximately 90 per cent of their total income over the last five or six years). This income has been donor grant (in the case of BRAC) and government allocations (in the case of TRDEP). Interest income from lending operations and institutional investments have constituted only 10 per cent of total income for BRAC, and less for TRDEP. The income which both programmes raise from other sources is minimal in relation to overall income (for example, BRAC's cost recovery from training, and TRDEP's Provisional Fund which is made up of deductions from loans to members).

TRDEP's reliance on government allocations appears to have led to severe financial instability. Cumbersome fund release procedures led to the dramatic fall in income over two years (in 1988–9 and 1989–90, see Table 12.9). The decreased annual allocation for these years increased the significance (proportionately) of the programme's loan interest income, but in absolute terms this type of income has remained small. In relative terms interest income on loans disbursed, as a proportion of total income, has been only half that generated by BRAC.

Regarding expenditure, staff remuneration is by far the most significant cost of both programmes. Tables 12.10 and 12.11 show BRAC staff costs as nearly 40 per cent, and TRDEP's as nearly 60 per cent of total expenditure over the last six years. Additionally, non-staff head office

Table 12.10 Programme-level operating expenses: BRAC RDP (Tk million)

Expenditure category	1986	1987	1988	1989	1990	1991	Total
Staff costs	10.00	15.04	23.95	33.31	66.78	88.72	237.80
	(45.9)	(37.8)	(41.8)	(37.5)	(36.9)	(38.9)	(38.6)
Target group training	2.59	10.69	18.73	13.99	39.99	48.61	134.60
	(11.9)	(26.9)	(32.7)	(15.8)	(22.1)	(21.3)	(21.8)
Recurring exp. (inc. capital exp. & depreciation)	9.16	14.07	14.56	13.61	59.70	72.41	183.51
	(42.1)	(35.4)	(25.4)	(15.3)	(33.0)	(31.7)	(29.8)
Head office[a]	—	—	—	27.91	14.60	18.47	60.98
				(31.4)	(8.1)	(8.1)	(9.9)
Total	21.75	39.80	57.24	88.82	181.07	228.21	616.89
	(99.9)	(100.0)	(99.9)	(100)	(100.1)	(100)	(100.1)
Revolving Fund	5.27	34.32	42.33	33.93	13.66	14.87	

Source: BRAC Audit Reports, various years
Notes
Figures in brackets are percentages.
[a] Figures for 1986–8 not available.

Table 12.11 Programme-level operating expenses: TRDEP (Tk million)

Expenditure category	1986–7	1987–8	1988–9	1989–90	1990–1	1991–2	Total
Staff costs	0.1	1.51	1.59	2.5	4.5	5.25	15.45
	(5.1)	(75.0)	(75.0)	(49.1)	(57.2)	(81.3)	(59.9)
Target group training	0.095	0.095	0.09	0.03	0.01	0.01	0.33
	(4.8)	(4.3)	(4.3)	(0.6)	(0.1)	(0.2)	(1.3)
Recurring exp. (inc. depreciation)	0.276	0.645	0.44	0.99	0.63	0.57	3.55
	(14.0)	(20.8)	(20.8)	(19.5)	(8.0)	(8.8)	(13.8)
Capital exp.	1.50	—	—	0.11	0.03	—	1.64
	(76.1)			(2.2)	(0.4)		(6.4)
Head office[a]	—	—	—	1.46	2.70	0.63	4.79
				(28.7)	(34.3)	(9.8)	(18.6)
Total	1.97	2.25	2.12	5.09	7.87	6.46	25.76
	(100)	(100.1)	(100.1)	(100.1)	(100)	(100.1)	(100)
Revolving Fund	1.00	6.80	2.3	2.46	2.46	4.02	

Source: TRDEP head office file data
Notes
Figures in brackets are percentages.
[a] Figures for 1986–7 to 1988–9 not available.

costs are much lower in the case of BRAC than TRDEP (averaging 9.9 per cent and 18.6 per cent, respectively, over the three years for which data are available). However, while BRAC spends a significant proportion on targeting group mobilisation and training (22 per cent) this cost is minor in the case of TRDEP (only 1.3 per cent). For both programmes recurring and capital expenditures accounted for substantial proportions of their budgets (almost 30 per cent of BRAC's and 20 per cent of TRDEP's).

On average, BRAC's actual total expenditure over the last six years has been almost twenty-four times that of TRDEP. Recalling the difference between the actual incomes of the two programmes noted above, this suggests a higher rate of resource utilisation by BRAC.

Programme-level efficiency

Trends in unit costs per member and the costs of delivering credit provide indicators of financial efficiency and the potential for long-term viability. Table 12.12 presents comparative figures for the two programmes over the last six years for which figures are available.

On average, over the last six years the cost of coverage per member is significantly lower in the case of BRAC (Tk398) than TRDEP (Tk656). However, this average figure appears to be more representative for TRDEP – if the lack of any trend in costs is taken into account. For BRAC the average cost of coverage is more of a distortion – recent higher costs per member were incurred because of the transfer of members from RDP to RCP; before this time, costs per member were substantially lower (for example, Tk250 in 1989). These comparative figures suggest that the BRAC RDP is more efficient, particularly when considering the high training input which the programme provides, in contrast to TRDEP's more minimalist approach. Undoubtedly, a deciding factor in TRDEP's high coverage and delivery costs is the (government) staff remuneration levels, which are much higher than those of BRAC.

For BRAC, the costs of credit delivery have been falling notably: from a high point in 1987 during which the cost per Taka loaned was Tk0.86, to a more reasonable level of Tk0.07 in 1991. For TRDEP, such delivery costs have been consistently higher, and though some sort of downward trend is discernible it is clear that these costs are much too high. On average over the last six years, TRDEP has spent Tk1 for each Taka loaned, while in the case of BRAC, this average is much lower (Tk0.4 per Tk1 loaned).

These averages suggest that neither programme is in a position to cover its costs by the interest rates that they are charging (20 per cent by BRAC and 16 per cent by TRDEP). However, while TRDEP has not yet approached a delivery cost capable of being borne by interest income, the fall in BRAC's delivery costs in the last two years shows more potential for financial viability in the long term. These conclusions are further

Table 12.12 Comparative financial efficiency indicators for BRAC RDP and TRDEP

I BRAC

	1986	1987	1988	1989	1990	1991
A Total exp. (Tk million)	21.75	39.80	57.24	88.82	181.07	228.21
B Revolving Fund (Tk million)	5.27	34.32	42.33	33.93	13.66	14.87
C No. of members (cumu-lative)	121,747	168,828	251,668	355,675	276,839[a]	270,274[a]
D Cost of delivery (B/A, in Tk)	0.24	0.86	0.74	0.38	0.08	0.40
E Cost of coverage (A/C, in Tk)	178.65	235.74	227.44	249.72	654.06	844.37

II TRDEP

	1986–7	1987–8	1988–9	1989–90	1990–1	1991–2
A Total exp. (Tk million)	1.97	2.25	2.12	5.09	7.87	6.46
B Revolving Fund (Tk million)	1.0	6.80	2.30	2.46	2.46	4.02
C No. of members (cumu-lative)	—	3,068	4,555	4,791	10,049	10,228
D Cost of delivery (B/A, in Tk)	0.51	3.02	1.08	0.48	0.31	0.62
E Cost of coverage (A/C, in Tk)	—	733.38	465.42	1,062.41	783.16	631.60

Note: [a] The fall in RDP membership in 1990–1 is due mainly to the transfer of members from RDP to RCP

supported by a computation of the hypothetical break-even interest rates for the past years, indicating the contrasting degrees of viability of the programmes (note that this calculation does not account for the high explicit and hidden subsidies on which both programmes are reliant).

The estimates for break-even interest rates required for viability are calculated on the basis of the following equation, in line with other case-studies in this volume (see Mosley 1993):

$$r = \frac{i + a + p}{1 + p}$$

where:

i = interest rate per unit of borrowed principal
a = administrative cost per unit of funds loaned out
p = default rate

The application of the equation to the BRAC and TRDEP data (see Table 12.13) results in average break-even interest rates of 52 per cent for the former programme and 100 per cent for the latter over the past six years. As with other data, the trend has been much more favourable for BRAC RDP than for TRDEP.

BRAC's hypothetical break-even interest rates during 1990 and 1991 fell to 10 per cent, well below the actual rate (20 per cent) charged to borrowers, indicating a significant degree of viability.

TRDEP's hypothetical break-even interest rates have not yet fallen to a level below their 16 per cent actual rates, suggesting that this programme has yet to prove its long-term viability. This is despite the fact that TRDEP claims 100 per cent repayment – a performance which is unlikely in the long term. However, BRAC also claims high repayment rates, which may also be difficult to sustain consistently over the future. Thus, the crucial difference in the performance of the two programmes lies in the trend in delivery costs of funds loaned out (the key difference already identified above).

Table 12.13 Estimates of break-even interest rates for BRAC RDP and TRDEP

Years	i	BRAC RDP a	p	r	Years	i	TRDEP a	p	r
1986	0	0.24	0.14	0.44	1986–7	0	0.51	0	0.51
1987	0	0.86	0.12	0.11	1987–8	0	3.02	0	3.02
1988	0	0.74	0.11	0.96	1988–9	0	1.08	0	1.08
1989	0	0.38	0.05	0.45	1989–90	0	0.48	0	0.48
1990	0	0.08	0.02	0.10	1990–1	0	0.31	0	0.31
1991	0	0.07	0.03	0.10	1991–2	0	0.62	0	0.62
Average	0	0.40	0.08	0.52	Average	0	1.00	0	1.00

Table 12.14 Estimates of SDIs for BRAC RDP and TRDEP

Years	A (Tk.m)	m (%)	c (%)	E (Tk.m)	P (Tk.m)	K (Tk.m)	LP (Tk.m)	i (%)	S (Tk.m)	SDI = S/(LP*i)
BRAC RDP										
1988	67.25	8	0	16.73	−40.52	0	101.32	20	47.23	233.07
1989	138.71	8	0	16.06	−72.76	0	213.18	20	85.14	199.69
1990	268.33	8	0	32.83	−148.24	0	159.77	20	172.33	539.31
1991	382.32	8	0	40.88	−187.33	0	169.56	20	221.19	642.25
Average	214.15	8	0	26.63	−112.21	0	160.96	20	131.47	408.39
TRDEP										
1988–9	4.43	8	0	1.50	−0.62	0	6.33	16	1.09	107.62
1989–90	1.99	8	0	1.11	−3.98	0	8.50	16	4.23	311.03
1990–1	33.10	8	0	2.41	−5.46	0	19.11	16	8.30	271.45
1991–2	17.70	8	0	2.77	−3.69	0	25.46	16	5.33	130.84
Average	14.31	8	0	1.95	−3.44	0	14.85	16	4.75	199.49

Despite BRAC's better performance over the last few years, it is still fully dependent on subsidies. The application of the SDI (see Yaron 1992) also shows that subsidy dependence is higher for BRAC than for TRDEP. Given the available data, the SDIs for the two programmes for the last four years are possible to calculate (Table 12.14).

Subsidy (S) is defined as:

$$A(m - c) + [(E * m) - P]K$$

where

S = annual subsidy received by the programme
A = concessional borrowed funds outstanding
m = interest rate the programme would be assumed to pay for borrowed funds if access to concessional borrowed funds was eliminated
c = concessional rate of interest actually paid on concessional borrowed funds outstanding
E = average annual equity
K = sum of all other subsidies received

Subsequently, the Subsidy Dependence Index is estimated as:

$$SDI = \frac{S}{LP * i}$$

where

LP = average annual outstanding loan portfolio of the programme
i = average on-lending interest rate paid on loan portfolio of the programme

Table 12.14 shows that during the four-year reporting period BRAC RDP received average annual subsidies of Tk131.47 million (US$3.46 million), while TRDEP received Tk4.74 million (US$0.13 million). BRAC's annual subsidies have increased steadily – from Tk47 million in 1988 to Tk221 million in 1991, as the programme has expanded under RDP II. TRDEP's government allocations have been more erratic.

In the case of BRAC, the SDI estimate suggests that an average increase of 408 per cent in the RDP lending rate would have been required to eliminate all subsidies during the reporting period, that is, a rise from 20 per cent per annum to 102 per cent per annum on loans disbursed to members.

The available data suggest that TRDEP would have required an increase of only 199.5 per cent on its present 16 per cent annual lending rate, that is, a rise to 48 per cent per annum on loans disbursed to members.

These average SDIs conceal a worrying upward trend in the case of BRAC, which appears to be increasingly dependent on subsidies; the TRDEP figures are more erratic, and are therefore difficult to interpret.

Overall, taking the average SDIs, the calculation shows TRDEP in a better position relative to BRAC's RDP – in contrast to the other measures of financial efficiency. In particular, there is a discrepancy with the results of the break-even interest rates (calculated as an average over the last six years of 52 per cent for BRAC and 100 per cent for TRDEP). This discrepancy is due to the fact that the Mosley method takes the actual rate of interest paid on borrowed funds (which for both programmes has been zero), but the Yaron method uses the hypothetical cost of raising capital on commercial terms which would be necessary if subsidies were discontinued (8 per cent from the Bangladesh Bank, during the relevant period). Also, the Yaron calculation takes into account other implicit subsidies (such as income generated by concessional funds held by the programme as deposits in other institutions).

Conclusions on financial performance

Much of the above analysis of the financial operations of the two programmes has to be interpreted in the light of their continued expansion. This process has been more rapid for BRAC under phase two of RDP than in the case of TRDEP, which remains a much smaller programme. In 1993 and 1994, TRDEP was scaling-up with the aid of ADB funds, and an SDI analysis of the programme during this phase could provide a better comparison with BRAC's position in the 1988–91 period.

Overall, despite BRAC's enhanced performance over time through reducing delivery costs and increasing profitability, RDP has been increasingly dependent on subsidies, and will remain so for the foreseeable future. The extent of TRDEP's reliance is even more pronounced, and this programme suffers from extremely high costs. TRDEP needs to follow the BRAC example in reducing these costs, and possibly to raise its interest rates. However, increasing interest rates by the hypothetical amounts suggested by earlier calculations would be impractical. For TRDEP, at least, the exemplary repayment performance which it claims is insufficient to guarantee viability.

The lack of any evidence to show that TRDEP is viable in the foreseeable future questions its role as a supply-side intervention in the rural credit market. For BRAC too, the claim of viability remains unresolved. One lesson that may be drawn from the above analysis of financial operations is that both programmes, and particularly BRAC's, have been expanding too rapidly. They need to slow down, avoid the large 'start-up' costs implied by continued scaling-up, and seek to generate interest income from branch-level operations in order to gain the stability which is necessary for their long-term survival. From the financial performance of these credit programmes for the poor, their justification is not obvious. This raises the question of their role in the rural credit market, and the benefits which they bring to their target groups.

ROLE IN THE MARKET

There are four broad categories of credit market participants in rural Bangladesh: the formal banks, orientated primarily to collateralised borrowers; government-targeted credit schemes, such as the BRDB RD 12; NGOs such as BRAC, RDRS and Proshika; and informal lenders of various types. Within each of these categories considerable variety exists, especially amongst informal lenders; and some institutions are difficult to categorise. (For example, the Grameen Bank is a parastatal, and is somewhere between a formal bank and the more flexible and experimental 'NGO' organisations; and because of TRDEP's design and aims, it is closer to BRAC and the Grameen Bank than most other government and formal finance institutions.) This section seeks to situate the roles of BRAC and TRDEP in this diverse financial and organisational environment.

BRAC and TRDEP in relation to other sources of credit

As the introduction noted, both BRAC and TRDEP aim to provide credit for those without access to other formal credit institutions, because of their target groups' difficulty of providing collateral. Informal discussions with VO and *kendra* members, and the results of our survey, confirmed that involvement with formal banks is extremely rare. Only three BRAC interviewees (out of 156) and five TRDEP interviewees (out of 160) said that they had taken a loan from a formal bank sometime in the past – all these eight borrowers were men. It therefore seems clear that these targeted programmes are not in competition with other formal credit institutions.

However, two particular concerns were raised by our fieldwork: first, the extent of overlap and potential competition amongst targeted credit schemes (working in the same localities); and second, the informal credit market contexts in which both the programmes and their borrowers are situated.

During our Dhaka discussions with academics, government officials and donor representatives it became clear that the sheer number of targeted credit schemes, both government and NGO, is causing some concern about the need to encourage co-ordination and avoid potential competition. There are political connotations to this Dhaka debate, which have been raised by Sanyal (1991), particularly in relation to government–NGO relations – which he maintains are characterised by an atmosphere of 'antagonistic co-operation'.

At a national level, the government maintains that targeted programmes should not overlap. Underlying this policy is an understandable concern that resources should be spread across the poorest half of the rural population as much as possible. In fact, often for logistical reasons, several programmes may be working in the same areas.

During our fieldwork, it was common to find BRAC, TRDEP and Grameen Bank offices and branches in close proximity. Local managers maintained that they always sought to operate in different villages; but since such boundaries are blurred in the high-density settlement patterns which characterise the countryside, such separation was not always evident in practice. For example, on visiting several BRAC VOs, it was found that one half of a village was deemed a Grameen Bank area, and the other half was 'BRAC's territory'; the boundary was often arbitrary (such as a track).

This 'competitive' atmosphere which seemed to be implicit when talking to field staff was more symbolic than substantive. As was outlined on pp. 99 and 106–10, there are few differences between the credit terms and delivery systems of all these organisations; and the presence of another programme in a working area does not, in itself, have an impact on the way the programmes provide services for their members. (However, branch and regional competition for members may be fuelling the speed of programmes' expansions, as executive and head office staff vie for larger size and therefore more justification for official and donor support; and programme expansion often affects smaller NGOs whose members are 'captured' by the larger organisations such as BRAC and the Grameen Bank.)

It also seemed to be the case that few people successfully maintained dual membership of different programmes. Both BRAC and TRDEP field staff seemed to be quite strict about this, overtly because of practical rather than policy reasons. Field staff commented that if one of 'their' members also belonged to another programme they feared it would allow the member to take too much credit – to use loans from one to pay off loans from the other programme. Such reasoning is questionable (it could work the other way round, because a borrower's additional credit line could *help* the field staff's own repayment collections).

However, the presence of several targeted programmes in a single area does raise questions about impact (which are discussed further in the following sections). Ideally, the larger the number of microcredit borrowers, the greater the injection of capital into a local economy: possibly increasing the likelihood that extra-household multiplier effects will occur. Our field study was not sufficient to investigate such hypotheses properly.

The limited involvement of programme members in informal markets

During discussions with groups of members of both programmes, people stated that their membership allowed them easier access to loans, on better terms, than those locally available on the informal market. In various groups in all the four district localities, members claimed that better-off people in their communities (such as richer cultivators, landlords and 'large' traders) and nearby markets (shopkeepers) were reluctant to extend them credit. Poor people, they said, are only offered loans at high interest rates, or with additional conditions attached (most commonly the pawning or mortgaging of assets such as livestock or household goods; or the pledging of labour in the coming seasons).

However, they also admitted that taking such loans was often necessary to meet contingencies caused by illness in the family or the costs incurred by social obligations such as dowries, marriage celebrations and funeral rites. There are also additional forms of minor credit transactions commonly occurring between kin and neighbours. These types of credit, which are sometimes interest-free, are often in kind (for example, paddy); but due to their size and nature do little more than help meet temporary consumption needs, and do not help solve long-term household financial problems.

Despite the involvement of our interviewees in informal credit transactions, there is also evidence to suggest that such forms of access are limited and insufficient in relation to the target groups' needs. In the case of BRAC borrowers, all said that the programme loan had financed over 75 per cent of their enterprise, and TRDEP borrowers maintained that their loans were over 80 per cent of their start-up capital. No interviewees stated that they were borrowing from other (informal) sources to help finance their income-generating activities. Two potential conclusions arise from this information: either the programme participants are substituting programme loans for informal loans, or most do not have sufficient creditworthiness to raise the necessary amounts of capital to start up their present activities.

Our survey results confirmed that most members of the two programmes are involved in informal credit transactions. The survey allowed

126

collection of data on (informal) loan amounts over the year preceding the last loan, and subsequently. For both surveys, the results imply that reliance on informal credit has decreased since joining the programme. Over the *year* preceding the last loan, BRAC borrowers took an average of Tk425 from three different sources; but since the programme loan they took only Tk110 from two different sources. In the case of TRDEP, members took an average of Tk865 from two different 'informal' sources in the year before their last programme loan, and since had taken only Tk120. Thus, BRAC members were borrowing, on average, smaller amounts from more sources than TRDEP members.

In order to show the significance of these results, it is necessary to note that TRDEP's members are, on average, significantly better off than BRAC's members. (Even though the target group definitions are almost identical, BRAC appears to be reaching more 'poorer' people, while TRDEP is tending towards the relatively better-off within the broad target population; the actual results of BRAC and TRDEP targeting are outlined in detail on pp. 129–31 and 139–41.) The data on informal borrowing may therefore be interpreted as reflecting the better creditworthiness of TRDEP borrowers compared to BRAC's (poorer) members; but in both cases, programme involvement appears to be reducing a previous reliance on informal loans.

It should not be surprising that both programmes are 'competing' successfully with informal creditors. Arguably, in the Bangladesh context, the factor of transaction costs (which are traditionally low for those borrowing from informal lenders) are much less significant than interest rates and loan sizes. Both BRAC and TRDEP are offering loans which are larger (for example, approximately Tk2,000 for a first loan) than the informal credits reported by borrowers for an annual period; interest rates of 16 per cent and 20 per cent, even when inflated by other conditions such as security deposits, are considerably better terms than informal rates, which are commonly around 10 per cent per month or tied to unpalatable conditions. In the context of capital scarcity, low creditworthiness, and high interest rates, the type of services offered by BRAC and TRDEP to the poor are far more attractive than those of informal lenders. There is also evidence to show that the members of these two programmes do, in fact, bear very high transaction costs, partly because these costs are in kind rather than in monetary form.

Despite 'taking the bank to the people', both TRDEP and BRAC impose high costs on members – though they are higher for the latter. BRAC's emphasis on education and VO mobilisation over a three to six month period, the weekly (one or two hour) meetings, and the need to collect loans from the local AO (rather than from a field worker at the VO meeting) mean that each loan requires a considerable investment of time, effort and discipline by BRAC members. TRDEP places less emphasis on the initial 'conscientisation' phase, but also requires borrowers' attendance at (somewhat smaller and shorter) weekly meetings. Thus, the transaction costs of these two programmes are certainly not small, and are surely greater than those incurred when going to a local landholder or trader for a loan. What is clear, however, is that borrowers are prepared to bear these disciplinary and temporal costs in order to gain access to much larger amounts of capital, on better terms, than would otherwise be available to them.

Competitive impact of BRAC and TRDEP on informal markets?

Given the successful provision of credit by BRAC and TRDEP, what effects do these schemes have on local informal credit markets? This is a complex issue, for which our data are limited.

We came across no evidence of resistance from local informal lenders to either BRAC or TRDEP, suggesting that such people do not regard themselves as being in competition with the programmes. As noted above, the work of Atiq Rahman (1992) on the informal sector over the last few decades suggests that its size has not been diminished by the growth in formal sector credit.

Until proved otherwise, it would be safer to suggest that the supply of informal credit is low compared to the demand for capital. In other words, while BRAC may be taking clients away from some moneylenders, programme coverage is still sparse enough to ensure that there are plenty of other potential customers. It is also evident that programme members still borrow from informal lenders, and will continue to do so. Neither BRAC nor TRDEP provides consumption credit, and both have relatively lengthy loan disbursement procedures. Thus, the informal sector is still the main recourse when people need credit in small amounts quickly.

There were some examples in our village visits of some slightly more negative attitudes held by lenders who were lending for reasons other than the purely economic – for example, richer cultivators securing labour for future seasons by lending to poor households in their neighbourhood. Such negative attitudes were not pronounced. Just as capital is scarce in relation to demand, so is labour abundant in relation to demand. Thus, even richer cultivators were not particularly concerned that BRAC members were becoming less reliant on the wage-labour market. (As noted on pp. 139–47, most TRDEP clientele appear not to have been reliant on wage-labouring before joining the programme.)

While BRAC and TRDEP provide a 'competitive' financial service for the poor, they are far from being a substitute for the informal sector. Informal lenders still retain advantages of local and timely access, speedy disbursement and fewer conditions on loan use. There is thus little real competition between these programmes and the informal sector at present.

THE IMPACT OF BRAC

BRAC's targeting

Our survey results suggest that BRAC's targeting is largely successful – most respondents meet the membership criteria laid down by RDP rules. However, the results also show social and economic differences amongst the programme's clientele. There are also indications that the most recent members are somewhat 'better-off' than longer-term members were when they originally joined. The reasons for this apparent shift towards slightly better-off borrowers are related to the expansion process and staff and VO leadership practices.

A brief socio-economic profile of the BRAC borrowers in our survey indicates successful targeting, and is suggestive of a central role of loan-financed activities in their livelihoods. At the time of our interviews, the 'average' BRAC borrower came from a household of about five and half members, with just under two income earners, had multiple sources of income, relied only partially on wage labouring, and had little or no formal education (only 13 per cent state that they can 'read and write'). The economic data suggest that this hypothetical 'average' BRAC household has just over 30 decimals of land, a recent (1992) monthly median income of Tk3,471 and an expenditure of Tk3,065, and that the median value of their total assets is Tk28,159. By far their most valuable asset is the little land which they own (both homestead and kitchen gardens, or other small plots); and their major sources of income are the loan-financed activities (over 40 per cent of total monthly income) and wage-labouring (a further 20–25 per cent of income).

However, this 'average profile' hides significant intra-membership differences. There is a minority of respondents who appear to be economically better-off than others to a significant degree. Perhaps the key indicator of this is that over 20 per cent of borrowers own more than 50 decimals of land (one of the main membership exclusion criteria). While some of these respondents (under 5 per cent of the total sample) purchased land after becoming members, and may therefore be using returns from BRAC credit to do so, approximately 15 per cent held more than the 50 decimals target criterion when they joined.

Conversely, nearly 10 per cent of respondents are totally landless, not even owning their homestead plots; and nearly 10 per cent of BRAC members are widowed or divorced women, another highly vulnerable social category. These contrasts between differentially endowed respondents indicate that the BRAC membership is far from homogeneous in

129

socio-economic terms, and that BRAC is reaching at least some of the extreme poor.

As outlined on pp. 101–12, the survey methodology allows for comparisons between two categories of borrowers (sixty-three recipients of one loan, and thirty-three recipients of three), and on the basis of household positions (a) at the interview time, and (b) 'before the last loan' in each borrower group. A comparison (or control) group is provided by the sixty recently recruited members who had received no loans at the time of the interview. The validity of using this non-borrower BRAC member group as a control depends partly on the assumption that their economic status is comparable to the previous positions of the other two borrower groups before taking any programme loans. However, some of the results of our survey indicate that such an assumption is debatable.

Indicators which support the assumption include the fact that land-ownership amongst the survey's three membership categories differs little; also, the incidence of female-headed households amongst the recent non-borrower members is almost identical to the proportion amongst first-time loanees. However, certain social and occupational indicators contest the comparability of the groups' starting positions.

Take for instance the indicator of access to education – one which Gustavsson (1990) correlates clearly with economic and social status in rural Bangladesh. As noted above, of the borrower respondents only 13 per cent of borrowers claim to be literate, the rest state that they had no schooling at all; but almost 27 per cent of the new members (yet to take any loans) are able to read and write, and almost half of these respondents have at least some secondary education.

More revealing is the asset situation of the three sample groups. While third-time borrowers reported an average total value for household assets of Tk26,230 at the time of the interview, the figure for first-time borrowers is Tk30,088. For the 'comparison group' non-borrower members total household assets averaged at Tk35,649.

In occupational terms, the recently joined non-borrower members also appear to be more advantageously placed than the borrowers (who had joined BRAC from two to four years ago). In the former category there are more people undertaking activities which involve fixed capital. For example, 8 per cent are shop trading, while there are no such shop-owners in the borrower categories; 10 per cent are doing some form of rural industry compared to under 5 per cent of the borrowers; and the frequency of regular waged 'service' employment amongst the new members is twice that of the borrower group. These figures add weight to the data on assets and the educational indicator, suggesting that the economic status of many newer members is somewhat better than those who joined in the past.

The survey results for the different membership categories suggest that a shift in the membership profile may have been taking place, that is, that

RDP has been less effective in reaching the poorest more recently. Throughout BRAC's expansion under RDP phase II (1989–) there has been a concern amongst donors and head office to maintain 'performance'. It appears that two major performance concerns – targeting and repayment rates – are potentially conflicting. At the field level, targeting is less emphasised than the need to keep repayment rates high. Quantitative targets impinge more on the perceptions of area office (branch) managers and their Programme Organisers, whose performance is more readily measured by such statistical indicators (assessing targeting is more time-consuming and the results are sometimes ambiguous).

Conversations with field staff suggested that these performance pressures result in POs and *Gram Shebaks* (and *Shebikas*) being more selective when recruiting new members, preferring the slightly better-off amongst the poorer 50 per cent of local target populations. Such people are more likely (at least, in the perceptions of the field staff) to be able to repay their loans on time than the less-well-endowed and assetless. Some BRAC field staff in one of our survey areas commented that VO leaderships will also be selective in this way (and probably especially so when POs and GSs are so inclined).

Rutherford (1993) has also stressed the problem of self-exclusion. Many targeted programmes raise social barriers to entry by using a highly disciplined approach. The rituals of membership (such as the regimented recitations of 'promises', rigid attendance rules and public discussion of loan applications and repayment) may enhance the fears and timidities of the extreme poor, including widows and women household heads, who are already partially excluded from 'normal' social life in a village environment. Rutherford's observations were made originally with reference to procedures of Grameen Bank Centres, but are just as applicable to BRAC's VOs.

Thus, a shift in the membership profile is understandable for operational reasons at the level of BRAC's field staff and Village Organisation leaderships. In particular, performance pressures may be resulting in a shift from a previous emphasis on the quality of service provided to the poorest, to a present concern with the fulfilment of quantitative targets. However, despite this targeting shift, most of the recent (non-borrower) respondents in our survey still fall within BRAC's definition of eligibility for RDP membership.

Because of the doubts about the comparability of the sample groups' economic starting positions, our analysis must rely predominantly on interviewees' 'before the last loan' and 'now' responses to questions about economic status.

Loan use and types of assisted enterprises

Most loans are being used for identifiable 'enterprises', but these are complementing a range of existing activities. Households are reliant on a diversity of income sources – a diversity which is necessary in the resource-poor and seasonal economy, plagued by under- and unemployment. In the entire sample of 156 BRAC members, less than 20 per cent had only one source of household income. (The significance of the loan-assisted activities for overall income is discussed further on pp. 134–6.)

Table 12.15 suggests that the types of activities financed by BRAC loans are similar for both first- and third-time borrowers, with petty trading dominating. Transport (mainly rickshaws, but also cart-pulling) and livestock (milk cattle, goats and poultry) both make up a similar proportion of the activities undertaken by the two borrower groups. Note that paddy husking is more significant for the more established borrowers. The lack of any major differences between the two groups, and the continued dominance of petty activities amongst third-time borrowers, suggests no graduation process with successive loans to alternative larger enterprises. However, across these sectoral activities, there is some evidence of a qualitative shift occurring.

Loan use appears to differ significantly amongst first-time and third-time borrowers. While thirty-seven out of sixty-three respondents (59 per cent) who had taken only one loan stated that it was used for 'working capital', this was true for a smaller proportion of the third-time borrowers (42 per

Table 12.15 Loan-assisted activities of BRAC borrowers

Activity	First-time borrowers	Third-time borrowers	All borrowers
Petty trading	21	9	30
	(33.3)	(27.3)	(31.3)
Livestock	11	6	17
	(17.5)	(18.2)	(17.7)
Transport	9	4	13
(mainly rickshaws)	(14.3)	(12.1)	(13.5)
Paddy-husking	4	6	10
	(6.3)	(18.2)	(10.4)
Crop cultivation	2	4	6
	(3.2)	(12.1)	(6.3)
Rural industries	5	—	5
	(7.9)		(5.2)
Shop trading	3	—	3
	(4.8)		(3.1)
Others	6	3	9
(including	(9.5)	(9.0)	(9.4)
consumption)			
Repaying other loans	2	1	3
	(3.2)	(3.0)	(3.1)
Totals	63	33	96
	(100)	(99.9)	(100)

Note: Figures in brackets are percentages

132

cent). Conversely, 'fixed capital' uses were more frequent amongst these more established members than among the first-time borrowers (39 per cent and 27 per cent respectively). These results suggest that successive loans increase the likelihood of acquiring productive assets.

Also, there is less fragmentation and diversion of loans amongst third-time borrowers. First-time borrowers appear more likely to use their loans for more than one purpose (13 per cent of respondents), while only one out of thirty-three third-time borrowers stated that the loan was used for multiple purposes. As with the positive correlation between number of loans and fixed capital investment, this result suggests that more established members are bearing more risk by concentrating their investment.

Only six out of the total ninety-six borrowers admitted to diverting the whole loan to consumption needs or to repaying other loans, but a further six said that they used some part of the loan for such needs. This means that just over 10 per cent of our sample are using their credit for consumption purposes to at least some extent. The survey results may under-represent the real extent of loan diversion – because BRAC's application process requires that the borrower states a specific 'productive' use for the loan (in all but exceptional circumstances) which may have discouraged interviewees from admitting consumption uses.

Eight out of the ten respondents who admitted consumption diversions were women (who are 67 per cent of the total borrower sample), suggesting that women are more susceptible than men to pressures to meet household consumption needs. Such a finding fits with existing analyses of household economics amongst the poor in Bangladesh. Kabeer (1989) has illustrated how the burden of poverty falls more harshly on women because they often have to use the meagre resources under their own control to ensure food and other basic daily needs are met. Men have fewer such daily responsibilities, and tend to have much greater freedom to dispose of cash as they wish.

Other data also suggests that women have particular problems in fulfilling the investment potential of credit. Although women dominate BRAC's RDP/RCP membership (they were 74 per cent of the total by the end of 1992, and are 67 per cent of our borrower sample), 10 per cent of our survey's women respondents reported no personal income despite being borrowers. For these nine women, who are different individuals from those using the loan partly or entirely for consumption needs, the loan use was determined by male kith and kin, who are also the first-hand beneficiaries of the returns (though the repayment burden remains with the women). The constraints facing BRAC's women borrowers, and the issue of who controls loans, have since been the focus of another, more detailed study (Goetz and Gupta 1994).

Changes in incomes and assets

Within households generating income from various sources, and because of the fungibility of credit and money in general, it is difficult to posit causal links between loan use and changes in income. However, correlating average figures for the borrower groups' household incomes before the last loan and at the time of the interview shows only marginal changes. These correlations suggest that the impact of credit on BRAC members' monthly incomes has been limited, particularly when rises in the price of rural commodities are considered. Table 12.16 summarises income changes for the two groups.

Given that the interviews for the above figures were undertaken in December 1992 to January 1993, and respondents took their last (one-year term) loan in the preceding one to four months, 1991–2 inflation figures can be used to approximate 'real' income changes. However, two Bangladesh Bureau of Statistics (BBS) indices could be used: the general rural consumer price index (6.7 per cent in the year), and the rise in the retail price of rice (12.6 per cent in the year). The latter figure is likely to be a more realistic measure of inflation. Because most BRAC households are functionally landless they buy their staple food on the market (and food constitutes 80 per cent or more of the total monthly expenditure of the BRAC members surveyed – see p. 48). Adjusting the survey income figures

Table 12.16 Monthly income changes 'before the last loan' and at the time of the interview: BRAC

Borrower group	Average monthly income 'before' (Tk)	Average monthly income 'now' (Tk)	Percentage increase
First-time borrowers (N = 63)	1,575	1,792	13.8
Third-time borrowers (N = 33)	1,401	1,679	19.8
All borrowers (N = 96)	1,513	1,752	15.8

Table 12.17 Real monthly income changes (actuals adjusted by general rural consumer and retail rice inflation indices): BRAC (%)

Borrower group	Nominal increase	Adjusted by rural consumer price index (6.7%, 1991–2)	Adjusted by retail rice price index (12.6%, 1991–2)
First-time borrowers	13.8	6.6	1.1
Third-time borrowers	19.8	12.3	6.4
All borrowers	15.8	8.6	2.8

above by these inflation indices, it appears that average real income increases of the first-time borrowers are very marginal. For third-time borrowers the increase is more – but still insufficient to constitute major growth (Table 12.17).

Nevertheless, the importance of the income from loan-assisted enterprises in relation to total household income is clear. Both types of borrowers reported similar income structures, in which loan-assisted enterprises accounted for around 44 per cent of the total, and are by far the most significant single source (the next most important is wages from casual labouring, which constitutes between 22 per cent and 26 per cent of the total for first- and third-time borrowers, respectively; and agriculture, which is 11 per cent and 10 per cent; other minor sources include returns from household livestock, remittances and various types of 'rental income' such as petty cash and kind loans).

Respondents' details of enterprise costs and proceeds suggest that successive investment is yielding higher absolute gains. Third-time borrowers investing in livestock reported absolute net profits twice those of first-time borrowers, and petty-trading and paddy-husking third-time borrowers reported substantially higher returns than first-time investors. However, profit as a proportion of gross proceeds is low in these cases of both petty-trading and paddy-husking (16 per cent and 40 per cent respectively), and much higher in the case of rickshaws and livestock holders (63 per cent and 93 per cent, respectively). However, diminishing returns over time in activities such as transport and petty trading are suggested (inconclusively) by our data, and were claimed by some respondents interviewed informally – see pp. 138–9 for further comments on poverty impacts.

Additional data on income generated by the loan-assisted enterprises suggest that successive loans have enhanced their centrality within the overall household livelihood strategies. Before the last loan, third-time borrowers reported that their enterprise generated over 35 per cent of their total monthly income (as opposed to the present proportion of 44 per cent); while first-time borrowers reported that the same activity which they were now undertaking with credit had generated only 19 per cent of their total household income. These results indicate an increasing dependency on the credit-assisted activities, but also reinforce the fact that such activities remain only a part of the total livelihood pattern of the households.

Somewhat more interesting (and significant) changes in household economic status appear in the data on assets – both business and total household (Table 12.18).

While changes in total household asset values before and after respondents' last loans have been marginal, there has been an increase in the value of 'productive' assets (that is, those employed in the loan-assisted enterprises). This is particularly noticeable for third-time borrowers (reporting a

Table 12.18 Changes in average household and enterprise asset values from 'before the last loan' and at the time of the interview: BRAC RDP

	Asset values 'before' (Tk)	Asset values 'now' (Tk)	Percentage increase
First-time borrowers (N = 63)			
Household	28,717	30,088	4.8
Enterprise	2,468	3,070	24.4
Third-time borrowers (N = 33)			
Household	24,408	26,230	7.5
Enterprise	2,956	5,777	95.0
All borrowers (N = 96)			
Household	27,234	28,760	5.6
Enterprise	2,635	3,999	51.8

massive 95 per cent increase in the value of such enterprise assets). The table also shows a noticeable difference in the absolute values of third-time borrowers' enterprise assets when compared to first-time borrowers – despite the fact that the value of the latter's total household assets is greater than those of the 'older' members. These results, when correlated with the differential investment in fixed capital and working capital by the two groups outlined above, suggest that successive loans do lead to a 'build-up' of productive assets over time.

While real income is increasing only marginally, the underlying asset and investment trends imply that some form of structural change is occurring – the main impact being an increase in the security, rather than in the absolute value, of income. However, what is clear from the general data is that this process is slow and gradual, and that the returns from such investments are marginal (see income changes outlined on p. 134). The implications of this structural shift (but marginal returns) are discussed further on pp. 138–9, in relation to the petty nature of most of the activities of BRAC members. There are indications that small trading, paddy-husking and rural transport – three of the key activities – have limited growth potential, being constrained both by their inherent nature and by contextual conditions such as market demand. These constraints are more evident when the limited impact of credit on other dimensions of borrowers' activities are considered, particularly the limited additional employment which is generated, and a lack of many changes in the intra-household organisation and methods (or 'management') of productive activities when loans are taken.

Productivity, employment and enterprise management

The increasing concentration of assets committed to the loan-assisted enterprises, together with the marginal increases in incomes reported by third-time borrowers, suggests no significant impacts on productivity can be argued from our data.

Also, even though the survey data suggest that successive loans increase the importance of enterprises as a part of overall household livelihoods, there is little evidence of any process of 'rationalisation' of these activities over time. As with the other case-studies in this volume, interviewees were asked whether borrowing had influenced their management practices. This question appeared to be inappropriate here. All except six of the ninety-six BRAC borrowers kept no written records of their business operations. The handling of cash returns did not change as a result of taking credit: both 'before' and 'after' loans, 40 per cent of all borrowers (mostly men, and a small proportion of the women) said that they kept their earnings separate from other household members, and 60 per cent (mostly women) said that such cash balances became 'mixed with other household cash'. Thus, the returns from loan-assisted enterprises appear to fit into existing household cash-handling practices, which help to reinforce male dominance in these matters – practices which fail to illustrate any clear separation of these 'enterprises' from households' other income-generating activities.

Employment impacts appear to be minimal, mainly because most enterprises are firmly rooted in the household. Sixty out of sixty-three (95 per cent) first-time borrowers did not employ anyone on a wage basis; and twenty-eight out of thirty-three (85 per cent) third-time borrowers have never used paid labourers. There appears to be a very slight correlation between successive loans and incidence of employment creation: of the four out of the ninety-six respondents who said that they were using more paid labour (all men) since their last loan, three were from the third-time borrower group (that is, 10 per cent of this category). However, quantitatively this employment generation by four households, who are each employing one man full-time, is tiny in relation to the total sample. While several respondents did say that they occasionally employed a temporary helper or got someone to do some 'piece-rate' work, these additional forms of employment were also quantitatively insignificant. Overall, the answers on extra-household employment show that BRAC's loans are not generating additional incomes for the non-borrower poor to any significant degree.

In the Bangladesh context, where underemployment of the functionally landless is chronic and exacerbated by the seasonality of the agrarian economy, BRAC's loans are more important for ensuring productive employment for the borrower and her (or his) household members. Since receiving the last loan 29 per cent of first-time and 33 per cent of third-time borrowers said that their activity is taking up more of their time. Only two out of the total ninety-six respondents claimed that they were spending less time on their activity. These responses, while not quantifying the actual hours spent on the activities, do suggest that successive loans lead to increasing absorption of household labour – just as the asset changes suggest increasing borrower commitment to the enterprise over time (see Hossain 1988 for similar conclusions relating to the impact of Grameen Bank loans).

Poverty impacts

The ideal impact of BRAC borrowers 'graduating out of poverty' is not clearly observable in our survey results. While marginal income and household asset increases were in evidence, the expenditure patterns of the two borrower groups (and these patterns before and after the last loans) were remarkably similar.

If income changes were having a significant impact on economic statuses it might be expected that essential expenditure on foodstuffs would fall as a proportion of the total. However, in all cases, households were and are spending over 80 per cent of their total expenditures on food, and between 6 per cent and 7 per cent on clothing. The remaining items (such as transport, medical, education and other expenses) remained minor in proportional terms.

Thus, while marginal income increases may have resulted in slightly improved food access and intakes, they have not been sufficient to change the structure of household consumption.

To put these changes in more concrete terms, the post-loan levels of income of the two borrower categories can be compared with data provided by the most recent (and comprehensive) study of poverty trends (Rahman and Hossain 1992). This study suggests an average 1989–90 figure for poverty-line expenditure of Tk2,567 per month (or Tk399 per capita). Present monthly *income* for BRAC's borrower households average Tk1,792 and Tk1,679 (or Tk340 and Tk303 per capita) for first- and third-time borrowers respectively, and their average monthly expenditures are slightly below these figures. These comparisons suggest that BRAC's clientele are still below the 1989–90 poverty line, and any adjustment for inflation up to the 1992 period would emphasise the gap between present borrowers' income–expenditure and the official poverty line.

Gauging the importance of the changes in assets is more difficult. As noted in Table 12.18, the total value of household assets increased only marginally, by 5.6 per cent on average, over the preceding year. In real terms (adjusting for inflationary changes), these increases are minimal or perhaps even negative. However, the structure of household assets does seem to have changed, with an average increase of over 50 per cent in the value of loan-assisted enterprise assets. This implies that BRAC borrowers are gaining a better income-generating base over time, and may therefore be achieving greater *security* of income. Yet enterprise assets remain a small proportion of the total (around 14 per cent), and are much smaller (almost half the value) than those of TRDEP households. It is thus far from clear that the BRAC borrowers' asset changes are fundamentally changing their economic status.

In brief, the quantitative data provided by our BRAC survey suggest that the impact of a few loans over several years is marginal, and the impact on poverty must be deemed very gradual. As yet, there is little evidence that BRAC's clientele are altering their structural position within the rural economy. These findings for the BRAC sample are somewhat different from those found for the TRDEP respondents. Explaining these differences is the subject of pp. 147–53, before which the data on TRDEP's impact is presented.

THE IMPACT OF TRDEP

TRDEP targeting

TRDEP's membership criteria are similar to those of BRAC; but the survey data shows that this government programme is reaching fewer 'very poor' people and includes many more men than women. The absence of more vulnerable categories of women (divorced, widowed and female heads of households) is marked. Instead, the programme is catering for better-endowed households, relative to BRAC. Also, both social and economic indicators suggest that there is a significant proportion of borrowers who are not from the target group.

Women make up only 28 per cent of the sample (44 out of 160), and only three of the borrower households are female-headed. Whereas the BRAC sample contained ten divorced or widowed women, only two amongst the TRDEP respondents were captured in the random survey. This bias towards men in TRDEP's clientele has been found in the other available field studies (Talukdar and Islam 1992; Rutherford 1993).

Educationally, the TRDEP sample appears to be of higher status than the national average for rural areas. Over 40 per cent of the interviewees stated that they can read and write, and forty-two of them (26 per cent) have had some secondary schooling. The average rural literacy rate is 24 per cent, and the proportion of people gaining secondary education is estimated as 17 per cent. This latter statistic is particularly revealing, because there is certainly a strong positive correlation between secondary schooling and higher socio-economic status in rural Bangladesh.

The economic data confirm the social indicators for TRDEP clientele's status. Average landholding of the 160 respondents, at 46 decimals, is only

139

slightly below the maximum 50 decimal ceiling. Average landholding for the first-time borrowers is higher (66 decimals), while the non-borrower members acting as our comparison group have average holdings of 31 decimals. In all, thirty-three households (21 per cent) have landholding above the 50 decimals ceiling.

Average total household asset values and occupational data are also indicative of an overall resource endowment significantly better than that of BRAC's clientele. TRDEP's borrowers reported average total values of Tk50,230 before their last loan, which is 84 per cent higher than the relevant figure for BRAC households and slightly above the level prescribed by the programme (Tk50,000); and occupationally, TRDEP members are involved in a range of activities which are generally of a more substantial nature than those of BRAC interviewees. Most notable is the limited involvement of TRDEP respondents in wage-labouring. Only four of the 160 said that they had done any casual labouring in the last thirty days. While trading is the main sectoral activity, the incidence of shop ownership is high amongst TRDEP borrowers (12.5 per cent), and the volume of commerce carried out by the 'petty traders' is also high (see the discussion of profits on pp. 151–3).

The survey data outlined above suggest that TRDEP's targeting is qualitatively different from BRAC's. Crudely stated, while the latter is reaching some of the very poor and disadvantaged, TRDEP is catering to the relatively better-off within the broad target group, and there are strong indicators that a substantial number of the programme's members are actually better-off than the rules stipulate they should be in order to be eligible for loans.

Reasons for the nature of TRDEP's targeting are similar to those which seem to be operating in BRAC's expansion process, but they are perhaps more intrinsic to the attitudes of government project staff and the organisational culture of the programme. Group Animators are under pressure from their branch managers to ensure timely repayment. (A recent government circular stated that GAs risk losing their jobs if their centres perform poorly.) Such pressures create incentives for GAs to select the more 'creditworthy' amongst the target group, that is, those relatively better-off; and indeed, it is officially stated (and reiterated by field staff during our informal discussions) that one of the criteria for membership is 'respectability'. Since this ambiguous quality is often determined by economic as well as social capabilities and may disadvantage women in the Bangladesh context, TRDEP's targeting outcomes are understandable. The relative absence of women and female-headed households, and the tendency to cater to the 'more respectable' members of the poor, confirms TRDEP's image as a somewhat 'conservative' programme compared to other credit programmes such as the BRAC RDP (which has an explicit 'empowerment of the disadvantaged' rhetoric) and the Grameen Bank (which extols the virtues of lending specifically to women).

Loan use and enterprise profiles

Out of ninety-six TRDEP borrowers, only one reported using part of their loan for consumption purposes, and none reported a need to pay off any outstanding debts with their new credit. The lack of any significant loan diversion to non-enterprise and contingency needs suggests that TRDEP households are in a relatively secure economic state compared to many (amongst the poorer 50 per cent of the population).

While the range of sectoral activities undertaken by borrowers is similar to that found in the BRAC sample (see Table 12.19) there are some important differences. The low number of women in TRDEP's clientele is reflected in the relative absence of activities such as paddy-husking (which is never a male activity). Apart from such gendered differences, there is strong evidence to show that TRDEP borrowers are running much larger enterprises than those of BRAC borrowers.

Most TRDEP respondents are using the credit to re-finance existing activities. Working-capital purchase is by far the most significant type of loan use (78 per cent of first-time, and 75 per cent of third-time

Table 12.19 Loan-assisted activities of TRDEP borrowers

Activity	First-time borrowers	Third-time borrowers	All TRDEP borrowers
Petty trading	26	13	39
	(40.6)	(40.6)	(40.6)
Livestock	18	8	26
	(28.1)	(25.0)	(27.1)
Shop trading	5	7	12
	(7.8)	(21.9)	(12.5)
Rural industries	7	1	8
	(10.9)	(3.1)	(8.3)
Transport (mainly rickshaws)	7	—	7
	(10.9)		(7.3)
Crop cultivation	—	2	2
		(6.3)	(2.1)
Paddy-husking	—	1	1
		(3.1)	(1.0)
Consumption purposes	1	—	1
	(1.6)		(1.0)
Totals	64	32	96
	(99.9)	(100)	(99.9)

Note: Figures in brackets are percentages

141

borrowers). Fixed capital investments are slightly more frequent amongst the third-time borrowers (22 per cent) than the first-time loanees (16 per cent), with the remaining respondents reporting mixed (fixed and working) types of capital purchases. The large proportion of borrowers involved in trading (53 per cent) is one explanation for this pattern of loan use: 50 per cent of all borrowers reported purchasing 'goods for sale' with their loan. Petty trading and even small shops (once established) need little or no fixed capital.

The size of enterprises is only partly due to loan size. TRDP first loans averaged Tk2,300 as opposed to Tk1,800 for BRAC; but third loans in each programme appear to be comparable (Tk2,765 for TRDEP, and Tk2,965 for BRAC). However, data on the average value of enterprise assets show significantly greater capital deployment in TRDEP activities. Before the last loan, for the ninety-six TRDEP borrowers 'business asset' values averaged Tk3,521 (while the comparable figure for BRAC borrowers is Tk2,635). Data on business expenses show even greater differentials in *all* sectoral activities. Average recurrent business expenses in the month 'before the last loan' averaged Tk7,053 for TRDEP borrowers, and only Tk1,225 for BRAC members (a differential of 5.7). These data show TRDEP borrowers as having much greater turnover than BRAC's members.

This larger scale of activities amongst TRDEP borrowers does not appear to be due to 'pooled investment' by the five-person joint-liability groups. As noted on p. 106, one of TRDEP's general operational principles is that of 'family' groups, to allow more concentrated investment by related members taking loans at the same time. Only one respondent of the ninety-six borrowers stated that this had been the case.

Informal discussions with *kendra* members confirmed that the five-person groups are rarely full families. The presence of two related persons (such as husband and wife) is quite common, and in such cases loans may be (but are not always) pooled in one enterprise. However, full families are rare, and when several kith and kin make up a joint-liability borrowing group, they are often from separate households and are using their loans in a similar way to BRAC members. These findings clearly indicate that TRDEP's aim of concentrating investment capability is not being achieved. This suggests that the reasons for larger enterprises lie in the existing economic statuses of borrowers prior to joining the programme.

Changes in income and assets

Data on income changes suggest that TRDEP borrowers are experiencing significant 'real increases'; and that these increases are, on average, greater for third-time borrowers than for first-time borrowers. These results are notably different from those reported by BRAC respondents, which suggested that the impact of credit on income was minimal. Tables 12.20 and

12.21 present the TRDEP sample data; the calculations of 'real income' changes rely on the same inflation data used in the section on BRAC borrowers. Not only are the amounts of monthly income both before and after the last loan significantly higher than those of BRAC's members (by between 30 per cent and 90 per cent for the different borrower categories), there is also a clear trend of income growth correlating with the number of loans. In contrast to the BRAC data, there are also clearer indications suggesting a causal role for the credit if the proceeds of TRDEP-assisted enterprises are taken into account (proceeds in absolute terms, and as a proportion of total income).

The data on the structure of household income clearly suggest that successive borrowers are becoming more dependent on their loan-assisted enterprises. For third-time borrowers, the enterprises contributed around 70 per cent of their monthly household income both before and after the last loan, for first-time borrowers their enterprises contributed 40 per cent of their monthly income prior to taking TRDEP credit, but this proportion has risen to 50 per cent now. These proportions are much greater than the comparable ones for BRAC borrowers (44 per cent for both categories), and indicate that TRDEP members' relatively larger-scale enterprises are a far more dominant part of households' overall livelihood strategies. Rather than diversifying, TRDEP members appear to be becoming

Table 12.20 TRDEP households' monthly income changes 'before the last loan' and at the time of interview

Borrower group	Average monthly income 'before' (Tk)	Average monthly income 'now' (Tk)	Increase (%)
First-time borrowers (N = 64)	2,027	2,648	30.6
Third-time borrowers (N = 32)	2,662	3,691	38.7
All borrowers (N = 96)	2,237	2,996	33.9

Table 12.21 Real monthly income changes (actuals adjusted by general rural consumer and retail rice inflation indices): TRDEP (%)

Borrower group	Nominal increase	Adjusted by rural consumer price index (6.7%, 1991–2)	Adjusted by retail rice price index (12.6%, 1991–2)
First-time borrowers	30.6	22.4	16.0
Third-time borrowers	38.7	30.0	23.0
All borrowers	33.9	25.5	18.8

Table 12.22 Changes in TRDEP borrowers' average household and enterprise asset values from 'before the last loan' and at the time of the interview

	Asset values 'before' (Tk)	Asset values 'now' (Tk)	Percentage increase
First-time borrowers (N = 64)			
Household	48,802	53,920	10.5
Enterprise	2,505	5,033	100.9
Third-time borrowers (N = 32)			
Household	55,230	63,084	14.2
Enterprise	5,549	10,011	80.4
All borrowers (N = 96)			
Household	50,943	56,976	11.8
Enterprise	3,521	6,693	90.0

more specialised. Given the relatively favourable economic status indicators for TRDEP respondents, this suggests that they are able to bear greater risks than poorer BRAC members.

Combining data on net profits with the data on income structure strengthens the argument that TRDEP credit is playing a causal role in the improvements in income averages. Net profits are significantly higher for TRDEP entrepreneurs than for BRAC members. For example, BRAC 'shop traders' reported average net profits per month of Tk706, while TRDEP shop traders reported an average of Tk2,418; the respective figures for petty traders are Tk884 and Tk1,884, and for livestock holders Tk268 and Tk1,055.

Does this mean that TRDEP members are gaining higher rates of return, or are these profit differentials merely a reflection of the larger scale of TRDEP activities? Our data are incomplete on this issue, but what there are suggest that the latter conclusion is more likely to apply. For example, profit as a proportion of gross monthly proceeds is similar in the case of both BRAC and TRDEP shop traders, livestock holders and those involved in transport activities. On average, BRAC petty traders report higher profit margins than TRDEP petty traders; but the eight TRDEP borrowers involved in rural handicrafts and industries report higher margins than the five BRAC members doing such work. Overall, it appears that profit margins (and therefore relative returns on household labour and capital) are broadly similar, and that the effect of TRDEP credit is greater because of the larger scale of the activities which they are helping to finance.

Not surprisingly, the increases in average household and enterprise asset values mirror changes in income, and again indicate third-time borrowers building up their business capital. As noted on p. 140, TRDEP household

144

assets are much higher than BRAC's, and as Table 12.22 shows, average values for both first- and third-time borrowers are now greater than the eligibility criterion lays downs (a limit of Tk50,000). These figures, combined with the data on income change, provide a general picture of favourable changes occurring that are at least partly due to access to credit.

Employment and enterprise management

Most TRDEP borrowers are operating their enterprises with the help of household members. A small minority of borrowers (five out of ninety-six) are working with non-kin in co-operative ventures of some form or the other (that is, partnerships). While there is some evidence of rationalisation occurring, there is little to show that TRDEP is creating additional (non-domestic) employment.

Eighteen members now keep records of their business activities (as opposed to eight before their last loans); 28 per cent of the third-time loanees keep such records (as opposed to 14 per cent of first-time loanees), and some of these records are highly detailed (including expenses, stock details, credit-in-kind given out, sales and profit calculations). Given that 40 per cent of the sample said that they can read and write, the number keeping records is fewer than might be expected. However, the data on increasing book-keeping combines well with the data on increasing business scale, suggesting that at least some TRDEP-assisted enterprises are becoming more discrete and well-managed. It is possible that such rationalisation is enabled by the overall more secure economic status of the borrower household, which gives an ability to withstand consumption and contingency needs from non-enterprise resources (which otherwise cause contractions in the enterprises of poorer borrowers, as input or stocks fall, due to diversion of resources).

Impact on local labour markets through TRDEP's credit provision is also minimal, according to our survey results. While eighty-seven out of ninety-six TRDEP borrowers stated that they had never employed paid labour, of the remaining nine, five are in the third-loan category. In proportionate terms, this means that nearly 16 per cent of the thirty-two third-time loanees are employing people, and only 6 per cent of the sixty-four first-time loanees are doing so. All these nine respondents said that they are using more such paid labour since receiving their last loan. This suggests that a small number of the loan-assisted enterprises, and in particular the more established ones of third-time borrowers, are beginning to generate employment for other, non-borrower poor.

However, as with the BRAC data, the number of employees involved is small, especially in relation to the total number of borrowers. Further increases in employment will not, of course, be supported by TRDEP credit (after three loans in rapid succession the *kendra* is closed down).

Thus, despite the fact that TRDEP loan-assisted enterprises are of larger scale than the BRAC ones, there is little evidence to suggest that the programme is having a major multiplier effect on the local economy through extra-household employment generation.

Poverty impacts

TRDEP's borrowers, on average, appear to be benefiting notably from credit. They are experiencing significant increases in both real incomes (by 16 per cent to 23 per cent) and the value of their household assets (by 10.5 per cent to 14.2 per cent); for both these dimensions of economic status, third-time borrowers appear to have experienced more increments than first-time borrowers.

In concrete terms, the comparison with the poverty trends analysis figures of Rahman and Hossain (1992) confirms the positive nature of the TRDEP results. In 1991, households of first-time borrowers had per capita incomes of Tk347, and third-time borrowers per capita incomes of Tk448. Both groups, and certainly third-time borrowers, were below or very near the official poverty line (estimated at Tk399 in 1989–90). Since receiving their last loans, first-time borrower households' per capita income has increased to Tk453 on average. This is surely close to any inflation-adjusted poverty line based on the 1989–90 figure. More significantly, third-time borrowers on average have crossed this line (they now have per capita incomes of Tk621). Our survey results therefore suggest that TRDEP borrowers, on average, are graduating out of poverty.

Data on the structure of household expenditure give a more practical illustration of the results of this graduation process. Before their last loans, both first- and third-time borrowers stated that they spent over 70 per cent of their monthly income on food (this is the average expenditure for rural households, according to the Rahman and Hossain study). While this proportion has remained constant for first-time borrowers since receiving their last loan, third-time borrowers report that they now spend only 59 per cent of their monthly income on food. They also report a marked jump in expenditure on 'incidental major expenses', on items such as improved housing and meeting social obligations. Thus, it appears that TRDEP third-time borrowers have more than is necessary to meet food consumption needs and that the degree of income increases is allowing previously unaffordable expenditures.

Thus, while it is clear that TRDEP credit is not generating significant extra-household employment, it does seem to be the case that programme borrowers are graduating out of poverty. However, the contrast between these survey results and those of BRAC requires explanation. Reasons for the differences may lie in operational differences between the programme, but arguably there are more fundamental causes. A more likely explanatory factor is the contrasting economic statuses of the two groups prior to programme intervention. If this is so, the findings of our field study suggest important conclusions about the limitations of credit as a poverty-alleviation strategy in Bangladesh.

EXPLAINING THE DIFFERENTIAL POVERTY IMPACT OF BRAC AND TRDEP

Our survey results suggest that credit is playing a promotional role for TRDEP borrowers. The graduation of third-time loanees implies that the poverty-cycle of low investment, low returns, low income and therefore low investment does appear to be broken. Yet for BRAC borrowers our evidence is less optimistic – graduation is not occurring and the changes in household economic positions are much more marginal.

If, as can be argued, the credit delivery systems of BRAC and TRDEP are so similar, then the reasons for these contrasting results must lie in targeting and contextual variables. If this is so, it implies that credit has different implications for different types of poor people. To support this argument, a better understanding of the Bangladesh rural context and the structural and process variants of poverty is necessary. Arguably, even if credit is not playing a promotional role for many of the poor, it may still provide important benefits which 'protect' the existing statuses of households, perhaps providing a form of safety net, by contributing to crisis-coping capabilities. However, the possibility that credit creates additional risks for the extreme poor also has to be considered. Credit may be insufficient and inappropriate for alleviating extreme poverty.

Comparing the BRAC and TRDEP credit delivery systems

From the perspective of borrowers, the way in which both BRAC and TRDEP operate in the field is very similar. *Shomitis* and *kendras* are formed, weekly meetings are held by either GSs or GAs. Loans are sanctioned (if not disbursed) on-site, and are mostly of fifty-two weeks repayment duration. Weekly savings and repayment procedures are identical in form (even if the amounts of savings differ slightly). Loan sizes appear to be similar, averaging approximately Tk2,000 for first loans and Tk3,600 for third loans.

The key difference lies in TRDEP's attempt to lend to household (joint-liability) groups, rather than BRAC's more individualistic approach. However, we have already noted in preceding sections that full family-based groups amongst the TRDEP clientele appear to be rare, though husbands and wives are quite common. Other kin-based groups do not lead to concentrated investment of loans because such kin are often from different households, and therefore economically separate entities.

147

In the case of BRAC, too, some degree of loan-pooling does occur. Visits to various villages where both male and female VOs had been formed provided many examples where both wives and husbands are taking loans from BRAC at roughly the same time. These cases, which are quite prevalent, suggest that the amount of household loan-pooling which occurs in both programmes is much more comparable than the different programme 'rules' would suggest.

This brief comparison of the way in which BRAC's and TRDEP's credit systems operate in practice suggest that the contrasting impact of the two programmes has to be explained by contextual factors. Before elaborating this argument in greater depth, a brief comparison of the economic statuses of the programmes' clientele provides clearer illustration of differences.

Economic differences between the programmes' clientele

A schematic selection of comparative data highlights some of the contrasts between the BRAC and TRDEP interviewees. Table 12.23 speaks for itself, and shows significant differences not only in income and asset values, but also in indicators such as landholding and labouring reliance which are

Table 12.23 Comparative economic status of BRAC and TRDEP borrowers

Economic indicator	BRAC RDP borrowers (N = 96)	TRDEP borrowers (N = 96)
Average income before last loan (Tk)	1,513	2,237
Average income now (Tk)	1,752	2,996
Average household assets before last loan (Tk)	27,234	50,943
Average household assets now (Tk)	28,760	56,976
Average enterprise assets before last loan (Tk)	2,635	3,521
Average enterprise assets now (Tk)	3,999	6,693
Average percentage of monthly expenditure spent on food	80 (all)	70 (first-time borrowers) 59 (third-time borrowers)
Average landholding (decimals)	30	46
Average percentage of income derived from daily labouring		
before loans	32	5
after loans	23	5
Percentage of divorced and widowed women (N = 96)	10	1

suggestive of the different relational position of the clienteles to their economic context.

Not only do BRAC's clientele appear to be less well endowed than TRDEP borrowers (before as well as after taking credit from the programmes), but there are also indicators of greater vulnerability (for example, expenditure on food; proportion of divorced and widowed women) and dependency on extra-household sources of livelihood (such as reliance on wage-labouring; lower landholding). These dimensions of poverty – vulnerability and dependency – are key issues in understanding economic status and the variant experiences of poverty.

Constraints on (and conditions for) graduation

The poverty trends analysis report outlines some of the key (broad) constraints facing the poor in contemporary Bangladesh (Rahman and Hossain 1992). They have to overcome two problems: insufficient income (and assets) to sustain an adequate livelihood; and a series of 'downward mobility pressures' which constrain improvements, or eradicate them when they occur temporarily.

These downward mobility pressures include: (a) structural factors in the social and economic environment, including seasonality; (b) crisis factors such as family contingencies (such as illness) and natural disasters (such as floods); (c) life-cycle factors and the developmental cycle of domestic groups (households may become poorer or better-off over time due to changes in the number of very young, older dependent and economically active members).

Perhaps the most evident of the structural factors impinging on poor people is the limited availability of employment in a depressed economy with over-supply of labour. The introduction to this chapter noted how agricultural growth in most of Bangladesh has been slow and unable to absorb new entrants into the labour market. The result has been a limited availability of wage work, depressed real wage rises in the last few years, and severe seasonal fluctuations in wage rates, averaging 30 per cent in a single year according to 1991 data (Rahman and Hossain 1992). Other structural factors include inflation and constrained market demand.

In general, poorer people depending on the market for access to basic foodstuffs experience higher inflation than better-off people (note the difference between retail rice price inflation and the general consumer price index, discussed on p. 134 above). Erosion of real income over time is difficult to assess and may be less significant than the more crises-inducing sporadic spurts in inflation which occur in different seasons. Pre-harvest-time rises in food prices can severely restrict poorer households' ability to purchase enough food, these seasonal price fluctuations coinciding with slack periods in the wage-labour market. Such temporary shortfalls can be

149

sufficient to cause distress conditions, leading to informal debt and sales of assets.

Constrained market demand is more difficult to define and assess, and differs according to regional economic conditions. If the rural economy were growing rapidly through rising production, generating increased disposable incomes, markets for goods and services would expand. We have already noted the low growth in Bangladeshi agriculture and it is probably realistic to argue that the growth that has occurred has been concentrated in a limited number of regions (see Hossain 1989 on the still low proportion of the countryside in which modern varieties and green revolution farming has been adopted). This means that credit-assisted petty enterprises will do better in high-growth areas, but are likely to face demand constraints in many others. Indeed, this raises questions about the limitations of credit in areas where programmes such as BRAC RDP and Grameen Bank are lending to large numbers of people. Does concentrated lending increase competition amongst petty entrepreneurs due to limited market demand for their products, thereby depressing prices and reducing real returns? Our own data are insufficient to provide any firm answer, but the possibility of these market-demand constraints operating in specific contexts cannot be discounted.

These structural factors mean that functionally landless households throughout rural Bangladesh need to earn livelihoods from a variety of sources – not just wage-labouring, but also from informal credit and savings-in-kind, petty enterprises of various types and, when cash is short, 'expenditure-saving' activities. These latter include gathering materials for housing and gleaning minor edibles and fish from (increasingly depleted) common access resources. Cutting down on food is a necessity for many in deficit periods each year.

Structural factors and phases in the developmental cycle of domestic groups contribute to crises brought on by the dimensions of poverty which derive from limited incomes. As Chambers (1983) notes, poor nutrition both increases susceptibility to disease and decreases working (and therefore income-generating) capabilities. Social and political vulnerabilities (for example, those deriving from poor education and disadvantageous relations with 'patrons' and officials) exacerbate isolation and powerlessness. These various dimensions of deprivation and vulnerability both enhance the probability of crises occurring and reduce the ability of households to cope with them. When they do occur, illnesses, marriages and deaths in the family can all lead to extraordinary demands on existing resources, causing distress sales of livestock or other household goods. Such crises act as 'ratchets', decreasing further the likelihood of graduation out of poverty, or wiping out what small gains may have been made prior to the crisis event.

Taken together, the various factors outlined briefly here constitute constraints which are difficult to overcome. Our survey material on BRAC and TRDEP borrowers suggests that it is only the former who appear, on average, to be able to surmount the obstacles which keep incomes at depressed levels. Some more specific discussion of income-generating activities is useful to illustrate these contrasts and to help identify some of the conditions necessary for credit-supported 'graduation' to occur.

Over 40 per cent of BRAC's borrowers are involved in petty trading or paddy husking, both activities favoured by women because of their flexibility. Such activities can be expanded or contracted relatively easily depending on the need to carry out other (for example, domestic) duties, and the availability of cash to buy inputs (either paddy or trading goods). They are also relatively attractive because both activities involve rapid returns on investment, which makes them safer ways of investing in an inflationary environment. However, the very characteristics which make them attractive can also create vulnerabilities. When contingencies arise, it is easy to switch cash which would have been invested in paddy or trading goods to cope with other non-productive demands. Profits over time can therefore be low unless the size of investment is maintained.

Many BRAC women taking loans for paddy husking claimed that they could get only limited returns. When receiving the loan, and investing it all in paddy, profits after the first husking can be ploughed back into buying more paddy quite rapidly (for example, Tk2,400-worth of paddy in 1992 was approximately 12 maunds (1 maund = approx. 0.37 kg), which could be husked and cleaned within 20–25 days, yielding a total return of approximately Tk2,880, that is, a profit of Tk480 after re-investing the original loan amount in more paddy). Yet growth in this activity (that is, buying greater amounts of paddy to be husked) is constrained both by lack of labour time and more fundamentally the frequent occasions on which cash returns have to be diverted to household consumption needs. This problem is particularly acute for women, who have to ensure there is enough food every day for family meals, and who are expected to use their own income for such needs before calling on the income of other (male) family members. Thus, there is often a limit to which paddy husking can generate income, and rapid turnover and domestic demands on returns means that women often have to reduce the volume of their work. For petty traders similar constraints operate, particularly if the lack of other household income sources and consumption requirements create sporadic demands on cash returns.

Another 30 per cent of BRAC borrowers in our survey use their loans for relatively 'fixed' and less-flexible investments, namely livestock and rickshaw purchases. The latter, especially, can generate a respectable income – perhaps twice as much as wage-labouring. However, with this activity a labour and time limit is placed on the amount of income which is feasible. The main benefit is that the investment is protected on a day-to-day basis, thereby providing a more secure income source. Once the ceiling on income is reached, further boosts to household income will have to come from additional sources (perhaps, if the constraining factors outlined here allow, through investment of rickshaw earnings – but because of the ceiling such building up of resources will be very gradual). Livestock investments are also 'lumpy' and therefore relatively protected sources of income (though here, of course, risks include loss through disease). However, net returns to livestock in the short term (through products such as eggs and milk) are low, averaging Tk268 per month for BRAC interviewees, compared to Tk795 from rickshaw drivers. Long-term returns (through breeding or sale of adult animals) are much more significant, and may constitute major re-investable sums; but by their very nature such returns are sporadic. Protecting lumpy assets such as rickshaws and cows and realising future re-investment potential are dependent on avoiding the crises and contingencies mentioned above.

When comparing BRAC and TRDEP borrowers (pp. 148–9) it was noted that there were major differences in scale of operation; but it is also notable that activities such as rickshaws and particularly paddy husking were much less in evidence (only 7 per cent and 1 per cent of TRDEP borrowers were using loans for these activities, respectively). By far the most important activities are petty and shop trading (together constituting 53 per cent of borrowers) and livestock investments (27 per cent).

On average, TRDEP's traders are operating with turnovers and returns over twice those of BRAC petty traders (for example, average monthly net profits were Tk1,884 for the former, and Tk1,010 for the latter). The value of livestock held by TRDEP borrowers was more than double that of BRAC borrowers, there being a major difference in pre-loan holdings. Returns were therefore much higher for TRDEP livestock investors than for their BRAC counterparts (Tk1,055 and Tk267, respectively). These contrasts suggest that for these two activities, at least, inherent limits on returns by household labour constraints do not apply: it is the scale of operation which is crucial, and the ability to protect profits for re-investment from daily consumption needs and the assets from more major demands caused by crises.

In summary, characteristics of different loan-assisted activities and the constraints outlined here lead to the argument that households need to have achieved a certain economic level in order to use loans successfully, protect their investments and (where limits do not apply) enhance the scale of their operations to achieve a sustainable level of higher income (see Rutherford 1993). While this 'economic level' is difficult to specify in quantitative terms, given the various dimensions of poverty, it can be defined by minimum characteristics such as: the existence of a reliable income; freedom from pressing debt; sufficient health to avoid incapacitating illnesses; freedom from imminent contingencies (such as family marriages); and sufficient resources such as savings and non-essential convertible assets to cope with problems when they arise. Other factors may also be important, such as levels of household creditworthiness which enable access to short-term informal loans – a creditworthiness which TRDEP's borrowers seem to have more of than BRAC's members (see pp. 126–7). For those households which are unable to achieve a combination of factors that provide this 'minimum economic level', credit alone is unlikely to enable the graduation process to occur.

Protectional and promotional credit impact

Credit may still play a crucial role for households poorer than our hypothetical 'minimum economic level'. Precisely because of the need to access various types of income sources and support, credit can contribute to the process of enhancing household security. The fungibility of monetary resources means that credit can enable diversion of existing (pre-loan) cash incomes to meet needs which would otherwise have led to reduced economic activity (such as cutting down on paddy-for-husking purchases or on trading goods) or the more critical sale of assets. In this way, credit can play a protectional rather than a promotional role.

These concepts of protection and promotion are used by Dreze and Sen (1989 and 1991) in their discussions of different forms of 'entitlement' and 'social security' which influence access to resources. While it is not necessary to go into this debate in detail, the concepts of promotion and protection are heuristically useful for categorising the different roles which credit can play as a strategy for poverty alleviation. Our own discussion of the different variables perpetuating poverty, and the pre-conditions for credit-assisted graduation, suggest that most, though not all, credit is protectional; but only some credit is promotional. The analogy of a safety net is also useful – because while credit can prevent further decline into poverty for some and propel others upwards, the mesh which it weaves may not be sufficient to catch all poor people.

Limitations of credit as a poverty-alleviation strategy in Bangladesh

Credit is also debt, and for those who are subsisting far below the 'minimum economic level' described above, taking loans constitutes considerable risk. Both TRDEP and BRAC (and the Grameen Bank) require their loans to be repaid in weekly instalments. Borrowers therefore need some form of regular cash flow to service their loans. For activities such as paddy husking, petty trading and rickshaw driving, returns may be regular and yield income which is sufficient to meet the weekly demands. For other activities, such as livestock husbandry, returns may be more irregular. All borrowers at various times may have to service their loans from non-assisted enterprise sources. For those without regular incomes, even the small amounts required can be a burden.

A loan of Tk2,000 requires weekly repayments (under BRAC) of over Tk40 – the equivalent of (or slightly more than) a day's labouring wage in several of the areas in which our survey was carried out. During informal discussions with some BRAC members and several of the poorest TRDEP members, it became apparent that household cash flows are not always sufficient to meet even these demands. While the repayment ratios of both organisations are high, this is because of their loan classification system (loans are not deemed overdue until one year after the final instalment should have been paid). What is hidden by the 'official' figures is a much more flexible reality. Borrowers do not always pay every instalment on time. Informal lending between members does occur; some field staff come to *ad hoc* arrangements with their *shomiti* or *kendra* member, allowing partial payment one week in return for additional payments in the next. Rutherford (1993) even found TRDEP Group Animators making 'informal loans' to *kendra* members to enable on-time repayments, because unless such figures appear in their repayment books their jobs are at risk. Thus, household cash flow is sometimes not sufficient, and when successive instalments are missed the consequences can be serious.

We came across several BRAC VOs in which defaulting members had been the object of peer-group pressure due to consecutive defaults at weekly meetings. In these VOs, most members appeared willing to 'help out' those with financial problems for the first few weeks; but such mutual support is limited. Successive defaulting has implications for the whole membership – and POs freely admitted that VOs were threatened with the withdrawal of future loans, or even closure, if defaulting members were not 'persuaded' to repay. This persuasion, however, sometimes has to take the form of quite aggressive action on the part of the VO leadership or majority. Examples included the forced acquisition of defaulters' assets (for example, livestock purchased with the loan, or household goods such as cooking pots) and their sale in order to raise the necessary repayments.

The negative results of peer-group pressure are rarely discussed in the literature on credit for the poor. However, references to this issue do exist, even in BRAC's own research documents. For example, Khan and Stewart (1992) recount a conversation with BRAC women in which 'they told us with pride that they had pulled down a member's house because she did not pay back her housing loan'. For poorer members on the receiving end of such an experience, inability to service debt and the forced sale of assets acts as a 'ratchet' like any other. For the poorest, credit may not be appropriate for alleviating their situation.

There is also evidence to suggest that both VO members and field staff of both TRDEP and BRAC are well aware of these risks to the poorest households – risks which are translated into risk to the VO (because of joint liability) and to field staff (who depend on good performance for their careers). We have already noted the nature of TRDEP's targeting, which is partly caused by staff concerns to deal mostly with the 'better-off' amongst the poor; and even though BRAC appears to be reaching relatively poorer people, it may still be leaving out the very poorest. An indicator of this is that while nearly 10 per cent of our BRAC sample are from female-headed households, the proportion of the population living in such domestic units is estimated at around 23 per cent. Thus, according to our survey, this most vulnerable category is under-represented in BRAC's membership.

It should also be noted that BRAC's targeting appears to have shifted in recent years as RDP has expanded. We have noted (pp. 143–4) that our survey comparison group (members who have most recently joined) appeared to be better endowed than the first-time borrowers, who in turn are better endowed than the third-time loanees (who joined three to four years ago). This shift, which we understand as being caused by both VO leadership and staff concerns about repayment discipline, supports the argument that credit for the poorest is not as practical as programme rhetoric suggests.

CONFRONTING THE POLITICAL ECONOMY OF POVERTY: BRAC'S ATTEMPTS TO EMPOWER WOMEN AND THE POOR

BRAC goes beyond the economistic definition of poverty alleviation by focusing on village-level institution-building as well as providing loans (see pp. 101–3). Ideally, VOs (*shomitis*) are not merely vehicles for credit delivery, but are potential mutual support groups which, as collectives of poor people, may also provide enhanced status and greater bargaining power in local communities.

The ultimate policy aim of this institution-building component of RDP is empowerment of the poor: the formation of separate VOs for women and the increasing focus on women during RDP's expansion mean that this empowerment objective has both gender as well as class implications. RDP's approach is in contrast to that of TRDEP. The latter's *kendras* are temporary bodies, closed down after the four-loan cycle. Unlike BRAC, TRDEP has no additional specialist staff such as institution-building and sectoral Programme Organisers to help develop the *kendras* beyond being credit groups. Additionally, TRDEP's emphasis on family principles has led to a relatively small representation of women. This section, on the wider extra-economic impact of credit integrated with other social development input, therefore concentrates on BRAC's RDP.

BRAC is not alone in advocating empowerment of the poor. Case-studies suggest that changes have occurred in the rural power structure as a result of the Grameen Bank's injections of capital into poorer social strata (see, for example, Rahman 1989). The supportive argument is that targeted credit is a way of enhancing a poorer individual's or household's economic status (and power), reducing existing socio-economic dependencies, therefore altering the relations of gender and class, to the benefit of the weaker parties. It is particularly the NGOs such as BRAC and Proshika who have emphasised the 'empowerment' objectives of their development interventions (see Korten 1989).

The argument for credit combined with institutional development relies on several assumptions. The link between enhanced economic well-being and socio-economic power may be seen empirically in many cases, but it is not an inevitable causality. Marginal increases in income and assets, while enhancing well-being and security, may be too small to alter entrenched political and economic relations.

In relation to gender, credit supporting traditional activities (such as paddy husking and petty trading) which are already structured by existing gender relations of labour and rights, may actually strengthen those relations rather than alter them. White (1991) maintains in relation to Action-Aid's Bhola Island project, organised in a way similar to BRAC's, that credit programmes have 'an overall contradictory character in relation to gender'. The introduction of credit into existing socio-economic relations might alter those relations, but it might also reinforce them.

The 'empowerment' of the poor through institution building?

The need for an empowerment strategy became a BRAC priority because of its early research into the political economy of rural Bangladesh. In particular, BRAC's *The Net: Power Structure in Ten Villages* (1983) clearly illustrated how various types of local elites form 'interlocking networks to gain control over local and external resources'. This led Abed (BRAC's Executive Director) to write in the Preface that 'without the resolution of the problems of power, genuine development in rural Bangladesh will continue to elude us' (1983).

However, the meaning of 'empowerment' in BRAC's case is not entirely clear, despite recent attempts by a working group to define the content of their strategy. This strategy is described by a list of activities under the RDP (BRAC 1992a), namely:

- institution-building (forming village organisations);
- a functional education course (given to all VOs before they start taking credit);
- human and skills training (primarily through the Non-Formal Primary Education Programme for the children of BRAC members; but also

through the training components of the sectoral programmes for poultry, livestock, irrigation, pisciculture, and sericulture);

- savings, both personal and group trust fund (compulsory savings);
- credit;
- issue-based meetings for village organisations (nominally held once every month);
- a paralegal programme, in which trainers explain legal stipulations relating to marriage, divorce, land rights, and so on, to VO members.

Education (functional and paralegal) may play an important role by providing clearer knowledge of rights, and by enhancing an individual's knowledge of how to go about securing such rights. The ability to attain these rights may also be increased through basic skills such as reading and writing. Additionally, technical training can provide borrowers with skills enabling more productive use of credit, and increase the likelihood of a livelihood less dependent on local patronage links.

However, the components of BRAC's strategy listed above are indirect methods of altering economic and social structures of power. Credit and savings are ways of empowering only if their effects ensure a relative improvement in the position of the poor *vis-à-vis* wealthier classes.

Such structural changes in social and economic relations affecting BRAC's clientele are unlikely to be effected in the short term, given the analysis of marginal economic benefits outlined on pp. 134–9 and 148–53.

The most significant component of the empowerment strategy is the institution-building, aimed at creating collective solidarity amongst the poor. This organisational strategy is potentially threatening to existing dominant individuals and groups, by giving the poor greater (physical) security and bargaining power in local affairs.

The forming of a village organisation starts, using BRAC's rhetoric, with a 'conscientisation' process through a functional education course run by specific trainers. According to Lovell (1992), this course consisted of thirty lessons (now reduced to twenty) aimed at developing 'villagers' political consciousness and awareness of their own environment and possibilities'. Course content includes 'lessons' on 'development . . . resource allocation . . . leadership . . . exploitation . . . social activities . . . participatory decisions . . . women's rights' (BRAC 1992a). After finishing the compulsory FE course, there are further optional lessons on literacy and numeracy – although these now appear to be quite rare in the present context of BRAC's rapid expansion. However, this same report acknowledges that 'participation in the discussion and implementation of decisions taken in FE class were not recognised [as] important either by FE teachers or POs' – suggesting conversely that members are not enthusiastically involved.

Certainly, when discussing FE courses with VO members during fieldwork, respondents remember these lessons as highly structured and passive experiences. In some *shomitis* respondents remembered few of the lessons or their content; nor could they explain the relevance of the 'grander' subjects (however, issues such as women's rights were acknowledged, especially marriage and dowry laws). There were also respondents who pointed out that the lessons did not seem very relevant (see also Khan and Stewart 1992). Our own impression, therefore, is that this stage of institution-building is in most cases highly pedagogical and didactic, rather than dialogical and participatory; and that members are not always in agreement with what is being preached.

When middle-class and university-educated staff come to 'instruct' the poor about their own 'situation of exploitation' and 'anti-social practices' (all quotes from discussions with field staff), without any real participation by the listeners, it seems unlikely that this method reverses the patronising tendencies already entrenched in a status-conscious and highly stratified society. Certainly, rural people are highly critical and sceptical (although not often openly) of lecturing outsiders, whose life-styles and priorities are so different from their own. Given the predominance of male field staff, the hierarchical interaction between BRAC and its clientele appears (to the outsider) even more pronounced in the case of women's *shomitis.*

Thus, our own observations of the impact of 'conscientisation' and level of participation accord with the conclusions of a previous study of six Bangladeshi NGOs (Hashemi 1990). Hashemi notes that despite a participatory and awareness-raising rhetoric amongst NGOs such as BRAC and Proshika, which both draw on the ideology of Freire, the reality is much less impressive. Meetings are organised and led by NGO workers; the agenda is usually set by them and not by the members of the *shomitis;* and the mode of interaction is teacher–pupil (ironically what Freire strongly condemns).

The most obvious result of BRAC's functional education course is the oft-repeated seventeen promises which VO members learn by rote. These promises are supposed to be recited collectively at the beginning of every weekly VO meeting, led by the *Gram Shebak* as chorus master. Yet in older VOs, and especially in male VOs, such recitations are often poorly done, implying that many members neither take these promises seriously nor see them as a useful ritual to encourage feelings of solidarity.

Thus, in practice, there are many more apparent similarities between TRDEP centre meetings and those of BRAC VOs than the latter organisation's rhetoric implies, particularly in terms of staff–clientele relations. One might expect that NGO and government staff interact somewhat differently, because of the added status which government service bestows (and receives from others); NGO staff, it might be expected, would be able to reverse such hierarchical principles to a greater extent than government staff. However, TRDEP Group Animators and BRAC Programme Organisers are, in fact, remarkably similar in terms of their social identities. They are all middle class and urban educated, with BA and MA degrees from the same universities, and are of roughly the same age; and quite a number of Group Animators whom we met had previously been BRAC POs. Additionally, the organisational weight and reputation which BRAC POs 'bring' to VO meetings is not very different from TRDEP as a government organisation: both are seen as large, powerful and rich institutions by village borrowers.

Our survey results do imply that BRAC *shomitis* have a better weekly attendance level than TRDEP centres, which can be taken as an indicator of higher personal commitment to such village organisations. The high level of absenteeism at the *kendras* is because many TRDEP borrowers make their repayments through family, friends and other members – a practice which GAs are quite happy with as long as the repayment and savings instalments are made. BRAC's field staff are, however, much more concerned about attendance as an indicator of discipline (an attitude which may affect an oft-absentee member's access to further loans).

However, the survey results on attendance do not support the idea that BRAC *shomiti* members become more committed and enthusiastic over time – which might be expected if these *shomitis* are becoming more rooted village 'institutions'. Average attendance at the older VOs in our sample is approximately 70 per cent, and for the newer VOs the average is approximately 80 per cent.

In addition, we came across a key issue illustrating some dissatisfaction amongst the members. In nearly all the thirty *shomitis* which we visited, men and women were deeply unhappy about BRAC's savings rules. Personal savings were on open access to members during the early years of BRAC's operations. In the last couple of years the rules have changed. A member is only allowed to withdraw one-quarter of his or her savings after five years of membership; and one-half after ten years of membership. Many members in the older *shomitis* were concerned that this change was imposed unilaterally. BRAC staff state that this reduced access means that a 'long-term asset' is being built up by the members – though savings need to be on open access if they are to play a role in enhancing the crisis-coping capabilities discussed on pp. 152–3.

As a result of these rule changes, savings are perceived as an added cost of borrowing – along with the 10 per cent (total) deductions at source from every loan for the Group Trust Fund, life insurance and security deposits. Thus, saving with BRAC is perceived by members as one of the conditionalities of accessing credit, not as an independent financial service which can be of immediate practical use. The (strong) expressions of unhappiness with this situation which we heard during our informal field visits are clearly affecting members' commitment to BRAC and their VO.

Another indicator that many BRAC VOs are unlikely to become well-rooted institutions is the high turnover indicated by respondents and BRAC AO managers. During 1992–3, the older VOs categorised under the Rural

Credit Project lost 25 per cent of their membership – in a 'clean-up' operation intended to weed out undisciplined members. During our fieldwork, BRAC branch and area office managers also admitted during informal discussions that they expect an annual turnover in their membership of between 10 per cent and 20 per cent of their (normally 6,000) local clientele. This is a considerable drop-out rate, which must surely militate against the collective solidarity of *shomitis*.

Finally, only in early 1992 were institution-building Programme Organisers allotted to every RDP area office (and RCP branches). Yet these individuals are overburdened. There are approximately 120 VOs under every AO, which means the key 'IB' staff can only spend, on average, two working days per year with each village organisation. BRAC's present expansion, leading to staff resource and training constraints, seriously restricts the likelihood that institution-building will become more effective in the foreseeable future.

These findings on the 'mobilisation process', attendance, drop-out, savings rules and the limited (functional) nature of participation suggest that there is a strong tendency for BRAC *shomitis* to become 'credit delivery units' rather than bodies with more comprehensive aims and purposes. 'Institution-building' efforts are prominent only at the time of VO formation, when FE classes are held and promises learnt. After the initial formation and 'conscientisation' stage, the personnel with whom VOs come into most contact are the credit *Gram Shebaks* and POs. Over the lifetime of a *shomiti* fewer efforts are made by staff (or members) to stimulate independent activities by the *shomiti*, and VOs become more exclusively focused on credit. The processes and conditions described above imply that village organisations are unlikely to become more rooted institutions unless collective solidarity and commitment comes from the members themselves, rather than through the instructions of paid outsiders.

Collective solidarity?

The formation of *shomitis* does not guarantee collective solidarity *per se*, and indeed, the main *de facto* purpose of VOs – as units for the delivery of individual loans – *may* encourage the opposite.

Some commentators on Bangladeshi NGOs that emphasise collective solidarity for poor people have argued that loans to individuals and their households inherently mitigate against the cohesion of groups by encouraging 'diversified work patterns and individual entrepreneurial attitudes' (Wood and Palmer-Jones 1990). While this identification of contradiction was aimed at Proshika's attempts to mobilise rural people, the same principles apply to BRAC's VOs.

Additionally, even within BRAC's target group there are significant differences deriving from the ownership (or not) of assets such as land.

160

During fieldwork, it was notable that the poorest members of BRAC VOs were more likely to be petty trading or paddy husking and rice trading, all activities with the lowest margins of return, than the slightly richer members. This implies that those who are already better off are more able to capitalise, literally, on the loan (as in the case of many of our TRDEP respondents).

Collective solidarity of BRAC *shomitis* does sometimes seem to suffer because of slight wealth differences between members. In one *shomiti* visited during fieldwork, there was tension between two groups, in effect leading to the practical exclusion of the poorer members from the main benefits of the VO.

This case consisted of a large women's VO with around sixty-five members. Fifteen of the members were from a small *para* (hamlet) at some distance from the main settlement. The latter was where the *sabhapati* (chairwoman), cashier and most of the other women lived; and households in this settlement were visibly better off than those in the small *para*. Some of the small *para* women were given the jobs of being guards of young mulberry trees in BRAC's sericulture programme; payment is in wheat, and the richer women of the main settlement did not want to do this work for this type of payment. The women in the small *para* complained to us that because of their sericulture appointments they were excluded from getting loans (and at this point they also mentioned the problem about their compulsory weekly savings being useful only if they led to loans).

Conversely, the main settlement women had been taking loans, though not repaying them very regularly. This infuriated the women in the small *para*, because in their eyes poor repayment reduced the likelihood that they themselves would get credit later. Also significant is the fact that the small *para* women, except one individual, were not given any positions as subgroup leaders. It was the main *para* women, who received their loans first.

An indication of the intra-VO economic divide is that the brother-in-law of the female *sabhapati* (both living in the same *bari*) had five acres of paddy land (a fact honestly admitted by himself during a discussion about changing paddy yields over the last few years). Technically the woman herself is landless, and therefore might appear to BRAC officials as a target group member – but her family clearly is not.

The main *para* women (interviewed separately) took some time before they admitted, through oblique comments, that 'the society is not going very well' – they initially claimed that only women from their own settlement were involved in the VO. After realising that we knew that others were involved, they then tried to claim that it was the small *para* women who were not repaying their loans (though they have not received any).

This case may be an unusual one, in that the VO seems to be dominated by really quite 'wealthy' middle-peasant people – which is certainly not the case in most VOs. There is also the geographical (*para*) division, which is much more clearcut in this example than in many other *shomitis*. However, this case is highly suggestive of the potential conflicts over control, distribution of loans and other benefits that can be fuelled by existing wealth differences within the membership. Where conflict is real or latent, then collective solidarity is unlikely to evolve.

Collective action?

There are forms of collective action which do occur that are not reflections of empowerment at all. An important example of this was provided earlier (pp. 153–4) when discussing the operation of the joint-liability mechanism and the effects that it can have on the extreme poor. Thus, some forms of 'collective action' are not always benign, and can worsen some people's positions rather than provide additional support. This exertion of collective power against individuals on behalf of the lending institution is, at least in the short term, contradictory to the aim of empowering the poor against other interest groups.

Collective actions by and *on behalf* of the poor are unlikely to evolve without at least a perception of mutual solidarity. Yet there are claims made of BRAC VOs undertaking such actions. Perhaps the major issues on which empowerment of BRAC VO members should be evaluated are the reactions and perceptions of local elites and the extent to which VOs engage in collective action for members' collective interests.

Comparative experiences of these issues are to be found in a text by Kramsjo and Wood on Proshika called *Breaking the Chains* (1992). Proshika's theory of group organisation is similar to BRAC's – emphasising a strong link between group unity and the ability of the poor to engage in activities which change their material dependence on others (effected through labour and tenancy relations, informal credit, and access to local resources such as land, water and their products). Proshika staff have tried to act as facilitators, encouraging groups to acquire (often on lease) government (*khas*) land for cultivation, stretches of water for fisheries, and market-place management contracts. Kramsjo and Wood's series of case-studies of such collective actions by rural poor are impressive examples of what is possible. BRAC staff too have some similar stories to tell, but their examples seem to be limited in number, and not really representative of the majority of *shomitis*. None of the thirty *shomitis* which we visited during fieldwork gave examples of such collective action, or of any major conflict (such as over land and wages) between themselves as-a-group and local elites.

Several BRAC AO managers claimed that the VOs in their area have negotiated with landowners about sharecropping terms and wage rates, but we could find no examples of such collective action in the *shomitis* we visited. Land and labour relations appear to be standardised across localities, and rarely susceptible to negotiation; they also appear to be highly personalised by quite long-term and resistant 'patronal' associations between households of particular *samajs* (socially linked homesteads, often connected to the same mosque, revolving around particular leaders (*matobars*)). The poorer parties to these arrangements are often not prepared to break such links since employment and access to tenancy land remain crucial sources of actual or potential security. The continuing commitment of many BRAC members to their previous patronal ties may also explain the rarity of antagonism between *shomitis* and elites.

This is not to argue that antagonism does not occur. In Rajbari district we were told that in one case POs were stoned by henchmen of a local landlord, and told that their motor cycles would 'go missing', when they were in the initial stages of forming a *shomiti*. BRAC field staff also mentioned that wealthier individuals often try to ensure that their younger or female family members are given a place in the VO when it is being formed. The presence of such people can perpetuate (and extend) existing patronal links, so staff claim that they strongly resist such attempts – a claim we would support since BRAC 'targeting' appears to be relatively successful.

One case, in which local elites had effectively sabotaged a *shomiti*, involved conflict over education. In a village in Sherpur district, some of the wealthier households had objected to a BRAC NFPE school being set up in the village because they felt it would take pupils away from the *madrassah* (religious school). The argument was couched in religious and social rather than financial terms. A few of the local elite families were paying for the *madrassah's* '*maulana*' (an Islamic cleric), so there was no need for pupils financially (in the sense that pupils' parents might be encouraged to make contributions to the *maulana's* upkeep at festival time). Rather, the argument against the NFPE school was that it had no religious focus.

Yet there was obviously more to this than the overt arguments. The two (male and female) VOs in the village were spilt into two groupings, one of which supported the *madrassah*, and the other which claimed that the NFPE school would be better for their children. However, the case did not involve poor versus wealthy, but was closer to a classic case of factionalism, with some wealthy families also supporting the BRAC school. Here, it appeared that intra-elite conflict was the cause, and the effect was to divide the poor through their different patronal loyalties to conflicting wealthy families. The *shomiti* is now considered by BRAC staff to be inactive, and the situation too tense to continue their activities in the village.

From our understanding of cases of conflict which we did identify, they occur most commonly in the early stages of BRAC's operations in a particular area. As an area office establishes itself with its impressive offices, many staff and bright red Honda motor cycles, and after it has created a network of VOs in its catchment area, it ceases to attract so much opposition from local elites. In one case, a BRAC AO manager explained that they worked in three Unions, with a total population of approximately 25,000 voters, of which approximately 7,000 were VO members. This, he says, means that BRAC is not an easy target for the local elite.

Yet this is a contradictory statement: with such a large proportion of members in a given area (from disadvantaged households) the threat to local elites, just in terms of sheer numbers, appears formidable. So why, given the rhetoric of empowerment, are there so few challenges to the status quo?

BRAC's institutional imperatives: local elites, avoiding conflict and the need for discipline

One interpretation is that BRAC cannot afford, from a perspective of institutional preservation, to be in conflict with other powerful groups (either locally or nationally). The manager quoted above claimed that politicians do not attempt to interfere with or manipulate BRAC's potential vote-bank; BRAC staff will not allow meetings to be used as electioneering occasions. Yet the same manager admits that local politicians do visit the area office to discuss local issues, suggesting that BRAC is regarded by such people as an important institution which cannot be ignored in local politics. BRAC is in constant danger of being caught up in local disputes, and assiduously attempts to remain neutral.

In order to remain neutral in the eyes of the powerful, BRAC must retain good relations with local notables and government. During the period of our fieldwork, the organisation's twentieth anniversary was celebrated across the country in each area office and branch, involving invitations to local notables and the most important local government officials. The latter made speeches of congratulation and together with staff watched a commemorative video. No VO leaders, let alone ordinary members, were invited to these events. This occasion seemed symbolic of where some of BRAC's *de facto* priorities lie: institutional self-preservation and a mode of operation which is not entirely in line with its participatory rhetoric.

As a credit institution, BRAC has had to weather some difficult political conditions in recent years. The loan-forgiveness announcements of parties fighting the 1991 election did not go unnoticed by some of the BRAC membership. This situation also affected BRAC repayment rates for a short period, since many members, seeing their neighbours being 'let off', wanted BRAC to do the same for them. In a local election in Nattore one of the political candidates unilaterally announced that under his tenure BRAC members would have their loans waived. Repayments at the weekly VO meetings stopped overnight, even though the result of the election was not yet known, causing a dramatic halt to the AO's cash flow. It took strenuous efforts by BRAC staff to reiterate that local office-holders do not have any authority over a non-government organisation, and that if repayments stopped then BRAC would 'run out of money', depriving the VOs of any future credit. Given the threat to financial viability which political interference can constitute, it appears that BRAC does require an active policy of negotiation and good relations with local elites. The expansion of RDP, which, as was shown on pp. 123–4, has led to an increasing dependence on donor subsidies and a delay in the RCP transition, exacerbates BRAC's need for conflict-avoidance to sustain repayment discipline.

It is perhaps inevitable that as BRAC has grown some priorities are derived from *internal* considerations rather than through its previous 'learning organisation' methods (see Lovell 1992 for an elaboration of this out-of-date image). Relations with its clientele appear to have become increasingly credit-orientated, and there are now more restrictive rules (such as for savings), all of which mitigate against the feasibility of participatory procedures. The likelihood, therefore, of BRAC facilitating empowerment of poor people seems to have diminished during RDP's expansion phase.

Avoiding federations

This discussion of collective empowerment ends with a note on the idea of federations of *shomitis*: an option which BRAC considered and experimented with in the past, but has not pursued.

Technically, there is still a federation of village organisations in the Manikganj area (first initiated in the early 1980s), although we were not able to make field enquiries about this network. Our understanding at the time of writing is that some people in BRAC regard federations as one way of increasing the level of participation by members, leading to higher-level representative (elected) committees which could also take on some managerial and organisational roles to co-ordinate common interests across several villages and *shomitis*. However, this idea does not seem to have wide support within BRAC's own management.

Several reasons for this lack of enthusiasm may be valid (from the perspective of a credit institution). First, if BRAC were to organise its membership into a democratic co-operative system it could give rise to apprehensions amongst onlookers that a political process was under way, therefore inviting political conflict and interference. Second, such a shift in emphasis towards more costly and time-consuming federation-building would inevitably reduce the resources presently being directed into BRAC's expansion and the 'BRAC Bank'; and those resources might become the focus of competition between different sections of the membership. Third, it is highly possible that a more active (and a higher level of) members' representation would lead to pressures on BRAC from below to change its policies, and to provide different services (for example, savings rules). These are all reasons why BRAC RDP, as a large credit institution, may be reluctant to 'empower' its members *vis-à-vis* the organisation itself.

The 'empowerment' of women

In what ways do loans to and the collective organisation of women affect gender relations? Such changes as there may be cannot be easily measured, and any analysis must rely extensively on qualitative information. Our fieldwork was much too brief to claim any substantial findings, but we do have indicative data and illustrations.

It is evident from secondary literature that the debate on women in Bangladesh is fraught with confusion and contradictions (see White 1992: 15–26). Bangladeshi society is renowned for its restrictions on women: familial and purdah norms limit mobility and ways of behaving in public (including market access); marriage and dowry practices disadvantage women and create dependency on males; inheritance laws discriminate against major assets being held in female hands; and the domestic division of labour constrains access to and use of the more valuable resources.

Perhaps the most obvious contradiction raised by the 'women and development' agenda is the inverse relationship between wealth and gender equality, when measured by conventional indicators such as the mobility and visibility of women. It has been observed that richer women are more likely to practise purdah, while poorer women can rarely afford to do so. Economic advancement therefore has implications of decreasing gender equality. Women going out to work is likely to be a reflection of, and be seen by others as, a reflection of distress, and not an indication of either higher status or reduced dependency or therefore empowerment of women.

Our argument in this section is that there is no guarantee that credit provision *per se* will change gender relations in ways that 'empower' women in any simple sense. It is somewhat easier to argue that some degree of social status is gained as a result of increased economic contribution to, and 'centrality' in, the household. However, those women who do particularly well as a result of credit are much more likely to be empowered *vis-à-vis* other (less-well-off) women, rather than *vis-à-vis* the menfolk in their household (or in wider society).

Greater evidence exists to support the hypothesis that the provision of credit encourages rather than contests the existing sexual division of labour and the concomitant predominance of male authority. This is particularly seen in types of activities for which women take loans, and the issue of how the proceeds of economic activities are shared and controlled within the household. When the division of labour and distribution of authority over resources remains uncontested, it is not easy to argue that there has been a positive change in women's degree of 'empowerment'. This is especially evident when the burden of women's work increases as a result of credit-supported activities but the control over the proceeds of that work remains in the hands of male kin.

BRAC researchers write of the organisation's 'strategy of empowering women' as well as their wider strategy of 'empowerment of the poor' (Ahmad *et al.* 1990: iv; Ahmad 1988: 1). Credit to women is seen as a potential means for affecting gender relations, which is complemented by group organisation and 'conscientisation'.

It might be thought that simply organising women into separate *shomitis* contradicts existing gender norms relating to purdah. However, precisely because of existing gender norms women often 'should' (and do) congregate separately at social functions such as marriages, village meetings, and during economic activities (such as fuel- and fodder-gathering and in labour groups). Thus in most respects BRAC's 'mobilisation' of women into separate *mohila shomitis* follows prevalent gender norms rather than contesting them.

It is the emphasis on 'conscientisation' which, in theory, challenges many prevalent practices that are symptomatic of women's lack of power. The initial functional education course and also monthly 'issue-based meetings' are aimed at promoting new social norms. Existing practices such as child marriage, dowry, domestic violence and sudden divorce are criticised. Yet the evidence of BRAC's own case-studies shows that such promotional efforts have limited impact on the practices which are verbally denigrated. Arguments against dowry and child marriage have not been accepted as *possible options* by women (Khan and Stewart 1992; Sattar 1991); no differentiations in patterns of violence have been found between members and non-members of BRAC (Roy 1992); knowledge about health and nutrition has not been translated into behaviour which counters the 'woman eats last and least' pattern, and women continue to conform to traditional sexual divisions of labour and space (Sattar 1991). The conclusion may be that processes of re-education do not have observable effects over the medium term, but this is also an admission that we cannot claim (yet) that they happen at all.

A problem which arises in evaluating the status and powers of women derives partly from assumptions inherent in the 'empowerment' approach. Women are seen as passive, restricted and subjugated. In this depiction, just about any action on the part of women is taken as evidence of empowerment. An illustration of this was provided by discussions with a women's *shomiti* and BRAC field staff concerning a divorce incident a couple of months before our visit.

A husband's ability to inflict sudden divorce on his wife is one of practices which BRAC attempts to combat through conscientisation. In this case a divorcée was supported by the other *shomiti* women, who spread stories about the husband's moral misbehaviour and pressurised their own male kin to get the husband to rescind his *talaq*. The social pressure generated seemed to have been successful, since the wife returned to her marital home. Both the BRAC PO and the women (at the weekly meeting) provided this as an example of the new 'strength' which the *shomiti* has given them.

However, on further questioning about these sorts of incidents (without the presence of the PO, on a second visit), the women admitted that many 'divorces' which had occurred prior to the *shomiti*'s formation had been resolved in similar ways. Two conclusions arise: first, the example is not a sufficient indicator that the *shomiti* has made any major difference; and second, women are not in any simple sense powerless, and have ways and means of contesting (individual) male behaviours through 'petty weapons of resistance' – similar to those which Scott (1985) illustrates as prevalent between those of different economic classes in a village. Evaluating, therefore, 'changes' in the position of women can only be done by recognising pre-existing practices and relations; indeed, most of our impressions concerning the impact of credit on gender relations is that pre-existing practices within the household are perpetuated.

In an overview of four Bangladeshi credit programmes White (1991: 101) pointed out that the vast majority of loans to women are financing traditional activities, involving simple technology, entailing market participation 'only at the lowest rung', and are heavily compromised by the persisting responsibilities of women to cover the consumption needs of the family. This argument applies to BRAC as well. RDP and RCP loan disbursement reflects traditional divisions between those sectors considered appropriate for men and women. Over 70 per cent of men take loans for petty trading, transport (mostly rickshaws) and agriculture-related activities; approximately 80 per cent of women take loans for livestock (including poultry), food processing (mainly paddy husking) and petty trading (BRAC Statistical Report 1992: 19).

It must be emphasised that 'petty trading' is not a uniform category in terms of gender: men's and women's trading tend to take distinct patterns, involving differing clienteles and use of social space. Women tend to trade with women (whoever the final user of the commodity may be); men trade with men. Women rarely go to periodic markets (*haats*) held on specific days in most villages, or to permanent ones (*bazaars*) – these are strictly male spheres. While men move more freely, women are often constrained to selling only to women in their own social network, going from house to house in the village and its *paras* (hamlets).

Additionally, rather than discrete activities of individual borrowers, trading often involves several individuals in a household or kin network which relies on a sexual division of roles. Husbands purchase goods at the *haats* for their wives to sell in the village; women get their sons and young daughters to do intermediary tasks in the process of carrying out various economic activities.

The reality of intra-household mutual reliance between the sexes (and those of different age groups) also applies to other loan-assisted activities. Men take loans under the label of food processing, but would not be seen husking paddy under a domestic *dheki,* which is culturally determined as a woman's task. Some women borrowers take loans for rickshaws – the plying of which is always left to male relatives. In just about any activity undertaken by women, including involvement with a *haat* or *bazaar,* the role of male kith and kin (or children, irrespective of gender) is critical, with crucial implications for a woman's control of the cash proceeds and her authority over how they are spent. BRAC has recently been experimenting with '*mohila* hotels' – tea shops and tiny restaurants to be run by women. This is an adventurous departure from tradition, facilitating a business that is generally a male preserve, not least because they are, by their very nature, public places often situated near markets frequented mostly by males. However, in the two cases when we visited such restaurants, the husbands were sitting in the front (while the women cooked at the back). Thus, even in this adventurous example, gender conventions had not been broken and real changes were not observable. This example reinforces our conclusion that loan use is rarely individualised. The existing gender division of labour is the pattern through which most loan-assisted activities are carried out.

A theme in BRAC's research papers and in the wider literature is that if credit enhances women's access to resources their social status is enhanced, their 'bargaining position' in the household becomes stronger, and their role in decision-making becomes more pronounced (see, for example, Ahmad *et al.* 1990; cf. Sen 1990). These changes are difficult to observe, and some have denied this bargaining model for gender relations.

The changes that result from women's access to credit and (potential) control over income cannot be ignored, even if they are difficult to 'measure'. As Kabeer (1989: 10) notes, women's conventional 'roles and responsibilities are led to a far greater extent in the non-monetised sector than those of men'. Women borrowing cash and generating cash income tend towards a contradiction of existing norms.

Control over cash is an important indicator of whether or not a woman's potential bargaining power has been enhanced. Our data, along with that of other surveys, suggests that cash more often falls under male authority than that of the households' loan-taking women.

Researchers writing on credit provision to women have noted the prevalence of intra-household transfers from the formal (female) borrower to their male kin (Hossain and Afsar 1989; Goetz and Gupta 1994). One survey of 151 Grameen Bank women borrowers found that 25 per cent transferred half or more of their loan to male family members (Rahman 1986). A study of BRAC women borrowers found that, in approximately one out of every four cases, males decided whether the woman should take the loan and also decided what the loan would be used for (BRAC 1990). More interestingly, the Grameen Bank study found a tendency for women to transfer a greater proportion of successive loans (Rahman 1986).

There are severe constraints on women's control over cash deriving from conceptions of who should spend money on what (relating to ideas of masculinity and femininity). Women's spending tends to be directed more to consumption needs and essentials, while men are relatively privileged with wider options. The larger the amount of cash the more likely it will be perceived to be under male spending authority. These constraints are further legitimised by the marketing norms discussed above, which give men control over higher value exchanges and wider choice.

Our survey was not designed to uncover direct transfers from women to men, but our data do confirm the conventional gender pattern of loan and cash utilisation described above, and hints at the tendencies identified in the studies on female to male transfers. One out of every eight BRAC women borrowers in our sample diverted some or all of their loan into consumption expenditures, while this was true for only one out of every fifteen male borrowers, none of whom used all the amount for consumption. Additionally, while most respondents reported that the source of their loan repayments was the activity for which they had taken credit, the only people who said that they relied on family and friends for the weekly cash were women.

One of the few potentially positive indicators which came out of the survey results was the fact that control over the loan-assisted activity seems to be higher for successive female borrowers than for first-timers; however, caution is required because of what seems to have been happening economically to these households over the recent past. Of the BRAC women who had taken only one loan, only 9 per cent said that they were 'in charge' (the *malik*) of the income-generation activity; 87 per cent said that their activity was a 'family partnership'. In the case of male first-time borrowers, 33 per cent said that they have sole authority over the loan-assisted enterprise; while 56 per cent said that it was a family partnership. For women who had taken three loans, 14 per cent said they were the *malik*, and 77 per cent said that their activity was a partnership with the other household members (and men). Answers from male successive borrowers also suggested a trend towards more individual loan use (half said that they were the *malik*, half said that the activity was a family partnership). While these ratios are tantalising – in their support for the idea that successive loans to women may give them more control – the margin for error in our sample is too large to draw conclusions.

That the small number of changes in control over use of productive assets (in favour of women) are of ambiguous significance is reinforced by indications that women's control over cash does not change after taking credit. Respondents in our survey were asked how they 'keep' the cash proceeds of the loan-assisted activity, allowing multiple responses and therefore combinations of practices, such as banking, mixing such income

Table 12.24 Household cash-holding practices of BRAC women borrowers
(double responses allowed) (*N* = 67)

Cash-holding practice	At time of interview (%)	Before taking BRAC loans (%)
Keep cash proceeds to themselves	24	25
Mixed with other household cash	40	37
Give cash to male kin or husband	7	5

with other household cash, keeping it individually, or giving it to someone outside the household; the questionnaire required the interviewer to explain the answer in words. Respondents were then asked to compare these present practices with their previous ones (before taking loans). Just over half of all male BRAC members said that they keep all their income themselves, the rest stated that they mixed it with other household cash (with the implication that it is pooled; but still under predominant male authority). Just over one-third of the sixty-seven women borrowers said that they keep their cash proceeds themselves, while six out of ten said that it was mixed with other household cash. One out of ten said that they gave all the proceeds to their husband or other male family member (see Table 12.24). Interestingly, there was no significant change in patterns of cash-holding practices when comparing the present situation to the period before respondents started taking loans from BRAC. This was true for both male and female respondents.

This comparison of cash-holding practices 'before' and 'after' loans suggests that, according to women themselves, these practices have not significantly changed; and those few changes which appear in the table are, in fact, negative indications of women's control over cash. This implies that when women bring cash loans into, and generate income for, the household unit, their *control* over these forms of cash does not increase: it merely flows into an existing set of relationships and practices.

As the discussion above suggests, control over income and assets is not (and never has been) exclusively in male hands. It appears true that only a minority of women control cash individually, and the most common practice of cash-handling is pooling it (normally under the authority of male family members, but women certainly have some say, or indirect influence over its disposal). There are also ways in which women counter male privilege, even though they may not be obvious. Women often on-lend small amounts of cash and paddy to neighbours and friends, constituting small and dispersed debts which provide future security; they tend to invest in small livestock such as ducks and chickens, which they care for and effectively control; and

171

they may 'share-out' a calf or goat, which is one way of keeping them out of the direct control of male kin. White's (1992) ethnography shows that there are many such practices through which women are effectively strengthening a social network which is a crucial resource for both women themselves and their households. However, there is another critical dimension to such activities, in that they constitute savings for women (normally amongst women). Such practices are protective of 'female assets' because they are withdrawn from the immediate sphere of male kin's control. While women often ultimately lose control over even small assets at the time of exchange transactions carried out by men, they can at least influence when this exchange takes place.

Because of the existence of such practices it seems reasonable to argue that cash injections into the household are likely to strengthen women's control over at least some assets, and therefore their position in the household. Yet these assets (and this control) are likely to remain small (and fragmented) in relation to those of men. Additionally, what cannot be presupposed is that increasing control over more assets by women affects gender relations within the household as long as the household as a unit is getting richer. Male members are still likely to retain control over the larger and more valuable assets, which reduces the significance of women's marginal benefits to gender relations.

Sen (1990) suggests that positive changes in a woman's status would be evident if any of the three following characteristics were observed: first, and most fundamental, if the woman gains a better 'breakdown' position (that is, what entitlements she would be left with if the household unit disintegrated); second, a clearer perception by the woman of her own individuality and interests; and third, a clearer perception amongst all members of the household of female members' contributions to their joint welfare.

Women's access to cash *per se*, and especially when this gives women a more pronounced role or more centrality in the income-earning activities of the household, may induce heightened recognition of their contribution to joint welfare. Enhanced control over at least some income and assets through the practices identified by White suggests that recognition of personal interests are more likely to evolve. But both these changes are likely to be limited, given the persistence of both the sexual division of labour and the sustained male control over cash which invested credit and its proceeds can actually strengthen. A household's increasing market involvement leads in most cases to increased cash flow – but most of this cash flow is through the hands of men.

Finally, a woman's 'breakdown position' is unlikely to be radically altered unless assets more substantial than those acquired through credit are gained, and retained, in solely female hands.

Using Sen's criteria it is possible to argue that women's status is likely to be enhanced to a small degree because of access to credit and increased household-based income generation. However, while the centrality of a woman in the household may increase as a result, the interests of women are not sufficiently divergent from those of male kin, and indeed of the household as a whole, for women to wish to controvert the existing division of labour, nor to threaten openly the male–female distribution of privileges. Given these conditions and practices, it is difficult to reconcile such grand terms as 'empowerment of women' with the reality of everyday domestic lives.

This rather negative argument about the effects of loans to women on gender relations should include a note on one of the common problems arising from treating gender as a phenomenon divorced from other social structures.

Where credit appears to have a major effect on a household's economic position, such as in the case of the more 'moderate poor' TRDEP sample, we cannot argue that *gender* relations are more equal as a result (even though the women may have a higher standard of living). The sexual division of labour, roles and responsibilities certainly persists; though more TRDEP women (compared to BRAC women) seem to handle their investments' proceeds themselves. It seems safest to argue that this cash control is a reflection more of the increased liquidity in these moderately poor households, than a reflection of transformed gender relations. It is also significant that one of the main results of TRDEP women's liquidity is that they are able to on-lend (to other households in their community) much larger sums of cash than BRAC female borrowers. In the month before our interviews TRDEP women on-lent nearly 70 per cent more than BRAC women. This raises the uncomfortable question (which we cannot answer) of whether or not moderately poor women are providing a beneficial or harmful service to women of similar or poorer households.

In conclusion, BRAC's approach to women by organising and 'educating' them does not seem to have major observable impacts. Credit *per se* has clearly contradictory implications for gender relations, since its use for conventional activities, undertaken according to conventional patterns, may actually strengthen the intra-domestic distribution of power which is heavily in favour of male members. It may be possible to hypothesise that women's 'social status' in the eyes of male kin is somewhat enhanced by bringing more credit into the household, performing more work, and generating additional income. But this does not necessarily give them any notable increase in power.

CONCLUSIONS

Credit for the poor in Bangladesh is a strategy strongly supported by both donors and government. The reputation of Bangladeshi schemes, and particularly the Grameen Bank, has provided impetus to the spread of aid-financed microcredit schemes across the developing world. Yet our own study has generated mixed findings about both the performance and impact of our case-study programmes – both of which are adaptations from the successful Grameen model, and both of which have been praised as 'successful' in their own right.

However, this success has been defined by limited criteria. Both BRAC and TRDEP, like the Grameen Bank, claim remarkable repayment rates; both claim successful targeting (in terms of the broad 50 per cent of the Bangladeshi population below the official poverty line). When assessing the performance of the two programmes with more detailed financial efficiency indicators, less-comforting conclusions arise. Also, the results of our field studies on credit impact seem to suggest the uncomfortable conclusion that credit may fuel differentiation amongst the poor; the results certainly point to some of the limitations of credit as a poverty-alleviation strategy.

Performance in the context of rapid expansion

BRAC RDP and TRDEP differ in their own developmental cycle. The former started to expand rapidly in the late 1980s, the latter's expansion started after our fieldwork; both expansions have been fuelled by enthusiastic ideological support and finances from major aid donors. Given these different stages of transition into large-scale rural financial institutions, the two schemes are not directly comparable. Neither programme has cause for complacency. While the data on BRAC suggest that RDP is in danger of over-extension, the data on TRDEP suggest that expansion has come too soon and has been too rapid.

TRDEP costs are extremely high, and even with sustained high repayment rates it is unlikely to be profitable without massive subsidies. The decision of the Government of Bangladesh and the Asian Development Bank to expand the programme without finding ways of altering its cost structure seems premature. Effective internal management was not in place at the time of study. Branch-level data were practically impossible to collect, and head office data were not compiled in an accessible form. The absence of internal monitoring systems raises questions about how representative certain types of data (including repayment rates) actually are. In these conditions, the ADB-supported expansion entails considerable organisational and financial risks. The burden of start-up costs, as new branches and a new zonal structure come into place, and with the existing financial efficiency ratios, will further delay any transition to viability. Certainly, subsidies will be required far into the future, and TRDEP's viability has yet to be proved.

For BRAC's RDP, having started to 'go to scale' in the late 1980s, the situation is somewhat different. Costs per unit of credit disbursed, and per member reached, have been falling. These are encouraging signs from the financial perspective. Yet the prospect of unsubsidised operations is obscured by the expansion process, the financial burden of which is considerable. Because of the rapid and large-scale nature of this expansion, the SDI calculation for RDP is higher than TRDEP's. Thus, we cannot conclude that RDP has achieved a greater degree of sustainability than TRDEP. The implication is that donors will be required to continue financing RDP in the foreseeable future, if only to avoid collapse; any reduction of subsidies will depend on BRAC slowing down, consolidating and reducing the drop-out of older members borrowing larger loans.

From quality to quantity

The need for consolidation is also suggested by the qualitative costs which BRAC has incurred: expansion has made the credit operations more crucial to the organisation's stability and the priorities of both head office and field staff. This means that the original BRAC approach of providing more diverse financial services (that is, savings) and integrating these services with institution-building has become overshadowed by the demands of credit disbursement and repayment discipline. With members' savings closely controlled (partly to protect area office-level finances), and VO support staff highly stretched (to enable an extension of staff across the new BRAC regions), BRAC's going to scale has not been a simple replication process, but has seen a transition from quality to quantity.

This conclusion is in contrast to BRAC's persisting reputation. Authors such as Korten (1989) and Lovell (1992) characterise BRAC as a 'learning organisation'. Yet members' dissatisfaction with savings, and the reluctance of BRAC to facilitate federations of BRAC groups, suggests that learning from the target group has lessened in recent years. The dilution of services which expansion has caused means that BRAC's effectiveness, as recounted in the existing published literature, should now be re-evaluated.

The constraints of credit discipline

Both BRAC and TRDEP concentrate primarily on 'productive' credit. Neither programme offers easy-access consumption loans or flexible and accessible savings facilities – which would contribute to poorer households' coping strategies. The emphasis on small weekly instalments to repay loans may appear to be geared to the limited cash flow of the poor, but it does impose constraints of discipline. In crisis situations, borrowers have few choices (if they wish to avoid the hostility of peers and field staff) but to 'pay up' or drop out. As recent BRAC statistical reports have revealed, the drop-out and turnover of the membership has been substantial in recent years. Not all borrowers, it seems, are able or willing to cope with the constraints imposed on them.

The centrality of credit also constrains the way in which both BRAC and TRDEP operate in relation to their clienteles. Repayment discipline is the foremost indicator of village- and branch-level performance. In both cases, despite the programmes' rhetoric, this concern with discipline results in a practical organisational culture which discriminates against the less credit-worthy amongst the poor. The targeting of TRDEP – towards the relatively well-endowed amongst the poor – and the shift in BRAC's targeting during its recent expansion – away from the poorest – suggest that field staff in both organisations recognise the importance of the 'minimum economic level' necessary to use productive credit effectively.

The impact of credit on the differentiated poor

Our data provide evidence of credit's promotional impact for some, and a protectional impact for others. However, taken together, the surveys of BRAC and TRDEP borrowers suggest that the better-off amongst the poor benefit more from credit than the poorer. To use credit effectively, households need to have already reached a 'minimum economic level' (see pp. 150–5). This is an uncomfortable conclusion for advocates of credit as a widespread, country-level, poverty-alleviation strategy, for it has simi-larities to the earlier debate on the differentiation of agricultural households in the green revolution process. Credit, like new technology, is far from scale neutral; if it benefits better-off households more dramatically (and quickly) than others who are worse-off, it may lead to increasing relative disparities in the countryside.

Also, our field studies suggest that credit can pose severe risks for the extremely poor. For households without regular cash flow, repayment obligations can contribute to other more structural downward mobility pressures which continually impair (already limited) crisis-coping capabil-ities. For this category of households, many of whom are still (and perhaps increasingly) excluded from even BRAC's targeted RDP, credit has severe limitations as a poverty-alleviation strategy. This confirms the hypothesis raised in the Re-thinking Poverty Report (Rahman and Hussain 1992) that the differentials within the bottom half of the Bangladeshi population suggest that poverty-alleviation strategies need to be suitably devised to address the different needs of particular 'poverty groups'. BRAC and TRDEP credit does not seem to address the needs of the extremely poor, who require other forms of financial intermediation and other poverty-alleviation policies to make their livelihoods more secure.

13

MUTUAL FINANCE AND THE POOR

A study of the Federation of Thrift and Credit Co-operatives (SANASA) in Sri Lanka

David Hulme, Richard Montgomery and Debapriya Bhattacharya

INTRODUCTION

Co-operatives in developing countries have a weak record for helping poor people to improve their living standards and for assisting micro-entrepreneurs (Lele 1981; UNRISD 1975). The experience of thrift and credit co-operative societies in Sri Lanka stands in marked contrast to this general situation and supports the case for a reconsideration of the role of credit co-operatives in rural finance (Huppi and Feder 1990). Since 1978 the thrift and credit movement (known by its Sri Lankan acronym, SANASA) has pursued a strategy of rapidly expanding its membership and activities, and of shifting from an orientation towards middle-income households to a greater focus on poorer rural people. A key element of this strategy has been the establishment of the Federation of Thrift and Credit Cooperative Societies (FTCCS). This is the apex organisation for the movement's twenty-seven district unions, 7,500 primary societies and 700,000 members (as of 1992).

The basic unit of SANASA is the primary thrift and credit co-operative society (PTCCS or 'primary society') composed of a number of members (from as few as ten to as many as 700) who contribute initial share capital, attend meetings, make regular savings, and are expected to manage the society democratically. Savings create the basis for a lending programme from which a PTCCS can earn income because of an interest rate spread. Some societies are content with simple savings and loan activities, while

Many thanks to Dinal Fernando, Upali Jayawardena, Mrs Jayalakshmi, P.A. Kiriwandeniya, R. Hettiarachi, S.B. Divaratre, L.B. Dassanayaka, Richard Bond, the Marga Institute Moneragala IRDP, and the staff and members of SANASA.

others set up rural 'banks' and employ staff. Primary societies associate at the district level into District Unions (DUs), which in accordance with co-operative principles, elect a management board. Each DU elects seven representatives to the FTCCS General Body which in turn elects a representative from each of the country's nine provinces to the FTCCS Board.

The evolution and contemporary achievements of SANASA have been heavily influenced by its social, economic and political context, and so we commence by outlining these.

Although a low-income country, with a per capita income of only US$470 (World Bank 1992), Sri Lanka has an enviable reputation for the social condition of its population with a life expectancy of seventy-one years, an infant mortality rate of nineteen per 1,000 and a literacy rate of 88 per cent (ibid.). Despite these favourable social indicator scores, a considerable part of the country's population has low and vulnerable levels of income and limited entitlements, although the exact proportion is a subject of heated debate. IFAD (1992) estimates that 46 per cent of the rural population are below the official poverty line. By contrast, the World Bank (1992) estimates that only 20 to 25 per cent of the population are 'truly poor' using the criterion of inadequate calorific intake. Whatever criterion is used, there is much evidence that poverty has been on the increase and the economic and political context of the 1980s – ethnically based civil war in the north and east, growing numbers of refugees, the JVP insurgency in the south, burgeoning military expenditure, escalating national debt, a downturn in primary product prices, the polarisation of incomes (Institute of Policy Studies 1992) and pervasive political decay – has not been conducive to poverty-alleviation.

A fierce and unresolved debate has developed about the relationships between government policy and the incidence of poverty (Moore 1990). Despite regular democratic changes in government up to 1977, all governments opted for a welfarist orientation in policy and emphasised the role of the state in meeting citizens' basic needs and promoting economic equality. However, in 1977 the right-of-centre United National Party (UNP) came to power with a manifesto emphasising liberalisation. Its gradual liberalisation of the economy in the 1980s rapidly intensified after 1989 following the negotiation of a structural adjustment facility. Since then parastatals have been privatised, there has been a deregulation of industrial, trade and financial policies, state subsidies have been reduced, welfare expenditure has been partially capped, export production has been highlighted and the civil service is being 'downsized'.

Sri Lanka's banking system has long been characterised by its conservative lending policies and particularly its reluctance to provide credit to small borrowers and the non-plantation rural sector. In response, both colonial and independent governments have attempted to stimulate the development of rural financial institutions. The origins of the thrift and credit movement, almost ninety years ago, lie in the colonial regime's concern that commercial banks focused only on plantation and urban financial markets. This trend has persisted to the present with old-established foreign banks, indigenous private banks and newly established banks all concentrating on trade financing, large-scale industrial activities and pursuing high-value/low-volume business. In an attempt to provide financial services to smaller borrowers and rural people the government helped to create the Bank of Ceylon in 1939. In 1961 under a socialist-orientated government, this bank was nationalised and the state-run People's Bank was also established. While both of these banks deepened the financial system, successive governments believed that further interventions were necessary and both banks have been heavily involved with the disbursement of subsidised loans for 'small farmers'.

The centrepiece of these efforts has been the Central Bank's New Comprehensive Rural Credit Scheme (NCRCS), which succeeded the Comprehensive Rural Credit Scheme (CRCS) in the mid-1980s, providing loans to small paddy farmers. These schemes have achieved very mixed results and at times have closely mirrored the picture of specialised farm credit institutions painted by the Ohio School. They have only been accessed by a limited part of the population. In the mid-1980s, the NCRCS granted between 40,000 and 50,000 loans per annum to a target group of 1.8 million small farmers (that is, less than 3 per cent coverage). The Bank of Ceylon and the People's Bank have been unimpressed by government incentives to participate in this on-lending of 'cheap' Central Bank funds (funds at 3 per cent per annum and loan guarantees), and have been pressurised into on-lending. Private banks have kept clear of the schemes. Collection has been highly politicised and recovery rates have averaged out at only 65.5 per cent over the period 1970–91, and for 1990–1 they were only 45.1 per cent (Central Bank 1992). The twenty-seven similar schemes targeted on other products (such as chillies, coconuts, pyrethrum) have had limited take-up and been equally problematic.

Off-farm enterprise received little attention until the early 1980s, partly because of the 'myth of the small farmer' dependent on subsistence rice production that characterised planners' thinking, and partly because it had little political significance. In 1979 the Small and Medium Industries Loan Scheme (SMI) was started. However, with an average loan size of Rs550,375 (that is, in excess of US$20,000), it is evident that such loans are for businesses that are well-established.

For the co-operative rural banks (CRBs) operated by state-dominated multi-purpose co-operative societies (MPCSs) and quite distinct from the thrift and credit co-operatives, the subsidised schemes were a mixed blessing. Being able to lend funds at low cost attracted custom, but defaults on loans meant that by the late 1970s many CRBs were ineligible for further funds. They responded by concentrating on savings mobilisation and pawnbroking. Pawnbroking, with its easy access and low borrower transaction costs, proved popular and by 1980 83 per cent of CRB advances were based on pledges (Bouman and Houtman 1988: 78). It was also profitable for the CRBs despite its unorthodox nature in conventional banking terms.

By the mid-1980s it was evident that the Bank of Ceylon and the People's Bank had extended the formal financial system to only a small minority of rural people and the government, influenced by Indian experience, decided to establish Regional Rural Development Banks (RRDBs). The first of these commenced in 1985, and by 1992 fourteen were operating. However, even these decentralised banks are beginning to converge with other banks (that is, to look for larger loans) and they are heavily subsidised (see pp. 225–31).

A consequence of the reluctance of private banks and the difficulties of state-controlled banks to service the needs of small borrowers is that informal finance remains of great significance in Sri Lanka. Although its 'share' of the rural credit market has slipped in recent decades, the official statistics (which indicate a reduction from 92 per cent in 1957 to 44 per cent in 1976) are widely believed to underestimate the scale of informal loans. Senanayake's (1984) review found no evidence that the informal sectors' 1962 'share' of the rural credit market (66 per cent) had declined over the 1960s and 1970s. Case studies of localised situations (see, for example, Zander 1991: 9) continue to indicate that around two-thirds of funds borrowed by villagers come through informal sources. Sanderatne and Senanayake (1989) identify a wide range of intermediaries in the informal market, including professional moneylenders, pawnshop operators, friends and relatives, traders, commission agents, *cheetus* (a form of rotating savings and credit association) and special-purpose credit groups.

Given the differing motivations, objectives and *modus operandi* of such intermediaries the informal market is characterised by widely ranging explicit and implicit interest rates, as well as widely varying terms and conditions (Zander 1992). Crude estimates of the charges levied by informal lenders suggest that around one-third of loans are interest-free (that is, a negative real rate), around one-third are between 1 and 25 per cent per annum (that is, charging below and around a real rate) and one-third are above 25 per cent per annum. For a proportion of the latter, rates are very high running into hundreds of per cent. In common with trends in other countries, the informal finance market's image has been rehabilitated in the last decade. Government policies now view such intermediaries as providing a useful service, in contrast to earlier policies that saw moneylenders as 'usurious' and sought to displace them entirely.

It is against this background of unsuccessful interventions in the rural finance market that the country's thrift and credit co-operatives have expanded in numbers and activities since the late 1970s. They have become increasingly important as a rural financial institution, meeting a demand that other intermediaries could not.

THE RISE, FALL AND RISE OF THRIFT AND CREDIT CO-OPERATIVES

Sri Lanka's first credit co-operatives were set up in 1906 by the colonial administration. Over the early decades of this century new co-operatives were established and by 1940 there were 1,302 credit co-operatives. The main concentration was in the 'advanced' wet zone area and the bulk of the membership comprised middle-income villagers and people on salaries.

At that time the only real competition that PTCCSs faced was from the informal sector. However, during the Second World War consumer co-operatives were established to ensure food security across the country. Following independence in 1948, the government took a keen interest in these state-controlled co-operatives and in 1957 developed them into a nationwide network of multi-purpose co-operative societies (MPCSs). These were retailers, wholesalers, produce marketers and also provided financial services. Competition from the MPCSs, and later their affiliated co-operative rural banks (CRBs), hit the thrift and credit movement badly. Members' interests and business shifted to the MPCSs which could offer a wider range of services and heavily subsidised loans and inputs, and which had to be visited regularly by all rural Sri Lankans in order to claim their state-subsidised 'rice ration'. Between 1964 and 1978 the number of PTCCSs dropped from 4,026 to 1,300 and the remaining societies suffered from problems of morale, ageing leaderships and increased incidences of poor management.

In 1977 a social activist with considerable experience in the voluntary sector, P.A. Kiriwandeniya, became involved with the movement in his home village of Walgama in the Kegalle District. Over a year he reactivated the village's PTCCS from a savings club for old men into a 'village bank' with its own premises and a wide membership. In 1978, Kiriwandeniya organised a seminar at Walgama to 're-awaken' the thrift and credit movement. Some seventy-nine PTCCSs from Kegalle District attended. They were addressed by notables, including the Governor of the Central Bank, and studied the operations of the Walgama PTCCS. The response was rapid and many of these societies became active and dynamic almost overnight. Representatives agreed to form a District Union (DU) to promote co-operatives, provide services and permit inter-lending between societies. A second seminar, in 1979, was attended by delegates from across the country. This seminar sought to extend the movement socially as well as geographically, so representatives of 'encroacher' villages and low-caste representatives were included. Again the results were galvanising and by 1980 five District Unions had formed and these agreed to finance the Federation of

Thrift and Credit Co-operatives (Table 13.1). This was to represent the movement to government and external agencies (particularly donors), develop management systems and provide technical assistance and training. Between 1980 and 1985 the number of PTCCSs almost doubled, the number of District Unions rose to nineteen and financial activities expanded rapidly (Table 13.2). Many new societies formed in areas, particularly the dry zone, where the movement had not operated before and, following the spirit of the Walgama seminars, societies made efforts to incorporate lower-income households and women in their activities.

However, by the mid-1980s the movement's expansion was encountering a number of constraints:

Table 13.1 The structure of the SANASA movement

	Level	Status	Functions
Federation of Thrift and Credit Co-operative Societies (FTCCS)	National	Legally registered body – district unions are members	Interlending between districts; technical assistance; education; communication; negotiation with government agencies and external agencies
District Union of Thrift and Credit Co-operative Societies (DU)	District	Legally registered body – PTCCSs are members	Interlending between PTCCSs; representation of PTCCSs in FTCCSs; technical assistance; promotion of TCCSs; sale of stationery; bank for PTCCS deposits, negotiation with provincial and local government agencies
Divisional Office	Division	Recognised by DU bye-laws, but no legal status	Administrative duties delegated from DU; 'bank' for PTCCS deposits
Primary Society Cluster	6–10 villages	Recognised by DU bye-laws, but no legal status	Unit for training and education of leaders and members. Since 1993 taking on promotion and technical assistance activities
Primary Thrift and Credit Co-operative Societies (PTCCS)	Village	Autonomous legally registered bodies	Savings and loans for members; other functions (e.g. nursery schooling) as determined by members
Individual members	Village	Member	Involvement in management of PTCCS, saver and borrower

1 a lack of technical and managerial capacity;
2 the organisational structure was inadequate for an expanded movement. In particular, the link between DUs and PTCCSs was too remote and it was not practicable for a single DU to oversee several hundred PTCCSs;
3 the movement's success meant that it began to attract increasing attention from politicians and political parties;
4 The growth of societies was hindered by the scale of their lending activities being closely related to the savings they could mobilise locally.

The first of these was responded to by recruitment and training, much of which was financed by donor grants. This was effective, at least in part, but it commenced a process that has seen the movement's dependence on external subsidies rise rapidly (see pp. 188–94). For the second, the movement

Table 13.2 The growth of thrift and credit co-operatives in Sri Lanka

Year	No. of primary societies[a]	No. of District Unions	Member-ship[a]	Total deposits in PTCCSs, savings and shares		Total loans disbursed by PTCCSs	
				Rs millions	US$[b] millions	Rs millions	US$[b] millions
1981	1,448	7	20,786	113	5.5	68	3.3
1982	1,570	11	16,920	153	7.2	117	5.5
1983	1,685	14	220,651	172	6.9	220	8.8
1984	2,166	16	241,615	188	7.2	141	5.4
1985	2,420	19	340,100	220	8.0	188	6.9
1986	4,387	24	470,200	310	10.9	407	14.3
1987	5,215	26	545,100	352	11.4	408	13.3
1988	5,885	26	568,320	388	11.7	594	18.0
1989	6,761	27	633,000	418	10.5	601	15.0
1990	6,821	27	675,000	491	12.2	448	11.1
1991	7,245	27	702,238	622	14.6	637	15.0
1992	7,632	27	730,980[c]	622	13.5	715	15.5

Sources: Kiriwandeniya (1992) and FTCCS Reports
Notes
[a] Not all PTCCSs are members of DUs and FTCCSs. Around 84 per cent of PTCCSs have joined the SANASA movement, representing about 63 per cent of the total membership of thrift and credit co-operative societies in the country. Non-member societies are generally PTCCSs that were operating before the 1978 reawakening, or very recently established societies that are awaiting the approval of their membership application.
[b] Computed from the average exchange rate for the year in question. The Sri Lankan rupee (Rs) has depreciated significantly over the last fifteen years from US$ = Rs15.51 in 1978 to US$ = Rs46.00 in 1992.
[c] In 1992 some 460,500 people were affiliated to FTCCS. If it is assumed that half of these came from households with two FTCCS affiliates and an average household size of five people, the FTCCS coverage was a little over 10 per cent of total households or 12.5 per cent of total rural households.

determined to introduce a divisional-level tier of administration between the DU and the PTCCS. In some areas, such as Kegalle, divisional offices are now well established with buildings and several staff, but in others they are non-existent. Divisionalisation has increased SANASA's costs and dependence on external grants, and has extended the role of professionals, rather than volunteers, in the movement.

The interest of politicians and political parties in SANASA has been a major concern as 'capture' would undermine the financial viability, autonomy and credibility of the organisation. It has been dealt with in a number of ways. First, SANASA's leadership consciously seeks to avoid contact with politicians at all levels. Second, it has become an organisational norm that individuals who are active in party politics cannot hold office in the movement (and co-operative law bans politicians from holding office). Third, the leadership has been successful in performing a 'juggling act' when coming under political pressure by appeasing politicians while minimising their impact on the movement. Mistakes have occurred, though, as is illustrated by the Million Houses Programme (see next paragraph).

The fourth problem on our list was financial, in that the SANASA resource base was limited to members' savings and this was insufficient to meet demand for loans. This problem has been tackled in three main ways. First, rates for deposits have on average been increased so that primary societies now pay rates at around those of the National Savings Bank, rather than lower as was the case in the late 1970s and early 1980s (Table 13.3). Second, deposits are now being taken from non-members. In 1992 this increased PTCCS saving levels by 8.5 per cent and DU total savings by 10.7 per cent. Third, and most significantly, the movement has been receiving donor funds for on-lending to DUs and PTCCSs. These have come from a variety of sources including IFAD, CIDA, SIDA, NORAD, the Dutch government and NGOs. However, the most significant on-lending programme in terms of its impact on SANASA has been the USAID-financed 'Million Houses Programme' (MHP) operated by the National Housing Development Authority (NHDA). In 1985 SANASA agreed to act as the rural delivery mechanism for this programme. This decision came after intense political pressure, but it was also influenced by the opportunity MHP created for earning income at Federation, DU and PTCCS levels.

Altogether around Rs170 million of NHDA loans were distributed through the movement in 1986, 1987 and 1988 (Mercier 1990: 21). This resulted in the number of societies and the total value of loans disbursed more than doubling over the period 1985–8. It had other effects of a less positive nature, however. The first was that many of the new societies were formed exclusively to access subsidised credit. Such members did not develop the financial disciplines that characterised SANASA membership and they had little interest in savings and unsubsidised credit schemes. They

Table 13.3 Savings deposit rates: PTCCSs and the National Savings Bank compared (%)

Year	Average rate for PTCCSs[a]	National Savings Bank
1978	8.0	8.4
1982	10.0	12.0
1986	12.0	12.0
1990	14.0	14.0
1992	14.0	14.0

Sources: SANASA (1993) and Central Bank, *Annual Report* (1993)
Note: [a] PTCCSs set their own rates and these vary. This is FTCCS's estimate of the average rate

also tended to come from middle-income backgrounds and were often keen to exclude poorer villagers. Second, involvement in MHP loans meant that both local- and national-level politicians sought to make arrangements for their supporters to get access to loans through PTCCSs. These strains were intensified when the JVP threatened to assassinate SANASA staff and members for working on a government programme. Finally, the event that SANASA leaders had feared most of all occurred. Shortly before the 1988 elections the ruling party announced that 'poor people' would not need to pay instalments on their MHP loans. Although not as badly hit as other lenders, SANASA experienced an immediate downturn in repayments and widespread default (see pp. 228–9). Initially this appeared to threaten the existence of the movement, but the problem seems to have been contained as the NHDA has not pressed SANASA to cover the defaults, and MHP non-repayment has not contaminated other loans. The experience has left SANASA wary of involvement with financial arrangements that involve the government, however.

Since 1993 the movement has begun to introduce a further tier of paid staff into its structure. This is termed the 'cluster' and seeks to link together the operations of four to six PTCCSs and to mobilise higher levels of savings. The cluster unit is planned to be self-financing within a short period and there will be strong incentives for staff to achieve this goal. If successful, the cluster will professionalise the movement further by including paid insurance officials and technical assistance officers and through this diversification attract activity away from CRBs. It will also mark a further shift in SANASA's organisational culture from 'welfare' to 'enterprise'. During the establishment phase of 'clusters', donor grants are being heavily relied on: it remains to be seen whether or not such units can become self-financing.

SANASA's features differ markedly from all the other institutions studied in this volume (Table 13.4). Its primary groups are very varied and highly autonomous in their financial activities (they are not 'branches'); it is heavily

Table 13.4 SANASA: design features

	PTCCS	DU	FTCCS
Operational level	Village	District	National
Number of members	10–700	1,500–1,50000	500,000
Borrowers	Individual members	Member PTCCSs	DUs
Loan size (Rs)	200–50,000 (approx.)	50,000–500,000 (approx.)	100,000–10,000,000 (approx.)
Source of finance	Member savings and shares, non-member savings, DU loans and profits	PTCCS savings and shares, non-member savings and FTCCS loans	DU savings and shares, government loans, donor loans and grants
Maturity	1–24 months	12–24 months (approx.)	12–60 months (approx.)
Repayment frequency	Monthly	Monthly	Monthly
Collection method	At PTCCS 'office' in village	At DU office	At FTCCS HQ or by cheque
Interest rates (1992)			
Loans (actual) (%)	20–80	18–22	16
Loans (FTCCS recommended) (%)	20–24	18–22	16
Deposits (%)	12–17	13–17	10–15
Savings mobilisation	Compulsory and voluntary member savings, term deposits, non-member savings	Compulsory and voluntary PTCCS savings, member and non-member savings	Compulsory and PTCCS savings
Insurance arrangements	No	No	No
Incentives to repay	Peer pressure	Inter-society pressure	Unclear
Collateral and guarantors	Compulsory savings of 10% of loan value and two guarantors	No	No
Criteria for approval	Variable with PTCCS – regular meeting attendance and good character	Approval by the DU Board and a satisfactory repayment record	Approval by the Federation Board and a satisfactory repayment record
Repeat loan eligibility	Yes – no fixed ratio but usually graduated	n.a.	n.a.

Table 13.4 Continued

	PTCCS	DU	FTCCS
Appraisal method	By PTCCS finance committee – savings, proposal, past record and guarantors	Savings and past record	Savings and past record
Women members (%)	51% (some evidence that women emphasise savings and men loans)	n.a.	n.a.
Loan use	Any – including consumption	Productive or housing, varies with donor preferences	Productive or housing, varies with donor preferences

reliant on voluntary contributions to underwrite its services; it emphasises savings as much, if not more, than loans; it has a long history, has evolved over decades and is deeply rooted in society; it has an open membership and does not exclusively target the poor; it is a significant financier of smallholder agriculture; and SANASA and its constituent parts are ultimately accountable to its membership, not to a board of shareholders or NGO trustees. Understanding how these features have influenced its performance is the main analytical task of this chapter.

THE INTERNAL FINANCIAL PERFORMANCE OF SANASA AND ITS ROLE IN THE MARKET

Analysing the internal effectiveness of the SANASA movement is a more complex task than for other case-studies in this volume as the movement is comprised of thousands of separate legal entities, operating at three geographical levels. The nature of the organisation at each level is very different. In particular, the scale and functions of the national and district bodies demand full-time professional staff with a range of specialisations to complement elected office bearers. This means that administrative costs of DUs and the Federation are much higher (proportionally) than at village society level. Such costs are a key determinant of financial viability.

A main finding of the analysis is that the financial viability of the SANASA network is strongest at the primary society level. The District unions are in a weaker financial position while the Federation's finances are highly dependent on support from donors. The financial fragility of the Federation is due to the costs incurred by organisational expansion in the 1980s and early 1990s, along with problems of loan recovery from war zones. While this financial fragility is a serious problem requiring action, it must be noted that much of the financial strength of grassroots societies derives from externalities conferred by DUs and the Federation.

The Federation's financial performance

Since its formation in 1981, the Federation has massively expanded in financial terms, particularly between 1985 and 1989. During these five financial years the Federation's reserves grew by twenty-eight times, from Rs230,302 to Rs7,465,540 (Mercier 1990: 33–4). However, growth in both reserves and credit disbursement was largely fuelled by external assistance, while expenditures exceeded income from own activities – an imbalance which continues, according to more recent audited accounts. In each of the last five years the Federation has recorded a deficit. This type of growth, dependent on donors, raises questions about the long-term financial viability of the institution.

Federation: sources of finance

Total funds employed by the Federation (Table 13.5) increased fivefold between 1988 and 1992 from about Rs28 million to more than Rs149 million (approximately US$3.2 million). However, the flow of equity capital, basically membership shares, played only a minor role in this growth and share capital has averaged under 3 per cent of total funds employed for the last four years. The other important source of 'internally generated' resources, the compulsory and voluntary deposits made by DUs, have also decreased in importance from more than 40 per cent in 1988 to only 8 per cent of funds in 1992. DUs have increasingly moved to holding their excess deposits in commercial banks, rather than with the Federation.

The declining share of equity capital has coincided with annual income-expenditure deficits, particularly after 1988. On average, over the last five years, the deficit has amounted to 5.5 per cent of total funds employed (after adjusting for statutory reserves and gratuity). However, the deficit decreased from a peak of Rs9.35 million in 1991 to Rs6.76 million in 1992 and SANASA staff report further decreases in 1993 and 1994.

In contrast to the early 1980s the Federation has been overwhelmingly dependent on foreign grants and concessional credits for its recent expansion. The main forms of donor contributions are special projects and funds for specific heads of expenditure. Such resources also contribute indirectly because of the surpluses generated from these projects and bank interest accruing to temporarily 'idle' resources. Funds originating from international donors constituted about 70 per cent of the Federation's total annual deployment over the 1988–92 period and rose from around Rs13 million to Rs120 million (Table 13.5).

Table 13.5 FTCCS: annual sources of finance, 1988–92 (Rs millions)

	1988	1989	1990	1991	1992	*Average*
A Share capital	—	1.57	2.25	2.98	3.84	2.66
		(2.67)	(3.30)	(3.29)	(2.57)	(2.86)
B Project funds	16.38	47.66	59.82	89.29	140.40	70.71
	(59.18)	(81.07)	(87.79)	(98.54)	(93.93)	(89.57)
1 International	2.69	8.48	9.86	19.31	51.67	18.40
project funds in hand	(9.72)	981.07)	(14.47)	(21.31)	(39.57)	(23.31)
2 Internationally	10.47	30.39	34.80	46.57	70.89	38.64
generated funds	(37.83)	(51.86)	(51.07)	(51.40)	(47.43)	(48.95)
3 Funds created	0.13	4.01	5.35	8.50	16.88	6.97
through project expenditure	(0.47)	(6.82)	(7.85)	(9.38)	(11.29)	(8.83)
4 Funds created	3.08	4.68	8.82	13.46	0.95	6.20
through project and fixed funds	(11.13)	(7.96)	(12.94)	(14.85)	(0.64)	(7.85)
5 Other funds	0.003	0.003	0.96	1.45	—	0.49
	(0.01)	(0.01)	(1.44)	(1.60)		(0.62)
C Reserves	0.01	−4.37	−4.48	−9.27	−6.64	−4.93
	(0.04)	(−7.43)	(−6.57)	(−10.23)	(−4.44)	(−6.25)
1 Statutory	0.01	0.01	0.01	0.01	0.01	0.01
reserves	(0.04)	(0.02)	(0.01)	(0.01)	(0.01)	(0.01)
2 Gratuity	0.01	0.03	0.05	0.07	0.11	0.05
	(0.04)	(0.05)	(0.07)	(0.08)	(0.07)	(0.63)
3 Accumulated	−0.01	−4.41	−4.54	−9.35	−6.76	−4.36
surplus/deficit	(−0.04)	(−7.50)	(−6.66)	(−10.32)	(−4.54)	(−5.52)
D Deposit made by	11.29	13.93	10.55	7.61	12.13	11.10
the district unions	(40.79)	(23.69)	(15.48)	(8.40)	(8.12)	(14.06)
E Funds employed	27.76	58.79	86.14	90.61	149.35	78.91
(A + B + C + D)	(100)	(100)	(100)	(100)	(100)	(100)

Source: FTCCS audit reports
Note: Figures in brackets are percentages

Federation income and expenditure

Analysis of annual income structure shows that the most important source is from interlending activities to DUs, which accounted for about 57 per cent of average annual income between 1988 and 1992 (Table 13.6). However, as an income share this is declining. The share of 'other income', which includes derived earnings from foreign funds (for example, investment in fixed and ordinary deposits with other financial bodies) is

189

steadily rising, and for the reporting period it constituted more than 37 per cent of annual average income. Noticeably, the Federation derives minimal income from the 'other services' (that is, technical assistance and education) that it provides to DUs.

Federation costs can be divided into three categories: general administration, financial, and educational/extension expenditures. Administrative expenditure has remained more or less steady at around 37 per cent of the total during the 1988–92 period (Table 13.6). A larger share of expenditure is incurred by the FTCCS's educational and extension programmes and was 48 per cent by 1992. These costs include the operation of a large educational campus at Kegalle, the management of country-wide educational programmes with the DUs, and the production and dissemination of promotional materials including a monthly newspaper.

Table 13.6 FTCCS: income and expenditure, 1988–92[a] (Rs millions)

	1988	1989	1990	1991	1992	Average
A Income (total)	0.70	1.80	2.65	2.88	8.49	3.30
	(100)	(100)	(100)	(100)	(100)	(100)
1 Interlending section	0.37	1.53	2.02	1.63	3.79	1.87
	(52.86)	(85.0)	(76.23)	(56.60)	(44.63)	(56.67)
2 Stationery section	0.06	0.01	0.07	0.21	0.003	0.07
	(8.57)	(0.56)	(2.46)	(7.29)	(0.03)	(2.12)
3 Publication section	—	—	0.27	0.07	0.05	0.13
			(10.19)	(2.43)	(0.58)	(3.94)
4 Other income	0.27	0.26	0.29	0.97	4.60	1.28
	(38.57)	(14.44)	(10.94)	(33.68)	(54.76)	(37.27)
B Expenditure (total)	3.21	4.01	4.45	4.93	11.88	5.69
	(100)	(100)	(100)	(100)	(100)	(100)
1 Administration	1.22	1.51	1.44	1.95	4.55	2.13
	(38.01)	(37.66)	(32.36)	(39.55)	(38.30)	(37.43)
2 Educational and extension services	1.99	2.50	1.25	1.65	5.71	2.62
	(61.99)	(62.24)	(28.09)	(33.47)	(48.06)	(46.05)
3 Finance	—	—	1.54	1.05	1.31	0.78
			(34.61)	(21.30)	(11.03)	(13.71)
4 Sundry	—	—	0.22	0.27	0.31	0.16
			(4.94)	(5.68)	(2.61)	(2.81)
C Annual surplus/ deficit	−2.51	−2.21	−1.80	−2.05	−3.39	−2.39
D Expenditure–income ratio	4.59	2.23	1.68	1.71	1.40	1.73[b]

Source: FTCCS audit reports
Notes
[a] We have classified external grants to FTCCS not as income but as an addition to assets. Hence they are incorporated in Table 13.5. This practice differs from that of Mercier (1990) who treated them as part of the income flow.
[b] Weighted average.

The Federation also acts as an apex supervisor and manager of special projects across the DUs; in addition, it runs a small monitoring and evaluation unit. Lobbying the government (and other non-government organisations) in the interests of the membership is also part of the Federation's activities.

Although the average expenditure to income ratio for 1988–92 was worryingly high at 1.73:1 (that is, the Federation covered only 58 per cent of its expenditure from earnings) a steady improvement occurred and in 1992 the ratio was down to 1.4:1 (Table 13.6). However, part of this 'improvement' derives from the inflow of substantial subsidised funds so the decline reflects only a partial move towards financial viability.

A crucial qualification to the financial situation outlined above is that the FTCCS is still a 'young' institution incurring 'start-up' costs. The Federation's managerial and educational services have high costs, but have been essential for the rapid establishment (and sixfold expansion) of Thrift and Credit Societies across the country since the early 1980s. The key issue is to identify the present problems encountered by the Federation and examine its future prospects.

FTCCS financial weakness and interest rate policy

The major structural factor influencing the financial situation of the Federation is the narrow interest rate margin between its loan portfolio and total deposits. The bulk of loans to District Unions are made at 16 per cent per annum. In addition some 13 per cent of loans go to 'Low Income Earners' projects at 8 per cent per annum, and 5 per cent of loans are 'rehabilitation loans' at 3 per cent per annum. The weighted real interest rate on the Federation's portfolio is 14.31 per cent per annum.

Conversely, DU compulsory savings (loan security deposits) earn only 10 per cent, ordinary savings earn 13 per cent, and fixed (term) deposits earn 15 per cent per annum. Fixed deposits are approximately 45 per cent of the Federation's member deposits, compulsory savings are approximately 38 per cent, and ordinary savings about 17 per cent of the total. This yields a weighted deposit interest rate of 12.76 per cent. While the real interest rate margin of 1.55 per cent is sufficient to meet the costs of the interlending programme, it does not cover the considerable educational and extension activities of the Federation nor does it provide the basis for generating surplus – an issue which we return to below.

FTCCS financial weakness and the political situation

The main reason for the Federation's weak financial situation is poor repayment by member District Unions. Out of Rs59.59 million outstanding loans at the end of 1991, Rs27.38 million (46 per cent) constituted

191

overdue loans. By the end of 1992 overdue loans had dropped to 39 per cent of the portfolio, but the absolute figure was stable at Rs28.7 million. A part of this amount arises from Million Houses Programme Loans (see pp. 184–5) but the bulk of overdues originates from loans made during the 1989–91 period of political strife. Around one-third of total overdues lies in the DUs of the war-torn north and east, particularly Jaffna. As the overdue loans are not repaying interest they have reduced Federation income significantly. Given that recovery is unlikely from the war-devastated areas, FTCCS could well have written-off these loans. This has not been done as it might 'set a precedent'. On the positive side, it must be observed that the return of peace to much of the country and the cessation of loans to civil war areas means that this source of non-repayment is unlikely to occur in the future.

FTCCS interest rate margins and subsidy dependence

Given the features of the Federation's financial performance outlined above, independent viability is clearly some way off. To substantiate this conclusion two aspects of sustainability require further elaboration: the prospects for future interest rate policy, and the degree of present dependence on (and future requirements for) subsidy.

The most obvious way for the Federation to improve its financial position is by lowering its deposit rates or increasing its loan interest rates. The former is infeasible in the competitive financial market that exists. The *hypothetical* lending rates at which the FTCCS costs and incomes would have broken even between 1988 and 1992 are very high (Table 13.7).

This calculation, assuming the 'worst scenario' situation in which loans overdue define the default rate, suggests that the Federation would have to

Table 13.7 FTCCS: estimates of break-even lending rate of interest

Year	i	a	p	r
1989	0.02	0.14	0.40	0.93
1990	0.01	0.16	0.40	0.95
1991	0.01	0.10	0.45	1.02
1992	0.01	0.27	0.39	1.10
Average	0.01	0.17	0.41	1.00

Source: FTCCS records

Notes The break-even lending rate (r) per unit of on-lent principal $= \dfrac{i + a + p}{1 - p}$

i = borrowing interest rate (weighted average) per unit of principal;
a = administrative cost of per unit of principal;
p = default rate (assuming that all overdue loans are defaults);
r = break-even lending rate.

charge around 100 per cent interest to the District Unions to cover costs. Interest rates of that magnitude are not feasible, but the calculation points to the Federation's need to reduce overdues and minimise administrative costs. The former is already happening, but requires a much more concerted approach. The latter is problematic, as there is little room for slimming down the small interlending division and the Federation is vehemently opposed to reducing its educational and extension expenditure because it believes this is essential to long-term performance and the achievement of its mission.

The fact that the Federation is expanding its activities, under internal financial constraints, has made it increasingly dependent on donor support. External subsidy has risen from Rs13 million in 1989 to Rs33 million in 1992. The magnitude of this dependency is illustrated by the Federation's Subsidy Dependence Index (SDI) which increased from 190 in 1989 to 308 in 1992 (Table 13.8). If the Federation had to function without subsidy from external sources, then the lending rate, other parameters being the same, would have to be increased more than three times (that is, a subsidy-free interest rate would be almost 50 per cent). If indirect subsidies (for example, 'second round' income from bank deposits which originated from earlier grants and concessionary credits, and so on), and subsidies from public sources were included in the calculation (in which case k will not be

Table 13.8 FTCCS: estimates of Subsidy Dependence Index (SDI)

Years	A (Rs.mil)	m (%)	E (Rs mil)	P (Rs mil)	LP (Rs mil)	i (%)	S (Rs mil)	SDI
1989	47.66	14.0	1.57	−2.21	46.04	14.5	9.10	136.3
1990	59.82	17.0	2.25	−2.34	53.92	14.5	12.89	164.9
1991	89.29	19.5	2.98	−2.16	59.58	14.5	20.17	233.5
1992	140.40	20.5	3.84	−3.84	74.09	14.5	33.05	307.6
Average	84.29	17.75	2.66	−2.55	58.41	14.5	17.89	212.3

Source: FTCCS records. The concept of a Subsidy Dependence Index is taken from Yaron (1992)

Notes

Annual subsidy received = $A(m − c) + [(E*m)] + K$, where:

A = concessional borrowed funds outstanding and grants

m = interest rate the institution would be assumed to pay for borrowed funds if access to concessional borrowed funds were eliminated

c = concessional rate of interest actually paid on concessional borrowed funds outstanding (for FTCCS 1989–92 = 0)

E = average annual equity

P = annual profit

K = sum of all other subsidies received (for FTCCS 1989–92 = 0)

S = annual subsidy received by the Federation

SDI = index of subsidy dependence = $\dfrac{S}{LP * i}$

LP = average annual outstanding loan portfolio of the institution

i = average on-lending interest rate paid on the loan portfolio of the institution

zero as assumed in Table 13.8), then the SDI would be higher, and the hypothetical break-even interest rate would move closer to the estimates in Table 13.7.

In practice, the Federation's interest policy faces constraints. The FTCCS's rates on deposits at the time of our fieldwork were already slightly less than those of some of the banks, which implies that a reduction in savings rates (to widen interest rate margins) would be uncompetitive as many DUs already place a growing proportion of their funds in commercial banks.

There is more opportunity to raise lending rates because commercial bank rates are well above Federation levels. However, doing this would prove unpopular because DUs receive highly concessionary funds from Provincial Councils and government IRDPs. This has created a perception that downloaned funds should be cheap and so some DUs are reluctant to borrow funds at market-related rates. An alternative to this would be a move towards charging DUs the full cost of all services provided. There is opposition to this, however, as DUs perceive (probably correctly) that there are presently several aid donors around who will meet a high proportion of such costs. Continued external assistance during the coming decade will be essential to continue the management training and educational extension programmes which strengthen the network of DUs and PTCCSs and facilitates improvements in their own financial efficiency. Continued inputs from the Federation are also likely to enable recovery of overdues in the future. Without consolidation through such activities, District Unions and societies will also be more vulnerable to political and economic pressures arising from involvement in provincial government-sponsored credit programmes and national initiatives such as the *Janasaviya* Programme (see p. 242). Such programmes tend to conflict with the self-reliant ideology of primary societies, which is the basis of their credit discipline, good repayment rates and financial viability. The crucial question for the future is whether the Federation can use its external subsidies to mobilise more deposits (at all levels) and the generation of other 'internal' resources from the District Unions and their PTCCS members. In the medium term the Federation can probably rely on donor assistance, as donors are keen to work with it. To have long-term financial sustainability, however, the Federation must gradually move to being 'financed from below' once its 'start-up' phase is over.

District Union financial performance

The twenty-seven autonomous District Unions affiliated to the Federation are similar in their aims and operations. They mobilise equity and borrowed capital using the same procedures as the Federation and their functions are similar to the Federation, involving the administration of credit and savings services, and the provision of educational and managerial services. Generalisations about DU finances are difficult because DU financial data are not comprehensively collated at Federation level and significant variations exist between DUs at different stages of development. Further difficulties arise from the inconsistency of the data held by individual DUs.

Sources of finance

DUs have seen a phenomenal growth in deposit mobilisation. From a base of Rs0.3 million in 1982 deposits rose to Rs149 million in 1992. The most important source (more than 40 per cent) of DUs' deposits is in the form of 'ordinary savings' by member PTCCSs (Table 13.9). However, there are clear indications that the shares of the more recently introduced 'fixed deposits' and 'children's deposits' are on the rise. Moreover, the proportion of 'non-member' deposits is also increasing. These innovations reflect the increasing maturity of constituent primary societies and their growing capacity for 'product' diversification.

The volume of loan disbursements from DUs to primary societies has increased at a lower rate than the increase in deposit mobilisation between 1990 and 1991 (Table 13.10). However, the total amount of credit disbursed in each year far exceeded the deposits, indicating the significance of external financing for DUs. In 1991, for instance, the value of all deposits held by DUs amounted to only 44.6 per cent of the value of the total loans disbursed. The general trend has been for internal resourcing to become more significant, as in 1986 only 35.9 per cent of loans were based on deposits (Mercier 1990: apps 1, 4). However, these consolidated figures

Table 13.9 District Unions: structure of deposits

Type of deposit	Amount (Rs mil)		Rate of interest (%)	
	1990	1991	1990	1991
Shares	14.14	20.38	—	—
	(16.26)	(15.86)		
Ordinary savings	39.04	44.83	13.0	14.0
	(44.89)	(34.88)		
Compulsory savings	15.07	23.36	12.0	13.0
	(17.33)	(18.17)		
Fixed deposits	11.48	22.79	16.0	17.0
	(13.20)	(17.73)		
Children's deposits	0.15	4.26	14.0	15.0
	(0.17)	(3.31)		
Non-member deposits	7.08	12.91	12.0	13.0
	(8.41)	(10.04)		
Total	86.96	128.53	—	—

Source: FTCCS audit reports
Note: Figures in brackets are percentages.

195

Table 13.10 District Unions: structure of loans

Type of loan	Amount (Rs mil)		Rate of interest (%)	
	1990	1991	1990	1991
Agriculture	51.88	73.51	19.0	20.0
	(25.94)	(25.53)		
Animal husbandry	9.48	13.92	19.0	20.0
	(4.74)	(4.83)		
Small industry and self-employment	33.97	29.20	19.0	20.0
	(16.98)	(10.14)		
Housing	85.90	125.63	17.0	18.0
	(42.94)	(43.62)		
Others	18.80	45.72	21.0	22.0
	(9.40)	(15.88)		
Total	200.03	287.98	—	—
	(100)	(100)		

Source: FTCCS audit reports
Note: Figures in brackets are percentages.

hide considerable variations between District Unions. For example, Moneragala DU's total member deposits constituted under 15 per cent of the finance for its 1991 lending operations; Galle DU's member deposits financed just over 46 per cent of loans to PTCCSs in the same year.

In the four case-study DUs dependence on external sources of finance was very high, averaging 83 per cent of total assets employed. The main reason for this was the Million Houses Programme, which constituted 33 per cent of down-lending for these DUs. This leads to an over-statement of the present position as the writing-off of a significant proportion of these loans (at least 60 per cent) by NHDA has been under discussion for a long period and is likely to occur in the future. Other significant sources of external finance include the Provincial Councils' 'Self-employment Support Scheme', Swiss Inter-Co-operation in Kurunegala and the IRDP in Moneragala.

District Union income and expenditure

Countrywide data on DU income and expenditure are not available so this section focuses on the four case-study unions. It provides a pessimistic picture of their financial status. For the years 1988–91 the major source of income for these DUs was interest earnings from the 'Bank Section' which takes PTCCS deposits and on-lends them and which also down-lends external funds and takes a margin. On average more than 60 per cent of income came from this source (Table 13.11). The 'Trade Section', largely involved in sales of stationery, earned around 9 per cent of income on average. A further 30 per cent of income is from miscellaneous sources including fees and fines, service charges and grants from donors. The full

Table 13.11 Average annual income, expenditure and budgetary balance for four District Unions, 1988–91 (Rs '000)

	1988	*1989*	*1990*	*1991*	*Average*
I Income					
Bank Section	97.12	344.94	471.09	140.06	263.30
	(38.1)	(60.3)	(73.3)	(53.5)	(60.8)
Trade Section	9.63	60.83	57.20	31.83	39.87
	(3.8)	(10.6)	(8.9)	(12.2)	(9.2)
Other	148.27	165.92	114.55	89.61	129.59
	(58.1)	(29.1)	(17.8)	(34.3)	(30.0)
Total income	255.02	571.69	642.84	261.50	432.76
	(100)	(100)	(100)	(100)	(100)
II Expenditure					
Administration	288.00	410.00	475.00	287.00	265.00
	(75.2)	(54.3)	(31.0)	(54.3)	(45.6)
Depreciation	26.00	78.00	104.00	82.00	72.50
	(6.8)	(10.3)	(6.8)	(15.5)	(9.1)
Other expenditures	69.00	79.00	105.00	65.00	79.50
	(18.0)	(10.5)	(6.9)	(12.3)	(9.9)
Vehicle Section	—	37.00	60.0	95.00	48.00
		(4.9)	(3.9)	(18.0)	(6.00)
Interest paid	—	151.00	788.00	—	234.75
		(20.0)	(51.4)		(29.4)
Total expenditure	383.00	755.00	1,532.00	529.00	799.75
	(100)	(100)	(100)	(100)	(100)
Budgetary balance	(127.98)	(183.31)	(889.16)	(267.50)	(366.99)
Expenditure–income ratio	1.50	1.32	2.38	2.02	1.85

Source: Selected District Union audit reports (Galle, Kegalle, Kurunegala and Moneragala)
Note: Figures in brackets are percentages.

extent of donor support for DU recurring costs is not known but a 1992 survey by the Canadian Co-operative Association (CCA) found that for DU salary bills 52 per cent of costs at Hambantota were met by donors, 48 per cent at Kurunegala, 31 per cent at Kulliyapitia, 27 per cent at Puttalam but under 10 per cent for three other DUs. Continued assistance will clearly be needed by many DUs if they are to maintain and expand operations.

The DUs' main expenditures are on administration (mainly salaries and allowances) and interest payments on deposits, averaging around 45 per cent and 30 per cent of total costs respectively. While both income and expenditure fluctuate considerably from year to year it is evident that even in 'good' years income fails to cover annual costs (Table 13.11). The expenditure–income ratio for the four case-study societies has risen over recent years, and the average figure, at 1.85:1 indicates that DUs have earned only 54 per cent of their total expenditure in 1988–91. This negative trend is discernible in the assets–liabilities situation of the four DUs. Their stock of working capital has been eroded and there is evidence of a gradual depletion of total assets (fixed and working capital).

Systematic data on loan repayment from primary societies are not available and this provides evidence of a weakness in the management of DUs. However, the information that is available indicates that repayment rates are at levels much better than those achieved by the Federation and other rural lenders. For the four DUs examined in the field only 3 per cent of loans had not been repaid on time. The CCA survey of 1992 reported outstanding loans, as a percentage of total loans, for six DUs as follows: Matara 2 per cent; Moneragala 8 per cent; Puttalam 12 per cent; Kurunegala 13 per cent; Hambantota 18 per cent; and Nuwara Eliya 19 per cent. Given that the bulk of these overdues are the politically problematic MHP loans, a large proportion of which are expected to be written-off by NHDA, then the loan recovery position of the DUs at present is relatively healthy in comparison to the Federation.

District Unions: interest rates and subsidy dependence

With a weighted average borrowing interest rate (i) of 0.14 (see Table 13.7 for equation), an administrative cost per unit of principal (a) of 0.02 and assuming that there was total default on the outstanding loans indicated in the above study, Matara DU would need to charge an interest rate on loans of 18.4 per cent to break even and Nuwara Eliya of 43.2 per cent. The DUs are much closer to these rates than the Federation is to its current 'break-even' rate of almost 100 per cent, indicating that they are closer to financial viability than the apex body. Although it was not possible to compute SDIs it is evident that most DUs will continue to rely on subsidised credits and grants for some time. District Unions' financial viability will depend on the further growth of PTCCSs, whose mobilisation of resources and high degree of financial self-sufficiency are already impressive.

The financial performance of primary thrift and credit co-operatives

By 1992 the FTCCS reported that there were 7,632 primary thrift and credit co-operatives (PTCCSs), with a total membership of 730,890 and aggregate shares and deposits of Rs696.83 million. However, about 15 per cent of PTCCSs were not yet affiliated to District Unions and the Federation. Total loans granted by PTCCSs in the year amounted to Rs715.12 million, indicating that the PTCCSs' own resources amounted to more than 90 per cent of disbursements.

Ideally, an analysis of PTCCSs would include a detailed discussion of the different levels of financial and organisational maturity, to show the developmental stages through which they pass. However, a unilinear model would be misleading. Although all PTCCSs have similar bye-laws they also have considerable autonomy and follow local priorities. Thus there are many differences in their terms and conditions. In particular, upper limits of loans, as well as their repayment and interest conditions, vary from society to society. The diversity of PTCCSs is one of the outstanding features of the thrift and credit co-operative network and an important contributing factor to their performance.

Sources of finance and portfolio structure

PTCCSs' capital is constituted by membership shares, ordinary and compulsory savings, fixed and children's long-term deposits, and in some cases 'non-member' deposits (Table 13.12). The table also shows the schedule of interest rates recommended by the Federation. The basis of a society's growth comes from mobilising deposits, and diversification into children's accounts and term deposits has become increasingly important. Ordinary savings from members and compulsory savings remain the most important sources of finance.

By building up deposits PTCCSs enhance their ability to borrow from the District Union, which gives members access to a variety of loan schemes under different terms and conditions.

There has been a steady growth of aggregate outstanding loans since the late 1970s (Tables 13.2 and 13.13). Housing appears to be the single most important category with over 34 per cent of all loans 1990–2. However,

Table 13.12 Structure of deposits of PTCCSs (as of 31 December)

Type of deposits	Amount (Rs mil)			Federation-recommended rates of interest (%)		
	1990	1991	1992	1990	1991	1992
Shares	80.29	86.37	90.46	—	—	—
	(16.34)	(13.88)	(12.98)			
Ordinary savings	152.90	235.61	261.72	12.0	13.0	13.0
(i.e. on demand)	(31.13)	(37.87)	(37.56)			
Compulsory savings	157.82	177.57	195.35	12.0	12.0	13.0
(i.e. security for loans)	(32.13)	(28.54)	(28.03)			
Fixed deposits	46.91	43.72	52.93	15.0	16.0	17.0
	(9.55)	(7.03)	(7.60)			
Children's deposits	13.99	26.07	35.40	13.0	15.0	15.0
	(2.85)	(4.19)	(5.08)			
Non-member deposits	39.32	52.74	60.98	11.0	12.0	12.0
	(8.00)	(8.48)	(8.75)			
Total	491.23	622.08	696.84	—	—	—
	(100)	(100)	(100)			

Source: SANASA Federation reports
Note: Figures in brackets are percentages.

Table 13.13 Structure of loans granted by PTCCSs

Type of loans	Amount (Rs mil)			Federation-recommended rates of interest (%)		
	1990	*1991*	*1992*	*1990*	*1991*	*1992*
Agriculture	94.75	164.00	188.46	21.0	23.0	22.0
	(21.10)	(25.75)	(26.35)			
Animal husbandry	19.73	31.51	45.97	21.0	22.0	22.0
	(4.39)	(4.95)	(6.43)			
Small industry and self-employment	77.98	116.67	126.32	20.0	21.0	21.0
	(17.37)	(18.32)	(17.66)			
Housing	155.94	224.27	249.21	19.0	20.0	20.0
	(34.73)	(35.21)	(34.85)			
Others	100.56	100.52	105.16	22.0	23.0	24.0
	(22.40)	(15.78)	(14.71)			
Total	448.96	636.97	715.12	—	—	—
	(100)	(100)	(100)			

Source: FTCCS audit reports
Note: Figures in brackets are percentages.

such loans have the longest terms of repayment (normally five years), and it is evident that much of this lending constitutes disbursements outstanding from MHP loans in earlier years. Uncertainty about the recording of housing loans on PTCCS's official accounts means that caution is needed with these figures. The interest rates recommended by the Federation are also shown (though, as with deposits, these interest rates are discretionary).

Income, expenditure and performance

The growth in an individual PTCCS's credit portfolio is usually gradual, and relies mostly on the efforts and financial resources of the membership. Since the Million Houses Programme in the 1980s, during which new PTCCSs were given large external loans in comparison to their members' deposits, the Federation has encouraged District Unions to avoid providing financial assistance to young PTCCSs until they have mobilised their own share capital and deposits. This present policy of a gradual and relatively 'non-interventionist' approach to young PTCCSs seeks to ensure that office holders and members learn the importance of savings mobilisation and credit discipline. Savings mobilisation is an essential element of the movement's co-operative ideology of member ownership, self-reliance, as well as the peer-group pressure by which those who are in arrears are persuaded to avoid default. Most of the case-study societies exhibited financial and social features which show the influence of this ideology. Certainly, the repayment rates of the case-study societies are evidence of impressive credit discipline (Table 13.14). Five of the nine societies had

Table 13.14 Repayment rates, net profit, administrative costs and financial costs of nine PTCCSs

Code[a]	Year of establishment[b]	Rank of loan portfolio[c]	Repayment rates at time of audit (%)	Net profit as % of total income[d]	Administration costs as % of outstanding loans[e]	Financial costs as % of interest earned on loan[f]
K	1933	1	99.9	24.4	2.3	72.1
D	1940	2	97.6	14.2	2.8	42.2
B	1983	3	96.5	7.4	3.4	74.2
MG	1986	4	68.5	30.0	3.1	36.3
M	1983	5	99.9	2.5	2.6	79.6
N	1986	6	100.0	76.8	1.0	7.0
MW	1943	7	100.0	46.6	2.2	34.4
E	1983	8	100.0	49.5	5.0	19.7
L	1986	9	95.1	23.0	8.1	60.7
Weighted average			96.0	31.9	2.8	59.0

Source: Audited Accounts

Notes

a Codes E, L and M are Moneragala societies, the rest are in Kurunegala; most Moneragala societies' accounts were not available due to severe delays by the government Co-operative Auditors.

b The year of establishment shows year of initial formation.

c Rank is given according to the total value of loans disbursed in the audit year.

d Net profit is the deduction of financial, administrative and other expenses from interest earned on loans and other income (called 'surplus' in cooperative audits).

e Administration costs are given by the co-operative audits, separate from financial and other costs.

f Financial costs consist predominantly of interest payments on members' deposits, but also include interest paid by the society on external loans from District Unions.

virtually perfect repayment rates at the time of study. Only one society appeared to have severe problems, and these were related to 'old' MHP loans which remain on their books. A reasonably well-established society, probably around ten or more years old, will provide a variety of loans. Such credit is commonly categorised by purpose – consumption loans, short-term agricultural production loans and other types of working-capital credit, larger loans for off-farm and farmers' fixed-capital investments, and longer-term loans for 'non-productive' purposes such as house construction or school fees. The terms and conditions for different credit services vary (Table 13.15). In most societies, consumption and seasonal farm loans are most in demand. They are also the smallest loans (typically, between Rs500 and Rs1,000). These types of loans are often the ones which a new society will offer, before it has developed the capability to

Table 13.15 Credit facilities of a mature PTCCS: a typical example from Kurunegala District, 1992

Types of credit	*Terms and conditions*
1 Small consumption loans called 'instant credit': Rs500–Rs1,000	Minimum of formalities Repayable in 1 month High interest (4–5% per month equal to 60–80% per annum)
2 Seasonal farm loans	Repayable in 6 months (after harvest); 18% p.a.
3 Farm production loans	Repayable in 2 years (at 19% p.a.); or in 5 years (at 20% p.a.)
4 Manufacturing loans	Repayable in 2 years (at 21% p.a.); or in 5 years (at 23% p.a.)
5 Trade loans	Repayable in 5 years, at 26% p.a.
6 Repayment of other debts	Repayable in 3 years, at 24% p.a.
7 Housing, electricity and water loans	Repayable in 5 years at 22% p.a.
8 Self-employment loans	Repayable in 2 years at 18% p.a., or if beyond 2 years, at 20% p.a.
9 Releasing mortgaged assets	Repayable in 5 years, at 20% p.a.
10 Welfare (funerals, weddings etc.)	Repayable in 3 years, at 20% p.a.
11 Externally financed loans such as 'special project credit' (or in the past, NHDA loans) from Provincial Councils, IRDPs or foreign donors	Depends on donor. Often at concessionary rates, e.g. 8% p.a. Members view such 'special credit' as different from loans made out of the society's own funds, or those borrowed at commercial rates from the District Union

offer larger and longer-term loans. However, reiterating the diversity of PTCCSs, some long-established PTCCSs have stuck to a simplified format: offering credit for all purposes at a uniform interest rate except consumption loans and occasional large investment loans.

In Kurunegala, societies charging uniform interest on loans adopted quite different rates, ranging from 16 per cent to 20 per cent per annum, according to what members felt was 'fair' rather than through systematic analysis. However, the Kurunegala DU will only provide credit at 2 per cent less than the rates listed in Table 13.13 in an attempt to influence the interest rate policies of individual societies. (In practice such influence is only partial as societies automatically apply for the cheaper types of DU credit, and substitute their own funds to provide for those purposes for which the DU charges higher rates.) Societies are increasingly following DU guidelines on credit interest rates, since they reflect understandable differences in risk and profitability of different types of investments.

Just as costs of credit differ between societies, so do the rates of interest paid on savings deposits. While the Federation has suggested rates (Table 13.12) societies determine their own, and in one case-study society the spread between loans and deposits had been set at 12 per cent. Interest rate policy tends to reflect the priorities of a co-operative's members and often relate to the society's stage of development. Wider margins between savings and loans rates obviously generate surplus (profit) for future expansion of credit facilities and are favoured by young PTCCSs. At initiation, societies start with low maximum loans for all members (as little as Rs1,000) and graduate to larger loans every one or two years. It can thus take many years before a full range of credit facilities and a diverse loan portfolio are built up, theoretically enabling mature societies to have narrower interest rate spreads.

Significantly, all the case-study societies in Kurunegala and Moneragala Districts were reported to have made profits from their operations in 1991, even those with the narrower interest rate spreads. Low administrative costs are central to profitability. Recent audited accounts for nine out of fifteen case-study societies were available, and despite important differences, the financial viability of these societies is clear (Table 13.14).

Consolidating these accounts and averaging them provides a crude picture of selected financial performance indicators (Table 13.16). The audited accounts show an amount of 'loans disbursed' greater than the total supply of funds (internal savings and external borrowings) because of the turnover of these 'revolving funds'. It is not possible, therefore, to calculate a realistic ratio between internal and external funds. Treating the figures as 'stable' would give a savings to borrowing ratio of 1:1.1, indicating that the PTCCSs are much more self-reliant than District Unions. However, the turnover of the societies' own funds (out of savings deposits) is likely to be much faster than the longer-term credits given by the DUs to the PTCCSs. This implies that the 'real' ratio of loan financing would reveal that societies' internally generated funds finance many more loans to individuals and households than external funds taken from the District Unions. The significance of external credit for different societies varies widely and for seven out of the nine co-operatives in Table 13.15, 85 per cent or more of the money lent out to members was financed by locally generated funds – a remarkable achievement in self-reliance.

An attempt was made to estimate the break-even interest rate (r) of the PTCCSs for the year 1991, based on the nine audited accounts. The borrowing rate of interest (a weighted average) for the societies (i) was Rs0.14 per unit of principal, and the administrative cost of lending a unit of principal (a) was Rs0.03. With a default rate (p) of 4 per cent, the break-even

Table 13.16 Selected PTCCS financial performance indicators (1992 averages and annual averages, $n = 9$)

1	Number of members	137
2	Total savings deposits (Rs)	44,100.97
3	Total external borrowing (Rs)	47,458.00
4	Total amount of loans disbursed during the year (Rs)	460,232.00
5	Total amount of arrears (Rs)[a]	18,634.00
6	Total annual income (Rs)	77,632.00
	(a) Interest income on loans (Rs)	71,941.00
	(b) Other income (Rs)	5,691.00
7	Total annual expenditure (Rs)	64,302.00
	(a) Financial expenditure (Rs)[b]	42,551.00
	(b) Administrative expenditure (Rs)[c]	13,723.00
	(c) Other expenditures (Rs)	8,028.00
8	Net profit (Rs)	13,330.00
	Memo items	
	(a) Per capita savings (Rs)	321.90
	(b) Per capita loan disbursed (Rs)	3,359.36
	(c) Internal–external ratio in loan sourcing	1:1.08
	(d) (i) Total cost of loan delivery per unit of principal (Rs)	0.14
	(ii) Administrative cost per unit of principal (Rs)	0.03
	(iii) Financial cost per unit of principal (Rs)	0.09
	(e) (i) Total income per unit of principal (Rs)	0.016
	(ii) Interest income per unit of principal (Rs)	0.06
	(f) Default rate (%)	4.05
	(g) Rate of net profit (on income) (%)	17.17

Source: Audit reports of PTCCSs
Notes
[a] The bulk of the arrears relates to Million Houses Programme loans from the 1980s. These have not yet been written off by NHDA and so societies must keep them on their books.
[b] Financial costs consist predominantly of interest payments on members' deposits, but also include interest paid by the society on external loans from District Unions.
[c] Administrative costs are given by the co-operative audits, separate from financial and other costs.
[d] Net profit is the deduction of financial, administrative and other expenses from interest earned on loans and other income (called 'surplus' in co-operative audits).

interest rate (r) was estimated to be 0.21 per unit of principal, that is, a 21 per cent interest rate on loans. This calculation, which compares favourably with the actual rates charged by PTCCSs, provides further evidence of their financial viability.

Low administrative costs are clearly an important factor and the administrative costs of seven out of the nine societies in our study are less than 3.5 per cent of the value of credit disbursed. This is significantly lower than other innovative rural banking schemes and even the society with the highest administrative costs (8.1 per cent of the total value of loans disbursed) compares favourably with other banking institutions (see Vol. 1, Chapter 3, for a comparison).

The two PTCCSs with higher administrative cost–loan portfolio ratios are both more recently formed than the others, and are therefore still meeting 'start-up' costs. Even when these cost ratios are included in a weighted average calculation, this average is still remarkably low – suggesting that administrative costs average out at only 2.8 per cent of the value of outstanding loans.

While economies of scale are undoubtedly achieved by larger societies, small co-operatives are able to avoid administrative costs by using voluntary labour and 'no-rent offices' (usually donated by a committee member). As the volume of financial operations increases at least one paid staff member is usually required. This is often a transitional stage in a society's development as administrative costs increase but financial operations take a period to yield their returns. The two case-study societies with lowest profit margins (ranks 3 and 5 in Table 13.14) were going through this transitional phase of setting up an office with only a limited turnover.

It is clear from the case-study societies that the difference between interest earned on loan portfolios and interest paid out on members' savings deposits is a major contributor to the profit margin, estimated as 17.17 per cent on average for the nine societies.

An interesting aspect of PTCCS financial performance, evident from the audited accounts, is the lack of a clear relationship between administrative costs and repayment ratios (Table 13.14). Discussion of banking institutions in less-developed countries has often cited such a relationship as one of the key policy dilemmas. This is because (as discussed in Vol. 1, Chapters 2 and 3) high administrative costs are incurred by banks using intensive loan supervision procedures – which are seen as a way of reducing the risk of arrears and defaults; higher repayment rates may generate interest income to compensate. A relationship between high administrative costs and high repayment rates is therefore often assumed. SANASA co-operatives do not, however, illustrate such a relationship because of their capacity to defer direct costs by voluntary contributions and the fact that peer pressure within groups is not reliant on continuous inputs from paid employees.

Federation, district unions and primary societies: fitting the pieces together

The SANASA movement has clearly achieved Yaron's (1991) criterion of effectiveness in terms of outreach (Table 13.2). However, in terms of achieving a 'commercial approach' it is evident that while this is the case for primary societies, the upper tiers of the structure, and particularly the Federation, are a long way from financial viability at present and are heavily dependent on donor subsidies. The ending of the insurgency in the south of the country, the lull in fighting in the east of the country and the anticipated writing-off of Million Houses Programme loans all mean that repayment problems should be less significant in coming years than in the late 1980s and early 1990s. Although an array of donors appear willing to continue to support SANASA with direct and indirect subsidies, there is clearly a need for the Federation to adopt a more commercial approach and to encourage DUs to do the same. The solidarity and support that keeps PTCCSs running so effectively – voluntary contributions, peer pressure to repay, guarantors – is much weaker at the District Union and Federation levels. In part this reflects the fact that the greatest beneficiaries of DU and FTCCS activities are new societies, which have the least capacity to contribute to higher tiers. Efficient, mature societies need much less assistance, but have a much greater financial capacity to support a DU or FTCCS.

Treating the Federation and DUs as discrete entities is useful when analysing finances, but it should not obscure the fact that they are constituent parts of the country's thrift and credit movement and confer significant benefits at the primary level. They have successfully stimulated PTCCS formation, have encouraged the mobilisation of a great volume of savings, promote the redeployment of those resources in rural areas from which finance is usually extracted (see pp. 227–9) and can provide access to external resources. If an SDI were computable for the entire movement it would be at much lower levels than those for the Federation or DUs. A more systematic approach to cost recovery from lower levels will be required in future, but it would be unfortunate to make the full financial viability of the Federation and DUs a primary objective in the short or medium term. Both tiers have done a great deal to stimulate the overall rural financial market with PTCCSs and DUs holding significant funds with commercial banks, the copying of SANASA approaches by RRDBs and the creation of competition in a market where monopoly profits could previously be taken. These are valuable externalities. From an 'interventionist' perspective, relatively small sums of money (in terms of the large amounts of aid disbursed for rural development) have induced amounts of self-reliant grassroots financial mobilisation and poverty alleviation of an order with which comparative programmes in the country cannot compete (see pp. 225–33).

IMPACTS ON INCOMES, EMPLOYMENT ACTIVITIES AND PRODUCTION ORGANISATION

This section looks at the role of credit; particularly its impact on incomes and asset formation, productivity, employment and technology adoption. While the focus here is on loans, the 'thrift' dimension of primary societies is not ignored. Assessing the economic impact of credit is notoriously difficult. Changes to both individual enterprises and local economies often occur gradually. Distinctions need to be drawn between (a) more 'structural' and sustained changes ('impacts'), and (b) immediately observable, but possible short-term 'effects'. Ideally, impact is observed over the long term, and is often cumulative rather than immediately evident. Borrowers in this survey were asked about their present situation, and then asked to compare it to immediately before their last (non-consumption) loan: a period of between one and two years for different respondents. So the changes documented below are only for a short time period.

Ascribing a causal role to credit is complicated by the nature of household economics, involving multiple sources of (and seasonal variations in) incomes. The difficulties of documenting these microprocesses and the intrinsic 'fungibility' of money often obscure an exact link between a loan and a change in a household's situation (for example, loans not directly used for a clear investment purpose may be releasing other resources for new investments). The economic context is also a major factor determining the relative impact of credit on borrower households. The survey data shows that Kurunegala's local economy is more diverse and vibrant than Moneragala's, providing a more favourable investment environment.

The socio-economic composition of PTCCS members, loan size and use

The survey sample indicates that PTCCS membership reflects the socio-economic composition of wider society. This is illustrated using a crude poverty-line analysis building on data used by the Central Bank (1989), defining a poverty line income as Rs1,400 per month (per household) in 1988.[1] Adjusting this figure for inflation, a comparable poverty-line definition for our survey respondents is Rs2,100 for the last quarter of 1991, one year before the interview (and Rs2,239 at the time of the interview). Some seventy-nine (52 per cent) SANASA members interviewed had incomes below Rs2,100 in late 1991. This is higher than the FAO's most recent (1988) estimate of 46 per cent of the rural populace being below this poverty line (IFAD 1992: 37). Only twelve (8 per cent) of the sample households had monthly incomes in excess of Rs10,000, placing them in what might be termed a position of being, in relative terms, 'wealthy'.

Other indicators from the interviews also suggest a correspondence between membership and communities in general. For example, 13 per cent of Moneragala respondents were illiterate, which correlates with government statistics for the area. Additionally, the number of single and widowed women members, some 15 per cent, is the same as the official figures for Kurunegala and Moneragala Districts (Census of Population and Housing 1981, in Rasanayagam 1993: 150) and indeed, slightly higher than the Central Bank's (1989: 25) more recent estimate of 13 per cent. Lastly, SANASA societies overall include slightly more women than men (51 per cent and 49 per cent, respectively), as does our sample.

The predominance of farming households in our sample, with 70 per cent of respondents primarily agriculturalists, reflects a general feature of the PTCCS membership which is Federation-affiliated. It is therefore not surprising that most respondents' productive loans were for an agricultural activity (Table 13.17). However, it must be noted that in such households credit is often used for a series of interdependent income-generating and subsistence activities rather than for a specific 'micro-enterprise'. In several of the PTCCS case-studies, the most numerous type of loan disbursed is seasonal agricultural production credit. These loans tend to be small, and thus their effects are difficult to observe in the short term. Nevertheless, access to seasonal production credit is important both for the introduction of new crops (such as sugar cane in Moneragala) and the adoption of 'green revolution' inputs in the paddy sector. SANASA credit therefore plays a crucial role in the agricultural sector as is reflected in many of the survey's results.

Average loan size amongst sample respondents was Rs5,094, but the median was Rs3,500 – a small number of high-value loans (Rs15,000–20,000) having pushed up the mean value. Only 27 out of 151 loans (18

Table 13.17 Use of last loan by respondents

Type of activity (product or service)	Number of respondents	Percentage
Paddy cultivation	66	44
Various other crop cultivation	27	18
Sugar cane cultivation	14	9
Trading (shop)	12	8
Petty trading	9	6
Petty industry	8	5
Agro-processing	3	2
Service	3	2
Poultry husbandry	2	1
Other activities	7	7
Total	151	102

Table 13.18 Sizes of loans by District in fifteen case-study societies

Loan size	Kurunegala District	Moneragala District	All borrowers
Under Rs2,000	6	39	45
	(8.5)	(48.8)	(29.8)
Rs2,001–5,000	43	35	78
	(60.6)	(43.8)	(51.7)
Rs5,001–10,000	12	2	14
	(16.9)	(2.5)	(9.3)
Above Rs10,000	10	4	14
	(14.1)	(5.0)	(9.3)
Total	71	80	151
	(100.1)	(100.1)	(100.1)

Note: Figures in brackets are percentages.

per cent) were higher than Rs5,000, and most of these (22) were disbursed by societies in the more developed Kurunegala area (Table 13.18). Most borrowers did not use loans for the acquisition of fixed assets: manufacturing machines, mini 'land-master' tractors (which cost around Rs30,000) or even a new pair of buffalo (approximately Rs3,000) are difficult to finance from such small loans. In our sample, 85 per cent of respondents had used their recent loans to acquire working capital.

Impact on income

The survey shows that taking co-operative credit is commonly associated with increases in household income. SANASA members could often identify causal links between access to credit and their income flows. Aggregate survey figures show impressive average increases in monthly household income, from Rs3,582 before the last loan to Rs4,680 during the month preceding the interview. Adjusting by the Central Bank's (1992) average annual percentage change in prices of 11.4 per cent for the twelve months preceding the interviews, household incomes have risen by 15.8 per cent in real terms. However, these average figures mask considerable variation within the sample. Kurunegala members' average monthly income rose from Rs4,026 to Rs5,407, while Moneragala members' rose from Rs3,232 to Rs4,098 over the reporting period. These figures constitute real income increases of 19 per cent for Kurunegala members, and 12.3 per cent for those in the Moneragala societies. Both figures are impressive, but they indicate the importance of the local economic context as a determinant of credit impact.

The most important factor correlating with increased income was labour. There is a moderate correlation (0.39) between increases in the number of employees paid by a respondent and increases in income (however, the effect of loans on aggregate paid employment seems to have been very small, as discussed on pp. 211–13). More significant was the level of intra-household employment, that is, the number of members working 'in' the loan-assisted activity. This labour–income correlation (0.61) is not only relatively high, but is statistically significant. Such a finding, along with the moderate correlation between increases in income and the number of paid employees, suggests that credit is creating an increased demand for labour. As labour is a key to higher outputs and incomes amongst rural households in the South Asian context, this is an important finding.

Variations within the sample are masked by the averages. While a section of the sample registered very high income increases, particularly those already in the middle-income bracket, 20 per cent of those interviewed said either that their income had not changed (nineteen persons), or that their income in the present month was less than during the month preceding their last loan (eleven persons). Of those reporting negative changes, all except one were farmers.

However, there is evidence that income benefits have accrued to members across the different economic strata and have not simply been confined to those who were already relatively 'well-off' (Table 13.19). Thus, poorer households have benefited, and the sample results suggest significant 'graduation' above the adjusted official poverty lines. Before their last loans, 52 per cent of households were below the relevant poverty line (Rs2,100), while only 40 per cent had such low incomes at the time of the interview (when the poverty line was adjusted to Rs2,239). In other words, nearly *a quarter* of the seventy-nine 'poor' households graduated above the official income-defined poverty line during their investment of a SANASA loan.

Table 13.19 Households in different monthly income brackets over time (*n* = 144)

Monthly household income	No. of households before loan	No. of households 12–18 months after loan[a]
Under Rs1,500	55	40
	(38.2)	(27.7)
Rs1,501–3,000	46	39
	(31.9)	(27.1)
Rs3,001–5,000	23	30
	(16.0)	(20.8)
Rs5,001–10,000	14	23
	(9.7)	(16.0)
Above Rs10,000	6	12
	(4.2)	(8.3)
Total	144	144
	(100)	(99.9)

Note: [a] Adjusted to October 1991 values.

Asset acquisition

Most co-operative members use credit primarily for working capital, and the proportion acquiring major productive assets recorded by the survey was very small. However, when asked to give details about, and estimate values for, their overall household assets, a large number of borrowers reported major changes. It is possible that access to credit is releasing funds normally used for recurrent expenditures and enabling households to build up their assets (a process illustrating the importance of fungibility in household economics) but more research would be required to substantiate this.

Prominently, the asset formation is mainly non-productive. Eighty-five out of 151 borrowers (56 per cent) claimed that the value of their overall household assets had increased by more than Rs10,000, from the time before their most recent productive loan and the time of the interview.[2] A further 26 per cent reported enhanced values, but below the Rs10,000 threshold. Only 18 per cent reported negative or unchanged values. When asset values are broken down into their constituent items, investment on housing stands out. Of the eighty-five respondents, thirty-three had invested substantially in their dwellings (purchasing bricks, timber, and so on). A further forty respondents had acquired household equipment and consumer durables (including one respondent who purchased a television). While these improvements may certainly be seen as enhancing living standards, obviously the priority for SANASA members, they are the least productive assets in terms of economic output.

Only five people specified productive capital assets relating to their existing agricultural activities or off-farm businesses. Another five people said that their families had acquired sewing machines and livestock – assets with both 'consumption' and income-earning potential. These figures do not include those borrowers who had bought minor tools for petty manufacturing (another eight people).

Effects of loans on production methods, employment and enterprise management

The most important technological changes were in the agricultural sector, in which green revolution inputs were made accessible due to seasonal production loans from the societies.

Only 8 per cent of respondents reported an increase in the number of paid employees in their loan-assisted activity (and four households reported decreases in the number of people they employed). Half of these respondents were farmers, who reported the largest increase in numbers of employees (Table 13.20). Only eight borrowers reported employing other family members in their loan-assisted activity. Overall, therefore, SANASA

Table 13.20 Respondents reporting increases in employment in loan-assisted activities

Activity	Increase in paid employees			Increase in family employees		
	No. of respondents	Average increase in number of employees	Sample % (n = 151)	No. of respondents	Average increase in number of employees	Sample % (n = 151)
Paddy	5	5	3.3	5	2.2	3.3
Sugar cane	1	3	0.7	1	1	0.7
Other crops	3	5.3	2.0	—	—	—
Agro-processing	1	3	0.7	—	—	—
Petty trade	2	1	1.3	1	1	0.7
Cottage industry	—	—	—	1	1	0.7
Total	12	4.1	7.9	8	1.8	5.3

credit appears to have had little impact on employment outside of the borrower's household.

Nearly all (eleven out of twelve) respondents who reported increased paid employees had been SANASA members for more than three years. This was a more significant factor than, for instance, the size of loans, for which there is only a small positive correlation (0.4). Farmers employed nine out of every ten new employees taken on by survey respondents. Such increased labour use is most prominent for paddy cultivation. Thus, the effects of SANASA credit on employment creation are most marked in the agricultural sector.

Although 57 per cent of respondents said that they had used their loans to make technical changes in their enterprise, few of these changes actually involved the acquisition of new fixed capital (that is, equipment). Most technical changes were made by farmers, who referred to their adoption of 'new techniques' rather than to tools or machinery. Only seventeen respondents (11.3 per cent) had acquired 'new equipment' as a result of the loan, and fourteen of these were farmers (Table 13.21).

Most respondents making technical changes were referring to their using credit to adopt green revolution practices such as HYV seeds, fertilisers and pesticides. Additionally, some Moneragala farmers said that access to credit had affected local labour patterns. They have started to transplant rather than broadcast their paddy but this entails having cash available to pay for the extra labour required. *Attam* (labour exchange) can be unreliable, since the labour team is not always available at the right time for individual farms. Thus, adopting 'new' transplanting labour practices was directly connected to access to credit.

Table 13.21 Respondents acquiring new equipment as a result of loans

Type of activity	No. of households	Sample number	As % of sample no.
I Agricultural			
Paddy	5	66	7.6
Sugar cane	3	14	21.4
Other crops	6	27	22.2
II Off-farm			
Petty industry	1	8	12.5
Other	1	7	14.3
Service	1	33	3.3
Petty trade	0	9	—
Agro-processing	0	3	—
Retail trade	0	12	—
Poultry	0	2	—
Total	17	181	11.3

Off-farm technology changes for productive purposes were rare, largely because most of such loan-assisted activities are 'petty' in scale, and there were few agro-processors in our sample. Only one of the twelve 'large shop' operators in the sample reported any technological changes in their enterprise. This was the purchase of a motor cycle for transporting goods.

Surprisingly, there appeared to be no relationship between loan size and technological changes (a correlation of only 0.07). During informal discussions with members about loan use, people said that they could not use SANASA loans to purchase machinery because of their small size. This constraint was clearly illustrated by the story of one petty manufacturer who wanted to expand his business.

A member of a Kurunegala society had applied for a large loan (Rs20,000) to purchase a machine tool for brass ornament making (a 'craft' commodity for which there is a considerable urban demand). However, the society's official loan limit was Rs10,000 – and such loans were rare because their disbursement reduced the society's ability to provide a larger number of members with smaller loans. The brass maker circumvented these rules by agreeing with a friend that they would both lobby for Rs10,000 loans, pool them in his own business, and he would pay the colleague back in the future. Apparently, the society office holders were prepared to turn a blind eye to this arrangement (for it is unlikely that such a 'coincidence' would go unnoticed). This brass maker now runs an impressive 'industry' in the back room of his house, has employed two more full-time workers to increase his production, and his wife has taken responsibility for keeping the books and marketing the products.

Enterprise diversification

Almost 30 per cent of borrowers reported a diversification of their income sources in the last three years. These are of two types: the starting of a new income-generating activity, or the addition of another facet to an existing enterprise. Respondents reporting this latter type were the majority, mainly farmers adopting new crops, usually sugar cane, but also citrus fruits and market-orientated vegetables. Those starting new off-farm activities, such as paddy milling, poultry, cottage industry and petty trading, were in the minority.

Diversification was much commoner for female borrowers than male borrowers. Twenty-eight women had taken up new activities, as compared to only sixteen men claiming such diversification. The majority of these women have taken up petty industry or trading – flexible activities that are compatible with their other domestic responsibilities (Epstein 1990). In the few cases where women had taken risks to invest in fixed assets, returns were impressive. One of the most successful female interviewees had taken a Rs4,000 loan to buy chickens and build a coop. By producing eggs and chicks commercially she had achieved a 25 per cent increase in her monthly income, and had generated assets from the loan and its profits to the value of Rs7,000 (the coop, hens and minor utensils).

However, most women's enterprises were extremely small-scale in terms of both working and fixed capital. For example, a popular petty industry in the Kurunegala societies is the weaving of small coconut palm boxes for sale to urban packing companies. The only equipment needed are an iron and scissors. Women petty traders deal mostly in single commodities, such as fruit or cashew nuts, bought in tiny quantities from local households, processed, and then sold in bulk to larger, town-based merchants. Some of the enterprises taken up by women borrowers are highly vulnerable to market fluctuations and women cashew traders suffered in 1991–2 when the world price slump made Sri Lankan trading intermediaries switch to alternative commodities.

Because local demand is limited, enterprises such as poultry farming cannot be widely adopted in the same community without additional marketing and transport facilities. Indeed, in many of the villages which we visited, and particularly in Moneragala, one of the most commonly cited constraints on economic activities was poor transport facilities.

Five of the nine petty traders said that 'competition had increased', reinforcing the comments heard in several communities that having too many traders or producers in one activity leads to excessive competition, falling prices and reduced returns over the long term. In communities with poor road access, such competition is accentuated due to the smaller marketing area. Nevertheless, the provision of start-up credit for these activities is important, particularly for widows and single women.

In Moneragala, the major on-farm diversification identified by the survey and group interviews was the adoption of sugar cane by small farmers. This relatively new crop for the region is one of the most remunerative. Interviewees reported that although an acre of paddy was often worth around Rs9,000 for a crop, the costs of sugar cane production are less than for paddy over several years. Although sugar cane requires an initial investment in quality seed and agro-chemicals, the perennial nature of the crop (successive ratoons from the same root system) determines that the higher profit margins come in the second and third years, when no outlay on seed and few field operations are necessary (Vitebsky 1992: 167–9). Paddy production costs, during our fieldwork, were around Rs4,000–5,000 per acre, while the costs of sugar cane in ratoon years are minimal, making the Rs6,000 income almost entirely profit. These features of sugar cane's production cycle makes credit for the initial inputs essential if poorer farmers are to adopt this crop. Co-operative societies in Kurunegala have also been important in providing small farmers with an opportunity to diversify. Credit has permitted farmers to plant citrus fruits and buy seeds for better varieties of chillies and new vegetables – all of which are in demand.

Despite these positive indications of diversification there were differences between case-study societies. In some of the co-operatives dominated by farmers, the provision of credit for off-farm activities appeared to be sidelined in the interest of the majority. The seasonal provision of short-term agricultural production loans produces a simultaneous demand on a co-operative's resources and cash flow, reducing its ability to disburse the larger loans normally needed by potential capital-investing entrepreneurs. However, this institutional constraint is not always the main cause of a failure of co-operative members to diversify. It is just as often a reflection of the lack of opportunities for new enterprises. In Moneragala, Galle and Matara districts, for instance, transport and marketing problems were constantly cited by petty traders and producers as the major constraint on their business. Exogenous constraints, such as the absence of infrastructure, lack of investment opportunities and marketing facilities, and weak demand, limit the contribution that credit *per se* can make to income-generation.

POVERTY IMPACTS: CAN CREDIT CO-OPERATIVES HELP THE POOR?

Co-operatives have been widely criticised as institutions unsuited to 'reach the poor'. Lele (1981: 56) argues, for instance, that these 'open' institutions reflect the composition of the society in which they are situated, and ultimately serve the interests of already dominant groups. Numerous studies of agricultural co-operatives show how larger farmers capture control by using their economic power and status to become the elected leaders (UNRISD 1975). Such situations rarely lead to an effective channelling of resources to poorer members. The power of local elites can actually be increased by control over co-operative resources, a situation which may exacerbate the predicament of the poor.

In order to evaluate the anti-poverty role of the thrift and credit societies in Sri Lanka, four questions are addressed in this section.

1 To what extent are poor people included in thrift and credit co-operatives?
2 Are financial services differentially available to richer and poorer members?
3 What are the economic impacts of credit provision on the livelihoods of poorer members?
4 Do societies bring about progressive changes in political and social relations within communities?

Society membership

One of the few published accounts of Sri Lanka's thrift and credit co-operatives, based on limited fieldwork, takes the view that the poor are rarely included in a society's membership (Fernando *et al.* 1989: 25). Our survey clearly shows that this is nonsense. PTCCS aggregate membership includes a higher proportion of people below the official poverty line than the national average (see pp. 207–8).

When thrift and credit co-operatives were first established, they were largely orientated towards middle-income rural people. Societies were located mainly in the wealthier wet zone, especially in Kurunegala's 'coconut triangle'. These types of associations have also been historically popular amongst salaried employees (subscribing to save-as-you-earn schemes) both in Sri Lanka and other South Asian countries such as India. This historical background has created an impression amongst some observers that thrift and credit co-operatives cannot provide services to poorer people. Such a position is invalid for the majority of contemporary SANASA societies.

During the last decade, as the SANASA network spread, there has been a significant reorientation of the movement. A special system of down-lending funds for low-income earners has been set up, which has encouraged societies to follow the policies of the apex institutions. Also, these bodies have run special programmes to establish co-operatives amongst poorer groups, such as urban shanty dwellers, and the dry-zone colonies established by poorer migrant groups. There is also a programme targeting tea estate workers, who remain one of the most economically and socially disadvantaged groups on the island (see Samarasinghe 1993). Beyond these

216

specific initiatives the movement's leadership has constantly transmitted the message that SANASA societies must include and assist poorer villagers. This has been highly influential.

The 'reawakening' has encouraged both a socio-economic deepening of existing societies and the establishment of new societies by poorer people. Many of the Kurunegala case-study societies and most Moneragala societies are composed of very small farmers, who constitute the largest group amongst Sri Lanka's poor. Members of these societies are visibly less well off than members in some of the older and wealthier societies in Kurunegala District. But even in the latter area, where the middle-income dominance is established, informal fieldwork discussions confirmed that there has, in general, been a 'downward' expansion of membership.

A key change has been the modification of society rules and regulations so that they are more appropriate for poorer people. Societies have always had rules for joining which entail an initial cost for new members. This normally consists of a membership fee (Rs10–20), the purchase of one share (on average Rs240 in 1992), and a deposit of Rs5–10 to open a savings account. Some societies also require new members to open a long-term savings account using a minimum of, say, Rs25. An individual's total 'entrance' cost is therefore around Rs300. While these conditions may appear strict, they are now made flexible in most societies by allowing new members to pay up their share capital in instalments, often over a twelve-month period or even longer. Given that wages for a labourer during 1992 in both Kurunegala and Moneragala were between Rs50 and Rs75 per day, the 'entrance' cost is not discriminatory and the ability to pay in instalments enables even the very poor to join. Claims that contemporary PTCCSs have procedural rules which discriminate against the poor (Fernando et al. 1989: 25) are thus largely unfounded.

One of SANASA's major achievements over the 1980s was the increasing inclusion of women, who often have little collateral in their name, fewer income-earning opportunities than men and less access to the formal banking system. Rural credit systems have rarely been effective in countering such traditional male bias. In Sri Lanka, only 17 per cent of the New Comprehensive Rural Credit Scheme's borrowers are women (Central Bank, *Annual Report* 1988: 133).[3] This is partly because of long-standing ideas that formal credit and financial matters are a male preserve (see Wickramasinghe 1993: 172). Since land and other forms of collateral are commonly registered in the names of men, the channels for attaining financial services are open only to them. Lump sums of money are often controlled by male household members, and when women do hold cash, they are expected to spend it on the daily subsistence needs of their family (ibid.).

Three of the older case-study societies in Kurunegala had been started in the 1930s and 1940s by men, and originally had no or few women members. The membership of most of these societies has equalised between men and women over the last fifteen years. In contrast to these 'traditional' PTCCSs, one of the case-study societies in Moneragala had been initiated by women, all its committee members in the first years had been women, and men had only started to join when the benefits of the society became evident.

The general conclusion that thrift and credit co-operatives include poorer people in their membership, including some particularly disadvantaged groups such as single women, does not deny the existence of great differences between societies. In Kurunegala, there were reports of several PTCCSs which were refusing to expand their membership – the existing members believed that the poorer people in their community were 'bad risks', and therefore not suitable borrowers. In an earlier survey by one of the co-authors, several societies specifically formed to acquire loans from the Million Houses Programme openly admitted not granting membership to poorer villagers.

By contrast, in the same district, another older society had established a special scheme to encourage poorer members of the village to join, and was concentrating on organising them into a group venture for paddy processing and milling. A neighbouring society, consisting entirely of food-stamp holders (that is, people officially regarded as below the poverty line), had specifically concentrated on providing women with loans for cashew nut processing and petty trading. In another Kurunegala village, members pointed out that the richest farmers (with around twenty acres of paddy land) had refused to join the society, believing it to be below their dignity due to the predominance of poorer members, and preferring to acquire their credit from formal banks. Thus, while the dominance of middle-income people may have been common in the past, SANASA has done much to reorientate the network, and throughout the 1980s (and with the exception of societies purely set up to access the Million Houses Programme) new members have come from poorer rural groups and more disadvantaged rural areas.

Nevertheless, it does seem that society office-holders are predominantly middle-income or wealthier people. Tilakaratna et al. (1992: 12) found that 'the vast majority of the members [of 226 societies surveyed] are much poorer than their leaders'. This gives the impression that the leadership of a society commonly reflects the unequal distribution of economic resources and concomitant status within the community. There is, however, an important qualification to this statement. The office-holders of societies commonly come from a specific section of the rural elite, namely the 'respectable professional class', such as teachers, Ayurvedic doctors and retired civil servants rather than landlords or traders. There was no society amongst the fifteen studied which was clearly dominated by large farmers, and only a few (in Kurunegala) led by trading families. Indeed, leadership

218

by members of the 'professional elite' is often very marked, and is seen as beneficial by poorer members because of the respectability of such persons. This feature of 'trust in' and the 'image of' leaders is important to many local-level institutions, and must be recognised as an important factor contributing to the viability of co-operative societies.

Access to financial services

Sri Lankan thrift and credit co-operatives are successful partly because they satisfy a real need of rural communities. Although the formal banking system has increasingly penetrated the countryside, informal sources 'continue to dominate the rural credit market' (Fernando 1988: 249). Amongst the PTCCS borrowers surveyed in Moneragala and Kurunegala, only 20 per cent had taken loans from banks, 70 per cent had never applied, and a further 10 per cent had applied but been refused. More importantly, this lack of access to banks was much more pronounced amongst poorer interviewees: 85 per cent of those with monthly incomes less than Rs3,000 had never applied to banks, while only 64 per cent of wealthier households had never applied. Co-operatives undoubtedly provide poorer people with greater access to credit from 'non-kin' sources at reasonable rates of interest and with limited transaction costs.

Societies are based, in principle, on equality of membership, in the sense that there are uniform membership rules, an elected committee and chairman, and monthly open meetings in which all members may participate and are given the opportunity to express their views. Yet intrinsically, and perhaps paradoxically, these co-operatives are based on highly individualistic principles of creditworthiness and ability to repay, which may sometimes place poorer members and women at a disadvantage relative to wealthier and male members. While the number of loans taken may not be differentiated in terms of class or gender, the quantity of credit available may be influenced by these factors. Thus, for instance, the average loan size of male borrowers in our survey was Rs5,979, while for women it was almost 30 per cent smaller, at Rs4,307.

Collateral in the form of assets is waived in most societies as a method of risk alleviation, being replaced by a system of guarantors and security deposits. But borrowers still have to meet several conditions which are harder for poorer members to fulfil. Borrowers must graduate from small (for example, Rs1,000) to larger loans (Rs3,000, Rs5,000 and above). Each graduation is dependent on repaying the previous loan. Additionally, over and above the initial share purchase, most societies insist on a member purchasing another share for loans above a certain value (sometimes as low as Rs3,000, but normally Rs5,000).

This process of graduation to higher-value loans undoubtedly reinforces credit discipline by ensuring that an individual's access to larger loans is dependent on a good repayment record. Credit discipline reduces risk to the society, increases turnover and profit, and ultimately a society's ability to offer larger loans to more members in the long run. However, the gradua-tion rule can lead to a situation whereby poorer members are more likely to be taking smaller loans than richer members. This can arise because wealthier members are more able to repay initial loans before their final due date in order to gain access to larger loans (a practice which occurred in several societies visited during fieldwork). This differential access is also understandable in a common-sensical way: neither office-holders nor many poorer members wish to create impractical indebtedness, and larger loans are a higher risk for poorer households than for more wealthy ones. As von Pischke (1992) maintains, credit needs also to be seen as debt and a potential burden in situations of distress.

Survey work demonstrated that wealthier respondents, on balance, received larger loans than lower-income borrowers (Table 13.22).

However, the finding that the co-operative system of loan provision has an inherent tendency to favour wealthier members needs to be qualified with examples of the egalitarian management principles operated by several case-study societies. In one of the six Kurunegala societies and three in Moneragala, there was an explicitly egalitarian policy of distributing the same amount of credit to nearly all members (other than in exceptional cases). In these societies, the principle of graduation is applied collectively: larger loans are not available until the society has increased its reserves.

This type of egalitarian distribution of credit was common amongst the younger (and poorer) societies, and less evident in the older (more often relatively wealthy) ones. It also appeared to correlate with relatively homo-geneous memberships, and especially when a society was dominated by agriculturalists. In these cases, the provision of seasonal production loans was the highest priority, and 'sharing out' the credit available appeared to be the most acceptable approach to disbursing funds. Societies with a number of shop traders commonly displayed a different pattern, with this occupa-tional group often receiving significantly larger loans for their businesses

Table 13.22 Borrowers' loan size (%) by household income group (*n* = 144)

Household income group:	Rs1,000–3,000 (n = 80)	Rs3,001–5,000 (n = 30)	Rs5,001–10,000 (n = 23)	Above Rs10,000 (n = 11)
Loan size				
Rs500–5,000	91	80	65	65
Rs5,001–10,000	6	—	22	18
Above Rs10,000	3	20	13	17
Total	100	100	100	100

than the (majority) small farmer members. It was not clear whether the younger, more homogeneous and poorer societies will move towards a more diverse portfolio (in terms of loan sizes) as their resources and membership grow larger or whether they will retain their egalitarian principles.

The savings side of the financial market must also be given some consideration. For poorer households, with limited capacity to save, credit co-operatives offer an interest-bearing deposit facility that formal institutions cannot match. This is a new service for most of the poor, for whom depositing with banks often has high transaction costs. For over 65 per cent of our sample, the only savings account which they operated was with their PTCCS. For households with monthly incomes below Rs3,000, this figure rose to 80 per cent. Village-based societies solve the logistical problems of 'piecemeal' saving, that is, successively depositing small amounts. Savings with formal institutions are normally the preserve of wealthier groups, who save in larger amounts and hope to use banks for their credit facilities. Accumulating savings (even small amounts) with SANASA is one important mechanism by which poorer households can reduce their vulnerability to family crises and sudden falls in income due to economic shocks.

The impact of credit on poorer members

Advocates of credit as a poverty-alleviation measure see the poor as trapped in a 'vicious circle': low incomes cause low savings, constraining investment, thereby reinforcing low incomes. Credit gives poor people a means of investing and breaking out of this circle. This economistic view appears to be valid for at least some SANASA borrowers.

The survey indicated (see p. 210) that increased income was a benefit accruing to both poorer and richer borrowers. A quarter of households below an official 'poverty line' at the time preceding their last productive loan had graduated above the line by the time of interview. We also identified the significant number of poor women using credit for working capital to establish petty enterprises, thereby gaining an independent income. Co-operative credit was also seen as the prime cause of reduced dependencies on informal 'tied' credit with crop traders, implying an increased profit margin for farmers. There is also evidence to show that credit has increased intra-household employment, thereby increasing households' output and income generation. A disappointing result of the survey was the lack of evidence of job creation outside the household (and therefore income generation for other members of the community who were not SANASA members). However, there are other ways in which, arguably, thrift and credit co-operatives play a significant and effective 'anti-poverty' role.

The economistic view of credit (propelling borrowers out of poverty in an investment cycle) may not always reflect the priorities of those who are poor. Southwold-Llewellyn (1990: 201), in her anthropological study of two Kurunegala villages, argues that poor households want regular credit for consumption rather than investment. Increased productivity by coconut- and paddy-producing smallholders has not led to increased incomes in the past, largely because increased output has depressed farm-gate prices (ibid.: 205–6). For these households, a more critical need is to fill the seasonal gap between agricultural incomes and their production costs, daily consumption requirements, and expenditure on the festive occasions which strengthen social bonds.

Meeting the short-term consumption and production needs of poor people has been the traditional role of informal sources of credit. Whereas formal banks rarely provide small amounts of seasonal credit (too costly), and are even less likely to lend for non-productive purposes, traders, moneylenders and other big men often supply credit to those they know in a local community. However, even such informal sources are not ubiquitous, and they are often 'costly', not only in terms of interest rates, but also in terms of social and political costs: to be 'indebted' is not just a monetary relationship.

Thrift and credit co-operatives perform a role similar to informal lenders in two ways. First, they provide small loans as consumption credit repayable within one month, which can be used for expenditures on food, social occasions or any such 'non-productive' costs – thereby protecting a household's existing assets and future income. Second, they provide the small amounts of seasonal production credit which other formal credit institutions are rarely able to provide.

The provision of these types of credit has advantages over other informal sources because of their ease of access, and the fact that co-operative membership gives an explicit entitlement to these loans. Unlike traditional informal sources, a co-operative committee is rarely justified in refusing a member's application. Thus, co-operatives increase a poorer member's entitlement in a way that a bank (or local moneylenders) can never do.

All the societies surveyed placed a high priority on 'instant' (consumption) loans. These are regarded as a financial service distinct from production loans, and they are uniformly popular, despite their high interest charges (sometimes the equivalent of 80 per cent per annum). They can be taken regardless of outstanding production loans, thereby ensuring that these are not diverted to meet distress or ritual requirements. The security which access to this type of credit provides should not be underestimated: this is one of the major qualitative impacts of co-operative credit provision. As Chambers (1983) has demonstrated, the slide into poverty of many households is associated with having to respond to emergencies that operate as a 'ratchet', that is, the response causes a permanent loss of entitlement. Thus, instant loans give poorer members an additional option, other than informal credit or distress sales of assets, that will protect a household's existing situation.

Effects of co-operatives on socio-political relations

A convincing evaluation of the effect of co-operatives on socio-political relations would require more in-depth fieldwork than is covered by this study. However, there is sufficient information to make some tentative comments.

In cases where the poor predominate, the formation of a society provides a financial system which not only decreases members' insecurity, it also provides them with a greater degree of independence from other socio-economic groups. One of the major changes which SANASA co-operatives have brought about is the reduced dependency which members have on credit tying them, in disadvantageous relationships, with economically more powerful traders. In some communities, this appeared to have constituted a fundamental shift in a long-standing class relationship.

Additionally, SANASA co-operatives have been successful in providing an increasing number of women with access to finance. This is particularly important for female-headed households, but it is also significant for women belonging to other family units. In the latter case, what women most often lack is access to an independent source of income, which loans for petty enterprises can provide. Through access to credit and income-generating activities, women can enhance their status within the household, and potentially gain more bargaining power in their relations with male family members (Sen 1990).

The degree to which poorer members of a society increase their bargaining power with wealthier people in their community depends on several factors. Not least are the degree to which and the type of relations determining how a community is stratified by differential access to resources. These factors are ones which demand in-depth study. Yet our tentative conclusion is a positive one, deriving principally from observing the way in which societies conduct their affairs in a participatory manner, in which poorer members debate issues with wealthier members. The combination of small-scale and open and participatory procedures makes it difficult for elites to misuse societies and capture them for their own ends.

Many 'co-operative' development institutions have not fulfilled the ideal of democratically controlled business associations formed to promote the interests of their members. From Tanzania, to India, to Peru, agricultural marketing and credit co-operatives have been the focus of much critical literature (see, for example, Braverman and Guasch 1989: 352; Lele 1981: 60). Wiggins and Rogaly (1989: 230) have documented a typical case of government interference in agricultural co-operatives in an Indian state, and the 'increasing appropriation' of agricultural co-operatives by political parties in India. More commonly, these types of institutions have suffered from dominance by wealthier groups such as larger farmers (Batra 1988: 106). Sri Lanka itself has a network of government-controlled multi-purpose co-operative societies (MPCSs) characterised by malpractices arising from politicians' and local big men's patronal influences. References to this 'politicisation' were a common complaint made by ordinary members of the MPCSs during fieldwork, a complaint barely heard in relation to SANASA.

The small size of individual PTCCSs distinguishes them from these other 'co-operative' institutions. Whereas the five MPCSs in Moneragala District have an average membership of 50,000 people, the 100 SANASA societies in the same region have an average membership of around ninety-five persons. The scale of MPCSs' activities means that they need to be bureaucracies. In contrast, thrift and credit co-operatives remain rooted in individual communities. These features of scale encourage several characteristics which, in the Sri Lankan context, reduce the prevalence of elite capture. Face-to-face contact is maintained between members, enabling individuals to participate to a greater extent than is possible in MPCSs. Even the largest PTCCSs are able to operate effectively with only a few staff, and maintain continual interaction between leaders and members and hold regular, well-attended monthly meetings. Such small membership enables each PTCCS to be rooted in a single community, and rarely includes people farther away than neighbouring hamlets. This provides a knowledge advantage both for office-holders (evaluating credit applications) and for members, who are better able to judge the activities of their leaders.

Meetings amongst members, in small societies, provide the basis for relatively egalitarian contributions to debates about a society's policies and specific problems such as cases of arrears, or disagreements about whether loan applications should be approved. In the case-study societies, meetings followed a clear agenda. The longest and often most important part of a meeting was usually an 'open forum' consisting of public loan applications, queries and discussions started by ordinary members from the floor. The ability of ordinary members to contribute is also based on the 'openness' of accounts and books, with the office-holders of most societies providing a financial summary of the last month's business at each meeting. Many societies display financial summaries on the walls of their offices. The small number of members makes it difficult for office-holders to conceal information about individual cases or overall financial affairs. This 'transparency', facilitated by the high literacy rates in Sri Lanka, reduces the likelihood of malpractices by those in positions of responsibility.

In conclusion, such open and participatory procedures make it unusual for societies to be manipulated by elites or managed in a blatantly discriminatory fashion. Given their participatory nature, it is appropriate to see

SANASA co-operatives at least as forums in which poorer people can voice their concerns and priorities, and at times strengthen their social cohesion and capacity to articulate and press for their interests.

THE WIDER PICTURE

The comparative performance of SANASA

While the previous sections have identified problems in some aspects of SANASA's operations and performance, they have produced favourable indicators of SANASA's capacity to reach low-income households, provide them with a valued service and cover operational costs at the primary level. To more fully appreciate SANASA's performance, a comparative perspective is useful.

Despite the continuing dominance of the informal sector in credit activities for poorer people and micro-enterprises (see p. 180), a growing number of formal organisations compete with SANASA for small-scale rural loans and savings. A dense network of banks is spread across the country, averaging out at one bank branch per 22,000 people (Sanderatne 1990: 2). The initiative for such activity comes mainly from the state, as the formal private sector has proved persistently reluctant to enter this market and remains a minor player (Finance and Banking Commission 1991). Historically, the main agencies involved have been the two state-owned banks (the Bank of Ceylon and the People's Bank) along with the Co-operative Rural Banks (CRBs) that are part of the state-controlled Multi-purpose Co-operative Society system (MPCSs). More recently the government-initiated regional rural development banks (RRDBs) have commenced activities. The operations of all these banks have been heavily influenced by state policies to provide subsidised credit to small farmers through Central Bank re-financing (the New Agricultural Credit Scheme, later the Comprehensive Rural Credit Scheme, and most recently the New Comprehensive Rural Credit Scheme), to link the formal and informal sectors by the *Praja Naya Niyamaka* (PNN) scheme of 1988 and to provide loans for productive enterprise to the poor on the basis of collateral granted by the *Janasaviya* programme or loans from the *Janasaviya* Trust Fund (JTF).[4] These policies have increasingly sought to draw NGOs, community groups, traders and moneylenders into the provision of financial services. Information on the comparative performance of SANASA's competitors is often limited, but in the following paragraphs we examine the available data.

Despite stated objectives, the People's Bank and Bank of Ceylon have pursued orthodox banking approaches based on collateral, established client repayment records, a preference for larger loans and an aversion to activities that involve a significant degree of risk (that is, smallholder agriculture). It is only through 'moral suasion' and political pressure that they have been pushed into lending to small farmers and lower-income groups. The main device for this has been the Central Bank's rural credit schemes, but these schemes have not performed well (FAO 1988). Funds have often 'leaked' out to non-target groups and recovery rates have been poor for both agencies, ranging from 32.4 per cent to 89.5 per cent, and averaging out at only 67.6 per cent, over the 1967–8 to 1991–2 period (Central Bank, *Annual Report* 1993). The low interest rate spread offered to the banks and high operational costs have meant that they have incurred persistent losses through these schemes and reinforced their antipathy to rural lending and microcredits.

The People's Bank and Bank of Ceylon have more recently been drawn into on-lending for *Janasaviya* recipients. Being a component of President Premadasa's electoral promise to rid the country of poverty, the banks' senior management have little choice in this matter. Despite reports from the *Janasaviya* Secretariat that repayments are running at 100 per cent on time, independent research (Table 13.23) has revealed recovery rates of under 60 per cent, indicating that both banks are incurring losses from the scheme. In contrast to the rural credit schemes the available evidence does indicate that a significant proportion of such loans are to poorer households. In sum, both the People's Bank and Bank of Ceylon are reluctant to enter the market niche that SANASA meets, and when forced into it they have performed poorly, with the exception of pawn-broking activities (see pp. 179–80).

Recognition that the two state-controlled banks and the established private banks were unlikely to operate effectively in the microcredit field culminated in the establishment of RRDBs from 1985. By 1992, fourteen

Table 13.23 Loans by banks to *Janasaviya* recipients

	Bank of Ceylon	People's Bank	CRB	RRDBs
Round 1				
No. of loans	29,346	20,602	3,525	—
Amount of loans (Rs mill.)	248.9	159.2	22.5	—
Average loan size (Rs)	8,482	7,727	6,386	—
Recovery rate (%)	55	57	n.a.	—
Round 2				
No. of loans	6,144	11,067	26,582	3,640
Amount of loans (Rs mill.)	41.5	70.6	188.2	17.1
Average loan size	6,755	6,379	7,080	4,498
Recovery rate	n.a.	n.a.	n.a.	n.a.

Source: Fernando (1993)

RRDBs were in operation. These were to fill the perceived 'credit gap' in the formal financial system and 'were expected to be a new species of banks which would bring about a new culture in banking' (ADB 1990: 16). They were not to compete with existing financial institutions but would supplement them by serving small farmers, rural artisans, petty traders and micro-entrepreneurs. By being locally based and directed, working closely with other agencies, concentrating on small loans, simplifying administrative procedures, providing mobile services, using field staff and by the sale of equity in them to private interests, they would innovate and develop programmes appropriate for their clientele. Although the 'privatisation' objective has not been realised and in 1993 all RRDBs were still fully owned by the Central Bank, the RRDBs have been innovative. In particular, most have utilised group approaches to lending, market-related interest rates and intensive loan supervision.

There is some evidence that this has paid off as RRDBs make smaller loans than other banks (Table 13.23) and, for example, Hambantota RRDB has produced better recovery rates under NCRCS than the Bank of Ceylon and the People's Bank. Its average recovery rate for such loans (1987–9) was 85 per cent against the Bank of Ceylon's 78 per cent and People's Bank's 71 per cent (Jayamaha 1990: 46).

Despite this information there is a growing consensus that RRDBs have failed to fulfil their mandate.[5] They have not attracted private-sector equity, have a very high-cost structure, have high staff to borrower ratios, relatively small turnovers (Sanderatne 1990: 5), and incur substantial defaults. For example, in 1990 and 1991 the average recovery rate of the Matara RRDB was only 60 per cent (Ryan 1992). Although some have reported profits, this is only because of 'a high level of both explicit and hidden subsidisation' (Finance and Banking Commission 1991: 54) from the Central Bank and other public agencies. Interviews with board members of Kurunegala, Moneragala and Kegalle RRDBs revealed that the banks' response to these problems had been orthodox, that is, to compete directly with other banks for urban-based, larger, secured loans. For the RRDBs it is time to 'go back to the drawing board' and the Finance and Banking Commission (ibid.) has concluded that the RRDBs must be totally 'restructured'.

The Co-operative Rural Banks have been operating since 1964 as elements of multi-purpose co-operative societies and there were almost 1,000 by 1990. For a long period they were linked to the People's Bank as its local-level agency, but this link was unsatisfactory and in the 1970s the bank decided to lend directly in rural areas. CRBs are not full 'banks' and can only mobilise savings, lend funds for specific purposes and pawnbroke. Their major contribution in the provision of financial services to low-income households is to offer a convenient savings service. CRBs have dominated the rural savings scene for many years, with SANASA consistently lagging well behind in second place (Table 13.24). While they clearly

Table 13.24 Deposits and advances by major rural sector financial agencies, 1989–92 (Rs million)

		Co-operative Rural Banks	SANASA	Bank of Ceylon ASC sub-offices	RRDBs
1989	Total savings	2,211.9	418.0	203.9	159.6
	Total advances	238.7	416.0	22.5	135.0
	Difference	1,973.2	2.0	181.4	24.6
1990	Total savings	2,497.3	514.3	196.5	313.9
	Total advances	434.7	485.3	24.6	429.8
	Difference	2,062.6	29.0	171.9	−115.9
1991	Total savings	3,448.5	588.0	220.1	437.5
	Total advances	583.7	608.6	208.8	595.4
	Difference	2,864.8	−20.6	11.3	−157.9
1992	Total savings	4,333.1	696.8	287.3	666.6
	Total advances	595.6	715.1	134.2	703.2
	Difference	3,737.5	−18.3	153.1	−36.6

Source: Central Bank Annual Reports

Table 13.25 Comparison of the targeting and recovery of Million Houses Programme loans to PTCCSs and CRBs, December 1990

	Income group of borrower[a]	Rural PTCCSs	Rural CRBs
Total number of loans granted	Below median	1,964 (83)	1,204 (49)
	Above median	405 (17)	1,272 (51)
	All	2,369 (100)	2,476 (100)
Total value of loans granted (Rs million)	Below median	8.65 (82)	9.50 (35)
	Above median	1.90 (18)	17.53 (65)
	All	10.55 (100)	27.03 (100)
Average loan size (Rs)	All	4,450	10,900
Loans in arrears in excess of 90 days as % of total for the agency	All	47	91
Loans in default[b] as % of total for agency	All	39	59

Source: USAID documents
Notes
[a] As estimated by USAID for rural areas.
[b] Defaults were defined as all loans in excess of one year in arrears.

provide a valuable function for rural savers, the 'imbalance' of their portfolio is a cause for concern. In effect, the CRBs mobilise rural savings for transfer to Colombo where they have helped to finance the growing budget deficit. They are a major contributor to making finance scarce in rural areas: in 1992 for every Rs100 they took on deposit, only Rs14 was lent out. Perhaps this is just as well, given that their recovery performance for NCRCS has been poorer than the state banks (Panditha 1988: 12). A direct comparison of CRB performance against PTCCSs is possible for the Million Houses Programme (Table 13.25). It confirms the widely held view that CRB lending is orientated to the more affluent in rural areas and that the financial discipline of CRB members is much lower than that of PTCCSs.

The most recent entrants into the market for microcredits and savings have been an array of NGOs. The largest of these is the Sarvodaya Shramadana Movement. This agency moved into credit and savings activities (REP), with much support from donors and along 'Grameen Bank lines' in the mid-1980s. During 1992–3 it issued Rs46.5 million credit to around 20,000–25,000 borrowers.

Total member savings reached Rs28.7 million by late 1993. Its plans for expansion were hampered, however, by President Premadasa blocking its access to donor funds under the pretext of an 'investigation', along with the recognition by Sarvodaya and donor staff that the REP programme needed to consolidate because of loan recovery problems. A donor consortium report in 1990 noted that repayments were running at only 68 per cent of programmed levels and that only 15 per cent of total administrative costs were being recouped by REP. Zander (1992: 13) has described the targeting and repayment problems of a Sarvodaya group he studied. Data on the comparative performance of Sarvodaya and PTCCSs, along with other agencies, are available for the IFAD/CIDA Small Farmers and Landless Credit Project which provides loans to marginal farmers and the landless in four districts (Table 13.26).

SANASA societies have a 100 per cent on-time recovery rate in contrast to Sarvodaya's 80 per cent, RRDBs' 86 per cent, and other NGOs ranging from 79 per cent to 94 per cent. With Premadasa dead, Sarvodaya is now in a position to compete with SANASA, but it will need to enhance its village-level group mobilisation processes if it wishes to achieve even a partially satisfactory cost-recovery basis. Donor-financed subsidies are running at much higher levels than the SANASA movement with operating costs of Rs113 for every Rs100 loaned (Sarvodaya Donor Consortium 1993).

Finally, mention must be made of the PNN scheme, by which formal financial institutions lend funds to registered informal sector traders and moneylenders at 18 per cent per annum for on-lending at 30 per cent per annum to villagers. Rs470 million were disbursed in 1989 and 1990 to 7,000 PNNs under this scheme, but a study revealed little evidence of this being

Table 13.26 Agency performance on IFAD/CIDA Small Farmers and Landless Credit Project, December 1992

	RRDBs	IFAD/CIDA project offices	LMS[a]	Women's Bureau	Sarvodaya	PTCCS (SANASA)	UNICEF	CARE	DVF[a]	Total/average
Number of loans	4,742	4,448	159	319	893	1,058	492	90	317	12,518
Average size of loans (Rs)	6,703	6,390	6,001	7,111	5,237	8,024	7,712	7,328	6,301	6,634
OT recovery rate (%)	86.5	90.3	94.3	85.7	80.0	100.0	98.9	76.9	84.7	88.9

Source: Files at Canadian International Development Agency, Colombo
Note: [a] Sri Lankan NGOs.

on-lent to the poor or micro-enterprises (Finance and Banking Commission 1991: 49). This is not surprising given that PNNs were selected on political grounds (Zander 1991), and there were widespread reports of PNNs using credit to finance their own enterprises or larger businesses. It seems likely that this 'dream scheme' to link the formal sector with private moneylenders will be abandoned in the near future.

It must be concluded that SANASA has performed well when compared to other institutions involved in rural finance. This is supported by the analyses of many government and donor agencies (National Planning Division 1984; SIDA 1991; IFAD 1987a). Although subsidised, it has a self-financing potential that exceeds its formal-sector competitors because of its loan recovery performance and low administrative costs at field level. It manages to recirculate and attract funds to rural areas, rather than extract them, and it provides services to a wide socio-economic range of villagers and reaches more low-income people than other financial institutions.

SANASA's role in the market

Assessing the extent to which SANASA has affected informal credit markets is difficult to quantify, but there is direct evidence that co-operative credit has reduced members' reliance on more costly sources of loans. In Puttalam District there was one society which had definitely 'captured' the local credit market, leading two moneylending traders to leave the village for more profitable environments (the establishment of the society was given as the explicit reason for the departure of these two households). In Kudagammana PTCCS in Kurunegala, reliance on *mudalali* (moneylenders) had been almost eradicated by the society. There were still some villagers who went to such traders in the town, but with relatively high monthly interest rates of 20–30 per cent, this was now rare and a sign of real distress. The impact of SANASA on moneylenders' terms and conditions is not clear, but there has clearly been an impact, given evidence collected in Puttalam, Ratnapura and Moneragala that moneylenders actively seek to undermine the establishment of PTCCSs in 'their' areas.

SANASA fulfils the main functions of informal lenders. It provides a secure source of local credit, easily accessible, therefore with relatively low transaction costs. More importantly, SANASA societies provide for two types of purposes that are offered by informal lenders and avoided by formal financial institutions. These are small seasonal agricultural expenditures, and 'consumption' needs. It is not surprising, therefore, that SANASA competes effectively with informal moneylenders.

Decreased reliance on informal credit relations was particularly evident in Moneragala District – where seasonal credit tied to crop harvests is common and becoming more widespread because of macro-economic conditions (Central Bank 1989: 6). All farmers who referred to these relationships saw them as exploitative. The high costs of paddy and sugar cane inputs at the start of the production cycle, in conjunction with low incomes experienced by most farming households at this time, makes credit essential. Crop traders provide 'in kind', supplying necessary inputs (such as seed and fertiliser) at high nominal prices, to be repaid 'in kind' immediately at harvest time, when the crop's market value is at its lowest. This also forces farmers to sell more than they might otherwise do, reducing their subsistence stock of paddy and leading to a reliance on the market for consumption at a later date, when the price of rice is higher.

In Moneragala, within the case-study villages, co-operative society members were much less involved in tied production-harvest credit than non-members. In those villages with no society, most small farmers had no alternative to traders' credit. In contrast, SANASA farmers stated that avoidance of these tied transactions often led to significant increases in their harvest profits.

In terms of the formal sector it must be recognised that SANASA competes directly with the CRBs, RRDBs, and the People's Bank and Bank of Ceylon sub-offices for deposits. This market became increasingly competitive over the 1980s in part because of SANASA's expansion. However, having 'driven' the competitive process in the 1980s SANASA now finds itself searching for policies to defend its market share in the early 1990s. The movement has been under pressure to compete against other lenders in the provision of state-designed lending programmes (NCRCS, MHP and JTF). However, given its MHP experience, SANASA has opted to keep clear of NCRCS and been reluctant to commit itself to JTF because of the high risks associated with state programmes.

In terms of financial policies, specific impacts cannot be identified but a broader influence over certain issues is discernible. First, SANASA has demonstrated to Sri Lankan policy-makers that villagers, and particularly large numbers of poorer villagers, are 'bankable'. Information from overseas about this matter has been reinforced by the SANASA experience. Second, SANASA has demonstrated that group-based lending schemes can work (in contrast to CRB and MPCS lending experiences) so that the use of forms of 'social collateral' by intermediaries in Sri Lanka has been validated. Thus, virtually all the RRDBs have committed themselves to experimenting with forms of group lending for part of their portfolio. The other main actors in rehabilitating group lending in Sri Lanka have been external donors (notably IFAD, CIDA, Redd Barna and the four-nation Sarvodaya Consortium) pushing the 'Grameen Bank' approach. The recognition of the potential role of group schemes by Sri Lankan policy-makers is positive. Unfortunately, this still needs to be matched by an understanding of the alternatives that exist within group approaches. Sarvodaya staff already openly question whether they should have opted for a different approach to group formation while both donors and government have found that developing a capacity for group mobilisation and formation in state agencies (for example, the Women's Bureau, the National Youth Service Council and IRDPs) is highly problematic.

The final contribution of SANASA has policy implications, but these also have an ideological dimension. SANASA has demonstrated to Sri Lankan policy-makers that financial intermediation need not be solely provided by private, for-profit agencies. It has shown that local-level collective action has a useful role in the 'pluralistic approach' (Finance and Banking Commission 1991: 25) to rural financial provision that is now being pursued.

EXPLAINING SANASA'S ACHIEVEMENTS

The earlier sections have examined the performance of the thrift and credit movement and have demonstrated its considerable contribution to the livelihoods of many rural people. When compared to other organisations involved in rural finance in Sri Lanka, the movement's performance might be regarded as exceptional. To what factors can this relative success be attributed? Proponents of the Ohio School usually ascribe the achievements of financial institutions that are not purely market-driven to exceptional contextual factors such as the predisposition of certain societies to 'co-operative behaviour' or the emergence of a charismatic leader. According to this line of argument, such institutions have little policy relevance as contexts cannot be replicated. Undeniably the Sri Lankan context has provided a number of supports for SANASA. Ideas of voluntarism, reciprocal transactions and collective action are long-established in the practice of *attam* (labour exchange), *dhansala* (community gifting of food for festive occasions) and *shramadana* (voluntary labour for community schemes). Kiriwandeniya's charisma and commitment was also fundamental to the 'reawakening'.

However, there is a deception in such an argument because contexts are important in all cases, as in the Ohio School-favoured case of Indonesia.[6] For SANASA the Sri Lankan context and 'personality' factors provide only a partial explanation at best. Within the SANASA experience are a range of potential 'lessons' that have relevance for those who design and manage rural finance schemes and institutions (Table 13.27). These can be summarised in terms of factors that contribute (a) to institutional financial viability; (b) to making services attractive to borrowers and savers; (c) to effective internal management; and (d) to the effective management of external relationships.

Institutional financial viability

Although the upper tiers of SANASA remain a long way from a sustainable financial situation the movement's 7,000 PTCCSs are generally in a healthy

233

Table 13.27 SANASA: characteristics that contribute to performance

Variable	Characteristics
1 Institutional financial viability	
High recovery rates	Joint liability groups
	Members' savings serve as loan capital
	Quasi-collateral mechanisms
	(compulsory deposits and guarantors)
	Graduation to larger loans
Low administrative costs	Simple procedures and systems
	Voluntarism
	Affordable professionalism on a phased basis
	Externally subsidised training
Operational margins	Market-related interest rates
	Tapered interest rates (i.e. higher rates for smaller loans)
	Product diversification
2 Attractiveness to customers	Competitive total borrowing costs
	Savings facilities
	Proximity
	Consumption and production loans
	Instant loans
	Flexibility of repayment schedules
	Timeliness
3 Effective internal management	Distance from government
	Primary society autonomy
	Leadership vision and influence
	Gradualistic approach to group formation
	Emphasis on training
4 Management of external relationships	Avoidance of contacts with politicians
	Politically active officials not permitted
	Grouping of donors into a consortium
	Long-term relationships with key donors

financial position. This can be attributed to a complex of design features that keep recovery rates high, depress administrative costs and make operational margins profitable.

Recovery rates

The low loan default rates typical of most PTCCSs can be understood in terms of four main features. Prime amongst these is the group structure and procedures mechanism that makes PTCCS members responsible for the defaults of other members. Regular meetings and open procedures (allied to the fact that those wishing to borrow must regularly attend meetings) permit peer screening of new members and of proposed loan activities and facilitate peer pressure to repay and peer support when difficulties are encountered. The latter is reflected in the common practice of rescheduling the loans of members who face genuine problems. While other studies in this volume (BancoSol, BRAC, KREP) bear out the finding that regular, well-attended, open meetings facilitate 'social collateral', the SANASA experience differs in that groups are of a *heterogeneous* social and economic composition. Evidently group homogeneity is not a generalisable requirement for the effective operation of joint-liability mechanisms.

A second important factor is the requirement that all borrowers must first make savings. This instils financial discipline, screens out unsuitable borrowers and reinforces group cohesion. SANASA members distinguish between group-mobilised resources (hot money) and external resources (cold money). Defaulting on loans from the former is universally recognised as something that will invoke more serious social consequence than the latter, as evidenced by the Million Houses Programme credits. Huppi and Feder's (1990: 199) finding that members' propensity to repay is closely related to the extent to which members' own funds 'are at stake' is supported by the SANASA data.

A third feature of PTCCSs that fosters recovery is the quasi-collateral mechanism which requires borrowers to make compulsory savings of at least 10 per cent of the value of a loan and to have two loan guarantors with savings of a similiar level. Although we found little evidence of the seizure of compulsory savings, this device does mean that around 35 to 40 per cent of the value of a loan is held in a PTCCS as borrower and guarantor savings and shares.

Fourth, PTCCS borrowers go through a loan graduation process in which access to larger loans is dependent upon having satisfactorily serviced smaller loans. This is a common practice in other high-recovery schemes (BancoSol, BRAC, KREP, BRI, BKK) although in SANASA it is not a uniform set of steps but is determined by the individual society.

Administrative costs

PTCCSs have low administrative costs (less than 3 per cent of the value of outstanding loans for our sample). The main features to which this can be ascribed are simple procedures and systems and voluntarism. The former is characteristic of all the successful schemes examined in this volume. The latter is not (although it must be noted that the small groups involved in BancoSol, BRAC, KREP, MMF and TRDEP all involve an element of unpaid management). Successful societies not only rely a great deal on the efforts of 'initiator-leaders' within the community who are prepared to shoulder the responsibility for organising its affairs, sitting on committees and responding to members' needs, but also individuals donating services such as book-keeping or the use of a room as an office. Additionally, societies grow faster and are more effective financially if members are prepared to put in time at monthly meetings, when problems affecting all are discussed and collective agreements to policies can be made.

Such behaviour is not understandable within the confines of public-choice theory, given that it involves a combination of private interest and interest in the well-being of others. While Sri Lanka may be a good context for such behaviour it cannot simply be treated as a quaint, case-specific deviance from some general law. Uphoff's (1992) writings are illuminating in this regard, pointing out the way in which ideas and behaviours (such as donating time or energy to a community organisation) create an environment in which it becomes more likely that other individuals will involve themselves in partially selfless behaviours. SANASA's leadership and the ideology transmitted in its training sessions and meetings strengthen the belief of members in the value of co-operation and voluntarism. Indeed, the 'reawakening' of SANASA since the late 1970s could be interpreted as a self-sustaining diffusion of co-operative ideals from the Walgama seminar.

Necessary as voluntarism is for the establishment of new societies, once a PTCCS expands a process of affordable professionalisation occurs as a bank worker and premises are required and, if expansion continues, eventually a manager and a book-keeper. The local roots of each PTCCS permit this professionalisation to be undertaken at low cost, although each 'step up' that a society takes increases its overhead costs and reduces profitability until a corresponding increase in turnover has been generated.[7] Finally, it must be noted that the administrative costs of PTCCSs are held down by the subsidised training, advisory and mobilisation services that they receive from the DUs and Federation. To a very high degree the 'start-up' and institutional development costs of PTCCSs are borne by the other tiers. Developing mechanisms to recoup these costs will be an important activity for SANASA in coming years if the movement is to be weaned off subsidies.

Operational margins

The profitability of PTCCSs is closely related to the margins on which they operate. Over the 1980s these have widened and now stand at around 6 per cent for ordinary loans and around 40–50 per cent for the increasingly important 'instant' loans. This greater commercial orientation in pricing policy is underpinned by a process of organisational cultural change from a break-even orientation to an enterprise orientation. In the 1970s the idea of charging poorer members rates of 80 per cent per annum would have been repugnant to most societies; by the late 1980s, however, most societies regarded it as 'meeting member needs'.

Allied to the move to market-orientated interest rates is the process of product diversification. Over the 1980s a growing proportion of societies have extended their resource mobilisation activities by introducing non-member deposits, fixed deposits and children's savings schemes. On the lending side they have moved into the profitable instant mini-loan business. Potentially this is only the start of such diversification and since 1992 a number of societies have started insurance operations.

While this move to market-orientated pricing has helped SANASA to expand, it must be noted that the commitment of a number of aid donors (SIDA, CIDA and IFAD) and provincial councils to subsidised interest rates for poor people is creating confusion within the movement about appropriate interest rates. In particular, PTCCSs receiving low-interest aid agency/provincial council funds on-lent by DUs perceive that the higher interlending rates charged by DUs are 'too expensive'. This reduces demand for the market-priced interlending funds which are available in greater volume than intermittent external 'rural credit' schemes. Not on-lending subsidised funds would be a wise policy for SANASA, but it is difficult to refuse members access to such 'handouts'.[8]

Providing an attractive service to rural people

On the demand side SANASA's relative success must be understood in terms of its capacity to provide hundreds of thousands of villagers with a valued service which competitors cannot match (see also pp. 225–31). While the rural population has access to savings facilities through the CRBs, access to formal-sector loans is very limited for lower-income households and those who lack collateral. In the informal sector, friends and relatives are the preferred source of credit but they rarely have funds available. Money-lenders and traders may make loans, but their rates are likely to average out at high levels.[9] In terms of both the total costs of borrowing and a set of non-quantified factors that encourage/discourage the use of a source of credit, PTCCSs demonstrate a clear advantage, except over friends and relatives (Table 13.28). Fieldwork revealed that for all except small amounts the funds available from friends and relatives were very limited and that often even minor borrowings (Rs100–500) were not possible.

So in terms of loan costs, access and the option to use loans for consumption (a service particularly valued by poorer members) SANASA has clear advantages. Over and above these it must be noted that involvement in a PTCCS has additional benefits. In some cases this relates to specific non-financial services such as societies running nursery schools, winning contracts for planting trees and maintaining plantations and transporting inputs. In other cases it relates to the fact that for many

Table 13.28 Comparative costs of rural lenders and a comparison of other features (based on a Rs5,000 loan for 12 months)

	PTCCS[a]	Bank[b] (commercial terms)	Bank[c] (government-subsidised schemes)	Moneylender[d]	Trader[e]	Friends and relatives[f]
Interest charges	1,100	1,200	450	7,500	2,500	0
Documents and fees	0	220	220	0	0	0
Borrower time	75	327	327	75	75	75
Travel expenses	0	168	168	10	10	0
Total costs	1,175	1,915	1,165	7,585	2,585	75
Effective interest rate (%)	23.5	38.3	23.3	151.7	51.7	1.5
Closeness to home	Very close	Distant	Distant	Close	Close	Very close
Restrictions on access	Must be member and have 2 guarantors	Collateral required	Collateral required	—	—	Unlikely to have funds available

Flexibility on payments	Flexible	Inflexible	Inflexible	Flexible	Flexible	Flexible
Timeliness	High	Moderate	Moderate to poor	High	High	Low – unlikely to have funds
Restriction on uses	None	Not for consumption	Not for consumption	None	None	None
Consequences of default	Negotiable – loss of access to future loans and seizure of savings	No further access to loans	No further access to loans	Seizure of assets or land	Seizure of assets or land	Variable

Notes

[a] Assuming 22% interest rate and one day's labour forgone (a high assumption).
[b] Assuming 24% interest rate and transaction costs as FAO (1988) study.
[c] Based on FAO (1988) study.
[d] Assuming interest rate of 150% (Zander 1992), one day's labour forgone and nominal transport costs.
[e] Assuming interest rate of 50% (Zander 1992), one day's labour forgone and nominal transport costs.
[f] Assuming one day's labour forgone.

villagers attendance at a monthly meeting, and the informal social activities that follow, is a social event that is much valued.

Effective internal management

Central to effective management in SANASA has been the movement's autonomy from government. This has permitted the many organisations within the movement to define and pursue their goals and has ensured that the top-down control orientation which has weakened co-operatives in many parts of Asia (including Sri Lanka) has not weakened SANASA (Yun 1987). The organisational dynamic of SANASA is based upon autonomous PTCCSs that are influenced (through argument, rhetoric, persuasion, example and training) by a strong leadership with a clear vision for the movement. Over the years the national and district leadership has encouraged societies to professionalise, modify interest rate structures and become more concerned about servicing the needs of poorer members. As mentioned earlier, this leadership has also been successful in activating voluntarism at the local level.

At the PTCCS level, management capacity is developed by a slow and careful process that fosters the formation and expansion of groups but ensures that the groups 'belong' to the members (and not to the parent organisation as in BRAC, TRDEP, MMF and so on). Training is provided for both leaders and members by the District Union, and increasingly the division and cluster. In turn the FTCCS has built up the DUs in terms of training professional staff and the volunteer boards and installing systems. As Esman and Uphoff (1984) have demonstrated, the vertical linkages of a federal structure have greatly strengthened local activities. These upper tiers have been largely financed by external grants, and the question of how to recoup their costs by internal charging remains unanswered.

Inevitably, an understanding of how SANASA's structure has evolved requires a discussion of the role of P.A. Kiriwandeniya: he initiated the reawakening, was the first general manager of the Federation and has been president of it for more than ten years. Does Kiriwandeniya's role (along with that of Yunus in the Grameen Bank, Abed at BRAC and Romero in BancoSol) lead us to what David Leonard (1991: 255) has termed the 'great man theory of organisational accomplishment'? If this is the case then such performances can be lauded but not learned from. Such a position is too negative and too narrow. First, as this section has shown, there are a whole series of design lessons that can be drawn from the SANASA experience. Second, and perhaps even more importantly, the potential leaders of innovative finance schemes are not simply 'born' but develop and take inspiration (and sometimes lessons) from other leaders. The achievements of Kiriwandeniya (as with Yunus, Abed and Romero) increase the likelihood of similarly dynamic characters emerging, and developing new approaches and organisations for financial services (or indeed for other services for poorer people and micro-entrepreneurs). Under Kiriwande-niya's guidance SANASA has activated a cadre of young and energetic co-operative leaders and managers. There is no guarantee that any of them will successfully take over the management of SANASA or create new 'high-performing' organisations, but their existence increases the likelihood of both these outcomes.

The management of external relations

Coincident with the expansion of SANASA has been Sri Lanka's slide into 'democratic decay' (Moore 1992). This has been associated with politicians and political parties seeking to manipulate public and private organisations for their personal gain and to strengthen their political position. At the same time there has been civil war, a major guerrilla insurgency and a state response involving tens of thousands of extra-judicial executions. This is no environment in which to establish a mass, democratic, grassroots structure, and yet SANASA has succeeded. A full appreciation of how this has been achieved would require a more detailed study than this. However, the key elements of the SANASA strategy can be identified:

1 the movement's leaders have systematically avoided direct contact[10] with politicians to retain its image of neutrality in terms of party politics and to minimise the opportunity for politicians to ask or offer 'favours';
2 SANASA officials and staff at all levels are expected to give up their position in the movement if they become actively involved in party politics.

On the one occasion on which SANASA became closely involved with a government programme – the Million Houses Programme – the move-ment's entire viability was threatened when a moratorium was arbitrarily declared. In consequence, the policy of keeping 'distant' from (but not openly critical of) government has been reinforced.

In terms of external relations, SANASA has a wealth of contacts which at times has become overwhelming in relation to their demands on manage-ment time.[11] In an attempt to reduce the amount of time spent negotiating with donors and to facilitate donor co-ordination, a SANASA-convened 'consortium' has been meeting since 1989. This is an interesting variation on the conventional aid consortia which are donor-convened. Of central importance in SANASA's external linkages are the continuing relations with the World Council of Credit Union (WOCCU) and the Canadian Co-operative Association (CCA). These linkages bear similarities to those described in the Indonesian case-study (Chapter 11) in which relatively long-term relationships have been formed, donor advice has been stable and both donor and recipient personnel are comrades rather than contestants. They add further strength to the argument that donors may best assist recipient organisations by conceptualising their activities in terms of a relationship rather than a discrete investment.

And the future?

The achievements of SANASA in Sri Lanka's rural financial market should not obscure the considerable challenges that it faces. The most pressing of these at the time of study in 1992 and 1993 concerned the *Janasaviya* Trust Fund (JTF) which was keen to use thrift and credit co-operatives as an on-lender of its funds. The JTF's managers were under great pressure to disburse. The World Bank wished to see expenditure targets met (US$57.5 million in three years to show its commitment to its recent poverty 'agenda') while the UNP, facing an election before early 1995, was keen to pump credit into the villages. The FTCCS was reluctant to engage with JTF, seeing the situation as potentially a repeat of the Million Houses Programme loans on which a moratorium was declared just before the 1988 election. As a result, the JTF bypassed the Federation and started to work directly with a number of DUs. Such moves threatened to undermine the federal structure that has permitted the reactivation and expansion of thrift and credit co-operatives: in effect the World Bank had begun financing institutional destruction (Hodson 1996). Ultimately the FTCCS's stalling tactics worked as JTF (and the government) have reduced their pressure on the movement following a change in government and a critical mid-term evaluation of JTF.

The second challenge concerns the financing of the administrative structures that have been developed at Federation, district and now cluster level. These are heavily reliant on external grants. SANASA's performance may permit it to continue to attract such support for some years to come, but in the medium term it must develop a greater internal financing capacity. For the FTCCS this will mean persuading DUs to deposit more of their funds into the Federation (perhaps through bye-law changes or more attractive interest rates) or to pay higher fees. Neither will be easy. The financing of clusters will depend on the ability of cluster officers to mobilise additional savings and sell insurance: little is known of their performance in these areas to date.

A further challenge facing SANASA is succession. In the medium term the movement will need to find a successor to Kiriwandeniya with the capacity, credibility and contacts to manage both donors and the domestic political environment, and the ability to provide a vision that will maintain SANASA's momentum. Ensuring that the 'successor generation' is prepared remains a strategic task for the current leadership.

We end this section with a speculation: what if the worst happened and the government interfered in the Federation, donors hastily withdrew, internal cost recovery failed and the succession was ineffective? No doubt SANASA, as currently constituted, might collapse, but the operations of thousands of PTCCSs would continue. Unlike the other group schemes described in this volume (BRAC, TRDEP, MMF, KREP, BancoSol, SACA), SANASA has genuinely institutionalised itself at the village level and its primary societies have an autonomous capacity to function (albeit on a reduced scale) without the higher tiers.

CONCLUSIONS

Although the thrift and credit co-operative movement does not have an exclusive focus on poverty alleviation, it confers a number of benefits on several hundred thousand low-income households in Sri Lanka. Poorer households join primary societies; through membership they gain improved access to loans and savings services for income-generation and consumption; the use of these services is associated with increased incomes and economic diversification for a significant proportion of poorer members and provides most members with an extension to entitlements that reduces vulnerability; more tentatively, it can be argued that SANASA contributes to socio-political change because of the opportunities it offers to female members, and more broadly by the open forum it creates to discuss individual and community issues at the village level.

While the upper two tiers of the SANASA pyramid are reliant to a great extent on donor subsidies, our case-studies of village co-operatives largely verify the Federation's claim that their network is a genuine grassroots movement which is sustainable because it mobilises resources which are, in turn, reinvested in those communities. Repayment levels at the PTCCS level are excellent and most PTCCSs are profitable.

In addition SANASA has generated externalities for other players in the market by demonstrating the 'bankability' of lower-income rural people and the potential of group lending schemes. When set against the comparative performance of other rural finance institutions and a background of civil war, insurgency and political decay SANASA's performance is remarkable.

For the designers of rural finance schemes, SANASA throws up a number of potentially important lessons:

- Lending for agriculture can be viable if it is only part of an organisation's portfolio, is demand-led and is closely monitored.
- Cooperative structures can be effective in generating joint liability mechanisms that foster loan recovery. However, the process of primary society development needs to ensure that societies are not hastily created and that both leaders and members are trained.
- Co-operatives can provide financial services to poorer people.
- Market-related interest rates must be pursued to permit resource

mobilisation allied to organisational financial viability. Tapered interest rates for smaller loans (see Vol. 1, Chapters 3 and 8) can permit sustainable poverty-focused lending. Product diversification strategies should be pursued once co-operatives are stable.

- The use of borrower savings to finance loans provides a secure capital base, serves as a strong incentive for repayment and helps to insulate institutions from political manipulation.
- Administrative costs can be kept at low levels by strategies to foster voluntarism and phased professionalisation at affordable rates.
- The 'taboo' on consumption loans must be challenged. Small, accessible consumption loans can assist in income and welfare protection for poorer households and can be commercially viable.
- Keeping courteously 'distant' from the state and its agencies is an effective strategy to avoid co-option in some environments.

For aid donors and external agencies seeking to assist poverty-focused financial institutions to establish there are additional lessons:

- Subsidies are desirable but they should be concentrated on institutional development (systems, training, research) rather than interest rate subsidies.
- Assistance is best conceptualised in terms of a long-term relationship entailing a continuous review of policies and achievements and agreements on policy changes rather than as the 'investment' of a capital sum.
- Helping indigenous organisations and their leaderships to evolve gradually (SANASA, BRAC, BancoSol) may be a slower strategy but is more likely to yield results than trying to rapidly establish new organisations with 'recruited' leaders (MMF and TRDEP).
- The desire of external agencies to 'shift funds' (USAID and the World Bank in SANASA's case) is highly detrimental to financial institutional development. Such actions are damaging in their own right and encourage domestic governments to behave in ways that are inimical to institutional development.

The expansion and performance of SANASA over the last fifteen years point to the need for the rehabilitation of credit co-operatives (Huppi and Feder 1990) as part of a pluralist institutional strategy to develop rural financial markets that can meet the needs of poorer people. The thrift and credit movement still faces great challenges (particularly in terms of covering the costs of its upper tiers and the marauding activities of agencies pursuing disbursement targets) but its achievements stand in marked contrast to its competitors in the Sri Lankan countryside.

NOTES

1 There is considerable debate about how a poverty line should be defined in Sri Lanka, about the accuracy of official statistics and about trends in poverty in the country. We do not have space to explore these debates in this chapter and the reader should refer to Moore (1990) for a review of the materials. We have utilised the Central Bank (1989) definition which we believe to be superior to the criterion used for food stamps eligibility.

2 Figures provided by respondents on asset values must be treated with caution. The major asset of most respondents was their residence. Respondents perceived that a real increase in property prices was occurring, but the valuation of such property, which is rarely openly marketed, is highly problematic.

3 In India only 15 per cent of IRDP beneficiaries are women (Bennett 1992: 31).

4 The *Janasaviya* programme and *Janasaviya* Trust Fund are discrete entities. Each has a different programme, they are separately administered and while the former is domestically financed, the latter is World Bank-funded.

5 The Banking Development Division of the Central Bank has taken great pains to ensure that indicators of RRDB performance are kept confidential. The picture provided here is thus partial and may well not indicate how costly and ineffective RRDBs have been.

6 Where else in the world is economic liberalisation at a revolutionary pace likely to occur without political instability, where a team of US advisers can be openly involved in running the economy, where there is a vast natural resource base available for 'mining' and a location on the Asian Pacific Rim fostering East Asian investment?

7 Low-cost professionalisation is facilitated in Sri Lanka by the large pool of educated but unemployed persons seeking white-collar work in most rural areas.

8 Evidence from field research indicates that such funds do not increase poor members' access to loans nor is it clear that the subsidy element accrues only to poor members.

9 See Zander (1992) for recent estimates. His estimates are consistent with interview data collected during the course of this study.

10 This practice went as far as politely declining several invitations to 'take tea' with the president.

11 For example, in 1992 SANASA was receiving 'support' from thirteen different foreign agencies.

14

INDIA

The regional rural banks

Paul Mosley

THE POLICY AND INSTITUTIONAL
BACKGROUND

It has been typical in studies of institutions in developing countries, including rural banking, to treat the case of India as *sui generis*. This is unfortunate, as the problem of rural poverty is universal, and there is much which both India and other countries can learn from a comparative study. The practice of state-sponsored rural development banking, pioneered by the Reserve Bank of India (RBI) in 1948, has been adopted by very many developing countries with widely varying results. In particular, the structure of intervention in rural credit markets worked out by the RBI and by Bank Indonesia (as described in Chapter 11) is in externals virtually identical, but the outcomes could scarcely be more different. In this chapter we want to explore the reason why.

The institutions with which this chapter is concerned – the regional rural banks – are but one component in the network of institutions by which finance reaches the Indian farmer and rural entrepreneur; they are, however, the institutions most directly concerned with direct poverty relief. Since independence in 1948, the Government of India, acting through the RBI, has been concerned to provide affordable loan finance for the rural producer in competition with the private moneylender.[1] To this end it has:

1 created Land Development Banks (LDBs) for long-term finance and Co-operative Banks (CBs) for short-term finance at the state, district and locality level for support to rural producers' co-operatives;
2 nationalised the twenty major commercial banks, in 1969 and 1980; these banks had the field to themselves for the ensuing twenty years but since

Particular thanks are due to S.M. Sant, Director, and R.V. Sindagi, Faculty Member, of the State Bank Institute of Rural Development, through whom sample surveys reported on in this chapter were carried out; also to the Chairmen of Manjira and Sangameshwara Regional Rural Banks for agreeing to be interviewed, and to R. Krishnamurthy for major assistance with the crop insurance research discussed on pp. 269–70.

1992 have been subject to competition by those foreign private banks allowed to operate in India since the liberalising reforms of the early 1990s;

3 set up a regulatory framework specifying, *inter alia*, maximum interest rates for particular categories of loan, minimum 'statutory liquidity ratios' for assets deposited with the RBI, and minimum shares of commercial bank portfolios which must go to specified priority sectors, including agriculture;

4 set up a number of lines of credit in favour of rural and urban low-income groups at a price even cheaper than the statutory minimum interest rate for each sector. The most important of these is the Integrated Rural Development Programme (IRDP), initiated in 1979 and the subject of a number of studies summarised in Pulley (1989), which now serves some 20 million rural families – more than the entire population of Nigeria. IRDP provides capital assets such as livestock and irrigation equipment to the rural poor and landless through a mixture of government subsidy and loans from the banking system (in the ratio of 1:2). Through IRDP and through the credit component of twenty-four other poverty-alleviation schemes[2] the Government seeks to fulfil a commitment to what it calls 'social banking', or lending as an instrument of poverty-reduction;

5 created a lender of last resort, initially known as the Agricultural Refinance and Development Corporation and since 1982 as the National Bank for Agriculture and Rural Development (NABARD), which provides refinance at between 6.5 and 8.5 per cent to all the banks above mentioned in respect of their 'agricultural and rural' business. This term in recent years has been defined ever more elastically and now embraces not only conventional agro-processing and trade but also high-tech rural manufacturing such as artificial fibres and electronic assembly and even services such as travel agencies.

The network of state credit provision and regulation into which the regional rural bank fit – operating, it must be remembered, alongside an established network of moneylenders and the emergent private banks – is summarised in Figure 14.1.

By virtue of its large home market and diversified export base, India was late in being hit by the macro-economic and debt crisis, originally provoked by oil price increases, which engulfed the developing world in the 1980s; but hit it finally was, in the summer of 1991, when inflation rose to nearly 20 per cent and foreign exchange reserves dwindled to two weeks' cover. Under the threat of default on its overseas debt, India was forced into accepting a Washington-supervised adjustment programme, of a kind which it had not experienced since the mid-1960s and had hoped never to experience again. One facet of this adjustment programme was that the government was forced to make changes to the elaborate structure of state

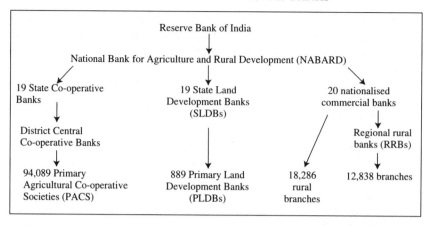

Figure 14.1 Structure of Indian rural banking system as at December 1994

ownership and regulation of the banking system as described in 2 and 3 above: changes for which banking interests had been clamouring for some while.[3]

These changes are summarised in Table 14.1. Interest rates were liberalised on large loans, but on small (less than Rs200,000) loans it remains a criminal offence to lend at more than half the true cost of credit;[4] statutory minimum liquidity ratios were relaxed, reducing the proportion of total assets which banks were required to hold with the central bank at penally low rates of return; and foreign banks were allowed to operate in India for the first time. But Indian banks, at the time of writing (end 1994), remain subject to controls on their freedom of manoeuvre of a type that have been blown away in most other developing countries, many of which the Government of India continues to justify as being essential to enable it to fulfil its mandate of delivering 'social banking' to the poor. Whether this justification is valid is a central question for this chapter, and the entire book, to try and answer.

How do the regional rural banks fit within this system and its reform process? According to the report of the Agricultural Credit Review Commission of 1989, gaps on the coverage and efficiency of the co-operative system, the spearhead of the Reserve Bank of India's market intervention in the 1950s and 1960s, had become apparent by 1969, and the RRBs were the chosen instrument for filling the gap. Specifically, they 'were intended to combine the local feel and low-cost profile of the co-operatives with the business organisation, ability to mobilise deposits, access to central money markets and modern outlook of the commercial banks with the view to reach the rural disadvantages more effectively' (Government of India 1989: para. 5.09); their invention thus marked a stepping-stone along the road of

Table 14.1 Regulatory environment for Indian rural banking and its liberalisation, 1989–94

Policy instrument	Restrictions on use	Modifications since 1989
Interest rate	12% on loans below Rs200,000	Raised from 10%
	16.5% on loans of Rs200,000–1 million	None
	Unrestricted on loans Rs1 million	Until 1990, maximum = 16.5%
Loan portfolio	Commercial banks: at least 40% to 'priority sectors'[a]	
	Regional rural banks: at least 60% to 'target groups'[b]	Until 1993, 100% to 'target groups'
	Statutory liquidity ratio 30% (to be invested in low-yield government securities)	Until 1991, 38.5%
Lending operations	'Lead bank scheme' (*aka* 'service area approach'): one commercial bank or RRB designated as credit supplier to each rural locality	

Notes
[a] Agriculture and small-scale industry.
[b] Households with land holdings not in excess of 6.5 acres; annual income not in excess of Rs10,000.

Indian Government disillusion with the co-operative movement in favour of the commercial-bank route to rural development. Each regional rural bank is capitalised and owned 50 per cent by the Government of India, 15 per cent by the state government and 35 per cent by the (state-owned) commercial bank which agrees to 'sponsor' it, and until July 1993 they were authorised to lend only to those below the poverty line, defined in 1993 as maximum family income of Rs10,000 ($400) per annum. On the surface, the RRBs bear a strong resemblance to the poverty-focused lending institutions of Indonesia discussed in Chapter 11, which also were intended to drive the rural moneylender out of business (he is actually illegal in Indonesia); which also are in many cases sponsored by 'parent' institutions (in the Indonesian case the BPDs, or provincial development banks); and which also administered a supply-driven programme of sub-sidised credit designed to place modern agricultural inputs in the hands of poor farmers (in the Indonesian case BIMAS or 'mass mobilisation').

However, even if the target and the instrument were the same in both countries, the outcome, as we shall see, was very different.

DESIGN FEATURES

It will be useful to continue to use the Indonesian rural credit system as a benchmark when enumerating the basic design features of RRBs. As in Indonesia (but untypically in relation to our sample as a whole) loans are made to individuals, not groups of borrowers. As illustrated by Table 14.2, regional rural banks differ from the 'Ohio School stereotype' of pervertible rural finance institutions by mobilising savings deposits and by having access to a fully fledged crop insurance scheme (for details of which, see Mosley and Krishnamurthy 1995). In both these respects the institutional achievements of the RRBs surpass, we shall later argue, the achievements of the Indonesian BPD institutions. However, among more worrying features we note, over and above the interest rate curbs mentioned in the previous section, appraisal of some loans by non-bank staff (namely the local government officials entrusted with the allocation of IRDP loans);[5] loan size rigidly dictated by the nature of the borrower's enterprise (for example, all loans for one hectare of irrigated rice are the same size); 'balloon' repayments at the end of the loan period; and the absence, indeed prohibition, of material incentives to borrowers to repay on time or to bank staff to achieve good financial performance.[6] Worse, under a Union Government decision of 1991 regional rural banks are forced to pay their staff the same salaries as prevail in commercial banks, thereby forcing their cost structure upwards and aggravating their already serious financial situation.

The political environment surrounding the repayment of loans to RRBs requires separate discussion because it has so often been presented as the Achilles' heel, not only of the Indian credit system but of government-sponsored rural finance in general.[7] There are at least three levels of this environment to consider. At the lower level, village councils frequently take the side of debtors and thus, by contrast with the Indonesian system where they act as debt-collection agents, frequently obstruct creditors in the event of any concerted attempt to recoup overdues, particularly if the council chairman (*sab panch*) is himself a major defaulter, as was the case with one of the RRBs studied in the following sections.[8] At the second level, state governments may write-off all loans in default from particular categories of debtor, as in the case of the governments of Maharashtra (1978), Tamil Nadu (1979) and Andhra Pradesh (1987). Most damagingly, the Union Government of V.P. Singh declared an amnesty in October 1989 on all overdue agricultural debts with a value of less than Rs10,000 (the Agricultural and Rural Debt Relief Scheme, ARDRS), thereby writing-off a portfolio of some Rs130 billion ($5 billion). The combined effect of these past actions is very nearly to nullify the credibility of any threat from a creditor (not only an RRB) to take punitive action in respect of small

250

Table 14.2 Regional rural banks: design features

Design feature	India RRBs	Indonesia: BPD institutions
Interest rates and other charges	Fixed by law for 'small' loans (see Table 14.1)	At lender's discretion
Collateral requirement	Only for 'large' loans (>Rs100,000)	No
Savings facilities	Yes (deposit rates determined by sponsor bank)	Yes (deposit rates at lender's discretion)
Persons eligible for loans	60% (until 1993, 100%) must be 'poor' (annual income <Rs11,000; land holding <Rs10,000)	'Any productive enterprise'
Loan size	Determined by nature of enterprise (minimum: Rs500)	Determined by previous loan repayment performance (see Table 11.2)
Loan repayment arrangements	For crop farmers, annually after monsoon, at bank. For dairy farmers and small enterprises, usually monthly	Weekly at mobile office in borrower's village
Insurance arrangements	For farmers of cereals, pulses and oilseeds, formal insurance is bought from a private company by sponsor bank	10% compulsory savings deposit is paid into 'loan insurance fund' by lender
Material incentives	Illegal, except token payments to *panchayats*	Available for borrowers, bank staff and appraisers (see Table 11.2)

Source: Indonesian data from Chapter 11; Indian data from NABARD, *Statistics on Regional Rural Banks*, various years

agricultural overdues. This shadow will overlie, and for a few years dilute the effectiveness of, any measures of whatever type that may be made to improve loan recovery in the future.

INTERNAL EFFECTIVENESS AND 'ROLE IN THE MARKET'

By conventional financial criteria, the performance of the 196 regional rural banks, as a mass, has been dismal ever since their inception. By 1994 their accumulated losses had risen to Rs13 billion ($0.5 billion), completely wiping out their share capital and reserves, and they were continuing to lose $40 million per day; 171 of them, or 84 per cent, were unprofitable; 70 per cent of them had negative net worth; but to this day no regional rural bank has ever been allowed to close, nor, as shown by Table 14.3, have savings deposits ceased to accumulate at a healthy rate. The fundamental reason for this financial failure is that RRBs have never been allowed to charge for their services at rates which compensate them for the costs of operation and in particular for the costs of bad debts. As shown by Table 14.3, the conventional measure of these costs – the three months overdue rate – was running in 1993 at 32.8 per cent; but the overdue rate of the RRBs was not significantly in excess of that suffered by other institutional lenders in the rural areas of India, so that, as the Khusro Committee put it, 'there is little to choose between Tweedledum and Tweedledee' (Government of India 1989: para. 1.35). Profitability data, of course, often conceal a great deal of hidden subsidy, and to expose this and make possible comparisons with other lenders we proceed to estimate Yaron's Subsidy Dependence Index (SDI), the multiple by which the average lending rate must be raised to enable the RRBs to operate free from subsidy. The data required for this calculation, taken from NABARD's *Statistics on Regional Rural Banks*, are given in Table 14.4. In their raw form they give an SDI of only 81 per cent, a moderate figure by the standards of Table 14.3 , but the raw accounts contain an average loan-loss of provision of 4.7 per cent, which bears no relation to actual default rates.[9] If we assume that half of declared 1992 overdues of 33 per cent of portfolio will eventually have to be written-off – a charitable estimate[10] – the SDI for RRBs as a whole rises

Table 14.3 Regional rural banks: deposits, loans and overdues (Rs millions, year ended March)

	1976	1981	1986	1992	1993
Deposits	70	3,360	17,140	58,698	69,090
% annual growth rate		113	38	23	18
Loans issued	10	4,060	6,720	40,118	52,530
% annual growth rate			9	34	30
Overdues	—	540	4,120	12,527[a]	
% overdues to demand	—	48	51	33	
for comparison:					
commercial banks	—	47	43	—	
primary agricultural		43	41	—	
co-operative societies					
land development banks		46	39	—	

Source: National Bank for Agriculture and Rural Development, *Statistics on Regional Rural Banks,* September 1993
Note: [a] As at 30 September 1991.

Table 14.4 Regional rural banks: calculation of the Subsidy Dependence Index for 1992

Symbol	Item	1992 value (Rs millions) for:	
		All RRBs, average	Two sampled RRBs
A	Value of borrowings outstanding	18,956	114
m	Cost of borrowing on 'open market'[a]	16.0	16.0
c	Rate of interest paid on borrowed funds outstanding[b]	10.2	9.7
E	Average annual equity	1,128	12
P	Annual profit	(2,445)	(18)
	(Adjusted for 'realistic' loan-loss provision)[c]	(7,297)	(54)
K	Value of non-interest subsidies[d]	2,000	20
L	Value of outstanding loan portfolio	40,118	448
n	Average on-lending interest rate[e]	16.6	17.0
$SDI = \dfrac{A(m - c) + (Em - P) + K}{Ln}$		80.5	57.8
	(with P adjusted for 'realistic' loan loss provision)	153.4	106.6

Sources: All India data from NABARD, *Statistics on Regional Rural Banks*, 30 September 1992, subject to Notes below; data for individual RRBs from Sanagameshwara and Manjira RRBs, *Annual Reports*

Notes

[a] Specified lending rate for non-export bank credit over Rs200,000, as given by Government of India, *Economic Survey 1991–92*, part II: *Sectoral Developments*, table 3.6.

[b] Interest payment on deposits and concessionary loans as percentage of loan portfolio: the same concept as i in Figure 14.2.

[c] Uses the loan-loss provision that would be required to maintain the RRB's capital at its current level, given the rates of default estimated in Table 14.5: II.

[d] IRDP subsidies, plus concessional support (training, etc.) from commercial banks, plus technical assistance supplied by aid donors (estimated as the value of such assistance pro-rated across the institutions specified).

[e] Interest earned divided by value of loan portfolio (L above).

to 153 per cent for 1992.[11] Otherwise put, we estimate their break-even interest rate at 42 per cent against an average lending rate of 16.6 per cent, so that it would be necessary to more than double lending charges or more than halve overdues to make the system cover its accounting costs. However, it may be that the RRB system conveys external benefits, to the weaker sections and others, which justify such losses being subsidised by banks, government and aid donors. It will be the task of later sections to determine whether this is the case.

The composition of costs over time is given in Figure 14.2 for both the RRB system as a whole and for the two 'sample institutions' which are the subject of our field survey. These sampled institutions are Manjira and Sangameshwara Grameena Banks, respectively 50 km west and 100 km

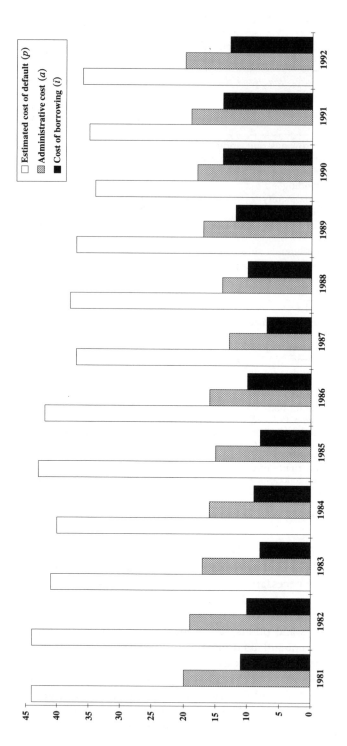

Figure 14.2 Regional rural banks: components of lending costs, 1981–2
Source: NABARD, *Statistics on Regional Rural Banks*, various years

Data for Figure 14.2 (percentages of total lending)

	1981	1982	1983	1984	1985	1986	1987	1988	1990	1992
Interest cost of borrowing	10.5	9.3	7.4	7.8	6.9	7.9	6.1	8.4	10.5	10.2
(a) Administrative cost,	8.9	8.9	8.9	7.9	7.7	7.8	7.2	6.3	8.2	9.7
of which: salaries:	6.9	6.8	6.9	6.1	5.8	5.6	4.9	4.5	6.0	7.1
insurance:	0.2	0.3	0.2	0.2	0.3	0.6	0.8	0.5	0.6	0.7
(p) Cost of default:										
(p^1) formal loan-loss premium	4.6	4.6	4.6	4.6	4.6	4.6	4.6	4.6	4.6	4.6
Declared overdue rate	48.0	50.0	48.0	50.0	52.0	51.0	49.0	50.0	31.0	32.9
(p^2) estimate of % of portfolio written off = 50% of declared overdues	24	25	24	25	26	25	24	25	16.5	16.4
Total cost of lending:										
$i = a + p^1$										
$\dfrac{i = a + p^1}{1 - p^1}$ using formal loan loss premium	25.1	23.7	21.5	21.1	20.0	21.1	18.6	20.1	24.2	25.3
$\dfrac{i + a + p^2}{1 - p^2}$ using measure p^2 as estimate of default rate	56.9	57.6	53.7	54.2	54.1	55.6	49.0	52.9	39.6	42.5

Source for all data: NABARD, *Statistics on Regional Rural Banks*, various years.

south of Hyderabad in a semi-arid, rainfed agricultural zone of Andhra Pradesh.[12] As RRBs have expanded and average loan size has increased, there has none the less been only an insignificant decline in total costs (that is, break-even premium); indeed, there would have been none at all in the absence of the 1989 amnesty (ARDRS), which caused some $5 billion of small agricultural overdues to be declared no longer due by Union Government fiat. Although the cost of overdues is throughout the period the largest element in cost, it is none the less also apparent from Figure 14.2 that the RRBs' average lending rate of 16.6 per cent would have failed, in 1992, to cover even the borrowing and administrative elements in cost; that is, it would have led to losses even if overdues had been zero.

The squeeze imposed on RRBs by the small margin between their operating costs and the maximum legal rate at which they can lend has led to some grotesque distortions of resource allocation. In particular, it has made lending an unprofitable activity for many, and encouraged them to invest as much of their portfolio as possible in financial assets rather than the loans to the poor which it is their function to provide. The chairman of Gorakhpur Grameena Bank, a profitable RRB 200 km east of Lucknow in Uttar Pradesh, explained the underlying rationale of this behaviour in the following way:

> My bank was one of the first RRBs to be set up, in October 1975. The catchment is a fertile sugar-growing area, where previous to 1975 many of my customers had no banking facilities available to them whatsoever. Deposits have grown much faster than advances, and they are now worth 200 crores [$64 million]. At present 65 crores [$21 million] is lent out in the form of advances; 90 per cent of these advances are to target groups with an income below the poverty line. My average recovery rate on these advances was 45 per cent over crop years 1990–2 inclusive, but it is currently down to 35 per cent; it is particularly poor, about 15–20 per cent, for IRDP borrowers, who mainly invest in milch animals and [motor cycle] rickshaws. Anyhow, the remaining 135 crores [$43 million] is invested in financial assets: mostly thirty-day notice accounts in my sponsor bank [the State Bank of India], but we also have some shares in a telephone company. These investments earn a secure 13.5 per cent, by contrast with an insecure 12 per cent on most loans to target groups; hence it is the bank's financial interest to keep lending down as far as possible, and invest as much as possible in the short-term money markets. By doing this, I have managed to keep the bank profitable.[13] Would you not do the same as me, in my position?
>
> (Interview, Chairman, Gorakhpur RRB, 3 September 1992)

It is possible, then, to make a profit with a recovery rate of 35 per cent, a financial sleight of hand second only to Milo Minderbinder's achievement in making a black market profit out of buying eggs at seven cents and selling them at six cents.[14] The secret is not to lend; or if you have to lend to satisfy an externally imposed social obligation, to lend as little as possible, preferably to activities already covered by one or other insurance scheme.[15] Until the triple constraint of externally imposed interest rates, balloon

Table 14.5 Determinants of repayment performance of RRBs

I Regional average data

		Possible determinants			
Region	*Average repayment rate, 1983–91[a]*	*Crop income per ha per capita (1983–91)*	*Savings deposits per capita (1989)*	*% of area irrigated (1990)*	*Average rainfall (1901–90)*
North	56.7	2,413	563	39.4	798
Punjab	82.6	5,476	983	77.5	591
Himachal Pradesh	60.4	914	916	21.4	1,328
Northeast[b]	33.7	680	134	—	2,321
East	46.3	2,827	160	20.8	1,330
Central	47.6	2,346	141	27.3	1,075
West	53.1	2,026	266	13.4	994
South	61.6	3,822	228	26.9	1,425
All India	52.5	2,149	277	20.9	1,444

II Results of statewise regression analysis

Dependent variable: average repayment rate of all RRBs in state
Number of observations: 23
$r^2 = 0.63$ s.e.e. $= 8.59$

	Regression coefficients on independent variables (Student's t-statistics below coefficients in brackets)				
	Crop income per ha per capita (1983–91)	*Savings deposits per capita (1989)*	*Percentage irrigated area (1989)*	*Percentage scheduled castes (1989)*	*Average rainfall (1901–90)*
Constant					
28.38*	0.006*	0.028*	−0.062	−0.329	0.631
(3.46)[c]	(2.85)	(3.15)	(0.24)	(0.98)	(1.55)

Sources: Repayment rates from National Bank for Agriculture and Rural Development, *Statistics on Regional Rural Banks*, annual. All other data from Indian Banks' Association, *Rural Development: Selected Statistics*, 1989, table 140: 'Key indicators of development'

Notes
[a] Repayment rate is defined as proportion of due loan instalments actually paid six months after due date.
[b] Data for Manipur, Nagaland and Tripura only.
[c] Figures in brackets are Student's *t*-statistics.
* Denotes significance at the 1% level.

repayment of loans and political reinforcements towards non-repayment is removed, it is unlikely that this perverse incentive will disappear.

Within these constraints, however, we can derive useful information about the determinants of repayment performance on a comparative basis, before going down to the level of the individual bank, by using the same regression techniques first adopted in Table 3.4 (Vol. 1). The independent variables used to explain the repayment performance of the RRBs in Table 14.5 are the same as those used in the earlier table, with the exception of the proportion of women borrowers (no data available) and the design features of group organisation, loan collection method and incentives to repay (no variation between states or RRBs). As shown by Table 14.5, repayment performance in most RRBs is clustered around the all-India average of 52.2 per cent, with significantly better than average performance in the agriculturally richest state of Punjab and significantly worse performance in the poor north-eastern states of Mizoram and Nagaland. However, the regression analysis in the second part of the table makes it clear that what is associated with better repayment performance is not so much higher borrower income as higher per capita savings deposits: states with low per capita income and high levels of personal savings, such as Himachal Pradesh, tended to have relatively high rates of repayment. These data buttress the general conclusion of Vol. 1, Chapter 3, that the existence of effective savings facilities is a valuable, possibly an essential, means of bringing about high repayment rates, even in a country where the overall policy environment is not favourable.

Even at the purely financial level, however, other criteria are important, apart from subsidy dependence and recovery rates. Crucial is *additionality*, the ability of RRBs to compensate for imperfections in the capital market by reaching people who would otherwise have been unable to borrow. On this criterion, our two sampled RRBs score only moderately, by the standards of the other institutions surveyed in this volume: 61 per cent of borrowers had taken a loan from a source other than the RRB, and of this previous borrowing about half came from informal moneylenders. This 61 per cent contrasts with an average of 38 per cent across the ten other institutions providing data on this matter for Table 3.3. Of the 37 per cent of sampled borrowers who remained below the poverty line throughout the observation period (mid-1992 to mid-1993), most – over three-quarters – had never borrowed before, and those who had borrowed used exclusively family and friends or traditional moneylenders. By contrast, 82 per cent of borrowers above the poverty line had borrowed from some other source; and as income increased this was increasingly likely to be a formal institution rather than a moneylender or relative. The moneylender is, in the economist's sense, the provider of an 'inferior good', whereas the services of commercial banks have a very high income elasticity of demand. This point is further taken up on pp. 266–7 below.

Table 14.6 Borrowers from sampled RRBs: extent of previous borrowing, analysed by income[a]

Previous participation in capital market	Family income (Rs/month)			
	<1200 (i.e. below poverty line)	1,200– 2,000	>2,000	Total
No previous loan from any source	28	7	4	39
Loan from moneylender	4	12	3	19
Loan from family or friends	5	10	2	17
Loan from commercial bank or co-operative	—	9	10	19
Loan from other source (e.g. NGO, ROSCA)	—	4	2	6
Total	37	42	21	100

Source: Author's survey, May 1993 (see p. 259 for details)

Notes
1 Sample size = 280.
2 $1 = Rs31 at time of survey.
3 In computing income, on-farm consumption of own produce is valued at prevailing market prices.
4 The poverty line used is Rs14,400 per family per annum ($39/family/month) which includes an allowance for the average consumption of non-food items by below-poverty-line families.
5 For further discussion of the methods used, see Datt and Ravallion (1994) and p. 259 below.
Figures in each cell are percentages of total sample.

IMPACT ON INCOMES AND PRODUCTION METHODS

We now try to assess the influence on income and other dimensions of family welfare achieved by our sampled regional rural banks. As explained on p. 255 above, these banks, Manjira and Sangameshwara, are both located in areas of rainfed agriculture in inland Andhra Pradesh,[16] and many of the conclusions drawn for these banks cannot be generalised to RRBs operating in regions of the country with a different infrastructure or agro-climatic environment. However, as shown by Table 14.7, both in financial performance and in the social composition of borrowers, the two banks come close to the all-India average; however, the average size of loans and deposits is a little larger than the national average in the sampled banks.

A sample of 140 borrowers was taken at random in each of the two RRBs, with one-quarter of each sample consisting of new borrowers who had been approved for, but had not yet taken, a loan. As in our other country surveys, these 'novice' borrowers are treated as a control sample for the purpose of

Table 14.7 Summary statistics: sampled RRBs in relation to the all-India average, 1990–2

	Manjira and Sangameshwara GBs	*Regional rural banks, all-India average*
Average borrower income ($/family/month)	42.1[a]	
% scheduled castes	22.7[a]	23.3
Average loan size ($)	136.3	99.5
Average savings deposits ($)	79.6	50.1
Overdue rate (%)	31.5	33.0
SDI (%)	106.6	153.4

Sources: Statistics on Regional Rural Banks, September 1991, except data on borrower incomes and per cent scheduled castes, which are from our survey data

Note: [a] Figure based on survey sample data, not on the total of borrowers from the RRB. Borrower income includes an allowance for on-farm consumption of own produce.

separating out those income changes which are loan-induced. The distribution of income changes by production category, income group and gender within the sample is as given in Table 14.8. The overall impact of lending, even when measured correctly as the difference between the income change of loan beneficiaries and the control group, is positive (at Rs727 or $23 per family per year), but amongst borrowers below the poverty line it is on

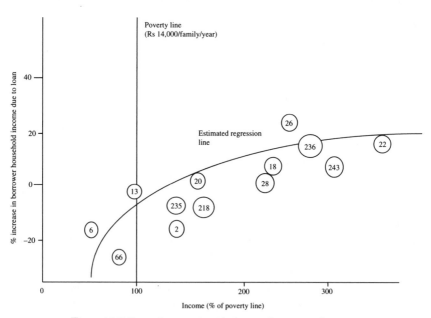

Figure 14.3 Loan impact in relation to borrower income

Note: Only some illustrative data points are shown: number in circles represent sampled households

average negative. For the sample as a whole, the relationship between a borrower's income and the benefit he or she derived from a loan is an upward-sloping but flattening curve, as for the other illustrations we have studies, as illustrated by Figure 14.3. Around this curve, however, the dispersion of outcomes (coefficient of variation) within the 'poor' group is very wide – wider than it is for the richer groups. In particular, a significant number of borrowers in the sample – thirty-four, of whom eight were

Table 14.8 Estimated loan impact on family incomes

I Before versus after[a]

	Monthly family income one year ago (Rs)			
	1,200	*1,200–2,000*	*>2,000*	*Total*
Income change since last loan:				
Decrease/no change	19+9	3+3	1+0	35
Increase 0–50%	5+3	24+13	13+0	58
Increase >50%	0+2	5+1	2+0	9
(1) Average change since previous year (Rs)	−218	750	6,550	
(2) Standard error	531.8	805.7	5,032.9	
(3) = (2)/(1) Coefficient of variation	243.9	107.4	76.8	

II With versus without

	Increase in annual net income (Rs)	
	Recently approved borrowers (no previous RRB loans)	*Experienced borrowers (one or more completed RRB loans)*
Main activity agriculture		
Borrowers below poverty line (Rs1,200/month)($n = 97$)	−511	−173
Borrowers above poverty line ($n = 123$)	1,358	3,076
Main activity non-agriculture		
Borrowers below poverty line ($n = 15$)	−116	−4
Borrowers above poverty line ($n = 45$)	1,862	925
Average income increase (Rs/family/year)	712	1,439
($/family/month)	1.9	3.86

Source: Author's survey, May 1993. For details of sample selection, see p. 255. Poverty line of Rs14,400 per family per annum ($39/family/month) includes an allowance for the average non-food consumption of poor families; for further details, see p. 262 below.
Note: [a] Figures in each cell are percentages falling within each category; entries to the left-hand side of the + sign are male and entries to the right are female.

female – crossed the estimated poverty line of Rs14,400 or $39 per family per month during the year under review.[17] This is 12 per cent of the sample; the percentage of borrowers who crossed the poverty line was, interestingly, lower among those who received loans through the Integrated Rural Development Programme (IRDP: the government-subsidised programme designed explicitly for this purpose, described on p. 247 above).

It is worth pausing at this point to consider in more detail the role and achievements of the IRDP within the portfolio of the regional rural banks. In India as a whole IRDP currently accounts for 22.6 per cent of new lending issued by regional rural banks (*Statistics on Regional Rural Banks*, September 1991); within our sample the rate was 29 per cent. Its aim is to select appropriate poor people as loan recipients (during the 1985–90 Seventh Plan period official guidelines suggested that no IRDP loan should be given to a household earning more than Rs4,800 per annum, against a poverty line of Rs6,400 per annum) and move them across the poverty line by placing in their hands (literally: until very recently all IRDP loans were transferred in kind rather than in cash) an appropriate asset. Classically this would be a buffalo or milch cow, and as recorded by Table 14.9 livestock was a far more important source of income for the IRDP borrowers in our sample than it was for the sample as a whole. The programme was relatively successful in its targeting in our sample, as it has been nationwide: 79 per cent of IRDP loans were made to families existing below our selected $39 poverty line at the beginning of the survey year, and 74 per cent of Scheduled Castes borrowers as well as 89 per cent of female borrowers were financed through IRDP. As noted earlier, the IRDP-financed element of the portfolio was less successful in pushing borrowers across the poverty line, and achieved a smaller increase in borrower income, than the less targeted and less overtly subsidised non-IRDP component. But the achievements of IRDP in the sample, in moving an estimated 10 per cent of borrowers across the poverty line in one year, suggest a more optimistic outturn in the sampled regions of Andhra Pradesh than in the country as a whole, where 'no more than one in five and possibly closer to one in twenty' eligible households succeeded in crossing the poverty line (namely, throughout the entire period of the 1985–90 five-year plan) (see Copestake 1995: 5). Critics of the IRDP approach to poverty reduction, who have for a long time drawn attention to the inefficiencies latent in its supply-led, subsidised, government-appraised, in-kind design technology,[18] will find here one small additional piece of evidence of those inefficiencies. But inefficient as IRDP has been, it has not been ineffective – no other programme in the world has taken an estimated million people across the poverty line in the last five years. It may, as Copestake (ibid.: 3–4) suggests, even be fairly efficient in relation to the other poverty-alleviation measures used by the Government of India; and in common with other aspects of the operation of regional rural banks, its design features are now being quite

Table 14.9 IRDP in relation to non-IRDP borrowers

	IRDP borrowers (n = 81)	Non-IRDP borrowers (n = 199)
Average income (Rs/household/annum)	11,389	17,400
Composition (%)		
agriculture	19.8	67.9
livestock	38.2	14.5
business	25.2	10.2
labour	16.6	9.1
Average loan size (Rs)	8,763	11,565
Percentage female	74	2
Estimated loan-induced increase in income[a] (Rs/household/annum)	103	150
Percentage of borrowers crossed poverty line[b]	11	15

Notes

[a] The 'estimated loan-induced increase in income' is the measured change in income between mid-1992 and mid-1993 as recorded in Table 14.8: I, corrected for the proportion of that change in income which was not induced by the loan, as estimated by the ratio (0.494) of the increase in the income of the control group to the increase in income of the borrower sample as recorded in Table 14.8: II.

[b] The poverty line we use is $39 per family per month, which is slightly above the threshold used by the Indian Planning Commission: for discussion see note 17.

rapidly changed as a part of the global pressures towards liberalisation and experimentation which have penetrated the Indian banking system in the last four years. We return to these issues on p. 265.

The logical next step is to ask what, if anything, differentiated the lending operations, both IRDP and non-IRDP, which induced significant income increases for the poor compared with those which did not. (We use this criterion rather than 'crossing the poverty line' because a given increase in income for a borrower which none the less fails to carry him or her across the poverty line has at least as much value as an increase of the same absolute value which does take borrowers across the poverty threshold.) Table 14.10 suggests that:

1 loans allocated to individuals with a 'diversified portfolio' (several sources of income) tended to have higher impact than loans allocated to families with a single income source;
2 loans with a low ratio of 'leakage into consumption' (that is, with a low ratio of asset purchases to loan size) tended to have *lower* impact than those with a high leakage into consumption.

The second of these findings is superficially bizarre, and appears to undermine all the efforts made by lenders and donors to maximise the investment (contribution to future income) component of their lending. Our own interpretation, of both findings, is different. We believe that the major

263

Table 14.10 Poor[a] RRB borrowers: comparisons

Increase characteristic	*Income change*	
	Positive income change (n = 43)	*Negative income change* (n = 54)
Average change in income (Rs/annum)	265	−580
Percentage female	60	41
Percentage with >1 source of income	72	45
Percentage of loan value committed to asset purchases (average)	37.4	64.2

Source: Author's 1993 survey
Note: [a] 'Poor' is defined as an income less than Rs14,400 per annum, including the value of subsistence consumption, over the measurement period mid-1992 to mid-1993.

contribution which lending to the poor can make is to reduce their vulnerability, and that although this can be done through some varieties of investment lending, in particular through varieties which diversify the number of income sources available, it can also be done through consumption lending *inasmuch as it moves the borrower closer to a position in which he can profitably commit resources to capital investment*, as argued in Chapters 4 and 5 (Vol. 1) above. Much of the RRBs' lending to poorer people, although switched into consumption, appeared to do this, in the sense that they experienced an income increase larger than the control group: for example, it put them in a position where they could commit some of their own resources to small capital purchases such as fertilisers, tools and water-pipes. The switching of loan resources by poor people, hard fought though it may be by donors, is not necessarily dysfunctional.

We now examine the contribution of different potential income sources to borrowers' livelihoods, both above and below the poverty line, in more detail. Table 14.11 decomposes both borrowers' initial incomes, and in particular the income change revealed in Table 14.8 (of which about half, on the evidence of the second part of the table, can be treated as loan-induced) into its constituent parts. As household income increases, relative dependence on livestock income diminishes (which is almost certainly connected with the high dependence of IRDP borrowers, who are mostly poor, on milch cattle) and, a little surprisingly, relative dependence on labour income increases. The strong and significant correlation which was apparent between labour income and the rate of income increase in the Sri Lanka study (Chapter 13, p. 210) is also in evidence here. There would appear, on evidence from interview material, to be two separate effects at work. In the first place, as businesses (both agricultural and non-agricultural) grow successfully, they take on some family labour, which is often paid a cash

Table 14.11 Decomposition of income increases received by borrowers[a]

Income source	Income category		
	<1,200	1,201–2,000	>2,000
Agriculture	−81 (49.0)	396 (52.8)	3,733 (56.9)
Livestock	−128 (24.9)	74 (9.9)	458 (8.9)
Non-farm enterprise	−26 (15.7)	160 (21.4)	589 (6.9)
Labour and other	17 (10.2)	118 (15.8)	1,703 (26.0)
Sub-sample average	−218	750	6,550
Number in sub-sample	112	122	51

Source: Author's survey, May 1993
Note: [a] First figure in each cell is average increase in rupees received by each sub-group; bracketed figure is the average share (%) of the income source named in the sub-group's total income.

wage. Second, successfully growing enterprises often received income from off-farm labour which could be invested in, or at least serve as an insurance against ups and downs in the income of, the family business. As Table 14.11 shows, borrowers themselves tended not to hire significant amounts of labour from *outside* the family until they reached a certain threshold income, which on the evidence of the table is around Rs2,000 per month. This has an important implication for poverty reduction: very small loans to people at the bottom of the income spectrum (for example, most of IRDP) cannot be expected to reduce poverty indirectly through taking on poor people into wage employment: at best, they will lead to increased intra-family employment, some of it unpaid. This parallels similar findings from the case-studies on Bolivia (Chapter 10, p. 19) and Malawi (Chapter 16, p. 392).

Table 14.12 relates these changes in employment to asset accumulation and technical change, which however was a minority activity: most loans (88 per cent across the sample) were not used to embody technical change (defined as the purchase of capital equipment or materials not previously used on the farm or business). Rather, they were used to buy equipment and materials within the currently prevailing technology, although average loan size exceeds asset accumulation by a large margin,[19] suggesting the presence of major leakages of the loan finance provided into consumption. Within income groups, asset accumulation and the propensity to technical change are substantially higher amongst male than female borrowers, but amongst borrowers with a monthly income below Rs2,000, female borrowers have a higher propensity to take on labour.

THE WIDER PICTURE

Particularly in India, the impact of relatively recent financial institutions such as the regional rural banks cannot reasonably be looked at in isolation

Table 14.12 Changes in employment and technology by gender and income group of borrowers

Income category (Rs/month)	Changes in employment and technology		
	Average increase in employment (numbers)	*Average increase in assets (value in) (Rs '000)*	*Percentage implementing technical change*
<1200[a]			
male (*n* = 74)	0.2	1.7	8
female (*n* = 38)	0.5	1.9	0
1,201–2,000			
male (*n* = 97)	0.4	9.2	16
female (*n* = 25)	0.8	1.4	0
>2,000			
male (*n* = 51)	1.7	8.8	25
female (*n* = 0)	—	—	—
Whole sample average	0.6	5.6	12.2

Source: Author's survey, May 1993
Note: [a] That is, below poverty line.

from the rural financial market as a whole. Although long intended to 'remove the rural moneylender from the forefront and put him in his place' (RBI 1954: II, 151) state intervention in rural capital markets has by no means abolished competition in the market for lending to the rural poor,[20] and part of the influence of the regional rural banks must therefore be measured in terms of the indirect impact which they exerted on the availability of credit provided by others. We now examine that influence.

In his survey of the interrelationship between formal and informal rural financial markets, Bell (1990: 306) reports that contrary to the official evidence of the Reserve Bank of India, 'although the moneylender did lose ground relative to institutions over the period 1951 to 1981, he remained a very important source of finance to rural households, and the expansion of aggregate debt was almost surely so great as to imply that his volume of business grew'. This was certainly the case for all of the five moneylenders (all men) on whom the data for Table 14.13 are based, who are from Vepur village near Mahboobnagar in Andhra Pradesh, within the catchment of the Sangameshwara Grameen Bank. These lenders are all part-timers; two were large farmers, two traders, one a teacher. All concurred that their agricultural business had been squeezed after the arrival of a branch of the RRB in the village eight years previously, which had forced them to bring their rates down (one of them claimed to have brought his average nominal lending rate down from 30 per cent to 24 per cent between 1985 and 1993) and to focus on loans for purposes for which RRBs would not lend, that is, very small loans (below Rs2,000) or consumption loans. 'For a daughter's marriage an individual will always go to the moneylender', the chairman of the Sangameshwara RRB told me, a

Table 14.13 Vepur, Andhra Pradesh: relative transaction costs of a Rs5,000, one-year loan, August 1993

| | *Percentage of principal sum per annum* | |
	Sangameshwara RRB (official rates)	*Five moneylenders (average costs)*
Direct financial costs	12[a]	18–50
Transactions and accessibility costs		
negotiation with lender	8	5
appraisal and inspection charges	2	—
travelling time	7	4
asset pledge	—	0–10
Total cost of borrowing	29	27–60

Sources: Direct financial costs from interviews, Vepur, 26 August 1993; transactions and accessibility costs from survey, June 1993
Note: [a] RRB lending rate rises to 16.5 per cent for loans up to Rs1 million and can be any figure for loans more than Rs1 million. (No loan made to any of the sampled borrowers was anywhere near as large as this.)

perception which was echoed by the borrowers and the moneylenders themselves. The striking finding emerging from Table 14.13, by contrast with evidence from other countries, is the enormous range of variation which would be applied by *any one* moneylender to a loan of given size, depending on his relationship with the borrower: less would be charged to men than to women, long-term borrowers than short-term borrowers, borrowers of small than large sums and, above all, to individuals whom the moneylender knew personally. Some moneylenders would ask for an asset pledge (usually gold or jewellery), but only on a minority of loans. The upshot of these inter-loan cost variations is to make the balance of competitive advantage between RRB and moneylender absolutely contingent on these personal characteristics.

CONCLUSIONS

'The aim of serving the poor', the Khusro Committee concluded in 1988 with particular reference to the regional rural banks, 'has ended up in giving poor service' (Government of India 1989: para. 1.68). Many might like to use that as an epitaph for the 'traditional' approach to credit for the poor, in which subsidised credit is supplied to a defined target group on terms largely defined by the state; and certainly the financial record of the RRBs is not impressive. But the RRB model is not without merit, and in its externals bears a considerable similarity to the much-admired institutions created for micro-enterprise by the regional development banks of Indonesia, of which the BKKs and KURKs, studied in detail in Chapter 11, are the most famous. These also recycle subsidised central bank credit (and

267

offer savings facilities) to small producers through an institution with local expertise in an environment where the activities of private moneylenders are officially suppressed. These also have served as agents for national programmes for the diffusion of simple agricultural and small-business technology to the rural poor (BIMAS in the Indonesian case, IRDP in the Indian). But there are also vital differences, of which the most important are probably the existence of free-market interest rates, intensive loan supervision (without loan waivers) and incentives to staff and borrowers in the Indonesian environment only. But those features were not designed into the Indonesian institutions from the beginning: they were grafted on in an environment of macro-economic and institutional crisis between the mid-1970s and the early 1980s. The macro-economic crisis of the 1980s took a longer time to hit the less open economy of India, but hit it finally did in 1991, and the repercussions on the banking system are now beginning to be felt: freer (but not yet completely free) interest rates from 1992 onward, a relaxation of the strict targeting rules in 1993, and at the time of writing (February 1995) it has been announced that fifty of the RRBs are to be comprehensively restructured, involving the clearing of their balance sheets and infusions of fresh capital; and there is the prospect of the RRBs being reabsorbed into their sponsor banks or into NABARD and being subjected in the process to much tougher financial disciplines (Mudgil and Thorat 1995). In time, this may bring about a turnaround as dramatic as that which occurred in Indonesia.

It must also be remembered that, as our survey of two RRBs has helped to demonstrate, the RRB instrument has been successful in mobilising rural small savings, in bringing down the interest rates charged by moneylenders and in raising the incomes of many poor people, some of whom it enabled to enter the capital market for the first time; some of what RRBs lose in efficiency, therefore, they may gain in effectiveness. Seldom, however, were these income increases associated with significant technical change. Effectiveness seems to have been greater for that part of RRBs' lending that was conducted outside the IRDP and therefore appraised directly by bank staff. The effectiveness of lending was at its lowest in relation to the poorest borrowers, but within this group loans with a consumption component to people with diversified sources of income seem to have been more successful than investment-only loans to individuals depending on one source of income. These ideas reinforce our general argument that very small loans to very poor people need to be appraised and administered on a different basis from loans to well-established and experienced borrowers.

NOTES

1 The most important of these schemes are summarised in Copestake (1995: table 1).

2 In 1954 the *All-India Rural Credit Survey* described the objective of government intervention in rural credit markets as being 'to provide a positive institutional alternative to the moneylender himself, something which will compete with him, remove him from the forefront and put him in his place' (Government of India 1954: II. 481–2).

3 The Agricultural Credit Review Committee set up by the Reserve Bank of India in 1989 (known after its chairman as the 'Khusro Committee') had recommended two years previously that 'the over-administered structure of interest rates must be corrected, and the determination of interest rates must be left substantially to the forces of demand and supply, in a freely competitive environment . . . and that only in the case of mandatory programmes and policies focused on the weaker sections and low income groups in society, administered and concessional interest rates and prices should be permitted' (Government of India 1989: para. 1.12).

4 Analysis to be presented below estimates the average break-even rate of interest $(i + a + p/1 - p)$ for a regional rural bank at 23.89 per cent (see Figure 14.2).

5 The Khusro Committee (Government of India 1989: para. 1.78) comments that 'at present the banks are involved neither in the selection of beneficiaries [under IRDP], nor in the identification of viable activities, nor in the matching of activities with the beneficiaries, nor indeed in helping the beneficiaries to prepare feasible projects. The net result is that the banks do not regard the IRDP as their programme and are only involved in it in a mechanical manner. This affects the quality of credit, the goodness of the project, its operations and the recovery.'

6 Under Union Government law it is illegal for banks to make non-salary payments to staff or to reward borrowers who repay on time. However, it is permissible for regional rural banks to reward *villages* whose loan repayment performance is outstanding by presenting them with a collective reward such as a well, schoolroom or water filter. Even here, some RRB chairmen place an upper limit of Rs500 on rewards which can be offered in this way (Interview, Sangameshwara Grameen Bank, 26 August 1993).

7 For example, the Khusro Committee argues (Govenment of India 1989: para. 1.76) that 'depoliticisation of banks' lending and recovery activities is an important precondition for successful recoveries'.

8 Sangameshwara RRB, Mahboobnagar, A.P.; see p. 255.

9 The provision for bad debt of 4.7 per cent of outstandings is criticised by the World Bank as 'not accurate and made without any assessment of the borrower's ability to ultimately repay' in the World Bank's Overview of the Khusro report (World Bank 1988: para. 8).

10 For each crop year overdues are quoted for the end of the year on 31 March. Most crop loans will have fallen due on 31 December and thus be three months overdue at that time. The proportion of these overdues that can eventually be collected will vary according to the motivation of, and resources available to, individual RRBs but we have estimated it here as 50 per cent nationwide.

11 The internal NABARD estimate of the RRB's SDI for 1992, using the same data as those given in Table 14.3.I is 109 per cent (interview Y.C. Nanda, 27 August 1993) suggesting that their lending rate would have to rise to only 35 per cent to make them viable. The difference between their estimate and ours almost certainly arises either from a more optimistic estimate of the percentage

of overdues that can be recovered or a different method of estimating non-interest subsidies.

12 Average annual rainfall in Mahboobnagar District (the catchment for Sangameshwara GB) over the period 1901–90 was 701 millimetres per annum and in Sanga Reddy District (the catchment for Manjira GB) was 802 millimetres per annum. Indian Banks' Association, *Rural Development: Selected Statistics* (annual, 1992 edition: table 140: 'Key indicators of development').

13 In the year to 31 March 1992 Gorakhpur RRB made a net profit of Rs534 lakhs ($1.72 million) (NABARD, *Statistics on Regional Rural Banks*, September 1992).

14 Joseph Heller, *Catch-22* (1961).

15 The existence of these insurance schemes (the Comprehensive Crop Insurance Scheme for certain categories of crop loan and the Deposit Insurance and Credit Guarantee Scheme for loans to priority sectors such as scheduled castes and other weaker sections) exposes banks to the temptation of making loans which they know will not be repaid in order to collect on the insurance premium. In 1989 RRBs were thus tempted to lend to Andhra Pradesh rice farmers in the middle of a flood and in August 1990 to Gujerat groundnut farmers even though no monsoon rain had fallen since June. For further detail of these scandals, see Mosley and Krishnamurthy (1995: 443) and General Insurance Corporation of India: *Fifth Annual Report, 1989–90*: 13.

16 Average rainfall in the catchment of Manjira and Sangameshwara RRBs (Medak and Mahboobnagar Districts) over the period 1901–90 was 820 millimetres, by comparison with an all-India average over the same period of 1,374 millimetres. Indian Banks Association, *Rural Development: Selected Statistics* (1989 edition: table 140: 'Key indicators of development').

17 The poverty line we are using for 1993 is the standard poverty line for the 1986–90 Seventh Plan period (Rs6,400 per family per annum) with two adjustments: first, it is updated for inflation over the period 1988–93 (to give Rs11,300/family/annum); and second, since the Planning Commission poverty line contains only food requirements, it is further adjusted upwards by Rs3,100/family/annum, which is the average 1993 expenditure on non-food items, within our sample, of individuals below the food poverty line (*Source*: author's 1993 survey, data as in Table 14.8). This approach of adjusting the poverty line for non-food necessities (as suggested by Datt and Ravallion 1994) brings the Indian poverty line to $38.7 (Rs1,199) per family per month, a figure very close to our estimated 'adjusted' Indonesian poverty line (see Chapter 11) and well below those estimated for Bolivia, Kenya and Malawi (see Chapters 10, 15 and 16 respectively).

18 Copestake (1995: 2) writes that 'viewed purely as a credit programme, IRDP breaks nearly every rule for successful development of rural financial services known to neoclassical economic man'. A further sympathetic and empirically based critique is provided by Pulley (1989). On the tendency of the supply-led approach of IRDP to impose adverse selection problems on the costs and rates of return of IRDP borrowers, see Seabright (1991).

19 Average loan size across our sample was Rs6,954 per houshold ($221, cf. $136 for the two RRBs as a whole from Table 14.7 above). Average asset accumulation over the previous year for the sample was Rs4,712 per household.

20 Interview, chairman, Sangameshwara Grameen Bank, 26 August 1993. For more information on the trend of informal lending rates, see Government of India (1989: para. 1.25).

15

FINANCING THE JUA KALI SECTOR IN KENYA

The KREP Juhudi scheme and Kenya Industrial Estates Informal Sector Programme

Graeme Buckley

You cannot tell a defaulter until the money is in the pocket
– Juhudi member

THE KENYAN ECONOMY AND THE INFORMAL SECTOR

Kenya has traditionally relied on the agricultural sector as the mainstay of its economy. This remains the case, but since independence in 1963 successive governments have attempted to diversify the economy and, with ample assistance from donors, this policy has met with some success, such that Kenya now has one of the most important industrial sectors of any black African country and tourism has become the major source of foreign exchange.

Without shying from nationalisation and direct intervention where it saw fit, Kenyan governments have repeatedly placed faith in the private enterprise system and guaranteed to protect foreign investment at the same time as promoting the 'Africanisation' of the economy. The result has been a fairly stable economy with a substantial amount of foreign investment and an extensive range and number of small to medium-sized businesses. However, the process of Africanisation has not developed as many would like. The Asian community controls a disproportionately large share of the private sector and the prospects for Africanisation have been severely

Especial thanks to Kimanthi Mutua, General Manager, and C. Aleke-Dondo and H.O. Oketch, researchers, at KREP; James Tomecko at Kenya Industrial Estates; and Hugh Scott of the British High Commission, Nairobi, for assisting with research permissions and logistics.

constrained by one of the highest birth rates in the world. With a correspondingly slower growth in output – in 1991 the population growth rate was 3.5 per cent compared to the GDP growth rate of 2.2 per cent – it is not surprising that as the opportunities for modern sector employment have been squeezed, the informal sector has expanded.

A worsening economic climate in the 1980s served to exacerbate this trend. In 1991, real per capita gross domestic product (GDP) declined for the third consecutive year, and the inflation rate has followed a deteriorating trend, rising from 12.3 per cent in 1987 to 15.8 per cent in 1990, 19.6 per cent in 1991 and 27.5 per cent in 1992 (Economist Intelligence Unit 1993). Employment growth in the modern sector has been sluggish, averaging about 2.4 per cent over the period 1988–91, compared to about 14.5 per cent in the informal sector (Government of Kenya 1992a). This informal-sector growth has interesting regional and sectoral components. The distribution of employment by province in the informal sector is given in Table 15.1.[1]

Urban centres accounted for almost two-thirds of total informal sector employment, with Nairobi accounting for almost a quarter of this total. In contrast, the relatively poor and underdeveloped Western Province had less than 7 per cent of total informal sector employment in 1991. Although one can assume that these figures – and those in Table 15.2 – give a good indication of relative contributions to informal sector activity, they are likely to underestimate the true size of the sector. A recent informal sector study claimed that: 'discussions with CBS personnel in charge of *their* survey [that is, the data presented in Tables 15.1 and 15.2] suggest that employment in these types of firms might be as high as 20–30 per cent more than what is currently captured in their published statistics' (Tomecko and Aleke-Dondo 1992).

Table 15.1 Kenya: informal sector, 1988–91. Number of persons engaged, by province

Province	1988	1989	1990	1991
Nairobi	83,350	89,856	104,952	122,308
Central	56,507	61,949	69,949	78,325
Nyanza	43,023	47,756	53,917	61,034
Western	23,382	26,422	29,936	33,675
Rift Valley	63,093	71,674	81,852	94,048
Eastern	35,937	39,609	43,639	48,403
Coast	41,070	46,245	52,349	59,364
Total	356,362	383,511	436,594	497,157
urban	233,057	245,636	284,812	331,542
rural	123,305	137,875	151,782	165,615

Source: Government of Kenya (1992a)

Table 15.2 Informal sector, 1988–91. Number of persons engaged, by activity

Activity	1988	1989	1990	1991
Manufacturing	66,096	73,167	84,876	101,109
Construction	128	144	170	200
Wholesale, retail trade, hotels and restaurants	219,131	242,574	274,585	308,455
Transport and communications	5,540	6,187	7,047	8,015
Community, social and personal services	55,456	61,439	69,916	79,378
Total	346,351	383,511	436,594	497,157

Source: Government of Kenya (1992a)

Table 15.2 shows the sectoral contribution to employment in the informal sector. The size of the growth in manufacturing employment, at 53 per cent over the period, is somewhat surprising. To an extent it may reflect the slowdown in growth of the formal manufacturing sector, the saturation of opportunities to work in the wholesale, retail, hotels and restaurants subsector and the increase in demand for cheap basic goods that is likely to occur when consumers are forced to become increasingly price-sensitive under recessionary conditions. The figure is also inflated by the inclusion of tailoring as a manufacturing activity. In practice many tailors remain in business by retailing clothes, so their inclusion under the manufacturing heading may be a bit misleading.

There is little interface between the informal sector and the formal banking sector in Kenya. Collateral requirements tend to deter informal sector entrepreneurs from seeking commercial bank loans, although the Banking Act does not stipulate collateral as a legal requirement for obtaining credit. However, the Central Bank Act does constrain the provision of non-governmental organisation (NGO) financial services to the informal sector inasmuch as NGOs are permitted to lend but not to obtain deposits directly. This problem can be, and is, circumvented by NGOs acting as proxies or intermediaries for their clients' funds which are held on deposit at commercial banks.

In July 1991, interest rates in Kenya were deregulated, allowing commercial banks and non-bank institutions to set their own interest rates. Thus, in 1991, there was a substantial increase in the cost of loans compared to previous years. The maximum (controlled) rates in 1989 and 1990 were 18 and 19 per cent respectively, but in 1991 market forces took this to 29 per cent. Although in theory this allows commercial banks to set interest rates in line with the cost of lending to individual groups of customers, for a variety of reasons it has not led to any significant increase in lending to the informal sector.

273

Although few informal sector business people have access to bank loans some hold bank accounts. Those that do have experienced a decline in the value of their savings. Although interest rates on loans and advances have remained above the inflation rate throughout the past five years, this has not been the case with deposits which have consistently yielded negative real interest rates.

Finally, in this brief discussion of the political economy as it affects the informal sector, mention must be made of the legal and bureaucratic impediments that abound. As in most other countries, informal sector businesses in Kenya operate in a very uncertain environment, on the margins of legality and vulnerable to official harassment. Much legislation that affects the informal sector is antiquated (Vagrancy Act) or inappropriate or unrealistic (Employment Act); other legislation is more logical but tends to invite corruption, such as the local government bye-laws. Thus, micro-entrepreneurs live in a very unstable environment that necessitates short-termism, which in turn has important implications for credit policy. Clearly, much legal and bureaucratic reform is needed but even assuming this, attitudes of officialdom may be stubbornly resilient to change, as Box 15.1 illustrates.

FROM RHETORIC TO REALITY? PROMOTING THE SMALL AND INFORMAL SECTOR IN KENYA

It is now widely recognised that small-scale and informal sector businesses, the latter usually referred to as *jua kali* enterprises,[2] have a vital role to play in the economy of Kenya. But this is a fairly recent view, given official sanction and popular support only since the mid-1980s. In the 1960s the sector was effectively overlooked, in the 1970s it was 'discovered' but largely ignored, and in the 1980s it was given extensive attention but little direct support. Finally, the 1990s appears to be the time when rhetoric is translated into reality and the sector not only gets the attention but also the support that it so obviously deserves. In the immediate post-independence era, the Government of Kenya was primarily committed to industrial development of the large-scale modern sector. It was implicitly assumed that only large industrial and commercial enterprises, supported by traditional import substitution policies, could generate the employment and economic growth necessary to countervail foreign-owned businesses. The potential of the small-scale and informal sectors was largely disregarded.

Those initiatives that did exist came from the government and met with little success. For example, the Rural Industries Development Centres which provided an integrated approach to rural industry promotion centred on extension services, was credited with creating a total of 3,376 jobs, less than 0.4 per cent of the 911,561 formal sector jobs at the time (Livingstone 1981).

Box 15.1 The insecurity of informality

In 1978 Mr M. obtained a licence from the Nairobi City Council to operate a food kiosk near a local cinema off River Road. Mr M. acknowledged that he was only able to get the licence with the help of the then mayor of the city. His first encounter with the city authorities was in December 1982 when, without notice, his kiosk and thirteen others in the neighbourhood were demolished.

The kiosk owners went to City Hall to protest to the authorities concerned. They explained that they had all the necessary licences to operate businesses on their respective premises. The city officials admitted that the demolitions had been a mistake, but this did not result in compensation for the loss of property. The fourteen kiosk owners then petitioned the Nairobi Provincial Commissioner who also acknowledged the mistake in the demolitions.

Following these admissions, they reconstructed their businesses with their personal savings and went back to business. In 1985, however, the demolition squads returned and they flattened all the business premises once again. The kiosk holders again petitioned the City Hall authorities and the Provincial Commissioner. As in 1982 they were told the demolitions were a mistake. Again no compensation was given for property destroyed nor were any of the city *askaris* (police) or their supervisors reprimanded for the mistake. As a way of making up for the mistake, however, they were told that they would not be required to have licences for their businesses.

In 1989 they got a rare visit from the Deputy Director of the Inspectorate of Services who, on hearing that they had been operating for three years without licences, told them to pay the fees for the past three years. All the fourteen kiosk holders raised the money and took it in one sum to the City Hall. No receipt was issued. It took the kiosk owners five months of daily visits by at least one of the fourteen kiosk owners to City Hall to get the receipts. Soon after they had got the receipts their kiosks were demolished once again. The reason given for the demolition this time was that the land on which they operated their businesses was required for another project. Since September 1989 when the demolitions took place no development has taken place on the site of the demolitions.

Source: Tomecko and Aleke-Dondo (1992)

Of a more enduring nature is the Joint Loan Board Scheme (JLBS), a parastatal which was set up in 1955 with the purpose of furthering the cause of indigenous entrepreneurs, particularly those in the service and trade sectors. The JLBS covered each district and made use of the local government apparatus to disburse essentially character-based loans at 6.5 per cent interest. The JLBS still exists, yet its inefficiency has been publicly acknowledged. According to the 1989–93 Development Plan, 'the JLBs have faced numerous problems mainly due to poor management, false accounting, the issue of fictitious loans, etc. As of 1987, the JLBs had loaned out a total of KSh87.5 million covering over 30,000 loanees of which, regrettably, 11,000 were in default involving a total of about KSh45.0 million' (Government of Kenya 1989b: 159). A Ministry of Commerce Task Force was constituted to investigate how the JLBS could be reformed. It was dissolved, its recommendations ignored, further disbursements have continued and the total arrears have risen.

In 1967 Kenya Industrial Estates (KIE) was established as a subsidiary of the Industrial and Commercial Development Corporation, which had been set up by the colonial administration in 1954. The KIE was set up to provide the type of subsidised services that industrial planners of the 1960s ensured was all the vogue: extension services, 'blueprint methods' training, provision of raw materials, marketing and procurement support, the construction of premises for rental at sub-market prices and, of course, subsidised credit. Such prescription approaches to industrial promotion in Kenya received substantial donor support and were focused on the major urban centres of Mombasa, Nakuru, Eldoret, Kisumu and Nairobi.

The KIE mandate was to assist the development of essentially medium-sized formal sector businesses. However, since 1988, a separate Informal Sector Programme (ISP) has been in existence, focusing exclusively on small businesses and providing loans averaging about KSh25,000 to businesses with growth potential. This programme is one of the two case-studies which will be discussed in detail later in the chapter.

Thus, as Kenya approached its second decade of independence, there was little in the way of small business promotion and even less in the way of support to the informal sector. The dawn of change was heralded in 1972 with the publication of an influential International Labour Organisation (ILO) policy paper on *Employment, Incomes and Equity in Kenya*, which served to popularise the term 'informal sector' and to give the concept international attention. The study outlined the importance of the informal sector as a generator of economic growth and as a mechanism for redistributing the fruits of growth in an equitable manner. For the first time, the informal sector in Kenya was identified and its development potential described. The Government acknowledged the findings of the ILO team and expressed agreement but reaction remained confined to the rhetoric of various policy statements and there was no demonstrable change in practice.

The Government remained suspicious of the informal sector and continued to promote industrial and commercial development through the existing aforementioned channels.

Interest in the informal sector waned until rekindled by a government sessional paper in 1986. Not only was the informal sector returned to the spotlight but a serious examination of current enterprise and industrial policy was undertaken. But perhaps the most pertinent observations made in this sessional paper concerned employment. The labour force was forecast to grow by 6.2 million by the year 2000 and the formal sector was projected to absorb up to 200,000. The balance of 6 million employment opportunities was expected to be provided by the agricultural and informal sectors. The sessional paper projected that the informal sector could generate over 2 million new jobs via the creation of about 1.3 million new enterprises. Such an optimistic scenario required a national strategy for small enterprise development and the foundation for this was laid in 1988 with the creation of the Centre Project.[3]

The Centre Project was a planning forum set up by the Government of Kenya in collaboration with the ILO, United Nations Development Programme (UNDP) and the German development agency (GTZ). It succeeded in setting the agenda for a national strategy on *jua kali* and small business development and in so doing created a national awareness and broad consensus on the importance of the sectors. The Centre Project turned out to be a watershed for small business development in Kenya by providing an agenda for change.

Against the background of the national projections on demographic trends, the demand for employment and the type and volume of current industrial activity, numerous documents were published throughout the 1980s stressing the significance of the small business and informal sectors. There emerged a general acceptance of the following *perceived* benefits of the small enterprise/*jua kali* sector(s) (Government of Kenya 1992c):

- it makes a significant contribution to the economy in terms of output of goods and services;
- it creates jobs at relatively low capital cost, especially in the fast-growing service sector;
- it develops a pool of skilled and semi-skilled workers who are the potential base for future industrial expansion;
- it strengthens forward and backward linkages among socially, economically and geographically diverse sectors of the economy;
- creating demand as well as supply, it has been established that 90 per cent of rural enterprise products are marketed directly to rural households;
- the sector contributes to the increased participation of indigenous Kenyans in the economic activities of the country;

- it offers excellent opportunities for entrepreneurial and managerial talent to mature;
- the sector supports industrialisation policies that promote rural–urban balance;
- the sector increases the amount of domestic savings and investment and other local resources;
- the sector can adapt quickly to market changes.

Although some of these points have not been tested empirically, there is a consensus that they are plausible. But a number of constraints also face the sector. Among those most frequently cited are:

- an unconducive legal framework, especially concerning security of tenure on business premises;
- poor infrastructure;
- demand constraints;
- limited access to managerial and technical skills and training;
- A lack of available, accessible and effective institutional credit.

In addressing these constraints, most enterprise support initiatives have focused on the latter two points. Indeed, there is now a plethora of bodies involved in small business promotion in Kenya, most of which have credit as a major component of their assistance. A Kenya Rural Enterprise Programme (KREP) survey in 1991 listed thirty-four non-governmental programmes administering various types of credit programmes (Aleke-Dondo 1991) and a government publication claims that 'other sources of limited credit to this sector have been from over 600 non-governmental organizations (NGOs) registered in the country' (Government of Kenya 1992c: 17). In addition, there are credit schemes administered by the Government, traditional development finance institutions and commercial banks.

Financial support for small and informal sector businesses

The Government of Kenya

Despite paying lip service to fulfilling a 'facilitative' rather than interventionist role, the Government remains actively involved in promoting the small enterprise sector. Apart from the KIE-ISP programme and the JLBS, the Government launched a new scheme, the Rural Enterprise Fund, in 1990.

The Rural Enterprise Fund is a nationwide rural-focused loan scheme using a character reference from chiefs (senior local government officials) as the sole proxy for collateral. There is a subsidised interest rate of 8 per cent, a one-year grace period and a repayment schedule of between two and five years. The maximum loan size is KSh100,000, though most of the individual disbursements from the total KSh400 million allocated in the first year (1990–1) have been for substantially less. Although no official recovery rates have yet been published, they are not expected to be good. The Fund has been openly politicised and is run by the same local government officials who administer the JLBS. Overall, the conditions for effective delivery of credit do not appear good but, nevertheless, the Government remains committed to the Fund.

Traditional development finance institutions

With Government participation but mostly private-sector funding, the Small Enterprise Finance Company (SEFCO) was established in 1983 with a similar mandate to KIE. However, in 1989 with funding from the Friedrich Ebert Foundation, a Double Credit Guarantee Scheme was set up to provide loans to micro-enterprises. This programme uses peer pressure, within associations of on average about twenty-two businesses, as the basis for disbursing loans, which average about KSh10,000. If the peer pressure breaks down and the association fails to honour the SEFCO loan, then a guarantee fund can be accessed by SEFCO to recover losses. With a relatively high incidence of bad debts and high operating costs the scheme has begun to flounder, and at the time of this study there was some doubt as to the continued operation of the Double Credit Guarantee Scheme.

Apart from this scheme and the KIE Informal Sector Programme, the traditional development finance institutions remain committed to the promotion of medium and large-scale industries. This is largely the case with the commercial banks, although even in these bastions of conservative lending practices glimmers of light have begun to shine out on to the small business sector.

Commercial banks

The country's commercial banks have traditionally avoided the small business sector because of the relative inadequacy of small business collateral and the high transaction costs of lending to the sector. A Central Bank directive banning banks from charging for non-financial services has also acted as a disincentive to lend to small businesses. However, a breeze of change is beginning to blow through the corridors of some commercial banks as knowledge and interest in the sector increases. But it is questionable whether this interest in small businesses has much to do with the banks' commercial interests or is more to do with the latest fashions, the desire to derive some public relations kudos and the willingness of donors to subsidise such lending programmes. Most involvement has come from the country's two biggest banks: Kenya Commercial Bank (KCB) and Barclays Bank of Kenya. The KCB is 70 per cent Government-owned and it would appear that its interest in the small business sector is determined largely by the Government's direct involvement in setting the bank's policy. To date, the most sophisticated and varied approach to small-scale business/informal sector finance appears to have come from Barclays Bank.

Barclays Bank claims that the guiding principle for their lending to these sectors is the viability of the businesses rather than their ability to offer collateral as security. Nevertheless, in all the schemes they operate they receive substantial direct or indirect subsidies from donors or donor-funded NGOs. All the schemes are targeted at specific groups such as disabled people, polytechnic graduates or women, and are mostly located in specific parts of the country.

Barclays distinguish between formal sector loans to businesses employing between ten and fifty workers and informal businesses with up to nine employees. All loans are made at commercial rates of interest. Barclays extend the greatest financial exposure to the formal sector group but the informal sector programmes are the most innovative. Although the bank's financial exposure to these schemes is negligible they do represent the beginning of a challenge to conventional bank wisdom that views such clients as beyond the remit of commercial banks. The approach may still be at arm's length but perhaps the length of the arm is shortening. At present, Barclays are reaping the benefits of good public relations but they have also begun to build a new client base and have capitalised on training opportunities for their staff. To support these programmes and to provide a fund for NGOs involved in small business/*jua kali* development Barclays have established the Barclays Bank Development Fund which is funded from a provision of 1 per cent of their annual pre-tax profits.

Non-governmental organisations

NGO lending to small businesses and especially micro-enterprise has exploded since the United States Agency for International Development (USAID) set up the Kenya Rural Enterprise Programme (KREP) in 1984. KREP was set up as an umbrella organisation for channelling money to and supervising existing NGOs involved in business promotion through credit. From the beginning KREP developed effective staff development, loan monitoring systems and planning methods, and sought to propagate these through a network of NGOs. Initially, the emphasis was on 'credit plus' activities, with credit being only one component of a wider enterprise support package. But by the late 1980s questions were being asked as to the effectiveness of the non-credit components of the NGO programmes. More particularly, there was a mounting body of opinion that favoured the minimalist approach to lending (finance-only or finance with minimal non-credit support activities) or the type of lending popularised by the Grameen Bank in Bangladesh. Thus the focus has shifted to developing effective and efficient lending institutions – what KREP calls a financial systems approach – rather than on providing a wide-ranging and by implication less easily quantifiable support package.

There are a large number of NGOs that lend small amounts of money as part of a broader poverty-alleviation programme such as those schemes administered by CARE-Kenya, Partnership for Productivity, Action Aid, Food for the Hungry and numerous religious bodies. These schemes usually serve a relatively small number of borrowers in a specific area. They are motivated by social welfare concerns and their lending schemes are usually of the revolving-funds type and tend to subsidise their social welfare functions. Thus, operational costs per loan tend to be high, and with recovery rates insufficient to maintain capital bases these schemes are likely to be completely donor-dependent.

KREP has attempted to steer the main NGO *jua kali* lending programmes towards a focus on business creation or business expansion rather than poverty alleviation. Their lending procedures follow classical group-based, minimalist guidelines, with nominal membership, loan application and annual subscription fees, compulsory weekly savings and an insurance fund. Members are usually obliged to save for a specified period of time prior to getting a loan. First loans are most commonly for KSh10,000 and repayments are made at weekly meetings, where core groups of five members called a *watano* (meaning 'the five') come together with six other groups to form what are called KIWAs (*Kikundi Cha Wanabiashara*, meaning 'group of entrepreneurs').

Table 15.3 presents information on some of the most prominent micro-enterprise credit programmes, all of which are monitored by KREP. Some of these programmes still include significant welfare components in addition to their credit operations and sometimes this appears to compromise financial discipline and, in some cases, has led to conflict over organisational objectives, particularly concerning policy on defaulters and the application of market-orientated interest rates.

One scheme of particular note is the Promotion of Rural Initiatives and Development of Enterprises (PRIDE) scheme, which was established by an enterprising American and is largely funded by USAID. This scheme is a fairly rigid copy of the Grameen Bank, with fixed loan sizes of KSh5,000, KSh10,000 and KSh15,000 for first, second and third loans respectively. Repayable over one year, loans are advanced to individuals in groups of five (with loan security resting on peer pressure within the groups). A loan insurance fund exists and there are compulsory weekly savings. The scheme operates in five districts, though most loans have been disbursed in just one of these districts (South Baringo). A distinct feature of the PRIDE loan

281

Table 15.3 KREP-supported minimalist credit schemes

	Total no.	No. of borrowers	Total amount saved	Members' loans disbursed	Repayment rate[a] (%)
KWFT[b]	300	247	1,340,000	418,400	100
PCEA,[c] Chogoria	1,080	1,878	12,492,500	3,151,895	96.2
Tototo					
Mariakani	550	397	2,112,500	611,482	91.4
Ukunda	545	383	1,980,000	608,244	91.2
Gongoni	450	327	1,790,000	278,271	90.2
PRIDE[d] (Baringo)	306	2,481	16,724,500	879,857	95.8
NCCK[e] Credit Programmes					
Kakamega	410	367	3,670,000	164,720	67
Kisumu	759	375	3,468,000	990,110	70
Nakuru	956	664	6,658,500	1,439,513	100
Mombasa	952	923	9,113,000	1,603,700	76

Source: KREP *Monthly Statistical Report,* November 1992

Notes
[a] Qualitative measure of repayment rate, i.e. total repayments received less pre-payments/ total amount due.
[b] KWFT = Kenya Women's Finance Trust
[c] PCEA = Presbyterian Church of East Africa
[d] PRIDE = Promotion of Rural Initiatives and Development of Enterprises
[e] NCCK = National Council of Churches of Kenya

scheme is a credit-rating mechanism which is based on repayment punctuality and which encourages good borrowers to open accounts with Barclays Bank. The scheme, therefore, is aimed at graduating micro-entrepreneurs into the formal banking system and it projects that 5–10 per cent of its clients will 'graduate'. Although only in existence since September 1989, PRIDE lives up to its name in having a vibrant, expansionist policy. With donor funding, it has already expanded to Guinea and plans were afoot in late 1992 to open an office in Tanzania. But in Kenya its high growth projections have resulted in a high client attrition rate with KSh3,444,321 of compulsory savings forfeited to defray defaults, as at November 1992, which represented 21 per cent of total disbursements (KREP *Monthly Statistical Report,* November 1992).

An internal document (PRIDE 1992a) indicates that each PRIDE branch is expected to extend 2,460 loans over a three-year period (1,000 first loans, 1,000 second loans and 460 third loans). These multi-sectoral loans are expected to finance business expansion, diversification and a limited number of start-ups and to generate real income increases of about 40–50 per cent over two years. A model branch requires approximately KSh1.8 million to utilise as a loan fund to on-lend to clients at the level cited above and a further KSh800,000 to cover operational and initial capital costs until it can cover all its costs from operating revenue. Together with a contribution to head office costs and assuming thirty branches, this is forecast to occur after five years.

A PRIDE evaluation carried out in South Baringo in 1991 revealed that a typical PRIDE client is thirty-five years old, married, with five dependants and with a few years of primary school education. He/she is a sole proprietor with a business started with KSh5,500, owns a rural micro-enterprise that makes a net profit of less than KSh2,000 per month on sales of less than KSh10,000, and has average business assets of less than KSh15,000. Year-on-year waged employment creation was estimated at 10 per cent. Female clients (42 per cent) tended to be less educated than male clients, started their businesses with less capital, were more likely to be dependent on their business as their only source of income and reported a higher return on their investments (Noballa in KREP 1992: 19).

Except for the KREP Juhudi Scheme, which is one of the two case-studies to be discussed later, the PRIDE programme is probably the most ambitious and arguably the most dynamic of the minimalist lending schemes in Kenya. The PRIDE programme also represents the most blatant attempt to replicate the Grameen Bank model – for example, it seeks to bring about changes in the attitudes and values of its members through group 'education', in addition to its central concern with business development. The PRIDE approach is undoubtedly very ambitious and perhaps over-ambitious. At present, it seems to suffer from a desire to grow (*à la* Grameen Bank) at a rate which seems to outstrip the ability or willingness of its clients to respond. As previously mentioned, PRIDE clients have had to forfeit a large volume of savings to keep the programme afloat and this has resulted in the low savings to disbursements ratio shown in Table 15.3.

Irregular informal credit sources

Finally, mention should be made of irregular or spontaneous informal sources of credit. By implication, informal economies operate in tandem with traditional social and cultural forces that predicate economic behaviour. Any discussion of credit in Kenya, therefore, must refer to the communal nature of economic activity in the context of a tribal society. Whether in a rural or urban setting the Kenyan entrepreneur operates in a competitive but sharing community, where obligations extend beyond the household to the broader kinship group. Such obligations, of course, are usually bound by the principle of reciprocity.

Probably the most prominent type of community-organised finance is the *Harambee* movement which was set up following independence as a purely indigenous mechanism for bringing about *uhuru* (independence). *Harambee* is a self-help movement that takes the form of cash, labour or materials contributions from all sectors of the *wananchi* (people) and also

Table 15.4 Juhudi Kibera and ISP: institutional features

Feature	Juhudi	ISP
Date established	1990	1988
Institutional status	NGO	Parastatal
Source of funding	Mostly USAID	Mostly GTZ
Funding	(USA)	(Germany)
Eligibility	Kenyan micro-entrepreneurs operating in the catchment areas, with less than KSh200,000 in assets	Licensed and viable businesses
Requirements	Group (*watano*) members must not be related	Owners must be able to develop a business plan and furnish collateral to cover 40 per cent of any loan. They must complete a client orientation programme, be owner-managers, employ less than 9 people and have existed for more than one year. Preference given to manufacturing or service enterprises
Target group (actual)	Micro-entrepreneurs, small traders who operate in a Nairobi slum	Small businesses operating in trading centres or urban areas nationwide
No. of borrowers	1,177	1,717
Female borrowers (%)	51	23
Lending method	To groups of 5 No collateral Payment by bank cheques	To individuals Collateral required Payment by purchase order
Loan size	Fixed: KSh10,000 (1st loan) KSh15,000 (2nd loan) KSh20,000 (3rd loan)	Variable: Average KSh25,170 Min: KSh10,000 Max: KSh50,000 (1st)
Repayment period	12 months	2–3 years
Repayment method	At weekly meetings	Monthly, collected by field officers
Incentives to make early repayment	Interest calculated on weekly declining balance for 13, 17, 26 or 39 week repayment cycles. But savings must correspond to a full 52 week cycle	None

Table 15.4 Continued

Feature	Juhudi	ISP
Savings	Compulsory and voluntary each week	None
Interest rate (%)	27 (declining balance)	18 (declining balance)

Sources: KREP and ISP internal documents

from firms and government. Initially the focus was on infrastructural projects but in the past decade emphasis has shifted to social development projects in health, education and welfare. The contribution of *harambee* to national development since independence has been significant: 'the total nominal value of *Harambee* projects between 1965 and 1984 accounted for 11.8 per cent of Gross Fixed Capital Formation' (Government of Kenya 1989b: 31). If a micro-entrepreneur gets into financial difficulties, the chances are that he will think about organising a type of *harambee*. This means that he will call on relatives and kinfolk to provide money or labour for him to get over his difficulties. The organising of a *harambee* is often an entrepreneur's first strategy for raising finance.

If a *harambee* is not possible or does not solve the problem, moneylenders may be used. However, the practice of lending money for pecuniary gain is not common in Kenya. The fieldwork uncovered only one case of a respondent having used an African moneylender and the few other cases uncovered involved Asian moneylenders. When asked about moneylenders, respondents gave the impression that such practices would be shunned by the community: one respondent remarked that, 'Asians could do it because they were not African'. However, as economic pressures grow such views may change and, especially in the urban setting, moneylending may become more prevalent. Indeed, some respondents in the shanty town sample (see Appendix 1), felt that this was already beginning to occur, as they knew of people who would provide such loans. It appeared that moneylender loans were likely to be short-term, often for about a month and typically incurred a 25 per cent (per month) interest rate. As so few of the survey respondents admitted to having had any experience of moneylenders, it proved impossible to ascertain any relationship or 'impact' between the case-study institutions and moneylender behaviour.

Of far greater significance were the ubiquitous ROSCAs (Rotating Savings and Credit Associations) which are commonly referred to as 'merry-go-rounds'. The fieldwork in the shanty town revealed that almost 20 per cent of respondents were in a merry-go-round. These are groups of between five and thirty people (in rare cases there may be less than five or more than thirty) who have something in common, such as living in the same neighbourhood or working in the same type of business. They are based on the important values of trust and honour. Each member of the group agrees to contribute the same fixed sum each week or month into a savings pool. In the sample, slightly more contributed monthly and, not surprisingly, the average amount contributed was substantially greater for monthly contributions than for weekly ones. Each time a contribution is made, one member receives the pool of money (a loan), which is subsequently repaid in the form of the weekly or monthly contributions. Each member gets a turn to receive the pool of money, the last recipient successively acting as a creditor until he receives the final pool. Thereafter, a second cycle is begun. For example, in a group of ten members, each contributing KSh100 per week, each member would receive KSh900 (plus his KSh100) at his turn then contribute KSh100 each week for ten weeks before receiving a second loan in week eleven, when the cycle is repeated.

Default on repayments was rare but some respondents remarked that the group required the pledge of an asset as security before becoming a member of the group but there was no case of this security having been foreclosed. The time value of money was generally ignored but some groups changed the order of rotation for each cycle, thereby introducing an extra element of equity. Although ROSCAs generate savings and loans out of deferred consumption, the tendency appeared to be to translate this deferred expenditure into non-productive capital consumption rather than income-generating investment, typified by the large number of ROSCA pools that went into the purchase of hi-fi equipment. Nevertheless, ROSCAs in Kenya – as in many other places – operate successfully, they represent a vital source of voluntary financial intermediation and a traditional solution to financial needs that is likely to comprise features crucial to the successful delivery of modern credit systems. At the time of fieldwork (1993) KREP was exploring a programme to lend to ROSCAs.

This chapter focuses on two lending institutions: the Juhudi Kibera Credit Scheme (Juhudi), which is run by the Kenya Rural Enterprise Programme (KREP), and a government lender, the Informal Sector Programme (ISP) of the parastatal Kenya Industrial Estates. A summary of their main institutional features is presented in Table 15.4.

THE KENYA RURAL ENTERPRISE
PROGRAMME: JUHUDI KIBERA
CREDIT SCHEME

KREP was established in 1984 as a USAID-funded Private Voluntary Organisation (NGO) project and incorporated locally as a company limited by guarantee and with no share capital in 1987. Its mission is to 'serve as a catalyst for facilitating people's participation in the development process and enhancing their standards of living', by strengthening informal sector credit programmes with the objective of generating employment and

Box 15.2 KREP: some problems of success

At the core of KREP's success is a particular management or organisational culture. Employing competent, committed and motivated individuals attracted by market-based salaries and performance-linked bonuses, KREP has propagated a long-term perspective founded on an holistic approach to staff development. The focus is on a 'financial systems approach', with an enterprise culture among its staff (as distinct from a welfare-orientated focus) and the institutional objective is to achieve long-term financial sustainability rather than to adopt a project or programme focus.

The participatory and creative management style is something that the KREP staff are rightly proud of. Its very existence, let alone success, is somewhat surprising in an environment invariably characterised by the 'big man', hierarchical approach to management. However, the very style and success of KREP is starting to place serious strains on the organisation's ethos and operational capacity.

First, due to a high workload, there are feelings that time for 'discussion and debate' has been reduced and that this is threatening to stifle the organisation's acclaimed dynamism and creativity. Second, the steady flow of visitors who want to analyse or replicate KREP's approach serves to further disrupt operations and places greater demands on management time (the author's study is, of course, guilty on this count).

Third, the quality of KREP's staff leaves the organisation exposed to headhunters, especially from international organisations which may be able to offer motivated individuals inducements that KREP cannot match. Fourth, KREP is likely to have to refine its role by concentrating on what is does best, as ultimately it is likely to be difficult to reconcile the objectives of operating a micro-enterprise 'bank' with acting as an umbrella support organisation for NGO credit programmes. If, as is likely, the latter function is phased out, KREP may well find it difficult to disentangle itself from its past successes. For example, in certain activities (such as the propagation of relatively sophisticated management information systems among NGOs) KREP may have created a degree of dependency on its technical assistance and operational support.

increasing incomes (KREP n.d.: 1). Initially, KREP acted as an umbrella organization concerned with supporting other NGOs to develop sustainable credit programmes, but it has diversified into a number of related activities (see Figure 15.1) and it is with KREP's own lending programme (Juhudi) that this study is concerned.

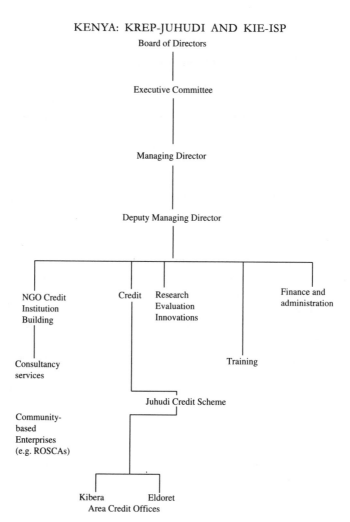

Figure 15.1 KREP organisation chart

KREP was a donor creation and it remains totally dependent on donor finance for funding operations but not for technical assistance. Since May 1992 when the American managing director was succeeded by a Kenyan it has become fully staffed by an efficient, well-qualified and well-paid local staff. The main financial input has come from USAID and amounts to about $13.5 million over the period 1984–94. Additionally, there are a number of smaller donor inputs, including almost $500,000 from the Ford Foundation. The success and high profile of KREP has attracted further donor interest, principally from the British Overseas Development Administration (ODA), which at the end of 1992 finalised a £1 million, five-year project to open two new Juhudi branches. Thus, in 1989 KREP relied on donors for 87.8 per cent of its income, for 98.5 per cent in 1990 and for 90.6 per cent in 1991. The Juhudi Credit Scheme in particular has attracted considerable donor interest, following the success in piloting the scheme in what is seen as a very difficult area – there is a view (probably mistaken) that if Juhudi can succeed in Kibera, it should succeed anywhere. USAID specifically allocated $700,000 to fund the Juhudi Eldoret branch and the ODA funds are specifically for the Juhudi part of KREP. As at the end of 1992, KREP was forecasting that a Juhudi branch (Area Credit Office), which operates as a distinct profit centre, could become profitable (*not* sustainable) after two years. This projection is based on a branch costing KSh1.7 million per year to run and covering 1,800 members. Sustainability – distinct from profit-ability in that it implies planned growth in lending volumes – is forecast to occur after five years when revenue from members' savings will cover profitable on-lending. KREP is keen to expand the Juhudi Credit Scheme as a means to generate income to cover its *own* sustainability. This income comes via the profit at which KREP on-lends funds to its 'subsidiary' (Juhudi Credit Scheme) and it is estimated that KREP could become fully sustainable when 15–20 Juhudi branches are operational.[4]

The Juhudi Credit Scheme operates in two areas: Kibera (since September 1990) and Eldoret, Kenya's sixth biggest town, located in the northern Rift Valley (since September 1991). Piloting the scheme in an area of high-density urban settlement like Kibera guaranteed substantial economies from minimising transaction costs but carried the risk of exposure to a potentially transient and unwieldy population. In each area credit office, which covers an area with a radius of about 5 kilometres, there are six credit officers who are directly responsible for KIWA operations and who report to the area credit officer, as shown in Figure 15.2. Each credit officer is ultimately expected to be responsible for ten KIWAs or sixty *watanos*, each with 300 borrowers.

The Juhudi Credit Scheme adopts and adapts the group-based structures popularised by the Grameen Bank and it is the *watano* which serves as the unit for the screening and processing of loan applications. But Juhudi (meaning determination) is a minimalist lending programme and the groups are mandated to serve only a banking function and have none of the credit-plus activities associated with the Grameen Bank 'centres'. Targeting pro-cedures are fairly non-specific and any Kenyan citizen over eighteen years of age, who has or intends to start a micro-enterprise located within the designated catchment area (Kibera) and who has (business) assets of less than KSh200,000 is eligible to join. Initially, credit officers will publicise the credit programme by holding a *baraza* (meeting) to encourage interested entrepreneurs to form a *watano*. After a short period of induction training from the credit officer, the *watano* chairperson and treasurer are elected and they are responsible for upholding group and financial discipline. Each member must pay a membership fee of KSh100 and purchase a passbook

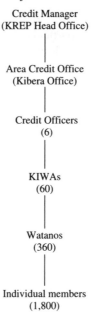

Credit Manager
(KREP Head Office)

Area Credit Office
(Kibera Office)

Credit Officers
(6)

KIWAs
(60)

Watanos
(360)

Individual members
(1,800)

Figure 15.2 Juhudi organisation chart

costing KSh50. *Watano* members must understand and agree to the principle of co-guarantee, which extends from the *watano* to the KIWAs. They must meet weekly and each member must make their compulsory savings of KSh50, which are deposited in commercial bank accounts and held in the joint names of designated signatories of both the Juhudi Credit Scheme and the particular KIWA. The KIWA members christen their KIWAs with some emotive and pertinent names such as: 'Let's try'; 'Hope'; 'Success'; 'Togetherness'; 'Let's not perish'; 'Help ourselves'; 'Defend yourself'; and 'Discipline' (obviously, the names appear in the vernacular and these are approximate translations). After eight weeks, three members of the *watano* become eligible for loans of KSh10,000 and after a further four weeks and subject to satisfactory savings and repayments, the next two members (usually the chairperson and treasurer) become eligible for their loans. Each loan is issued following the completion of a simple loan application form for each borrower, which has to be accompanied by a fee of KSh100. Loans are successively approved by the *watano*, the KIWA and finally the credit officer, and they must be secured against the savings and any tangible assets of the individual (first level), against the savings of the other four *watano* members (second level), and finally against the savings of the other twenty-five KIWA members (third level). Each loan is disbursed in the form of a cheque and repayment is made weekly over fifty-two weeks to the KIWA treasurer, who, after

290

verification by the credit officer, is responsible for banking the money. The loan sizes are fixed at KSh10,000 for a first loan, KSh15,000 for a second loan and KSh20,000 for a third loan (at the time of the research nobody had yet obtained a third loan) and repayment can be made in thirteen, seventeen, twenty-six, thirty-nine or fifty-two weeks (in practice all loans are initially scheduled to be repaid over fifty-two weeks) and the interest charged is calculated on a weekly declining balance equivalent to 27 per cent simple interest.[5] Apart from the intention to simplify the lending process to minimise transaction/appraisal costs, a further motivation behind the fixed loan amounts was the desire to have systematic savings configurations. If members in the same KIWA had different loan amounts, different savings rates would have to be calculated to ensure that the benefits and risks of group loan guarantee were equitably distributed. As the scheme expands and borrowers graduate to bigger loans this will obviously become necessary, but the Juhudi experience suggests that when a group-based credit programme begins and its target clients are fairly homogeneous, fixed loan amounts are likely to be most appropriate.

The real costs of a Juhudi loan amount to considerably more than the published interest rate. The true cost is made up of a number of financial commitments that each member must make in order to get a loan, most of which have already been mentioned. In addition there is a Reserve (insurance) Fund for loans that fall into default because of some unforeseen calamity such as illness or death. Such loans are written off as bad debts without affecting members' savings, but the costs of this are borne collectively by all members as the Reserve Fund is a sinking fund financed from a 1 per cent levy on each borrower's monthly loan repayments. Thus, the real cost of a Juhudi loan for KSh10,000 comprises a number of different elements and is shown below.

With a principal of KSh10,000 the total interest payable is (KSh20 × 52 weeks) = KSh1,440, which implies a flat interest rate of 14.4 per cent, equivalent to 27 per cent simple interest on a declining balance. But, imputing the following costs yield a different figure:

	Ksh
Membership fee	100
Loan application form fee	100
Passbook	50
Reserve/Insurance Fund	52
Total	302

Therefore, the total sum payable on the loan is KSh1,440 + KSh302 = KSh1,742. This implies an effective flat rate of 17.42 per cent which is equivalent to 32.66 per cent simple interest on a declining balance.

Everybody in the sample was repaying on a fifty-two-week cycle but for

Table 15.5 Juhudi Credit Scheme accounts: performance statistics

	Juhudi Kibera	*Juhudi Eldoret*
No. of months in operation	24	12
No. of members	1,177	1,260
Male:female ratio	579:598	649:611
No. of *watano* groups	235	252
No. of KIWAs	40	42
No. of loans disbursed	1,777	1,026
Amount disbursed (KSh)	19,346,000	10,295,000
Amount due (KSh)	18,080,499	4,961,656
Amount paid (KSh)	16,464,139	4,745,975
Amount of outstanding loans (KSh)	5,325,282	5,908,391
No. of loans in arrears	270	121
Amount in arrears (KSh)	97,362	47,015
Amount prepaid (KSh)	129,636	276,152
No. of loans in default	452	203
Amount of defaults (KSh)	1,291,492	168,665
Amount declared as bad loans (KSh)	0	0
Quantitative repayment rate (%)[a]	91.1	101.2
Qualitative repayment rate (%)[b]	90.39	5.7
No. of repeat loans	237	28
Branch operating cost (KSh)	2,720,094	2,008,634
Cost per loan on branch cost (KSh)	1,531	1,958
Cost per KSh lent on branch costs (KSh)	0.14	0.20
Investment income (interest + fees) (KSh)	2,176,837	800,168
Sustainability index on branch cost (%)[c]	80.0	39.8
Total amount saved (net) (KSh)	2,818,694	1,607,227
Amount forfeited to defray defaults (KSh)	1,244,628	127,883
Average savings per member (KSh)	2,395	1,276
Savings/amount of outstanding loans (%)	53.0	27.0

Source: KREP *Monthly Statistical Report*, November 1992
Notes
[a] Quantitative repayment rate = total repayments received/total loan amount due.
[b] Qualitative repayment = total repayments received less prepayments/total amount due.
[c] Sustainability index = investment income/branch operation costs.

those who choose to repay on a shorter cycle, the burden of these fixed costs is inversely related to the length of the repayment cycle.

Furthermore, Table 15.5 shows that each Kibera borrower had, on average, forfeited KSh1,057 of savings to defray defaults (KSh1,244,628/ 1,177), and if this is imputed into the above equation, the effective flat interest rate becomes 28 per cent, still assuming a KSh10,000 loan (that is, double the published rate).

Table 15.5 shows the in-house performance statistics for the Juhudi Credit Scheme at the two branches in Kibera and Eldoret at the time of the fieldwork. Generally, the figures appear quite consistent between the two branches, one half the age of the other. Membership and group formation at Eldoret appears to have risen quickly in its first year of existence, overtaking the number of members, *watanos* and KIWAs that have been built up over two years at Kibera. The same does not hold for disbursements, which have shown a more conservative growth. The older Kibera scheme has twice as many arrears and double the amount of loans in default (but over seven times the total *value* of defaults and almost ten times as much in savings has been forfeited to defray defaults) which is reflected in the lower repayment rates. Only half as much prepayment of loans is occurring among Kibera borrowers. These figures appear to illustrate the typical 'growing pains' that so many innovative lending programmes experience. However, the Kibera branch has good sustainability indicators relative to the Eldoret branch: with costs per KSh lent at 0.14 compared to 0.20 at Eldoret and almost three times as much investment income, which contributes to a sustainability index of 80 per cent compared to 40 per cent at Eldoret. The implication of these figures appears to be the simple rule that the key to institutional success rests on minimising default and maximising cost efficiency. Details of the Juhudi Credit Scheme accounts are given in Table 15.5.

In 1991, the Subsidy Dependence Index (SDI) for the Juhudi Credit Scheme was 217 per cent, implying that the scheme would have to raise its interest rate by a factor of 2.17 or to 59.68 per cent in order to eliminate the subsidy. For details of the SDI see Yaron (1991 and 1992).

THE INFORMAL SECTOR PROGRAMME

The ISP began operations in 1988 and is housed in the Nairobi head office and regional offices of its parent body, Kenya Industrial Estates. But apart from sharing office space and some 'consumables' and, at the policy level, reporting to the KIE managing director and board, the ISP seeks to operate as autonomously of its parent as possible. Field stations are manned by one or two field/credit officers depending on their size, and these are grouped into their respective provinces, for which there is a designated field supervisor (see Figure 15.3). The ISP is a nationwide programme seeking to provide loans to informal sector businesses that are able to demonstrate growth potential. Specifically, the programme is concerned with increasing the value added that this sector makes to the Kenyan economy. Although the name suggests otherwise, clients are more accurately classified as small businesses rather than *jua kali* or informals. Indeed, all clients must have a licence to be eligible for a loan, which is clearly at variance with usual definitions of the informal sector.

The ISP is another donor creation (like KREP), financed largely from German (GTZ) funds. Since it was created in 1988, GTZ has contributed Deutschmark 2.4 million, representing almost 75 per cent of total capitalisation and has supplied additional inputs in the form of technical

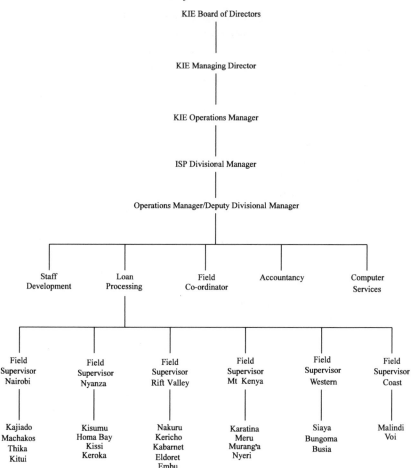

Figure 15.3 ISP organisation chart

assistance. Further sums have come from Belgian, Swedish and Norwegian overseas development assistance. The ISP also received a small sum of capital funding from its parent KIE (that is, the Government of Kenya) amounting to less than 2 per cent of total capital funding and it receives an indeterminate but possibly negligible amount of cross-subsidisation on its recurrent budget from the KIE. The ISP income account runs at a recurrent loss, the loanable funds account is continuously being depleted and there is no savings function, so the ISP is not in a position to seek sustainability in terms of being self-financing. The ISP is a parastatal and although it has sought to distance itself from its parent it suffers from a lack of operational independence. Thus, it has been prone to political interference and undoubtedly some clients perceive ISP loans as 'political money' which does not have to be repaid. The ISP cannot hire and fire staff independently or offer them performance-based contracts (currently, periodic incentive schemes are run for field staff and they feature token 'prizes' such as penknives or T-shirts). Any revenue-generating activities must first be approved by the Government, which also controls the ISP interest rate. Thus, the ISP operates with the implicit objectives of minimising costs and maximising impact. See Table 15.6 for a summary of the financial accounts for the Informal Sector Programme.

An approximate Subsidy Dependence Index for 1992 is 267 per cent, which implies an increase in the lending rate by a factor of 2.67, equivalent to a rise to 48.08 per cent to eliminate the subsidy.

Table 15.6 provides a snapshot of statistics relating to the four stations (or branches) of the ISP covered by this study and the aggregate figures for the whole programme. In terms of repayment rates, Nakuru and Murang'a tend to perform above average, while Bungoma and Kakamega are a little below average. However, the overall repayment rates are dragged down by four particularly poorly performing stations in Western

Table 15.6 ISP: performance statistics

	Overall	Kakamega	Bungoma	Murang'a	Nakuru
Loans disbursed	1,717	73	100	106	125
Loans disbursed in past year	655	26	55	33	30
Loans closed in past year	162	14	16	15	23
Total amount disbursed (KSh)	43,216,835	1,736,500	2,685,147	2,794,000	3,219,000
Total outstanding (KSh)	29,311,503	1,144,153	1,813,447	1,610,419	1,569,813
Total payments to date (KSh)	23,390,249	968,641	1,372,152	1,699,436	2,280,982
Advance payments (KSh)	950,042	69,441	71,398	47,091	59,210
Total arrears (KSh)	6,871,296	354,113	472,523	156,152	474,870
Average loan size (KSh)	25,170	23,788	26,851	26,358	25,752
in group A (%)[a]	38	34	40	49	48
in group B (%)	29	30	26	31	31
in group C (%)	11	5	16	11	5
in group D (%)	23	30	18	8	16
matured loans (%)	21	36	10	8	34
Repayment rate (quantitative) (%)	79.8	77.3	77.4	94.0	84.6
Repayment rate (qualitative) (%)	76.6	71.7	73.4	91.4	82.4

Source: KIE/ISP *Monthly Management Report,* January 1993
Notes [a] Due to rounding, these figures do not always add up to 100. See also notes to Table 15.5.

and Nyanza Provinces which have repayment rates in the low sixties. The classification into groups is an in-house monitoring tool and the groups are defined as follows (legal action against default is instituted against those in group C):

Group A borrowers are completely up to date with their repayments;
Group B borrowers are one to two months in arrears;
Group C borrowers are three to six months in arrears;
Group D borrowers are more than six months in arrears.

With approximately a third of all borrowers in groups C or D, Kakamega and Bungoma stations appear to be in considerable difficulties, especially the former, which has 30 per cent of its borrowers more than six months in arrears. The four poorly performing stations alluded to above each have in excess of 50 per cent of their borrowers in group D. Thus, it is a little surprising that so many new loans were disbursed in Kakamega and Bungoma over the preceding year. This had not been the case with the four poorly performing stations, where there were few new disbursements over the preceding year, reflecting ISP policy to concentrate on better-performing regions. However, the ISP will have to be cautious in following this path as there is a strong correlation between region (and by implication, ethnic group/tribe) and repayment rates and any perceived bias in credit allocation is likely to invite political interference.

ISP loans are targeted at manufacturing or service enterprises rather than retailing activities. Each field station is given an ambitious target of loans to be disbursed each year and clients should be clustered in and around specified locations. This cost-effectiveness measure is a recent adaptation introduced because, when the programme was first launched, the objective was to spread the loans as widely as possible to ensure equality of opportunity and maximise geographical coverage, but the high costs of this approach rendered a change of course necessary. Additionally, each assisted business must have existed for more than a year and should not employ more than nine people. The owner should be of 'good character' and must also manage the business, but at least one business surveyed did not qualify on this latter criterion: the owner, a politician, had apparently no involvement in the running of his business and had delegated all operations to an employee.

Loans range from KSh10,000 to KSh100,000, the average being about KSh25,000; the maximum for first-time borrowers is KSh50,000. The current interest rate is 18 per cent simple interest on a declining balance, but at the time of the survey the ISP was petitioning its parent ministry to allow an increase to 22 per cent. Considering that repayment is phased over two to three years and the 1992 year-end inflation rate was in excess of 25 per cent, the current rate is highly favourable to borrowers. Thus, the ISP believes that raising the interest rate to 22 per cent will not affect demand for loans and is likely to generate extra revenue amounting to KSh50 per loan per month or over KSh1 million per year at the current portfolio size. Loans can be used for either working capital or fixed capital.

To get a loan, clients have to complete a fairly rigorous application procedure which increases the transaction costs associated with each loan but ensures effective screening of applicants. The process of candidate selection is termed a 'self-selection process' by the ISP because candidates disqualify themselves during the process if they do not meet the basic minimum criteria. Initially, the process is likely to begin with a *baraza* (public meeting) after which prospective clients are asked to complete a 'Sales and Raw Materials Form' (which has to be bought for a nominal fee). From this point onwards applicants go through a process of close monitoring. This form is assessed by the field officer during a visit to the entrepreneur's business place. If successful, the prospective borrower will then have to attend a Client Orientation Programme (COP). This is a gathering of between ten and fifteen potential clients who come together to receive an introduction to the ISP, to learn how to make a business plan and to correctly estimate the size of the loan for which they wish to apply. The COP is conducted by the field officers usually for a total of about ten days spread over four or five weeks. After the COP, the field officer completes approval forms for successful participants which are passed on to an Approvals Committee. The business plan is also a vital output of this stage as it is supposed to be adopted by the entrepreneur as a type of operational blueprint for his or her business (it also comprises useful baseline data for in-house client impact studies). Successful completion of the COP paves the way for a loan. But the applicant must first furnish a chattel mortgage to cover 140 per cent of the value of the loan (the loan can be offset against this) and obtain two guarantors who serve to underwrite the loan. Assessment and supervision of these requirements rests with the field officer. Finally, a letter of recommendation from the chief (a senior local government official) is needed. Thereafter, loan agreements are drawn up at the head office and loans are disbursed in the form of cheques in favour of a certain supplier (a type of purchase order). Additionally, a small sum of cash can also be disbursed at the discretion of the field officer. Repayment by standing order is encouraged but most borrowers prefer to deliver the monthly repayments personally to the field office or to have the credit officer collect the instalments from his/her business, for which a fee is charged. The whole procedure involves the field officers in making a detailed assessment of the applicant's business and loan application, and contrasts strongly with the simple Juhudi loan application procedure, which involves minimal loan appraisal and is largely based on client demand.

Once the loan has been disbursed, the clients are closely monitored using a client performance report. Each client will also be ascribed a credit rating, as described previously, which will determine his or her chances of receiving a subsequent loan in addition to being the main indicator for taking action against those in arrears. When arrears persist and debtors cannot be persuaded to repay, the first recourse for field officers is seizure of the chattel securities. Thereafter the guarantors will be approached and, failing this, legal proceedings will be instituted. But difficulties have plagued these strategies. First, the policy of asset seizure has resulted in the ISP being overwhelmed with repossessed goods, the value of which often fails to cover the cost of default, and the seizure has often been treated by the defaulter as an indication that the loan obligation has been written off. Second, the legal option is a cumbersome last resort that is severely constrained by a legal system riddled with backlogs and bottlenecks.

Although the ISP is first and foremost a lending institution, it has a policy of 'non-interventionist client development'. This means that field officers will provide 'information' services to clients. One mechanism for this consists of business information sheets, which are practical instruction sheets on various aspects of business management, originally prepared by two British volunteers and provided for a nominal fee. However, the uptake of these has been disappointing. Client help stops short of extension services, which are seen as interfering in the decision-making process of individual entrepreneurs. Thus, the ISP explicitly aims to generate business growth – the creation of a business plan at the client induction stage is another feature aimed at business development – in contrast to the Juhudi Kibera Scheme, where the nature of the market limits (but does not prevent) business growth and where success may more accurately be measured in terms of poverty alleviation.

In addition to the standard loan programme, the ISP has also piloted two other lending programmes. For those areas with lower potential for manufacturing and service businesses there is a Small Retailers Scheme which provides loans of KSh5,000 to KSh25,000 on terms similar to those above. Also, in response to requests from entrepreneurs, a Short-term Working Capital Scheme has been set up for existing clients with a consistently good repayment rating. This scheme provides loans of up to KSh50,000 for bulk purchases of working capital. Once again, chattel mortgages to the value of 140 per cent of the loan are required but repayment is made in a one-off lump-sum payment after three or six months. The interest charged is 2 per cent per month plus an administration fee of 4 per cent of the amount of the loan. Neither of these schemes falls within the remit of this study but they do demonstrate flexibility on the part of the ISP to respond to entrepreneur demands and to diversify its product portfolio and, by implication, its revenue sources.

ENTREPRENEUR PROFILES

The two programmes target two different types of business. For Juhudi, the target group is shanty town dwellers who are essentially involved in 'survival economics'. Their income-generating activities are usually for the purposes of short-term sustenance, few entrepreneurs are in a position to develop their businesses for longer-term growth and capital accumulation, which is obviously especially difficult and risky in an environment like Kibera. For those more-successful business people, any sustained surplus is likely to be repatriated to their rural homes, so measuring credit impact is very difficult as the actual impact may be 'transferred' elsewhere. The typical ISP client is somewhat more sophisticated, has a bigger business (both in terms of capitalisation and in terms of employees) and is more likely to be reliant on his business for his sole source of income. Overall, as we shall see below, ISP clients appear to have a greater potential for business development but Juhudi clients, by virtue of the low levels from which they start, have a greater *potential* for growth *per se*.

The entrepreneur profiles presented in Table 15.7 show that the two sets of clients (as distinct from their business activities) are fairly similar except for the male bias among the ISP sample. The average ISP client is likely to be slightly older and better educated than the average Juhudi client but both groups have relatively high levels of formal education. For example, 10 per

Table 15.7 Entrepreneur profile

	Juhudi Kibera	KIE-ISP
Average age (years)	5.5	39
Age range (%)		
<20 years	1	0
>19 and <30	31	15
>29 and <40	45	46
>40 years	23	39
Marital status (%)		
married	83	93
single	15	4
Male/female ratio		
% female	54	18
Average household size	4.48	6.82
Educational status (%)		
tertiary	1	10
secondary >2 years	40	33
secondary <3 years	13	17
primary	40	40
non-formal	6	<1
Head of household (%)	59	88

Source: Author's survey
Note: Percentages are rounded to the nearest whole number.

Box 15.3 Gender dimensions to the credit programmes

Although Juhudi groups are self-selected, the credit staff, half of whom are female, are responsible for ensuring a gender balance in membership, and this is achieved. At the time of the survey, 51 per cent of members were female. Watano and KIWA groups tended to be mixed and there was no evidence to suggest that either male or female members were consistently better or worse repayers. However, from those surveyed, female-owned enterprises tended to have fewer assets (about three-quarters of the value claimed by male respondents), to have sales averaging about two-thirds of those reported by male members and to employ on average about three-quarters of the average number employed in male-owned enterprises. The range of activities undertaken by men and women was similar within the obvious gender divisions (all beauty parlours and hair salons were run by women and all shoemakers/repairers were men, for example). Given the research methodology employed, there was no evidence to suggest that differences in the gender of the borrower were correlated to enterprise efficiency or loan impact.

The ISP professes gender neutrality and adapts its delivery mechanism so as not to disadvantage women. For example, the ISP permits the use of non-land collateral (in view of the dearth of land titles held by women) and does not prevent women from borrowing money independently of their husbands (commercial banks usually require the husband's signature before lending to women). Despite this, the ISP appears to be biased towards male entrepreneurs. This is principally because its target of manufacturing and service industries is likely to embrace more male-owned enterprises.

Given this, the *actual* gender distribution may be fairly representative of the target population. At the time of the survey about a fifth of borrowers were female and most were either involved in tailoring or allied activities or owned hair salons. Among those surveyed, the average-sized loan to a female business was KSh24,190, compared to the overall average of KSh28,795, while female-run businesses were generating average sales of KSh18,881 compared to the overall average of KSh23,597. The survey found no evidence to suggest a significant gender difference in repayment rates but an in-house survey in 1991 concluded that women had a slightly better repayment rate than men from a sample of 100 (twenty women) (Eigen *et al.* 1992).

It is also notable that the staffing of the organisation is heavily biased in favour of male employees: from a total of about forty field officers and supervisors, there were only two women (see ibid. for further details).

cent of the ISP sample had some tertiary education and 41 per cent of Kibera entrepreneurs had completed three or more years of secondary schooling. Only one ISP respondent had no formal education, but this is not surprising as it is a condition of acceptance that ISP borrowers be literate (for the purposes of understanding the various documents needed to get a loan and in order to prepare a proper business plan).

The difference in average household size is not as significant as it appears – 4.48 in Kibera as against 6.82 for the ISP sample – due to the fact that the Kibera residents had an average of 2.36 dependants not resident in Kibera but in their rural home. If these people (usually children) are added to the figures for household size, the actual average household size of the two sets of respondents is almost identical. But there was a noticeably greater chance of the typical ISP client being the head of the household – 88 per cent of ISP respondents said they were heads of their household compared to 59 per cent among the Juhudi sample. This reflects the gender distribution of the two samples: 54 per cent of Juhudi respondents but only 18 per cent of ISP respondents were female. This, in turn, largely reflects the targeting policy of the ISP towards production and service activities which men dominate compared to the preponderance of hawkers/traders in the Juhudi sample, which is more likely to exhibit a more even gender distribution.

ENTERPRISE PROFILES

The typical enterprise financed by the two programmes is presented in Table 15.8 which provides clear evidence to demonstrate the difference between the two target groups. The most obvious difference is in the types of enterprise financed. At least 58 per cent of Juhudi clients were exclusively traders, most of whom sold either clothes or foodstuff. In reality this figure is likely to be considerably higher, as many respondents who claimed to be in the service and/or production sectors were likely to get a considerable percentage of their income from retailing activities, such as the dressmaker (production) who gets most of her income from selling secondhand clothes (retailing) or the restaurants (service) that are basically in the business of retailing drinks and 'fast foods'. In contrast, only 4 per cent of the ISP sample were wholly traders and two-thirds had some element of production in their business. Also, the ISP sample covers a greater range of types of activity, evidenced by the data for those activities listed and by the fact that 32 per cent of the ISP clients were classified as 'other' type of enterprise, compared to 18 per cent for the Juhudi sample.

The age profile of the businesses sampled was fairly consistent between the two programmes with the majority of businesses being between three and ten years old: 67 per cent in Kibera and 56 per cent of the ISP sample. Interestingly, almost 20 per cent of the Juhudi sample had been in business

Table 15.8 Enterprise profile

	Juhudi Kibera	*KIE-ISP*
Category of enterprise (%)		
production	2	26
service	21	17
trade	58	4
production & service	1	18
production & trade	10	6
production, service & trade	10	18
service & trade	3	11
Type of enterprise (%)		
retailing	58	4
tailoring	17	26
carpentry	1	13
metalwork	3	20
shoemaking/repairs	3	5
other	18	32
Average age of enterprise (years)	6	9
of which (%):		
1–2 years	16	10
3–5 years	31	25
6–10 years	36	31
11+ years	17	34
Nature of premises (%)		
rented	58	84
owned	25	14
other	17	2
Location of premises (%)		
same building as home	39	18
urban	100	13
rural town	0	53
rural trading centre	0	34
Record keeping: with some	60	89
written records (%)		

Source: Author's survey

Note: Percentages are rounded to the nearest whole number.

for ten or more years and one business had existed for thirty-seven years, which suggests that there is a substantial body of permanent businesses in Kibera. Overall, the average age of a business was six years for Juhudi businesses and nine years for ISP-funded businesses.

The remaining information in Table 15.8 confirms the greater degree of sophistication of the ISP businesses. Although the question concerning written records largely relied on the truthfulness of the respondents (it was rarely possible to verify physically whether there really were records or what the records represented), which is likely to lead to an exaggeration of actual practices, it is reasonable to assume that the relative proportions of those who claimed to keep some written records (60 per cent for Juhudi and 89 per cent for the ISP) reflects reality inasmuch as one would expect bigger, more-sophisticated businesses to keep more (and better) records than smaller, less-sophisticated businesses. Finally, Table 15.8 gives an indication of the type of premises from which the respondents carried on their businesses. Some 84 per cent of ISP respondents had designated premises that they rented (58 per cent for the Juhudi respondents) and 39 per cent of Kibera residents operated their businesses from the dwelling where they lived, compared to only 18 per cent of ISP clients.

The typical ISP client has a bigger enterprise than the typical Juhudi client, so it is not surprising that ISP clients tend to be more dependent on their business for their only source of income (80 per cent for ISP sample and 62 per cent for Juhudi sample) as shown in Table 15.9. The same holds true in terms of the main source of income, but the difference is slightly smaller: 97 per cent of ISP respondents relied on their enterprise for their main income (compared to agricultural sources, for example) which was slightly greater than the 89 per cent of Juhudi respondents. In nearly all cases, the remaining 11 per cent of the Juhudi sample relied on another enterprise for their main source of income and appeared to be using the Juhudi loan to build up a second or alternative business. This may well be an enlightened strategy of diversification in the face of limited or saturated markets for many lines of activity. The figures for the distribution of household sources of income (which, for the Juhudi clients, refers only to the Kibera household) shows that 12 per cent of ISP households had three or more sources of income, which in most cases comprised agricultural and livestock income from *shambas* (family farms) and not other enterprises. The fact that almost half of the Juhudi households had more than one income source (that is, enterprise) makes it extremely difficult to

Table 15.9 Income sources for ISP and Juhudi respondents (%)

	Juhudi Kibera	KIE-ISP
Borrowers with only one source of income	62	80
Borrowers whose main source of income is the target business	89	97
Household sources of income		
households with 1 source	55	60
households with 2 sources	39	28
households with 3 sources	6	7
households with 4+ sources	0	5
Average no. of household members with a cash income	1.51	1.59

Source: Author's survey
Note: Percentages are rounded to the nearest whole number.

trace the impact of the loans to a specific enterprise: there is likely to be a high degree of loan fungibility between enterprises (a practice that does not contravene any Juhudi rules and is accepted provided timely repayments are made).

SAVINGS AND CREDIT HISTORIES

This section will analyse the credit and savings situation of the two target groups of borrowers, specifically in terms of their relationships to the two lending institutions. There are many different types of credit and one that is often overlooked is credit between businesses. Many larger-scale businesses 'survive on credit' by juggling their creditors and debtors, but the survey found this option to be unavailable for most entrepreneurs in both samples. In the ISP sample 71 per cent extended credit to their customers but only 29 per cent ever obtained credit from their suppliers. Among the Juhudi members, 67 per cent gave credit (mostly to customers from Kibera) but only 24 per cent received it (from suppliers usually from outside Kibera). To make sales, it often appears necessary for the respondents to provide credit but their relative lack of bargaining power places them at a disadvantage when it comes to getting credit from suppliers, who are likely to have far greater leverage.

In terms of the two lending programmes, the first point to note is that in neither case has Juhudi or the ISP made a significant contribution to new business start-up. This is not surprising with the ISP as their loan conditions are supposed to preclude funds for business start-up – yet 6 per cent of respondents still claimed to have used their loan to start their business – but with the Juhudi Scheme operating in an area of massive under- or unemployment, it is surprising that only 3 per cent had used their loan to fund a new income-generating activity. Possibly, the *watanos* are attracting like-minded people – that is, existing business people – who may well be risk-averse when it comes to sanctioning *and* guaranteeing new ventures. In both the ISP and the Juhudi samples, most business people had started principally with personal savings (Juhudi 66 per cent and ISP 81 per cent) and any additional funds were likely to have come from family members or friends.

Respondents cited the importance of the credit officers in publicising the respective schemes, especially among ISP clients, one-third of whom attended public meetings organised by the credit officers precisely because the credit officer had first visited them and told them of the event. Almost half of all Juhudi members had first heard of the credit scheme through friends or neighbours, over a quarter directly from credit officers and a similar number from enumerators. The KREP Research Department is prolific and has conducted many data-collection exercises among Kibera residents and in the process the enumerators have directly and indirectly

Table 15.10 Savings and credit profile of Juhudi and ISP clients

	Juhudi	ISP
Credit		
never applied to any formal lending institution for a loan (%)	96	72
obtained a loan from a formal lending institution (%)	2	13
obtained finance through membership of a ROSCA (%)	20	4
used a moneylender (%)	<1	3
Savings		
personal savings in formal bank accounts (%)	59	95
average savings for borrowers with deposits (KSh)	6,865	8,327
average savings for all borrowers (KSh)	3,227	7,962
Range of savings (%)		
<2,500	25	28
>2,499 <5,000	25	13
>4,999 <10,000	30	29
>9,999 <20,000	13	17
>19,999 <30,000	6	11
>29,999	0	<1
Average date of first deposit	mid-1984	mid-1986
Range by year of first deposit (%)		
1990–2	38	38
1985–9	18	43
1980–4	21	9
before 1980	23	11

Source: Author's survey
Note: Percentages are rounded to the nearest whole number.

publicised the Juhudi Credit Scheme. Both programmes have adopted the philosophy that the best grassroots publicity is through the grapevine, especially if it comes from satisfied borrowers. Most clients obtained their loans *because* they are made available rather than because of particular features of the lender's 'package' (most borrowers seemed very interest rate inelastic, for example). Nevertheless, when pressed to name the most attractive features of the lending institution, ISP borrowers tended to place most importance on the repayment terms (30 per cent), followed by the training and support given in the preparation of a business plan (17 per cent) and the rate of interest (15 per cent). The ease of application and the use of peer-group pressure as a substitute for collateral were cited by Juhudi members as being the most attractive features of the credit scheme (55 per cent), followed by the opportunity to make compulsory regular savings (20 per cent) and the repayment terms (16 per cent).

Conventional lending institutions appear to have quite different approaches to the two groups of borrowers, which tends to reflect the different economic status of the two groups. Among the informals of the Juhudi Scheme, 96 per cent had never applied for a loan from a formal lending institution, three respondents had applied but had been refused and three had been successful in getting a loan (see Table 15.10). All three successful applicants were women and they had obtained their loans from three different commercial banks. Others had sought financial help from family and friends (56 per cent) or from membership of a ROSCA/merry-go-round (20 per cent). There was also one case of a Juhudi borrower getting a loan from another NGO, one recipient of a JLBS loan and just one case of a respondent having used a moneylender. A moneylender is taken to mean somebody who lends money on a regular basis for personal, pecuniary gain and not simply a family member/friend/business associate or some other person who makes an *ad hoc* loan to a business person in difficulties. Although some may have used a moneylender and preferred not to admit it, discussions with KREP staff confirmed the paucity of moneylending activity in Kibera and it seems reasonable to conclude, perhaps for the reasons stated above, that moneylending to urban informals in Kenya is relatively uncommon.

From the ISP sample, 72 per cent had never applied to any formal lending institution; but 13 per cent had succeeded in getting a commercial bank loan and half of these had obtained their loans from the Kenya Commercial Bank. A further 7 per cent had loans from an NGO (in some of the surveyed areas there had been a history of donor-funded NGOs making loans for income-generation purposes, usually as part of a broader welfare-focused poverty-alleviation project). There were four cases (3.5 per cent) of borrowers having obtained government loans (two JLBS loans and two Rural Enterprise Fund loans). Membership of ROSCAs was much less common than in Kibera, perhaps reflecting the difficulty of partaking in a ROSCA when businesses are widely dispersed throughout rural areas. Less than 3 per cent of respondents had used a moneylender and in each case the loan had come from an Asian wholesaler. Again, as with the Juhudi sample, the incidence of loans from family and friends was high. Thus, it seems reasonable to conclude that many borrowers had loans from the ISP and particularly from Juhudi because of an absence of alternatives.

The other side of the banking equation involves formal savings (bank account deposits) and in this respect the picture is quite different. As ISP clients are encouraged to have bank accounts for making loan repayments, it is not surprising that 95 per cent had funds on deposit at a bank and 15 per cent had deposits in two different banks. More surprising is that 59 per cent of Juhudi clients had savings in a bank account. Additionally, of course, *all* Juhudi members will have savings on deposit at commercial banks as part of the compulsory Juhudi savings fund. This money is not in

---

Box 15.4 The sample frames

Juhudi-Kibera sample

Type 1 (T_1) = borrowers servicing their first loan ($n = 50$)

Type 2 (T_2) = borrowers servicing their second loan ($n = 50$)

Type 3 (T_3) = Juhudi members who have not received a loan, but are due to receive one soon ($n = 34$)

Type 4 (T_4) = a similar questionnaire for randomly selected non-borrower informal sector entrepreneurs, i.e. not members of Juhudi ($n = 26$)

ISP sample

Type 1 (T_1) = borrowers who had completed repayment of their first loan or completed 12 months-plus of repayments on their first loan ($n = 65$)

Type 2 (T_2) = borrowers repaying a second loan ($n = 14$)

Type 3 (T_3) = borrowers who had got their first loan within the last three months or those applicants who had undergone a Client Orientation Programme (COP) and were waiting for their loan disbursement ($n = 20$)

Type 4 (T_4) = borrowers servicing their first loan but who had made fewer than 12 months repayments and more than 3 months ($n = 15$)

Type 5 (T_5) = a similar questionnaire for randomly selected, comparable non-ISP borrower informal sector entrepreneurs ($n = 26$)

---

individual accounts and is not readily accessible. Furthermore, these savings make up a substantial cumulative fund for commercial banks which are unlikely to on-lend to the sector. Thus, the savings fund constitutes a net transfer from the informal sector to the formal banking sector. There was evidence to suggest that getting loans with Juhudi was correlated with opening a bank account. Of the sample that had not yet obtained a loan (T_3) 44 per cent had a bank account, this figure rose to 60 per cent for those servicing their first loan (T_1) and to 68 per cent for those servicing their second loan (T_2), all of which compared favourably to the non-Juhudi, non-borrower control group (T_4), where only 38 per cent had bank accounts (see Box 15.4 for definitions). Clearly, rather than directing loans at entrepreneurs who already had bank accounts, Juhudi membership appears to be encouraging greater use of banking accounts among its members. A similar situation exists for ISP clients. The figures referring to year of first deposit in Table 15.10 show that 81 per cent of respondents had opened accounts since 1985 and of the 47 per cent who had opened accounts during the period 1989–92 (ISP started in late 1988) it would be reasonable to assume that a large proportion did so *because* of their ISP loan. Correspondingly, only 58 per cent of the non-borrower (T_5) sample had bank accounts. Both schemes, then, appear to play a facilitative role, graduating their clients into the savings side of the formal banking sector.

Table 15.10 also shows that the average Juhudi member *with* savings on deposit had KSh6,865 compared to KSh8,327 among the ISP sample.[6] The comparatively small difference between the two groups is widened considerably when we consider the whole sample for each group – this is due to the greater number of Juhudi members who do not have any savings (41 per cent) compared to the ISP clients (5 per cent). Focusing on the Juhudi members with savings, only 19 per cent had savings greater than the value of a first Juhudi loan and half had less than KSh5,000. Men were likely to have almost twice as much savings as women – KSh9,477 compared to KSh5,029.

LOAN PROCESSING: INDIVIDUAL AND GROUP-BASED APPROACHES

The Juhudi scheme is very efficient in terms of disbursing loans. The process of loan appraisal is a simple one largely devolved to peer approval, and most loans should be disbursed in the standard format that requires an eight-week wait before the first three members receive loans, followed by a further four weeks before the last two receive their loans. Thus, it is not surprising that most respondents had less than eight weeks to wait between applying for and getting their loans. The Juhudi credit officers are likely to assist members throughout the process of loan application, approval and disbursement but ultimately it is the members of each *watano* who must have the prime responsibility. However, the credit officer is likely to play a greater role in appraising the needs of second-time borrowers. This process contrasts with the thorough and usually lengthy screening process adopted by the ISP. The author's survey found that the average borrower waited thirty-five weeks for his or her loan. Almost 8 per cent of respondents waited over a year to get their loans, the modal time between application and disbursement was fifty-two weeks (23 per cent of respondents) and the shortest period was ten weeks, claimed by just one respondent. The ISP management is aware of this problem and estimates the average turn-around time between loan appraisal and disbursement for the whole programme to be about 180 days. This has been identified as a major weakness and the plan is to halve this figure.

Table 15.11 shows loan disbursal by amount among ISP clients (the Juhudi loans are for predetermined amounts, so cannot be analysed in

Table 15.11 Frequency distribution of ISP
loans by size

Average loan size (KSh)	28,795
Range of loan (%)	
<20,000	26
>19,999 <30,000	31
>29,999 <40,000	21
>39,999 <50,000	6
>49,999 <75,000	13
>74,999	3

Source: Author's survey
Note: Percentages are rounded to the nearest whole
number.

the same way). The average loan is KSh28,795, slightly larger than the overall programme average of KSh25,170, which may be explained by the sample distribution drawing on greater numbers of respondents in Bungoma and Murang'a, which are stations with above-average loan sizes. Over half the sample got loans between KSh19,999 and KSh40,000 and only 14 per cent and 5 per cent got loans comparable in size to the normal first and second Juhudi loans respectively. As ISP loans are given in kind via purchase orders, it is fairly easy to trace their use by type: 61 per cent were for working capital items only; 22 per cent were for a mixture of working and fixed capital; and 17 per cent were for fixed capital only. Although some purchase orders may be abused, the ISP management believed this was of an insignificant magnitude, primarily due to the close supervision of clients by credit officers. In contrast, it is very difficult to trace the actual use of Juhudi loans, although in virtually all cases the loan was ostensibly for working capital.

In keeping with the overall institutional performance figures, the ISP sample demonstrated a worse repayment record than the Juhudi sample. Of the latter, 88 per cent claimed to be fully up to date with their repayments and the remaining 12 per cent were in arrears largely because of unforeseen calamities such as the destruction of business premises (by fire, flood and so on) or a family death (which, for funeral expenses alone, usually places a considerable financial burden on the remaining family members). Among the ISP sample 19 per cent admitted to arrears. This figure is undoubtedly an underestimate for the stations surveyed, as the research failed to capture a representative number of defaulters. Although suitable respondents were identified, defaulters usually refused to co-operate with the research or in some cases ran away (literally) when they saw the researchers coming. It would be reasonable to assume that the figure above may underestimate the true number of defaulters by as much as 50 per cent (cf. Table 15.6).

The loan processing method and collateral requirements of the two programmes are very distinct and imply significant variation in institution transaction costs. Unfortunately, data do not exist to quantify and compare the actual differences in transaction costs but a good proxy is the staff to borrower ratio. For servicing 1,177 members, the Juhudi Kibera branch employs eight staff (excluding secretaries, watchmen, messengers, and so on) or 147 borrowers per branch worker. In comparison, the ISP branch network serves 1,717 borrowers and employs about forty field officers and supervisors, giving a ratio of forty-three borrowers per branch worker. Furthermore, the administrative to field staff ratio for the ISP is nearly 1:1, a figure which the ISP is planning to reduce to 1:2. It is also obvious that substantially greater travelling costs are incurred by the ISP field workers, as borrowers are dispersed throughout each district and monthly repayments are normally collected by the field workers; this contrasts with the Juhudi approach which shifts the repayment costs onto the borrower groups (the ISP makes a charge for loan collection but this does not cover the actual cost).

The dynamics of group-based lending

The creation of *watanos* rests with individuals motivated to obtain credit so they tend to form and register quickly. The *watanos* are then grouped into KIWAs by the credit officers and this can take some time; it also means that there are two distinct levels of peer pressure and responsibility, with the *watanos* being more closely knit and harmonious than the KIWAs. Indeed, there were some respondents who felt uncomfortable about guaranteeing the loans of people in the KIWA who were strangers even though, in the case of default, the financial costs to the KIWA may be negligible, as it is the individual defaulter's savings that are forfeited first, those of the other *watano* members next and finally, if necessary, those of the KIWA members. Among those surveyed, 32 per cent had experienced forfeiture of *watano* savings to cover a defaulter and over a third of these members had responded to this by curtailing or stopping their contributions to voluntary group savings and some had even tried (but were obviously prevented from) stopping their compulsory savings contributions. As the financial exposure of *watano* members is potentially high, many groups have made verbal (and sometimes written) agreements to pledge some property as security against default. Usually this is a fixed asset such as a sewing machine, tools or radio, and seizure of this is obviously designed to prevent members having their savings fund affected by a defaulter. Obviously, most groups preferred to use moral pressure before resorting to asset seizures and if there was good reason for someone getting in arrears, such as illness or death in the family, it was common for other members to help out. Occasionally, those in arrears had their repayments paid for them by other members of the *watano* or KIWA in exchange for work. An in-house survey of KIWAs found that slightly more than a third of KIWAs had resorted to the use of police and legal mechanisms in dealing with default and slightly less than a third had set aside a common fund among themselves to cover defaults (Oketch 1992).

The importance of ensuring *watano* discipline and solidarity is stressed from the beginning when potential members have to undergo a thorough orientation and induction process. When the programme was first launched this process was not fully developed and a number of teething problems centring on group solidarity and cohesion were evident. A number of *watanos* broke up and there were cases where *watano* officials had to be replaced for being either inactive or dictatorial (KREP 1992). It is a requirement of membership that clients forming *watanos* should be known to each other; this, it is believed, is likely to solidify peer pressure. Thus, many *watanos* tend towards some form of homogeneity whether it be in terms of gender, tribe, religious or enterprise similarity, and in most cases *watano* members tend to be neighbours. But at the KIWA level membership is mixed. One KIWA in the survey comprised people from nine different tribes. Most respondents felt that multi-tribal groups would reduce faction-alism and bring balanced views on business options and skills. It was found that certain activities, such as food selling, shoe-shining or *jiko* stove-making, for example, are practised predominantly by particular tribes, so if KIWAs were mono-tribal it was likely that there would be less diversified activities, and thus experiences, than if the KIWAs were multi-tribal. This is probably why KIWA members were keen to claim that groups should comprise people from different tribes. Interestingly, one group comprised Kikuyu and Kamba members plus one Luo, who was the chairman. However, some Juhudi members pointed out the benefits of being in a group where everyone spoke the same mother tongue and more than one KIWA had experienced disputes because some members communicated in their local language and not the *lingua franca*, Kiswahili. Overall, there was no evidence to suggest that any particular type of group composition is any better or more effective than any other. The overriding criteria for effective group dynamics appeared to be that members knew each other and were fully aware of the purpose of group solidarity and joint liability.

Each KIWA meeting takes place at a set time and place each week and is conducted by the KIWA chairperson (who is elected by the members) in the presence of a Juhudi credit officer. Meetings often begin and end with a prayer but otherwise the formal agenda comprises loan disbursements (by cheque) and repayments (which includes contributions to compulsory savings and the loan insurance fund). Most meetings take about an hour and rarely are all thirty members present. One-third of the surveyed KIWAs did not have a full complement of registered members and on average only slightly above two-thirds of members were present at each meeting. This average may underestimate the usual norm due to the heavy rains at the time of some of the survey work, but an in-house evaluation concluded that over half of the surveyed groups contained at least one member who hardly ever attended meetings (Oketch 1992).

Most groups seemed to function fairly well. There were occasional misgivings among some members, especially concerning the compulsory savings, covering for defaulters in other *watanos* (as mentioned above) and group/meeting discipline. On the first point, it was evident that many members did not know either the value of their cumulative individual contribution or the total value of their group savings. In some cases, even the treasurers of some KIWAs – those who are responsible for collecting and banking monies – seemed unclear on this issue. One group wanted to employ an 'auditor' to check their accounts and there were a few groups where the treasurer had clearly defrauded other members. Surprisingly, few people complained about access to their savings even though, in normal circumstances, they can only be accessed when a member leaves the credit scheme. Most people seemed to regard it as a price they had to pay to get their loans. In addition to the compulsory savings, virtually all groups had tried to set up a voluntary savings club but almost half of them had failed due either to a lack of commitment or because of a lack of trust in those responsible for managing the funds. A number of respondents claimed that the Juhudi repayment terms were too restrictive and suggested that grace periods be introduced to match enterprise cash flows. The common example quoted was of a vegetable seller being able to turn over sales and generate income in a much shorter time period than a carpenter. A similar number also favoured fortnightly (or, in a few cases, monthly) repayments, implying that weekly repayments carried a high opportunity cost in terms of the time taken in attending weekly meetings. Another often-repeated request was for variable-sized loans to match business needs and entrepreneur abilities rather than a blanket-sized loan. However, none of those who suggested this appeared to realise the added transaction costs (and possible increases in rates of interest) that this would imply.

The issue of group/meeting discipline inevitably reflects the different levels of commitment that different people bring to the groups. Most groups operated a fines system for lateness or absence from meetings, with the monies collected used for group costs, such as photocopying, buying stationery or to add to group savings. Inevitably, however, the amounts involved were negligible and in many cases it was evident that late-comers or absentees were able to justify their behaviour and thus avoid the fines. It was quite common for absentees to send somebody else with their weekly repayments. There was also evidence of some members habitually delaying repayments for some weeks before paying up, a practice which clearly reduces an individual's effective interest rate.

Within the obvious cultural parameters, meetings did not appear to be dominated by any particular groups in a systematic way. There were a few cases of members with bigger businesses dominating meetings and at least one case of members appearing inhibited by these 'bigger guys'. There were mixed views on the group size – most seemed to think that thirty was just about manageable – but some wanted bigger groups because they felt that this would entitle them to bigger loans and others sought smaller groups in the belief that this would facilitate quicker disbursement of loans.

Overall, the KIWAs and *watanos* were operating successfully and were fulfilling their primary purpose of securing loans for a hitherto neglected group of poor people. However, the groups have none of the systematic welfare and educational inputs of the Grameen model. Of course, the groups serve as forums for the exchange of advice and ideas among business people – what this may mean in tangible terms, though, is not clear. There were cases of a group having used voluntary savings to buy property for rent (but there was subsequent disagreement over the allocation of rental income among the group); one group planned a *harambee* to raise funds for a nursery school and another was collecting to start a 'youth polytechnic' for Kibera residents. There was a high incidence of intra-group lending (with, presumably, many cases where one or more members of a *watano* had provided the cash for another member's loan repayment) and generally an impressive degree of participation in decision-making within groups. However, it is unclear how far *watano* and KIWA activities are likely to extend beyond their immediate credit and savings functions. Although the survey of Juhudi groups referred to above concluded that: 'Perhaps one of the greatest contributions of the Juhudi Scheme may eventually turn out to be the creation of an opportunity for the clients to come together and to pool resources . . . [and] the main impact of the scheme on the entrepreneurs might eventually turn out to be its positive influence on group dynamics and performance' (Oketch 1992: iv), it may well be that tangible returns to this scenario require a little more in terms of systematic credit plus inputs and a general improvement in the economic environment in which Juhudi members operate.

CREDIT IMPACT ON BUSINESS ACTIVITY

This section focuses on income, assets, sales and employment and seeks to identify how these variables have changed in the context of a borrower's relationship to a lender. It is, of course, exceedingly difficult to obtain reliable data on the above quantities using direct responses from entrepreneurs whose records usually come from their heads, and virtually impossible to attribute changes in these variables to a particular loan or loans. Nevertheless, this section attempts to draw some conclusions by making the assumption that the loan(s) from the respective institution is the major exogenous variable to impact on the business over the period covered by the research.

Enterprise employment

The average number of employees varies considerably between the two programmes, as can be seen in Table 15.12, which shows the levels of employment at the time of the survey. It is clear that the average ISP client is generating over twice as much employment as the average Juhudi client. Indeed, six ISP businesses had ten or more employees compared to the Juhudi businesses, of which only six (four of which were 'hotels') had five or more employees. However, there is an important caveat to enterprise employment for the Juhudi sample. The survey revealed a tendency for entrepreneurs in Kibera to be employees themselves in addition to running their own enterprises. In about a fifth of cases this employment was more or less concurrent with running the enterprise. This is obviously a risk-spreading strategy and the Juhudi Credit Scheme does not discriminate against such part-time entrepreneurs, but clearly such behaviour may ultimately compromise business efficiency, meeting attendance and possibly loan repayment.

The gender distribution of the Juhudi sample shows that female-owned businesses were twice as likely as male-owned businesses to have no employees. Indeed, the average number of employees per female business was 0.9, compared to 1.56 in male-owned businesses. The gender composition of the ISP sample makes valid comparison on this point difficult, but the relative difference between employment generation in male and female businesses follows a similar pattern.

One of the most important indicators of success for micro-enterprise lending programmes is the impact on employment. Unfortunately, it is very

Table 15.12 Employment in ISP and Juhudi-funded businesses

	Juhudi Kibera		KIE-ISP	
Average number of full-time employees (paid & unpaid)	1.20		3.18	
Those with (%)	All	All	M	F
0 employees	42	7	66	34
1 employee	31	15	45	55
2 employees	12	26	75	25
3 employees	7	25	56	44
4 employees	4	11	60	40
5+ employees	4	6	50	50

Source: Author's survey
Note: Percentages are rounded to the nearest whole number.

Table 15.13 Changes in full-time paid employment for Juhudi borrowers

| | Employees per enterprise | | Growth rate |
	One year ago	At time of survey	(%)
T_1	0.84	0.92	10
T_2	1.30	1.56	20
T_3	0.62	0.56	−10
Overall	0.96	1.07	12
male	0.69	0.77	11
female	0.26	0.30	14
T_4	0.81	1.08	33
male	0.62	0.88	44
female	0.19	0.19	0

Source: Author's survey
Note: Percentages are rounded to the nearest whole number.

Table 15.14 Changes in full-time paid employment for ISP borrowers

| | Employees per enterprise | | Growth rate |
	One year ago	At time of survey	(%)
T_1	3.03	3.15	4
T_2	3.07	4.14	35
T_3	2.20	2.45	11
T_4	2.67	3.00	13
Overall	2.84	3.13	10
Nakuru	2.68	3.09	15
Bungoma	3.46	3.91	13
Murang'a	1.75	1.88	7
Kakamega	4.35	4.53	4
T_5	2.47	3.05	23

Source: Author's survey
Note: Percentages are rounded to the nearest whole number.

difficult to measure properly changes in real employment. It is notoriously difficult for many micro-entrepreneurs to distinguish between full-time, part-time and casual employment because one employee can successively qualify for each category in any given time period. The equation gets even more complicated when one tries to include family members as employees. There is also extensive underemployment in many businesses and it is extremely difficult to ascertain the extent of productive employment, even assuming one could define such a thing. Nevertheless, Tables 15.13 and 15.14 contain some interesting findings on what the respondents regarded as changes in total full-time paid employment over the preceding year.

The first point to note is that 78 per cent of all Juhudi respondents had not experienced any change in employment in their businesses over the previous year and a further 8 per cent had experienced a decline in employment, so the relatively impressive growth figures in Table 15.13 should be interpreted in the context of applying to only 14 per cent of the sample. The overall growth rate in employment of 12 per cent is derived from a heavily skewed distribution with a few respondents reporting particularly impressive increases in employment. Although those members who have been with Juhudi the longest (T_2) demonstrate highest growth rates among the sample of Juhudi members and the incidence of negative growth is recorded for members yet to obtain their first loan, there is nothing to suggest that Juhudi members are doing any better at employment generation than non-Juhudi entrepreneurs (T_4). In fact, the contrary seems to be occurring. However, the Juhudi respondents appear to be more inclined to employ females (in absolute and growth terms) than their non-Juhudi competitors.

Unfortunately, it is beyond the scope of this research to enter into a detailed analysis of the cause-and-effect relationships on employment changes within micro-enterprises but there are a number of significant observations which can be gleaned from the data collected. First, employment was positively related to income and assets. Those businesses with above-average income employed on average more than twice as many people as those businesses with below-average income. Similarly, those businesses with above-average total assets employed on average 1.55 employees compared to those with below-average total assets employing on average 0.79 employees. Retailing businesses employed on average a third of those employed in non-retailing businesses. And finally, on an anecdotal note, virtually all respondents who had experienced a growth in employment and income also kept records.

There was evidence to suggest that wage rates for Juhudi member employees tended to be lower than for the corresponding non-borrower group. The male/female wage rates were fairly similar between Juhudi member groups, but the lower wage rates for Juhudi members compared to the non-borrower (T_4) group may be accounted for by the fact that there was a greater tendency for Juhudi members to employ women (even then, only 1 in 3.5 employees were women compared to 1 in 6.5 in the T_4 group) which may have deflated average wage rates. However, this analysis should be interpreted in the context of the sample distributions: for Juhudi members there was an even balance between men and women while the non-borrower sample largely comprised men. In contrast, the ISP sample was 82 per cent male which reflects the male bias of the programme and 1 in 5 employees were female, compared to 1 in 7 among the non-borrower group. The survey found that ISP clients paid 13 per cent more to their employees than the non-borrower group and, on average, ISP clients paid their male employees 16 per cent more than their female employees.

Employment in the ISP sample is shown in Table 15.14; although ISP clients have significantly higher levels of employment per enterprise, the overall employment growth rate is slightly less than in the Juhudi sample. The particularly high employment growth rate of 35 per cent within the T_2 group may be attributable to the fact that to get a second loan a borrower must have successfully repaid a first loan and have by implication demonstrated potential for business growth, which among small business is likely to be correlated with employment creation. Although ISP clients are likely to employ more people than respondents in the non-borrower group, the latter experienced higher employment growth – 23 per cent compared to 10 per cent. Only 53 per cent of ISP clients had not experienced a change in the number of employees over the preceding year, 18 per cent had shed labour and two-thirds of the 29 per cent who had increased employment had taken on one extra person. The rate of employment creation in the T_5 non-borrower group was above the overall ISP client average and there was not one case of a non-borrower reducing employment. Once again, non-borrowers appear to be doing better at generating employment growth than the target borrower group. The ISP sample displayed the same trend as the Juhudi sample in terms of demonstrating a positive relationship between the volume of assets, size of income or sales and the level of employment.

One of the major determinants of performance for the ISP is location. It has already been noted that repayment rates vary between regions, and this is strongly correlated to ethnicity/tribe; Table 15.14 provides further evidence on the importance of client location. The average business in Murang'a (predominantly Kikuyu) employs just 1.88 people compared to 4.53 employees in Kakamega (predominantly Luhya). Although the following logic is somewhat terse, these two branches present a dilemma in that the relationship between number of employees and successful loan repayment is an inverse one. There are, of course, many other factors which should be considered to fully understand this illustration which is not simply an anecdotal case. Above all, it probably indicates the importance of understanding culture as a precondition to understanding Kenyan (and African) entrepreneurial behaviour.

Enterprise capitalisation

Tables 15.15 and 15.16 present information on fixed, current and total business assets. This was probably the most 'difficult' area of the questionnaire and the findings should be treated with caution. The two biggest difficulties in collecting reliable data involved the correct valuation of assets and the proper separation of assets. First, there was a noted tendency for respondents to overestimate the real value of their assets (especially fixed assets) by ignoring depreciation and *appreciating* the value to correspond with the current purchase price of the particular item. Second, there was

Table 15.15 Frequency distribution of business assets: Juhudi scheme (%)

	Current assets	Fixed assets	Total assets
Range:			
<5,000	26	39	13
>4,999 <10,000	18	13	10
>9,999 <20,000	22	17	18
>19,999 <30,000	16	9	15
>29,999 <40,000	11	5	8
>39,999 <50,000	3	5	10
>49,999 <100,000	4	7	19
>99,999 <200,000	0	4	6
>199,999	0	<1	<1

Source: Author's survey
Note: Percentages are rounded to the nearest whole number.

Table 15.16 Frequency distribution of business assets: ISP scheme (%)

	Current	Fixed	Total
Range:			
<5,000	7	2	0
>4,999 <10,000	6	4	3
>9,999 <20,000	9	10	3
>19,999 <30,000	18	9	2
>29,999 <40,000	10	12	5
>39,999 <50,000	9	15	9
>49,999 <100,000	18	25	39
>99,999 <200,000	8	9	21
>199,999 <400,000	4	10	7
>399,999	<1	4	11

Source: Author's survey
Note: Percentages are rounded to the nearest whole number.

the inevitable difficulty in distinguishing between household assets and business assets, especially when the business was undertaken at the person's home.

Table 15.15 shows that two-thirds of the Juhudi clients operated with less than KSh20,000 in current assets and slightly more operated with less than KSh20,000 in fixed assets. There were thirty respondents (22 per cent) who claimed to have no fixed assets (these were retailers essentially operating without premises by hawking their wares from the passageways of the slum or retailers operating from very basic rented premises). In keeping with the nature of their businesses, both in terms of their activity (retailing) and in terms of the employment of short-term horizons, most respondents operated with a high current to capital asset ratio. Although 56 per cent had less than KSh30,000 in total assets, there were a few comparatively large enterprises: the biggest was an 'hotel', with assets valued at about KSh250,000, which, in theory, should have debarred this particular businessman from taking a Juhudi loan.

Table 15.16 clearly shows the larger scale of the ISP borrowers. These respondents had a greater range of capitalisation, with 39 per cent claiming total assets of between KSh49,999 and KSh100,000 and another 39 per cent with assets in excess of KSh99,999. Three respondents had total assets in excess of KSh500,000: an electrician, a chalk manufacturer and a doctor who had a clinic which he valued at slightly over KSh1 million.

Tables 15.17 and 15.18 show asset growth using respondent recall with the data adjusted to cover inflation at 20 per cent. Not surprisingly, those enterprises that started with a low level of capitalisation had the highest rates of growth following loan disbursement, but as most growth was in terms of working capital (current assets) it is not clear how sustainable these changes are likely to be.

Table 15.17 shows asset growth among Juhudi members. It is noticeable that the T_3 group – those members who had not yet obtained a loan – reported low levels of assets compared to the two groups who had a loan. Indeed, their asset holdings appeared to be losing value at a worrying rate (negative growth of 11 per cent on total assets), so they clearly needed a loan simply to shore up their businesses. Not surprisingly, Juhudi loans have little effect on borrowers' fixed assets and we can question the sustainability of the 7 per cent increase in borrowers' current assets as there is little difference between the current assets of the T_1 and T_2 groups – if the additions to stock accruing from the loan were sustained, the current-asset situation of the two groups would presumably not be so similar. The Juhudi loans may lever businesses up but only so long as it takes for the business person to off-load increased stock. Any increased

Table 15.17 Asset growth among Juhudi members

	Current assets (KSh)	Growth rate (%)	Total assets (KSh)	Growth rate (%)
T_1	14,973	8	37,439	4
T_2	13,843	5	27,576	1
Overall: T_1 & T_2	14,408	7	32,508	2
T_3	9,805	−17	20,663	−11
Overall: T_1, T_2, T_3	13,240	1	29,502	0
T_4 (NB)	17,421	10	45,057	3

Source: Author's survey

Notes

1 Percentages are rounded to the nearest whole number and the T_4 data have been smoothed by removing four outliers.

2 The growth rate measures the respondent's estimate of asset growth over the preceding year, adjusted for inflation at 20%.

Table 15.18 Asset growth among ISP clients

	Current assets (KSh)	Growth rate (%)	Total assets (KSh)	Growth rate (%)
T_1	36,272	22	99,958	4
T_2	32,691	11	103,214	4
T_3	27,733	−4	121,705	−1
T_4	51,488	2	128,762	5
Overall	36,337	13	107,963	3
T_5 (NB)	23,176	8	64,909	−5

Source: Author's survey
Notes:
1 Percentages are rounded to the nearest whole number.
2 The growth rate measures the respondent's estimate of asset growth over the preceding year, adjusted for inflation at 20%.

profits do not appear to be reinvested in the business as evidenced by the low asset growth rates for the two borrower groups. The asset sizes give a good indication of the borrower's financial exposure: the typical Juhudi borrower appears to be 25–50 per cent geared, in terms of the proportion of total assets financed by loanable funds. Finally, it is noticeable that the non-borrower group has significantly more business wealth than the Juhudi members. Once again, the evidence suggests that Juhudi is attracting the poorer sections of the Kibera business population.

Among the ISP sample shown in Table 15.18 there is a significant increase in current assets, especially for those borrowers who had repaid or serviced a considerable portion of their first loan (T_1). It is surprising that the T_3 group demonstrates negative current asset growth as many of those respondents should have recently received an ISP loan, which should imply an increase in their assets. As with the Juhudi data above, the overall growth rates should be interpreted in light of the gearing ratio of a typical borrower: assuming an average loan of KSh28,795 and total assets of KSh107,963, this stands at 27 per cent. This leverage will feed into the entrepreneur's 'income statement' but its true impact will only be known once the loan has been amortised. From the data given here this is not possible to ascertain at this stage, but intuitively at least a significant short-term impact on business income would be expected (see pp. 321–4). In contrast to the Juhudi borrowers, the typical ISP client appears to have a more capitalised business than the average non-borrower (T_5) and also, in terms of asset growth, appears to be doing better.

Capital/labour ratio

On average, ISP clients tend to have over three times more capital invested in their businesses than Juhudi clients (the actual ratio is 1:3.66) and they tend to have almost three times as many employees (the actual ratio is 1:2.93). The crucial question is how much capital the businesses employ to maintain one job. On the basis of this survey, each job in a Juhudi-funded enterprise 'costs' KSh27,572 and each job in an ISP-funded enterprise 'costs' KSh34,493. These gross figures should be treated with considerable caution, as they are derived from (probably) quite accurate employment figures but (possibly) exaggerated capital-employed figures. However, the error may well be reduced if we attempt to include only those 'productively' employed in the respective enterprises – although crucial to any analysis of the impact of credit on business growth, the author is not aware of any study that has attempted to do such an exercise. However, it seems safe to conclude that the smaller-scale entrepreneurs serviced by Juhudi credit are more efficient at generating employment than are those entrepreneurs serviced by the ISP, but they do not generate as much employment in absolute terms and the quality of the employment may be suspect.

Enterprise sales, expenditure and profits

Most respondents complained of 'tough times' and believed that the political uncertainty in 1992 had adversely affected their businesses. The effects of this were particularly strong towards the end of the year when Kenya experienced its first multi-party elections, so expectations were particularly depressed at the time of the survey. Despite this, 58 per cent of respondents considered that sales in 1992 were as good or better than the previous year but, in real terms, with inflation running at 20+ per cent, this figure is likely to be misleading. Table 15.19 shows the size distribution

Table 15.19 Size distribution of monthly sales (%)

Range	Juhudi	ISP
<2,000	2	2
>1,999 <4,000	8	2
>3,999 <6,000	11	2
>5,999 <8,000	13	5
>7,999 <10,000	14	15
>9,999 <12,000	8	5
>11,999 <14,000	7	7
>13,999 <16,000	12	7
>15,999 <18,000	4	5
>17,999 <20,000	3	3
>19,999 <25,000	6	12
>24,999 <30,000	3	9
>29,999	8	25

Source: Author's survey
Note: Percentages are rounded to the nearest whole number.

321

of monthly sales between the two sets of borrowers. Almost half the Juhudi respondents had sales of less than KSh10,000 compared to about a quarter of ISP respondents.

There were notable differences in sales between different borrower types. In the Juhudi sample, the T_1 and T_2 groups' average sales were very similar, but for the T_3 group of Juhudi members who had not yet obtained a loan average sales were about 43 per cent less. This could be due to a number of factors. Perhaps it shows the positive impact on sales of a Juhudi loan. This may be the most likely reason, as most loans translate into goods for sale and thus, assuming there is demand for extra supply, this will translate into greater sales. Alternatively, this difference could be interpreted as showing that Juhudi's initial intakes were from more-successful businesses in terms of sales and that future borrowers will be drawn from less-successful businesses. If this is the case, there may be significant implications for future repayment rates. Sales among the non-borrower group (T_4) were broadly comparable to the sales reported by existing borrowers. On the basis of sales, it would seem reasonable to infer that Juhudi members form a representative cross-section of Kibera microbusinesses. As a final caveat to sales among the Juhudi borrowers, it is interesting to note that none of those in the top quartile of sales and only two from the top two quartiles were in arrears. Also, all but two respondents in the top decile of sales had completed primary education and all the rest had completed at least four years of secondary education.

The ISP sample produced less-interesting results on sales. There was a large spread among respondents with some exceedingly high estimates of monthly sales: two borrowers reported sales in excess of KSh100,000. Thus, although the average monthly sales for all borrowers was KSh23,597, 63 per cent of borrowers fell below this figure. In contrast to the findings in Kibera, the non-borrower (T_5) group reported average sales 25 per cent below the figure reported for all borrowers. The average ISP client appears to be doing better, in terms of sales, than his typical competitor.

Table 15.20 compares estimated profit, expenditure and sales for the Juhudi sample. Although reported profit growth was similar for all borrower groups, the non-borrower (T_4) group had reported a notable downturn in business fortunes (−18 per cent growth). However, those Juhudi members who had not yet obtained a loan were reporting considerably lower sales, expenditures and, to a lesser extent, profits than any of the other groups of respondents. For Juhudi borrowers (T_1 and T_2), average profit was 34 per cent greater than for those Juhudi members who did not yet have a loan (T_3) and only slightly lower than the non-borrower T_4 group. If one assumes that the T_1 and T_2 groups were once comparable to the T_3 group, then a Juhudi loan seems to contribute to loosening the cycle of poverty and elevating the enterprise to higher levels of expenditure/sales and profits.

Table 15.20 Enterprise monthly profit (net income): expenditure and sales of Juhudi members

	Estimated profit (KSh)	Annual growth (%)	Current expenditure (KSh)	Annual growth (%)	Current sales (KSh)
T$_1$	6,285	−1	7,074	0	14,111
T$_2$	5,428	−2	7,650	3	14,829
T$_3$	4,358	0	3,677	4	8,244
Overall: T$_1$ & T$_2$	5,856	−2	7,362	1	14,470
T$_4$	6,154	−18	9,231	0	13,580

Source: Author's survey

Notes

1 Percentages are rounded to the nearest whole number, and the T$_4$ data have been smoothed by removing one outlier.

2 The growth rates measure the respondent's estimate of growth over the preceding year, adjusted for inflation at 20%.

The trend on expenditure was either zero or marginally positive. As all respondents come from relatively low-income groups, the decision whether or not to purchase inputs basically translates into running the business or not. (For most micro-enterprise traders who are operating on a knife-edge, what they buy is similar to what they sell as there is little if any product transformation, turnover is fairly fluid, margins are tight, and if items are not bought, business dries up; so maintaining expenditure at least at existing levels is imperative.) If input prices go up, it may be difficult to pass on these increases to consumers because the type of market in which they operate is usually near to saturation and consumers are likely to be extremely price sensitive. Thus, for many micro-entrepreneurs operating on a knife-edge, as margins trickled downwards, expenditure crept up and their already weak position in the economy was exacerbated. Because 1992 was a year of ever-rising inflation and price decontrol, both of which have a disproportionately negative impact on the poorest, these events may partially explain the worsening position of profits to expenditure for many entrepreneurs in Kibera.

Table 15.21 shows comparable data for the ISP sample which performs, universally, on a higher scale than the Juhudi sample. As a result, these borrowers are more able to curtail expenditure under recessionary conditions because their businesses have some inbuilt flexibility by virtue of operating on a bigger scale. The data for the T$_4$ group are interesting in that they seem to confirm that these respondents were at a fairly early stage of repaying their first loan. This group experienced particularly high growth in expenditure which may be accounted for by increased expenditure on inputs following recent receipt of an ISP loan. Assuming that this had not yet fed through fully into increased sales and profit, which will lag behind expenditure, this would also explain the comparatively lower levels

Table 15.21 Enterprise monthly profit (net income): expenditure and sales of ISP members

	Estimated profit (KSh)	Annual growth (%)	Current expenditure (KSh)	Annual growth (%)	Sales (KSh)
T$_1$	9,464	−1	12,877	−11	24,609
T$_2$	9,253	2	10,684	−5	22,099
T$_3$	9,109	19	13,867	−3	26,601
T$_4$	5,866	−1	9,044	21	16,740
Overall	8,902	2	12,277	−7	23,597
T$_5$	8,033	34	8,849	−8	17,646

Source: Author's survey

Notes

1 Percentages are rounded to the nearest whole number.

2 The growth rates measure the respondent's estimate of growth over the preceding year, adjusted for inflation at 20%.

of net income and sales experienced by this group. Although the sales, expenditure and profit figures for the T$_5$ group fall below those for the borrowers, the non-borrowers appear to be experiencing particularly impressive growth in profits. The ISP selection process is a fairly rigorous one and, in the context of targeting enterprises with growth potential, the data for the T$_3$ group appear to vindicate current targeting practice, as this group demonstrates sound business behaviour: strong sales figures, controlled expenditure growth and rapid growth in profits.

The household economy

Respondents in the two samples had fairly consistent domestic expenditure profiles. The major monthly expense per household was on food, which usually constituted at least half of total expenditure, followed by education (school fees and equipment purchases) and rent. The average ISP borrower was likely to have twice as much disposable household income as the average Juhudi borrower. This reflects the higher individual income of the ISP respondents and the greater number of income sources among ISP respondent households (almost half, for example, had at least one regular wage earner) and is only partially offset by the higher average household size of ISP respondents. For most households, income sources comfortably covered average expenditure but the latter calculation took no account of irregular or unforeseen expenditure, such as the purchase of capital items or costs associated with ill-health, death or marriage. It was also found that average household expenditure was growing at a rate of 33 per cent (for Juhudi members) and 25 per cent (for ISP clients) faster than

Box 15.5 Technology: the missing link?

The research sought to ascertain the impact of credit on the internal operations of businesses in terms of changes in technologies used or techniques applied. Such change is considered necessary to increase labour and/or capital productivity which, in turn, is necessary to bring about economic diversity and real growth. Unfortunately, there appeared to be very few indications that this had occurred.

Over three-quarters of Juhudi-supported enterprises were exclusively or largely based on trading and most were 'copy-cat' ventures and, not surprisingly, most entrepreneurs were happy doing what they knew best. Changes imply risk, and the margins for error are precariously slim for informal sector entrepreneurs, so it is not surprising that most were content to seek credit solely for working capital, perhaps believing that technology changes required investments that were especially risky in the highly unstable environment of the informal sector. Although a few respondents had a rather simplistic view of the path to business growth, believing that increases in their stock would equate automatically with ever-higher profits, most did not share this view. Virtually all surveyed respondents wanted to increase their skills via training, and most indicated that they would pay to acquire additional skills. However, in virtually all cases the demand was for business skills (book-keeping, marketing, etc.) rather than technical skills (tailoring, metalworking, etc.). Officials of the credit scheme, aware of the danger of financing the same types of business and thereby contributing to market saturation, have recognised the significance of education and training. It seems reasonable to hypothesise that this could be the missing bridge linking credit and changes in technology or technique. Additionally, it is to be expected that as the Juhudi scheme expands, it will be the repeat borrowers with their larger loans who will begin to make changes in the way they operate their businesses. Thus, technological change may become more noticeable as the credit scheme matures, especially if Juhudi develops appropriate new financial products.

The ISP specifically targets manufacturing and service sector enterprises and this is reflected in the fact that 17 per cent of loans are for fixed capital items and 22 per cent are for a combination of fixed and working capital. The type of activities financed by the ISP are more diversified than those financed by Juhudi but a heavy dependence on a limited range of enterprise types is still evident. The survey came across a few cases where respondents had introduced new technology, such as the purchase of a new sewing machine, a different type of fabric or a metalwork tool. There were also a couple of cases of striking ingenuity, demonstrated by one entrepreneur who had transformed a motor bike engine into a circular saw and another who had devised a bellows for furnace work largely from a bicycle wheel, chainset and large spool. But in neither case was credit the catalyst for this inventiveness, as both respondents, while recognising the importance of their ISP loans, considered their initial business improvements to be independent of their credit.

Officials of the ISP were aware of the need for technology changes among their clients and there was a recurrent belief in the need to foster both productivity changes and improvements in product quality. However, although credit alone is unlikely to have much effect on technological adoption, it may not be prudent for lenders to mix wider enterprise development inputs with financial services. The ISP management was also of the opinion that improvements in technology and methods of running businesses were most likely to come from certain types of enterprise and entrepreneur and that this would require specific screening and appraisal techniques in addition to those employed for the purposes of delivering credit.

average household income. Among the Kibera respondents, average household income was 89 per cent of the comparable non-borrower group, and for the ISP respondents average household income was 146 per cent of that reported by non-borrowers. This appears to be a further indication that the Juhudi scheme is reaching the poorer cohort of Kibera entrepreneurs and that the ISP is reaching the better-off cohort of comparable entrepreneurs.

The research attempted to collect data on household/domestic assets but it proved very difficult to get meaningful information. The typical Kibera resident lives in a semi-permanent house on which it was difficult to put a value. Household assets were of a bare minimum sufficient to sustain existence and little additions were reported over the preceding year. Most respondents had a rural home on which they were usually prepared to place a value in terms of real estate, farms, livestock, and so on, but such values were highly subjective and it was impossible to verify them. The ISP respondents reported total household assets on average four or five times greater than the Kibera residents, but once again verifying this was virtually impossible. ISP respondents tended to live in a better dwelling than those from Kibera and in most cases tended a *shamba* (small farm) to which they usually ascribed a greater monetary value than for their businesses. As mentioned above, in both samples it was often difficult for respondents to demarcate between business and household or domestic assets and in many cases between business expenditure and household or domestic expenditure. Thus, it is quite likely that loanable funds or the proceeds from activities financed by the loans not only feed in to enhance household consumption and investment but also enable entrepreneurs to release funds for domestic purposes that would otherwise have gone into recurrent business expenditure.

CONCLUSIONS

The foregoing analysis has attempted to appraise the two lending programmes in terms of two broad criteria: institutional efficiency and effectiveness, and the socio-economic impact on the businesses financed *vis-à-vis* non-borrower groups. The evidence is mixed and is conditional because both programmes are relatively new and longer-run time-series data are clearly required for a more thorough understanding of the full impact of credit.

It is clear that both programmes have had a positive impact on the businesses to which they lend. The degree of impact, however, is variable and is probably more dependent on the abilities, aptitudes and attitudes of individual borrowers than on any particular feature of the respective lending programmes. Undoubtedly, the most significant feature of these two innovative lending programmes is simply their very presence in areas hitherto neglected by credit institutions.

What the two programmes clearly demonstrate is the need to correctly target borrowers with the right 'products'. The two programmes are operating in very different areas serving different clients and they cannot use the same delivery mechanisms. For example, it would be inappropriate for the ISP to use group lending in areas where clients are widely dispersed and the Juhudi scheme could not operate an individual collateral-based lending programme in Kibera because few borrowers would have the collateral. Thus, given their respective target groups, a group-based lending programme is probably best for Kibera and an individual-based lending programme is probably best for the type of entrepreneurs targeted by the ISP.

The importance of correct targeting is also evident in terms of the need to match loan size with business needs. By offering flexibility in loan size and repayment terms the ISP is directly responding to the different capital needs of businesses with different production patterns and cycles. Businesses in Kibera are more homogeneous in terms of their methods and modes of production and operate on the type of short time-frames commensurate with a relatively small loan, repayable weekly. The lesson, then, is that successful lending requires successful matching of 'products' and targets.

In turn, the target group defines the criteria on which the lending programme can be evaluated. The ISP is clearly concerned with business growth. The effects of ISP loans on household economies, gender relations or even non-borrower business competitors are of little direct importance. The ISP is designed to foster growth in employment, assets, sales and value added. The Juhudi Credit Scheme is more closely aligned to poverty alleviation through income generation and employment creation. Thus, this credit scheme is concerned *not only* with business growth but such issues as gender equity, client empowerment and emancipation and it seeks this without compromising financial discipline in its lending programme.

In formulating policy, then, it is necessary for micro-enterprise lenders to segment the market correctly for their loans and to determine their primary objective, which could be poverty alleviation or business growth. The two are not mutually exclusive but business growth does not necessarily mean poverty alleviation, and poverty alleviation may be a necessary condition for business growth but it is not a sufficient condition. Successful lenders will be able to prioritise these two goals, but in either case, considerable donor support appears axiomatic at least at the initial institution-building stages.

Both programmes have adopted a professional approach to institutional development, stressing staff development and propagating an atmosphere of competence and commitment. The Juhudi scheme has gone the furthest in this respect as the ISP has less autonomy given its parastatal status. Both institutions have developed efficient and effective management information systems and *use* them in controlling and planning. This also constitutes an effective early warning mechanism to ensure a responsive and dynamic approach to portfolio management. In both organisations reporting functions are married to organisational learning and both are striving to become increasingly 'bank-like'.[7]

The Informal Sector Programme and the Juhudi Credit Scheme are doing well. A lot is expected from them and they are breaking new and tough ground with a flexible and efficient approach to small/informal enterprise credit. But it is important to remember that they cannot turn the tide on an ailing economy. The 1990s have brought increased economic hardship and heightened political and ethnic instability to Kenya, and there are indications that poor people are becoming increasingly preoccupied with survival rather than with the long-term benefits of developing savings and fostering business growth; this does not augur well for either of the two lending institutions. Thus, performance and impact can only be judged in the context of the broader environment. It is clearly wrong to expect that credit for micro-enterprise can produce overnight results: there are no easy solutions to complex problems; or that it can change the cultural context in which business takes place; for example, in respect of the mutual obligations of kinship that may transcend conventional business behaviour. Therefore, given the environment into which these two institutions have been baptised, their achievements are especially commendable. In terms of institutional development and the provision of financial services for small and micro-enterprises they provide very useful organisational models. In terms of client impact, the lessons are still being learnt and the definitive conclusions must await further analysis using a longer time-series; but, to date, the indicators augur well.

APPENDIX 1: RESEARCH METHODOLOGY

The fieldwork on which this study is based took place in October, November and December 1992 and focused on two informal sector lending programmes. First, Kenya Rural Enterprise Programme (KREP) Juhudi Kibera Credit Scheme, which is an NGO group-based lending programme that provides financial services for micro-entrepreneurs located in Kibera, a large shanty town in West Nairobi. And second, Kenya Industrial Estates Informal Sector Programme (ISP) which is a parastatal with offices in twenty-two locations throughout the country and a target of small business/micro-entrepreneurs with growth potential. The two institutions were chosen because they are examples of innovative, well-organised micro-enterprise/small business lending programmes that have achieved apparent success with dissimilar approaches and very different lending procedures.

The primary data sources comprised structured and unstructured interviews with staff from the two lending institutions, clients of the institutions, comparable non-client entrepreneurs, donors, government officials, bankers and other lending institution staff. A number of secondary data sources were also used, such as documents and statistical data provided by each institution, donor reports and Government of Kenya publications.

The main survey instrument was a detailed structured questionnaire backed up, in the case of the Juhudi scheme, by observation and informal discussion at eighteen KIWA meetings (comprising 108 *watanos*). The structured (main) questionnaire comprised six sections: an entrepreneur and enterprise profile; credit and savings; group savings and credit (not for ISP); management practices and the business environment; credit impact on the business operations; and credit impact on the household. Each questionnaire, which took about an hour to complete, was translated into the vernacular *in situ* by each enumerator. In the field and subsequently in Nairobi, both sets of questionnaires went through a very thorough data-cleaning exercise. Thereafter, the data were entered on to a database for detailed analysis.

In the case of the Juhudi data collection, a stratified random sample was selected from client/member lists. The project enumerators then identified each respondent at the respective KIWA meeting and thereafter made arrangements to conduct the interview with the respondent.

A structured questionnaire was given to 134 Juhudi members (representing 11 per cent of total membership) comprising:

Type 1 (T_1)	=	borrowers servicing their first loan	($n = 50$)
Type 2 (T_2)	=	borrowers servicing their second loan	($n = 50$)
Type 3 (T_3)	=	Juhudi members who have not received a loan, but are due to receive one soon	($n = 34$)
plus			
Type 4 (T_4)	=	a similar questionnaire given to randomly selected non-borrower informal sector entrepreneurs, i.e. not members of Juhudi	($n = 26$)
Total sample =			($n = 160$)

Note: T_3 and T_4 were control groups.

All respondents were located at the Kibera slum. Kibera is situated 7 kilometres south-west of Nairobi (most other slums are to the east), close to Nairobi Dam and Wilson Airport. It comprises fourteen neighbourhoods, four of which are formal estates (upper income) and ten of which are densely populated slums (lower income). The purpose of the Juhudi scheme is to work with entrepreneurs in the low-income areas and all respondents in the survey operated in these areas. Virtually all respondents also lived in the low-income areas but there were a few who lived in the upper-income neighbourhoods and a smaller number who did not live in Kibera at all.

Kenya has seventy towns (or urban centres) with a population of more than 5,000 and a total urban population of 3.6 million (about 15 per cent of the total population), but almost 60 per cent of these live in just two cities, namely Mombasa with 500,000+ and Nairobi with 1,500,000+ (both figures may well be rather conservative estimates). Most of these residents are relative newcomers to city life, having arrived from the rural areas looking for a better life but almost inevitably ending up as slum dwellers. Kibera is possibly the largest slum or shanty town in Kenya, with a population estimated in the area of 300,000 (Aleke-Dondo and Parker 1991). The growth of Kibera has mirrored the growth of its parent, Nairobi, and the settlement has its origins in the racial jigsaw created by the colonial administration, when rights of settlement were granted to Nubians, who constituted an important group in the colonial army. Interestingly, of the entrepreneurs surveyed, eight of the ten longest residents of Kibera were Nubians yet they comprised less than one in ten of the total sample. Kibera has now grown to include many different tribal groups and has become an established settlement that appears to have outgrown the ability of officialdom to control it. Although slum settlement has no legal basis, the growth of Kibera has brought about *de facto* ownership of property, as evidenced by the survey findings: 58 per cent of respondents rented their business premises, 22 per cent owned them and only one respondent (from a sample of 160) acknowledged he had unauthorised use of his site.

The degree of permanency of residence in Kibera is not fully understood. Nubians still regard it as their 'patch' in Nairobi but for other groups there is conflicting evidence as to whether migrants arrive in Kibera to look for better urban opportunities and return to their rural home if opportunities do not arise, or whether most residents are permanent with little expectation of moving on to better things and little intention of returning to their rural home. It is generally believed that there is a substantial body of permanent residents and a much smaller transient population. From the survey findings, virtually all respondents referred to dependants 'up country' (in their rural home), which illustrates an attachment, but the average length of residency in Kibera was almost twelve years, and with almost 80 per cent having resided in Kibera for six or more years, clearly many people see Kibera as some sort of home. For a fuller description of settlement patterns and unofficial town planning in Kibera see Amis (1984).

The ISP data were collected using a two-tier stratified sample. First – within the constraints defined by time and budget – four of the twenty-two stations (branches) serviced by the ISP were identified as being broadly compatible with the sampling frame (see Box 15.4, p. 307) and 'representative' in terms of station performance. Those selected were: Murang'a, in a coffee-growing area of Central Province and in the heart of Kikuyu-land;

Nakuru, in the agriculturally prosperous Rift Valley; Kakamega, in the relatively poorer Western Province; and Bungoma, which, like Kakamega, is a Luyha-dominated region in the Western Province. The latter station was a late replacement for a station in an area which would have made the survey more ethnically representative. But this area was judged by our in-country research collaborators to be politically volatile, and as the research was taking place during Kenya's first-ever multi-party elections it was felt unwise to proceed with the planned fieldwork in this area. With the benefit of hindsight, the research could have taken place as planned but by the time the elections had been held and the results announced the fieldwork had already been completed. It should be noted that each station had an office based in the towns of Kakamega, Bungoma, Nakuru and Murang'a but the clients were widely dispersed throughout the *districts* of the same name. Most clients were located in towns or rural trading centres.

Once suitable locations had been determined, the second tier of stratification involved the actual classification of the target respondents as per the criteria below. Initial screening of client lists took place at the ISP head office in Nairobi and were then confirmed by the respective credit officers in each station. Thereafter, the respondents were identified and interviewed at their places of business. A structured questionnaire for 114 ISP clients was completed (representing 7 per cent of the total portfolio). The questionnaire format was essentially the same as that used for the Juhudi sample but the actual client stratification differed to accommodate the different lending procedures and repayment cycles:

Type 1 (T_1) = borrowers who had completed repayment of
their first loan or completed 12+ months of
repayments on their first loan ($n = 65$)
Type 2 (T_2) = borrowers repaying a second loan ($n = 14$)
Type 3 (T_3) = borrowers who had got their first loan within the
last three months or applicants who had
undergone a Client Orientation Programme
(COP) and were waiting for their loan
disbursement ($n = 20$)
Type 4 (T_4) = borrowers servicing their first loan but who had
made fewer than 12 months repayments and more
than 3 months ($n = 15$)

plus

Type 5 (T_5) = a similar questionnaire for randomly selected,
comparable non-ISP entrepreneurs ($n = 26$)
Total sample = ($n = 140$)

This sample was collected at over twenty sub-locations within the four stations, with the following distribution: Kakamega ($n = 28$), Nakuru ($n = 26$), Murang'a ($n = 45$) and Bungoma ($n = 41$).

NOTES

1 In official statistics, the informal sector refers to enterprises having fewer than ten employees and small-scale businesses having between nine and fifty employees. These are misleading definitions as few informal enterprises formally employ more than one or two people and small-scale businesses rarely have more than ten employees. There are, of course, numerous alternative bases on which to define the sectors and perhaps the best method may be to use a composite of indicators, including asset size, sales volume, income, employment and legal status, amongst others.

2 *Jua Kali* is Kiswahili approximating to '(out under) the hot sun' and was originally used to describe those artisans who worked without proper premises and were therefore exposed to the elements. It is a term synonymous with micro-enterprise or the informal sector and is sometimes erroneously equated with the small-scale business sector which, more accurately, comprises somewhat bigger and often 'registered' enterprises.

3 The Centre Project was responsible for numerous documents published during the period 1988–92. Two of the most notable ones are Government of Kenya (1989a and 1992c).

4 All these projections are to be found in the ODA/Ministry of Planning and National Development Project Memorandum entitled: 'Kenya Rural Enterprise Programme, Support for Juhudi Credit Scheme', October 1992 (unpublished). It should be noted that all the projects are based on what the author considers are favourable assumptions regarding such variables as recovery rates, inflation rates and client graduation figures (the numbers graduating to bigger loans).

5 Interest rates in Kenya are usually based on simple interest on a declining balance. To even out cash-flow requirements, these are often converted to a flat rate of interest which amortises the loan amount in equal instalments of principal and interest.

6 Responses referring to savings must, for obvious reasons, be treated with caution. The questionnaire was designed such that a simple question asking only if the respondent had money in a bank was followed by the more sensitive questions 'How much?', 'With which bank?' and 'Since when?' Among the Juhudi sample 20% refused to answer the second level of questions. Among the ISP respondents the figure was 16%. Additionally, many of the amounts given appeared to be quite rough estimates.

7 At the time of going to press KPEP has applied to the Central Bank for incorporation as a private bank. It plans to divide its financial and NGO institution-building activities into separate organisations.

16

RURAL AND AGRICULTURAL CREDIT IN MALAWI

A study of the Malawi
Mudzi Fund and the Smallholder
Agricultural Credit Administration

Graeme Buckley

THE MALAWIAN ECONOMY

Malawi is a small landlocked country in Central Africa, with a population estimated at 9.1 million growing at an annual rate of 3.6 per cent. It is one of the poorest countries in the world (estimated GNP per capita in 1991 was US$230: World Bank 1993b) and also one of the most densely populated countries in Africa (89 inhabitants per square kilometre of land surface or 170 inhabitants per square kilometre of arable land).

In the period from independence in 1964 through to the late 1970s the economy enjoyed strong economic growth, built on the expansion of estate agriculture, which benefited from favourable world prices for tobacco, tea and sugar. Simultaneously, the manufacturing base expanded, principally in response to major infrastructural developments like the construction of the new capital city in Lilongwe. Adverse shifts in the terms of trade, the war in neighbouring Mozambique which severed Malawi's transport routes to the sea and led to the influx of up to a million refugees, an over-extended public sector, high interest rates and a series of weather-related shocks scuppered the impressive growth rates and brought economic crisis to Malawi.

In response to these problems, the Government of Malawi undertook a broad-based structural adjustment programme throughout the 1980s. By the early 1990s the economy seemed to be back on course with favourable growth in output, the fiscal deficit brought under control, the rate of inflation slowed and a healthy expansion in private sector credit (World

Many thanks to Nwanze Okidegbe, Anne Conroy, James Ntupanyama, Clement Phiri, E.S. Malindi and the committed and enthusiastic teams of enumerators at SACA and Malawi Mudzi Fund.

Bank 1990a; Centre for Social Research 1990; Donovan 1992). However, in 1991–2 the economy was hit by a severe drought which reduced the average yield of the staple food crop, maize, by nearly 60 per cent and served to highlight the widespread poverty and food insecurity that is prevalent in the country. To compound the economic woes of the country, bilateral donors and the European Community imposed an embargo on further development assistance in May 1992, principally for reasons of governance. Not for the first time, the structural problems of the Malawian economy, with its fragile and narrow resource base, small domestic markets, widespread subsistence agricultural production and dependence on a few exports, had been exposed.

Poverty and the rural economy

Agriculture dominates the Malawian economy, accounting for over a third of GDP and 85 per cent of exports and employment. The agricultural sector is divided into two sub-sectors: the estate sector, which embraces land holdings above 10 ha, and the smallholder sector. The former serves the export sector, essentially tobacco, tea and sugar (only about a third of estate output is for domestic consumption), and the smallholder sector is dominated by maize production (75 per cent of total output). While the average hectarage of a smallholding is 1.35 ha compared to an average estate size of 51.78 ha, both figures mask large regional variations (Table 16.1). The differences between the two sectors – traditionally defined by institutional rules regulating crop production, marketing, pricing and tenure – have narrowed. The average size of estates has declined steadily and now incorporates a heterogeneous group of farms varying in size, capitalisation and in terms of the application of management and technology (Mkandawire *et al.* 1990). On the other hand, some of the institutional rules have been relaxed and, since the late 1980s, the smallholder sector has begun to compete with the estate sector on a more equal footing (smallholders are now permitted to grow burley tobacco, for example).[1]

About 90 per cent of Malawians live and work in the rural areas and 77 per cent of households survive principally from smallholder farming under customary tenure. Thus, poverty is essentially a rural phenomenon and is usually assessed through terms of land holding.

About 26 per cent of an estimated 1.3 million households cultivate less than 0.5 ha of land and are classified as 'core poor' because they are unable to subsist on food production from their land. This is the poorest and most vulnerable group dependent on selling their labour to the estates or large smallholders (a practice known as *ganyu*) and from operating micro-enterprise activities. Most of these latter sources of income are based on trading, usually of foodstuffs or basic commodities like matches, Vaseline and firewood, or on food and drinks processing. Only a very few activities

Table 16.1 A comparison of smallholder and estate agriculture[a]

	Smallholder sector	*Estate sector*
Contribution to GDP	25% (MK1,392 m)	9% (MK501 m)
Contribution to agricultural GDP	75%	25%
Contribution to agricultural employment	90%	10%
Contribution to exports	10% (MK76 m)	85% (MK645 m)
Contribution to total food production	80%	20%
Number of units	1,300,000	14,500
Total hectarage	1,750,000	750,000
Crops produced	Maize (75% of total cropped land, of which, 90%+ comprises local varieties), groundnuts, fire-cured tobacco, cassava, cotton, rice, various legumes and burley tobacco	Burley tobacco, tea, sugar, maize (34% of total)

Sources: Nwanna (1993) except figures in brackets which are derived from World Bank (1993c) and refer to 1991 estimates in millions of current Kwacha

Note. [a] Only 24 per cent of the 750,000 hectares of estate land is cultivated. This is due to rotational cropping patterns. The figures in this table imply that the estate sector is about three times more productive than the smallholder sector. Much of this can be attributed to higher applications of technologies, together with the market advantages for estate farmers.

involve much in the way of input transformation such as handicraft production, carpentry or metalwork. Thus, there is little in the way of economic diversification in the rural areas. Most of the time, the 'core poor' are underemployed and dependent on better-off relatives. Not surprisingly, female-headed households are disproportionately over-represented in this group. Although they constitute about a third of total smallholders, about two-thirds of all households cultivating less than 0.5 ha are headed by females and 72 per cent of all female-headed households cultivate less than 1 ha of land (Shanmugaratnam *et al.* 1992: 18), compared to the national average of 56 per cent cultivating less than 1 ha. About 30 per cent of the rural population farm between 0.5 and 1 ha and together with a further 20 per cent farming between 1 and 1.5 ha are classified as 'poor', meaning that they produce insufficient food to feed themselves in three out of five years. The remaining 24 per cent farm more than 1.5 ha of land, they are not classified as poor and many of this group are commercially orientated small-scale farmers and found in the Central Region.

Land holding is not the only indicator of poverty and attempts have been made to obtain income data to establish suitable poverty lines. Thus, the World Bank has defined a crude poverty line based on minimum nutrition

requirements while maintaining the households' food/non-food prefer-
ences. This is based on prices and data collected in 1988–9 and gives a
national poverty line of US$40 corresponding to the annual per capita
minimum nutrition requirement of 216 kg of maize. This corresponds to
about MK300 in mid-1993 prices,[2] but takes no account of significant
regional variations. This line corresponds to the poorest 55 per cent of the
population which is roughly the same number who farm less than 1 ha of
land. But as the data on which the poverty line figures are based are, by the
World Bank's own admission, somewhat dubious (World Bank 1990a: 19),
land holding rather than income remains the preferred measure of poverty
in Malawi.

Most smallholder farming is of a very rudimentary nature. Hand shelling
and pounding of maize and groundnuts is the norm. Ownership of farm
equipment is generally limited to simple hand tools and only about 5 per
cent of land is ploughed using oxen; about 7 per cent is ridged and about 20
per cent of farmers use their own oxen for transport (Nwanna 1993).[3] The
application of improved maize varieties is also low compared to other
major maize-growing countries in Africa (Table 16.2). There are also
significant regional variations in terms of the application of technologies
and average land-holding sizes, the Central Region being significantly better
endowed than either the highly populated Southern or relatively sparsely
populated Northern Regions.

There are many alarming statistics about Malawi but one of the most
pertinent for such an agriculturally dependent country concerns the per
capita land-holding ratio. Arable land declined from an estimated average of
0.86 ha per capita in 1966 to 0.63 ha in 1977 and 0.49 ha in 1985. It is
estimated to fall to about 0.26 ha by 2005. The situation in the Southern
Region is even worse, with estimates for 2005 suggesting just 0.18 ha for

Table 16.2 Areas sown to improved maize germplasm: six largest maize producers
in Africa, 1986–8

	Total maize area (ha)	Hybrids (improved) (%)	OPVs[a] (improved) (%)	Local (%)
Sub-Saharan Africa	15,000,000	22	11	67
Zimbabwe	1,300,000	100	0	0
Kenya	1,400,000	55	10	35
Nigeria	1,500,000	2	20	78
Tanzania	1,700,000	11	6	83
Ethiopia	1,000,000	6	10	84
Malawi	1,200,000	5	2	93

Source: CIMMYT (1990) as reported in Simler (1993)
Note: [a] OPV = open pollinating varieties.

each person (Shanmugaratnam *et al.* 1992). Inevitably, such pressures on the land have resulted in widespread rural poverty.

Other indicators of Malawi's socio-economic status portray a desperately poor country (Table 16.3). Indeed, Malawi is number 153 out of 173 countries listed on the UNDP human development index (UNDP 1993).

The plight of the smallholder sector in general and the 'core poor' and 'poor' sub-sectors in particular shows no signs of improving. The present agricultural system, of which credit allocation is a part, serves to exacerbate the condition of farmers in these latter sub-sectors. As this chapter will show, the smaller and poorer smallholders are trapped in a poverty cycle. They prioritise household food security by giving a higher priority to intensification of local maize than to hybrid maize production.

This is not the case for larger smallholders, who aim at generating marketable surpluses to maximise profit. They are able to do this because they have greater access to credit and fertilisers which enable them to cultivate hybrid maize more productively. Furthermore, the poor smallholder is obliged to seek *ganyu* employment or off-farm income, both of which work against the adoption of improved maize technology. Obviously, labour demand from estates and larger smallholders is highest at peak times of agricultural activity such as planting and weeding, and poor smallholders are often unable to plant or weed their own land and that of others at the same time. Usually the preference is to earn immediate cash rather than to work their own farm and receive the benefits some months later. The consequence is that subsistence planting and weeding may be delayed, with inevitable consequences for yields. The better-off smallholders may not be burdened by the opportunity cost of *ganyu* labouring but even if they do *ganyu* work they are likely to be able to offset at least some of the effects on their land by increased fertiliser adoption. The majority, denied access to fertiliser credit, cannot. Another problem is the tendency for part-time

Table 16.3 Malawi: basic indicators

Indicator	Malawi	Sub-Saharan Africa	Date
Life expectancy at birth (years)	48.1	51.8	1990
Completion of primary schooling as % of grade 1 entrants	47	62	1988
Population with access to safe water (%)	53	41	1988–90
People in absolute poverty (%)	90	n.a.	1991
Under-5 mortality rate (per 1,000 live births)	253	165	1990
Daily calorie supply as % of requirements	88	93	1988–90
Aid as % of GNP	29.1	10	1991

Source: UNDP (1993)

farmers to miss out on the potential benefits of extension because extension activities take place during the day when these farmers are working at off-farm activities. This problem is most acute in the Southern Region and especially near Blantyre, where part-time farming is most prevalent due to opportunities for regular off-farm employment.

Because of the unchecked biases of the credit system the result is an exacerbation of rural inequalities. As a number of studies have shown (see Shanmugaratnam et al. 1992; Conroy 1993), and this one confirms, gender of household head and size of smallholding are significantly associated with the adoption of hybrid maize varieties and with both the quantity and stability of income. Thus, male-headed households and those with larger smallholdings tend to determine access to smallholder credit and thus monopolise the efficient use of maize technology. The net effect for poor smallholders is a classic poverty trap, where low land endowment and lack of capital results in low yields and low incomes.

RURAL FINANCE

The financial system in Malawi is small and underdeveloped. It operates with relatively few distortions, especially since 1987 when the Government liberalized interest rates, giving financial institutions in Malawi the authority to make autonomous operating and lending decisions based on commercial considerations (Table 16.4).

The formal financial sector largely bypasses smallholders and especially the rural poor. Malawi has only two commercial banks (prime lending rate in 1993, 21 per cent) and they have limited rural outreach via mobile banking units. There are a number of financial institutions serving the estate sector but for the rural poor their financial needs are likely to go unfulfilled, except the better-off smallholders who may have savings accounts. These savings are most frequently held in post office accounts primarily because they have the largest network of offices and agencies of any financial institution and in 1993 earned a return of 10.75 per cent. Membership of credit unions, known as Savings and Credit Co-operatives (SACCOs), which fall under the umbrella of the USAID-funded Malawi Union of Savings and Credit Co-operatives (MUSCCO) is generally limited to the better-off and especially to those with regular waged employment. Indeed, MUSCCO requires savings first, and grants loans, at 12 or 15 per cent, on the basis of the amount saved, which effectively excludes most smallholders. The Small Enterprise Development Organisation of Malawi (SEDOM) is the principal lender to small enterprises (16 per cent lending rate in 1993) and requires prospective clients to provide 20 per cent collateral and to demonstrate skill or experience in running a small enterprise. Both the commercial banks and the Investment and Development Fund (INDEFUND) make loans to estate farmers but, apart from the

Table 16.4 Formal financial institutions in Malawi

Name of organization	Type of institution	Selected interest rates (1992)
Reserve Bank of Malawi	Central bank	20% (discount rate) 12.5% (treasury bill)
National Bank of Malawi Commercial Bank of Malawi	Commercial banks (nationalised)	21% (prime lending rate) 10% (short-term deposit) 19.5% (6-month time deposit)
Investment & Development Bank (INDEBANK)	Merchant bank	7.5% (short-term call deposit)
New Building Society	Building society	12.75% (minimum mortgage rate)
Post Office Savings Bank (PostBank)	Savings institutions	10.75% (savings rate)
Malawi Union of Savings & Credit Co-operatives (MUSCCO)	Credit union	12% or 15%
Mercantile Credit Leasing & Finance Company of Malawi	Finance houses	8.75% (short-term deposit) 25% (lending rate)
Malawi Development Corporation	Development finance institution	Negotiable
Investment & Development Fund (INDEFUND)	Development finance institution	Negotiable
Small Enterprise Development Organization of Malawi (SEDOM)	Development finance institution	16% (lending rate)
Malawi Mudzi Fund	Microfinance institution	18.5% (6-month lending rate)
Smallholder Agricultural Credit Administration (SACA)	Agricultural credit institution	18% (seasonal lending rate)

Source: World Bank (1993a) *inter alia*

Smallholder Agricultural Credit Administration (SACA), the financial needs of smallholders are largely unfulfilled and those of petty traders and micro-entrepreneurs are ignored altogether.

The informal financial sector is far more significant and includes money-lenders (known as *katapilas*), traders and grain millers, estate owners, employers, co-operative savings associations (or ROSCAs), community funds and, most importantly, friends, neighbours and relatives.[4] Estimates of the incidence of informal sector finance vary enormously but most commentators believe that it is considerably bigger than the formal sector (Chipeta and Mkandawire 1992). However, most informal sector finance is

Table 16.5 SACA and MMF: institutional features

Feature	MMF[a]	SACA[b]
Date of establishment	1989 registered 1990 operational	1968 Farmers' Clubs individual credit 1973 Farmers' Clubs group credit 1988 SACA created
Institutional status	Trust fund	Ministry of Agriculture Dept
Source of funding	IFAD	Multiple (SACA HQ funded by IFAD/World Bank)
Eligibility requirements	<1 ha of land or equivalent assets	Any 'trustworthy' smallholder (<10 ha of land) One credit package per household
Target group (actual)	Rural poor, petty traders, females	Better-off smallholders
No. of borrowers	223[c]	400,062
Female borrowers	82% (overall) 99% (of new borrowers)	28%
Average group size	3.79	25.74
Average loan size	MK222[d]	MK299
Repayment period	6 months (originally 12 months)	Seasonal (roughly 10 months)
Repayment method	At weekly centre meetings which comprise a maximum of 21 members in groups comprising 3–7 individuals	At point of sale of crop (usually via a single repayment)
Savings component	Group tax 5% of loan Compulsory savings of 20 tambala a week	None
Nominal interest rate	18.5%	18%

Source: SACA and MMF internal documents
Notes
[a] Data for 1992–3.
[b] Refers to 1992–3 season.
[c] Refers to borrowers as at March 1993 (at that time there were 337 active members out of a total membership of 1,400).
[d] Refers to off-farm loans only. In 1992–3 the MMF piloted a small number of small loans for agricultural inputs.

short term and for consumption purposes and, because the savings side of the finance equation is largely neglected, the informal sector does not appear to address the needs of the poorest in a sustainable manner.

This chapter focuses on two institutions (Table 16.5): the Malawi Mudzi Fund (MMF) and the Farmers' Club Movement or Smallholder Agricultural Credit Administration (SACA). The latter is a long-established countrywide group-focused credit delivery system, consolidated under a government department within the Ministry of Agriculture. Apart from a small amount of separately administered medium-term credit, all SACA farmers' club credit comprises seasonal packages of agricultural inputs given in kind not cash and made up of fertilisers (which average about 86 per cent of the value of the total credit package), seeds (13 per cent) and pesticides (1 per cent). In contrast, the Malawi Mudzi Fund is a new body (still in an experimental stage), set up in 1989 as a trust fund, modelled on the Grameen Bank and with very limited coverage. Loans are made to individuals within small groups for off-farm income-generation activities. Apart from the fact that they charge apparently similar rates of interest and ostensibly lend through groups, the two organisations have very little in common.

THE SACA: AN ORGANISATIONAL PROFILE

Before focusing on SACA and the current status of the farmers' club system, it is useful to outline the history of agricultural credit in Malawi, which is not untypical of the experience of other countries in anglophone Africa. Prior to 1958 African farmers had no access to formal credit as, excluding commercial banks, the only source of agricultural credit was from the Farmers' Loans and Subsidies Board which served white farmers. In 1958 the Nyasaland African Loans Board was established. Loans were issued in cash or more usually in kind for a variety of purposes including seed and fertiliser. Farmers did not have title deeds to pledge as security, so creditworthiness was based on character (which remains the fundamental criterion for current farmers' club loans) and consequently most loans were short-term. These features – character-based loans, often in kind, usually short-term – became guiding influences in smallholder credit and have remained to this day.

Another major feature, donor involvement, has its origins in 1962, when the Government of Malawi requested 'the United States of America to provide a consultant to study the credit facilities already available in the country and to make recommendations for an expanded credit programme' (SACA 1993: 2).

Following this consultancy, a Central Farmers' Loans Board (later, the Government Loans Board) was established in 1964 and superseded the Nyasaland African Loans Board. A central secretariat was set up in the

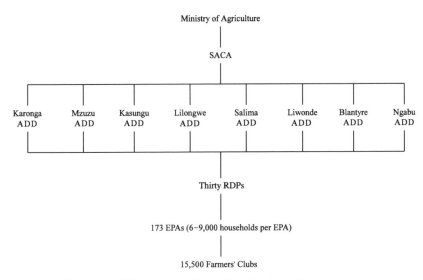

Figure 16.1 The National Rural Development Programme

Ministry of Finance and extension workers assisted the Loans Board in assessing loan applicants and monitoring their farming methods. The next major development occurred in 1968 when, partly with donor funding, the Government launched four Agricultural Development Projects in selected areas. One of these projects was the Lilongwe Land Development Project (LLDP) from which the farmers' club group credit system emerged in 1973 (see p. 345 below).[5] A smallholder credit component was integrated into each project and they were generally seen as successful. Consequently, in 1978, the National Rural Development Programme was created (Figure 16.1) to extend the benefits of the four Agricultural Development Projects to other areas of the country.

A priority for each National Rural Development Programme (NRDP) was the raising of smallholder productivity by the provision of input loans. However, because certain areas within the NRDP became the focus for particular donors, areas that did not receive donor funding were placed at a disadvantage. To counter this, the Government created a Central Credit Fund in 1982 (later the Smallholder Credit Fund) which was the precursor of SACA and it is from this Fund that all loanable funds (including those from donors) were consolidated and distributed. Thus, it is into this legacy that the Smallholder Agricultural Credit Administration was established as a Ministry of Agriculture department in 1987.

SACA fits into the National Rural Development Programme (NRDP) which divides the country into eight Agricultural Development Divisions (ADDs). Each of these ADDs has an average of four Rural Development

342

Projects (RDPs). The RDPs are sub-divided into Extension Planning Areas (EPAs) and each EPA comprises a number of farmers' clubs.

The Credit and Marketing Officer in each ADD manages a credit fund held at the Reserve Bank of Malawi and drawn down through a commercial bank. There are further layers of credit supervisors at both the RDP and EPA levels. In theory, it is the latter cohort known as Credit and Marketing Assistants (CMAs) who are responsible for assisting club officials and members with their loan applications, the processing of loans, the distribution of credit inputs, supervision and loan collection. But contact between CMAs and farmers' clubs is constrained by the fact that each CMA is responsible for between sixty and eighty farmers' clubs.

As SACA was fitted into the existing ADD framework many years after the latter was established, there has always been a blurring of responsibilities concerning the work of SACA employees and the ADD extension staff. In practice, field assistants (primary-level agricultural extension workers attached to the ADDs) have played a pivotal role in credit management and are usually the primary points of contact for farmers' clubs, each field assistant being responsible for between five and ten clubs. As farmers' clubs are supposed to be points of contact for extension work in addition to their credit role, it is quite legitimate for field assistants to be involved in forming clubs and advising on credit packages and their application and impact. However, field assistants, motivated by the fact that their superiors tend to evaluate their performance largely in terms of credit recovery, prioritise SACA work. In effect they cross-subsidise the operations of SACA to such an extent that it is virtually impossible to evaluate its cost structure.[6]

The Agricultural Development and Marketing Corporation (ADMARC) is a parastatal which has had a monopoly in the supply and distribution of inputs and a *de facto* monopsony role in the purchase of the smallholder maize crop. However, this monopolistic role has been greatly reduced under the structural adjustment programme. In the long run this is expected to bring about positive changes but in the short run of the past few years the erosion of this monopoly has coincided with a decline in the SACA annual repayment rate (see pp. 351–2 below). The major input used by smallholders is fertiliser and this is centrally procured by a national fertiliser revolving fund (all fertiliser is imported and due to the substantial transport costs is comparatively expensive).

Figure 16.2 illustrates the flow of credit operations over a seasonal cycle. First, SACA determines future credit allocation on the basis of information gathered from ADD fieldworkers during the current season. The seasonal inputs are procured on a national level by ADMARC and allocated to individuals within farmers' clubs as per each ADD allocation. The inputs are then distributed to ADMARC regional depots. From here the inputs are released to the farmers who obtain their inputs in exchange for an ADD-issued credit voucher (often the farmers' club officials will collect the

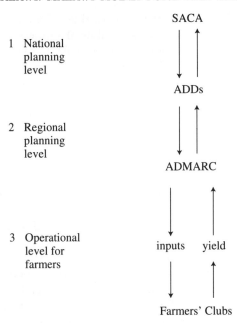

Figure 16.2 The transaction cycle: credit disbursement and collection

inputs on behalf of all their members rather than individual members turning up to the depot one by one for their inputs). ADMARC receives payment from the ADDs in respect of the credit vouchers. Each ADD finances this out of revolving funds established by either donors or the Government and managed separately by each ADD. About ten months later immediately following the maize harvest, the farmer will return to ADMARC with his crop for which he will be paid the (fixed) price. Thereafter, depending on his commitments, he can either pay for the inputs he had obtained on credit immediately or at some specified future date. In either case, the monies are paid to the farmers' club treasurer who issues a receipt to the farmer, consolidates the repayments and passes the monies to the relevant CMA, who issues one consolidated receipt to the treasurer. Thereafter, the respective ADDs replenish their revolving credit funds held with ADMARC. Clearly, if the monopoly position of ADMARC is broken this system is undermined, and that is precisely what has happened since the late 1980s (see pp. 354–5 below).

This process is effective but inefficient. Both the ADDs and ADMARC maintain a complete record of credit transactions thus doubling the administration cost. Ordinary extensionists spend 30 to 50 per cent of their time in credit administration (interviews with ADD officials). Not only does this cross-subsidise the lending operations but it also has a high opportunity cost of reducing the time they may give to other critical extension activities such as running demonstration plots and providing training and advice on fertiliser use. Indeed, there is a further potential 'cost' of this extension cadre input: namely, that they are required to perform two mutually inconsistent roles of providing assistance and learning about farmers' problems whilst enforcing credit discipline.

The farmers' clubs

At the base of the SACA pyramid are the farmers' clubs. They were developed in response to a failed attempt to promote rural co-operatives and with the objective of reducing the costs of lending (hitherto done on an individual basis).[7] The farmers' club group lending system was piloted in Lilongwe in 1973.[8] All groups are voluntary associations and number at least ten members. Under the LLDP most groups had about twenty members but as the scheme has expanded to embrace the whole country this average has gone up, and in 1993 a typical farmers' club had twenty-six members.

Under the LLDP the joint liability of group members was supplemented by a security fund which was initially conceived of as a prelude to a rural savings movement. Borrowers were required to pay 10 per cent of their loan amount as a deposit into a common group fund that was set up with a commercial bank under the supervision of the LLDP administration. Losses due to default were recoverable from this fund which then had to be replenished prior to the issuance of new credit. It was expected that this fund would gradually accumulate over a number of years so that an insurance fund against crop failure could be developed. However, this floundered partly because members preferred to disband their groups after each season and establish new ones before the next season so that membership could be kept flexible. Further criticism came from those who felt the idea of a security fund was too punitive and a deterrent to farmers wary of taking on a loan for the first time. There were also allegations concerning misuse of the deposit funds by the credit officials.

The LLDP was judged a success primarily due to the rapid uptake of group credit, which was presumably attributable to the fact that individual credit was charged at 15 per cent compared to 10 per cent for group credit. Although there was no significant difference between the repayment records of individuals and groups, there were indications that the almost equal repayment records were achieved with much greater effort in collecting payments from individuals than from credit groups (Schaefer-Kehnert 1982).[9] Since then, the farmers' club system has expanded to cover the whole country but the pecuniary benefits of group lending versus comparable individual credit have never been quantified. However, the farmers' club system has become institutionalised and by removing the need to secure loans against capital – which would be impossible as few farmers would have sufficient collateral to secure loans on commercial terms – has opened a window of opportunity that has embraced over a quarter of all smallholders through 15,500 groups.

As already mentioned, farmers' clubs exist almost solely for the purpose of obtaining packages of inputs on credit. They are voluntary associations with broad eligibility requirements: 'it is important to note that the responsibility for selecting an individual eligible to join the club lies with the club membership itself' (SACA 1993). Membership is open to any 'trustworthy' smallholder (anyone farming less than 10 ha) but occasionally non-smallholders receive loans (see p. 348 below). The farmers' clubs are usually formed with assistance from ADD officials and all members are supposed to have at least a day's training in leadership, conducting meetings, keeping payments and receipts ledgers, and credit procurement procedures. Although the author's survey revealed that most borrowers could remember having received some advice or training from the ADD officials, virtually none could remember exactly when this was given or what the training or advice was actually about. Recall was generally better among club office bearers but even for them there was little in the way of follow-up training on management. Membership of clubs appears to be flexible, with 87 per cent of sampled respondents reporting that membership of their club had changed since they joined: the usual practice is for successful clubs to expand up to the point where communication within the group and management of the group becomes too complex, then the group splits.

Farmers' clubs are managed by unpaid, elected officials (chairperson, secretary and treasurer) and sometimes by sub-committees, such as a discipline or a crop inspection sub-committee.[10] The elected officials are likely to be among the better-educated members of the community as they are supposed to be literate. Virtually all clubs had an annual membership fee which usually ranged from MK2 to MK10 (modal = MK5) and some clubs also had a monthly levy, usually of less than MK1. These funds were used for club expenses such as purchasing stationery or sometimes as a type of members' welfare fund. Meetings were held according to the wishes of members. The author's survey found that 38 per cent held fortnightly meetings, 29 per cent monthly, 24 per cent weekly and 5 per cent annually. Often the meetings were of an informal nature and rarely were all members present. It is estimated that, on average, over a year only about two-thirds of members were present at meetings. Attendance peaked in the weeks leading up to credit disbursement and at harvest time (repayment time) but fell off at other times. A typical meeting lasts two to three hours; in theory, fines are imposed for absence or late arrival (usually between 50 tambala and MK1) but in practice these are rarely imposed because members tend to have excuses or refused to pay.

Farmers' clubs comprise individuals from a particular locality and often represent a fairly heterogeneous mixture of smallholder and smallholding types. Within a particular region, for example, land-holding sizes and rates of application of technology can vary within groups as much as between groups. What is clear, however, is that groups are self-selecting and this means that the poorest farmers (a disproportionate number of whom are female), who are perceived to be a greater credit risk, are usually excluded from club membership (see Box 16.1, p. 357). Members are mature, with an average age of forty-four years;[11] tend to be male (official SACA data indicate that 72 per cent of borrowers are male); and to have an above-average land-holding size (combined average for all three ADDs surveyed was 1.96 ha for borrowers − range 0.2 to 12 ha − and 1.09 ha for non-borrowers − range 0.1 to 3 ha).

There is no evidence to suggest that any particular composition of farmers' club membership is better than another. In discussions with farmers, it was found that groups were formed largely on the basis of geographical proximity of members. Although credit officials are supposed to ensure that members are 'trustworthy, hard working and that they follow extension advice', the process of selection is devolved to the groups themselves and appears to be based on two levels: the social and the economic. In discussions with farmers' club members in one area, the following risk perceptions could be ascertained (Figure 16.3).

First (level 1), a potential farmers' club member is appraised on the basis

---

Level 2: Economic criteria

Sources and stability of household income

Assets of the household

Crops grown

Acreage of land holding

Level 1: Social criteria

High risk

PERSONS living in the village but farming outside the credit area

PERSONS living outside the credit area but farming in the village

PERSONS living and farming in the village but not born in the village. Connected to the village by marriage

WOMEN born, living and farming in the village but with no husband, a husband elsewhere or dead

MEN born, living and farming in the village

Low risk

Figure 16.3 Credit risk as perceived by the farmer

of social status criteria which concern his or her relationship to the village. A second level of appraisal (level 2) is based on economic criteria. The more of these things a household possesses, the lower is the potential liability to the club. The selection process, then, comprises an appraisal of these two closely connected sets of information. Thereafter, homogeneity of the same features is likely to solidify and stabilise the group but only so long as individual self-interest is met by the group. However, largely because of the nature of the credit system with its restrictive input and output options for farmers, there is no evidence to indicate that income homogeneity within groups will result in higher repayments than income heterogeneity within groups, *ceteris paribus*.

The main function of the farmers' clubs is for members to obtain seasonal credit by accepting mutual liability for the loans obtained for each member. Not only does the group screen borrowers and apparently provide the substitute for collateral but it is also charged with the responsibility of ensuring repayment of the credit packages. This has the effect of encouraging club officials to place importance on the ends (making sure each farmer repays his loan by the end of the season) rather than the means used to achieve this (suitability of the credit package and its appropriate application). Thus the farmers' club system successfully removes the need for securing loans on collateral and thereby increases access to credit and it also lowers the administration and monitoring costs of lending and until recently ensured high repayment rates (see p. 351 below) but questions exist as to the technical efficiency of the lending programme. There are also allegations from some smallholders that the devolution of membership of farmers' clubs to the local level results in political interference and exclusion on questionable grounds. For example, during the author's survey, a number of non-members of farmers' clubs claimed that they were prevented from joining their local groups due to hostility from chiefs or from representatives of the Malawi Congress Party.

SACA also makes available a small number of medium-term loans to individuals who may or may not be in farmers' clubs. These loans are usually repayable over five years at 20 per cent per annum and are made in kind for durable items such as farm carts, ploughs and sprayers. Loans are also made for livestock including dairy animals, oxen and poultry. At the end of 1992 there were 6,011 medium-term loanees owing MK1,211,072. The on-time recovery rate stood at 43.5 per cent. This poor performance is largely attributable to the fact that medium-term loans are not secured on the basis of group liability and are not integral to a closed input–output cycle like the seasonal credit packages. They are focused on the wealthier farmers, especially in the Central Region, and do not appear to be closely monitored. According to a senior SACA official, the demand for these loans is not great as farmers tend to perceive medium-term credit as high-risk. Many are deterred by the value of such loans, while others have a preference to use labour rather than capital inputs wherever possible because labour is usually cheaper and is multi-functional whereas capital is often uni-functional. Thus labour can be hired and fired and used for weeding, planting and harvesting whereas a plough, for example, is less flexible and remains unused for most of the year. Exceptions to this rule include dairy animals, poultry, oxen and farm carts. Getting dairy animals on credit is considered a viable option by many not only because they constitute a physical asset and are likely to yield a more regular and stable income than crops but also because of the status accruable from owning such animals. These loans – unlike any others – are also compulsorily underwritten with an insurance policy, guaranteeing the farmer and SACA against losses due to disease and/or death of the animals. Credit for farm carts and oxen is also popular because these items have many uses and can be hired out throughout the year to yield an income for the farmer. Indeed, the ownership of the means of transport in rural areas is a key to power.

Most farmers' clubs function as both supportive and disciplined bodies but the repayment objective is paramount and the exclusion sanction is most effective in ensuring credit discipline. If a particular member has a problem then other members are likely to see the danger signals earlier than SACA or ADD officials. Common problems may include incorrect use of inputs, neglect of fields, illness or death in the family. If these problems occur the farmers' club has a number of options, depending on the problem. Usually moral pressure will be put on the member to encourage him to overcome his problem. If there is a genuine reason, such as sickness or death in the family, other members may provide help in the form of labour or an emergency loan to hire labour. In most cases, the club officials are likely to alert the ADD officials to the problem. If a loanee refuses to repay his loan, there are basically three options open to the club officials: do nothing and become ineligible for credit the next year; repay the loan out of other members' savings or income (7 per cent of those interviewed had helped out other members of their farmers' club in this way); or, the most common approach, seize assets of the defaulter and sell them to recoup the costs of the loan. The defaulter is then, obviously, excluded from the club.

In theory if one group member defaults then the whole group is ineligible for a future loan. In practice this does not always happen because SACA has a policy of 'exclusion as last resort', essentially because it is believed that a heavy-handed policy would result in too many groups breaking up. Ministry of Agriculture policy also emphasises the importance of extending the opportunity to repay for as long as possible, believing that exclusion would be self-defeating in the long run as an ever-increasing number of farmers would simply be caught in the type of poverty trap experienced by most poor smallholders involving low technology adoption, low yield, low income and low food security. Thus, each ADD Programme Manager has the discretion to allow borrowers who have repaid 90 per cent

Table 16.6 Smallholder maize area planted, average yields and total production, 1983–4 to 1991–2

Season	Maize (all varieties)		
	Area cultivated ('000 ha)	Yield (kg/ha)	Production ('000 tonnes)
1983–4	1,183	1,182	1,398
1984–5	1,145	1,184	1,355
1985–6	1,193	1,085	1,295
1986–7	1,182	1,017	1,202
1987–8	1,215	1,174	1,427
1988–9	1,271	1,188	1,510
1989–90	1,344	999	1,343
1990–1	1,392	1,142	1,590
1991–2	1,362	482	657

Source: Third Crop Estimates (1992 price review) in Simler (1993)

of their current loan by 30 September of each season to be issued with new loans (SACA 1993). Further, in April 1992 SACA relaxed the rule on credit discipline by stating that any borrower who has repaid 100 per cent of his loan would qualify for further lending through his credit club irrespective of whether other members had repaid or not. This position was opposed by the World Bank.

Until 1991–2, most clubs had avoided defaulting and the repayment rates in all regions of the country were impressive but in that season there was a severe drought that plunged the country into a crisis and virtually wiped out the maize crop in many areas. The impact of the drought varied throughout the country and, according to Malawi Meteorological Department data, rainfall in 1992–3 (a typical year) for Blantyre ADD was over 50 per cent up on 1991–2; up by about a third in Lilongwe; and by about a fifth in Kasungu. As shown in Table 16.6, the maize yield for 1991–2 was only 43 per cent of the average yield for the previous eight seasons. As a result a large number of farmers simply did not have a crop to sell and so could not repay their loans. The Government (and hence SACA) responded to this by announcing that any borrowers who had suffered losses through no fault of their own and were therefore unable to repay would be granted a moratorium. Their seasonal loan for 1991–2 would be converted into a medium-term loan repayable over three years. The public announcement to this effect got distorted and the rumour spread throughout the countryside that a *general* moratorium on repayment had been declared. Once this belief became ingrained it was difficult to change, especially in an election year.[12] Thus, many farmers – whether able to

350

Table 16.7 Smallholder credit and repayment, 1968–70 to
1992–3, and yield data, 1983–4 to 1991–2

Year	Total disbursed (MK million)	Average yields (kg/ha)	Percentage repayment
1968–9	0.43		100.00
1969–70	0.13		99.78
1970–1	0.28		99.83
1971–2	0.63		99.58
1972–3	0.67		99.81
1973–4	0.80		99.83
1974–5[a]	1.21		98.70
1975–6	1.48		99.75
1976–7	1.67		98.26
1977–8	2.40		97.60
1978–9	2.87		98.49
1979–80	3.57		97.46
1980–1	5.68		97.58
1981–2	5.24		97.92
1982–3	8.34		97.19
1983–4	11.46	1,182	97.95
1984–5	15.56	1,184	96.67
1985–6	19.07	1,085	88.59
1986–7	18.28	1,017	92.18
1987–8[b]	26.87	1,174	91.00
1988–9	42.20	1,188	79.90
1989–90	56.00	999	85.90
1990–1	6.50	1,142	86.50
1991–2	87.97	482	20.84
1992–3	100.14	n.a.	n.a.

Source: World Bank (1993a) except yield data, see Table 16.6; 1991–2
figures obtained from SACA Quarterly Report, October–December
1992; 1992–3 figure from SACA internal document 5/3/93.
Notes
[a] First season of group credit under the LLDP.
[b] First year of group credit consolidated under SACA.

repay or not – were included in this moratorium and the repayment rate
plummeted (Table 16.7).

Thus, although the 1991–2 collapse in repayment is undoubtedly a
function of an exceptional drought which resulted in low yields, the
severity of the collapse has much to do with the democratisation of Malawi
that was under way in 1992 and 1993. The fact that 64 per cent of all SACA
credit goes to smallholders in Kasungu and Lilongwe (see Table 16.8) gives
validity to this hypothesis, for it is in these ADDs that smallholders were in
general least affected by the drought and also have the greatest security
against the risk of low maize yields due to the prevalence of drought-
resistant tobacco crops in these regions.[13]

351

Table 16.8 SACA credit allocation by ADD, 1992–3

ADD	Input value	Farmers' clubs	Total members	Average loan per member	Average loan per club
Lilongwe	40,197,388	3,634	116,038	346	11,061
Kasungu	36,500,625	3,887	104,544	349	9,390
Mzuzu	12,699,570	1,955	37,066	343	6,495
Liwonde	11,951,282	1,999	60,125	199	5,979
Blantyre	8,974,167	1,605	39,643	226	5,591
Salima	6,666,993	1,122	24,732	270	5,979
Karonga	1,359,100	603	6,469	210	2,254
Ngabu	1,209,963	740	11,445	106	1,635
Totals	119,559,040	15,545	400,062	299	7,691

Source: SACA internal documents
Note: All figures rounded to nearest MK.

SACA: organisational performance

Due to the way smallholder credit is organised it is virtually impossible to evaluate the organisational effectiveness of SACA without incorporating an analysis of ADMARC and the ADDs together with various agricultural and agronomic aspects, all of which is likely to lead us very far from a socio-economic investigation into smallholder credit. The determinants of successful smallholder lending have as much to do with SACA as they have to do with the ADDs and with ADMARC and with crop yields which are determined by factors beyond the control of SACA, as evidenced by the experience of the 1991–2 drought. Even the method of funding tends to sidestep SACA as individual donors fund specific rural development programmes in ADDs and the funds are allocated to ADDs and only 'administered' by SACA. SACA itself receives virtually all its HQ funds from the World Bank (45.5 per cent) and IFAD (45.5 per cent), with the Government contributing the balance (9 per cent) (SACA Audit Reports 5/02/93). Donor inputs tend to be directed at capital and recurrent costs in addition to loanable funds but do not generally support long-term technical assistance. It is extremely difficult to get a clear picture of the cost structure of SACA, principally because of the high degree of cross-subsidisation between SACA and the ADDs and the impact of price controls on the credit packages. Thus, a World Bank appraisal mission concluded:

> Given SACA's status as a government department, it is unable to operate along customary commercial principles. As all its field staff are Ministry of Agriculture personnel, it is currently impossible to accurately estimate its operating costs. Informed estimates, based on the work times spent by field personnel including agricultural extension staff on SACA's credit operations, when taken as a percentage of salary costs, indicate that 1990/91 operating costs approached 11 percent of total loan portfolio.

With annual interest rates fixed by the Government at 18 percent and 25 percent for short term and medium term credit respectively, it is evident that SACA is being subsidized by Government at an estimated MK4 million per year.

(World Bank 1993a: 16)[14]

Table 16.8 shows credit allocation by ADD. The two most important ADDs (in terms of yields of both cash crops and staple food crops) are Kasungu and Lilongwe which together account for 64 per cent of all SACA credit, 55 per cent of all borrowers and 48 per cent of farmers' clubs. As SACA is a national agricultural credit agency, it could be expected that credit allocation follows national demographic patterns. However, the figures in Table 16.8 can only partly be explained by demography. The Northern Region (Mzuzu and Karonga) is relatively under-populated (10 per cent of total smallholder population) and hence has a relatively small proportion of clubs, members and credit inputs, but the Southern Region with 55 per cent of smallholders has less than 19 per cent of credit inputs and 28 per cent of total membership. SACA's policy has favoured the richer Central Region (which has also been the heartland of Banda's Malawi Congress Party). This is, of course, justified in terms of the Central Region being the major agricultural producer and thus it has both the greatest requirement for credit (in absolute terms) and is the main contributor to the credit system, but it does nothing to address the needs of poorer Malawian smallholders in the Northern and Southern Regions. Although total membership stands at 400,062, this is only about 31 per cent of the total number of smallholder households in Malawi and included in this number are very few of the 'core poor' (<0.5 ha) and relatively few of the 'poor' (between 0.5 and 1.5 ha) (see Table 16.10).

If SACA does not appear equitable in terms of the regional distribution of credit, it has certainly achieved impressive growth in total credit disbursement having quadrupled total disbursements in its six-year existence (Table 16.7). Indeed, SACA was created to consolidate credit activities and to facilitate greater lending volumes in response to the demands from donors impressed by the very high repayment rates achieved by the farmers' club system but concerned about the capacity of the system to grow without a central executive. Thus, SACA has its origins in donor demands for greater accountability and owes its existence essentially to World Bank/ IFAD planning and funding. Thus, donor worries were placated and the volume of loanable funds increased enormously following the creation of SACA. Unfortunately, these extra funds brought problems for the ADDs as they often did not have the resources to deal with the greatly increased flows of money that accrued from donors and were allocated to them via SACA. Thus, screening practices slipped, more risky farmers got loans and the underlying trend to lower repayment rates accelerated. In response to this, there were accusations from some farmers that SACA or ADD officials (or their representatives) indulged in 'tough guy tactics' in an attempt to forestall the fall in repayment rates. Some farmers alleged that considerable intimidation and coercion were used, including the seizure of assets to repay debts, thereby ensuring that particular clubs did not lose their eligibility for future loans. It is difficult to get a clear picture of the extent of these practices but it seems that they were localised and were not officially sanctioned and it is clear that they did not redress the underlying downward trend in repayment rates which plummeted and reached a point of no return in 1991–2. Although attributable to a variety of factors, the root of which was a severe drought, 1991–2 will be remembered as the year in which the dreaded domino effect occurred leaving the Government as the 'underwriter of last resort'. However, these events have subsequently been overtaken by sweeping institutional changes which resulted in SACA being replaced by the Malawi Rural Finance Company (MRFC) in time for seasonal credit issues in 1993–4. At the time of the study, it was expected that the MRFC would take over all the assets and liabilities of SACA and be responsible for recovering old or doubtful debts including those incurred in 1991–2. However, the Malawian Government was expected to be responsible for underwriting the costs incurred by the MRFC in debt recovery (including any debt write-offs).

The MRFC was in the planning pipeline prior to 1991–2 and, following the creation of SACA itself, is the second major World Bank-induced attempt to restructure and upgrade the farmers' club system. The MRFC is the central component of a US$25 million World Bank-initiated Rural Financial Services Project and is expected to 'follow the normal commercial and private sector practices' of a bank (World Bank 1993a). It will comprise four divisions: small estates; smallholders; off-farm loans in rural areas for income-generation schemes; and deposit-taking. The farmers' club system will remain intact and function largely as it did under SACA except that each farmers' club will be encouraged to develop a savings fund to complement their credit activities. (For details see World Bank 1993a.)

The striking increase in disbursements of credit packages shown in Table 16.7 has not corresponded with a commensurate increase in yields. Rather, the productivity of smallholder maize production has stagnated over the past decade. There are a number of reasons that could explain this apparent discrepancy between the supply of inputs and output. First, an indeterminate but possibly large amount of fertiliser obtained through farmers' clubs is resold to estate farmers (who are not eligible for the subsidized credit inputs). This resale may be at a mark-up, or at the subsidised price, or it may be at a lower price with sale forced on smallholders by their need to resolve immediate liquidity problems. Mkandawire *et al.* (1990) estimated that 70 per cent of small estates (<15 ha) obtained fertiliser from ADMARC either through illicit participation in smallholder credit clubs or through direct purchase. In either case, it is likely to compound the problem of input availability for smallholders by crowding out those smallholders who do not participate in a farmers' club or those borrowers who wish to purchase additional inputs from ADMARC on cash terms. Sometimes individual smallholders will sell their 'surplus' fertiliser to estate farmers; on other occasions estate farmers may organise smallholders into 'phoney' farmers' clubs with the specific purpose of getting fertiliser on credit to transfer to the estate farmer.

During the author's survey, cases of the whole farmers' club credit package going to estate farmers were discovered. There were also numerous discrepancies between the official amounts of fertiliser disbursed to individual farmers and the amounts that these farmers claimed to have *used* on their land. In a few cases, it was found that farmers deliberately overstated the size of the land that they intended to devote to maize so as to get a larger credit package than was necessary. They would then sell the surplus fertiliser and use the excess land for an alternative crop (possibly tobacco) or leave it fallow. It is more difficult simply to claim a bigger plot than there is because the actual size of land is usually known to the field assistants whereas the actual cropping patterns are more easily manipulated.

The second major reason likely to explain the inconsistency between an increase in distributed inputs and a lower than expected increase in yields is the inappropriate application of fertiliser. Some commentators allege that the wrong credit packages are recommended to some smallholders because different soil and agro-ecological conditions are not adequately planned for when the Ministry of Agriculture determines its credit packages (Conroy 1993). It is clear from the author's survey that application rates and the timing of application varied enormously. Part of the problem is late delivery of inputs as confirmed by the 41 per cent of farmers surveyed who said they had experienced delays (from a few days to a few weeks) in getting their full credit package from ADMARC. But the major problem for smallholders appears to be in knowing when and how to apply fertilisers.[15] Although resolving these problems is outside the direct remit of SACA and even the farmers' club system, they obviously have a major bearing on the impact of the credit programme.

One criticism that can be levelled at SACA is that it has failed to build on the benefits of group lending and has not developed some of the innovative practices associated with group lending schemes in other parts of the developing world. This may well be because SACA is managed and controlled by the Government and thus operates along classic civil service lines, being highly bureaucratic and hierarchical. It has no independent policy-making function and all aspects of credit management are determined by a National Credit Committee which comprises senior civil servants. Inevitably this means that politics compromises commercial decision-making. An example of this was SACA's difficulty in persuading the Government to allow them to raise the interest rate on seasonal credit. Despite ever-escalating inflation and strong donor pressure it took a number of seasons before the National Credit Committee finally acceded to the request from SACA to raise the interest rate from 12 per cent to 18 per cent. Although not always in conflict, SACA often appears to have difficulty balancing the respective demands and influences of, on one hand, its donors, and on the other hand, the Government.

Thus, SACA does not have a 'proactive' role in credit recovery. In fact, it has little real control over its loans. Quantities and prices of inputs are determined exogenously to SACA's operations. Credit allocation is done at arm's length with screening devolved to the farmers themselves and distribution controlled by ADMARC and monitored by the ADDs. It has no prospect of independent financial sustainability, relying on a mixture of concessionary donor funds and government subventions for loanable funds, capital and recurrent costs. There is no savings component to raise capital and, by Government decree, SACA does not even earn income from its funds held on deposit in the Post Office Bank.

SACA does not operate incentive schemes for either its staff or its borrowers. At the end of 1992, SACA had an establishment of 433 staff (corresponding to 924 borrowers per staff member) assigned to work exclusively on SACA duties but none of the staff had previous banking experience. There are no official financial incentives to enhance staff performance other than via the usual civil service channels and, largely as a result of this, certain crucial departments, such as financial control and computing/data management, are very weak and constitute a significant structural weakness for the organisation. It is clearly very difficult for SACA to recruit or retain staff in these areas because of the competitive remunerative packages offered by private-sector organisations. For borrowers, there is no incentive scheme to encourage early repayment. In the early 1980s an incentive scheme was piloted in one ADD which stipulated that if a 100 per cent repayment were achieved the whole club would receive a 5 per cent rebate on their loan. This lasted for only a couple of seasons and was shelved because it was felt that it would drain the capital base of the ADDs, reducing their loanable funds. Furthermore, there is no incentive scheme for good individual repayers who are not rewarded with bigger loans or better terms, as credit packages are largely based on land-holding size, not farmer efficiency or a good repayment record. Thus, with more or less fixed land-holding sizes for most borrowers, there is little opportunity for farmers to graduate to bigger loans.

Targeting issues

From the survey data, the typical farmers' club member is male (79 per cent), in his forties, has a household of 6.8 members and will have above-

356

Box 16.1 Female participation in farmers' clubs

Although female-headed households constitute about a third of all smallholders they are disproportionately over-respected among those farming small plots. About two-thirds of all households cultivating less than 0.5 ha are headed by females and 72 per cent of female-headed households cultivate less than 1 ha (Shanumugaratnam *et al.* 1992), compared to the national average of 56 per cent. As smallholder credit is biased in favour of those with above-average sized land holdings, it is not surprising that traditionally relatively few females received credit packages. However, partly in response to donor pressures, there has been a concerted effort to increase the number of female members since the late 1980s. Thus, in 1992–3, SACA was able to produce data on female membership (see below) which demonstrate good coverage, especially in Blantyre. Data relating to previous years are not available but it is widely believed among SACA and ADD officials that female membership has risen dramatically over recent years. In contrast, and significantly, very few females get medium-term loans.

ADD	*Total membership*	*Female membership*	*% female*
Kasungu	104,544	27,263	26
Lilongwe	116,038	27,895	24
Blantyre	39,643	14,769	37
Overall	400,062	110,972	28

Among those female borrowers surveyed by the author (21 per cent of the sample), the average land holding was 0.9 ha compared to 2.24 ha for males; no female borrower had had more than eight credit packages yet a third of males had; and the average value of the credit packages for female borrowers was only half of the comparable figure for males. These figures do not necessarily reflect gender biases *per se* in the credit system but certainly illustrate the inherent disadvantages experienced by female smallholders.

None of the women surveyed were in female-only groups and none specified a preference for this. A number of cases appeared to exist where a female was obtaining a loan effectively on behalf of a male member of her family or household. The extent of this was, for obvious reasons, difficult to gauge, but as 60 per cent of female respondents were not heads of household, it may have been a fairly common practice which could serve to undermine the perceived or potential benefits of increasing the number of female loanees. Thus, it is not clear whether SACA is actually reaching its target of female-headed households and so it may not be achieving the expected impact from increasing the number of female loanees.

average levels of education (75 per cent with at least two years of primary school education and 62 per cent with four or more years), reflecting the fact that members are typically male heads of household and therefore likely to have had preferential access to education. Some 39 per cent of respondents had other income-generating activities at some time during the year (this figure excludes income-generating activities principally undertaken by other members of the respondent's household). These activities were usually irregular and seasonal and, in most cases, based on trading. As farming is a family activity, it is not too surprising to find that 8 per cent of the sampled farmers combined their farming with full-time waged employment, usually in the public sector. Additionally, there was a high incidence of *ganyu* labour, especially among those with comparatively smaller land holdings. Although it is exceedingly difficult to determine farm employment, the typical borrower estimated he had 5.84 people working on his land at the peak times of the agricultural season and 2.91 people at low times.[16] Only 6 per cent of respondents claimed to be more or less self-sufficient in terms of their own labour input to their land.

The non-borrower sample of smallholders was broadly comparable in terms of gender and age but had slightly lower levels of educational attainment (62 per cent with at least two years of primary school education and 52 per cent with four or more years). Only 21 per cent said they had other income-generating activities besides farming. As with the borrowers, this refers to the income-generating activities undertaken by the *individual respondent* and not by other members of the household. Reflecting smaller land holdings, the average non-borrower employed about 3.44 people at peak times and 2.28 people at low activity times. Some 10 per cent claimed to be more or less self-sufficient in terms of their own labour input to their land.

Table 16.9 Smallholder land holdings (average hectarage)

		Farmers' club members	Non-members
Total smallholding	Kasungu	2.38	1.16
	Lilongwe	2.33	1.06
	Blantyre	1.35	1.04
	Overall	1.96	1.09
Area under maize	Kasungu	1.36	0.68
crop: all varieties	Lilongwe	1.49	0.67
	Blantyre	0.92	0.88
	Overall	1.30	0.74
Area under tobacco	Kasungu	0.52	0.23
	Lilongwe	0.56	0.20
	Blantyre	0.00	0.00
	Overall	0.64	0.15

Source: Author's survey

Table 16.10 Credit for the wealthy?
Allocation by land-holding size

Size of holding (ha)	Farmers' club members (%)	Non-members (%)
<0.5	7	12
>0.49 <1.0	20	32
>0.99 <1.5	21	30
>1.49 <2	17	18
>1.99	35	8

Source: Author's survey

Of more significance are the data on land-holding size and use. This information is presented in Table 16.9. The agriculturally rich areas of Lilongwe and Kasungu show a notable difference in total land-holding size between farmers' club members and non-members, the former being approximately twice as big. For Blantyre the difference is not so great. The pattern for total hectarage is mirrored by the pattern for maize hectarage (all those sampled grew maize). However, the most pertinent figures are those for tobacco production: 85 per cent of all farmers' club respondents in Lilongwe and Kasungu grew tobacco, compared to just 42 per cent of the non-borrower respondents from the same ADDs. None of the respondents in Blantyre (farmers' club members or not) had tobacco crops; this is primarily because they do not have licences to grow tobacco and, in many cases, would not have smallholdings big enough to justify planting it. As tobacco is a major cash crop and source of income for those smallholders who are able to grow it, the already significant differences in land-holding size (and hence, wealth) between those smallholders in the Central Region and those from Blantyre are transformed into even bigger differences in income, as shown below in Table 16.16.

Returning to the definition of the poor given earlier, it can be seen from this sample that SACA credit is going to the top quartile of smallholders (that is, the non-poor). Table 16.10 shows just how far SACA is from reaching the poor. Only 7 per cent of those sampled are 'core poor' and 52 per cent are 'non-poor'. By comparison, 74 per cent of the non-borrower sample can be classified as 'core poor' or 'poor'.[17]

Credit and savings histories

A notable feature of farmers' club loans is the number of repeat borrowers. From those surveyed, the average borrower in Kasungu had obtained 4.44 loans; in Blantyre, 5.21 loans; and in Lilongwe, 9.26 loans. Overall the average number of seasonal loans per respondent was 6.38 loans. Only

Table 16.11 Credit and savings experiences of credit and non-credit farmers in the ten years prior to the survey

Type of institution	Credit farmers (%)	Non-credit farmers (%)
Credit		
Commercial bank	2	0
Credit unions (MUSCCO)	6	0
Shopkeepers	25	22
Friends/relatives	34	30
ROSCAs	3	0
Moneylenders	16	16
Savings		
Commercial bank	14	6
Post Office	14	8
Other formal savings	5	0

Source: Author's survey

5 per cent of those sampled were in receipt of their first seasonal loan, yet 21 per cent had had ten or more loans and one farmer in Lilongwe was servicing his twenty-ninth consecutive loan. It seems reasonable to conclude that the farmers' club system of credit allocation has a narrow focus on relatively better-off repeat borrowers. The system is a conservative one and makes no attempt to wean-off those farmers who are able to purchase inputs on cash.

Table 16.11 shows that few borrowers had any experience of other types of institutional borrowing. Two respondents had borrowed from commercial banks, six had taken loans from MUSCCO affiliates and one (not shown in the table) had obtained some sort of Government loan (the respondent could not remember the exact details). Informal credit was far more common. A quarter of the sample had obtained short-term credit from shopkeepers usually for a small amount of provisions which rarely totalled more than MK30. About a third of respondents admitted to borrowing from friends or relatives. Most of these loans were for less than MK200, but one was for MK5,000, so the average was skewed upwards to MK354. Loans from Co-operative Savings Associations (ROSCAs) were surprisingly few (only three cases).

Relatively few respondents admitted to having obtained loans from moneylenders. Only sixteen cases were recorded and the average amount borrowed was MK100; in all cases the loan was for consumption purposes. One can assume that this figure is an under-representation, as people considered that borrowing from moneylenders carried a social stigma. Respondents, whether they had used a moneylender or not, were unanimously of the opinion that moneylenders' behaviour was exploitative and that they should be avoided. Most reported that moneylenders generally got a 100 per cent return on their loans irrespective of the time-frame. Whether the loan was to be repaid in a week, a month or a season, the standard cost was a doubling of the original amount lent. Moneylending in Malawi apparently grew out of the practice of lending and borrowing commodities, as reported in Chipeta and Mkandawire (1992).

Most respondents reported that moneylenders were unlikely to give relatively long-term loans (for seasonal inputs, for example) and were usually most likely to make loans for consumption purposes, for distress consumption, such as funeral or medical expenses, and for the payment of school fees. Thus, there is little in the form of a competitive relationship between moneylenders and farmers' club credit, as the two forms of lending are in quite distinct markets. There was a general feeling that moneylenders would not lend to the poorer members of a community but only to those who could offer some form of surety, such as to a member of the family with a waged income or a particular asset (money-lenders often insist on loans being guaranteed by an *mboni* who is usually a trusted man or relative of the debtor who testifies as to the borrower's honesty and ultimately underwrites the loan). For those who had used a moneylender, the process of getting a loan was not as quick as is generally assumed. First-time borrowers are likely to incur a significant transaction cost measured in time-consumed travelling to meet the moneylender, negotiating with him and then waiting for his response. Once one loan has been paid back and a record established the procedure is quick, the average time taken between first approaching the lender and getting the cash was 2.28 days. Some reported having to make repeated visits to the moneylender to persuade him of their creditworthiness. Although the latter can foreclose on a borrower's assets, this is a course of action which carries a number of costs for the lender as well as the borrower, and the general feeling was that moneylenders preferred to avoid seizing assets as often as possible so were careful to undertake a thorough screening of potential borrowers. Nevertheless, asset seizure remained their principal sanction on default.

Although SACA does not provide a savings facility this does not mean that borrowers do not save. Surprisingly, 33 per cent of respondents had accounts with formal savings institutions. These accounts were held almost exclusively and in equal numbers with either the Post Office Savings Bank or the National Bank of Malawi. Almost a third of those with accounts held over MK1,000 on deposit and the average deposit (for those with accounts) was MK930. Of those without accounts, the overwhelming majority said that this was primarily because they did not have enough money to make saving worthwhile but 13 per cent were deterred because they felt that banks were not interested in having customers like them, citing, in partic-ular, the infrequency of visits by mobile banks to their areas and hostility from bank workers as major deterrents. Although it is very difficult to ascertain the extent of rural savings in non-formal institutions, 54 per cent of respondents admitted to holding cash balances above those required for normal day-to-day living expenses outside formal institutions. Additionally, a probably significant but indeterminate amount of 'wealth' is held in the form of physical assets which are likely to provide reasonable security but poor returns.

It seems clear that there are savable funds in the rural areas but it must not be forgotten that the sample of farmers' club members comprises the better-off sections of the rural community. In contrast, 54 per cent of the non-borrower sample felt they had no prospect of saving as they did not have sufficient funds and only 14 per cent had formal bank accounts with average cash holding in these accounts of MK249, which is little more than a quarter of the comparable borrower group figure. There is also a noticeable suspicion of formal savings institutions among many rural people, who repeatedly indicated a preference to hold 'wealth' (whether real or imagined) in traditional forms rather than in accounts.

Farmers' club credit experiences

In theory the choice of credit package is supposed to rest with the individual recipients as per the advice of the ADD officials. In practice the decision is largely made by the ADD officials in consultation with the farmers' club officials and is dependent on what is available at the ADMARC depot. Officially, there are over 170 different credit packages that are available to smallholders but in practice many will not be available and there is a much narrower range of input packages actually in use. Over half of the respondents complained that they did not get what they wanted, although this complaint invariably referred to quantity rather than to particular fertiliser or seed types. This finding was backed up by the fact that 42 per cent of respondents had purchased fertiliser on cash terms in addition to their credit package. A quarter of these cases had involved the farmer purchasing more fertiliser on cash than he had received on credit. Further, 25 per cent of respondents had purchased additional amounts of seed on cash terms. Therefore, either SACA is failing to supply some farmers with enough inputs on credit or, at some point in the system, there is extensive redistribution of credit packages to non-participants in farmers' clubs. As mentioned above, credit farmers are known to resell input packages to estate farmers who are supposed to obtain their inputs from separate marketing agents at a higher price. This two-tier pricing system operates with significant arbitrage. In practice, there is little to stop estate farmers purchasing inputs from ADMARC. Although the latter is supposed to give preference to smallholders, the price differential and the supply constraint combine to ensure ample opportunity for various parties to exploit the system with resultant 'crowding out' effects for some

Table 16.12 Loan transaction costs for individual farmers

Credit source	Time spent (days)	Visits to ADMARC depot (no.)
ADDs		
Blantyre	1.55	1.31
Lilongwe	2.71	1.91
Kasungu	4.19	2.15
Overall	2.68	1.74
Moneylender	2.28	n.a.

Source: Author's survey

smallholders. Also, some smallholder credit undoubtedly gets recycled among smallholder farmers. It is unlikely that much would end up with smallholders excluded from the farmers' club system because, by definition, they are likely to be resource-poor and not in a position to purchase fertiliser on cash. However, some credit may get recycled from poorer to better-off members of farmers' clubs and some is likely to be distributed to family members outside the household of the loanee (16 per cent of those sampled admitted to doing this).

For the borrower it is not only important that SACA provides an opportunity for smallholders to participate in the market for credit but that this opportunity is provided at reasonable cost. The most obvious cost is the rate of interest which, from the mid-1980s, had been 12 per cent. In 1992–3 the National Credit Committee, under increasing pressure from the World Bank, finally approved a rise to 18 per cent. As loans are usually repaid over a ten-month cycle, this makes for an effective rate of 21 per cent which is still well below the official inflation rate.[18] Added to this is the individual farmer's transaction costs which are principally made up of the time spent travelling, meeting officials (of the farmers' club and the ADD), waiting/idle time and any form filling. Table 16.12 shows the time attributed to obtaining a seasonal loan with comparable data from those respondents who had used a moneylender. The figures show a marked difference between ADDs, with the transaction costs in Kasungu being over 2.5 times greater than in Blantyre (this is partly compensated by the fact that the average loan in Kasungu is 1.5 times bigger than the average in Blantyre).

These borrower transaction costs compare favourably with the transaction costs reported by those respondents who had used a moneylender: 2.68 days for the typical farmers' club loan versus an average 2.28 days for the moneylender loan. However, although both figures refer to the time spent *seeking* the loan, in the case of the farmers' club loan there is an additional period of 'down time' waiting for delivery of the credit package, whereas for the moneylender loan the credit is issued immediately after the

Table 16.13 Late credit packages: the impact on yields of delayed planting

| | Yield (kg/ha) | |
	Local (purestand) maize	Hybrid maize
Kasungu		
early planting[a]	1,191	2,631
late planting[b]	838	1,550
Lilongwe		
early planting	986	2,023
late planting	815	1,315
Blantyre		
early planting	802	1,987
late planting	148	n.a.
Malawi		
early planting	938	2,275
late planting	639	1,600

Source: Malawi Government (1992a)
Notes
[a] Planting before mid-December.
[b] Planting after mid-December.

time incurred under transaction costs. This 'down time' for farmers' club loans is the time taken between the borrower completing all the formalities and being told that he will receive a credit package and the time when he has actual possession of it. On average this was almost sixteen weeks and in many cases can have serious implications because it may imply late planting or delayed application of fertiliser. The impact this has on yields depends on many factors including the types of seed and fertiliser used, topography, climatic conditions and husbandry practices, such as the number of times a plot is weeded. An analysis of these factors is obviously beyond the scope of this study but according to the survey results obtained by the *Annual Survey of Agriculture* a combination of early planting and weeding *without* fertiliser application can lead to yields as high as those unweeded later plantings to which fertiliser is applied for all varieties of maize (Malawi Government 1992a). The actual impact of late planting, *ceteris paribus*, for each of the ADDs in this study is shown in Table 16.13. There is a significant regional variation, but nationally, late planting (taken to mean planting after mid-December) can reduce yields by an average of 46 per cent for local maize and 30 per cent for hybrids. Clearly, delays in issuing credit packages carry a significant opportunity cost.

Aside from the 'down time', a major element of the actual costs of seeking a loan can be attributed to the time spent visiting the ADMARC depots and waiting for delivery of credit packages. Even though many clubs nominate their officials to collect the loan packages on behalf of the club members, it is not uncommon for individual members to make repeated visits to the ADMARC depot to check on progress. Again, those borrowers in Kasungu complained of having to make the most visits to ADMARC depots (an average of 2.15 visits compared to an overall average of 1.74). It is an often-repeated complaint that ADMARC is sometimes slow in distributing credit packages and 41 per cent of those sampled complained that they had experienced delays in getting their credit package.

Finally in this sub-section, it is interesting to note the views of non-credit respondents to farmers' club membership. Interestingly, 42 per cent of the non-credit group had in fact been in a farmers' club in the past. Over a third of these left when their group was excluded because of a defaulter; other common reasons included the desire to 'stand on one's own feet', illness, and disagreements within the groups leading to banishment of particular individuals. Of the 58 per cent who had never been in a farmers' club, about half wanted to join but complained that they were prevented from doing so by club officials or village headmen/chiefs, and almost a quarter were risk-averse, believing that credit implied a risk or burden that was too great for them. However, from the responses of the non-credit group, there does appear to be an unfulfilled demand for more farmers' clubs and more credit.

Technological impact of credit[19]

The ultimate objective of farmers' club credit is to increase food production. It seeks to achieve this by promoting the use of hybrid maize varieties and commercial fertiliser. Therefore, an obvious measure of its success is the uptake of hybrid maize seed and fertiliser by smallholder farmers. Although uptake still lags behind other comparable countries in Sub-Saharan Africa (see Table 16.2), the farmers' club system has progressively increased the supply of fertiliser and hybrid maize seed to smallholders, especially since the mid-1980s, and currently supplies about 65 per cent of all smallholder fertiliser: in 1992–3 this comprised 79,025 tonnes of fertiliser and 4,111 tonnes of hybrid maize seed (SACA internal communication). Although impressive, there is still resistance to new technologies from many smallholders. There are also problems concerning timing and application rates of fertiliser and a general need for better extension

Table 16.14 Maize type by credit and non-credit samples (average hectarage)

ADD	Credit farmers		Non-credit farmers	
	Hybrid	*Local*	*Hybrid*	*Local*
Kasungu	0.97	0.39	0.29	0.39
Lilongwe	1.01	0.48	0.29	0.38
Blantyre	0.72	0.20	0.20	0.68
Overall	0.93	0.37	0.26	0.48

Source: Author's survey

Table 16.15 Fertiliser use by credit and non-credit samples (average kg)

ADD	Credit users		Non-credit users		Average fertiliser per ha Credit users	Non-credit users
	Credit package	Cash	Total	Total		
Kasungu	317	230	547	138	402	203
Lilongwe	464	159	623	88	418	131
Blantyre	222	36	258	88	280	100
Overall	334	130	464	105	357	142

Source: Author's survey

support, together with supply-side constraints and pricing problems concerning the fertiliser (nitrogen):maize price ratios.

Table 16.14 compares maize variety uptake between smallholders with credit and those without, and Table 16.15 makes a similar comparison on the basis of fertiliser use. The data for maize type clearly illustrates that credit farmers (and by implication the better-off farmers) are more inclined to grow hybrid maize than are non-credit farmers. Indeed, 42 per cent of non-credit farmers did not grow any hybrid maize, compared to only 2 per cent of the credit group.[20] The difference is most pronounced in Blantyre where credit farmers grew slightly more than three and a half times more *hybrid maize* than local maize, compared to non-credit farmers who grew slightly less than three and a half times more *local maize* than hybrid maize. A similar but more significant trend is noticeable in Table 16.15 which compares fertiliser use between credit and non-credit groups. In Lilongwe credit farmers were likely to use seven times more fertiliser than non-credit farmers and overall the difference in fertiliser usage was over four times higher for credit farmers. This difference is partly accounted for by the bigger land holdings of the credit farmers. But when fertiliser usage is normalised in terms of average fertiliser usage per hectare, the difference is still striking with credit farmers using 2.5 times more fertiliser per hectare than non-credit farmers. However, these data refer to amounts of fertiliser farmers *claim* to use, which may differ to the amount *actually* applied to a farmer's smallholding (due to the resale/redistribution problem). Thus, it is assumed that these data for credit farmers may well overestimate their true fertiliser application rates. Although all credit farmers applied some fertiliser, 42 per cent of non-credit respondents did not use any commercial fertiliser and only 8 per cent used more fertiliser than the average volume disbursed on credit terms to the credit group (262 kg). Consequently if we consider only those non-credit farmers actually using fertiliser, who tend to be those with above-average sized smallholdings, their application per hectare is 235 kg, which compares more favourably with that of the credit group. Thus, the challenge of increasing national food security may be less about reducing the difference in application rates between credit and non-credit farmers *per se* and more about encouraging the uptake of fertiliser among the poorer smallholders who, as yet, are not applying any fertiliser to their maize. The interesting question concerns causality: does credit induce new technology in the form of maize type and fertiliser use or is it a function of land-holding size, wealth or income? It is the author's view that causality is established by the latter set of variables but that farmers' club credit has served to exacerbate the differences in technology between poor and less-poor farmer groups.

As these differences in fertiliser and hybrid maize uptake are so pronounced, it remains surprising that demonstration effects have not resulted in more non-credit farmers adopting the new technologies. Although much of the problem rests on the supply side of the equation, the solution is unlikely to be based on a simple increase in supply. Some farmers – especially the poorer ones hitherto outside the farmers' club system – will be deterred by risk because getting fertiliser requires a large capital liability whether it is obtained on cash or credit; and on the issue of seed varieties, there may well be a feeling of 'better the seed you know'. There is also likely to be resistance to change on socio-cultural grounds, as many people complain that hybrid maize does not taste as good as local maize, that it is not so easy to store or that the 'pounding quality' is not so good.

Although the following cannot be fully attributed to the farmers' club system, the fact remains that after over twenty years of operation most smallholders do not apply fertiliser and those who do tend to do so at low rates of application. Land productivity, as measured by average yields per hectare, has not increased and the majority of smallholder households remain net purchasers of their staple food (Conroy 1993; Shanmugaratnam *et al.* 1992). What benefits that have accrued to smallholders have largely benefited the better-off and there is evidence to suggest that farmers' club credit has negative externalities for non-credit smallholders. First, there is the displacement effect as often there are insufficient supplies of inputs available to non-credit smallholders, a problem which is exacerbated by the 'credit customers first' policy for input sales at ADMARC, whereby even if there are sufficient supplies, the option to purchase rests primarily with the farmers' club members, so by the time non-credit farmers are allowed to buy them it is too late in the season. Second, there is the 'planned price trap' for non-credit farmers, which has been exacerbated by recent devaluations and the phased fertiliser subsidy removals.

The planned price trap refers to the fact that in setting official input and output prices, the Government uses the prices that prevail during a particular season. Thus, fertiliser prices for 1991–2 are used to determine the official maize producer price for 1991–2 (or vice versa). This is fine for credit farmers who are able to pay for the fertiliser they acquired in 1991 with the maize they harvest in 1992. But the non-credit farmers have to pay for fertiliser in 1991 with the proceeds from their 1991 harvest. Assuming prices are not constant, non-credit farmers face a higher fertiliser to maize price ratio than credit farmers. The faster the growth in prices, the greater is the disadvantage to non-credit farmers, and with the current high inflation rate in Malawi, this disadvantage is significant. According to Simler (1993) a non-credit farmer in 1992 would have to sell about 45 per cent more maize at 1992 prices to buy as much fertiliser as the credit farmer who repaid his loan from maize sales at 1993 prices: alternatively, the non-credit farmer would only be able to buy 70 per cent as much fertiliser as the credit farmer, even if their harvests were the same.

Changes in yield income and assets

Two convenient measures of impact are changes in income (or output) and changes in assets. Within the confines of the study methodology and in the context of smallholder farming, neither proved easily measurable. However, as credit farmers have bigger smallholdings and grow more hybrid maize and tobacco than non-credit farmers it was not surprising to find that their yields and incomes were considerably larger. Table 16.16 shows estimated

Table 16.16 Yield income estimates for season 1992–3 (average MK by ADD and percentage of cases by range)

ADD	Credit farmers		Non-credit farmers	
	Yield income (MK)	Yield income per hectare (MK)	Yield income (MK)	Yield income per hectare (MK)
Kasungu	3,497 ($s = 5,009$)	1,469	845 ($s = 729$)	728
Lilongwe	2,503 ($s = 3,195$)	1,074	844 ($s = 1,037$)	796
Blantyre	723 ($s = 888$)	536	373 ($s = 543$)	359
Overall	723	536	373 ($s = 543$)	
Overall income ranges (%)				
<250	15		36	
>249 <500	13		16	
>499 <1,000	24		20	
>999 <2,000	19		16	
>1,999 <3,000	6		6	
>2,999 <4,000	9		2	
> 3,999	14		2	

Source: Author's survey
Note: s = standard deviation.

total income from maize and cash crops for season 1992–3.[21] The average credit farmer has an income three times greater than the average non-credit farmer. But this masks some striking differences at the two extremes. While almost a quarter of credit farmers expected a yield income over MK3,000, a fifth of non-credit farmers expected no yield income at all (subsistence production only). The income per hectare data confirm that not only are the credit farmers getting significantly higher gross incomes from their land but they are also more commercially productive, achieving about 71 per cent more income per hectare than non-credit farmers. (The actual productivity differential is much less, as a relatively larger proportion of non-credit farmers' land will be devoted to subsistence production and so the output will not yield an income.) The vulnerability of the non-credit farmers was evident during the drought of 1991–2 when the difference in yield income between the two groups increased. (Author's conversations with farmers and field assistants.) The survey attempted to quantify this but the results proved inconsistent and incomplete, with most respondents unable to estimate incomes for 1991–2 accurately (see note 22). But it was clear that those able to rely on tobacco crops fared significantly better than those wholly or largely dependent on maize production.

The most significant asset for most farmers is their land, but smallholders farm customary land which has no commercial value so it is infeasible to attempt to value this. However, credit farmers were asked if, as a result of their loans over the preceding five years (or less, if applicable) they had managed to increase the amount of land in productive use. A surprising 34 per cent said they had, and these positive responses were evenly spread across the three ADDs surveyed, averaging an increase of 0.74 ha. In comparison the non-credit group was asked if they had managed to increase the amount of land in productive use over the past five years; only 18 per cent had managed to do so and the average increase was 0.36 ha. If the responses of these farmers are valid and can be generalised across the country, it seems that farmers' club credit encourages farmers to increase the amount of land under cultivation.

Apart from land, smallholders are unlikely to have many other fixed assets. The richest smallholders may have a farm cart or cattle, those in the middle-income group may possess a bicycle and a radio, but the majority will have little more than basic essentials such as a mud hut (possibly with tin sheet roofing), cooking pot and eating utensils. Again, putting values to these assets is very difficult. Each respondent was asked to estimate whether he felt he had increased the value of his possessions over the previous two years. Most believed they had: 75 per cent in the case of the credit farmers and 80 per cent in the case of the non-credit farmers. What is more significant is the type and value of these additions. The latter is difficult to calculate but as the credit farmers have considerably more disposable income than the non-credit farmers, it would be reasonable to assume that their additions to their 'wealth' were of a greater value than those made by the non-credit group.

Dividing smallholder assets into productive and non-productive items, it was found that over the previous two years credit farmers had a higher propensity to purchase both productive and non-productive items compared to the non-credit group. However, the difference between the two groups of farmers was less for purchases of non-productive capital items like cooking utensils, radios and tin roofing than it was for productive items like livestock, carts and agricultural equipment. This may be explained as follows. First, the returns to productive investment are likely to be higher for those with larger land holdings; and second, additions to non-productive capital are likely to be higher among resource-poor households which will presumably seek to satisfy basic capital needs before making productive investments.[22]

A note on smallholder employment

Unlike other studies in this series, which have analysed lending institutions that focus either wholly or predominantly on micro-enterprise lending, it is not possible to ascertain employment impacts attributable to credit in the context of smallholder production. There are two main reasons for this. First, the nature of what is essentially a peasant economy does not permit an easy analysis of the employment function due to the variability and ambiguity of the concept of the smallholder labour input: for example, it is very difficult trying to distinguish between part-time, full-time and casual labour; employment within the household and from without; employment in cash terms or in kind or as part of a mutual exchange relationship; or to account for the seasonality of employment. To obtain indications of *changes* in the labour input, when it is such a nebulous concept to begin with, is fraught with difficulties. And thereafter, to try to apportion this to the impact of credit is absurd. Linked to this is the second difficulty which concerns the methodology used to undertake this research. In essence, using a one-off survey based on recall does not allow one to obtain data that have sufficient rigour or validity to even begin addressing these issues. Thus, the only tentative conclusions that can be drawn on the issue of employment impact are that credit is a determinant of changes in the demand for smallholder labour only to the extent that it causes the credit recipient to increase his land under cultivation and to change his production technology. Even then the precise impact on the demand for labour is hard to ascertain. However, it appears that labour is a very important variable in the smallholder production function as studies have shown that 85 per cent of gross margins on crops such as maize are attributable to labour inputs and only 15 per cent to land *per se*, and that a doubling of the land available to the poor would at best increase income by 13 per cent (World Bank 1990b). Nevertheless, it is technological impact rather than employment that is likely to constitute the key to increased food security.

THE MALAWI MUDZI FUND

Origins and planning

The Malawi Mudzi Fund (MMF) had its genesis in the IFAD/World Bank missions which visited Malawi in the mid-1980s and which gave rise to the Smallholder Agricultural Credit Project, bringing about the creation of SACA in 1987. The MMF became a component of this project with an exclusive focus on the hitherto neglected rural poor. Thus, the MMF fits into the broad Government policy of raising rural incomes through agricultural diversification and the development of off-farm income-generating activities. The MMF is focused on the 'poor' and 'core poor' and this distinguishes it from most other initiatives, which have tended to focus on either small businesses or better-off smallholders.

The MMF was created to fill an institutional gap. It was hypothesised that if finance were made available to the 'core poor', they would be able to generate off-farm employment which would increase their incomes and lead to improvements in farming practices and greater food security. For the purposes of targeting it was considered vital to identify the poor as poor and not as small, marginal or below-subsistence farmers. Under the Smallholder Agricultural Credit Administration, for example, the poor were identified as smallholders so the focus of intervention was agriculture and consequently the scheme came to be monopolised by the better-off smallholders. The MMF was to be an organisation with membership strictly limited to those with less than 1 ha of land or equivalent assets.

Smallholders with less than 0.5 ha of land tend to produce only about 25 per cent of their annual food requirements, and those with between 0.5 and 1 ha are usually able to produce 75 per cent of their food requirements (Shanmugaratnam *et al.* 1992). The residual food needs are satisfied by income from either self-employment or *ganyu* employment. In the absence of credit, it was felt that these options were at best irregular and unpredictable and at worst unavailable to the poorest. Thus, it was believed that credit could fill a gap and function as a catalyst for improved rural well-being. A simple production function was assumed: survival skills of the poor + credit = self-employment possibilities and productive survival. It was concluded that 'if credit can be rightly delivered and served, it can leave a profound impact on the life of the poor in terms of significant improvements in their output, income, consumption and saving' (IFAD 1987b: 5).

As mentioned, the MMF was to give preference to the poorest and most vulnerable groups which had largely been bypassed by most rural support

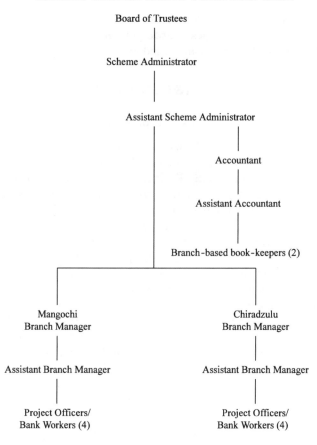

Figure 16.4 MMF organogram

institutions (although this objective appears to stand a little incongruously with the 1 ha upper limit). In particular, female heads of household, who are over-represented among the 'core poor' and 'poor', were specifically encouraged. It was felt that, compared to men, women would be 'more disciplined, hardworking, serious in their task and at the same time more concerned about household welfare' (IFAD 1987b: 5). The demand for credit was assumed, as were the multiplier effects of this credit. Thus, in 1989 the MMF was established as an IFAD-funded, Government-controlled trust fund with two pilot areas located in the Southern Region and a headquarters in Zomba, midway between the two areas of field operations and home to the Malawi Parliament. Operations did not begin until April 1990.

The project was one of the earliest attempts by an official aid donor to transfer the Grameen Bank model to another country. A seven-year, two-phase project was begun with the target of reaching 4,000 households through four branches. The first phase, involving the setting up of the headquarters and two branches, was to last five years and be funded by IFAD at a cost of Special Drawing Rights (SDR) 720,000, comprising SDR400,000 in grants and SDR320,000 in loans (this corresponds to MK2,801,592 at an exchange rate of SDR1 = MK3.8911). Funding for phase two had not been finalised at the time of study.

Organisation and terms of membership

As shown above in Figure 16.4, the MMF is a lean organisation with only a handful of staff, headed by a Scheme Administrator who is supported by an assistant scheme administrator, an accounts assistant plus deputy, a secretary and service staff. Each branch is headed by a branch manager and comprises an assistant branch manager, a book-keeper, four project officers and service staff.

Table 16.17 shows the financial implications of membership. In 1990–1 and 1991–2 the loan principal was repaid at 2 per cent per week for fifty weeks, with the 18.5 per cent interest consolidated and repaid in weeks 51 and 52, but for 1992–3 *pro rata* adjustments were made for the new six-month loans (see p. 382) and the Emergency Fund contribution was

Table 16.17 The terms of an MMF loan

Condition	Costs/benefits
Rate of interest	18.5% straight line on disbursed funds (15% pre-November 1992)
Emergency Fund	25% of the interest due is deposited in an Emergency Fund to insure against default by death, disability or other unforeseen calamity
Group tax	5% added to principal, then deducted from disbursed funds and deposited in Group Fund
Compulsory saving	20 tambala per week or MK10.40 per year deposited in Group Fund (originally 10 tambala per week). Loan issued after a satisfactory savings record has been established
Voluntary savings (personal savings)	Minimum requirement before a savings passbook is issued is MK2
Group-level fines (typical amounts)	Absence: 50 tambala Lateness: 20 tambala
Savings	10.75% paid on savings in Group Fund. Up to 50% of Group Funds can be on-lent within the groups.

Source: MMF internal documents

front-loaded and credited in weeks 1 and 2. The interest rate on loans (when expressed in terms of a declining balance rate and assuming no rebates for early repayment) is greater than that applied to commercial bank loans (more so following the decision to reschedule repayment over six months), while the interest applied to savings matches that offered by the Post Office (Figure 16.4). The various savings requirements are deposited in a Group Fund and at the end of 1992–3 about a third of funds accumulated had been on-lent (that is, withdrawn) within borrower groups. This is a surprisingly large amount considering the frugality of current savings (see p. 376). The fact that the Group Fund has not developed as it should has seriously handicapped the growth of the MMF. It is supposed to be the pivot on which the process of group solidarity and several liability is founded, but project officers have found it difficult to enforce or engender savings discipline and have been reluctant to confiscate monies in Group Funds to cover losses from defaulters, apparently due to a marked antagonism from good repayers to forfeiting their share of the Group Fund. Thus, few members and especially those likely to default have much financial exposure to the Group Fund and in many cases there has been little commitment to the group at all (see below).

Financial and operational performance

The MMF is wholly dependent on donor funding for all capital and operating expenses but has not received donor-funded technical assistance inputs (except at the planning and set-up stage). In addition, all loanable

Table 16.18 MMF financial data, 1990–1 to 1992–3

	1992–3	1991–2	1990–1
Income and expenditure account (Malawi Kwacha)			
IFAD grants receivable	621,537	400,893	500,000
Other income	77,807	52,003	10,584
Total income	699,344	452,896	510,584
Salaries/wages	210,291	129,894	126,807
Training	65,335	48,581	29,532
Other expenditure	373,780	287,881	247,486
Total expenditure	649,406	466,356	403,825
Surplus/(deficit)	49,938	(13,460)	106,759
Balance sheet			
Fixed assets	109,092	122,236	122,272
Net current assets	1,033,775	508,627	568,437
Total funds	1,142,866	630,865	690,709

Source: MMF annual reports

funds have come from the Malawi Government through a grant of MK500,000 which was made available to the MMF in 1990. Table 16.18 is a summary of accounts for the first three years of operations, excluding the grant for loanable funds. The small difference between IFAD income and total income comprises interest accruable which has gradually increased in each year of operation. The major item of expenditure is salaries/wages, followed by training of MMF staff (not borrowers). Until 1993, the MMF was wholly IFAD-funded but in January of that year USAID provided a grant of MK402,000 for further staff training (which, at the time of the study had not been utilised).

The financial analysis presented in Table 16.19 clearly shows the dependence on outside funding in terms of the proportion of total income received in the form of donor grants. Although the figure for 1992–3 implies that 10 per cent of income is internally generated, this income is almost wholly derived from the interest receivable from donor funds held in bank accounts. Thus, the calculation of a Subsidy Dependence Index (SDI) becomes a purely academic exercise. In 1992–3, the SDI was 577 per cent, which means that the MMF would have to raise its interest rate almost sixfold to offset the subsidy. However, the fact that the SDI is declining is simply due to the declining significance of sunk costs as a percentage of total costs and says nothing about the operational performance of the organisation. Total staff costs constitute a major proportion of total operating costs, 42 per cent in 1992–3, but most of these costs are largely unavoidable. However, the fact that for every kwacha lent, MK13 are consumed on operating costs is a striking one, even if we assume a high element of sunk costs. A major area of expenditure is on transport and especially mileage claims (almost a fifth of total branch costs are consumed in this way), which leads us to question the efficacy of both the mileage

Table 16.19 MMF: financial analysis

	1992–3	*1991–2*	*1990–1*
Donor income as % of total income	90	89	97
Subsidy Dependence Index (%)	577	1,330	3,746
Total staff costs as % of operating costs[a]	42.4	36.3	40.6
Mileage costs as % of branch operating costs[b]	19.5	16.1	5.6
Operating costs per MK lent	13:1	14:1	3:1

Source: MMF annual reports
Notes
[a] Total staff costs comprise: salaries and wages, leave grants, leave pay, hotel subsistence allowances, medical costs, pension and housing allowance.
[b] Mileage costs are paid to project officers in each branch primarily for petrol expenses for their motor bikes.

Table 16.20 MMF: operational performance indicators

	1992–3	1991–2	1990–1
Total amount disbursed (MK)	49,416	33,164	130,866
Total no. of new loans	223	168	478
Average loan size (MK)	222	197	274
Female borrowers (new loans) (%)	99	90	73
Total group savings (MK)	4,250	10,509	7,455
Total personal savings (MK)	4,379	2,189	1,259
Average savings per borrower (MK)	10	20	18
Cumulative repayment rate (%)[a]	64	55	54
No. of loans fully repaid	124	82[b]	
No. of members[c]	337	1,055	900
Staff:borrower ratio (approx.)	1:15	1:48	1:41

Source: MMF annual and quarterly reports

Notes

[a] Calculated at financial year-end and referring to those loans repaid within a month of schedule, expressed as a percentage of total outstanding loans.

[b] This figure represents the total number of loans completed for 1990–1 and 1991–2.

[c] Refers to all registered and active members.

allowance rates used and the decision to locate borrower groups so far away from branch offices and the project officers' homes (see pp. 376–8).

The operational performance of the MMF has not been impressive, as is shown in Table 16.20. The MMF got off to a bad start from which it has never really recovered and this is clearly shown by the data on total disbursements, number of new loans and number of registered members. In 1992–3, it is clear that the brakes were applied and there are expectations that the corner has been turned. However, the indicators remain worrying. After three fully operational years, the MMF has only 337 active members; only 206 borrowers have fully repaid loans; the cumulative repayment rate stands at a mere 64 per cent; and savings rates are strikingly low.

THE LIMITS TO CLONING: ORGANISATIONAL PITFALLS AND ADAPTATIONS

The MMF is a good example of an attempt to replicate the structures, systems and procedures of a successful organisation (the Grameen Bank) without taking into full consideration either the socio-cultural or geo-political context of the replication (Hulme 1993). Many of the following problems appear to have had their origin in the planning phase.

The location of the two branches was originally selected by the local District Development Committees (which are politically orientated) and not by the MMF management. Thus, operational efficiency was not given priority in selection, so project areas within each district are isolated from each other and some are based 50–70 km from the branch office. A significant variable used to determine the location of operations was population density and, by implication, land pressures and poverty. Overall, the Southern Region has a higher population density than the Central or Northern Regions, and Chiradzulu is the second most densely populated district in Malawi with 275 persons per square kilometre, so it qualifies on this criterion; but Mangochi is one of the least densely populated districts in the Southern Region and with 79 persons per square kilometre it falls below the national average of 85 persons per square kilometre (1987 Census). Clearly, Mangochi was chosen on grounds other than high population density. It may have been chosen because of its relatively low population density in comparison to other districts in the Southern Region (a contrasting test case to see if Grameen Bank replication could work under relatively sparse population density) or (according to one project officer) because in seeking Grameen Bank-like conditions, Mangochi was favoured because of its predominantly Muslim population.

True to Grameen Bank practices, a pilot study of the socio-economic characteristics of the two branch districts was undertaken prior to setting up the branches.[23] However, it was undertaken by university staff and students and not MMF employees. Thus, it constituted an academic exercise rather than serving as a learning experience for MMF workers. Unlike the research that precedes the opening of a Grameen branch, there were no familiarisation benefits for bank workers, no opportunity to generate trust, confidence and empathy between bank workers and local people. None of the vital institution-building externalities associated with socio-economic studies undertaken by Grameen Bank staff were obtained.

The overall responsibility for policy and financial control rests with a Board of Trustees which comprises six senior civil servants and one representative of a non-governmental organisation (NGO). In the main, the trustees are unfamiliar with the basic principles of rural banking for poverty alleviation. As the civil servant trusteeships are held by the particular incumbent in post, frequent changes in Board composition have occurred. In the first two years there were three different chairmen and two of the trustees who visited the Grameen Bank on a reconnaissance mission in 1990 left the Board within a year. The fact that the trustees are very senior members of the Malawi Government also means that they are very busy people whose time for MMF Board meetings is likely to be compromised. Thus, not only does the composition of the Board reflect a strong public-sector bias, which may not be the best approach for a grassroots rural bank supposedly independent of Government and striving for financial autonomy, but it has also entailed a high degree of instability.

The MMF has also suffered upheaval on the operational level. The MMF existed without an Assistant Scheme Administrator for virtually the first year of operations, the Scheme Administrator – on secondment from the civil service – reverted back from whence she came in 1992 and in the same year the Accountant died. Furthermore, a permanent replacement for the Scheme Administrator was not found and, over a year later, the Acting Scheme Administrator remained on temporary secondment from the civil service. Organisationally, the MMF has failed to distance itself from the Government and many rural people view it as a Government welfare-based agency, as shown by the findings of a study among first-year borrowers, 60 per cent of whom thought the MMF loans represented a grant from Government (reported in World Bank Project Review Mission *aide-mémoire*, June–July 1992).

Perhaps the biggest mistake concerned the rapid disbursements at the beginning of the project. It appeared that the scheme management, possibly due to the influence of donor pressures, was motivated more in terms of disbursement rates than in terms of ensuring high repayment rates in the future. The process of publicising the project, encouraging group formation, screening applicants, training them, registering and disbursing loans was undertaken with haste. Originally a 2-2-1 disbursement pattern was adopted for self-selecting groups of five, with the group chairperson being the last to receive a loan but receiving it within six months of the initial loan disbursements. All loans were unsecured and not covered by joint and several liability. This is, of course, a fundamental and apparently unplanned deviation from the Grameen model. It seems to have evolved from an inability to engender group discipline prior to loan disbursement, coupled with a lax attitude to the various savings requirements. Consequently, attendance at group meetings was irregular, there were very low savings rates and ultimately low repayment rates (see Table 16.20). The screening procedures were subsequently tightened and in 1992 all new groups were being required to save for three to six months prior to issuance of the first two loans, which depended as well on the project officer being satisfied as to the group's cohesiveness and commitment. Also, flexibility was introduced in terms of group and centre sizes, such that groups can number from three to seven individuals and centres should comprise a maximum of twenty-one individuals and not thirty as originally copied from the Grameen Bank. Nevertheless, the MMF still appears to take an ambiguous stance on the efficacy of trying to engender the practice of joint and several liability within groups (and centres). In the *Annual Report* 1992–3, it states: 'In future, access to subsequent loans will depend on full repayment of the outstanding loan. In addition, credit discipline within the group will also be considered.' This appears to lay the emphasis on the individual rather than the group as the focus for credit delivery and repayment (which mirrors the *actual* practice of the farmers' club system).

Once borrower groups have undergone a seven-day (later increased to eight-day) training exercise in MMF membership rules and procedures and have successfully completed the subsequent recognition test (carried out by the branch manager or his assistant), the members become eligible for

Box 16.2 A Mudzi Fund meeting observed

The weekly centre meeting was scheduled to begin in the mid-afternoon but actually started almost an hour late to accommodate latecomers. After all the waiting, the meeting was over very quickly once loan repayments had been made, which appeared to be the sole purpose of the meeting. There was little participation from the borrowers, all of whom were women, and it was clear that the project officer was in control and setting the pace of the meeting.

All those in attendance (only five people were missing out of a maximum twenty-nine) seemed very aware of the purpose of their weekly centre meetings – to make repayments and savings – but did not seem to understand the purpose of their individual groups (implying that the idea of group solidarity and co-liability was absent). Everyone at the meeting was able to make her loan repayment on this occasion, but some were in arrears and it was apparent that at least one borrower had borrowed her instalment from another member of the group. Liquidity problems are common and the practice of borrowing from within the group and from outside to make repayments seemed to be an accepted practice, although it was likely to be irregular one-off payments rather than the successive co-financing that leads to free-rider situations.

The economic condition of the members was precarious and fairly homogeneous and they felt they were not in a position to 'bale each other out' but, as they empathised with the problem of not having money, they were also reluctant to put pressure on someone with difficulties by forcing them to come up with repayments when it was clearly difficult for them to do so.

After the meeting, the members were asked their views on the Mudzi Fund and their general business experiences. One of the biggest complaints was the absence of a grace period for Mudzi loans, and some people complained of the difficulties of having to attend weekly meetings, implying a significant opportunity cost: some suggested a fortnightly repayment schedule. There was a unanimous feeling that successful repayment was dependent on the business climate and on factors largely beyond the control of the borrowers. The 2-2-1 system of disbursing loans to group members (with the chairperson the last to receive a loan) was not well appreciated because those who had to wait felt they were prevented from starting a good business at the right time. This seemed a justifiable complaint, as most businesses are highly seasonal and therefore have an optimal time of operation.

After prompting, members unanimously agreed that extension advice on health and welfare, literacy classes, and loans for agricultural inputs and school fees would be useful additional benefits to Mudzi membership.

loans. The decision on loan use is largely left to the individual borrowers to decide what activity they want to finance with their MMF loan but the project officers are responsible for determining the optimum amount for the chosen activity. The size of repeat loans is also largely left to the discretion of the project officers. However, it is not clear how systematically loan appraisal is carried out. Although it is recommended that a borrower cash flow is worked out (there are supposed to be models available to project officers outlining the most critical variables for financial success in the most common business activities), it appears that these practices have been relaxed in the interests of maximising loan disbursements. Inevitably this has resulted in some loans going to those either unable or unwilling to repay. The actual disbursement mechanism was originally inflexible and cumbersome. Initially, all loans had to have *de facto* Board approval as disbursement cheques had to be signed by a Board member. Loans were then disbursed as cash paid out at group meetings under the supervision of the Scheme Administrator and from the MMF's four-wheel-drive vehicle. Clearly, this was unlikely to convey the impression of a decentralised, grassroots organisation. This practice has subsequently been revised and the Scheme Administrator now approves disbursement and it is usually devolved to the branch level.

Once loans have been issued it is the responsibility of the chairperson and the project officer to monitor loan use. Loans are given in cash for a particular purpose and are supposed to be utilised within three days of issue. This guideline is usually followed and there is apparently little misapplication of loans. The project officers tend to maintain close relations with borrowers in the period immediately before and after loan disbursal and it is difficult for borrowers to misuse loan principals. Although this close relation is beneficial, it does have drawbacks. It tends to engender a dependency mentality on the part of the borrowers. This was noted by the first Scheme Administrator:

> most beneficiaries are desperate for a loan but do not comprehend what is fully involved. They expect to be spoon fed and may not take issues very seriously. This is reflected in some business proposals received which show inadequate market surveys and a lot of missing data. The beneficiaries expect the Project Officer to fill in this missing information because in most other programmes in the country, this is how things have been done. They find it strange and difficult to take charge of their own affairs.

The first Scheme Administrator also recognised a number of other constraints to the effective adoption of financial services for income-generation among the rural poor, including limited entrepreneurial skill, illustrated by a very high incidence of 'copycat businesses'; weak group leadership with its impact on group cohesion and dynamics; and (somewhat more contentiously) very low literacy levels.[24]

Socio-cultural or group discipline factors were not the only, or possibly even the major, causes of high default rates in the first two years of operation. A notable weakness of the whole lending programme was a failure to address the very nature of the rural economy. The first tranche of loans was distributed in June 1990, the cumulative repayment rate up to October was a satisfactory 91 per cent but thereafter it plunged and by financial year end stood at 54 per cent. The MMF had failed to adapt the one-year weekly repayment cycle to the seasonal nature of rural activity and incomes. Most rural people are first and foremost farmers (and not petty traders or micro-entrepreneurs). The months of October, November and December are the land preparation and planting times which generate high family labour demands and which in turn influence loan recovery arrangements and group meeting attendance. As loan recoveries slowed in late 1990, and anticipating that loan repayments would be diverted to consumption, the MMF was forced to suspend loan disbursements until April 1991. These difficulties were compounded by the drought in 1991–2, which was especially severe in the Southern Region, and which led to a scarcity of some business goods and thus forced the MMF to suspend loan disbursements for several types of particularly badly affected business activities.

The planting season is usually followed by the rainy season, which may come towards the end of the year and continue until about April. This is known as the 'hungry season' when food supplies dwindle and money is scarce. Inevitably, most of the activities financed by the MMF are seasonal and mirror the agricultural season, being buoyant when the crops are harvested and when there is liquidity in the rural economy. Thus, loan repayment schedules failed to match potential cash flows. It was not surprising, then, that group attendance and repayment fell off in the period immediately before and during the 'hungry season'. Although there are likely to be numerous cases of wilful default, for many the choice was between eating and repaying a loan. Attempts by the MMF management to obtain the assistance of traditional authorities in recovering debts met with little success for it was clear that, in practice, it was extremely difficult to distinguish between wilful defaulters and those who had no choice. Subsequently, the MMF endeavoured to keep year 2 borrowers totally isolated from year 1 borrowers. This has been accomplished but is likely to become increasingly difficult as and when the MMF expands its operational base.

To complement this approach, in late 1992 the Board of Trustees – under donor influence – gave approval to the Scheme Administrator to take legal action against defaulters. By the end of 1993 no defaulter had been taken to court because the MMF management remained suspicious of this course of action. On the logistical level, it was anticipated that legal action would be a prolonged process subject to many delays and involving a high cost–benefit ratio, as it is obviously a costly process and ultimately there may be little pecuniary gain from serving legal notices on very poor people. It was also felt that although legal action may show borrowers that the MMF was serious about loan recovery, it could alienate potential beneficiaries from joining the scheme. Thus, the *Annual Report* for 1992–3 concluded: 'Legal action is not the most effective means of achieving and maintaining high repayment rates in MMF'; rather, it could be better achieved by 'instilling credit discipline among its borrowers through continuous training amongst other mechanisms'. As part of this strategy, the Mudzi Fund management is keen to engender savings discipline among individual borrowers, partly to ensure that the Emergency Fund can operate effectively and partly so that individuals have a financial stake in the Mudzi Fund which they would forfeit if they defaulted on their loans. To date, in the main, members' savings have been inadequate to fulfil this function, and where there have been sufficient funds to offset against wilful default, there have been socio-cultural constraints preventing project officers from implementing this course of action (see pp. 390–1). Also, the use of traditional authorities has not been discounted, even though the sporadic attempts to use this option have met with little success. In conversation with project officers the author discovered the view that, if attempted in a systematic way with appropriate financial incentives, such people could play a useful role in enhancing loan-recovery rates.

The areas with the worst repayment records have subsequently been phased out. In year 2, borrowers were encouraged to 'front load' their loan repayments by making voluntary payments ahead of schedule, and this led to an improvement in repayment. In year 3, the following incentives were offered to those able to repay early: 50 per cent rebate on loans amortised in six months and a 75 per cent rebate on loans amortised in three months (introduced mid-1993). Also, six-month loans were phased in, with repayment (in most cases) scheduled to be completed before the onset of the 'hungry season'. It was felt that short-term loans would be easier for borrowers to manage and that they would more closely match their needs. This appears to have been vindicated as six-month loans have been popular and repayment has been high, so future MMF loans are likely to be of this type. The MMF also experimented with loans for agricultural inputs. As only twenty-eight of these loans were issued in 1992–3 and with repayment unknown at the time of this study, it is too early to judge this diversification in lending which was demand-driven and appears to service the type of 'core poor' smallholders which are largely bypassed by SACA farmers' club lending.

Table 16.21 is a summary of income-generating activities financed by the MMF in 1992–3. The table shows a strong concentration of loans in a limited range of activities. Almost half of all loans in Mangochi went to fish-trading activities and, excluding agricultural input loans, 86 per cent of

Table 16.21 Types of income-generating activities financed, 1992–3

Activity	Chiradzulu		Mangochi		Total	
	Loans (no.)	Av. size (MK)	Loans (no.)	Av. size (MK)	Loans (no.)	Av. size (MK)
Fish trading	20	261	43	187	63	210
Fritters	14	206	8	236	22	217
Flour trading	19	104	0	0	19	104
Bean trading	18	434	2	225	20	413
Clothes trading	8	466	6	318	14	403
Maize	6	168	8	150	14	158
Tea room/café	0	0	10	236	10	236
Scones	5	117	3	205	8	171
Rice trading	4	243	3	213	7	230
Kanyenya[a]	4	147	0	0	4	147
Groundnut trading	3	192	0	0	3	192
Tomato trading	3	63	0	0	3	63
Firewood	2	173	0	0	2	173
Hawker	0	0	1	600	1	600
Potatoes	0	0	1	340	1	340
Tinsmith	0	0	1	225	1	225
Sugar	0	0	1	200	1	200
Salt	1	60	0	0	1	60
Chickens	1	175	0	0	1	175
Agricultural input	18	109	10	96	28	104
Total	126	223[b]	97	200[b]	223	213[b]

Source: MMF, *Annual Report*, 1992–3
Notes
[a] Kanyenya is fried chicken pieces.
[b] Mean loan size.

loans went to just five types of activity. In Chiradzulu there is a somewhat broader range of activities financed, but still two-thirds of non-agricultural loans went to just four types of income-generation activity. These figures show very clearly the limited resource base and the dearth of income-generating activities open to people in these two districts (and in Malawi as a whole). Excluding food preparation, it is also notable that only one manufacturing enterprise is funded by the MMF (the tinsmith). The MMF appears sensitive to the need to diversify the range of income-generating activities and is especially keen to reduce the number of loans to fishmongering and processing activities (28 per cent of all loans in 1992–3) as there are clear indications that fish stocks in Malawi's lakes are falling at an unsustainable rate.

The MMF was set up with a number of objectives (as reported in successive annual and quarterly reports). Of primary importance is the provision of credit and savings facilities to the rural poor. There is also an aim of providing technical advice on business management. Although it is not clear in what form the technical advice is supposed to be delivered, other than as an uncosted externality associated with the banking functions, the actual provision of credit and savings facilities has fallen short of expectations and the MMF has had a very troubled first three years of operations. However, it should not be forgotten that the MMF is still in an experimental phase and has proved to be a very adaptive organisation. The changes it has made in its organisational and lending procedures augur well for the future. An associated objective concerns giving opportunity to the rural poor to run income-generating activities in order to improve their standard of living. It is to this objective that we now turn.

Targeting issues

The MMF has been reasonably successful in targeting the poorest. The criteria used to target them were not based on income but on assets (those with less than 1 ha of land or equivalent assets) and those excluded from existing institutional financial services (which effectively means exclusion from farmers' club agricultural credit). These criteria are not difficult to achieve as 70 per cent of all smallholder households in the Southern Region farm less than 1 ha and farmers' club membership is relatively low, with the Southern Region representing 55 per cent of all Malawian smallholders but only 28 per cent of total farmers' club membership.

Table 16.22 profiles the rural household and employment patterns for those micro-entrepreneurs sampled by the author. In terms of land holding, the MMF is generally reaching its target, but not always. Roughly a quarter of those sampled had land holdings of 1 or more hectares (mostly in Mangochi) and only a third could be classified as 'core poor' (with land holdings <0.5 ha). The average size of smallholding was 0.66 ha and less than 3 per cent had no smallholding at all. The non-borrower control

Table 16.22 Household and employment characteristics of samples

Characteristic	Surveyed members of the MMF	Surveyed non-members
Average size of smallholdings (ha)	0.66	0.49
Female (%)	96	28
Average age (years)	38	41
Average household size (no. of persons)	6.14	5.65
% with 4 or more years of schooling	38	58
% with only one regular source of household income	56	40
% with no regular employees	71	65
% with one non-household employee	11	28
% of activities based exclusively on trading	58	48

Source: Author's survey

Box 16.3 Female participation in the MMF

The Mudzi Fund began operations with a preference to lend to women but nevertheless accepted male membership. In its first two years of operations, male borrowers were found to be significantly more problematic than female borrowers so by 1992–3, when 99 per cent of all new loans went to women, the policy changed to one of *de facto* male exclusion. In the words of the Mudzi Fund *Annual Report* 1992–3: 'The overall performance of female loanees has been far better than men. In that connection, the future of the MMF depends upon women as their performance has duly demonstrated.'

In discussion with female members it was found that all-female groups were preferred because, in the absence of men, this facilitated openness and empathy. It was considered that, on average, men had 'more wants', were less likely to use the proceeds from businesses wisely and were therefore less likely to maintain timely loan repayments. Although 44 per cent of those sampled were heads of household and were likely to control the household economy (in theory, at least), they stood a good chance of reaping the benefits attributable to their loans; this was not always the case for loan recipients even if they had used their loan wisely and their business had succeeded, due to the inequality in household decision-making. For example, one woman, with an excellent repayment record, a successful business and now on her second loan had done so well, bringing so much money into the household, that her husband had been able to take a second wife.

Although the Mudzi Fund positively discriminates in favour of women members, as an organisation it has a strong male bias. At the time of the survey, only one of the eight project officers was female; in the head office, only two secretaries were female; and of the seven Board members, only one was female.

sample showed a tendency to have a slightly smaller average land holding size of 0.57 ha. About half of the sample were 'core poor' and a fifth had no smallholding at all.[25]

The female bias is clearly evident among the MMF borrowers. From the outset the scheme found that women were more regular attenders at meetings, had a higher savings rate and, most significantly, a much higher repayment rate compared to male borrowers. Thus, what was originally a distinct bias towards female members became a *de facto* policy to lend only to women in 1992–3 when 99 per cent of borrowers were female. However, when management sought to obtain Board approval to change MMF policy, making it a female-only credit programme, this was rejected. The vulnerability of rural households is illustrated by the data on sources of regular income. Over half of those MMF members sampled had only one regular source of income and typically this had to support a household comprising over six people. The data on extent of schooling are surprisingly high. No respondent had attended secondary school (Malawi has one of the lowest rates of secondary school attendance in the world: UNDP 1993) but over a third claimed to have had four or more years of primary schooling (which is especially surprising considering that the sample comprised virtually all women with an average age of thirty-eight years, factors which usually militate against achieving much in the way of formal education in low-income countries). Educational levels in Chiradzulu were generally higher than in Mangochi, but in both cases levels of functional illiteracy were estimated to be between 50 and 75 per cent, which appears to belie the reported years of schooling.[26]

The respondents' businesses appear fairly homogeneous (cf. Table 16.21) and were dominated by trading activities; 58 per cent of members and 48 per cent of non-borrower businesses were exclusively based on trading. Thus, over half of Mudzi loanees are purely retailers and do not transform products at all. Most of the rest are essentially retailers of prepared food. The size of the businesses is indicated by the data on employment. The majority of traders were sole proprietors: 71 per cent of members and 65 per cent of non-borrowers employed nobody on a regular basis. Most of the rest employed only one non-householder: 11 per cent among Mudzi members, 28 per cent among non-borrowers. Most employment – whether intra-household or from outside the household – was of a highly irregular nature and often for only a few hours at a time.

Credit and savings experiences

Mudzi Fund loans are usually a major determinant of enterprise activity because without a loan many borrowers would not be in business at all and most of the rest would be operating highly unstable businesses with considerably lower amounts of working capital. The respondents were asked to state the major source of their business start-up funds; 55 per cent cited the Mudzi loan (31 per cent cited personal or household savings and the rest referred to gifts). Three-quarters of all loanees had undertaken their business activity precisely because they got a loan. It would be incorrect to suggest that this implies a sudden release of entrepreneurial spirit among the rural poor as most loanees already had a history of involvement in income-generating activities but usually with low margins and little stability. Although the Mudzi loan cannot guarantee success, it does appear to offer some stability and it does fill a void by offering credit

Table 16.23 Credit and savings histories

Loan sources	MMF borrowers (%)	Non-borrowers (%)
Obtained loans from family or friends in past 10 years	44	28
Obtained credit from shopkeepers/traders in past 10 years	18	28
Obtained loans from farmers' clubs in past 10 years	25	40
Used moneylenders in past 10 years	3	22
Not used any source of credit in past 10 years[a]	16	43
Have personal non-banked cash savings	59	80

Source: Author's survey
Note: [a] In the case of the MMF borrowers this obviously excludes their MMF loan(s).

for off-farm income-generating activities to people hitherto neglected by other lenders.

Table 16.23 shows the credit and savings histories of the respondents. The Mudzi group are largely dependent on family and friends for loans, which tend to be short-term, without interest and for small amounts (average MK30). Less than a fifth had used shopkeeper credit and a meagre 3 per cent admitted to using moneylenders. The corresponding figures for the non-borrower group were 28 per cent and 22 per cent respectively. Many respondents (59 per cent of borrowers and 80 per cent of non-borrowers) regularly kept cash balances in some secret place. These sums (presumably quite small amounts) are usually kept for security reasons, for use in some emergency such as buying medicine or paying funeral costs or school fees. They may represent potential institutional savings but this is not necessarily the case as many respondents appeared suspicious of institutional saving and expressed reluctance to reduce their secret cash holdings. If this is the case, there is little prospect of institutionalising these savings as there is rarely any surplus above these cash holdings. Therefore, on the basis of this evidence, any prospect of extending formal savings services to the rural poor without significant improvements in the level of rural economic activity is likely to remain extremely limited. Currently, formal savings are rare: only one Mudzi member and a handful of non-borrowers had bank accounts and the average deposit was only MK81 (in all cases, funds were held in the Post Office).

Perhaps the most notable finding revealed in Table 16.23 concerns the high incidence of farmers' club credit among both borrower and non-borrower groups. Most Mudzi borrowers who had received farmers' club credit had done so for a number of seasons (one respondent in Mangochi had received ten seasonal credit packages) but none admitted to being currently in receipt of such credit. It appears that either they or someone in their farmers' club had defaulted, thereby removing eligibility for seasonal credit, and consequently they had turned to the MMF. It would seem reasonable to conclude that the MMF picks up a significant number of farmers' club 'drop-outs'. In contrast, many of the non-borrowers were currently in receipt of farmers' club loans and many of those who had borrowed in the past had not been excluded by default but had shifted their individual focus to off-farm income-generating activities, leaving other members of the family to pick up on farmers' club credit packages for their family smallholding. It appears that, in relation to farming, many of the non-borrower group had 'graduated' into off-farm self-employment, while many in the borrower group had 'fallen into' it.

Once again, the low incidence of moneylender use may reflect reluctance on the part of respondents to admit to using this socially stigmatised source of money. But it was also noted during the fieldwork that moneylender activity in some areas was minimal and sometimes totally absent (an observation confirmed by the project officers). Despite this, most respondents knew about moneylenders and their exploitative behaviour and felt that they would only turn to a moneylender in desperate circumstances. Many were fearful of the consequences of defaulting on a moneylenders' loan and a significant number felt that moneylenders would not make loans to them because of their poverty and lack of collateral (see pp. 359–62 for savings and credit histories of farmers' club respondents). In contrast, only occasionally did a respondent suggest she would be deterred specifically by the high rates of interest applied to moneylender loans. As mentioned above, although a moneylender can foreclose on a debtor's assets, this is likely to involve social, financial and time costs for the lender as well as the obvious financial costs for the borrower, and most respondents felt that moneylenders preferred to avoid these potential hassles as much as possible, so were careful to undertake a thorough screening of potential borrowers. But as foreclosure remained the moneylender's ultimate sanction on default it also constituted a major obstacle for either moneylender interest in the poorest (due to their lack of collateral) or interest from the poorest in moneylender credit (through fear of losing what little assets they have).

Most recipients of Mudzi Fund credit were generally supportive of its operations whether they were good repayers or not. Most recognised the originality of the scheme and the window of opportunity it offered to the poor and cited this as the main reason for approaching the MMF. The fact that the MMF was identified with the Government was also a major factor in attracting the poor, although conversely, so it was also a significant contributor to low repayment rates. Many rural people are fearful of the unknown and have little margin for error and for some the prospect of getting a loan that was repayable every week was a daunting one, assuaged only because, in the words of one respondent: 'I thought because the

Mudzi Fund is Government, they would approach me politely when asking for repayment' (author's survey).

Few respondents complained of having to wait long to get a loan. On average loans were issued 4.2 months after membership registration and were disbursed among the five members of a group on a 2-2-1 format, with established intervals between loan issues. If repayment is timely, loans will be issued systematically; if not, there will be delays or non-issuance. Provided project officers stick to the rules – and in some cases they appeared not to, with inevitable consequences – individual borrower transaction costs, measured in terms of the time taken to get a loan, are largely dependent on the commitment and efficiency of the group. However, maintaining good attendance has been difficult, as on average only two-thirds of members turn up to weekly meetings (author's survey). As the typical group size is 4.28 members, this means that usually at least one member is absent from each meeting. Admittedly, attendance at weekly meetings carries a significant opportunity cost in terms of the time spent at meetings (typically they last one to two hours), the idle time waiting for meetings to begin and, in some cases, the time spent travelling to and from meetings. For some respondents these costs contributed to low attendance but absence more usually reflected a lack of commitment and either an inability or unwillingness to repay (borrowers could always nominate someone else to make their repayments if they had other pressing matters to attend to and, in any case, meeting times are arranged to suit them).

The capable and incapable rural poor

The commitment issue appears to be of considerable significance. It was found that 39 per cent of respondents indicated that the actual membership of their group had changed since they joined. As the average length of membership was nineteen months, this represents a high turnover and in turn points to the issue of effective screening and borrower education which, to date, has been a debilitating weakness that the MMF has struggled to come to terms with. Ultimately the two main indicators of commitment are loan repayment rates and savings rates, neither of which has been impressive (cf. Table 16.20); but underlying this appears to be a failure to educate members to understand personal finance and management, although admittedly this is unlikely to be an easy task. However, common misunderstandings concerning the difference between grants and loans and the very role of the MMF as a rural bank and not a Government welfare agency point to the need for greater awareness-raising. Further, there appeared to be a lack of appreciation of the importance of saving. Rather than viewing the savings component of the Mudzi Fund as an opportunity to invest, it was viewed as a penalty or a necessary obligation. More than half the respondents did not know the actual balances on their loans (a clear

Table 16.24 MMF borrowers: arrears and defaulters, 1993

	In arrears (%)[a]	Defaulters (%)[b]
(%) of total borrowers	24	11
Main reasons for arrears or default		
business failure	42	55
distress consumption[c]	36	33
non-essential consumption	10	0
natural disaster	5	6
other/non-specified	7	6

Source: Author's survey

Notes

[a] 'In arrears' is defined as being behind by at least one repayment but not more than four.

[b] Default is defined as being more than four repayments in arrears.

[c] Distress consumption is unforeseen emergency consumption.

window for corruption and suspicion), over 90 per cent did not know the interest rate and barely half could state the difference between the money they received (principal) and the money they had to pay back (principal and interest). In the absence of awareness, discipline is likely to flounder and, as Muhammad Yunus puts it, 'credit without strict discipline is nothing but charity. Charity in the name of credit will destroy the poor, not help them'.[27] Again, the onus must rest with the MMF employees to counter misunderstanding and promote understanding and awareness of such issues.

Finally in this section, it is important to note the environment in which the MMF operates, as this is a major determinant of business performance and by implication of MMF member discipline and motivation. The limited range of income-generating activities currently evident in the areas of operation and the constraints imposed by the priority given by rural people to agriculture, together with the seasonality problem, have already been covered but a closer examination of those in arrears, and the few defaulters who were willing to co-operate with the author's survey reveal a further layer of constraints to which the MMF has to adjust. Table 16.24 presents data on arrears and default.

Although reasons may be many and quite convoluted ('I failed to repay because my business failed because my spouse fell ill and I had to pay for a doctor and there was little money because we had to buy more food than usual because our own supplies were limited by the drought'), the borrowers were asked to state what they considered to be the main reason for their arrears or default. Most cited business failure, which was often linked to the seasonality problem (supplies of inputs had dried up so the business was suspended) or to marketing problems (resulting from highly competitive markets and difficulties associated with transporting perishable goods from 'wholesale' to 'retail' markets). Some of these problems could have been overcome by effective business planning and business acumen. The question can always be asked, why do some traders succeed in the same markets where others fail? The MMF, as with other similar micro-enterprise lending schemes, appears to believe that the answer lies in the effective screening of the capable rural poor: those who have 'some little experience and drive to do business to improve their well being . . . to run their businesses at a profit . . . [to generate] extra income for reinvestment and other expenditure' (*Annual Report* 1992–3). This group would presumably be predisposed not to use their loan (or more accurately, the income derived from their loan) for routine or non-essential consumption but it would not exclude those affected by distress consumption. Over a third of defaults and arrears are due to this, which largely reflects the absence of formal social security and obligations to the extended family. Many of those citing distress consumption were afflicted by the significant financial costs of having to attend to funeral expenses, and for the poor such socio-cultural obligations weigh heavily on their economic survival. Nevertheless, identifying the capable poor appears vital to ensure financial discipline and good repayment and savings rates, thereby ensuring institutional efficiency and, by implication, significant economic impact, which is the focus of the next section.

THE IMPACT OF THE MALAWI MUDZI FUND

The MMF lends for working capital purchases to a small group of similar, often seasonally based trading activities (cf. Table 16.21). It has not actively sought to stimulate diversity in the range of income-generating activities it finances or to have any direct bearing on technology adoption or adaptation. Its impact tends to be short-term by levering recipients away from poverty during peak trading times. The degree to which this leverage is sustained is largely beyond the control of the MMF. The most direct impact concerns employment.

The employment impact

As already noted, MMF loans have a major bearing on enabling the poor to start (or re-start) businesses and to sustain them: three-quarters of borrowers attributed their business start-up to obtaining a loan. By implication, therefore, the employment impact is high if we assume that in the absence of a loan there would be no economic activity. This is clearly a restrictive assumption but it would be wrong to ignore this self-employment by simply focusing on derived employment: the demand for labour generated by the loanees' businesses. Even with a loan, self-employment for the rural poor is a vulnerable, fragile and very unpredictable experience. For much of the

Table 16.25 Employment in borrower and non-borrower businesses

Employment	Borrowers (%)	Non-borrowers (%)
No regular[a] paid or unpaid employees	71	65
Employs one unpaid family member[b] on a regular basis	20	28
Employs two or more unpaid family members on a regular basis	8	8
Employs one paid employee[c] on a regular basis	11	28
Employs more than one paid employee on a regular basis	1	5

Notes
[a] 'Regular' implies some consistency of employment, such as daily, certain days of the week, certain times of the day, but not irregular, one-off types of employment.
[b] 'Unpaid family labour' is defined as family employment (not just intra-household employment) without direct payment. The family member will be fed from the profits of the activity but this does not imply a monetised exchange relationship.
[c] If a monetised exchange relationship exists for a family member, then this person would be classified as a *paid employee*.

year most loanees are not in business; when they are, the returns are rarely sufficient for them to generate paid employment. Table 16.25 shows that 71 per cent of borrowers and 65 per cent of non-borrowers employed nobody, whether paid or unpaid. Among the borrower group there was a tendency to employ family members rather than non-family members among those who did employ people. From a sample of eighty, there was paid employment for a total of ten people (0.125 employees per business), two years previously there had been total employment for twelve people. Most employment was generated by tea rooms/cafés and, interestingly, over the two-year period employment had shifted in favour of women: two years previously for every woman employed there were two men; at the time of the survey this ratio had reversed. Due to the highly fluid nature of business activity and the small sample, it is unwise to generalise too much but it may be that MMF loanees have a tendency to employ females rather than males. However, there may be other reasons to explain this, such as female labour being cheaper or more flexible or the type of employment in the business activities may have an inherent gender bias (that is, the employment created may be in activities normally undertaken by women). Finally, the data in Table 16.25 show that although borrowers had only a slightly lower propensity to employ unpaid family members, the non-borrower group was significantly more inclined to employ paid labour, which may imply greater business stability on the part of non-borrowers.

Assets and enterprise worth

Mudzi loans are exclusively for working capital, and as the scheme is at such an experimental stage it would be inappropriate to assess loan impact on business assets. Quite simply, the impact on business worth is determined by the size of the loan and is measured wholly in terms of the addition to working capital. Very few respondents had any fixed capital assets at all and for those who did, they had very little monetary value. Respondents were asked to estimate the sale value of their businesses at that moment (a figure which approximates to the value of goods for sale in most cases) and the average was MK318. About a quarter of respondents were effectively inoperative, having no assets (the survey was undertaken at a reasonably good time of the year in terms of the general level of business activity). A more positive indicator came from the 29 per cent of the borrower group who believed that their businesses were worth more now than two years ago, compared to 50 per cent of non-borrowers. Most of the rest felt that things were more or less the same. The fact that the non-borrower group reported greater growth in enterprise worth is probably largely due to the proportionately higher incidence of non-seasonally based trading activities among this group.

Enterprise sales, household income and profits

As business activity is so seasonally dependent, it is with some caution that we analyse data on enterprise sales and household income.[28] Table 16.26 shows enterprise sales among different categories of borrowers. A very interesting trend is discernible. The Mudzi members yet to obtain a loan have low sales: barely half of the sales achieved by those servicing their first loan. Those who had completed repayment of a first loan (but who had not yet received a second loan) were doing better still, and those who were servicing a second loan were recording twice the volume of those servicing a first loan.

Finally, the stars of the lending programme, those who have completed repayment of a second loan, were achieving very high average sales of MK1,133. However, these data are biased towards MMF successes and say nothing about those drop-outs who troubled the scheme in its first two years. We can assume that sales are less buoyant for this group. However, it seems that the capable poor – those who can demonstrate good repayment and business skills – can directly benefit from Mudzi loans. However, due to the small samples, any such inferences can be nothing more than tentative.

The data in Table 16.26 relate to sales for the particular enterprise activity currently (or most recently) operated by the respondent. The data in Table 16.27 refer to total monthly income available to the respondents'

393

Table 16.26 Borrower enterprise sales (MK)

Borrower type or location	Sample size	Average monthly sales (MK)	Standard deviation
Overall average	$n = 80$ ($n = 40$)	383 (531)	394 (406)
Mangochi: $n = 47$	($n = 20$)	374 (613)	374 (297)
Chiradzulu: $n = 33$	($n = 20$)	396 (409)	396 (446)
Borrowers servicing first loan	$n = 24$	282	240
Borrowers who have fully repaid one loan	$n = 36$	345	365
Borrowers servicing a second loan	$n = 8$	591	499
Borrowers who have fully repaid a second loan	$n = 5$	1,133	264
Members who have not yet borrowed	$n = 7$	155	114

Source: Author's survey recording twice the volume of those servicing a first loan
Notes
1 Monthly sales figures will vary enormously throughout the year. These data refer to sales in the month preceding the survey and should not be interpreted as *typical* of any given month.
2 The figures in brackets refer to the non-borrower group.

Table 16.27 Borrower monthly household income

Borrower type or location	Average monthly household income (MK)	Standard deviation
Overall average	273 (279)	391 (255)
Mangochi	234 (335)	207 (299)
Chiradzulu	330 (195)	552 (131)
Borrowers servicing first loan	268	215
Borrowers who have fully repaid one loan	173	149
Borrowers servicing a second loan	655	970
Borrowers who have fully repaid a second loan	648	257
Members who have not yet borrowed	103	73

Source: Author's survey
Notes
1 Monthly household income figures will vary enormously throughout the year. These data refer to income in the month preceding the survey and should not be interpreted as *typical* of any given month.
2 The figures in brackets refer to the non-borrower group.

households. Once again, caution must be given to interpretations made about these data as income sources can vary enormously depending on many factors, such as the season and the opportunities for waged employment. Furthermore, it was not always known how much money particular members of the household were actually contributing to the household.

Only 44 per cent of the sample were heads of household and as most of the sample (96 per cent) were women, it was not surprising to find that many did not really know the full income obtained by their spouses and therefore were unable accurately to estimate monthly household income. Nevertheless, from the data given, in all cases the main source of income was from the respondent's enterprise and in 80 per cent of cases this was the only source of income in that month. Once again, the Mudzi members yet to get a loan appear to be significantly worse off than those with a loan history. Those borrowers servicing or who have repaid a second loan have considerably larger household incomes than those who have paid or are repaying a first loan. As with sales data, the impact of Mudzi Fund credit on borrower household income appears to be cumulative. It is worth noting that for this particular month, each member of a borrower household had an income of MK44 (average household size 6.14). The data do not give any indication of change over time – only between groups – but each respondent was asked to estimate household income for the same month two years previously. Almost a third of respondents felt that their current household income was actually lower than the same time two years ago, while virtually all those who noted an increase in absolute terms had in fact seen their incomes barely keep pace with inflation. More than anything, these figures probably reflect the dire economic environment into which the Mudzi Fund was born.

Most enterprises yield a considerable short-term profit but few offer a stable income. Nevertheless, the uses to which these profits are put is of considerable importance. The MMF management believe that by focusing on female borrowers loans are more likely to impact on productive investment (and 'useful' consumption) within households than if loans went to males. The survey findings tended to confirm this as most funds realised from borrower enterprise activity (96 per cent female) went on buying food (32 per cent) and paying for school fees (10 per cent), followed by repaying the Mudzi loan (9 per cent). In comparison, the non-borrower group (72 per cent male) had a slightly lower propensity to spend business profits on food (26 per cent) and a markedly lower incidence of expenditure on school fees (1 per cent). These findings compare favourably with those of a study of 319 pioneer loanees conducted by researchers from the University of Malawi in mid-1992.[29] They found that most funds realised from enterprise activity went on buying food and clothes (42 per cent), followed by paying school fees (14 per cent), repaying the loan (12 per cent), employing farm labourers (7 per cent) and buying fertiliser (6 per cent). The high incidence of expenditure on food is not surprising despite the prevalence of subsistence farming, as food security is a major issue facing Malawi and especially those in the densely populated Southern Region where many smallholders are not self-sufficient in food production. The same University of Malawi study found that only 14 per cent of respondents produced sufficient food to last the full year and over two-thirds had run out of food by the end of December and therefore had to rely on food purchases or, less likely, the benevolence of relatives for over a quarter of the year. Without adequate baseline data or annualised current income estimates it is impossible to ascertain impact on household food security and changes in consumption patterns attributable to income flows from MMF loans, but the objective of enhancing household food security is implicit in the MMF programme and has been given extra importance by the introduction of seasonal loans for agricultural inputs.

CONCLUSIONS

The SACA/farmers' club system

In evaluating smallholder credit in Malawi it is necessary to analyse essentially two institutions. First, the Smallholder Agricultural Credit Administration, a relatively new and ultimately short-lived administrative body, and second, the farmers' club movement, through which credit is delivered and collected. However, to make things even more complicated, both these institutions operate within a system defined by the Ministry of Agriculture. Thus, in evaluating these lending institutions we are looking at a process within a system, and it is the system that defines the process. The successes of SACA and the farmers' club movement are largely attributable to the system in which they operate. The same can be said of their respective weaknesses. Of course, the wider operating environment will have significant implications for the success or failure, strengths or weaknesses of any organisation, but smallholder credit in Malawi exists in a particular straitjacket principally defined by the Government of Malawi in the form of the Ministry of Agriculture, the regional Agricultural Development Divisions (ADDs) and the Agricultural Development and Marketing Corporation (ADMARC) and conditioned by the state of the economy and the commitment of donors, especially the World Bank.

The following is a summary of the major strengths, weaknesses, opportunities and threats facing the smallholder credit delivery system in Malawi.

Strengths

- There exists a well-established and effective system of farmers' clubs that are well respected and understood by those better-off smallholders who benefit from membership of them.
- Credit in kind reduces fungibility and, so long as recovery is integral to output, recovery rates are likely to be high.
- Demand for seasonal credit exceeds supply and demand for membership

of farmers' clubs exceeds opportunities for their creation. Thus, there exists undoubted potential for expansion.

- Credit delivery and collection is devolved to the local level and is backed by extension advice, thereby reducing borrower transaction costs and potentially improving the returns to credit.

Weaknesses

- The environment for smallholder credit is a precarious one. Malawi has a resource-poor economy with the majority of people dependent on subsistence agriculture but a system that is biased to estate production. Income levels are low, there is little agricultural diversification and the economy is highly prone to exogenous shocks which have their greatest impact on the poorest.
- Farmers' club credit bypasses the majority of smallholders, especially the poor and core poor groups.
- Smallholder credit is delivered within a civil service structure resulting in bureaucratic and hierarchical practices which stifle dynamism and innovation and lead to a blurring of responsibilities with other parts of the Government.
- There are a number of institutions responsible for credit delivery and collection and for policy making, such that a weakness in one is potentially a weakness for the whole system. In certain areas there is an unnecessary duplication of responsibilities.

Opportunities

- There exists great potential for expanding and solidifying the role of farmers' clubs beyond their current role as conduits for credit (for example, more and better extension support aimed at improving the technical efficiency of credit packages is required). This opportunity is probably best taken up by an institution other than the provider of credit, to avoid cross-subsidisation and conflicts of purpose.
- Opportunities exist to develop incentives for improving staff and borrower performance.
- Underdeveloped markets exist for non-seasonal credit including off-farm income generation, consumption credit and certain types of medium-term agricultural credit.
- The new World Bank-induced Rural Financial Services Project (see p. 354) presents opportunities for a streamlined, independent banking organisation to service clearly defined market segments, including a much-needed deposit-taking/savings-generation department.

Threats

- The evolving market liberalisation taking place in Malawi will remove many of the certainties concerning input purchases and maize sales for smallholders with access to credit and eliminate the monopoly control situation for credit delivery and collection.

- Dependence on donor funds and Government subventions is likely to remain for the foreseeable future. Until a smallholder lending institution has greater financial independence it will remain tied to donor and Government policy decisions.

- The rapid expansion in credit disbursements since the mid-1980s has coincided with some difficulties evidenced by a fall in repayment rates. Although reasons for this are many, there are indications that, as coverage expands, there are both institutional 'growing pains' and a likelihood that less able or less disciplined smallholders will get credit.

Although SACA and the farmers' club system has succeeded where most other similar institutions in Africa have failed, its major limitations are that it has embraced only the better-off smallholders, bypassing the majority, that its input packages have often been inappropriate and that it has failed to develop a savings function and thus remains dependent on external sources for concessional funds. The World Bank-designed Malawi Rural Finance Company (MRFC) is expected to address these problems. But doubts must remain whether SACA can be transformed (or usurped) in such a revolutionary way. Indeed, the MRFC is expected to build on the perceived success of the farmers' club group-based lending system but there is no evidence to suggest that this particular mechanism is the most effective one. Most commentators rest their faith in the farmers' clubs on the basis of their impressive repayment rates. It is a mistake to assume a simple cause-and-effect relationship: Table 16.8 shows that repayment rates were actually *higher* in the six years prior to farmers' club group-based lending when loans were made to individual smallholders. Rather than being the pivot on which successful lending is based, the role of the farmers' clubs, in the aggregate, is fairly indeterminate. The real success behind seasonal credit in Malawi has been the closed input–output relationship by which ADMARC has held a monopoly in the provision of smallholder inputs and in the procurement of smallholder output. If smallholders have nowhere else from which to get inputs and nowhere else to sell their maize they have little choice but to repay their loans. This relationship appears to be vindicated by the fact that repayment rates have declined as the ADMARC monopoly has been eroded. Thus, the big question is whether the farmers' club system can adjust to market liberalisation. This remains to be seen.

The Malawi Mudzi Fund

The Malawi Mudzi Fund is still in its infancy and in an experimental phase. However, its record to date has not been impressive and this is largely attributable to the misguided attempt to copy rigidly the Grameen Bank without creating a capacity for adaptations to local conditions. As the project is largely donor-driven, most of the blame in this respect must lie with the principal planners and funders of the MMF. However, as with other attempts at Grameen replication, such as the now largely successful Amanah Ikhtiar Malaysia, the Mudzi Fund is undergoing a learning experience and is gradually finding methods and ways of operation more suited to the particular circumstances in which it operates (Hulme 1993). Thus, it has experimented with incentives for voluntary early repayment of loans and with six-month loans to overcome the seasonality problem; it has introduced agricultural loans in response to borrower demands; it has focused on female members because of their greater financial discipline; it has introduced flexibility in group size; and it has introduced more effective screening of the capable poor. These are promising moves, but they may be too late to save the Fund.

The MMF still suffers from a public image too closely associated with the Government, and the problem of frequent changes of staff and director has not been overcome. It is also desperately in need of computerisation of its credit and savings ledgers and the development of an operations manual. Above all, it needs to establish the principle of joint and several liability within its borrower groups by educating members in the rules, procedures and benefits of Mudzi Fund membership. With enhanced group discipline, the incapable rural poor could be screened out, repayment rates will rise and savings discipline will be engendered, which is vital if the MMF is going to achieve self-sustainability. Although group discipline is the crucial factor in ensuring institutional effectiveness and efficiency, the Mudzi Fund appears to have recognised the importance of addressing its cost structure and particularly the costs associated with servicing widely dispersed borrower groups. It must not be forgotten, however, that as the Mudzi Fund is in its formative years it is still incurring significant sunk costs. The question of whether customary or formal courts should become a sanction of last resort remains a policy for scheme management to explore.

As with the Grameen Bank itself, the Malawi Mudzi Fund should not be expected to achieve success overnight as it is navigating uncharted waters in a hostile geographical and economic environment. After a troubled beginning, it has made a partial recovery; but it has little prospect of achieving financial sustainability even in the medium term so will remain dependent on donors and the Government. Even if the MMF continues to realign, adjust and improve its operational performance, its future remains tied to the patience of its funders and the identification of a leader to take it through its experimental phase.

APPENDIX: RESEARCH METHODOLOGY AND FIELDWORK

The survey results mentioned in the text were obtained from fieldwork conducted by the author in Malawi over the period March–June 1993. The main survey instrument was a detailed questionnaire completed on a one-to-one basis between an enumerator and a respondent. The formal interviewing was supplemented by informal interviews with selected credit and non-credit respondents both on an individual basis and (where possible) in a group discussion format; in addition, interviews were carried out with case-study institution officials, civil servants, various donor organisations and others, such as representatives of the private sector (both formal and informal).

The detailed questionnaire was piloted separately for each institution and appropriately customised, but in both cases followed a similar format:

Part A   A general profile of the smallholder/micro-entrepreneur
Part B   A focus on non-case-study credit and savings experiences
Part C   Detailed questions on the respondents' experiences with the particular case-study institution
Part D   Smallholder/micro-enterprise activity and credit impact on employment, income, wealth, and so on

The questionnaires were targeted at members of the two case-study institutions, and a similar questionnaire was used for comparable non-member/non-borrower respondents (the control group). A team of trained enumerators was used to collect the data. The sampling is detailed below.

Farmers' clubs/SACA

Three ADDs were chosen: Kasungu, Lilongwe and Blantyre. The choice of ADDs was designed to be broadly representative of smallholder farming by type and of the national distribution of farmers' clubs (within the obvious confines of time and budget). Thus, Kasungu and Lilongwe were chosen because they constitute almost two-thirds of the total credit disbursed through the farmers' club system and over half of the total membership. Land holdings are above average and there is a high incidence of cash crops in these areas. Lilongwe was also deemed suitable because it was the pioneer region from which the farmers' club system grew. In contrast, Blantyre was chosen because it is comparatively under-represented in terms of credit allocation as a proportion of total smallholder population and is characterised by below-average smallholdings, little smallholder cash crop production and a high incidence of off-farm employment. Within each ADD, the samples were drawn from a cross-section of randomly selected Rural Development Programmes (RDPs) and Extension Planning Areas (EPAs). The sample of credit farmers within each ADD was chosen at random from farmers' club lists.

A similar questionnaire was targeted at randomly selected non-credit farmers located within the same ADDs as the borrowers and drawn from the same RDPs. This group constituted the control sample. This group was chosen to be broadly comparable to the borrower groups in terms of agricultural activity and to comprise farmers who could potentially be members of a farmers' club. No attempt was made to further stratify these samples according to any criteria. Thus this group was not necessarily representative of the rural poor and, by definition, under-represents the 'core poor' of part-time farmers and the landless or near-landless. Farmers' club credit does not target the poorest, so it would be inappropriate to have a control group representing the poorest. This fact should be borne in mind when considering the standard against which the credit group is compared in the text.

The sampling was as follows:

	No. of credit farmers	*No. of non-credit farmers*
Lilongwe	34	17
Kasungu	27	17
Blantyre	39	16
Total	**100**	**50**

The Malawi Mudzi Fund

The sample was drawn from the two districts where the Mudzi Fund operates, with the following distribution:

	No.
Mangochi	47
Chiradzulu	33
of which:	
Mudzi borrowers servicing a first loan	24
Mudzi borrowers who have fully repaid a first loan but are without a second loan	6
Mudzi borrowers servicing a second loan	8
Mudzi borrowers who have fully repaid a second loan	5
Mudzi members awaiting their first loan	7
Total Mudzi Fund sample	80
Non-Mudzi Fund members	40
of which:	
Mangochi	24
Chiradzulu	16
Total sample	**120**

The actual distribution of this stratified random sample was effectively determined by the state of the Mudzi Fund membership. A further forty non-borrower micro-entrepreneurs were selected at random from the same or nearby areas in which the borrowers were located.

NOTES

1 See Kydd and Christiansen (1982) who argue that growth in the estate sector has been financed largely at the expense of the smallholder sector which has borne an implicit tax on its activities via the more favourable conditions of access to inputs, credit and extension services and the opportunity to obtain permits to grow certain cash crops denied to the smallholder sector.

2 The 1993 figure is an approximation derived from the composite consumer price index and US$/MK exchange rate prevailing in June 1993.

3 It should be added that these figures mask significant regional differences. Smallholders in the Central Region are far more likely to have oxen, use ridging, and so on, than smallholders elsewhere, for example.

4 For a good summary article on the informal financial sector in Malawi, see Chipeta and Mkandawire (1992). For an account of the role played by an urban moneylender in Malawi, see Bolnick (1992).

5 A small pilot project aimed at promoting the use of hybrid maize via the distribution of credit packages to groups of smallholders, using village headmen as the focus of distribution and repayment, was tried in 1970–1. Allegedly due to their low levels of literacy (and, presumably, in the absence of training) the headmen had to be closely supervised, so the system was found to be more expensive than individual credit and the pilot project was not continued.

6 According to the SACA Consolidated Accounts for 1991–2, total operating expenses amounted to MK2,897,473. With a seasonal loan portfolio of MK119,559,040 this works out at a very impressive MK0.024 cost per MK lent on operating expenditure, or with 400,062 borrowers (1992–3), a cost per borrower of only MK7.24. However, these figures are quite meaningless as they ignore the high cross-subsidisation of SACA by the central Ministry of Agriculture, the ADDs and ADMARC. Wages and salaries, for example, do not appear on the SACA accounts. It is important to appreciate that SACA is *completely* dependent on the ADD accounting staff for accounting information and these staff do not consider themselves to be credit staff, so they tend to give credit accounts a low priority.

The following is a summary of SACA Consolidated Accounts (all figures are in Malawi Kwacha and financial year-end is 30 September).

Balance sheet

	1987–8	1988–9	1989–90	1990–1	1991–2
Fixed assets	2,208	77,364	153,328	60,523	628,582
Loans	705,000	1,407,581	1,736,235	1,807,274	1,566,493
Current assets	39,303,873	50,607,856	88,785,744	96,058,629	138,113,788
Total liabilities	11,399,985	11,388,672	24,241,385	3,702,005	46,288,773
Total net assets					
(capital employed)	28,611,798	40,704,129	66,433,922	84,324,421	94,020,090
Financed by:					
Capital injection	13,252,780	21,924,944	42,701,134	57,413,895	59,621,011
Profit for the year	3,162,311	2,610,290	4,936,694	3,859,910	7,203,589
Retained earnings					
brought forward	12,196,707	16,168,895	18,796,094	23,050,616	27,195,490

Income Statement[a,b]

	1987–8	1988–9	1989–90	1990–1	1991–2
Turnover (loans)	0	0	55,881,210	79,319,437	89,520,556
Income	3,867,389	4,616,887	10,292,386	14,195,256	16,260,817
Expenditure	133,654	694,743	1,855,408	2,438,134	2,897,473
Profit (before prov.)	3,733,735	3,922,144	8,496,978	11,757,122	13,363,344
Less provisions for doubtful debts	571,424	1,311,854	3,500,284	7,897,212	6,059,754
Profit	3,162,311	2,610,290	4,936,694	3,859,910	7,303,590

[a] The figures obtained from SACA accounts for the 1991–2 income statement do not reconcile, so the author has had to interpret them in the apparently most logical way.
[b] Turnover figures for 1987–8 and 1988–9 are zero because the ADDs were not able to supply SACA with those data for those years.

7 See note 5 above. Apparently, the performance of the headmen had not been too much of a deterrent, as the LLDP was established only two years after the failed experiment and used village headmen for group lending.

8 For an account of the initial experiences with this pilot project, see Schaefer-Kehnert (1982).

9 The author was unable to obtain any information on the actual cost difference in administering the two types of credit.

10 The procedure for choosing officials is often rather elaborate. First, those interested put themselves forward and usually require a 'seconder'. If necessary, a vote is held which normally involves a straightforward show of hands (done in the absence of the nominees), but there were reports of more unusual practices such as blindfolding the nominees and having the voters file past them and indicating their vote by touching their chosen nominee, and the even stranger practice of blindfolding everybody, except the person doing the counting – voters and nominees (so that nobody knows who has voted for which candidate). The prevalence of crop inspection committees within farmers' clubs is undoubtedly influenced by the well-established and publicised annual Presidential Crop Inspections. They are encouraged by SACA/ADD officials as early-warning devices of crop failures.

11 This somewhat surprisingly high figure does not necessarily reflect exclusion from farmers' clubs for the under-forties. Rather, it reflects the pattern of transferring land under customary tenure. Farmers' club membership is likely to rest with the head of household (an older person) but the land is a family concern and will pass to younger members of the household only when the head dies. In the meantime, younger members of the household play their part in farming although they will not technically be the recipients of the credit packages.

12 In 1992 the ruling Malawi Congress Party was forced, principally by donors, to hold a national referendum on whether Malawi should remain a one-party state. The election was finally held in June 1993 and the ruling party was defeated.

13 The survey data contain information on maize yield and yield income for season 1991–2 (drought) as well as forecasts for 1992–3 (non-drought), but the validity of the recall data (1991–2) is not sufficient to justify comment on the ability of farmers to repay 1991–2 loans rather than take a moratorium. For obvious reasons, respondents were inclined to underestimate their yields and income for 1991–2, the extent of which is not known but, in the opinion of those enumerators who helped collect the data, the underestimation could be considerable in some cases.

14 Refer to note 6. In addition, the annual accounts do not reveal the cost of

concessional funds that go to each ADD for on-lending purposes. Thus, it is difficult to determine a meaningful Subsidy Dependence Index for SACA. The SDI is calculated as follows (for details see Yaron 1991, 1992). The amount of annual subsidy is determined by:

$$S = A(m - c) + [(E*m) - P] + K$$

where:

S = annual subsidy received
A = borrowed funds outstanding
m = interest rate for borrowed funds in absence of concessional funds (assumed figure)
c = average concessional interest rate on borrowed funds
E = average annual equity
P = reported profit
K = the sum of all other types of subsidies

Then:

$$SDI = \frac{S}{LP*n}$$

where:

SDI = subsidy dependence index
LP = average annual outstanding loan portfolio
n = average on-lending interest rate

Thus, for the record, the following approximates to an SDI for SACA for 1991–2:

$$S = 105,909,784(0.2 - 0) + \{(58,517,453 * 0.2) - 13,172,555\} + 9,676,700$$
$$S = 29,389,593$$
$$SDI = \frac{29,389,593}{61,580,936 * 0.12}$$

$$= 3.98 \text{ or } 398\%.$$

This means that SACA would have to raise its interest rate by 398% to cover the 1991–2 subsidy. The interest rate for farmers' club loans would have to rise to 47.76%.

Explanatory notes:
A = total liabilities + capital injection
m = 20% (assumed)
c = 0% (assumed)
E = [capital injection 1990–1 + capital injection 1991–2]/2
K = (operating) expenditure taken as 11% of loan portfolio
P = profit + provisions
n = 12% (the rise to 18% was effective from 1992–3)
LP = loanee debtors (as listed under current assets) (1990–1 + 1991–2)/2

15 For further details on these issues and others associated with maize and smallholder production in Malawi, see Conroy (1993).
16 These figures include family labour and refer to levels of labour during times of agricultural activity. Obviously, at some times of the year there is no agricultural work to be done and the labour input would be zero.
17 The author acknowledges that the surveyed areas are likely to bias these

findings due to the fact that smallholders in Kasungu and Lilongwe have above-average sizes of smallholding. However, the significance of these regions should not be forgotten as they accounted for 64 per cent of *all* credit disbursed in 1992–3.

18 Annual inflation rate as measured by the composite consumer price index for April 1993 was 29 per cent (*Monthly Statistical Bulletin*, April 1993).

19 As it was a one-off survey conducted just before the 1992–3 harvest, it is not able to ascertain changes in agricultural *output* per unit of land or per worker but can point to *a priori* changes in *inputs* accountable to credit, which, in shifting the nexus from traditional to non-traditional forms of agricultural production should, in theory, lead to increases in output. Measuring the real impact of this and the technical efficiency of the 'new methods and inputs' is beyond the scope of this study.

20 All farmers' club borrowers in the survey were issued with hybrid seeds so those who claimed not to use hybrids (two cases) presumably sold their credit package.

21 The survey was conducted just before the 1992–3 maize harvest. Farmers knew the prices they were likely to get for their crops and also the volume produced. The figures they gave were validated by extension workers so should be good estimates. Unfortunately, it proved impossible to obtain time-series data on yield income for the purpose of making 'before and after' comparisons. This was because estimating the previous season's yield income using recall would not have produced valid data for reasons associated with the 1991–2 drought, and trying to get smallholders to recall yield incomes for season 1990–1 proved infeasible.

22 It is obviously very difficult to classify asset purchases into productive and non-productive items. Smallholder households use the same item for productive and non-productive uses at different times (a good example is a bicycle); even an ostensibly non-productive item like a radio can become a source of increased productivity if the farmer uses it to listen to the many farming advice programmes that are broadcast by Malawi Broadcasting Corporation. The author, therefore, recognises the difficulties associated with this piece of analysis. For the record, the classification used and the survey results are given below:

Productive items All livestock, farm carts, sprayers, ploughs, ridgers and agricultural tools and equipment. Any capital item used principally for the purposes of running a micro-enterprise.

Non-productive items Household items such as chairs, tables, cooking and eating utensils. Any additions to the house structure such as tin roofing or installation of a latrine. Radios and bicycles.

Additions to capital in the previous two years (number of individual items).

	Productive items		Non-productive items	
	Credit group	Non-credit group	Credit group	Non-credit group
Kasungu	17	4	15	5
Lilongwe	15	7	11	5
Blantyre	10	3	11	7
Overall	42	14	37	17

The credit farmers made three times more productive purchases than the non-credit group but only twice as many non-productive purchases.

23 Nyanda (1990) contains a number of methodological irregularities, making its use as a baseline severely limited.

24 Nyirenda (1991).

25 The difference in size of smallholding may reflect the sampling methodology, as the non-borrower control group was selected at random from among micro-entrepreneurs whose businesses were operating on the days of the survey. The borrowers were selected from MMF members' lists and located either at their place of business or at their smallholding (which was unlikely to be the same place). As the survey was undertaken at harvest time, many rural folk would have been working on their plots. This was the case with many borrowers but, by definition, the non-borrowers were working on off-farm activities, which may imply that their income source is more likely to be biased towards off-farm activities and possibly that they have smaller plots. If the non-borrower survey had been undertaken a month earlier, more people with predominantly farm-based sources of income may have been engaged in off-farm activities and therefore would have been located at market places and trading areas. Thus, the survey of non-borrowers may be biased towards those with no landholding or smaller than average landholdings.

26 Respondents were supposed to state their final class or level of completed schooling. Answers may have been deliberately overstated to give a 'better' impression, in other cases the respondent may have misunderstood the question or misled the interviewer by giving their number of years of schooling rather than final class reached, thereby ignoring repeat years (very common) or including incomplete years as full years (mid-year drop-out is common). The interviewers were usually familiar with the respondents and, after each interview, were asked to cross-check the data collected. It was generally acknowledged that levels of functional literacy would be significantly overestimated on the basis of the respondent's answers on formal educational attainment. The majority of respondents were judged to be illiterate. This was partly confirmed by the virtually total absence of written records and the fact that project officers had to fill in loan application forms for most borrowers.

27 The meaning of this, of course, concerns the role of charity as a perpetuation of dependence, compared to credit as a generator of self-reliance. The quotation was obtained from Gibbons and Kasim (1990: 66).

28 It would be convenient to extrapolate the data on sales and income to determine average annual sales and income figures and then to compare this with a predetermined poverty line, but the author refrains from doing this for a number of reasons focused on the nature of the field research and the absence of valid and meaningful poverty-line income data. The methodological nature of the survey is such that these data refer to spot figures that are not representative of a typical month. Monthly income figures will vary enormously and it would be misleading to make any assumptions about what income flows may or may not be like at other times. These data tell us only about the month in question and therefore it is valid to compare effects within borrower groups and between borrower and non-borrower groups surveyed at the same time, but not to determine movement around a particular poverty line, partly because such a measure does not exist in either a useful or reliable form but most significantly because the poverty-line data that do exist are annualised and, as explained, the survey data cannot be annualised to make neat comparisons.

A further point concerns the validity of the recall data obtained. Although the research sought to make a 'before and after' comparison of income in line with other studies in this series, the results are of suspect quality. The first problem was that it was infeasible to get recall data based on the previous year because of the distorting impact of the drought, so an attempt was made to get respondents to recall their income for two years previously. Inevitably, the accuracy and validity of the data obtained fell and, in the opinion of the author, is such as to make any highly speculative inferences on changes in income that may or may not be attributable to Mudzi Fund credit.

29 Nankumba and Elias (1992) and Nankumba and Kapininga (1992): studies undertaken in Mangochi and Chiradzulu districts by the Rural Development Department, Bunda College of Agriculture, University of Malawi.

APPENDIX:
BORROWER QUESTIONNAIRE

INSTITUTE FOR DEVELOPMENT POLICY AND MANAGEMENT

Micro-finance Study, Sri Lanka

Fieldworkers were trained for three to five days in the use of this form, before commencing data collection. Questionnaires were reviewed on a daily basis.

Serial Number: _____

Researcher: _____

Interviewer: _____

Date: _____

Institution: _____

Place: _____

Additional details:

_____

_____

_____

_____

Part A: Entrepreneur and enterprise profile

A–1 Gender of entrepreneur: male   1
                                      female   2

A–2 Age: [_____]

A–3 Marital status: married   1
                                      single   2
          RING ONLY   divorced   3
          ONE CODE   widow/widower   4
                                  separated   5

A–4 Household size: [_____]

A–5 Number of household members with individual cash incomes?
                                                    [_____]

A–6 How long have you been working in this locality (in years)?
                                                    [_____]

DO NOT ASK: FROM OBSERVATION OR NAME
IDENTIFICATION ONLY

A–7 Socio-cultural group: Sinhalese   1
                                     Muslim   2
                                  Tamil (C)   3
                                  Tamil (I)   4
                                      other   5
      If 'other', specify:

_____

A–8 Educational status: tertiary   1
                                 secondary   2
          RING ONLY   primary   3
          ONE CODE   literate   4
                                non-literate   5

A–9 Type of enterprise supported by credit (specify products/ service provided)

_____

_____

_____

A–10 What type of enterprise is this?

production only	1
service only	2
trade only	3
production and service	4
production and trade	5
service and trade	6
production, service and trade	7

A–11 Does the entrepreneur have other income-generating activities besides that of the assisted enterprise?

RING ALL APPROPRIATE CODES

none	1
other production enterprise	2
other service enterprise	3
other trade enterprise	4
other combination of p/s/t	5
wage employment	6
livestock	7
agriculture	8

A–12 Is your loan-assisted enterprise your main source of income?

yes	1
no	2
don't know	3

A–13 If NO to Qu. 12: What is your main source of income?

other production enterprise	1
other service enterprise	2
other trade enterprise	3
other enterprise p/s/t in combination	4
wage employment	5
livestock	6
agriculture (farm)	7
don't know	8

A–14 How old is the enterprise?   Number of years   [_____]
                                     + number of months [_____]

A–15 What is the ownership 'structure' of the enterprise?

sole proprietor	1
family partnership	2
non-family partnership	3
cooperative/group	4
other	5 _____

411

A–16 What is the location of the business?

rural (countryside)	1
rural (town)	2
peri-urban	3
urban	4

A–17 Is your business located at the same place as your home?

yes	1
no	2

A–18 What is the nature of the business premises?

own (family) premises and land	1
own premises + leased land	2
rented premises	3
authorised use of site	4
unauthorised use of site	5
fully mobile	6
other	7

A–19 How many employees (paid and unpaid) are there in your business?

none	1
one person	2
two persons	3
three persons	4
four persons	5
five or more persons	6

If 'five or more persons', specify the number   [_____]

A–20 What are the average hours of operation of your business?

hours per day   [_____]

days per week   [_____]

A–21 Is the enterprise seasonal?

yes	1
no	2

A–22 If YES to Qu. 21: What are the seasons of high and low activity?

MONTHS: J   F   M   A   M   J   J   A   S   O   N   D
High activity [ ] [ ] [ ] [ ] [ ] [ ] [ ] [ ] [ ] [ ] [ ] [ ]
Low activity [ ] [ ] [ ] [ ] [ ] [ ] [ ] [ ] [ ] [ ] [ ] [ ]

A–23 To what extent do you keep records of your business?

LOOK AT THE RECORDS AND
MAKE A JUDGEMENT

none	1
basic	2
good	3

Part B: Credit and savings

B–1 What was the main source of your start-up funds?

project loan	1
other loan	2
household savings	3
personal savings	4
gifts	5
don't know	6
other	7

If 'other', specify:

_____

B–2 Did you use any other funds to start up your business (apart from your main source of start-up funds)?

none	1
project loan	2
other loan	3
household savings	4
personal savings	5
gifts	6

B–3 In the 5 years prior to the present loan, what other types of credit have you used?

SOURCE	USED	NOT USED	NUMBER OF TIMES
Banks' names	1	2	[_____]
_____			
_____			
_____			
Other lending institutions' names	3	4	[_____]
_____			
_____			
_____			
Local traders/ money lenders/ or landlords (Big Men)	5	6	[_____]
Family/friends	7	8	[_____]

FIELDWORKER: IF NO LOANS REPORTED IN Qu. 3 ABOVE,
→ GO TO Qu. 5

B–4   What is the total number of other sources of credit?

1 source	1
2 sources	2
3 sources	3
4 sources	4
5+ sources	5

B–5   Has a bank or lending institution ever refused you a loan application?

yes	1
no	2
'never applied'	3

B–6   Are any of your previous loans outstanding?

yes	1
no	2

B–7   If YES to Qu. 6: What is the total amount of your previous loans outstanding?   [_____]

B–8   When did you receive your project loan with the Thrift & Co-operative Society?   Month [_____]   Year [__19___]

B–9   How did you first come to hear about the possibility of getting a loan from this institution?

bank workers	1
family/friends	2
neighbours	3
advertisement	4
other	5
don't know	6

B–10   THERE IS NO QUESTION B–10 FOR SANASA RESPONDENTS

B–11   How long did it take between applying for the loan and receiving it (enter number of weeks)?   Number of weeks [_____]

B–12   What time did you devote to obtaining the loan?
        ENTER TIME IN HOURS   travelling [_____]
                                     meeting officials [_____]
                                     waiting/idle time [_____]
                                     form filling [_____]
                                     other (specify) [_____]

        _____

        _____

                               TOTAL ESTIMATE [_____]

B–13   Amount of loan (principal):   [_____]

B–14   Interest rate: [_____]

IF RESPONDENT CANNOT GIVE THE ANNUAL INTEREST
RATE, SPECIFY RESPONDENT'S ANSWER IN WORDS:

_____

_____

_____

B–15   Total amount of loan (principal + interest)   [_____]

B–16   Total repayment period (number of months):   [_____]

B–17   Regularity of instalments due   [_____] times per week
                               or   [_____] times per month
               or OTHER   _____

B–18   Amount due at each instalment   [_____]

B–19   Total interest and principal paid to date   [_____]

B–20   Amount of present loan outstanding: [_____]

B–21   Are there arrears (i.e. is the respondent behind in their loan repayments)?
                                                    yes   1
                                                     no   2

B–22   If yes: what are the reasons for the arrears?
                                business failure   1
                                natural disaster   2
                         consumption requirements   3
                            distress consumption   4
                                   other (specify)   5

_____

_____

B–23   What was the original intended purpose of the loan?
                                working capital   1
                                  fixed capital   2
                                          other   3
        SPECIFY PURPOSE IN WORDS:

_____

_____

415

B–24   What was/is the actual use of loan?

working capital only	1
fixed capital only	2
consumption only	3
both fixed and working capital	4
consumption and working capital	5
consumption and fixed capital	6

SPECIFY ACTUAL USE IN WORDS:

_____

_____

B–25   What is the source of income for loan repayments?

enterprise profits	1
wage employment	2
agriculture	3
livestock	4
other loans	5

IF OTHER LOANS, SPECIFY SOURCE IN WORDS:

_____

_____

gifts	6
asset sales	7
other (specify)	8

_____

B–26   In relation to the present loan, do you have any of the following arrangements?

RING ALL
APPROPRIATE
CODES

training	1
technical assistance	2
compulsory saving	3
voluntary saving	4
insurance provision	5
welfare provision	6
other	7

If 'other', specify:

_____

B–27   If you have savings linked to the present loan, what is the current value of these savings?   [_____]

B–28   What was the value of these savings when you first obtained the present loan?   [_____]

B–29   Do you have any other savings with another institution?

yes	1
no	2

FIELDWORKER: If NO to Qu. 29, go to → Qu. 31

B–30   With what institutions(s), what is the value of these savings, when did you first start saving with this/these institution(s) and what is the current interest rate you receive?

Institution (name)	Amount (now)	Amount of first deposit	Interest rate (p.a.) (current)
_____	[_____]	[_____]	[_____]
_____	[_____]	[_____]	[_____]

B–31   Do you have cash savings in your home?

                                        yes   1
                                        no   2

B–32   If YES to Qu. 31: Please give details of these cash savings held:

_____

_____

_____

B–33   Have you obtained any other loans during the lifespan of the present loan?

                                        yes   1
                                        no   2

FIELDWORKER: If NO to Qu. 33, go to → Qu. 36

B–34   If YES to Qu. 33: Specify by source and total amount borrowed:

Name of source	Number of loans	Total amount borrowed
Bank's name	[_____]	[_____]
_____		
_____		
Other lending institution name	[_____]	[_____]
_____		
_____		
Local money lender/ trader/landlord Local landlord	[_____]	[_____]
_____		
_____		
Family/friends	[_____]	[_____]

417

B–35   What was the purpose(s) of obtaining this credit?

working capital   1

fixed capital   2

consumption   3

SPECIFY_____

_____

_____

_____

B–36   Do you need more credit?

yes   1

no   2

B–37   If YES, Specify for what purpose_____

_____

_____

_____

_____

_____

_____

Part C: Group savings and credit

C–1   Are you a member of a borrower group?

yes   1

no   2

C–2   How many members does this group have?   [_____]

C–3   For how many years and months have you belonged to this group?

years   [_____]   months   [_____]

C–4   FIELDWORKER: THERE IS NO QUESTION C–4.

C–5   Since you joined the group, has the membership changed?

yes   1

no   2

C–6   How often does the group meet?

SPECIFY_____

_____

C–7   Does every member attend each group meeting?

yes   1

no   2

FIELDWORKER: Please do the necessary calculation for Qu. 8 and classify appropriately.

C–8   If NO to Qu. 7: Is attendance usually   80–100%?   1
                                               60–80%?   2
                                               40–60%?   3
                                               0–40%?   4

C–9   How often do you attend? For example, in the last year, out of every 12 SANASA meetings how many did you attend?

                                    [_____]   meetings out of 12

C–10   How long do the meetings last?
                                   under 1 hour   1
                                   1 to 2 hours   2
                                   2 to 3 hours   3
                              more than 3 hours   4
                                    varies a lot   5

C–11   FIELDWORKER: THERE IS NO QUESTION C–11.

C–12   How is the group's leadership selected?
                           by consensual selection   1
                                    by an election   2
                               by self-appointment   3
                             appointed by the PTCCS   4
                                      don't know   5
       (Explain if necessary)_____

       _____

C–13   Do you have an official role in the group?
                                             no   1
                                       chairman   2
                                      secretary   3
                                      treasurer   4
                              committee member   5
                                         other   6
       If 'other', specify:

       _____

C–14   As a member of the group have you received any training?
                                            yes   1
                                            no   2

C–15   If YES to Qu. 14, specify whether training in:

group motivation	1
group co-operation	2
book-keeping	3
general business skills	4
non-formal education (e.g. literacy/numeracy)	5
health education	6
other	7

If 'other', specify:

_____

C–16   Does your group have a savings scheme?

yes	1
no	2

C–17   If YES to Qu. 16, specify type/s of scheme:

compulsory only	1
voluntary only	2
both compulsory and voluntary	3

C–18   What is the total value of your group's savings?   [_____]

C–19   Have these savings been used to cover 'bad debts' of group members?

yes	1
no	2

FIELDWORKER: If NO to Qu. 19 go to → Qu. 23
If YES, continue with Qu. 20

C–20   How many individual bad debts have been covered by funds from the group's savings?   [_____]

C–21   How much money has been used to cover this/these bad debt/s?

    [_____]

C–22   Have the bad debts stopped you from saving, or reduced the size of your deposits?

stopped saving	1
reduced saving	2
no affect on saving	3

C–23 Besides dealing with loans and savings, does your group have any other activities?
(PLEASE LIST RESPONSES) _____

_____
_____
_____
_____
_____

Part D: Management practices and the business environment

D–1 Do you participate in any business organisation?

none	1
business or trade association	2
co-operative association	3
self-help committee or group	4
registered NGO	5
other	6

If 'other', specify:

_____

D–2 Do you participate in other social organisations?

none	1
religious bodies (e.g. temple society)	2
school committees	3
sports clubs	4
political groups	5
welfare groups	6
other	7

If 'other', specify:

_____

D–3 FIELDWORKER: THERE IS NO QUESTION D–3.

D–4 After receiving your project loan, have you changed the way in which you keep financial records for your business?

	Now	Before loan
none	1	4
intermittent	2	5
regular	3	6

D–5 What do these records show?

	Now	Before loan
sales	01	07
operating expenses	02	08
gross profits	03	09
net profits	04	10
stocks	05	11
assets	06	12

421

D–6   How do you control the credit you give to customers?

		Now		Before loan	
		Yes	No	Yes	No
only to trusted customers?		[___]	[___]	[___]	[___]
give credit freely?		[___]	[___]	[___]	[___]
do you keep records of people who owe you money		[___]	[___]	[___]	[___]

D–7   Has the amount of credit you give changed since you obtained the project loan?

more 1
less 2
about the same 3

D–8   To whom do you give this credit?

customers 1
suppliers 2
others 3

Specify_____

_____

D–9   What is the rate of interest you charge for this credit?
SPECIFY_____
(INCLUDE MONTHLY AND/OR ANNUAL RATE, AND SPECIFY WHICH)

D–10   How do you control your cash balances?

		Now		Before loan	
		Yes	No	Yes	No
is the cash banked?		[___]	[___]	[___]	[___]
is there a separate bank account for your enterprise?		[___]	[___]	[___]	[___]
are they mixed with other household cash?		[___]	[___]	[___]	[___]
are they mixed with other enterprise cash?		[___]	[___]	[___]	[___]

D–11   How has the level of competition in your enterprise changed since you obtained the present loan?

about the same 1
increased 2
decreased 3

D–12   Over the period of the present loan have you succeeded in doing any of the following?

increase the volume of goods/services	1
improve the quality of your goods/services	2
diversify into new goods/services	3
purchase new tools or equipment	4
move to better premises	5

D–13   Have you been successful in getting more customers over the period of the present loan?

yes	1
no	2

D–14   Is there any training you would like to receive for yourself and/or your employees?

yes	1
no	2

D–15   If YES to Qu. 14: Specify the type of training you would like:

_____

_____

_____

Part E: Credit impact on business operations

E–1   What changes in employment have occurred between now and the time immediately before obtaining the loan?

NOW:	Male	Female	Total
TOTAL NUMBER OF PAID EMPLOYEES of which:	[__]	[__]	[__]
total no. employed full-time	[__]	[__]	[__]
total no. employed part-time	[__]	[__]	[__]
total no. of unpaid family members employed	[__]	[__]	[__]
total number employed on a casual basis	[__]	[__]	[__]
BEFORE LOAN:	Male	Female	Total
TOTAL NUMBER OF PAID EMPLOYEES of which:	[__]	[__]	[__]
total no. employed full-time	[__]	[__]	[__]
total no. employed part-time	[__]	[__]	[__]
total no. of unpaid family members employed	[__]	[__]	[__]
total number employed on a casual basis	[__]	[__]	[__]

E–2 How have the rates of pay of your employee changed over the same period?

NOW:

	Male	Female	
full-time workers	[___]	[___]	per day
part-time workers	[___]	[___]	per day
casual rate	[___]	[___]	per day
piece-rate	[___]	[___]	

(IF PIECE-RATE, SPECIFY TERMS)

_____

_____

BEFORE LOAN:

	Male	Female	
full-time workers	[___]	[___]	per day
part-time workers	[___]	[___]	per day
casual rate	[___]	[___]	per day
piece-rate	[___]	[___]	

(IF PIECE-RATE, SPECIFY TERMS)

_____

_____

E–3 Has the loan been used to make technical changes in your enterprise?

yes 1
no 2

FIELDWORKER: If the answer is YES, please obtain a description of this technological change and the impact this has made on the enterprise (e.g. for farmers: fertiliser/pesticide/irrigation/traction and improved seed use).

_____
_____
_____
_____
_____
_____
_____
_____
_____

E–4 If YES: has this technical change meant that you use less labour?

yes 1
no 2

E–5   What relative changes have occurred in the asset structure of the business between now and the time before the present loan was disbursed?

(FIELDWORKER: enter a tick)

ESTIMATED RELATIVE VALUE

	Up	Down	About same
FIXED ASSETS:			
land	[__]	[__]	[__]
livestock	[__]	[__]	[__]
premises	[__]	[__]	[__]
tools & equipment	[__]	[__]	[__]
fixtures & fittings	[__]	[__]	[__]
other (specify)	[__]	[__]	[__]
Total	[__]	[__]	[__]
CURRENT ASSETS:			
raw materials	[__]	[__]	[__]
unfinished goods	[__]	[__]	[__]
goods for sale	[__]	[__]	[__]
cash at bank	[__]	[__]	[__]
petty cash	[__]	[__]	[__]
money owed by customers	[__]	[__]	[__]
supplier's credit	[__]	[__]	[__]
other (specify)	[__]	[__]	[__]
Total	[__]	[__]	[__]

E–6   What actual changes have occurred in the asset structure of the business between now and the time before the project loan was disbursed?

(FIELDWORKER: Enter a monetary value)

	Now	Before loan	(Change)
FIXED ASSETS:			
land	[____]	[____]	[____]
livestock	[____]	[____]	[____]
premises	[____]	[____]	[____]
tools & equipment	[____]	[____]	[____]
fixtures & fittings	[____]	[____]	[____]
other (specify)	[____]	[____]	[____]
Total	[____]	[____]	[____]

E–6   *Continued*

                                    Now   Before loan (Change)
        CURRENT ASSETS:
                    raw materials [_____] [_____] [_____]
                  unfinished goods [_____] [_____] [_____]
                    goods for sale [_____] [_____] [_____]
                      cash at bank [_____] [_____] [_____]
                        petty cash [_____] [_____] [_____]
           money owed by customers [_____] [_____] [_____]
                 supplier's credit [_____] [_____] [_____]
                    other (specify)[_____] [_____] [_____]

        _____

                       Total [_____] [_____] [_____]

E–7   What were the sales of your business last month?   [_____]
        Out of this figure, how much was profit?   [_____]
        (FIELDWORKER: MANY RESPONDENTS WILL NOT BE ABLE
        TO ANSWER THIS – DO NOT PRESS THEM)

E–8   What were your average monthly sales for the most recent three months?
                                                        [_____]

E–9   What were your average monthly sales for the first six months following
        receipt of the loan?   [_____]

E–10   What were your average monthly sales in the three months prior to the
        loan?   [_____]

E–11   What are your current business expenses, in the month prior to this
        interview?
        AND: What were these types of monthly business expenses before you
        received the present loan?
                                    Current   Expenses (Change)
                                    expenses before
                                              the loan
                tools/minor equipment [_____] [_____] [_____]
                              stocks   [_____] [_____] [_____]
                                rent   [_____] [_____] [_____]
                            utilities [_____] [_____] [_____]
                            transport [_____] [_____] [_____]

E–11 *Continued*

	Current expenses	Expenses before the loan	(Change)
licences, fees, taxes	[_____]	[_____]	[_____]
wages in cash	[_____]	[_____]	[_____]
wages in kind	[_____]	[_____]	[_____]
loan repayments	[_____]	[_____]	[_____]
others (specify)	[_____]	[_____]	[_____]

TOTAL EXPENSES [_____] [_____]

TOTAL CHANGE [_____]

E–12 Net average cash flow per month = [_____]
FIELDWORKER: NET AVERAGE CASH FLOW = AMOUNT ENTERED IN E–7 MINUS TOTAL CURRENT EXPENSES

E–13 FIELDWORKER: THERE IS NO QUESTION E–13.

Part F: Credit impact on the household

F–1 How many people are there in your household now, and how many were there before the project loan?

now [_____]
before the loan [_____]

F–2 Are you head of the household?

yes 1
no 2

F–3 If NO to Qu. 2: Who is the head of your household?

spouse 1
father 2
mother 3
other 4

If 'other', specify:

F–4 How many in your household have wage employment?
(ASK HOW MANY WERE EMPLOYED BEFORE THE LOAN)

now [_____]
before the loan [_____]

F–5   How many are of school age?

                                        now   [_____]
                              before the loan   [_____]

F–6   How many, including those of school age, are dependent on you for income?

                                        now   [_____]
                              before the loan   [_____]

F–7   How many members of your household are unemployed, but seeking employment?

                                        now   [_____]
                              before the loan   [_____]

F–8   Are there other members of your family beyond the household who are dependent on you?

                                        yes   1
                                        no   2

F–9   If YES to Qu. 8: How many members of your family beyond the household are dependent on you?

                                        now   [_____]
                              before the loan   [_____]

F–10   How many members of your household are employed in your enterprise at the moment, and how many were employed in the enterprise before the loan?

                                        Number employed
                                        Now   Before
                                               loan
                        full-time   [___]   [___]
                        part-time   [___]   [___]
                          casual   [___]   [___]
                        piece-rate [___]   [___]

F–11   Do you pay these family employees?

                                        yes   1
                                        no   2

        IF YES, SPECIFY RATES NOW, AND BEFORE THE LOAN
                                        Now   Before
                                               the loan
                        full-time   [___]   [___] per day
                        part-time   [___]   [___] per day
                          casual   [___]   [___] per day
                        piece-rate [___]   [___]

        (IF PIECE-RATE, SPECIFY TERMS) _____

_____

F–12 Compared to the time immediately before the present loan was disbursed how much time are members of your household now spending working for your enterprise?

more time	1
less time	2
about the same amount of time	3

F–13 Compared to the time immediately before the present loan was disbursed how much time are you now spending working for your enterprise?

more time	1
less time	2
about the same amount of time	3

F–14 What other economic activities are you and members of your household engaged in?

(FIELDWORKER: Enter a tick in the 'Others' column if any member of the household is engaged in the specified economic activity)

	You	Spouse	Others
wage employment	[__]	[__]	[__]
'exchange labour'	[__]	[__]	[__]
agriculture	[__]	[__]	[__]
livestock	[__]	[__]	[__]
other self-employment	[__]	[__]	[__]

F–15 Has the amount of time devoted to these activities increased, decreased or remained about the same over the life of the present loan?

	Increased	Decreased	About the same
FOR YOU:			
wage employment	[__]	[__]	[__]
agriculture	[__]	[__]	[__]
livestock	[__]	[__]	[__]
other self-employment	[__]	[__]	[__]
FOR YOUR SPOUSE:			
wage employment	[__]	[__]	[__]
agriculture	[__]	[__]	[__]
livestock	[__]	[__]	[__]
other self-employment	[__]	[__]	[__]
FOR OTHERS:			
wage employment	[__]	[__]	[__]
agriculture	[__]	[__]	[__]
livestock	[__]	[__]	[__]
other self-employment	[__]	[__]	[__]

F–16 What are your average monthly household expenses, and what were these expenses before the time of your loan?

	Current expenses	Before project loan
food	[_____]	[_____]
rent	[_____]	[_____]
transport	[_____]	[_____]
education	[_____]	[_____]
clothing	[_____]	[_____]
medical	[_____]	[_____]
household utensils	[_____]	[_____]
other major expenses	[_____]	[_____]

Specify_____

_____

TOTALS [_____] [_____]

F–17 Please estimate the value of your major household assets:

	Now	Before project loan
house	[_____]	[_____]
land	[_____]	[_____]
agriculture	[_____]	[_____]
livestock	[_____]	[_____]
other enterprises	[_____]	[_____]
savings	[_____]	[_____]
other (specify)	[_____]	[_____]

_____

_____

TOTALS [_____] [_____]

F–18 Please detail major household investments acquired since the project loan was first disbursed?

_____
_____
_____
_____
_____
_____
_____

430

F–19   Please indicate your household income per month from the following
        sources:

(FIELDWORKER: Annual or seasonal income should be averaged into
monthly income.)
(Give a total figure for all other members of the household in the 'Others'
column.)

	Entrepreneur	Spouse	Others

NOW:

	Entrepreneur	Spouse	Others
from assisted enterprise	[_____]	[_____]	[_____]
from other enterprises	[_____]	[_____]	[_____]
from livestock	[_____]	[_____]	[_____]
from agriculture	[_____]	[_____]	[_____]
from rents	[_____]	[_____]	[_____]
from wages	[_____]	[_____]	[_____]
from remittances	[_____]	[_____]	[_____]
other (specify)	[_____]	[_____]	[_____]

_____

_____

TOTALS [_____] [_____] [_____]

GRAND TOTAL (CURRENT) [_____]

BEFORE THE LOAN:

	Entrepreneur	Spouse	Others
from assisted enterprise	[_____]	[_____]	[_____]
from other enterprises	[_____]	[_____]	[_____]
from livestock	[_____]	[_____]	[_____]
from agriculture	[_____]	[_____]	[_____]
from rents	[_____]	[_____]	[_____]
from wages	[_____]	[_____]	[_____]
from remittances	[_____]	[_____]	[_____]
other (specify)	[_____]	[_____]	[_____]

_____

_____

TOTALS [_____] [_____] [_____]

GRAND TOTAL (BEFORE THE LOAN) [_____]

FIELDWORKER: Record any other useful comments or additional
information on the back of this sheet.

BIBLIOGRAPHY

Adams, D.W., D.H. Graham and J.D. von Pischke (1984) *Undermining Rural Development with Cheap Credit*, Boulder, Col.: Westview Press.

Adams, Dale and J.D. von Pischke (1992) 'Microenterprise credit programmes: *déjà vu*', *World Development* **20**, 1463–1470.

Ahmad, E., J. Dreze, J. Hills and A. Sen (eds) (1991) *Public Action for Social Security: Foundations and Strategy. In Social Security in Developing Countries*, Dhaka: University Press.

Ahmad, Z. (1988) *Subsistence Level Development Trap in an Empowerment Strategy: Is BRAC Coming Out of It?*, Dhaka: BRAC Research and Evaluation Division, unpublished paper.

Ahmad, Z., M.A.K. Chowdhury and H. Hasan (1990) *Gender Differences and the Role of Women in the Households* [sic]: *The Case of Female Loanees,* Dhaka: BRAC Research and Evaluation Division, unpublished paper.

Akerlof, George (1970) 'The market for "lemons": quality uncertainty and the market mechanism', *Quarterly Journal of Economics* **84** (August), 488–500.

Aleke-Dondo, C. (1991) *Survey and Analysis of Credit Programmes for Small and Microenterprises in Kenya*, Nairobi: KREP.

Aleke-Dondo, C. (1992) *A Guide for Evaluating KREP Funded Minimalist Credit Schemes*, Nairobi: KREP.

Aleke-Dondo, C. and J. Parker (1991) 'Kibera's Small Enterprise Sector: Baseline Survey Report', Nairobi: KREP.

Amis, P. (1984) 'Squatters or tenants: the commercialization of unauthorized housing in Nairobi', *World Development* **12** (1), 87–96.

Asian Development Bank (ADB) (1990) *Sri Lanka: Study of Crop Protection Incentives,* Manila: ADB.

Asian Development Bank (ADB) (1993) *Asian Development Outlook 1993*, Manila: Oxford University Press.

Asian Development Bank (ADB) (n.d.) *The Thana Resource Development and Employment Project*, Manila: ADB, mimeo.

Bangladesh Rural Advancement Committee (1983) *The Net: Power Structure in Ten Villages*, Rural Study Series, Dhaka: BRAC Prokashana.

Bangladesh Rural Advancement Committee (1992a) *A Report on BRAC's Empowerment Activities*, prepared by the Working Group on Empowerment and submitted to the Donor Consortium meeting, Dhaka: BRAC, unpublished paper.

Bangladesh Rural Advancement Committee (1992b) *Rural Development Programme and Rural Credit Project, Half Yearly Report, June 1992*, Dhaka: BRAC Printers.

Bangladesh Rural Advancement Committee (1992c) *Statistical Report, Rural Development Programme and Rural Credit Project, June 1992*, Dhaka: BRAC Printers.

Bangladesh Rural Advancement Committee (1992d) *Statistical Report, Rural Development Programme and Rural Credit Project, September 1992*, Dhaka: BRAC Printers.

Bangladesh Rural Advancement Committee (1992e) *Statistical Report, Rural Development Programme and Rural Credit Project, December 1992*, Dhaka: BRAC Printers.

Bank Rakyat Indonesia (BRI) (1990) *Kupedes Development Impact Survey*, Jakarta: BRI Planning, Research and Development Department.

Batra, S.M. (1988) 'Agrarian relations and sugar cooperatives in North India', in *Who Shares? Cooperatives and Rural Development*, D.W. Atwood and B.S. Baviskar (eds), Delhi: Oxford University Press, 91–111.

Bell, Clive (1990) 'Interactions between institutional and informal credit agencies in rural India', *World Bank Economic Review*, 4, 297–329.

Bennett, L. (1992) 'Women, poverty and productivity in India', Economic Development Institute Seminar Paper no. 43, Washington, D.C.: World Bank.

Bennett, Lynn and Michael Goldberg (1992) *A Review of Asia Region Projects Providing Enterprise Development and Financial Services to Women: A Decade of Bank Experience*, Washington, D.C.: World Bank Asia Technical Department.

Berger, Marguerite (1989) 'Giving women credit: the strengths and limitations of credit as a tool for alleviating poverty', *World Development* 17, 1017–1032.

Bhattacharya, D. (1990) *Rural Poverty Alleviation Through Non-farm Employment Programmes: Evaluation of Poverty Alleviation Programmes,* vol. 2, Dhaka: Bangladesh Institute of Development Studies, unpublished report.

Billetoft, J. and T. Malmdorf (1992) *Bangladesh: Addicted to Aid. Which Way Out?*, CDR Project Paper no. 93.2, Copenhagen: Centre for Development Research.

Binswanger, Hans and Donald Sillers (1983) 'Risk aversion and credit constraints in farmers' decision-making: a reinterpretation', *Journal of Development Studies* 20, 5–21.

Blount, Jeb (1992) 'Profit's not a dirty word at Bolivia's bank for the poor', *Wall Street Journal* 10 April.

Bolnick, Bruce R. (1988) 'Evaluating loan collection performance: an Indonesian example', *World Development* 16, 501–510.

Bolnick, Bruce R. (1992) 'Moneylenders and informal financial markets in Malawi', *World Development* 20 (1), 57–68.

Boomgard, James J. and Kenneth J. Angell (1990) *Developing Financial Services for Microenterprises: An Evaluation of USAID Assistance to the BRI Unit Desa System in Indonesia*, Gemini Technical Report no. 6, Bethesda, Md: Development Alternatives Inc.

Boomgard, James J., James Kern, Richard Patten and William Miller (1992) 'A review of the prospects for rural financial institution development in Bolivia', Gemini Technical Report no. 42, Bethesda, Md: Development Alternatives Inc.

Booth, Anne (1990) 'Indonesian agricultural development in comparative perspective', *World Development* 17, 1235–1254.

Booth, Anne (1992) 'The World Bank and Indonesian poverty: review article', *Journal of International Development* 4, 633–642.

Bouman, F.J.A. and R. Houtman (1988) 'Pawnbroking as an instrument of rural banking in the Third World', *Economic Development and Cultural Change* 37 (1), 69–89.

Braverman, A. and J.L. Guasch (1989) 'Institutional analysis of credit cooperatives', in P. Bardhan (ed.), *Economic Theory of Agrarian Institutions*, Oxford: Clarendon Press, 340–355.

Buckley, G. (1993a) 'Finance for the poorest in Malawi', University of Manchester/ University of Reading Working Paper on Finance for Low Income Groups no. 6.

Buckley, G. (1993b) 'Smallholder credit: the Malawian experience', University of

Manchester/University of Reading Working Paper on Finance for Low Income Groups no. 8.

Casper, K.L. (1992) 'A case study of the impact of group formation and credit on "social security" networks and exchange relations of women', Dhaka: BRAC Jamalpur Village Studies Project, unpublished paper.

Central Bank of Sri Lanka (1986) *Agricultural Statistics*, vol. 4, Colombo: Department of Agriculture and Central Bank.

Central Bank of Sri Lanka (1989) *Small Farmers and Landless Credit Project*, unpublished report in collaboration with CIDA and IFAD.

Central Bank of Sri Lanka (1992) *Sri Lanka Socio-economic Data, June 1992*, Colombo: Central Bank of Sri Lanka.

Central Bank of Sri Lanka (various years) *Annual Reports*, Colombo: Central Bank.

Centre for Social Research (1990) *The Effects of the Structural Adjustment Programme in Malawi*, report of a workshop held 26 February to 2 March 1990 at Club Makokola, Mangochi, Malawi, Lilongwe: University of Malawi.

Chambers, R. (1983) *Rural Development: Putting the Last First*, London: Longman.

Chambers, R. (1992) 'Spreading and self-improving: a strategy for scaling-up', in M. Edwards and D. Hulme (eds), *Making a Difference: NGOs and Development in a Changing World*, London: Earthscan.

Chavez, Gonzalo (1992) 'El BDI [Banco de Desarollo Interamericano] y el Banco Mundial en la economia boliviana', Ministero de Hacienda, Bolivia, unpublished paper.

Chipande, G.H.R. (1986) *Income Generating Activities for Rural Women in Malawi: A Final Report*, Lilongwe: Centre for Social Research, University of Malawi.

Chipeta, C. and Mkandawire, M.L.C. (1992) 'The informal financial sector in Malawi', *African Review of Money, Finance and Banking*, 2.

Conroy, A. (1993) *The Economics of Smallholder Maize Production in Malawi with Reference to the Market for Hybrid Seed and Fertilizer*, PhD dissertation, University of Manchester.

Copestake, James (1987) 'The transition to social banking in India: promises and pitfalls', *Development Policy Review* 6, 139–164.

Copestake, J. (1995) 'IRDP revisited', paper given to Conference on Finance Against Poverty, Reading, 27–28 March.

Craig, K. (1990) 'The PRIDE credit programme: an evaluation report for Baringo, Kenya', Nairobi: PRIDE.

Crow, B. (1992) 'Finance in context: exploring diverse exchange conditions', unpublished paper presented to the seminar on Financial Landscapes Reconstructed, Wageningen, The Netherlands.

de Soto, Hernando (1990) *The Other Path*, New York: Harper & Row.

Development Alternatives (1993) *Project Completion Report of Technical Support Provided to the Financial Institutions Development Project, Indonesia*, Bethesda, Md: Development Alternatives Inc.

Donovan, G. (1992) 'Malawi: structural adjustment and agriculture', Working Paper for the World Bank Sector Study, draft mimeo.

Drake, Deborah and Maria Otero (1992) *Alchemists for the Poor: NGOs as Financial Institutions*, ACCION Monograph Series no. 6, Cambridge, Mass.: ACCION International.

Dreze, Jacques (1991) 'Poverty in India and the IRDP delusion', *Economic and Political Weekly* 24, A95–A104.

Dreze, J. and A. Sen (1989) *Hunger and Public Action*, Oxford: Oxford University Press.

Dreze, J. and A. Sen (1991) 'Public action for social security: foundations and strategy', in E. Ahmad, J. Dreze, J. Hills and A. Sen (eds), *Social Security in Developing Countries*, Dhaka: University Press, 1–40.

Economist Intelligence Unit (1993) 'Kenya Country Report', 4th Quarter 1993, London: EIU.

Eigen, J. (1992) 'Assistance to women's business: evaluating the options', *Small Enterprise Development*, 3 (4), 4–14.

Eigen, J., E. Gacinah and M. Masyuko (1992) *Informal Sector Programme: Annual Impact Evaluation of ISP Clients*, Nairobi: Kenya Industrial Estates.

Epstein, T.S. (1990) 'Female petty-entrepreneurs in their multiple roles', in S. Vyakarnam (ed.), *When the Harvest is In: Developing Rural Entrepreneurship*, London: Intermediate Technology Group Publications, 254–265.

Esman, M. and N. Uphoff (1984) *Local Organizations: Intermediaries in Rural Development*, Ithaca, N.Y.: Cornell University Press.

Fernando, E. (1986) 'Informal credit and savings organisations in Sri Lanka: the Cheetu System', *Savings and Development* 10 (3), 253–263.

Fernando, N.A. (1988) 'The interest rate structure and factors affecting interest rate determination in the informal credit market in Sri Lanka', *Savings and Development* 12 (3), 249–269.

Fernando, P.S. (1993) 'Alleviation of poverty and Janasaviya', *Economic Review* 18 (11), 23–33.

Fernando, Sunimal *et al.* (1989) 'Thrift and Credit Cooperative Societies in Sri Lanka and the question of the appropriate economic background of its members', *Economic Review*, March, 25–27.

Finance and Banking Commission (1991) *Report of the Finance and Banking Commission*, Colombo: Government Printer.

Fischer, B. (1988) 'Rural financial savings mobilisation in Sri Lanka: bottlenecks and reform proposals', *Savings and Development* 21 (1), 35–61.

Fischer, William, Jeffrey Poyo and Ann Beasley (1992) *Evaluation of the Micro and Small Enterprise Development Project in Bolivia*, Gemini Technical Report no. 42, Bethesda, Md: Development Alternatives Inc.

Food and Agricultural Organisation (1988) *Sri Lanka: Rural Credit Review Phase II Report*, Rome: FAO.

Gaiha, Raghav (1992) 'On the chronically poor in rural India', *Journal of International Development* 4 (3), 273–289.

Gibbons, D.S. and S. Kasim (1990) *Banking on the Rural Poor*, Center for Policy Research, Universiti Sains Malaysia.

Gichira, R. (1991) *An Analysis of the Laws and Regulations Affecting the Development of the Informal Sector in Kenya*, Nairobi: KREP.

Glosser, Amy J. (1993) *BancoSol: A Private Commercial Bank. A Case Study in Profitable Microenterprise Development in Bolivia*, Gemini Working Paper no. 35, Bethesda, Md: Development Alternatives Inc.

Goetz, A.M. and R.S. Gupta (1994) 'Who takes the credit? Gender, power and control over loan use in rural credit programmes in Bangladesh', IDS Working Paper no. 8, Brighton: Institute of Development Studies.

Goldmark, Susan and David H. Lucock (1988) *Mid-term Evaluation of the Financial Institutions Development Project (Phase I)*, Washington, D.C.: Development Alternatives Inc.

Goldmark, Susan and Jay Rosengard (1983) *Credit to Indonesian Entrepreneurs: An Assessment of the BKK*, Washington, D.C.: Development Alternatives Inc.

Gonzalez-Vega, Claudio and Rodrigo Chavez (1992) *Indonesia's Rural Financial Markets*, Report for the Financial Institutions Development Project, Columbus, Ohio: Ohio State University.

Government of Bolivia (1989) *Encuesta Integrada de Hogares* [Integrated Household Survey], La Paz: Instituto Nacional de Estadisticas.

Government of Bolivia (1992) *Encuesta Integrada de Hogares* [3rd and 4th rounds, 1991 and 1992], La Paz: Instituto Nacional de Estadisticas.

Government of India (1981) *Report of the Committee to Review Arrangements for Institutional Credit for Agriculture and Rural Development (CRAFICARD)*, Bombay: Reserve Bank of India.

Government of India (1989) *Report of the Agricultural Credit Review Committee* (Khusro Committee), Bombay: Reserve Bank of India.

Government of Kenya (1986) *Sessional Paper no. 1 of 1986 on Economic Management for Renewed Growth*, Nairobi: Government Printer.

Government of Kenya (1989a) *A Strategy for Small Enterprise Development in Kenya: Towards the Year 2000*, Centre Project, GOK/ILO/UNDP, Nairobi: Government Printer.

Government of Kenya (1989b) *Sixth Development Plan 1989–93*, Nairobi: Government Printer.

Government of Kenya (1992a) *Economic Survey 1992*, Central Bureau of Statistics (CBS), Nairobi: Government Printer.

Government of Kenya (1992b) *Sessional Paper no. 1 of 1992 on Development and Employment in Kenya*, Nairobi: Government Printer.

Government of Kenya (1992c) *Sessional Paper no. 2 of 1992 on Small Enterprise and Jua Kali Development in Kenya*, Nairobi: Government Printer.

Grameen Bank (1992) *The Annual Report, 1991*, Dhaka: Grameen Bank.

Gustavsson, S. (1990) *Primary Education in Bangladesh: For Whom?*, Dhaka: University Press.

Hashemi, S.M. (1990) *NGOs in Bangladesh: Development Alternative or Alternative Development?*, Department of Economics, Jahangirnagar University, unpublished paper.

Henderson, Dennis and Farida Khambata (1985) 'Financing small-scale industry and agriculture in developing countries: the merits and limitations of "commercial" policies', *Economic Development and Cultural Change*, **22**, 349–373.

Hirschman, A.O. (1984) *Getting Ahead Collectively*, New York: Pergamon Press.

Hodson, R. (1996) 'Elephant loose in the jungle: the World Bank and NGOs in Sri Lanka', in A. Hulme and M. Edwards (eds) *NGOs, States and Donors: Too Close for Comfort*, London: Macmillan, chapter 11.

Holt, Sharon (1991) *Incomes in the BPD and Unit Desa Financial Services Programs: Lessons from Two Impact Studies in Indonesia*, Gemini Technical Report no. 19, Bethesda, Md: Development Alternatives Inc.

Holt, Sharon and Helena Ribe (1991) *Developing Financial Institutions for the Poor and Reducing Barriers to Access for Women*, World Bank Discussion Paper 117, Washington, D.C.: World Bank.

Holtsberg, C. (1991) 'Development of selected rural development policies and programmes', vol. VI: 'Evaluation of poverty alleviation programmes', Dhaka: Bangladesh Institute of Development Studies, unpublished (third draft).

Hossain, M. (1988) *Credit for Alleviation of Rural Poverty: The Grameen Bank in Bangladesh*, Research Report no. 65, Washington, D.C.: International Food Policy Research Institute.

Hossain, M. (1989) *Green Revolution in Bangladesh: Impact on Growth and Distribution of Income*, Dhaka: University Press; first published as International Food Policy Research Institute Report no. 67.

Hossain, M. and R. Afsar (1989) *Credit for Women's Involvement in Economic Activities in*

Rural Bangladesh, Research Report no. 105, Dhaka: Bangladesh Institute of Development Studies.

Hulme, D. (1991) 'The Malawi Mudzi Fund: daughter of Grameen', *Journal of International Development* **3** (4), 427–431.

Hulme, D. (1993) 'Replicating finance programmes in Malawi and Malaysia', *Small Enterprise Development* **4** (4), 4–15.

Huppi, M. and G. Feder (1990) 'The role of groups and credit cooperatives in rural lending', *World Bank Research Observer* **5** (2), 187–204.

Informal Sector Programme (1992) *ISP Procedures Manual*, Nairobi: KIE-ISP.

Informal Sector Programme (various) *Monthly Management Reports and Annual Accounts 1989–1992*, Nairobi: KIE-ISP.

Institute of Policy Studies (1992) *Review of the Economy*, Colombo: IPS.

Inter-American Investment Corporation (1991) *Report to the Board of Directors on a Proposed Equity Investment in COBANCO, La Paz, Bolivia*, Washington, D.C.: IIC.

International Fund for Agricultural Development (IFAD) (1987a), *Rural Indonesia: Socio-economic Development in a Changing Environment*, Rome: IFAD Economic and Planning Department.

International Fund for Agricultural Development (IFAD) (1987b), *Pilot Credit Scheme for the Rural Poor (Malawi Mudzi Fund)*, Smallholder Agricultural Credit Project Staff Appraisal Report Working Paper, Rome: IFAD.

International Fund for Agricultural Development (IFAD) (1992) *The State of World Rural Poverty*, London: IT Publications.

International Labour Organisation (ILO) (1972) *Employment, Incomes and Equity in Kenya*, Geneva: ILO.

Jayamaha, R. (1990) 'Innovative approaches to poverty-alleviation through banking and financial institutions: the case for Sri Lanka', *Staff Studies of Central Bank* **20** (1 and 2), 21–46.

Kabeer, N. (1989) *Monitoring Poverty as if Gender Mattered: A Methodology for Rural Bangladesh*, Discussion Paper no. 255, Brighton: Institute of Development Studies.

Kenya Rural Enterprise Programme (KREP) (1992) *Proceedings of the Conference on Microenterprise Credit Schemes: A Special Focus on the Group-based Method of Lending to Individuals*, Nairobi: KREP.

Kenya Rural Enterprise Programme (KREP) (n.d.), 'Juhudi Credit Scheme Operations Procedures Manual' (third draft), Nairobi: KREP.

Kenya Rural Enterprise Programme (KREP) (various) *Monthly Statistical Reports* and *Annual Reports*, 1990–2, Nairobi: KREP.

Khan, N. and E. Stewart (1992) 'Institution building and development in three women's village organizations: participation, ownership, autonomy', Dhaka: Research and Evaluation Division, BRAC, unpublished paper.

Khandkar, Shahidur R., Baqui Khalily and Zahed Khan (1995) 'Grameen Bank: what do we know?' paper presented to World Bank Conference, Dhaka, 19–21 March.

King, K. (1977) *The African Artisan: Education and the Informal Sector in Kenya*, New York: Heinemann/Teachers College Press.

Kiriwandeniya, P.A. (1992) 'The growth of the SANASA movement in Sri Lanka', in M. Edwards and D. Hulme (eds), *Making a Difference: NGOs and Development*, London: Earthscan, 111–117.

Korten, D.C. (1989) 'Bangladesh Rural Advancement Committee: strategy for the 1990s', Boston, Mass.: Institute for Development Research, draft for review.

Kramsjo, B. and G.D. Wood (1992) *Breaking the Chains: Collective Action for Social Justice among the Rural Poor in Bangladesh*, Dhaka: University Press.

Kydd, J. and R. Christiansen (1982) 'Structural change in Malawi since independence: consequences of a development strategy based on large scale agriculture', *World Development* **10** (5), 355–375.

Lele, Uma (1981) 'Co-operatives and the poor: a comparative perspective', *World Development* **9** (1), 55–72.

Lele, Uma (1987) *Structural Adjustment, Agricultural Development and the Poor: Some Observations on Malawi*, World Bank Discussion Paper, Washington, D.C.: World Bank.

Lele, Uma and Arthur Goldsmith (1989) 'The development of national research capacity: India's experience with the Rockefeller Foundation and its significance for Africa', *Economic Development and Cultural Change* **37**, 305–343.

Leonard, D. (1991) *African Successes: Four Public Managers of Kenyan Rural Development*, Berkeley: University of California Press.

Livingstone, I. (1981) *Rural Development, Employment and Incomes in Kenya*, Addis Ababa: ILO/JASPA.

Livingstone, I. (1991) 'A reassessment of Kenya's rural and urban informal sector', *World Development* **19** (6), 651–670.

Lovell, C.H. (1992) *Breaking the Cycle of Poverty: The BRAC Strategy*, West Hartford, Conn.: Kumarian Press.

Malawi Government (1981) *National Rural Development Programme: National Credit Study Phase 1*, Lilongwe: Ministry of Agriculture/Dusseldorf: GITEC Consult.

Malawi Government (1987) *Statement of Development Policies, 1987–1996*, Zomba, Malawi.

Malawi Government (1988) *Statistical Yearbook 1988*, National Statistical Office, Malawi.

Malawi Government (1992a) *Annual Survey of Agriculture 1982/83–1984/85*, National Statistical Office, Malawi.

Malawi Government (1992b) *Guide to Agricultural Production in Malawi 1992/93*, Ministry of Agriculture, Malawi.

Malawi Government (1993) *Monthly Statistical Bulletin, April 1993*, National Statistical Office, Malawi.

Malawi Mudzi Fund (various) *Annual and Quarterly Reports*, 1989–93, Zomba: Malawi Mudzi Fund.

Malhotra, Mohini (1993) 'Informal financial intermediaries in Bolivia', Bethesda, Md: Development Alternatives Inc., unpublished working paper.

Malindi, E.S. and W. Mlenga (1987) *Smallholder Credit Impact Study, Ngabu Agricultural Development Division*, Lilongwe, Malawi: Ministry of Agriculture Evaluation Report.

Maloney, C. (1989) *Credit to the Poor Through Groups: The RDRS Example*, Dhaka: Community Development Library.

Mercier, A. (1990) 'Sri Lanka institutional analysis: strengthening financial management capabilities of the Thrift and Credit Cooperative system in Sri Lanka', Colombo: World Council of Credit Unions and Federation of Thrift and Credit Cooperatives, unpublished report.

Mkandawire, R., S. Jaffee and S. Bertoli (1990) *Beyond Dualism: The Changing Face of the Leasehold Estate Sub Sector of Malawi*, Bunda College/Institute of Development Anthropology, Malawi.

Moore, M. (1990) 'Economic liberalisation, growth and poverty: Sri Lanka in long-run perspective', IDS Discussion Paper no. 274, Brighton: Institute of Development Studies.

Moore, M. (1992) 'Retreat from democracy in Sri Lanka?', *Journal of Commonwealth and Comparative Politics* **30** (1), 64–84.

438

Morales, Juan Antonio (1991) 'Ajustes estructurales en la economia campesina boliviana', *Debate Agrario* (Lima) **9**, 121–162.

Mosley, Paul (1993) *Credit for Low-income Groups: An Analytical Framework*, Working Paper on Finance for Low Income Groups no. 1, Universities of Manchester and Reading, Manchester: Institute for Development and Policy Management.

Mosley, P. and R.P. Dahal (1987) 'Credit for the rural poor: a comparison of policy experiments in Nepal and Bangladesh', *Manchester Papers on Development* **3** (2), 45–59.

Mosley, P. and R. Krishnamurthy (1995) 'Can crop insurance work? The case of India', forthcoming in *Journal of Development Studies* **31**.

Mosley, P., J. Harrigan and J. Toye (1995) *Aid and Power*, 2nd edn, London: Routledge.

MSI/HASFARM (1992) *The Development Impact of Financing the Smaller Enterprises in Indonesia*, Gemini Technical Report no. 26, Bethesda, Md: Development Alternatives Inc.

Mudgil, K.K. and Y.S.P. Thorat (1995) 'Restructuring of rural financial institutions: the regional rural banks' experience in India', paper presented to Conference on Finance Against Poverty, Reading, 27–28 March.

Müller and Associates (1991) 'Restucturación del sistema financiero boliviano', unpublished paper.

Mungai and Associates (1990) 'Kenya Industrial Estates Limited Informal Sector Programme short-term working capital lending package', Nairobi: Mungai and Assocs.

Mutiso, G.C.M. and E.H.A. Mugwanga (1991) *Evaluation Report to WEREP Ltd– Kenya Rural Enterprises Programme (REP) on the Promotion of Rural Initiatives and Enterprises Development (PRIDE)*, Nairobi: KREP.

Mutua, K. (1990) *A Guide to Developing Management Information Systems*, Nairobi: KREP.

Nankumba, J.S. and B. Eliasi (1992) *Pioneer Loanees of Malawi Mudzi Fund (MMF): A Case Study of Mangochi District*, Rural Development Department, Bunda College of Agriculture, University of Malawi.

Nankumba, J.S. and J. Kapininga (1992) *Pioneer Loanees of Malawi Mudzi Fund (MMF): A Case Study of Chiradzulu District*, Rural Development Department, Bunda College of Agriculture, University of Malawi.

Narasimham, M. (1992) *The Financial System: Report*, Delhi: Nabhi Publications.

National Planning Division (1984) *Rural Credit: Trends and Prospects*, Colombo: Ministry of Finance and Planning.

Newman, John, Steen Jorgensen and Menno Pradhan (1991) 'How did workers benefit from Bolivia's Emergency Social Fund?', *World Bank Economic Review* **5**, 367–393.

Nwanna, G. (1993) 'Rural financial markets in Malawi', Working Paper for the World Bank Sector Study, draft mimeo.

Nyanda, M.E. (1990) *The Pilot Credit Scheme for the Rural Poor: Final Report of the Findings of a Baseline Survey Presented to the Government of Malawi*, Centre for Social Research, University of Malawi.

Nyirenda, M.M. (1991) *Malawi Mudzi Fund Pilot Scheme*, Zomba: Malawi Mudzi Fund, mimeo.

Odada, J.E. and J.O. Otieno (1990) *Socio-economic Profiles . . . [of nine districts]*, Nairobi: Ministry of Planning and National Development of the Government of Kenya/ UNICEF.

Oketch, H.O. (1991a) *Hotels and Restaurants in Kibera: A Subsector Analysis of Functions, Organization and Dynamics*, Nairobi: KREP.

Oketch, H.O. (1991b) *The Kibera Juhudi Microbusiness Credit Scheme: A Profile of Proprietors and Assisted Enterprises*, Nairobi: KREP.

Oketch, H.O. (1992) *A Diagnostic Survey of the Workings of Group Based Lending: The Case of KREP's Juhudi Credit Scheme–Kibera*, Nairobi: KREP.

Oketch, H.O. and J. Parker (1991) *Furniture Making in Kibera: A Subsector Analysis of Functions, Organization and Dynamics*, Nairobi: KREP.

Oketch, H.O., A.K. Mutua and C. Aleke-Dondo (1991) *Microenterprise Credit, Employment, Incomes and Output: Some Evidence from Kenya*, Nairobi: KREP.

Okidegbe, N. (1992) *Malawi Rural Financial Markets: Strategic Options for Economic Development*, Washington D.C.: World Bank, mimeo.

Osmani, S.R. (1991) 'Social security in South Asia', in E. Ahmad, J. Dreze, J. Hills and A. Sen (eds), *Social Security in Developing Countries* Dhaka: University Press, 305–355.

Overseas Development Administration (Nairobi) and Ministry of Planning and National Development (1992) 'Project Memorandum: Kenya Rural Enterprise Programme (KREP) support for Juhudi credit scheme', October, unpublished.

Padmanabhan, K.P. (1986) *Rural Financial Intermediation*, Pune: Shubhada-Saraswat Publications.

Panditha (1988) 'The role of Cooperative Rural Banks in Sri Lanka's rural sector', *Economic Review,* **14** (8 and 9), 9–16.

Patten, Richard H. and J. Rosengard (1991) *Progress with Profits: The Development of Rural Banking in Indonesia*, San Francisco: International Centre for Economic Growth.

Pearson, Roland and Dallas Garland (1993) *Financial Institutions Development Project in Indonesia: Developing Financial Institutions to Secure Small Enterprises*, Gemini Working Paper no. 41, Bethesda, Md: Development Alternatives Inc.

Pitt, M. and S. Khandkhar (1995) 'Household and intra-household impacts of the Grameen Bank and similar targeted credit programs in Bangladesh', paper presented to World Bank Conference, Dhaka, 19–21 March.

Prabowo, Dibyo (1987) *Some Items on Informal Credit Markets in Indonesia*, Yogyakarta: Gadjah Mada University.

Prabowo, Dibyo and Sayogyo (1973) 'The importance of credit channelled through the BIMAS scheme compared to credit outside BIMAS', in *Changes in Rice Farming in Selected Areas of Asia*, Los Banos, Philippines: International Rice Research Institute.

PRIDE (1992a) *An Overview of Branch Credit Services and Funding Requirements* Nairobi: Council for International Development.

PRIDE (1992b) *The PRIDE Credit Manual*, Nairobi: Council for International Development.

Pulley, Robert V. (1989) *Making the Poor Creditworthy: A Case Study of the Integrated Rural Development Program in India*, World Bank Discussion Paper no. 58, Washington D.C.: World Bank.

Rahman, Atiq (1992) 'The informal financial sector in Bangladesh: an appraisal of its role in development', *Development and Change* **23**, 147–168.

Rahman, Atiur (reprinted 1989) *Impact of Grameen Bank Intervention on the Rural Power Structure*, Research Report no. 61, Dhaka: Bangladesh Institute of Development Studies.

Rahman, H.Z. and Hossain, M. (1992) *Rethinking Rural Poverty: A Case for Bangladesh*, Dhaka: Bangladesh Institute of Development Studies.

Rahman, Rushidan I. (1986) *Impact of Grameen Bank on the Situation of Rural Poor Women*, Working Paper no. 1, Grameen Bank Evaluation Project, Dhaka: Bangladesh Institute of Development Studies.

440

Rasanayagam, Y. (1993) 'Women as agents and beneficiaries of rural housing programmes in Sri Lanka', in J.H. Momsen and V. Kinnaird (eds), *Different Places, Different Voices: Gender and Development in Africa, Asia and Latin America*, London: Routledge, 146–158.

Reserve Bank of India (RBI) (1954) *All-India Rural Credit Survey*, 3 vols, Bombay: RBI.

Rhyne, Elizabeth (1991) *The Microenterprise Finance Institutions of Indonesia and their Implications for Donors*, Gemini Working Paper no. 20, Bethesda, Md: Development Alternatives Inc.

Roy, Rita Das (1992) 'Domestic violence against women' (translated from the Bengali), BRAC Research and Evaluation Division, unpublished paper.

Rutherford, S. (1993) 'Alternative credit systems', unpublished draft report for the Asian Development Bank.

Ryan, P. (1992) 'Regional Rural Development Banks', Bradford: University of Bradford, mimeo for Asian Development Bank.

SACA (1993) *SACA Technical Credit Manual 1993*, Ministry of Agriculture, Malawi.

Sadeque, S. (1986) 'The rural financial market and the Grameen Bank in Bangladesh: an experiment in involving the rural poor and women in institutional credit operations', *Savings and Development* **10** (2), 181–195.

Salloum, Douglas (1993) 'The business of lending to the smallest of the small enterprises', unpublished paper presented to BancoSol Workshop on 'The Commercial Approach to Micro-credit', 26–28 April, Santa Cruz, Bolivia, Toronto: Calmeadow Foundation.

Samarasinghe, V. (1993) 'Access of female plantation workers in Sri Lanka to basic-needs provision', in J.H. Momsen and V. Kinnaird (eds), *Different Places, Different Voices: Gender and Development in Africa, Asia and Latin America*, London: Routledge, 131–145.

SANASA (1992) *Statistical Report*, Colombo: FTCCS.

SANASA (1993) *Fifth Consortium of SANASA Partners: Briefing Papers*, Colombo: FTCCS.

Sanderatne, N. (1990) 'Banking for the poor', a paper presented at the Sri Lanka Association for the Advancement of Science Symposium on Banking for the Poor, Colombo.

Sanderatne, N. and S.M.P. Senanayake (1989) 'The structure of Sri Lanka's informal financial markets', *Upanathi* **4** (1 and 2), 125–160.

Sanyal, B. (1991) 'Antagonistic cooperation: a case study of non-governmental organisations, government and donors' relationships in income-generating projects in Bangladesh', *World Development* **19** (10), 1367–1379.

Sarvodaya Donor Consortium (1993) *Report of Twelfth Monitoring Mission*, Colombo.

Sattar, A. (1991) 'Primary education for older children: perceptions and attitudes of learners: an exploratory study', BRAC Research and Evaluation Division, unpublished paper.

Schaeffer-Kehnert, W. (1982) 'Success with group lending in Malawi', *Development Digest* **20** (1), 10–15.

Scott, J.C. (1985) *Weapons of the Weak: Everyday Forms of Peasant Resistance*, New Haven, Conn.: Yale University Press.

Seabright, Paul (1991) 'Identifying investment opportunities for the poor: evidence from the livestock market in South India', *Journal of Development Studies* **28**, 53–73.

Sebstad, J. (1989) *Expanding Off-farm Income and Employment Opportunities for Women*, Malawi Country Development Strategy Statement, Issues and Options for USAID/Malawi undertaken by Tropical Research and Development Inc., Gainesville, Fla.

Sebstad, J. and M. Walsh (1991) *Microenterprise Credit and its Effects in Kenya: An Exploratory Study*, prepared by consultants to Ernst & Young, under a sub-contract funded by USAID, Washington, D.C.

Sen, A.K. (1989) 'A study on moneylenders in rural informal financial markets', Informal Financial Market Study Project, Dhaka: BIDS.

Sen, A.K. (1990) 'Gender and cooperative conflicts', in I. Tinker (ed.), *Persistent Inequalities*, New York: Oxford University Press.

Senanayake, S.M.P. (1984) 'Sri Lanka', in Asian Productivity Organisation (eds), *Farm Credit Situation in Asia*, Tokyo: Asian Productivity Organisation, ch. 10.

Shanmugaratnam, N., A. Mossige, I. Nyborg and A.M. Jensen (1992) *From Natural Resource Degradation and Poverty to Sustainable Development in Malawi: A Study of the Population–Environment–Agriculture Nexus*, a report to the World Bank undertaken by the Agricultural University of Norway.

SIDA (1991) *Evaluation of SIDA-financed Rural Development Projects in Sri Lanka*, Colombo: SIDA.

Simler, K. (1993) 'Sources of growth in Malawi: past trends and future prospects', a World Bank Working Paper prepared for the Malawi Agricultural Sector Memorandum.

Snodgrass, Donald and Richard H. Patten (1991) 'Reform of rural credit in Indonesia: inducing bureaucracies to behave competitively', in D.H. Perkins and M. Roemer (eds), *Reforming Economic Systems in Developing Countries*, Cambridge, Mass.: Harvard University Press, ch. 13.

Southwold-Llewellyn, S. (1990) 'Household credit strategies for food security: a case-study from Sri Lanka', in J.I. Hans Bakker (ed.), *World Food Crisis: Food Security in Comparative Perspective*, Toronto: Canadian Scholars' Press, 201–228.

Stigler, George (1961) 'The economics of information', *Journal of Political Economy* **59** (June), 223–225.

Stigler, George (1967) 'Imperfections in the capital market', *Journal of Political Economy* **75**, 287–292.

Sutoro, Ann Dunham (1991) 'Market potential survey: survey of findings', Jakarta: Bank Rakyat Indonesia, unpublished report.

Sutoro, Ann Dunham, Don Johnston and Tim Litbank (1991) *Market Potential Survey: Some Quantitative Data*, Jakarta: Bank Rakyat Indonesia.

Swan, B. (1987) *Sri Lankan Mosaic: Environment, Man, Continuity and Change*, Colombo: Marga Institute.

Talukdar, R.B. and Mafizul Islam, A.F.M. (1992) 'Evaluation of Thana Resource Development and Employment Project', study prepared for the Department of Youth Development, Dhaka: Institute of Business Administration, draft.

Tilakaratna, W.M., Y.R. Amerasinghe and P.V.J. Jayaseker (1992) *Thrift and Credit Cooperatives of Sri Lanka: An Evaluation*, Institute for International Studies, Peradeniya University, mimeo.

Tomecko, J. (1990) 'Mainstreaming small enterprises in Kenya', *Small Enterprise Development* **1** (3), 17–26.

Tomecko, J. and C. Aleke-Dondo (1992) *Improving the Growth Potential of the Small-scale and Informal Sectors*, Nairobi: KREP.

Toye, J. (1987) *Dilemmas of Development*, Oxford: Basil Blackwell.

United Nations Development Programme (UNDP) (1993) *Human Development Report 1993*, New York: UNDP.

United Nations Research Institute for Social Development (UNRISD) (1975) *Rural Cooperatives as Agents of Change*, Geneva: UNRISD.

Uphoff, N. (1992) *Learning from Gal Oya: Possibilities for Participatory Development and Post-Newtonian Social Science*, Ithaca, N.Y.: Cornell University Press.

Vitebsky, P. (1992) 'Shifting cultivation comes to rest: changing values of land and the person in an area of Moneragala District', in J. Brow and J. Weeramunda (eds), *Agrarian Change in Sri Lanka*, New Delhi: Sage, 155–187.

von Pischke, J.D. (1992) *Finance at the Frontier*, Washington, D.C.: World Bank.

von Pischke, J.D. and D.W. Adams (1993) 'Fungibility and the design and evaluation of agricultural credit projects', in J.D. von Pischke, D.W. Adams and G. Donald (eds), *Rural Financial Markets in Developing Countries*, London and Baltimore, Md: Johns Hopkins University Press, 78–83.

Wade, R. (1988) *Village Republics*, Delhi: Cambridge University Press.

Wahid, A.N.M. (ed.) (1993) *The Grameen Bank: Poverty Relief in Bangladesh*, Boulder, Col.: Westview Press.

White, Sarah C. (1991) *Evaluating the Impact of NGOs in Rural Poverty Alleviation*, Bangladesh Country Study, ODI Working Paper no. 50, London: Overseas Development Institute.

White, S. (1992) *Arguing with the Crocodile: Gender and Class in Bangladesh*, Dhaka: University Press.

Wickramsinghe, A. (1993) 'Women's roles in rural Sri Lanka', in J.H. Momsen and V. Kinnaird (eds), *Different Places, Different Voices: Gender and Development in Africa, Asia and Latin America*, London: Routledge, 159–175.

Wiggins, S. and B. Rogaly (1989) 'Providing rural credit in Southern India: a comparison of commercial banks and cooperatives', *Public Administration and Development* **9** (2), 215–232.

Wood, G.D. (1992) 'Introduction', in B. Kramsjo and G.D. Wood (eds), *Breaking the Chains: Collective Action for Social Justice among the Rural Poor in Bangladesh*, Dhaka: University Press, 1–34.

Wood, G.D. and R. Palmer-Jones (1991) *The Water Sellers: A Cooperative Venture by the Rural Poor*, London: Intermediate Technology Publications.

World Bank (1987) *Staff Appraisal Report: Malawi Smallholder Agricultural Credit Project*, Washington, D.C.: World Bank.

World Bank (1988) *Indonesia, Rural Credit Sector Review*, 2 vols, Washington, D.C.: World Bank Asia Project Office (6917-IND).

World Bank (1990) *Bangladesh: Strategies for Enhancing the Role of Women in Economic Development*, Country Study, Washington, D.C.: World Bank.

World Bank (1990a) *Malawi: Growth Through Poverty Reduction*, Washington, D.C.: World Bank.

World Bank (1990b) *Malawi Food Security Report*, Washington, D.C.: World Bank.

World Bank (1991) *Women and Development in Malawi: Constraints and Actions*, Washington, D.C.: World Bank.

World Bank (1992) *Sri Lanka: Strengthened Adjustment for Growth and Poverty Reduction*, Washington, D.C.: World Bank.

World Bank (1993a) *Staff Appraisal Report Malawi Rural Financial Services Project*, Washington, D.C.: World Bank.

World Bank (1993b) *World Development Report 1993*, Washington, D.C.: World Bank.

World Bank (1993c) *World Bank Tables 1993*, Washington, D.C.: World Bank/ Baltimore, Md: Johns Hopkins University Press.

Worsley, P. (1971) *Two Blades of Grass: Rural Cooperatives in Agricultural Modernisation*, Manchester: Manchester University Press.

Wuyts, M., M. Mackintosh and T. Hewitt (1992) *Development Policy and Public Action*, Oxford: Oxford University Press.

Yaron, Jacob (1991) *Successful Rural Finance Institutions*, 2 vols, Washington, D.C.: World Bank (Agricultural Policy Division).

Yaron, Jacob (1992) *Assessing Development Finance Institutions: A Public Interest Analysis*, World Bank Discussion Paper no. 174, Washington, D.C.: World Bank.

Youngjohns, B.J. (1977) *Cooperative Organisation: An Introduction*, London: IT Publications.

Youngjohns, B.J. (1980) 'Agricultural cooperatives and credit', in J. Howell (ed.), *Borrowers and Lenders*, London: Overseas Development Institute.

Yun, K.H. (1987) *Agricultural Cooperatives in Korea*, Seoul: HY Publishers.

Yunus, M. (1987) *Credit for Self-employment: A Fundamental Human Right*, Dhaka: Grameen Bank.

Zander, R.C. (1991) 'Politics and rural financial markets in Sri Lanka', paper presented at Third Sri Lanka Conference, Amsterdam.

Zander, R.C. (1992a) 'Limits of the transaction cost approach in the comparative analysis of financial intermediaries', paper presented at a Conference on Financial Landscapes Reconstructed, Wageningen.

Zander, R.C. (1992b) 'Financial self-help organisation in rural Sri Lanka: responses to political and economic adversity', paper presented at Eighth World Congress for Rural Sociology, Pennsylvania.

INDEX